PUBLICATION DESIGN

PUBLICATION DESIGN

Fourth Edition

ROY PAUL NELSON
University of Oregon

wcb
WM. C. BROWN PUBLISHERS
DUBUQUE, IOWA

By Roy Paul Nelson

Publication Design
The Design of Advertising
Humorous Illustration and Cartooning
Editing the News (with Roy H. Copperud)
The Fourth Estate (with John L. Hulteng)
Articles and Features
Comic Art and Caricature
Cartooning
Visits with 30 Magazine Art Directors
Fell's Guide to Commercial Art (with Byron Ferris)
Fell's Guide to the Art of Cartooning

Interior Design: Roy Paul Nelson
Cover Design: Carol S. Joslin

Library of Congress Catalog Card Number: 87-70244

ISBN 0-697-00493-7

Printed in the United States of America
10 9 8 7 6 5 4 3 2

For JOHN L. HULTENG

Contents

Preface

Publication Design deals with a continuing problem in journalism: how to coordinate art and typography with content. Through text and illustration, the book suggests ways to make pages and spreads in magazines, newspapers, books, and other publications attractive and easy to read. As a book of techniques, it directs itself to potential and practicing art directors and designers and to editors who do their own designing.

It also directs itself to journalists in general and tries to build in them an appreciation for good graphic design. Even though these journalists may not be called upon to actually design and lay out pages, they may have the responsibility for hiring designers and approving their work. A goal of this book is to help editor and art director work together more harmoniously.

The first edition of the book noted a scarcity of material on publication design, especially magazine design, but soon afterward several excellent books appeared on the market. One came out just before this one and, by coincidence, bore the same title. The bibliographies at the ends of the chapters in this text list these books along with the scores of books on narrower aspects of design, such as typography and letterform, most of them published within the past ten years.

This book differs from other books on publication design and layout in that it concerns itself as much with editing as with design matters.

As a textbook, it documents its information, where possible, and tries to keep its author's biases in check. Where the author lays down rules, he tries to offer reasons. But these days the rules of design become increasingly difficult to defend as art directors experiment, often successfully, with exciting new arrangements and styles.

In its early chapters the book deals with publication design in general; later chapters narrow in on magazines, newspapers, books, and miscellaneous publications, including direct-mail pieces. Magazines get a little more attention than other media because the magazine look has so dominated the thinking of publication designers in recent years. Not that a newspaper should look like something other than a newspaper, or a book like something other than a book. There are differences to contend with, and the later chapters recognize them.

The book has been thoroughly revised and updated, of course. Illustrations that served well in earlier editions remain, but many new ones appear in each of the chapters. Much of what the book teaches comes from the captions, written from information supplied by the art directors and editors who granted reprint permission.

Since the publication of the first edition in 1972, the author has produced a monthly column on design for *IABC News* (renamed *Communication World* in 1982), a publication of the International Association of Business Communicators. More recently he has written design columns for *Northwest,* the Sunday magazine of *The Oregonian,* and *Magazine Design & Production,* a magazine for editors, art directors, and production people. An occasional section in this new edition draws from material appearing in these columns. Also, as was true of the first three editions, this one in its opening chapters relies in part on research conducted under a grant from the Magazine Publishers Association.

Publication Design serves as a textbook or supplemental reading for students in areas such as publication design and production, graphic design, graphic arts, typography, magazine editing, newspaper editing, picture editing, book publishing, publishing procedures, business and industrial journalism, public relations, and supervision of school publications. Previous editions found use, too, as a handbook for editors already on the job and, because of the numerous examples of innovative pages and spreads, as a source of inspiration for professional art directors and designers.

PUBLICATION DESIGN

A DREAM UP IN THE AIR

By Brian E. Albrecht

Distant thunder rolls from dark, sunset clouds, growing steadily louder as decidedly un-cloudlike shapes drop slowly toward Cleveland. Just enough light remains to define their ponderous dimensions in hues of purple and red; just enough darkness to veil their true identity.

Impact seems imminent. The once-distant thunder becomes a leaf-shaking roar, reverberating through the city. Traffic snarls; windows and doors burst open; eyes fix upward. Legions of pigeons on Public Square scatter in panic.

Holy helium! — The blimps are back!

Maybe. Ever since the Hindenburg's flaming demise in 1937, the rebirth of interest in airships has been spotty. But optimism soars among developers of a new generation of lighter-than-air (LTA) vehicle concepts launched in the past decade in the United States and Canada. CONTINUED ON PAGE 14

Illustration by Dennis Ziemienski

The article was about blimps, and so this art and design, although recent, took on a 1930s Art Deco look. A small box confined the copy to a left-hand page, starting up again later in the magazine. The article appeared in *The Plain Dealer Magazine* of the Cleveland *Plain Dealer* when Greg Paul was the magazine's design director. Dennis Ziemienski did the painting.

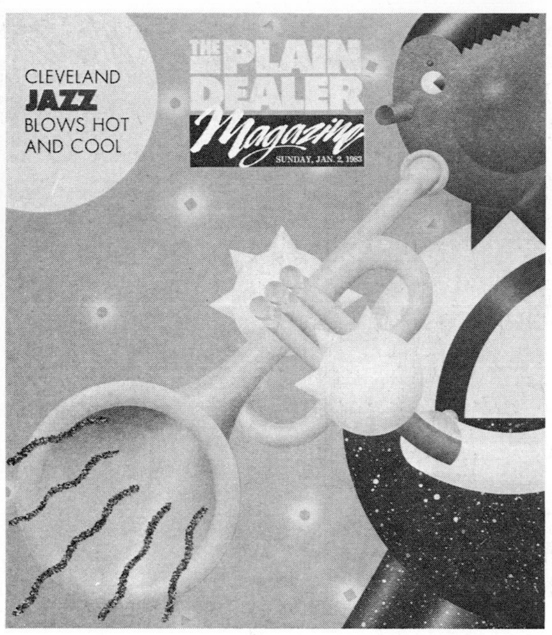

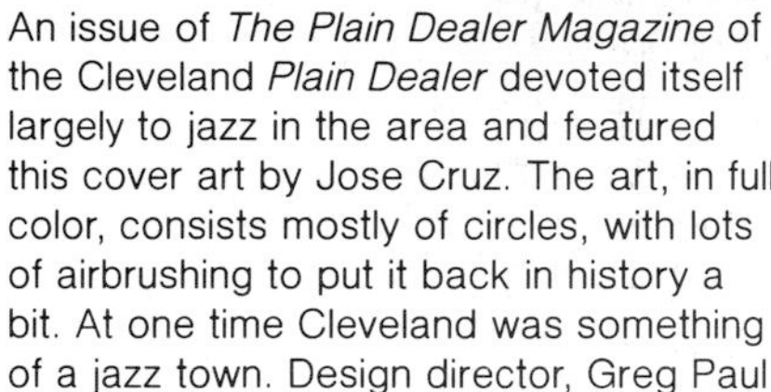
An issue of *The Plain Dealer Magazine* of the Cleveland *Plain Dealer* devoted itself largely to jazz in the area and featured this cover art by Jose Cruz. The art, in full color, consists mostly of circles, with lots of airbrushing to put it back in history a bit. At one time Cleveland was something of a jazz town. Design director, Greg Paul.

The emergence of publication design

Books produced in fifteenth-century Italy, after movable type was perfected by Johann Gutenberg in Germany, are prized today by museums and collectors as art of a high order. Bibliophiles see in these books a design and printing quality not found in latter-day publications. Their excellence is all the more remarkable when you consider that the men of incunabula had to design their own types, cut them, make their own inks and in some instances their own papers, write their own books or do their own translating of the classics, set their own type, do their own printing, and sell their own products.

Or maybe that explains the excellence. With so proprietary an interest in the product, fifteenth-century artisans gave appearance and readability all necessary attention. But when the demand for printing grew, printers found it expedient to subdivide the work. Some designed and cut types—exclusively. Others set type—exclusively. Others ran presses—exclusively. Others wrote and edited copy, while still others took care of business matters. Specialization set in and, inevitably, quality deteriorated.

By the time periodicals took their place alongside books as products of the press, page design was all but forgotten. Nobody elected to stay with the product through its various stages to see to it that it had, overall, the beauty and readability of earlier products of the press.

Then came photography and photoengraving. As art was combined with type on the page, the need for coordination of these elements became apparent. Because art, when it was used, tended to dominate the page, the people responsible for fitting type and art together became known, first, as art editors and, later, as art directors.

No one can say who functioned as the first publication art editor or art director. One of the first in this country, certainly, was Charles Parsons of the Harper & Brothers organization (now Harper & Row), publishers of books and magazines. It was Parsons who conceived the idea of gathering together a group of illustrators and schooling them in the needs of a publishing concern, also working with other artists on the outside as the need for art increased at certain times of the year. He became a director of art for both the book and magazine divisions of his company.[1]

Nearly all the illustrations in those days had to be hand engraved on wood. It was after Parsons resigned in 1889 that photoengraving became a reality and illustration—including photos—became a vital part of most magazines. *Harper's Weekly* and *Harper's Magazine* no longer stood alone as vehicles for illustrations. Every publication could run them.

Visual considerations for most publications then centered on the nature of the art they carried. The beauty and serviceability that could be derived from skillful and imaginative combinations of art with titles and columns of type had not yet been fully explored. Nor was the small page size any inducement to do more than give proper spacing to standard typefaces and center titles and other display faces. The first magazines, with single- or two-column pages, adopted a book look. And the newspapers' only design concern seemed to be their hunt for bolder types, the better to make headlines stand out on the page.

A major influence on all graphic designers in the 1920s and 1930s was the Bauhaus, a school that preached "form follows function." The architect Walter Gropius founded the Bauhaus at Weimar, Germany, in 1919. Young architects and artists from all over came to live and study there. The idea was to deal with materials "honestly" and to bring the arts—all arts—together to serve "the people." The school also sought to bring art and technology together. Socialism was fashionable at the time among those who taught, and the place was run as a sort of commune. Even diet was controlled.[2]

Hitler closed it down in 1933, but not before its austere, geometric, modular, highly controlled look had taken hold around the world. Its faculty members scattered, many to the United States, where they took up teaching and greatly affected architecture as well as graphic design.

Gropius became head of the architecture school at Harvard; Josef Albers started a Bauhaus-like school at Black Mountain College in North Carolina, then moved to Yale; Lazlo Moholy-Nagy opened the New Bauhaus in Chicago, which became the Chicago Institute of Design; Ludwig Mies van der Rohe became dean of architecture at the Armour Institute in Chicago, which became the Illinois Institute of Technology.

The style that grew out of the Bauhaus movement and took hold in America became known as International Typography. Even today "it is contemporary, cosmopolitan and sophisticatedly simple, and carries the impression of quality sought by corporations and institutions with a well-developed graphic image—primarily international corporations and cultural institutions," observes Professor David A. Wesson of the College of Journalism, Marquette University.[3]

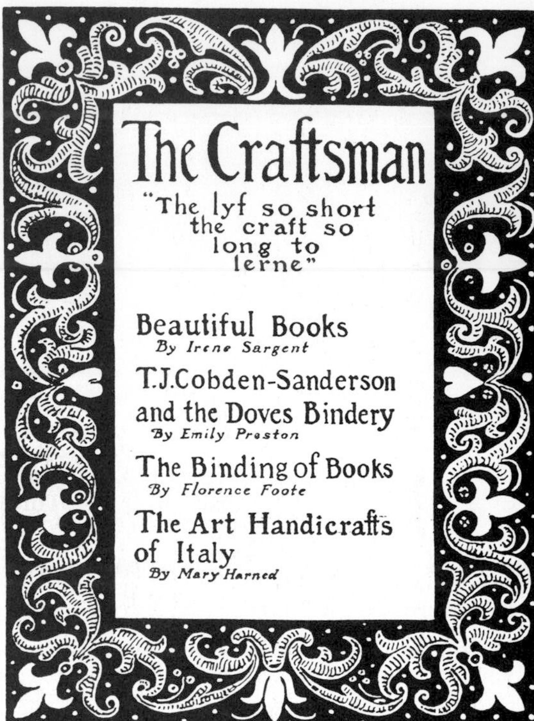

The cover of the April 1902 issue of *The Craftsman* has a hand-done quality to it. This was a magazine devoted to a return to arts and crafts in an industrialized society. Inside the magazine a forword promised that "no pains will be spared to make . . . [this] an acceptable and creditable issue."

The design of magazines

The magazines that, as a group, pioneered in good design were, understandably, the fashion books—especially *Harper's Bazaar*.[4] It was in 1916, after *Harper's Bazaar* had been purchased by William Randolph Hearst, that L'Aiglon Erté joined the staff. Erté was born Roman Tyrtov in Russia in 1892. (*Erte* comes from the French pronunciation of his initials: "Air-tay.") During his career he was widely admired as a fashion and set designer and artist as well as a graphic designer. An illustrator in the manner of Aubrey Beardsley, Erté introduced an entirely new visual sensibility to the magazine.[5]

In 1934 another Russian-born designer, Alexey Brodovitch, became *Harper's Bazaar* art director, a position he held until 1958. He sought to give the magazine what *Print* magazine later called "a musical feeling,

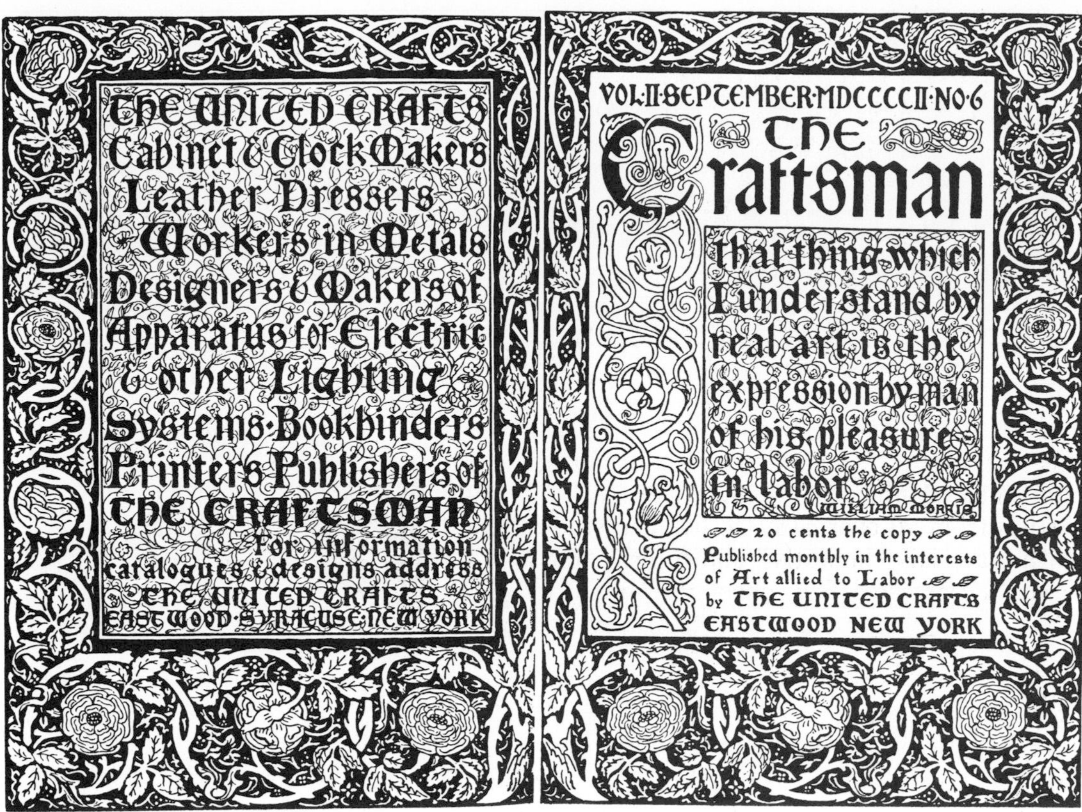

The back and front covers of a later 1902 issue of *The Craftsman* show the influence of William Morris. The back page is really a house ad for the publisher of the maggzine, United Crafts, Eastwood (Syracuse), New York.

a rhythm resulting from the interaction of space and time—he wanted the magazine to read like a sheet of music. He and [the editor] Carmel Snow would dance around the pages spread before them on the floor, trying to pick up the rhythm."

Brodovitch introduced to magazines the use of large blocks of white. For freshness, he used accomplished artists and photographers in types of work they had not tried before. At *Harper's Bazaar* he got Cartier-Bresson, Dali, Man Ray, and Richard Avedon to do fashions.

According to *Print,* Brodovitch "kept apprentices at his side much like an Old World master painter." He became famous not only as a designer but also as a photographer. He began teaching at the Philadelphia Museum in 1930, and among his students were soon-to-be magazine art directors Otto Storch, Henry Wolf, and Samuel Antupit and the photographer Irving Penn.

"This disarming, glum, elegant, shy, incredibly tough artist made an impact on the design of this country that eludes description to this day," said a writer for *U&lc.* "Measured on the quality of his graphic performances and his contributions to the modern magazine alone, he must be ranked as the towering giant of our time. . . . [He was] the master craftsman who began it all."[6]

At *Vogue* Heyworth Campbell was a force for innovative design. He served as art director from 1914 to 1928. Carmel Snow had been the editor at *Vogue* before taking over as editor at *Harper's Bazaar* in 1932, no doubt bringing some of Campbell's design thinking with her.[7]

Another leader in magazine design was Dr. M. F. Agha, who, with a degree in political science, became art director of *Vanity Fair* in 1929. Allen Hurlburt, director of design for Cowles Communications, said of Dr. Agha, "He entered areas of editorial judgment long denied to artists

274 THE CRAFTSMAN

The shaft, in these old monuments, is often carved with allusions to human life; the head with divine symbols. So here the patterns on the shaft form a kind of short pictorial biography, beginning at the bottom on the east, and going round with the sun.

The young Ruskin began as a poet, and attained some distinction as a verse-writer in magazines before ever he found his vocation as a writer of prose. Here under the arch at the foot of the stone is a young singer with his lyre and laurels, somewhat classical and not very passionately inspired. We rise through a tangle of interlacing before we come to his name, beneath his first great work, just as he had to live through some painful and perplexing years before he wrote himself large in "Modern Painters."

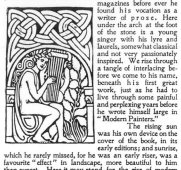

The rising sun was his own device on the cover of the book, in its early editions; and sunrise, which he rarely missed, for he was an early riser, was a favourite "effect" in landscape, more beautiful to him than sunset. Here it may stand for the rise of modern painting, the painting of Light in all its varieties. Sunbeams and level clouds, Turner's often repeated sky, are hardly a legitimate subject for sculpture, but this is not academic bas-relief; it is the kind of sketching in stone which the early carvers used, with complete disregard for what many take to be canons of art. It will be noticed

THE RUSKIN CROSS 275

that the surfaces are flat or nearly so; there is no modelling of the figures, and there is none of the usual flat ground out of which figures rise in true bas-relief. Incised outline and deep hollows for emphasis are alone used to tell the story; the intention being to preserve the simple decorative character of the work, considering the cross as a standing-stone fretted over with patterns like lace, not encrusted with sculptor's relief-carving. In this hard material and for this purpose and position the incised sketchy style has a use and legitimacy of its own, to which Mr. Ruskin has referred in a paragraph of "Aratra Pentelici:"—"You have, in the very outset and earliest stages of sculpture, your flat stone surface given you as a sheet of white paper, on which you are required to produce the utmost effect you can with the simplest means, cutting away as little of the stone as may be, to save both time and trouble; and, above all, leaving the block itself, when shaped, as solid as you can, that its surface may better resist weather, and the carved parts be as much protected as possible by the masses left around them."

The line of mountains from which the sun rises may recall the range of Mont Blanc from Geneva, and every reader of Ruskin knows how he has illustrated those aiguilles with pencil and pen, and how Geneva was the place where his book was first con-

This spread from *The Craftsman* makes room for a couple of inset illustrations. The article is about John Ruskin, the English art critic and social reformer.

and created a magazine that brought typography, illustration, photography, and page design into a cohesion that has rarely been equalled. After exposure to the severe test of more than thirty of the fastest changing years in history, the pages of *Vanity Fair* remain surprisingly fresh and exciting."[8] Hurlburt gave much credit, too, to Editor Frank Crowninshield for his "rare discernment and good taste."

Unfortunately, *Vanity Fair* became a Depression victim; but Dr. Agha continued his association with the Condé Nast organization until 1942 as art director of *Vogue* and *House and Garden.* Many of today's top designers trained under Dr. Agha.

A *U&lc.* writer said that Dr. Agha "forever altered the role of the editorial art director. . . . With innovative design, typography and layout, he shattered the restrictive style that was current." A native of Turkey, Dr. Agha was proud, arrogant, demanding. Nothing seemed to suit him. But he gained the respect of those who worked with him.[9]

Other trend-setters among magazine art directors in those days and later were Paul Rand, with *Apparel Arts,* and Bradbury Thompson, with *Mademoiselle* and several other magazines.

Still, the well-designed magazine was an exception. Well into the 1930s, most American magazines fitted themselves together, newspaper-style; when there was a column that didn't quite reach the bottom of the page, the editor simply threw in a filler. The job of any visually oriented person was primarily to buy illustrations, especially for the cover, and maybe to retouch photographs.

Two early-1930s books on magazine editing gave scant attention to art direction. John Bakeless in *Magazine Making* (Viking Press, New York, 1931) carried a six-page appendix on "Methods of Lay-Out." In it Bakeless discussed briefly a travel magazine that used "the daring device of

The Cosmopolitan of May 1895 was a far cry from Helen Gurley Brown's *Cosmopolitan* of the 1980s. Here's a spread from an article on "The Pleasant Occupation of Tending Bees." You see square-finish and vignette halftones, each with an all-caps caption. The two-column format was standard for 6 × 9 magazines in those days.

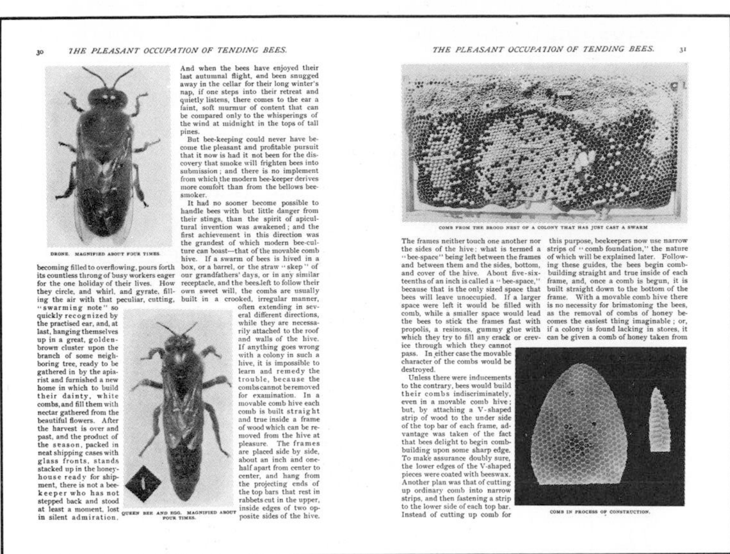

30 *THE PLEASANT OCCUPATION OF TENDING BEES.*

DRONE. MAGNIFIED ABOUT FOUR TIMES.

And when the bees have enjoyed their last autumnal flight, and been snugged away in the cellar for their long winter's nap, if one steps into their retreat and quietly listens, there comes to the ear a faint, soft murmur of content that can be compared only to the whisperings of the wind at midnight in the tops of tall pines.

But bee-keeping could never have become the pleasant and profitable pursuit that it now is had it not been for the discovery that smoke will frighten bees into submission; and there is no implement from which the modern bee-keeper derives more comfort than from the bellows bee-smoker.

It had no sooner become possible to handle bees with but little danger from their stings, than the spirit of apicultural invention was awakened; and the first achievement in this direction was the grandest of which modern bee-culture can boast—that of the movable comb hive. If a swarm of bees is hived in a box, or a barrel, or the straw "skep" of our grandfathers' days, or in any similar receptacle, and the bees left to follow their own sweet will, the combs are usually built in a crooked, irregular manner, often extending in several different directions, while they are necessarily attached to the roof and walls of the hive. If anything goes wrong with a colony in such a hive, it is impossible to learn and remedy the trouble, because the combs cannot be removed for examination. In a movable comb hive each comb is built straight and true inside a frame of wood which can be removed from the hive at pleasure. The frames are placed side by side, about an inch and one-half apart from center to center, and hang from the projecting ends of the top bars that rest in rabbets cut in the upper, inside edges of two opposite sides of the hive.

becoming filled to overflowing, pours forth its countless throng of busy workers eager for the one holiday of their lives. How they circle, and whirl, and gyrate, filling the air with that peculiar, cutting, "swarming note" so quickly recognized by the practised ear, and, at last, hanging themselves up in a great, golden-brown cluster upon the branch of some neighboring tree, ready to be gathered in by the apiarist and furnished a new home in which to build their dainty, white combs, and fill them with nectar gathered from the beautiful flowers. After the harvest is over and past, and the product of the season, packed in neat shipping cases with glass fronts, stands stacked up in the honey-house ready for shipment, there is not a bee-keeper who has not stepped back and stood at least a moment, lost in silent admiration.

QUEEN BEE AND EGG. MAGNIFIED ABOUT FOUR TIMES.

THE PLEASANT OCCUPATION OF TENDING BEES. 31

COMB FROM THE BROOD NEST OF A COLONY THAT HAS JUST CAST A SWARM

The frames neither touch one another nor the sides of the hive; what is termed a "bee-space" being left between the frames and between them and the sides, bottom, and cover of the hive. About five-sixteenths of an inch is called a "bee-space," because that is the only sized space that bees will leave unoccupied. If a larger space were left it would be filled with comb, while a smaller space would lead the bees to stick the frames fast with propolis, a resinous, gummy glue with which they try to fill any crack or crevice through which they cannot pass. In either case the movable character of the combs would be destroyed.

Unless there were inducements to the contrary, bees would build their combs indiscriminately, even in a movable comb hive; but, by attaching a V-shaped strip of wood to the under side of the top bar of each frame, advantage was taken of the fact that bees delight to begin comb-building upon some sharp edge. To make assurance doubly sure, the lower edges of the V-shaped pieces were coated with beeswax. Another plan was that of cutting up ordinary comb into narrow strips, and then fastening a strip to the lower side of each top bar. Instead of cutting up comb for this purpose, beekeepers now use narrow strips of "comb foundation," the nature of which will be explained later. Following these guides, the bees begin comb-building straight and true inside of each frame, and, once a comb is begun, it is built straight down to the bottom of the frame. With a movable comb hive there is no necessity for brimstoning the bees, as the removal of combs of honey becomes the easiest thing imaginable; or, if a colony is found lacking in stores, it can be given a comb of honey taken from

COMB IN PROCESS OF CONSTRUCTION.

Cartoons Magazine, published in Chicago early in this century, reprinted cartoons from around the world and ran illustrated articles on politics and social concerns. This right-hand page from a 1916 issue introduced a series of full-page cartoons by Louis Raemaekers, a Dutch artist who stood up to Germany during World War I. The French author of this short piece (the byline is at the end) said Raemaekers had "the verve of a Goya." The decorative border was characteristic of the period.

THE HEIGHT OF CIVILIZATION

A Series of Cartoons by Louis Raemaekers
Originally Published by the Amsterdam Telegraaf

HE is one of those who have shown the greatest ardor, the greatest courage—I would even say the greatest furor—in defending the cause of humanity and civilization, while mercilessly condemning the deeds that have forever branded Germany with the mark of the outlaw. Raemaekers is the Dutch artist who in the Amsterdam Telegraaf, and in a number of albums and separate prints, has unveiled in tragic visions the horror of murders, the unscrupulous breaches of faith, the atmosphere of death and suffering which the Austro-Germans and their accomplices have forced upon the world these weary months.

It was a bold act, especially during the early months of the war, to take the stand he did. Germany was angry and threatening, and Raemaekers was not safe, even in his own country. "Volunteers" ready to do murder for the sake of the "Fatherland" were as much in evidence there as in other neutral countries where conspirators are blowing up munition plants and firing ships.

Raemaekers' post cards have popularized valor. He has shown us in his phantasmagoric sketches victims of "Kultur" lifting their hands in vain appeals to heaven. He has made vitriolic attacks on the kaiser, especially in his sinister "wagon de marchandises" with its load of German corpses.

In brief, Raemaekers has done work, both as a thinker and an artist, for which France never can repay him. And it is with keen pleasure that French critics note his artistic debut among us. In "La Grande Guerre par les Artistes" he has given us a series of eight drawings that seem like dreams, but which breathe forth the most vehement satire. The verve of a Goya is displayed in them. The father and son galloping through the night, Wilhelm II and the crown prince—a curious counterpart to "Roi des Aulnes;" the big, ferocious general who assumes such an air of bravado and says jestingly: "I was the one who opened fire on the Rheims cathedral;" the ridiculous task of the official German painter who was obliged to change his picture of the triumphal entry into Paris for one into Belgrade; and finally, his superb and spirited "Advance of the Defenders of Liberty"—all masterpieces which should assure the artist the right of citizenship among us as he already has won it in the realm of art.—Arsene Alexandre in Le Figaro, Paris.

running a picture across all of one page and part of another." The book itself mentioned "art editor" twice and recommended at least one such person for "a large, illustrated periodical." Bakeless said that magazines using no pictures "obviously do not require an art editor."

Lenox R. Lohr in *Magazine Publishing* (Williams & Wilkins Company, Baltimore, 1932) devoted a chapter to illustrations and another to "Mechanics of Editing," but in them he gave only six pages to "Make-Up of an Issue."

One of the first nonfashion magazines to be fully designed was *Fortune,* introduced in February 1930 at a bold one dollar per copy. The designer was T. M. Cleland, who later set the format for the experimental newspaper *PM*.

In the 1940s Alexey Brodovitch designed a magazine that, with breathtaking beauty, showed other art directors what a well-designed magazine could be. Called *Portfolio,* it lasted three issues. That it was "ahead of its time" is probably an appropriate appraisal. In the late 1940s and early 1950s *Flair* (Louis-Marie Eude and later Herschel Bramson, art directors), although not universally admired by other art directors, encouraged format experimentation. That magazine also was short-lived. In the early 1960s *Show,* with Henry Wolf as art director, shook up magazine design thinking with imaginative covers and simple but elegant pages. *Show* soon died, too.

Stimulated by these thrusts, the well-established magazines began paying more attention to design. Allen Hurlburt took over as *Look's* art director in 1953 and gradually built the magazine, from a design standpoint, into one of the most admired in America. After the mid-1950s and "togetherness," Herbert Mayes, the new editor of *McCall's,* let his art director, Otto Storch, have a free hand: what Storch did with types and pictures prompted all magazines to make themselves more exciting visually. Prodded by what Arthur Paul was doing in design with the upstart *Playboy, Esquire* redesigned itself.

Hurlburt has noted a change in the art director's function with the coming of television. Before TV, the function of the art director, in an agency or on a magazine, was simply arranging things picked by others. With story boards for TV, the art director provided ideas, and the copywriter filled in with words. The art director became more important. As the art director's status improved in advertising agencies, it improved on magazines.

One of the important influences on magazine design in the 1960s in America was Push Pin Studios, New York. (A founder of Push Pin, Milton Glaser, was until 1977 design director of *New York.*) The organization was described by a magazine for the book trade as "one of the pioneering forces in developing an imaginative contemporary style that has had a major influence on the direction of current visual communications on an international scale."[10] The same magazine quoted the late Jerome Snyder, then art director of *Scientific American,* as saying that if imitation or plagiarism is any indication of flattery, Push Pin "is by far the most flattered group in contemporary graphics."[11] "The growing reputation has allowed Push Pin the luxury of a healthy snobbishness in their acceptance of assignments, and potential clients have been conditioned into calling on Push Pin only when they were ready to accept the excellence of their work without too many suggestions for 'improvement,' " Henry Wolf wrote in the foreword to *The Push Pin Style.*[12]

The individual who was most involved with the design direction taken by magazines in the 1960s and 1970s, most would say, was Herb Lubalin. Many younger designers can trace their design attitudes to his work. He was also a type designer and a typographer with an inventive flair, but he held readability to be more important than aesthetics. He designed or redesigned *Eros, Saturday Evening Post, Reader's Digest, Signature,* and *Sport,* among others. He also designed the logo for *Family Circle* and *Families.* He was editor of *U&lc.,* a magazine devoted to creative typography.

When he died in 1981, *The New Leader* devoted an obit editorial to Lubalin. He had redesigned the magazine in 1961, giving it a bold new look. He redesigned it again in 1969, to bring it up to date, making it one

Tadeusz Gronowski of Poland designed this busy Art Deco cover for the July 1928 issue of *Gebrauchsgraphik International* magazine.

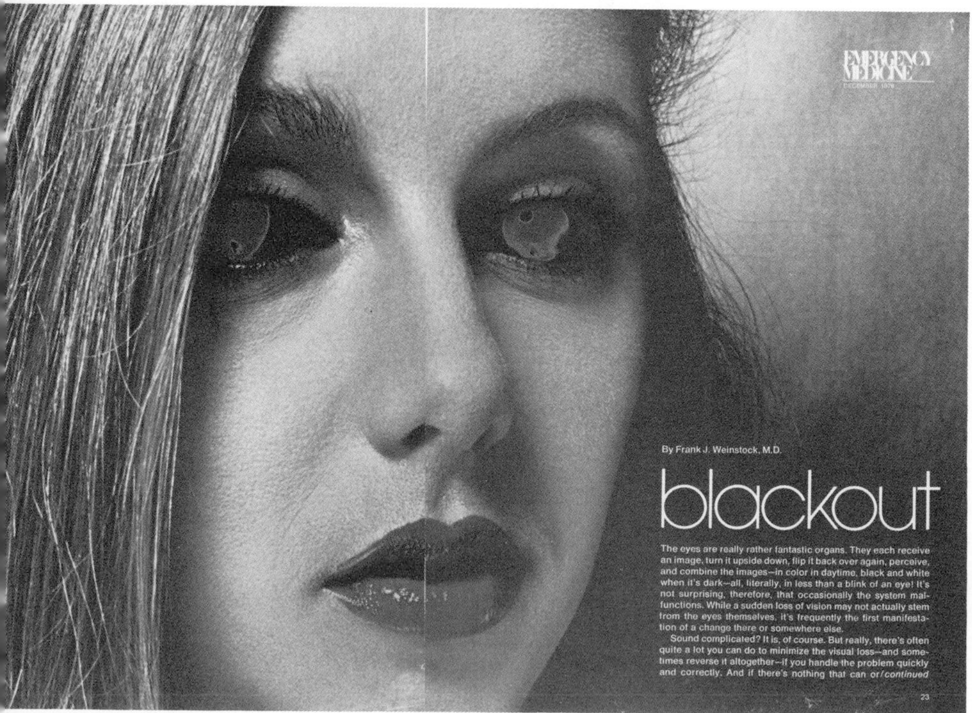

EMERGENCY MEDICINE

By Frank J. Weinstock, M.D.

blackout

The eyes are really rather fantastic organs. They each receive an image, turn it upside down, flip it back over again, perceive, and combine the images—in color in daytime, black and white when it's dark—all, literally, in less than a blink of an eye! It's not surprising, therefore, that occasionally the system malfunctions. While a sudden loss of vision may not actually stem from the eyes themselves, it's frequently the first manifestation of a change there or somewhere else.

Sound complicated? It is, of course. But really, there's often quite a lot you can do to minimize the visual loss—and sometimes reverse it altogether—if you handle the problem quickly and correctly. And if there's nothing that can or/*continued*

23

A dramatic and powerful spread from *Emergency Medicine* making use of a large face in full color. The face is large enough and cropped close enough to run across the gutter. The size was necessary to make the fogged-over eyes readable. The article starts out as reverse copy. Because this is an opening article occurring in the magazine after several pages of advertising, the editors ran a small logo at the top.

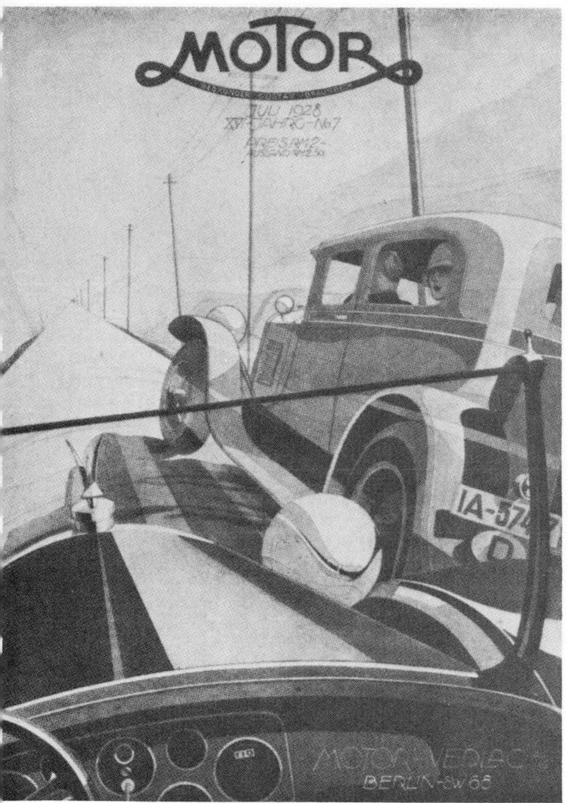

Bernd Reuters, a German, did this perspective illustration for the July 1928 cover of *Motor* magazine. The centered logo is designed to look a little like an automobile's hood and grill, complete with headlights.

of the handsomest of the struggling opinion magazines. Lubalin also helped the magazine with some of its special issues and covers. *The New Leader* commented: "He worked with a speed and ease that awed his contemporaries, his left-hand scratches producing tissues that put other people's finished pieces to shame. He could make type talk and turn its thousands of faces into pictures. His own type creations married the classical to the modern with powerful clarity, extending his reputation worldwide."[13]

Also wielding influence on magazine design in the 1960s was Willie Fleckhaus, who art directed two magazines published in Europe, *Tuyonne* and *Twen.*

Many magazines in the 1960s, especially those published by big corporations for public relations reasons, took on what became known as the Swiss Gothic look: clean, orderly, somewhat stilted. Some other maga-

PUBLISHER AND EDITOR-IN-CHIEF
LEDA GIOVANNETTI SANFORD
EDITOR
DONALD DEWEY
DESIGN DIRECTOR
PAUL HARDY
SENIOR EDITORS
GWENDA BLAIR, STEPHEN S. HALL, JOSEPH MANCINI
MANAGING EDITOR
ELLEN GOLDENSOHN
ART DIRECTOR
MARLOWE GOODSON
COPY EDITOR
KATE JENNINGS
ASSOCIATE EDITOR
JEAN GRASSO FITZPATRICK
ASSISTANT EDITORS
WENDY FISHER, CHRISTINE LORD
ASSOCIATE ART DIRECTOR
MILES ABERNETHY
ART ASSISTANTS
LINDA BEALE, ROSINE WEISBECKER
CONTRIBUTING EDITORS
NICHOLAS ACOCELLA, JULIAN BEES, MARGERY FRIESNER-BELLECCA, RICHARD GAMBINO, JOSEPH GIORDANO, THEODORA LURIE, ANTHONY MANCINI, CHARLES MANN, JOHN MARIANI, GEORGE SHEA, WILLIAM WEAVER
ASSOCIATE PUBLISHER
ALDO IAVARONE
PRODUCTION COORDINATOR
ROBERT SANFORD
PRODUCTION ASSISTANT
BARBARA ROSENFELD
CIRCULATION DIRECTOR
HARVEY SWAINE
FULFILLMENT MANAGER
SUZANNE OVAITTE
PUBLIC AFFAIRS COORDINATOR
LOIS TUREL
ASSISTANT TO THE PUBLISHER
VINCENZA GINA MAZZURCO
OFFICE MANAGER
BARBARA ZAPPA
BUSINESS COORDINATOR
RHODA LEVENBERG
BUSINESS ASSISTANT
LINDA GRECO
ADVERTISING DIRECTOR
MARY MEINELT

Jeno F. Paulucci, Chairman and Chief Executive Officer; Michael J. Paulucci, President; Robert E. Heller, Secretary and General Counsel; Robert L. Cotton, Treasurer; Leda Sanford, Chief Operating Officer

28 The tragic earthquake last November may prove to be the most important event in postwar Italy, focusing attention not only on the massive reconstruction effort, but also on the future of the impoverished Mezzogiorno.

36 Ever read a restaurant critic more interested in discussing antimatter than antipasto? Meet Fabian Plotnick (alias Woody Allen), who lampoons high-toned food reviewers in his short story "Fabrizio's: Criticism and Response."

58 For ailing teenagers Virin and Nick, life means an endless cycle of drugs, injections, and blood transfusions—all in a battle against a fatal genetic disorder whose very treatment hastens death.

38 All that glitters is not gold, and everything you buy at a bargain—watches, clothing, and luggage—is not always the real thing. How can you distinguish a fake from the genuine article?

2 FEBRUARY 1981

Attenzione

FEBRUARY 1981 VOL. 3, NO. 2

ATTENZIONE (USPS 482-930) is published monthly by Paulucci Publications, Inc., 10 East 49th Street, New York, NY 10017. Subscriptions: $24.00 a year, USA; $27.00, Canada; $30.00 foreign (surface mail only). Controlled circulation postage paid at Milwaukee, WI and New York, NY. POSTMASTER: Send address changes to ATTENZIONE, P.O. Box 943, Farmingdale, NY 11737. Copyright © 1980 by Paulucci Publications. Published in the United States. All rights reserved. Reproduction in whole or in part without permission is strictly prohibited. Member, Magazine Publishers Association. ABC membership applied for.

30 In an age when glass skyscrapers looked like the last word in architecture, Robert Venturi championed some unlikely sources of inspiration for design: Las Vegas and Levittown.

42 Italian grandmothers started a trend that has cooks across America making their own pasta. Turn to page 42 for our step-by-step instructions.

48 Pope John Paul II's denunciation of "adultery in the heart" is the take-off point for a free-wheeling Attenzione symposium on the effect of the church on Italian Americans. Six prominent Catholics give their views.

ATTENZIONE 3

Attenzione, a magazine for Italian-Americans, devotes two pages to its table of contents and includes on those pages a masthead (far left) and, on both sides of the listing of articles, pieces of art, large page numbers, and blurbs about major articles and features. Paul Hardy is design director.

FASHION

THE HOUSE OF MISSONI

BY GWENDA BLAIR

Question: When is a sweater more than just a sweater? Answer: When it is an ultrachic knit inspired by folk designs and produced by Ottavio and Rosita Missoni in a small factory outside Milan. When it has the Missoni name on it, a winter warmer could sell for three hundred dollars in Italy, fifty percent more abroad, or even end up in New York's Metropolitan Museum of Art. And unlike the peasant traditions which have influenced the husband and wife team, the Missoni fashion imprint shows no signs of fading. The next generation of Missonis (sons Vittorio and Luca, daughter Angela, and daughter-in-law Susanna) is already geared to carrying on the firm's unique ability to combine flair and simplicity for the style-conscious.

Rosita Missoni designs the garments and oversees the family operation.

Ottavio, known to all as "Tai," creates the fabrics.

Vittorio, the oldest of the Missoni children, is in the financial and marketing end of the business.

38 SEPTEMBER 1980

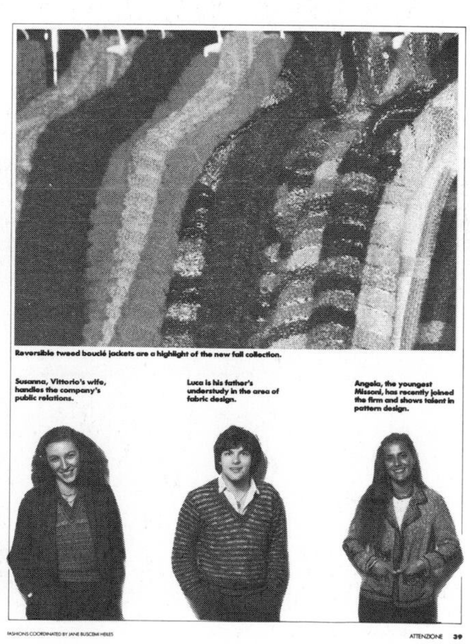

Reversible tweed bouclé jackets are a highlight of the new fall collection.

Susanna, Vittorio's wife, handles the company's public relations.

Luca is his father's understudy in the area of fabric design.

Angela, the youngest Missoni, has recently joined the firm and shows talent in pattern design.

ATTENZIONE 39

Full-color silhouetted figures, a couple of other smaller silhouettes, a large photo showing jacket textures, and an across-the-page blurb give this two-page opener for *Attenzione* its impact. The article settles down to a four-column-per-page format (not seen) after this opener. Missoni is a classy sweater maker of Italy. The people shown are principals in the firm—all members of the Missoni family. *Attenzione* on many pages, as here, combines a Speedball-pen-like sans serif title face with a lightweight slab serif body face.

zines during that period moved in an opposite direction. Influenced by the political and social unrest of the period, they became purposely chaotic. Some were dazzling and spectacular. But the design seemed *fitted on* rather than fully integrated. *Print* called the look "stupifying shallow."

In the 1970s magazines seemed to enter a new era: the emphasis was on content. *Communication Arts* and *Print* in 1970 both put out special issues on magazine design. Both were critical of what they had seen in the 1960s. The magazine industry, they agreed, was in a bad way because it had not adjusted to the times—not in content, not in design. Both agreed that flashy graphics often covered up a lack of solid content. And the graphics were not of a kind to delight the eye.

The chief problems were those of slickness and sameness. *Print* said major magazines looked alike because their art directors played musical chairs, moving from magazine to magazine, "spreading their best ideas and perpetuating their worst mistakes." Dugald Stermer, ex-art director for *Ramparts,* was quoted as saying, "This makes magazines very inbred, almost incestuous."

"On the whole," said Henry Wolf in 1978, "I don't think it's a terrific time for us designers. We're lucky if there's a magazine out today which is as good as it was if it's been around for more than 10 years. If you look at *McCall's,* at *Holiday,* at *Esquire,* nothing is as good. It's all scaled down, all unified. . . . It's all very much what happened to American cars. In the 30's, they were wonderful. They generally made their own motors—Dusenberg, Pierce Arrow, Reo. Now they make one motor, and it fits the Chevrolet and Cadillac alike."[14]

Art Direction noted a "new graphics" in the early 1980s, saying it originated in this country in *Wet* in the 1970s and in Andy Warhol's *Interview.* It was inspired by punk rock and by a design movement at Basal, Switzerland. *Essence, New York,* and *Mademoiselle* were among the magazines to pick it up. There were lots of lines and lots of dots, lots of mortises, lots of diagonals, lots of letterspacing. Designers of the old school saw it as a celebration of amateurism, with most of the standard rules of design gleefully broken.[15]

Just as the "new wave" defied design convention, it defied editorial convention by making editorial material nonexistent or secondary to advertising. The magazines' staffs designed much of the advertising—from

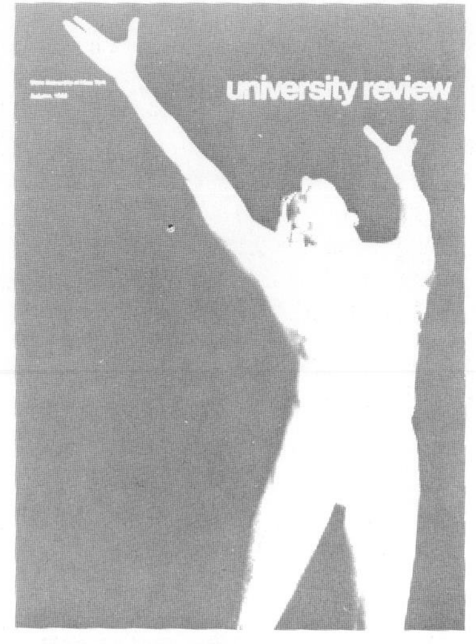

University Review, published by the State University of New York, was one of the best-designed alumni magazines in the country in the 1960s. For this issue the designer Richard Danne reused on the cover a portion of some inside art to tie the cover to a lead article. The cover is in dark blue and light green. The inside pages are in stark black and white. The bottom of the copy block area remains constant while the art goes through an evolution right before the readers' eyes. The photographer was Herman Bachmann.

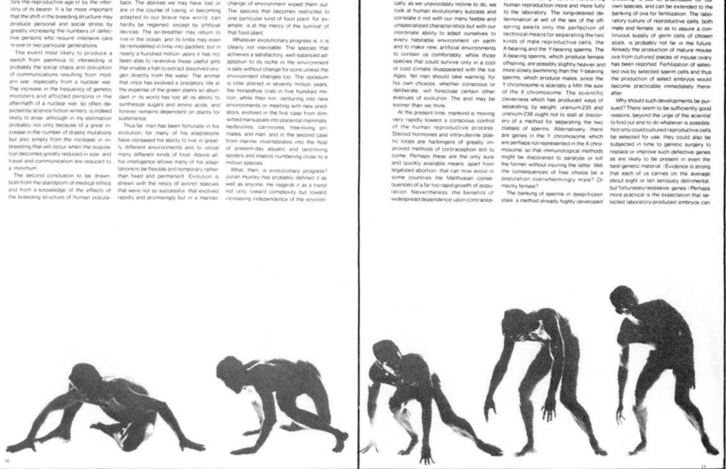
Bentley Glass

EVOLUTION and the Ethical Challenge

Rolling Stone introduces an "Inside the Gun Lobby" article on a red, white, and blue cover—actually starts it there—and continues it on inside pages. The big-type treatment for *GUN* on the cover repeats itself inside to help the reader get started again. (From *Rolling Stone* #343, May 14, 1981, published by Straight Arrow Publishers, Inc. © 1981. All rights reserved, Reprinted by permission.)

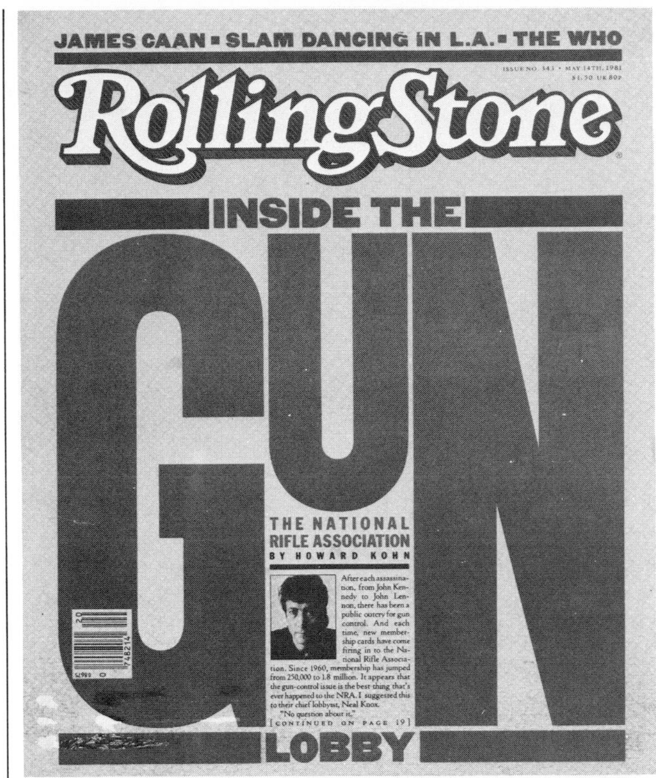

JAMES CAAN ■ SLAM DANCING IN L.A. ■ THE WHO

Rolling Stone

INSIDE THE GUN LOBBY

THE NATIONAL RIFLE ASSOCIATION
BY HOWARD KOHN

After each assassination, from John Kennedy to John Lennon, there has been a public outcry for gun control. And each time, new membership cards have come firing in to the National Rifle Association. Since 1960, membership has jumped from 250,000 to 1.8 million. It appears that the gun-control issue is the best thing that's ever happened to the NRA. I suggested this to their chief lobbyist, Neal Knox. "No question about it."

[CONTINUED ON PAGE 19]

specialty stores—and occasionally rejected ads that didn't meet design standards. Among these mostly-advertising magazines were *Manhattan Catalogue* (New York), *Boulevards* (San Francisco), and *Stuff* (Los Angeles). "People try to copy *Boulevards,*" its art director, Ross Carron, said in 1980, "and art students seem to use it as a Bible. If they only knew how little time we put into it."[16]

The "new wave" subsided somewhat in the 1980s, but the fashion magazines, at least, continued to be trendy and experimental. What you saw done with type and photographs in, say, *Mademoiselle,* you were not likely to see done in *Scientific American, Smithsonian,* or *Sports Illustrated.*

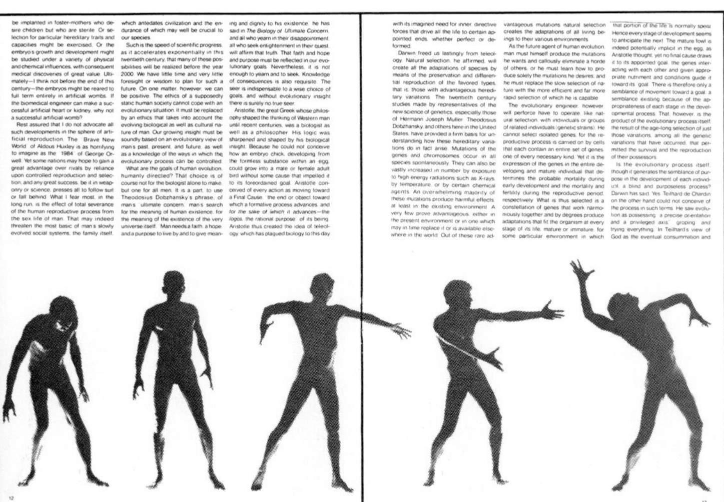

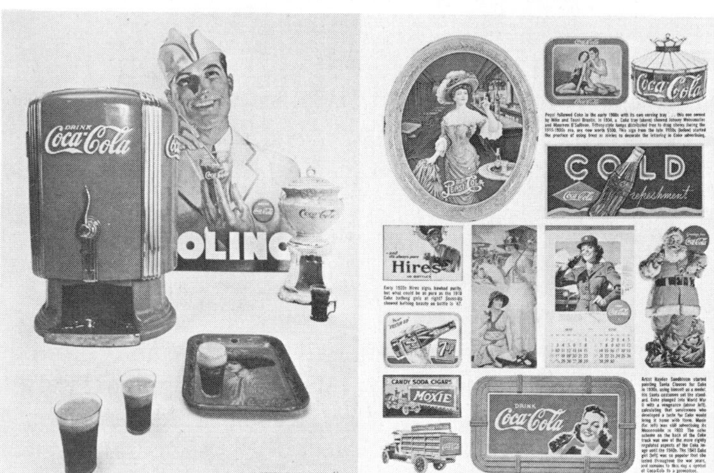

Long before launching its new Sunday magazine in 1985, the Los Angeles *Times* published a Sunday magazine called *West*. *West*'s art director, Mike Salisbury, flew from Los Angeles to Atlanta to dig up the art for this article on Coca-Cola and its advertising gimmicks. "The signs, bottles, matchbooks, and trays—some of which are now collectors' items—are as American as . . . well . . . Coke itself," says the blurb. (The article is copyrighted by Lawrence Dietz. Used by permission.)

"Fashion is concerned with style and change," said Judy Schiern Hecker, art director of *Young Miss*. It was not enough for an art director simply to go with current fashions in design. "You have to have a sense of what's in the air, a sense of what's coming. This has helped me to choose type with a special feeling."[17]

Les Line, editor of *Audubon,* noted the "cookie-cutter layouts" used by many magazines. Part of the problem lay with the economies that magazines had to take. "Magazines no longer have the luxury of taking a blank page, running a lettuce leaf in the corner and following that with a full page of salad," said Maxine Davidowitz, art director of *Redbook*. "Readers have less time. They want information, not just fluff."[18]

Some of the best design of the 1980s could be seen in specialized publications. The editors of specialized magazines, realizing that their readers were accustomed to exciting visuals from sources other than magazines, attempted to make their magazines just as exciting to look at as the new films, the new products, the new paintings. These editors didn't have to buck tradition. They served homogeneous audiences. They had less to lose.

One of the most exciting groups of magazines to watch were the company magazines—sometimes called "house organs." Some of the very best graphic design could be found in this group—and some of the very worst. In one respect, these magazines were an art director's dream. They car-

DESIGN

Not Just Jazz, a tabloid devoted to the artist, "whatever his chosen form," gave a page over to an interview with Tom Carnase, a graphic designer known especially for his logos and his imaginative use of typography.

The social sun shines on in Saratoga Springs each August. Joan Shipman Payson turns her binoculars from the pitching mound to the starting gate. John Galbreath trots out his racing stable. And Sonny and Mary Lou open up Cady Hill to the very blue of blood. Over at the Gideon, folks are paying $75 per for the colonial atmosphere and mineral water, and the robust ghosts of Nick the Greek, Diamond Jim Brady and Polly Adler and friends frolic about the elegant lobby.

SARATOGA SPRINGS: ONCE MORE, WITH BREEDING

By JOE FLAHERTY

A crowded two pages from the old *West* magazine (Mike Salisbury, art director). The art is by James McMullan of Visible Studios, Inc., New York.

Saving the Soil While Pumping Oil

Clean Water for an Iowa Community

The clean, orderly, and somewhat stilted Swiss gothic look of the 1950s and 1960s continues to be popular with many magazines in the 1980s, including *Soil and Water Conservation News.* For this and every spread in the magazine, the 2-inch sink and the thin horizontal lines remain the same. This spread accommodates two complete articles: one long, one short. The two heavy bars mark the articles' endings and lift out the legends about the authors. With organization this tight, it would be a good idea to add a line of copy to the second article and place the second legend parallel to the first legend. Also, the caption on the left-hand page would work better a little wider.

DON B. KATES JR.

GUN CONTROL:

Can it work?

States which have had the lowest homicide rates have had the most lax gun laws

'No research worthy of the name has been done on the issue of gun control'

Thick horizontal lines and thin ones work together with repetitious art here to create a highly organized but pleasant motif for an article in *National Review* on gun control. Note the "no guns" sign with bullet holes in it. James W. O'Bryan art directed.

ried no advertising around which editorial matter had to wrap. The design theme could run through without interruption. That many company magazines had no flair could be attributed to the fact that their budgets precluded hiring art directors; they remained undesigned. And many others were designed in outside shops, inhibiting thorough integration of design and editorial matter.

Of all magazine groups, the trade journals—or "businesspapers" as they are sometimes called—were probably the least design conscious. Excepting those going to physicians, architects, and similar professional groups, these magazines—especially the smaller ones—were "laid out" by editors rather than designed by art directors. Some of the magazines were so dominated by ads that art directors found few concentrations of space to use for extended editorial display.

Mary Lynn Blasutta, who studied with Milton Glaser in New York, nicely imitated the style of a colleague of Glaser's, Seymour Chwast, in executing this cover for *The Plain Dealer Magazine*. The butterflies coming from the stomach of the man tell you that, indeed, the poor fellow *is* "Scared Speechless." The cover and blurb refer to an article inside on "Speechmaking: How the Veterans Do It." Greg Paul was the art director for this magazine, published by the Cleveland *Plain Dealer*.

The design of newspapers

One man who helped give newspapers better design was Edmund C. Arnold, who was head of the graphic arts department of Syracuse University's School of Journalism and later taught at Virginia Commonwealth University. He redesigned a number of major newspapers and served as consultant to the Mergenthaler Linotype Corporation. Professor Arnold, in his frequent lectures to conventions of newspaper personnel and in his numberless articles and books, pounded home his admirable dicta: wider columns, no column rules, more white space, all-lowercase headlines.

Still, with Arnold and other more recent designers, consultants, and educators working with editors in a period of rapidly changing typesetting and printing technology, newspapers continued to hold onto many of their old practices. Publisher Gardner Cowles put his finger on the problem at a meeting of the William Allen White Foundation at the University of Kansas: "A good newspaper needs a good art director. When I say this, most editors don't know what I am talking about. On successful magazines, the art director ranks right below the top editor in importance and authority. He has a strong voice in helping decide how a story idea is to be developed. He suggests ways to give it maximum visual impact. He knows how to blend type and photographs so that each helps the other. His responsibility is to make each page come alive and intrigue the reader. Newspapers need this kind of talent. Too few have it."

SCIENCE ON PARADE

Join us for a million-year voyage from the interstellar dark to the luminous realm of the Earth and Sun

A RIDE ON A COMET

BY CARL SAGAN AND ANN DRUYAN

MR. HALLEY'S COMET RETURNS AGAIN

He was the first to predict accurately the return of a comet

Parade, with art direction by Ira A. Yoffe, presents a spread crowded with much type, several headings, two blurbs, captions, three initial letters, six pieces of art, lines and bars, and a sidebar (far right). Despite all that is involved, the spread is handsome and inviting. The titles for the article and sidebar use caps and small caps. The exceptionally large off-to-the-side initial letter (a sort of trademark of *Parade*) is followed by a line of body copy in all-caps. The photographs are in full color, and the sidebar carries a tan-pink tint to set itself apart from the article.

Newsweek International, sister publication of *Newsweek,* gathered three large photographs (two of them the same size) in this spread and ran them across the gutter, along with a red bar, to unite the pages. Small photographs below provide visual relief for the columns of copy. The titles for the short articles (these pages are part of a many-page feature on Japan) involve all-caps "kickers," underlines, and bigger-type lowercase lines of type, all flush left. Alfred Lowry is art director.

Shopping for fruit in the local market: 'I always wonder if it isn't possible, somehow, to live a different kind of life'

To the Grocery Born

'Young people today are too lighthearted'

Lord of the Streets

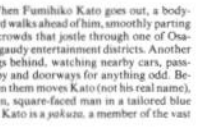

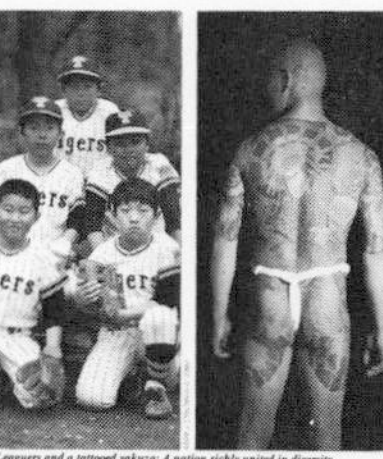

Little Leaguers and a tattooed yakuza: A nation richly united in diversity

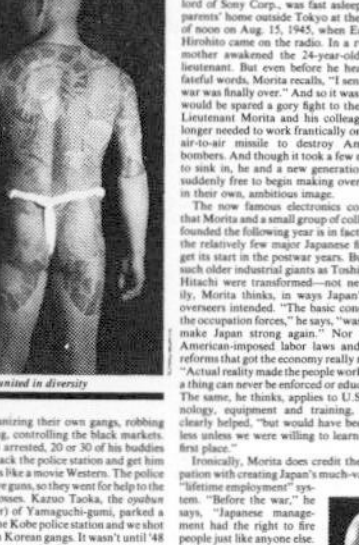

Out of the Ashes, Sony

A news day like this, with all its memorable photographs, cries for dramatic treatment, and it got it on a St. Cloud *Daily Times* front page. A severely horizontal photograph at the top contrasts with a larger, vertical photograph below, which contrasts with a small mug shot at the left. Two other small photographs complete the art on the page. The two heavy horizontal bars are in color. And some of the color shows up, too, in the insignia above *TUESDAY.*

Partly Cloudy

City waiting for response to sewer proposal/**1C**
School boards to fight joint bargaining plan/**1C**
Mille Lacs Indians won't contest fishing law/**1C**

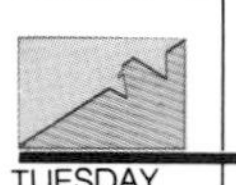

March, 31, 1981

St. Cloud Daily Times

St. Cloud, Minnesota 56301

TUESDAY

Reagan recovering quickly

Aide still in serious condition

Two secret service agents shove President Reagan into his limousine after he was shot outside a Washington hotel Monday.

Shooting disrupts routines

Hinckley called loner

More showers expected this week

Inside the Times TODAY

Outstanding parents

Assassination attempt

Index

Teller, published by the Royal Bank of Canada, combines colorful art and typography for lead articles with a more subdued look for standing features. This news section makes use of horizontal lines, sans serif headline faces, roman body copy, and numbered pictures and could be considered an example of Swiss gothic design.

Annual Meeting

President Raps Government White Paper

Among the first papers to employ art directors were the Chicago *Tribune*, New York *Times*, Providence *Journal* and *Bulletin*, Miami *Herald*, *Newsday* (Long Island), and *Today* (Cocoa, Florida). *The Bulletin* of the American Society of Newspaper Editors ran a report in the early 1970s on the duties of art directors and concluded that any newspaper with a circulation of more than 50,000 needed the services of one. *The Bulletin* correctly predicted that the idea of art directors for newspapers would spread.

Evidence of growing interest in design among newspaper people could be seen in the founding in 1979 of the Society of Newspaper Design. By 1983 the society listed 1,000 members. Also the American Press Institute at Reston, Virginia, held frequent seminars on newspaper design.

When design help came to newspapers, it came increasingly from outside the fraternity. It came from graphic designers with magazine or advertising agency experience who were fast enough and flexible enough to deal with multiple daily deadlines and late-breaking news and, more important, who were capable of making editorial as well as art and design decisions. It came from graphic designers who were verbally as well as visually literate.

The design of books

Although good design was very much a part of early books, it was forgotten as books became more readily available to the masses. Mechanical typesetting equipment and a great variety of new—and mostly vulgar—typefaces in the nineteenth century were partly to blame. Near the turn of the century, one man in England, William Morris, fighting the trend, revived the earlier roman types and brought hand craftsmanship back into vogue. But only a few books were affected. W. A. Dwiggins in 1920 observed that "all books of the present day are badly made. . . . The book publishing industry has depraved the taste of the public."

But design was returning to books. In England, people like Eric Gill and in America, people like Daniel Berkeley Updike, Bruce Rogers, Will Bradley, Merle Armitage, and Thomas Maitland Cleland restored bookmaking to the high art it once had been. Dwiggins himself became a design consultant to Alfred A. Knopf, a publisher who then and now has produced some of America's finest books, from the standpoint of both content and design. Adrian Wilson called Knopf "perhaps the greatest influence on the making of books in America after World War I." From 1926 to 1956 Dwiggins designed an average of ten books a year for the publisher. "His salty typography and ornament were additional hallmarks of the Knopf firm, the assurance of an inviting page and pleasurable reading."[19] Others who designed for Knopf were Warren Chappell, Herbert Bayer, Rudolf Ruzicka, and George Salter. These designers combined classic roman faces with appropriate decorative borders.

Still, to most publishers of popular books, design was not much of a consideration. In more expensive books design played a role, but often it looked as if it was an afterthought, something tacked on just before the book went to press. For many books no one designer took charge.

With the coming of television, with increased competition from other media, with a growing appreciation of visual beauty even among the less sophisticated book buyers, this situation changed. Textbooks, especially, took on a more exciting look both outside and inside. One reason textbook publishers were willing to devote extra effort to design was that mass

BEFORE THE DAWN

by TOYOHIKO KAGAWA

TRANSLATED FROM THE JAPANESE
BY I. FUKUMOTO AND T. SATCHELL

GEORGE H. DORAN COMPANY
ON MURRAY HILL : : NEW YORK

This 1924 title page spaces out its type to line up left and right margins and utilizes decorative borders and the publisher's trademark in its design. All the type is in caps. Note the punctuation used to separate *MURRAY HILL* from *NEW YORK*.

BEFORE THE DAWN

CHAPTER I

At Meiji University

⌘ ⌘ ⌘ ⌘ ⌘ ⌘ ⌘ ⌘ ⌘ ⌘ ⌘ ⌘ ⌘ ⌘ ⌘

THERE is a place near Shirokané in Shiba, Tokyo, where three valleys meet. There everything is fresh and green; only in the dank places of the ravine, where last year's rice-stubs have not been ploughed up, is the ground bare. In the depth of the valley nearest to Osaki, where grow innumerable cryptomerias, whose tops seem to reach above the clouds, stands Marquis Ikeda's mansion. On the hill nearest Shirokané there are one or two temples, but on the middle hill there are neither houses nor temples; only slender chestnuts and oaks grow in great profusion.

On a glorious day at the beginning of May, a youth was lying in the shade on the grass on the middle hill reading a book. He looked above the medium height,—a slender figure, dressed in a well-fitting black woollen uniform, the brass buttons of which were all marked with the letters "M.G." His face was dreadfully pale, his nose high, and his cheek bones a little prominent. His eyes were rather large and keen, and their shape showed their owner to be high-spirited.

He was in the habit of coming to this place at intervals and opening a book, though of late not reading it very attentively. Rather he would shut his eyes and fall into a muse,—not of long duration, for he soon became sleepy. His dream over he would quickly turn to his book again, repeat some three or four lines, and then hasten back towards Shirokané along the field paths.

17

The first chapter opening repeats the book's title before showing the chapter number and chapter title.

Literary Classics of the United States, New York, is republishing a series of important books by early American writers, all in a handsome, readable, standard format (5 × 8⅛) worked out by Bruce Campbell. This spread comes from the Herman Melville volume. Good book design often asks only for careful choice of type, usually of modest size, and subtle and consistent spacing, with maybe a thin rule used here and there. Illustrations often are not necessary; in fact they can intrude.

adoptions of these books were often dependent on their appearance. Furthermore, the average textbook enjoyed greater total sales than the average tradebook, which meant that more could be spent in anticipation of sales.

Some of the best design was found in the products of the university presses. Feeling less pressure than commercial publishers felt to show a profit, they could afford to devote a larger percentage of their budgets to design and printing.

The design of miscellaneous publications

Periodicals and books accounted for only part of the money spent for printing and only part of the activities of editors, writers, designers, and artists. There arose in the twentieth century a vast print medium subculture consisting of one-shots, infrequently issued publications, direct-mail pieces, newsletters, and shoestring operations.

The term "miscellaneous publications" hardly describes this array of printed pieces, but no other term functions any better. Every conceivable format was involved; and few persons associated with print media escaped producing such pieces. Nobody escaped reading them. Even regularly issued publications produced miscellaneous publications—to increase their audiences, to impress advertisers, to communicate with their employees, to comply with the law.

These publications ranged from elaborate printed pieces of cloth, leather, and materials other than paper to scruffy sheets of newsprint that were barely decipherable. They cost their sponsors anywhere from a penny or two to several dollars a unit. It is impossible to estimate the total funds that have gone into these pieces, but the amount, if it could be calculated, would be staggering.

Every one of these pieces had to be designed.

Many of them were designed by people who didn't know what they were doing. Others got the attention of the most accomplished designers.

Among these publications were some of the most beautiful and read-

234 TYPEE

plied. To read pathetic accounts of missionary hardships, and glowing descriptions of conversions, and baptisms taking place beneath palm-trees, is one thing; and to go to the Sandwich Islands and see the missionaries dwelling in picturesque and prettily-furnished coral-rock villas, whilst the miserable natives are committing all sorts of immoralities around them, is quite another.

In justice to the missionaries, however, I will willingly admit, that whatever evils may have resulted from their collective mismanagement of the business of the mission, and from the want of vital piety evinced by some of their number, still the present deplorable condition of the Sandwich Islands is by no means wholly chargeable against them. The demoralising influence of a dissolute foreign population, and the frequent visits of all descriptions of vessels, have tended not a little to increase the evils alluded to. In a word, here, as in every case where Civilization has in any way been introduced among those whom we call savages, she has scattered her vices, and withheld her blessings.

As wise a man as Shakspeare has said, that the bearer of evil tidings hath but a losing office; and so I suppose will it prove with me, in communicating to the trusting friends of the Hawiian Mission what has been disclosed in various portions of this narrative. I am persuaded, however, that as these disclosures will by their very nature attract attention, so they will lead to something which will not be without ultimate benefit to the cause of Christianity in the Sandwich Islands.

I have but one thing more to add in connection with this subject—those things which I have stated as facts will remain facts, in spite of whatever the bigoted or incredulous may say or write against them. My reflections, however, on those facts may not be free from error. If such be the case, I claim no further indulgence than should be conceded to every man whose object is to do good.

Chapter 27

THE SOCIAL CONDITION AND GENERAL CHARACTER OF THE TYPEES

I HAVE ALREADY MENTIONED that the influence exerted over the people of the valley by their chiefs was mild in the extreme: and as to any general rule or standard of conduct by which the commonalty were governed in their intercourse with each other, so far as my observation extended, I should be almost tempted to say that none existed on the island, except, indeed, the mysterious "Taboo" be considered as such. During the time I lived among the Typees, no one was ever put upon his trial for any offence against the public. To all appearances there were no courts of law or equity. There was no municipal police for the purpose of apprehending vagrants and disorderly characters. In short, there were no legal provisions whatever for the well-being and conservation of society, the enlightened end of civilized legislation. And yet everything went on in the valley with a harmony and smoothness unparalleled, I will venture to assert, in the most select, refined, and pious associations of mortals in Christendom. How are we to explain this enigma? These islanders were heathens! savages! ay, cannibals! and how came they, without the aid of established law, to exhibit, in so eminent a degree, that social order which is the greatest blessing and highest pride of the social state?

It may reasonably be inquired, how were these people governed? how were their passions controlled in their everyday transactions? It must have been by an inherent principle of honesty and charity towards each other. They seemed to be governed by that sort of tacit common-sense law which, say what they will of the inborn lawlessness of the human race, has its precepts graven on every breast. The grand principles of virtue and honor, however they may be distorted by arbitrary codes, are the same all the world over: and where these principles are concerned, the right or wrong of any action

235

able printed pieces ever produced. Some designers preferred working with miscellaneous publications rather than with periodicals because each miscellaneous publication represented a brand new challenge.

Rather than work with an established page size and an already-contracted-for paper stock, the designer often was free to set the size, pick the stock, and make any number of production decisions not usually made by the magazine or newspaper designer, or even by the advertising designer.

Some of what fell into the miscellaneous-publications category qualified as advertising, for it was meant to sell a product, service, or idea of the sponsor. Such pieces were called "direct advertising" or "direct-mail advertising." Other miscellaneous publications served public relations purposes: improving employee morale, for instance, or impressing stockholders. If published by a nonprofit organization, the piece solicited funds or provided advice.

The most handsome of the miscellaneous publications originated in advertising agencies or public relations firms or departments. The art directors there did the designing. In some cases it came from independent art studios or freelancers. But too many miscellaneous publications—especially folders—originated with public officials or business executives and their secretaries, with no help from professional designers.

Both sides of a three-fold, eight-panel folder show how handling of photographs can bring unity to a direct-mail piece. The chopped-corner look of the display type used for the title echoes the look of the heavy photo outlines. This is a two-color (black and brown) folder with a wood texture built into the paper. Western Forestry Center is a forestry and forest industry museum.

"At Your Service" is a regular feature of *The Quarterly,* published by the Lawrence Livermore National Laboratory, Livermore, California. Line drawings by Tom Gleason illustrate the short items. Printing is in black plus a second color, light brown. Lew Reed art directed.

An art director for every publication

Ideally, every publication should have an art director. An art director not employed full time can be employed part time. An art director not part of the publication's own staff can be a freelancer or a designer attached to a design studio. James W. O'Bryan, the late art director of *National Review,* ran a design studio in the building and treated the magazine as one client, although a very special one.

William Delorme handled *Los Angeles* from his studio, miles away from the magazine's editorial offices. The magazine took 70 percent of his "working" time. He spent the remaining 30 percent on other graphic design assignments and on fine arts painting. "I put 'working' in quotes . . . because at least three weeks out of the month my time is my own. . . . The magazine work can be done at home in the evenings or on weekends. One week out of the month is practically round-the-clock labor on the magazine in order to meet printing deadlines." He visited the magazine

John Whorral, illustrator and art director for the *California Dental Association Journal,* used the technique of Vincent Van Gogh to imitate a famous self-portrait, but with a slight change—Van Gogh is carrying dental tools on his pallet. The full-cover painting was used both on the cover and as a full page inside to illustrate an article by Woody Allen: "If the Impressionists Had Been Dentists," taken from the book, *Without Feathers.* From one of the "letters" to Theo: "I asked Cezanne if he would share an office with me, but he is old and infirm and unable to hold the instruments and they must be tied to his wrists but then he lacks accuracy and once inside a mouth, he knocks out more teeth than he saves. What to do?"

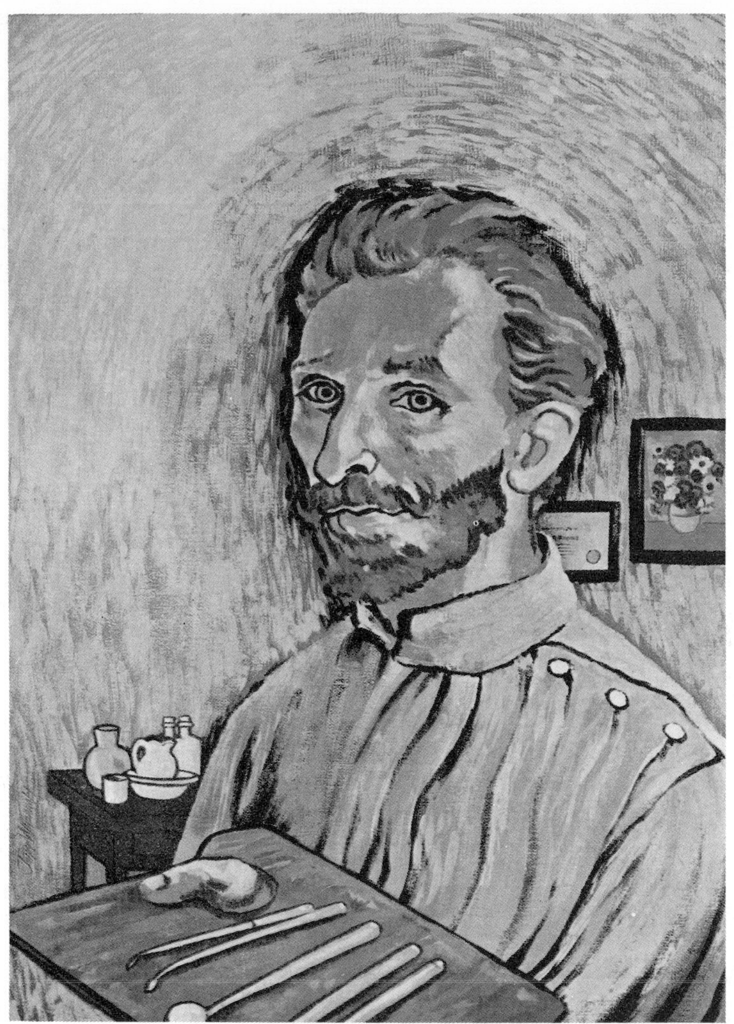

for editorial conferences and to present his rough ideas and finished layouts. He saw photographers and illustrators in his studio.

Salaries for staff art directors, like salaries for editors themselves, vary widely. For a small magazine the art director's salary might be as low as $14,000. For a big magazine it could go as high as $60,000.

If a magazine cannot afford either a staff or a freelance art director, it should hire a designer temporarily to set a simple, standard format that an editor can follow. At the least, an editor without design expertise or without an art director should avoid oddball typography, tricks with photographs, and complicated layouts.

An art director by any other name

As art directors have moved up on publication mastheads—on some magazines to a spot just below that of the editor—they have become vaguely dissatisfied with their titles. No one has yet come up with a title that fully describes the art director's several functions: to buy and edit illustrations and photographs, choose typefaces, make production decisions, and design and lay out the publication. Titles in use include art editor, designer, design editor, design director, design consultant, type director, production

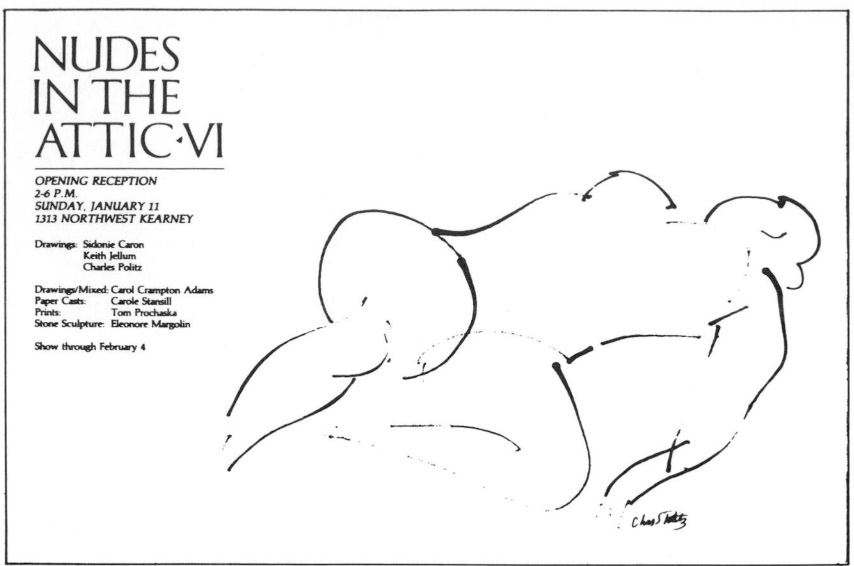

Drawing ability does not necessarily accompany graphic design ability. But the Portland designer Charles Politz has a sideline as a fine artist specializing in nudes, as this announcement demonstrates. It was for a showing at the Attic Gallery. The nude was one of several Politz works on display. His nudes sell regularly to collectors.

editor, graphics editor, picture editor. Art director remains the most common title.

But art director does not connote a concern with type and design. Art editor, the preferred title of the 1930s and 1940s, is worse: it brings to mind a person who runs a section of the publication devoted to a discussion of painting and other fine arts. The old terms no longer seem adequate, especially now that some art directors are making editorial and management decisions. Perhaps a publication should have two chief editors: a verbal editor and a visual editor. Maybe editorial director and design director, used on some magazines, represent the best combination of titles.

If a publication is large enough, its art director (or AD) is more an executive than a person who does the actual design work. A designer, working under the art director, designs and lays out the publication. Samuel Antupit, once art director at *Esquire* and now director of art and design for Henry N. Abrams, Inc., the book publisher, drew this distinction between a designer and an art director: "An art director, to distinguish him from a designer, must concern himself with converting the verbal into the visual by exploring and controlling the use of photography, drawing, painting, and typography within a magazine. By developing these elements he becomes a visual editor, interpreting and expressing the message of the magazine in visual terms. A designer is an arranger. He makes beautiful (if he's good) layouts which incorporate these elements. A designer's ultimate criteria, unfortunately, are the looks, not the meaning. A good art director may intentionally give the editor an ugly page if it best represents and expresses the material."[20]

Working with the art director or designer may be a pasteup artist, who puts type and art into final place for the printer. On many publications the art director, designer, and pasteup artist are rolled into one person, who usually takes the art director title. This book will use *art director* and *designer* interchangeably.

Some art directors are flirting with the term *communicator.* "I put design way down the list of what I do," says Greg Paul, former design director of *The Plain Dealer Magazine,* published by the Cleveland *Plain*

Dealer, and now art director of *New Age.* "I use design, but that's just a tool. I'm really interested in communicating with people."[21] Assigning a job to an illustrator or photographer, Paul tries to allow a great deal of freedom. He looks on his freelance artists as collaborators.

Art directors are moving into areas that involve more than visual sensibility. They are interested in bringing *all* the senses into play—not just the sense of sight. The feel of the paper, for instance, is part of it. So are smells. A magazine—or a book for children—may make use of encapsulated fragrances.

Milton Glaser, one of the world's most honored designers, does not confine himself to a single medium or even a single activity. And he is as well known for his illustrations as for his designs. Glaser was the cofounder of Push Pin Studios. He also cofounded and designed *New York,* which set standards not only for city magazines but for other magazines as well. His "I Love New York" insignia, with a heart standing in for *love,* has been appropriated by bumper-sticker makers to proclaim love for other locations, for various animals, and for just about everything else. He also redesigned the graphics as well as the interiors of the more than 500 Grand Union Markets. With Walter Bernard, Glaser redesigned the Washington *Post* in 1985.

The best of the art directors develop a mechanical aptitude as well as a design sense. Sometimes the effect the art director wants can't be had with ordinary photographs of ordinary props. For the first issue of the now-defunct *Careers Today,* published by *Psychology Today,* the art director Don Wright, to illustrate "The University Womb," cut a womb-shaped hole in a piece of plywood; put supports under the plywood to bring it up from the floor; nailed sheets of clear mylar around the hole to form a well; filled the well with water; put a nude male in the well; and photographed the setup from the top.

Art directors, like other journalists, have taken sides in the struggle for social, economic, and political changes. The art director for *National Review,* James W. O'Bryan, worked for free at first because he shared the philosophy of the *Review's* conservative publisher, William F. Buckley, Jr. Dugald Stermer played the important role he did on *Ramparts* because he believed in the leftist causes of that magazine. For the cover of one of its issues—in 1967—Stermer arranged for a photograph of four hands holding up burning draft cards. One of the hands was Stermer's. "If you're looking for an editorial in the usual place this month," said the magazine, "forget it. It's on the cover." The partners at Hess and/or Antupit, besides designing magazines and advertising and corporate pieces, handled a number of causes gratis or for low fees.

One thing becomes clear as you talk to art directors: they no longer are content merely to lay out pages. They argue—and the logic here is inescapable—that for a publication to be effective both verbally and visually, its art director must be involved in the planning as well as the production stages. Art directors on some magazines, major and minor, regard themselves as operating on the same level as their editors. Some art directors report that if they didn't have a say about the policy their magazines adopt and the articles and stories their magazines accept, they would resign.

Richard Gangel, as art director of *Sports Illustrated,* was part of a triumvirate that decided policy. He saw his role as primarily journalistic. Dugald Stermer, when he was art director of *Ramparts,* said he wouldn't be content to be "just an art director." He estimated that 80 percent of his time on the magazine was spent on editorial matters, including fund-raising. Kenneth Stuart, as art editor of *Reader's Digest,* checked articles before they were digested and suggested that certain sections be left in because they could be illustrated. Samuel Antupit on *Esquire* took an active role in accepting or rejecting manuscripts for publication.

Of course, someone has to have the final say, and that someone must be the editor. When Michael Parrish resigned in 1975 as editor of the weekly *City Magazine* of San Francisco, the San Francisco *Sunday Examiner and Chronicle* quoted a pleased art director, Mike Salisbury, as saying, "It's a really beautiful thing. We are all taking pictures, writing articles, and contributing in various ways. We don't have the traditional editorial hierarchy anymore." *City Magazine* didn't last long.

The big-name clothing designers are not part of our study, but it is interesting to note that many of them have branched out into the perfume business—or at least have lent their names to various fragrances. An AP writer noted that "perfume is not only profitable; it doesn't have to be redesigned each season."[22] One designer has put his name on a brand of chocolates.

The art director's background

Schools do not offer adequate training programs for magazine and newspaper art directors and designers of books. The art schools—the commercial schools—are mostly advertising-oriented. The fine arts schools seem mostly interested in developing painters. The journalism schools—many of them—still think in terms of routine newspaper makeup enhanced now by the computer.

So art directors come to publications by circuitous routes. In the early history of magazine art direction, when the job involved primarily the purchasing of art work, they came largely from the ranks of illustrators. Even when type direction became a more important part of the job, the illustrator's background served an art director well. A good illustrator is as interested in the design of a painting as in the draftsmanship. The feel for design can be transferred from the canvas board to the printed page.

Kenneth Stuart, former art editor of *The Saturday Evening Post* and later art editor of *Reader's Digest,* started out as an illustrator. But Stuart

Freelance artists and designers can be expected to draw and design their own Christmas cards, to keep in touch not only with friends but also with editors. Trina Robbins of San Francisco did this card, relying on a clean, crisp, 1940s style she has perfected for books she illustrates.

as art editor did not employ Stuart as illustrator. Those who use their own art in magazines have some misgivings about it; however, for some magazines there is no budget for outside work. Raymond Waites, Jr. prepared many of the illustrations for the religious magazine he art directed. Dugald Stermer did some illustrations for *Ramparts* while he was art director, causing Norman Rockwell to remark, "I didn't know he was a painter as well as an art editor. Boy, he has it both ways." In the 1970s Stermer made cover paintings for *Time*.

Jean-Claud Suares also illustrates as well as art directs. Once a week he does cartoonlike drawings for the op-ed page of the New York *Times*. He has illustrated (and designed) dozens of books as well, including a recent edition of *The Devil's Dictionary* by Ambrose Bierce. As an illustrator, Suares believes in a multiplicity of styles, even for a single assignment. *The Devil's Dictionary* shows his versatility. He started drawing at an early age, then stopped at twelve because "I didn't have the discipline," and later became an art director at the New York *Times*. He rediscovered drawing. "You know, art direction is working with other people's ornaments, and drawing is more yourself."[23]

But most art directors can't draw or paint well enough for publication. Samuel Antupit certainly does not consider himself an illustrator. "And I'm afraid to learn. I might be tempted to pick out people who did my kind of illustrating," he says.

Some art directors don't even design. They do only what their titles suggest: they direct. They feel their time is better spent working out solutions than actually executing them.

Art directors increasingly come to publications with backgrounds other than in illustration. They come with a more thorough knowledge of typography than their predecessors. A number get their training with advertising agencies.

Harris Lewine, an art director at Harcourt Brace Jovanovich, the book publisher, got into the business originally with a record company. He had no art background and certainly no ability to draw. "I'm not [even] really a designer," he says. "At my best I function as a ringmaster. I'm not about to save the world for the sake of design." He gets his kicks as an art director "from competing—not with other ADs but, strange to say, with a

His Christmas card read, "Royal wishes for a jolly good Christmas. Happy holidays from Brian Noyes (and friends)." And it carried this photo reproduction. That's Noyes, then art director of *Saturday Review,* standing between the royal couple, who had just visited Washington, D.C., where *SR* was being published. The prince and princess, of course, are plywood cutouts, made by entrepreneurs at Georgetown University, who charged $15 for a Polaroid shot and posing fee.

[Milton] Glaser or a [Seymour] Chwast or whatever. How much of my idea do they use? . . . It's a matter of helping, pointing . . . [these illustrators and designers] in the right direction."[24]

Brian Noyes, the young art director of the revitalized *Saturday Review* who moved to the Sunday magazine of the Washington *Post* in 1986, studied communications and graphic design at California State University, Fullerton before launching his career as a designer for several southern California newspapers. He worked for magazines in Tampa, Detroit, and Houston before going to the *Saturday Review* in 1984. His job there was to attract younger readers, and he gave the magazine a lively look it hadn't had before.

Editors vs. art directors

It is understandable that the relationship between the editor and the art director sometimes becomes strained. The one is word-oriented, the other visual-oriented, and the two orientations are not necessarily compatible. The editor may actually consider display typography and pictures intrusions on the text. Or the editor may expect the impossible of the art director, asking that a particular story and set of photos be fitted in too tight a space. The art director, on the other hand, may be more interested in showing tricks with type than in making the magazine readable. Or the art director may resort to the tired ways of laying out pages while the editor tries to move the magazine in some new direction.

Ideally, the editor and the art director should work as equal or near-equal members of a team, with the art director not only designing the magazine but also helping to make decisions on editorial policy and content.

Art directors seem unimpressed by, if not hostile to, editors who have design backgrounds. Samuel Antupit thinks such editors, because their knowledge of design is likely to be superficial, are harder to work with than editors who know nothing about design and admit it. Editors who know design know only design clichés, he says.

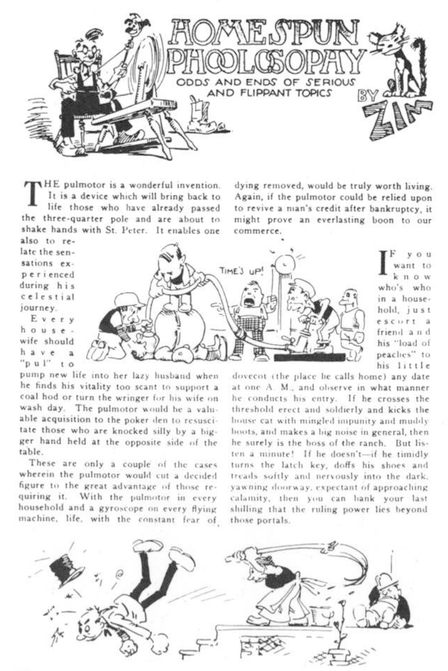

HOMESPUN PHOOLOSOPHY

ODDS AND ENDS OF SERIOUS AND FLIPPANT TOPICS

BY ZIM

THE pulmotor is a wonderful invention. It is a device which will bring back to life those who have already passed the three-quarter pole and are about to shake hands with St. Peter. It enables one also to relate the sensations experienced during his celestial journey.

Every housewife should have a "pul" to pump new life into her lazy husband when he finds his vitality too scant to support a coal hod or turn the wringer for his wife on wash day. The pulmotor would be a valuable acquisition to the poker den to resuscitate those who are knocked silly by a bigger hand held at the opposite side of the table.

These are only a couple of the cases wherein the pulmotor would cut a decided figure to the great advantage of those requiring it. With the pulmotor in every household and a gyroscope on every flying machine, life, with the constant fear of dying removed, would be truly worth living. Again, if the pulmotor could be relied upon to revive a man's credit after bankruptcy, it might prove an everlasting boon to our commerce.

IF you want to know who's who in a household, just escort a friend and his "load of peaches" to his little dovecot (the place he calls home) any date at one A. M., and observe in what manner he conducts his entry. If he crosses the threshold erect and soldierly and kicks the house cat with mingled impunity and muddy boots, and makes a big noise in general, then he surely is the boss of the ranch. But listen a minute! If he doesn't—if he timidly turns the latch key, doffs his shoes and treads softly and nervously into the dark, yawning doorway, expectant of approaching calamity, then you can bank your last shilling that the ruling power lies beyond those portals.

310

HOMESPUN PHOOLOSOPHY 311

ONE of our local butchers recently brought an action in the justice court against a prominent citizen to recover the price of a yard of link sausage which the defendant's dog had lifted from the market of complainant. All the legal talent of the town was pitted in the case, and after due deliberation, an intelligent jury rendered a verdict in the dog's favor. It was proven conclusively that a member of the aforesaid dog's family had mysteriously disappeared and circumstances pointed very strongly to the butcher as the cause, and that the dog's natural instinct led him to rescue his relative. Alas, blood is ever thicker than water!

DID it ever occur to you that being repeatedly drawn for jury duty is not the most desirable or convenient form of recreation? And have you never sought a remedy to avoid these legal drafts?

A city of considerable dimensions and enormous population would seem to afford one the greatest freedom from jury duty, but as long as you retain a house number and your name is inscribed in the directory, you're good for a call every time a panel is drawn. You must either keep moving or deny your identity when the census taker comes around. Not so in the country, however. There you simply join the Volunteer Fire Department, pay ten cents a month dues, and look pretty on annual inspection day. There are always plenty of non-member enthusiasts to pull the old machine to fires and carry out the manual labor connected therewith. It is your Christian duty to court good health so that you will be able at all times to decline to serve as a juror. In this you are backed by a handsomely engrossed certificate of active membership which exempts you for at least the first ten years of your connection with that heroic body, after which you become exempted for the balance of your natural lifetime. No important cases have ever been tried in my locality because of the lack of available timber to fill the jury box, though I have known the court to put off a case until the spring influx of new citizens arrived, then nail them to the cross before they had time to make application for membership in the fire brigade. In the country, jury dodging is an excusable crime, especially in the seasons when suckers are biting.

A TRAMP, having heard of the recent death of an old pal who was without family to mourn his demise, addressed a line of condolence to the deceased, as follows:

"Deer Pard: I em awfel sorrie to hear yer be ded, but you allus was a lucky dog in beetin yer pals in eny game yez ever plaid. Wen yer git settled in yer new quarters scribble me a lyne so as I kin git a idea how yoor komin onn and wen the game is over and I cash in me chips, I'll pay yez a wisit and praps iff ther climate and the cousine suit me and no work to

In 1916, as now, writers of humorous pieces sometimes acted as their own illustrators. This opening spread from *Cartoons Magazine* features the prose and drawings of Eugene Zimmerman, a popular cartoonist of the period who also ran a correspondence school in cartooning from his home in Horseheads, New York. The magazine ran Zim's full-page ad in the back, along with ads for other cartooning schools. The title for this article is hand drawn, and the art pieces are horizontal so that Zim can show a lot without taking up much space.

Here she is—the Gibson Girl of an earlier era, admired, desired, and, by a jealous few, despised. The magazine illustrator and cartoonist Charles Dana Gibson made her one of the nation's most known symbols. This pen and ink sketch is from the old *Life*.

Working with photographers and illustrators

Were you to become an art director or, as editor, play the role, you'd find yourself working part of the time as an art broker. It would be up to you to find the right illustrator or photographer for every cover, article, and story. Working for a magazine or book publisher, you'd deal mostly with talent outside the organization. This means you'd look at lots of portfolios put together by hopeful graduates of art schools. Perhaps you'd deal with artists' representatives. *Graphic Artists Guild Handbook: Pricing & Ethical Guidelines* (Robert Silver Associates, New York), which comes out periodically in a new edition, includes prices freelance artists—and freelance designers, too—would like to get for their work. Photographers' organizations have similar guidelines. But of course you are in a position to set your own prices. You must work these matters out in advance. If employed by a newspaper, you'd probably deal with staff artists and photographers rather than freelancers.

Some artists and photographers need a lot of direction. Others are more imaginative. You'll soon learn which freelancers need help, which ones should be left to their own devices. You will also learn that freelancers who perform well on certain kinds of assignments fail miserably on others. Your filing system will note strengths and weaknesses of your freelance contributors.

You will ask your photographers to give you full prints from their negatives so that you can, if necessary, do some cropping. Mike Salisbury, when he was art director of *West,* thought photos were easy to crop, retouch, or otherwise edit and often exercised his right to do so. But he thought that illustrations shouldn't be changed. Nor did he request an illustrator to make changes after submitting the work.

If the illustrator is sufficiently dependable, you will not even ask to see roughs first. Frank Kilker, former art editor of *The Saturday Evening Post,* told the story of his acceptance of an illustration from a regular contributor, painted to fit a large area set aside for it in one of the layouts. But clearly, the illustration was not up to that artist's standard. Rather than throw it out, Kilker revamped the layout to make the illustration occupy a smaller space in the spread.

Assigning a job to an illustrator, you often specify a size and shape to fit an already-existing layout. Seldom does the illustrator play a role in the selection of the typeface for the story title or in the placement of the title and body type on the page with the illustration. But of course art directors work differently with each of various illustrators. An illustrator like Al Parker could get away with designing the page or pages on which his illustration appeared and incorporating the title into his painting.

Working with writers

When freelance writers submit articles for publication they often submit photographs, too. The photographs may be of only routine quality. It is up to the art director to select those that are usable and perhaps to ask that others be retaken. Sometimes the art director can improve the composition of the photographs by cropping them. Occasionally the photographs go on to illustrators to use as guides for paintings or drawings.

But freelance writers almost never have anything to do with the way their articles are laid out. Maybe publications should make more of an effort to cooperate with writers on design matters. In gathering examples of page design to be included in this book, this author found it necessary,

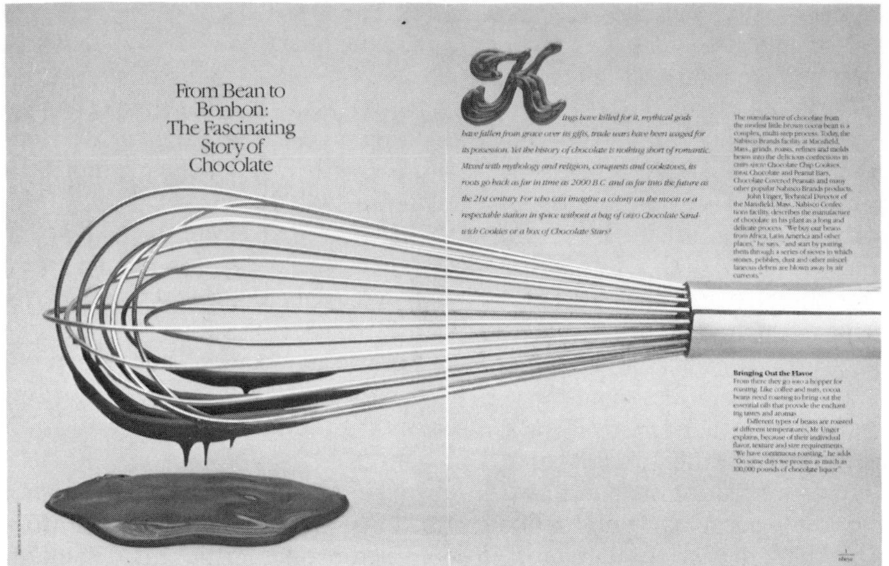

From Bean to Bonbon: The Fascinating Story of Chocolate

The opening spread and the last spread from an article in *nbeye* on chocolate use tinted pages, silhouetted art, and unusual initials built out of chocolate. Each spread in this six-page article is different, and each beautifully unites its two pages. *nbeye* is a quarterly company magazine published by Nabisco Brands, East Hanover, New Jersey.

after getting reprint permission from a magazine, to write to an author to get additional permission, even though the article would be reproduced in a size too small to read. It was a routine matter. But this is the note that came back: "I hope you don't think me a prig, but I must refuse your request. Each to his own taste—I happen to think the layout for my article . . . was an abomination. Title (not mine), blurb, pictures, and layout all worked together to violate the theme of my article. I cannot separate the layout from its purpose, and its purpose clearly was at odds with the text it supposedly was working with."

The freelancer's view of the art director

J. B. Handelsman, the cartoonist, showed what he thought of art directors (had one redesigned a magazine and closed out the gag cartoons?) with his picture of St. Peter standing at the gates of heaven, talking to a worried-looking man on the outside. In back of St. Peter was an art director (you could tell he was an art director by his hair style and mod clothes). St. Peter was telling the man outside, "I'm terribly sorry. The art director thinks your ears are too big."

A certain uneasiness prevails where art directors or designers work with people supplying art to publications. Sometimes the artist benefits from the direction given; sometimes the artist feels frustrated.

What is the photographer's idea of a good art director or designer? This question, among others, was discussed by three photographers at a meeting of the New York chapter of the International Association of Business Communicators.

Simpson Kalisher, whose work has appeared in many annual reports and other corporate publications, said, "For me, a good designer recognizes the integrity of an image. He doesn't crop and sacrifice an area either of color saturation or of grain. He also has a sense of the continuity of images when he puts a book together." Burt Glinn, whose photographs for the Magnum agency appear in many leading magazines, said, "You can be a good designer for the client and not for the photographer. But the best designer works for both of us." The designer should argue for what works, he added. "I want . . . a designer who does not cave in at the first sign of opposition. For when a client loses sight of where he's heading, it's our job to try to bring him back on track." William Rivelli, for twenty years a photographer for corporate publications, felt that often design fails at the printing stage. Little money is left after design and photography are budgeted. "So many jobs are ruined by the printing, and that seems to me foolish. It's like throwing away all the money you've spent." Watching over the printing is just one of the designer's jobs.

In the world of annual reports, company magazines, and other corporate publications, Glinn counts about thirty "top level" designers. "There are a lot of other good designers who are good with the scissors and they get their ideas from the first thirty."[25]

Realities of art direction

On some magazines the art director does not control the appearance of all the pages. James W. O'Bryan, for instance, used to do only the cover and the more important spreads for *National Review*. Recent art directors at *Esquire* did not do the covers: George Lois, an advertising art director and agency executive, did them. At *Newsweek* the art director, Fred Lowry, did not control the cover or the inside color section. When he was at *True,* Norman P. Schoenfeld, because of time limitations, found it necessary to leave back-of-the-book makeup to the printer, a practice common among magazines and newspapers. Raymond Waites, Jr. found it necessary to include in his magazine Polaroid shots taken by near amateurs. And when a magazine sees the need for a thorough revamping of its format, it is likely to call in an outsider.

That art directors do not oversee *all* the pages; that they give up control of the most important page of all, the cover; that they are willing to accept art and photography they know to be inferior; that it is some outsider who gets to remake the magazine when redesign is considered—all this is rough on the ego of art directors. There is, in addition, the problem of job burnout.

All too many art directors lack a feeling of job security. Between the time the author conducted his research into the role of art directors on American magazines and published his report with the Magazine Publishers Association, a two-year period, at least seven of the thirty art directors he interviewed had moved. "The job-switching among editorial art directors resembles a game of musical chairs," Alexis Gelber noted in *Art Direction.* Some of the changes obviously are forced by top management people looking for scapegoats for dwindling circulations and loss of advertising revenue.

Size of the design staff

On large magazines the art director employs several assistants. When he was at *Life,* Bernard Quint had a staff of about twenty, not counting the picture editors. That *Life* came out weekly made so large an art staff necessary. Several persons were there to carry out the rough sketches of the art director, others to do keylines and assembly, others to handle production matters. *Look,* the biweekly, had about fifteen. The big monthlies operate with smaller staffs. Herb Bleiweiss, when he was with *Ladies' Home Journal,* had four assistants, but he used them in a way different from that of most art directors: he let each assistant handle all the details for a single article or story. It made for unity within a feature but meant that the magazine lacked some unity overall.

Samuel Antupit, on his first stint with *Equire,* had two assistants and a secretary. In his opinion, "the smaller the staff the better." (These figures do not include artists and designers in the advertising and promotion departments.)

Emergency Medicine, one of the best-designed professional journals in the country, used only two designers for its 240 to 250 pages per issue. The art director, Ira Silberlicht, said it could be done because the magazine was a "formatted book. There are a couple of typefaces that we use . . . we don't sit and design headlines in beautiful type and go crazy." The aesthetics and excitement came from theme art. Silberlicht wanted a stay-the-same look each month to help readers segregate the magazine from the other couple of hundred in the field.[26]

The computer has eliminated the need for some people in design and art departments and especially in production departments of magazines as well as newspapers. Today the *writers* on some publications find themselves involved in matters of typography and design.

Bringing in a consultant

It was a single-sentence letter: "How much would you charge us to review the last 10 issues of ________ and then meet with us to make recommendations for improving our design and format?" "The trouble with you, Ron," the designer wrote back (he happened to know the editor), "is that you beat around the bush. I had to read through your entire salutation before I came to the meat of your letter. . . ."

A pleasant enough start for a consulting job, and as it turned out, the results pleased all persons involved. The editor changed a few things, and the designer had the satisfaction of seeing the changes come about. But

The Design Council, Inc., Portland, puts out an occasional promotional broadside (16 × 24) that folds down to an 8 × 8 mailer.

consulting jobs, both from the editor's and from the designer's standpoints, don't always work out as the principals hope.

No doubt editors who have used design consultants can catalog any number of complaints against them. Whether consultants are worth what they cost, in money and in the morale of the in-house designer, is subject to debate. But consultants have gripes, too. Among them, these:

1. The editor calls in the consultant not for fresh ideas but to substantiate some design biases.
2. A magazine is in desperate circumstances, and the editor thinks that redesign can work a miracle.
3. The editor has read a book about design or heard a lecture by someone like Milton Glaser or Samuel Antupit. And now the editor knows what's "in."
4. The editor has just seen a magazine whose appearance is appealing. Can the consultant duplicate those looks?
5. The editor doesn't really want to change the appearance of the magazine, a look traditional if not outdated, but would like to try a type like Avant Garde Gothic (with alternate characters) for the headline schedule or titles.

6. Finally, the editor buys a handsome, well-thought-out format along with elaborate instructions about what to do in every conceivable situation and accepts the new design enthusiastically. Within a couple of months, though, the editor adds a different display face for a new standing column, say, and drops some italic in favor of boldface and decides to try initial letters for some of the articles. What happens then to the look of the magazine is similar to what happens to the appearance of a new, well-designed building when somebody starts placing crude, hand-painted signs above doorways and in windows.

An editor paying for a new design program ought to stick to it and check back with the designer when changes have to be made. Anyway, a design program submitted by an outsider should provide for future adjustments.

Editors of magazines bring in consultants to (1) do a hit-and-run job involving a study of past issues and come up with advice for basic changes to be made by the editor or an in-house designer, (2) do a full-service job, involving the selecting of types and the setting up of a basic design pattern or grid for the editor or in-house art director to follow, or (3) do the actual issue-by-issue design and layout of the magazine. In this final instance the consultant becomes the art director, working for the editor on a freelance basis.

Freelance art directing

When the editor works with a freelance art director on a regular basis, as on a company magazine, frequent conferences may be necessary, not only to alert the art director to editorial complications but also to solicit advice. Art directors like to be involved in the editorial process. They do not want to be thought of as visual persons only.

But a great amount of the contact, typically, comes by phone. The art director may call in the middle of a pasteup to suggest a paragraph cut to make an article fit. This author, acting as a freelance art director, for some years designed a magazine 120 miles away from the editorial offices. Copy and photographs went back and forth by mail and Greyhound Express.

Lionel L. Fisher, editor of *Boise Cascade Paper Times,* had such a good relationship with his freelance art director, Joe Erceg, that he didn't even ask for thumbnails or roughs before final pasteup began.

Some art directors carry the work to only a rough-layout, comprehensive, or rough-pasteup stage, leaving the final pasteup to a pasteup artist or to the printer. Whoever does the pasteup, then, simply follows directions. Perhaps the rough that this pasteup artist works from has all kinds of measurements and arrows and instructions marked in the margins. On the other hand, some rough pasteups are so neatly done they can almost stand in as camera-ready copy. They do not need instructions marked in the margins.

At any rate, somewhere along the line, *somebody* has to bother with exact fitting of lines of type and headlines and art onto the page. An art director who really cares about the product may insist on doing this final pasteup. There are always some last-minute, precise fitting decisions to be made. To a real art director, a half point of space wrongly placed can ruin an otherwise good day.

Mr. Shepler cut the one hundred twenty pieces for each barn, and then he refused to do any more, ever again.

Phillip Wilson, who was the third-generation owner of one of the barns, said his grandfather liked his barn with the silo in the middle and the great curved feeder on the lower level. He explained to his grandson that a cow was pie-shaped, too—narrow in front, wide in the rear, and thus more of them could eat from a curved feeder than from a straight feeder of the same length. He didn't have to carry the feed very far, either.

The largest round barn in Ohio was built in Auglaize County, east of little New Hampshire, in 1908. It was built by a Yankee of few words, Jason Manchester, and was intended as a dairy. It is 102 feet in diameter, has three levels, and now is used and cared for by the fourth generation of Manchesters, who produce certified seeds. True to his taciturn origins, Jason Manchester never revealed why he built such a large and fancy barn.

Outside Wilmington, near the little crossroads of Gurneyville, is the McMillan barn. It is actually octagonal, but local residents, past and present, have always thought of it as round. The local Quakers, admiring perhaps the notion of ecclesiastical roundness, said there were "no corners for the Devil to hide in." Some of the Methodists, who had organ music and liked loud sermons, told newcomers a man died there. When pressed for details, the newcomers were invariably told, "Fellow ran himself to death trying to find a corner to p—— in."

The theory was less timber and more space. No interior roof supports, either, for the raised-seam tin roofs. The neighborhood story on the McMillan barn, however, is that whatever its builder considered, he built it finally to impress a lady. She was impressed, and they got married.

From the top: Fairfield Cty. Fairgrounds, Lancaster, built 1906 by J. E. Hedges. • Octagonal barn, Barlow, Washington Cty., 3½ mi NE of town; ¼ mi. S on Twnsp. Rd. 29 from CR 2. • Hocking Cty., between Chillicothe and U.S. 33 on St. Rte. 180. • Gilmore Farm, Somerset, 1932, 68′ diam. On Twnsp. Rd. 36, N of town.

76 April 1985

"Their alluring roundness confounded barn tradition and, sometimes, even the owners and builders."

John McGaughey Jr. bought a round barn near Junction City eighteen years ago and was so proud of it he painted the roof bright red. Mr. McGaughey says it was built in 1908 and that a tinner drove down from Baltimore, measured the barn under construction, and went home, where he cut all the diagonal tin for the roof. He returned with the rolls of cut tin in a buckboard, and it fit perfectly. He crimped the edges, walked around the barn and picked up a handful of clippings; then he went home.

The roofs were marvelous, but requiring of craft, not a notable modern virtue. When a big windstorm hit the two Kingston barns in 1980, it ruined both roofs. Present owner Charles Maxwell waited over half a year before his insurance company finally found a man to drive up from McArthur to repair his barn. Phillip Wilson, who has never visited Maxwell's barn, although it was identical to his and was just across the township, did not have as resourceful an insurance man and had to tear his barn down.

That leaves about two dozen or so around Ohio, artifacts in the museums of themselves, although most of those remaining are *working* museums. Their meager numbers tenuously hold out against the sober architecture of modern barns, and they are a lively testament to a time when—by careful eye and the luxury of material—the countryside still had a craftsman's symmetry.

From the top: John Hupman, owner, Darke Cty., 2 mi. E of Greenville on Requarth Rd. • Big J Farm, Junction City, 60′ diam.; 1 mi. E on St. Rte. 37 to Householder Rd. or CR 94A • Octagonal barn, Bryan, St. Rte. 15 and U.S. 127, just N of U.S. 6, 1½ mi. S of town. • Auglaize Cty., 102′ diam., built 1908 by Horace Duncan; 4½ mi. E of New Hampshire.

Additional research and photo identification by Dave Stephenson

Ohio Magazine 77

A three-page article on round barns in *Ohio magazine* makes a right-hand-page start and on the next spread features a number of small photographs, silhouetted and placed within the wide-set text matter, which is heavily leaded to accommodate the art and stay readable. Photos by Palmer Werner; design by Thomas E. Hawley. (From *Ohio Magazine*, April 1985. Reprinted by permission.)

The exercise of taste

A new art director taking over a magazine immediately makes changes. What to the casual reader would seem unimportant might greatly disturb an art director: length of ruled lines, choice of body type, the logo, placement of captions, etc. "A change of editor or art director is reflected instantly . . . [in a magazine's] pages," Henry Wolf points out. "A magazine is still largely the extension of an individual idea, a peculiar personal vision."

When Susan Niles moved up as art director of *Mademoiselle,* she changed the design to make it "cleaner, fresher, and younger." The covers became less posterlike, with colors more integrated. The *M* became much larger than the other letters in the logo. The January 1979 cover showed a woman wearing glasses, probably a first for fashion magazines. Niles was proud of the natural look among the magazine's models.

Although they would be slow to admit it, art directors in their choice of type and art and in their arrangement of these elements on a page lean heavily on what is fashionable. For a time the Bauhaus-inspired sans serifs are "in"; then the Swiss-inspired sans serifs. Everybody bleeds photographs for a time; then suddenly, everybody wants generous white margins around pictures. Letterspacing is thought to "open up" the typography, making it more pleasant to read; then close fitting of letters takes hold, to make it possible for the reader to grasp whole words rather than individual letters. For a time, all space divisions are planned so they'll be unequal; then spaces are divided equally, and new magazines come out in a square format rather than a golden proportion size. For a few years, the look is austere, simple, straight; then swash caps and column rules and gingerbread prevail. It is the rare art director who can resist adapting current art trends to a design: witness the psychedelic look on magazine pages at the end of the 1960s. A few art directors break away, rediscover old styles, come up with unused ones, and they become the leaders. In a few months others are following. "Let us . . . not delude ourselves that we are lastingly right," Henry Wolf once cautioned.

Occasionally an art director decides to go with the banal, the obvious, or the discarded. An illustrator has passed his prime, his style is outmoded. Very well, bring him back. He's the kind of illustrator who would never have appeared in that magazine even when he was on top. But that makes him all the more appealing now. His shock value is worth a lot to the art director.

Or the art director picks one of the typefaces that, even when it was first released, was dismissed as gauche by discerning designers. The art director uses it now, smugly, cynically even.

A little of this goes a long way. The trouble with some magazines today is that their art directors, caught up in an anything-is-art mood, are breaking all the rules of typography and design. They insist on doing their own thing. Some of their experiments succeed, and less self-indulgent art directors probably will incorporate them into magazines of the future. But most of the experiments fail. They fail because the experimenters do not recognize *readability* as the one overriding requirement of publication design.

BRIEFINGS

AUCTION BLOCK

A thirteenth-century stone head of King Herod (upper left), taken from the original choirscreen of France's Chartres Cathedral, sold for $198,000 at a recent Christie's, New York, auction.

The botanically accurate *The Lilies* (lower left) is one of Pierre-Joseph Redouté's (1759-1840) 468 paintings recording the Imperial Gardens at Malmaison. Commissioned by Empress Josephine, the collection is considered by many the most beautiful colorplate book ever produced. Sotheby's estimates it will bring five to seven million dollars at auction on November 20.

Also at Sotheby's, Claes Oldenburg's *Glass Case with 24 Open-faced Sandwiches* (lower right) went for $96,250.

Two leaves of seventh-century handwriting on vellum copied by an Irish monk (upper right), probably the earliest known piece of English writing still in existence, were sold for $112,000 at Sotheby's in London.

20 *Saturday Review* November/December 1985

Saturday Review runs a series of pages and spreads called "Briefings" up front each issue. This page, with an unusually wide copy block, combines an experimental style with a classic look.

Notes

1. Eugene Exman describes the operation in *The House of Harper,* Harper & Row Publishers, New York, 1967.
2. See Tom Wolfe's two-part series "From Bauhaus to Our House," *Harper's,* June and July, 1981, or the book *From Bauhaus to Our House,* Farrar, Straus & Giroux, New York, 1981.
3. David A. Wesson, *International Typography: From Abstract Art to American Graphics,* paper presented to the Visual Communication Division of the Association for Education in Journalism and Mass Communication, Gainesville, Florida, August 1984.
4. Some of what follows in this chapter appeared in a different form in the author's *Visits with 30 Magazine Art Directors,* published by the Education Committee of the Magazine Publishers Association, New York. Copyright 1969 by the Magazine Publishers Association. Reprinted by permission.
5. See "Harper's Bazaar at 100," *Print,* September–October 1967, pp. 42–49.
6. Jack Anson Finke, "Pro-File: Alexey Brodovitch," *U&lc.,* March 1977, p. 9. Beginning with this issue, *U&lc.* ran a series on famous designers and art directors.
7. From a letter to the author from Marcia R. Prior, instructor at Iowa State University Department of Journalism and Mass Communication, Ames, Iowa, Aug. 23, 1979.
8. Quoted from *Magazines: USA,* The American Institute of Graphic Arts, New York, 1965. See Cleveland Amory and Frederic Bradlee (editors), *Vanity Fair: A Cavalcade of the 1920s and 1930s,* Viking Press, New York, 1970.
9. Gertrude Snyder, "Pro-file: Dr. M. F. Agha," *U&lc.,* December 1978, p. 5.
10. "Louvre Holds Retrospective of Push Pin Studios' Graphics," *Publishers' Weekly,* April 13, 1970, p. 70.
11. Ibid., p. 72.
12. Published by Communication Arts, Palo Alto, California, 1970.
13. "Between Issues," *The New Leader,* June 1, 1981, p. 2.
14. Quoted by Gertrude Snyder, "Pro-File: Henry Wolf," *U&lc.,* September 1978, p. 8.
15. "The New Graphics," *Art Direction,* May 1980, p. 61.
16. Ibid., p. 64.
17. Quoted by Karen Jacobson, *Art Direction,* May 1981, p. 69.

18. "Many Magazines Today Look Alike, Designer, Editor Claim" *Folio,* April 1980, p. 24.
19. Adrian Wilson, *The Design of Books,* Reinhold Publishing Corporation, New York, 1967, p. 23.
20. Samuel N. Antupit, "Laid Out and Laid Waste," *The Antioch Review,* Spring 1969, p. 59.
21. Jean A. Coyne, "Greg Paul," *Communication Arts,* May/June 1981, p. 16.
22. AP dispatch, Eugene, Oregon, *Register-Guard,* May 3, 1978, p. 5D.
23. Kurt Wilner, "Too Much Isn't Enough: J. C. Suares," *Art Direction,* May 1979, p. 84.
24. Kurt Wilner, "View from Above—Harris Lewine," *Art Direction,* November 1978, p. 69.
25. Robert A. Parker, "A Panel Discussion of Corporate Photography," *Communication Arts,* January/February 1982, p. 79.
26. John Peter, "The Top Ten Business Magazines," *Folio,* August 1976, p. 77.

Suggested further reading

AIGA Journal, New York. (Quarterly.)
Art Direction, New York. (Monthly.)
Barthes, Roland, *Erte,* Franco Maria Ricci Publisher, Parma, Italy, 1972.
Beisele, Igildo G., *Graphic Design Education,* Hastings House Publishers, New York, 1981.
Berryman, Gregg, *Designing Creative Resumes and Portfolios,* William Kaufmann, Los Altos, California, 1984.
Bojko, Szymon, *New Graphic Design in Revolutionary Russia,* Praeger Publishers, New York, 1972. (Examples from the 1920s and 1930s.)
Bouillon, Jean-Paul, *Art Nouveau 1870–1914,* Rozzoli, New York, 1985.
Brackman, Henrietta, *The Perfect Portfolio,* Amphoto, Watson-Guptill Publications, New York, 1985. (Mostly about selling photographs.)
Carter, David, *Evolution of Design,* Art Direction Book Company, New York, 1985.
Chappell, Warren, *A Short History of the Printed Word,* Alfred A. Knopf, New York, 1970.
Chwast, Seymour, *The Left-Handed Designer,* Henry Abrams, New York, 1985.
Communication Arts, Palo Alto, California. (Bimonthly.)
Craig, James, *Graphic Design Career Guide,* Watson-Guptill Publications, New York, 1983.
Ferebee, Ann, *A History of Design,* Van Nostrand Reinhold Company, New York, 1970. (Covers Victorian, Art Nouveau, and Modern styles.)
Garner, Philippe, *Twentieth Century Style and Design: 1900 to Present,* Van Nostrand Reinhold Company, New York, 1985.
Glaser, Milton, *Milton Glaser: Graphic Design,* Overlook Press (Viking), New York, 1973.
Gold, Ed, *The Business of Graphic Design,* Watson-Guptill Publications, New York, 1985.
Gordon, Barbara, and Elliott Gordon, *Opportunities in Commercial Art and Graphic Design,* VGM Career Horizons, National Textbook Company, Lincolnwood, Illinois, 1985.
Heller, Steven, *Innovators of American Illustration,* Van Nostrand Reinhold, New York, 1986.
Jervis, Simon, *The Penguin Dictionary of Design and Designers,* Penguin, New York, 1984.
Jones, Gerre L., *How to Market Professional Design Services,* 2d ed., McGraw-Hill, New York, 1983.
Meggs, Philip, *A History of Graphic Design,* Van Nostrand Reinhold Company, New York, 1983.
Meyer, Susan E., *America's Great Illustrators,* Harry N. Abrams, New York, 1978.
Morgan, Ann Lee, ed., *Contemporary Designers,* Gale Research Company, Detroit, 1985. (Biographies of some 600 designers, along with essays and 400 illustrations.)
Morgan, Jim, *Marketing for the Small Design Firm,* Watson-Guptill Publications, New York, 1984.
Nelson, George, *How to See: Visual Adventures in a World God Never Made,* Little, Brown and Company, Boston, 1977.
———, *George Nelson on Design,* Whitney Library of Design, New York, 1979.
Nelson, Roy Paul, *Visits with 30 Magazine Art Directors,* Magazine Publishers Association, New York, 1969.
Perlman, Bennard B., *F. R. Gruger and His Circle: The Golden Age of American Illustration,* Van Nostrand Reinhold Company, New York, 1978.
Print, Washington, D.C. (Bimonthly.)
Prohaska, Ray, *A Basic Course in Design,* Van Nostrand Reinhold Company, New York, 1980.
The Push Pin Style, Communication Arts Magazine, Palo Alto, California, 1970.

Rand, Paul, *Paul Rand: A Designer's Art,* Yale University Press, New Haven, Connecticut, 1985.

Reed, Walt, ed., *The Illustrator in America, 1900–1960s,* Reinhold Publishing Corporation, New York, 1967.

Snyder, Gertrude, and Alan Peckolick, *Herb Lubalin: Art Director, Graphic Designer and Typographer,* American Showcase, distributed by Robert Silver Associates, New York, 1985.

Spencer, Charles, *Erte,* Clarkson N. Potter, New York, 1970.

Thiel, Philip, *Visual Awareness and Design,* University of Washington Press, Seattle, Washington, 1981.

Yorke, Malcolm, *Eric Gill: Man of Flesh and Spirit,* Universe Books, New York, 1982.

Starting this *Chocolatier* feature on a center spread allowed the art director, Dennis Andes, to run words across the gutter without worrying about any part of them being lost in the fold. The article title and the definable part of the art combine to make one powerful unit on the spread. The text wraps around this unit, and the last line of the title picks up one of its dimensions. The full-color photograph bleeds all around, further uniting the pages.

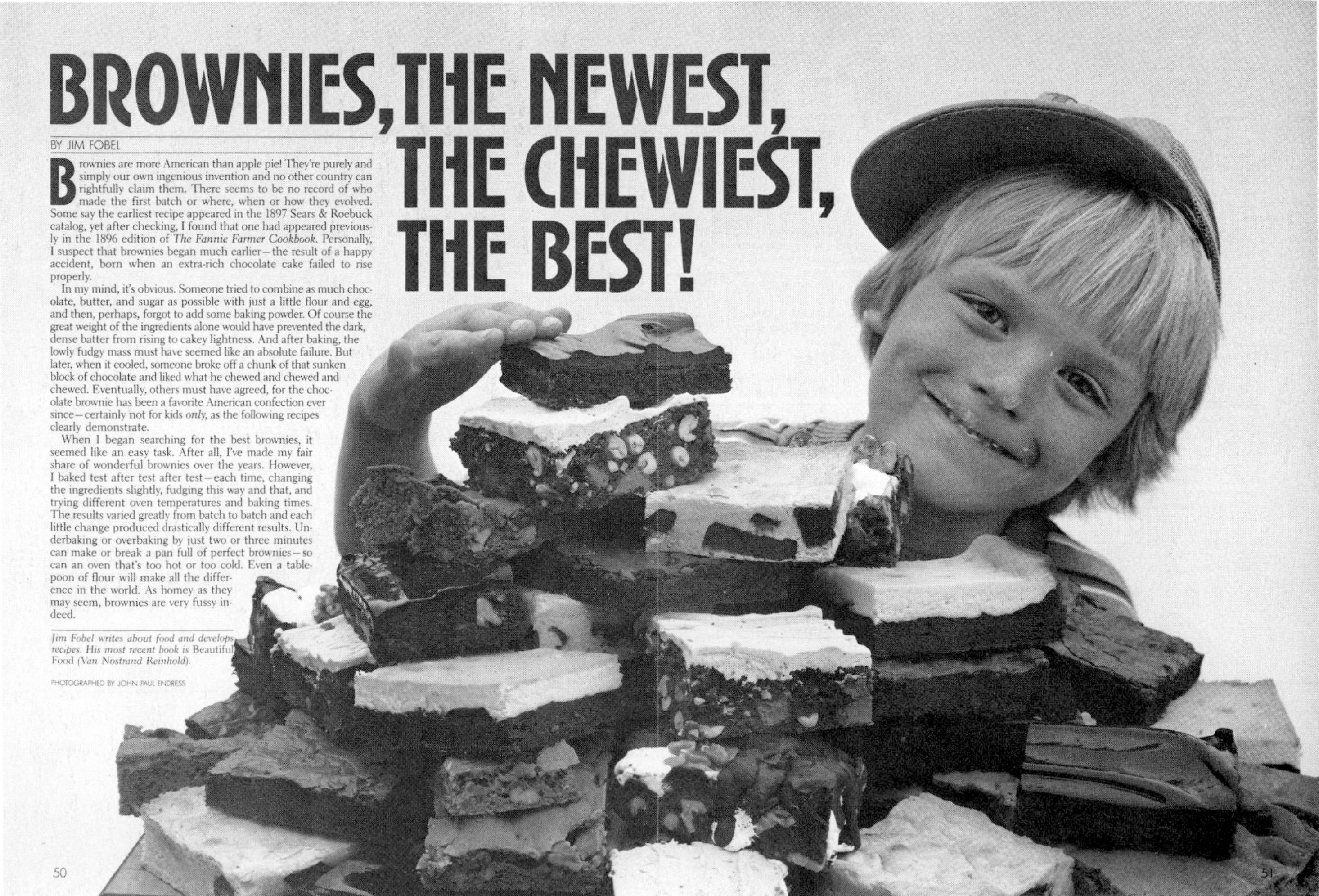

BROWNIES, THE NEWEST, THE CHEWIEST, THE BEST!

BY JIM FOBEL

Brownies are more American than apple pie! They're purely and simply our own ingenious invention and no other country can rightfully claim them. There seems to be no record of who made the first batch or where, when or how they evolved. Some say the earliest recipe appeared in the 1897 Sears & Roebuck catalog, yet after checking, I found that one had appeared previously in the 1896 edition of *The Fannie Farmer Cookbook*. Personally, I suspect that brownies began much earlier—the result of a happy accident, born when an extra-rich chocolate cake failed to rise properly.

In my mind, it's obvious. Someone tried to combine as much chocolate, butter, and sugar as possible with just a little flour and egg, and then, perhaps, forgot to add some baking powder. Of course the great weight of the ingredients alone would have prevented the dark, dense batter from rising to cakey lightness. And after baking, the lowly fudgy mass must have seemed like an absolute failure. But later, when it cooled, someone broke off a chunk of that sunken block of chocolate and liked what he chewed and chewed and chewed. Eventually, others must have agreed, for the chocolate brownie has been a favorite American confection ever since—certainly not for kids *only*, as the following recipes clearly demonstrate.

When I began searching for the best brownies, it seemed like an easy task. After all, I've made my fair share of wonderful brownies over the years. However, I baked test after test after test—each time, changing the ingredients slightly, fudging this way and that, and trying different oven temperatures and baking times. The results varied greatly from batch to batch and each little change produced drastically different results. Underbaking or overbaking by just two or three minutes can make or break a pan full of perfect brownies—so can an oven that's too hot or too cold. Even a tablepoon of flour will make all the difference in the world. As homey as they may seem, brownies are very fussy indeed.

Jim Fobel writes about food and develops recipes. His most recent book is Beautiful Food *(Van Nostrand Reinhold).*

PHOTOGRAPHED BY JOHN PAUL ENDRESS

50

51

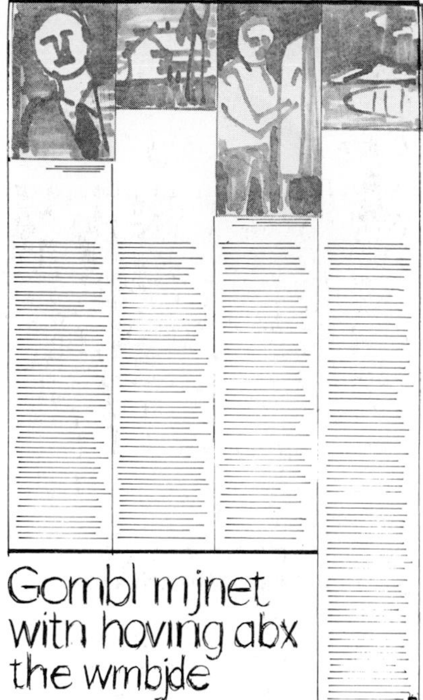

A rough layout by this author for a one-page article in a telephone company tabloid takes a tightly organized approach to design. The headline, not yet written, is "greeked."

The approach to design

The student of art and design finds a close correlation between art movements and trends in graphic design. The move toward abstraction after the turn of the century accompanied the experimentation going on with typography, especially in posters. Russian Constructivism, so much a part of the Russian Revolution, popularized photomontages and collages. Dadaism in Germany, an antiestablishment kind of art, inspired some interesting, even if unreadable, graphic design. In Holland the painters Piet Mondrian and Theo van Doesburg began the De Stilj movement with its highly controlled, geometric look. It was this movement that, according to Professor David A. Wesson of Marquette, had the most impact on modern graphic design.

Moreover, it is not difficult to see a correlation between the architecture of a period and its printed pieces. Fashion in clothes can also influence graphic design; for instance, the layered look relates to the boxes within boxes that some designers use.

Laughter is the Sun that Drives Winter from the Human Face

VICTOR HUGO

ILLUSTRATION BY STEVE HENRY

Seeing something funny can make you grin or chuckle or even laugh 'til tears roll down your cheeks.

Sometimes it's the instantly funny sight gag. Other times it's the slow, sly double-take which gradually tickles a laugh from you. However you define humor and its visual manifestation, it's one of the qualities that distinguishes human from beast and seems to peel away troubles, if only for a few moments.

This year's All-NBI Photo Contest offers the Company's amateur photographers a tremendous challenge: Have Fun! We're looking for photos that capture a mirthful moment expressing our theme: "Here's Something to Make You Laugh."

Rules

1. Only current and retired employees of Nabisco Brands, Inc., and its subsidiaries are eligible to enter. Spouses and relatives of employees are not eligible unless they are also employees or retirees of the Company. Entries submitted by on- or off-the-job professional photographers are not eligible.
2. Photos may be 35mm slides (large-format slides are ineligible), color prints or black-and-white prints. Prints must be no smaller than 3 x 5 inches and no larger than 8 x 10 inches. There's no limit to the number of submissions.
3. *Each* entry must be marked with the employee's name, work or home address and work or home telephone number. Any print or slide submitted without this information will be automatically disqualified. *Suggestion:* Use a peel-off label bearing the necessary information and affix it to the slide or print. Ballpoint, fluid ink and marker pens often leave damaging marks on prints, making them impossible to judge.
4. Prizes: $1000 First Prize, $500 Second Prize, $300 Third Prize.
5. All entries become the property of *NB Eye* and will not be returned. Send duplicates of irreplaceable photos.
6. Entries should be carefully packaged for shipment. Entries damaged in transit will be disqualified.
7. All entries must be received by *NB Eye* no later than October 1, 1985. Winning photos will be published in a future issue of *NB Eye*.
8. Photos previously entered in a Company employee photo contest, whether or not they won prizes, will not be eligible.
9. Send entries to:

   NB Eye Photo Contest
   Corporate Affairs
   Nabisco Brands Plaza 1
   7 Campus Drive
   Parsippany, N.J. 07054

Judging

Each entry will be judged according to these criteria:

1. Adherence to the theme, "Here's Something to Make You Laugh."
2. Technical quality (sharpness, color balance or contrast, lighting).
3. Creativity (uniqueness of approach, artistic treatment).

Winning Ways

How can you win this photo contest? Well, there are no sure-fire ways to capture a prize but we can suggest a few things to keep in mind which will improve your chances.

1. Keep your camera, loaded with film, handy at all times. Professional photographers agree that some of their best opportunities occur when they least expect them so they're always prepared to get that once-in-a-lifetime shot.
2. Keep the theme in mind. Each year we get a whole slew of stunning photos which are well-taken and very creative. But they have nothing to do with the theme and the judges eliminate them immediately. Here's a tip: sunsets, gondolas and sleeping squirrels will not make the grade in this year's contest.
3. Look through some photos you've already taken but have never entered in one of our photo contests. (See rule 8.) You may have the winner right in your photo album or slide carousel.
4. Worried that maybe your sense of humor might be different from the judges? Try out your photos on friends and family. If they laugh right away, you've got a possible winner.
5. Remember the limits of good taste. The winners will be printed in *NB Eye*, a publication which goes to readers' homes. Photos deemed vulgar or risque will automatically be eliminated.
6. Give yourself plenty of time. If you don't have a good entry on tap, allow yourself enough time to go out and stalk the winning photo, have it processed and then mailed to us in time to meet the deadline. If, for any reason, you encounter unusual problems, please let us know and we'll try to accommodate you.
7. Questions? Call: Dana Lee Wood, Editor, (201) 898-7766.
8. Lastly, *Enjoy yourself!* This is one contest which should be as much fun to enter as it is to win. If you get a few good chuckles out of photographing something funny, then you're already ahead.

Good Luck!

21
nbeye

nbeye, a company magazine published by Nabisco Brands, Inc., East Hanover, New Jersey, used a grey bar at the top along with big type and art to cross the gutter and unite two pages announcing a funny photo contest for employees. The headline is a quotation from Victor Hugo. The cartoon illustrations are by Steve Henry.

NAUTICAL QUARTERLY

ALFRED SØVIK-BOATBUILDER

THE SHOP OF ALFRED SØVIK, BOATBUILDER, CLOSED WHEN HE DIED IN 1977. HE REPRESENTED THE SEVENTH GENERATION OF HIS FAMILY TO BUILD THE WIDE-STRAKE DOUBLE-ENDERS COMMON TO THE HARDANGERFJORD ON NORWAY'S WEST COAST, AND HE WAS NORWAY'S UNDISPUTED MASTER BOAT-BUILDER. HE IS SHOWN HERE LITERALLY CARVING A GARBOARD TO SHAPE FROM AN OAK BLANK, MAKING WHAT PHOTOGRAPHER TED SPIEGEL DESCRIBES AS "A RADIAL SCULPTING WITH AN AXE." SPIEGEL WATCHED AND TOOK THIS PHOTOGRAPH WHILE SØVIK WORKED THE AXE WITH THE SKILL OF A SURGEON ON A STRAKE THAT SET INTO THE KEEL PERFECTLY WITHOUT STEAMBENDING. THE CHIP THAT CAME OUT WAS 4' LONG, THE RESULT OF 26 CLEAN STROKES OF THE AXE. TED SPIEGEL WAS OVERWHELMED BY THIS PERFORMANCE, AND HE SAVED THE CHIP. HE SAYS OF WHAT HE SAW IN THE SØVIK BOATSHOP: "YOU COULD NOT SEE THE MAN'S SKILL SOLELY IN THE BOAT; IN A WAY, THE REFUSE WAS THE MARK OF THE CRAFTSMAN." ALFRED SØVIK'S GENIUS WAS NURTURED THROUGH SEVEN GENERATIONS, AND HIS SKILLS WERE THOSE OF VIKING TIMES.

14

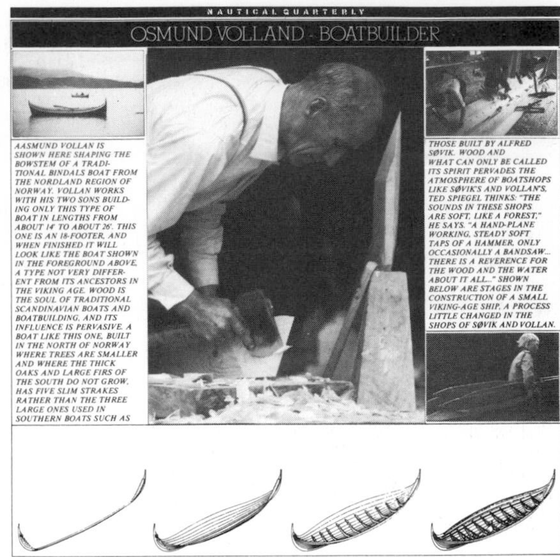

NAUTICAL QUARTERLY

OSMUND VOLLAND - BOATBUILDER

AASMUND VOLLAN IS SHOWN HERE SHAPING THE BOWSTEM OF A TRADITIONAL BINDALS BOAT FROM THE NORDLAND REGION OF NORWAY. VOLLAN WORKS WITH HIS TWO SONS BUILDING ONLY THIS TYPE OF BOAT IN LENGTHS FROM ABOUT 14' TO ABOUT 26'. THIS ONE IS AN 18-FOOTER, AND WHEN FINISHED IT WILL LOOK LIKE THE BOAT SHOWN IN THE FOREGROUND ABOVE, A TYPE NOT VERY DIFFERENT FROM ITS ANCESTORS IN THE VIKING AGE. WOOD IS THE SOUL OF TRADITIONAL SCANDINAVIAN BOATS AND BOATBUILDING, AND ITS INFLUENCE IS PERVASIVE. A BOAT LIKE THIS ONE, BUILT IN THE NORTH OF NORWAY WHERE TREES ARE SMALLER AND WHERE THE THICK OAKS AND LARGE FIRS OF THE SOUTH DO NOT GROW, HAS FIVE SLIM STRAKES RATHER THAN THE THREE LARGE ONES USED IN SOUTHERN BOATS SUCH AS THOSE BUILT BY ALFRED SØVIK. WOOD AND WHAT CAN ONLY BE CALLED ITS SPIRIT PERVADES THE ATMOSPHERE OF BOATSHOPS LIKE SØVIK'S AND VOLLAN'S, TED SPIEGEL THINKS: "THE SOUNDS IN THESE SHOPS ARE SOFT, LIKE A FOREST," HE SAYS. "A HAND-PLANE WORKING, STEADY SOFT TAPS OF A HAMMER, ONLY OCCASIONALLY A BANDSAW... THERE IS A REVERENCE FOR THE WOOD AND THE WATER ABOUT IT ALL..." SHOWN BELOW ARE STAGES IN THE CONSTRUCTION OF A SMALL VIKING-AGE SHIP, A PROCESS LITTLE CHANGED IN THE SHOPS OF SØVIK AND VOLLAN.

15

The handsome and expensive *Nautical Quarterly* was not afraid to take some chances on its square, glossy, full-color pages. This spread features two one-page profiles. Note the all-caps italic body copy (printed in a screened version of black) and the thin, slab serif all-caps titles. The name of the magazine in stenciled letters always appears at tops of pages. Creative director of the quarterly is B. Martin Pedersen.

The best graphic designers take their inspiration from outside their profession. Their study of the fine arts and the world around them carries over to the decisions they make about the printed page. They become the leaders in graphic design; others adopt their styles.

This is not to say that young designers should ignore what's going on in their own profession and refuse to be inspired by the printed pieces they admire. But inspiration is one thing; duplication is another. When *Conservative Digest* was taken over by another publisher in 1985, it became the "spitting image" of *Reader's Digest,* to use the words of *National Review,* which otherwise might have been expected to applaud the revamped magazine, considering its political views.

Neither should design be confined to any set of rules. But at the beginning an understanding of some generally accepted principles can be useful.

The principles of publication design

Consciously or unconsciously, art directors tend to operate by a set of basic design principles. These principles apply to all forms of art, not just to design.

1. *Balance.* We start with the most obvious of the principles—and the least important. It states, simply, that what is put on the left half of the page must "weigh" as much as what is put on the right half of the page. Or, what is put on one page of a spread must "weigh" as much as what is put on the facing page.

   If you are a designer who is overconscientious about this principle, you can take the easy way out: you can center everything—the heading, the photo, the text matter. If a spread is involved, you can run the heading across the gutter so half is on each side. You put a picture on the left page and a picture of equal size across from it on the right page. If you run two columns of copy under one picture, you run two columns of copy under the other. The

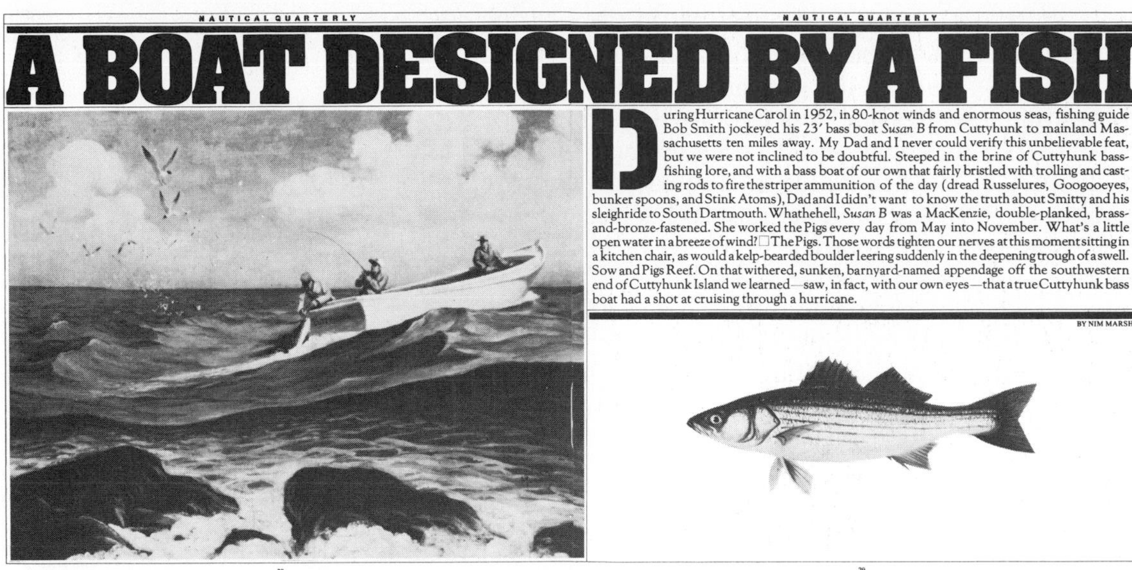
NAUTICAL QUARTERLY

NAUTICAL QUARTERLY

A BOAT DESIGNED BY A FISH

During Hurricane Carol in 1952, in 80-knot winds and enormous seas, fishing guide Bob Smith jockeyed his 23′ bass boat *Susan B* from Cuttyhunk to mainland Massachusetts ten miles away. My Dad and I never could verify this unbelievable feat, but we were not inclined to be doubtful. Steeped in the brine of Cuttyhunk bass-fishing lore, and with a bass boat of our own that fairly bristled with trolling and casting rods to fire the striper ammunition of the day (dread Russelures, Googooeyes, bunker spoons, and Stink Atoms), Dad and I didn't want to know the truth about Smitty and his sleighride to South Dartmouth. Whathehell, *Susan B* was a MacKenzie, double-planked, brass-and-bronze-fastened. She worked the Pigs every day from May into November. What's a little open water in a breeze of wind? □ The Pigs. Those words tighten our nerves at this moment sitting in a kitchen chair, as would a kelp-bearded boulder leering suddenly in the deepening trough of a swell. Sow and Pigs Reef. On that withered, sunken, barnyard-named appendage off the southwestern end of Cuttyhunk Island we learned—saw, in fact, with our own eyes—that a true Cuttyhunk bass boat had a shot at cruising through a hurricane.

BY NIM MARSH

28

29

In another spread—an opening spread—from *Nautical Quarterly,* the initial letter, in blue, is in stencil type to match the name running across the top. Oversize slab serif type makes the title stand out. The silhouetted fish contrasts nicely with the large painting on the left page. Designer Pedersen was willing to run the text type across a page as a single column. A new paragraph is set off with a small box instead of an indentation.

balance is bisymmetric. For some articles, for some magazines, this solution can be a good one, especially if you are after a classy look.

With a little more effort, however, you can achieve balance that is asymmetric and possibly more interesting. You can do this by putting a big picture on one page near the gutter and balancing it with a smaller picture at the outside edge of the other page. It is the same principle of balance involved when a parent and child use a teeter-totter; the parent sits close to the fulcrum while the lighter child sits way out on the end.

The balance becomes more complicated as graphic elements are added. We will not take the space here to consider the possibilities. Balance comes naturally enough as you move elements around and pull white space into concentrated masses. You feel the balance; and your intuition is all that is needed. Not confident, you can hold your design up to a mirror and check it in its reverse flow; this will quickly dramatize any lack of balance.

You work, then, with optical weights. You know from experience that big weighs more than little, dark more than light, color more than black and white, unusual shapes more than usual shapes. You know, too, that a concentration of white space, because it is unusual, can itself be heavy.

2. *Proportion.* Good proportion comes about less naturally. As a beginning designer you may be inclined to put equal space between the heading and the picture, between the picture and the copy, and between the copy and the edge of the page. Your margins then become monotonously the same.

   Better proportion comes from nature. The circumference of the tree trunk is greater than the circumference of the branch. The distance between the tip of the finger and the first joint is different from the distance between the first joint and the second joint.

   In designing publications, we also have the inspiration of the "golden section" (or "golden mean") of the fine arts. It provides that the lesser dimension in a plane figure is to the greater as the greater is to the sum of both; the dimensions are in a 0.616 to 1.000 ratio, roughly 2 to 3 or 3 to 5. We base page size—of typing sheets, of books, of magazines—more or less on this ratio. We find the ratio more interesting, less tiresome, less obvious than a simple 1 to 1. We avoid 2 to 1, 3 to 1, and 4 to 2 ratios because they are merely variations of 1 to 1. They divide into equal portions. We avoid cutting pages visually into halves or quarters. We avoid running pictures that are perfectly square because the ratio of width to depth is 1 to 1.

In designing an issue of a magazine, you might well vary the space between pictures as you move from page to page. And the space between title and article start on one spread might be different from what it is on another spread. But with these varying proportions you would maintain consistent spacing where distances are *meant* to be equal, as in the separation of subheads from the body of an article and captions from their pictures.

The page margin for many magazines is narrowest between inside edge of copy and gutter, wider between top of copy and top of page, wider still between outside edge of copy and outside edge of page, and widest between bottom of copy and bottom of page.

Total picture area for most publications takes up more space than nonpicture area; or it takes up less space. The ratio is seldom 1 to 1.

3. *Sequence.* You do not leave to chance the order in which the reader perceives the items on a page or spread. You know the reader ordinarily starts at the top left of a page or spread and moves to the bottom right. Arranging the elements so they read from left to right and from top to bottom is easy enough, but it limits design flexibility.

The reader also has a tendency to move from big to small, from black to white, from color to noncolor, from unusual shape to usual shape. You find it possible, then, to begin your design anywhere, directing the reader to the left, the right, the top, the bottom—in a circular motion, diagonally, whatever way you wish. Diminishing visual impact does the job.

You direct the reader, too, through the use of lines, real or implied, which carry the eye as tracks carry a train. The pictures themselves have direction or facing; they point the way as surely as if they were arrows. This is why you would nearly always arrange a major mug shot so that the subject looks into the text.

You try to arrange photographs so that an edge or a force from one photograph flows into an adjoining one. The curve of an arm, for instance, if carried over to the next photograph could merge into the roll of a hill. This happens without regard to what may be the outer dimensions of the photographs; one photograph may be considerably larger than the other and not aligned with it.

Or taking a line from within the picture—say the edge of a building—you extend it (without actually drawing it) and fit against it another item—say a block of copy. Or taking the hard edge of a picture and extending it, you fit another picture against it somewhere across the page.

And do not discount the possibility of actually numbering the pictures. If chronological order is all-important, as in a step-by-

You get a good idea of what makes for a set of pleasing proportions by observing the ruled lines, added by this author, in the margins of this decorative title page designed near the turn of the century by Charles Ricketts at the Vale Press.

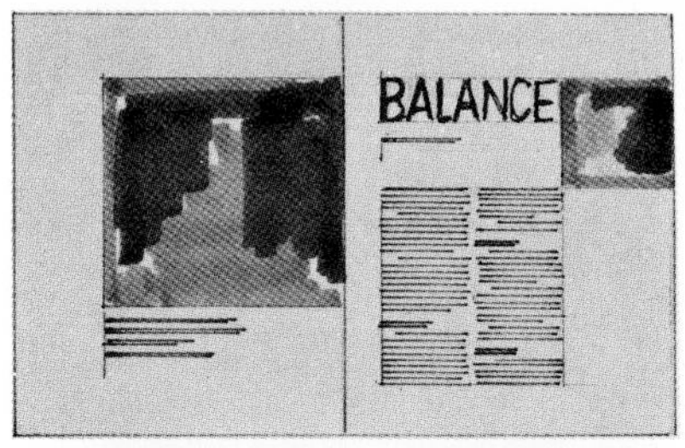

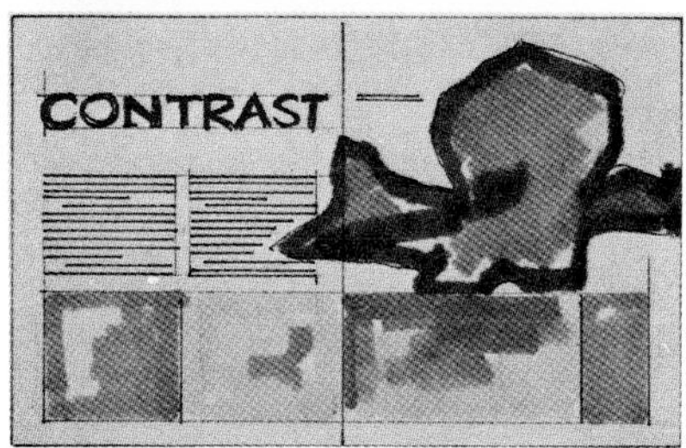

Each of these five rough sketches (thumbnails) of magazine spreads shows a design principle at work. (The sketches appeared originally in the author's *Communication World* column.)

step illustrated article on how to build a guest house, you may not find a better way for handling sequence.

Developing sequence from spread to spread is also part of the assignment—which leads to another principle.

4. *Unity.* The typeface must look as if it was designed to fit the style of the illustration. It must fit the mood of the piece. The overall effect of the spread, of the entire article or story, of the entire magazine must be one of unity, of harmony. The pieces, the pages belong together.

   Ideally, all typefaces in a magazine come from the same family. Ideally, all art is furnished by the same artist or photographer. Heavy rules or borders ordinarily call for boldface sans serifs. Bold sans serifs call for line drawings with plenty of solid blacks. Thick and thin rules call for modern romans. Modern romans call for well-ordered photographs, or clean line drawings, arranged in severe horizontal and vertical patterns.

   And pattern becomes important to the designer. Stepping back, you contemplate the overall effect. No longer looking for individual trees, you survey the forest. Does it all seem to fit together? The pattern can be loose, tight, bulky, smooth, rugged, soft, loud, dark, light, hard, straight, rolling, changing, any number of things—but the pattern is unmistakably there.

   You take a major step toward unity when you push your white space to the outside edges of your spreads. This teams photographs with other elements so that they work together. When large amounts of white space seep into the center, there is an explosion, sending the elements off in all directions. White space on the outside edges should be there in unequal concentrations, in conformance with the principle of pleasing proportion.

5. *Contrast.* Expressed negatively, the principle is contrast. Put positively, it is emphasis. Either way, something on the page or on the spread stands out from all else. What stands out is probably the most important item on the page. It is probably the item the reader sees first.

   You achieve contrast or give an item emphasis by making it bigger than anything else there—blacker, more colorful, or more unusually shaped. Or you get contrast/emphasis by causing all other items to point to the item or by putting it in a different setting, giving it different texture, or otherwise making it seem out of place.

   Only one item—or one cluster of items—dominates. When you give graphic emphasis to several items, they all compete for attention, frustrating the reader.

The principles in perspective

No doubt you would find that designing a publication is not as simple as the preceding section indicates. Nor do practicing designers pay a great deal of attention to these principles. Perhaps they could not state them if asked. Certainly they would not give them exactly as they are given here.

Both lists are worth contemplating. The beginning designer, especially, and the editor who has the design job by default would find the lists useful.

It may have occurred to you that the principles are contradictory. How can you have unity, for instance, when you insist on setting up one item to contrast with others? And doesn't use of unequal space divisions break up the sequence? The challenge in the list lies in knowing when to stress one principle, when to stress another. Obviously they can't all be applied in equal measure. When one principle does not seem appropriate, you should not hesitate to abandon it.

Edward Gottschall, editor of *U&lc.*, offers a slightly different set of design principles to consider. His list works out like this:

1. *Clarity.* Gottschall reminds us that legibility, readability, order, and emphasis all contribute to the clarity of design.
2. *Vitality.* The size of the page to begin with, the size of elements on the page, their shape and positioning, and the introduction of color give a design its vitality.
3. *Craftsmanship.* This shows up in the quality of the typesetting and art as well as in the skill and care with which they are arranged on the page. Gottschall mentions specifically letterspacing, word spacing, and alignment.
4. *Appropriateness.* The designer must consider the content and tone of the message, the sender's intent, and the needs and orientation of the reader. "As much as we need clarity, vitality and craftsmanship—if an exquisitely designed piece is misaimed it isn't an effective communication," Gottschall concludes.[1]

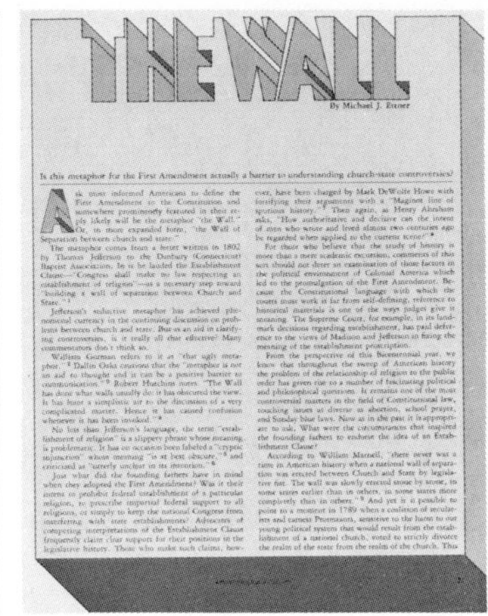
THE WALL

The boxing of articles appeals to many art directors, just for the visual order it brings. In this right-page opener the subject matter calls for a box—or wall—so the visual treatment is all the more appropriate. To tie the title to the initial letter, the designer used a chiseled-out style for both. The original employs a second color, maroon, in solid and two different tints arrived at by screening. Only the area outside the box—or wall—is white. (Courtesy of *Liberty,* "A Magazine of Religious Freedom.")

Two basic approaches to design

A designer takes one of two basic approaches to publication design. The first approach goes like this: Each picture, each caption, each title, each block of copy falls into a consistent pattern to unify the publication. The look is orderly. The reader feels secure and knows what to expect.

The second approach provides great variety, page after page. The look is lively. The reader prepares for a series of surprises. Using this approach, you would worry about unity, but only within a given article or story. You would feel that the nature of the article or story should dictate the choice of typeface and illustration.

One writer characterized the two styles as Bauhaus/Swiss design and Push Pin design. Bauhaus/Swiss design, as he saw it, was spare, functional, austere, uncluttered. It made use of a grid. It seemed particularly appropriate for corporate publications. The second style, popularized by Push Pin Studios, was more inventive, combining many styles, including decorative. In the Push Pin style there was often a touch of humor, a whiff of nostalgia. It seemed particularly appropriate to magazine covers, posters, and advertising.[2]

A magazine can have elements of both approaches, but one approach should predominate. One may be more appropriate than the other for a given magazine; but properly handled, either approach can work, regardless of magazine content.

It is safe to assume that visual pyrotechnics are not always necessary, even in an age when, having seen and experienced everything, people may be jaded. A return to the basics and a celebration of the simple pleasures on a page can be enough. The classic look still has a place in many magazines. G. K. Chesterton, writing in an earlier era, observed, "Nothing is poetical if plain daylight is not poetical; and no monster should amaze us if the normal man does not amaze."[3]

All the principles of design described in this chapter were incorporated by Don Menell, assistant art director of *Look,* in this single page. It is the opening page of a two-page article that starts on a right-hand page and ends on the (next) left-hand page. Menell combined roman display type with sans serif body type, added column rules, and carefully fit the type around the illustration. The illustration ties in beautifully with the title, carrying the reader down into the article and dividing the page pleasingly. Note that the hand both holds a pill and forms into the symbol for "OK." From *Look* June, 30, 1970. © 1970 by Cowles Communications, Inc. (Reproduced by courtesy of the editors.)

No medication is foolproof, but taken with your doctor's advice...

THE PILL IS SAFE

ONLY ONE birth-control measure is safer or more effective than the pill–total sexual abstinence. And that has never been too popular a choice. Any other method–rhythm, diaphragm, condom, foam, intrauterine device (IUD)–is either less effective or not as safe as the ubiquitous tablet more than eight million women swallow daily.

Unfortunately, the pill's benefits have been blackened, and its evils –real and imagined–have been magnified at the recent Senate subcommittee hearings chaired by Sen. Gaylord Nelson (D., Wis.). Contrary to newspaper and television reports, the hearings did not uncover new dangers in the pill but merely repeated old stories that the public had heard before and that had already been carefully weighed by responsible medical authorities.

So sensational were the charges, however, that a public-opinion poll suggests that more than a million women have been too frightened to continue using the oral contraceptive, although 87 out of 100 women said they previously were satisfied with it. Planned or not, the anti-pill hysteria has panicked these women into making–on their own–a complicated medical decision that demands a physician's guidance.

Dire predictions of death from blood clots and cancer frightened the women away. While the blood-clot danger is statistically small but real, the cancer scare is neither statistical nor real; it is simply conjectural.

Two years ago, a British survey showed that death from blood clots occurred nearly seven times more often among pill-users than among similar-aged women not on the pill. A smaller United States survey found that the risk was about four times greater. Sever or four, even the smaller number is significant and must not be ignored. Any woman taking the pill should be aware that there is the danger of blood clots.

Although the risk is real, it is equally important for every woman to know what the added danger actually means. The British study revealed that three women out of every 100,000 taking the pill died from blood clots. The toll involved was no greater than that among women who are killed while riding in cars or crossing the street. Certainly, such accidental deaths are deplorable, but no one suggests that the risk is so great women should stop riding in automobiles.

It is even more significant that pregnancy entails harsh risks of its own. Actually, the chance of death associated with pregnancy is 17 times greater than with pill-taking. Thus, the million or more women who reportedly abandoned the pill in fear because of the hearings may find their lives in greater jeopardy should they become pregnant as a consequence.

Although the blood-clot problem is relatively recent, hints of it appeared eight years ago. As an editorial consultant to the *Journal* of the American Medical Association, I recommended in 1962 that the *Journal* publish a report by a clinician linking the occurrence of blood clots with oral contraceptives. The *Journal* did so, and also asked me to write an editorial calling for definitive research on the how and why of the relationship.

To this date, no definitive research has been done. One reason may be the near-impossible task of evaluating the pill's role, when the basic mechanism of blood clotting is largely a mystery to scientists. Another is the unresolved argument over who should foot the bill for the research. Is it the drug companies' responsibility, because they stand to profit from the sale of oral contraceptives? Or should it be the Government's concern because, with eight million users, the pill has become a public-health problem?

During the Washington hearings, several witnesses advocated that women switch from the pill to one of the many intrauterine devices available. (One witness who was the pill's severest critic is the developer of an IUD that is now being manufactured and sold.) An IUD is a piece of plastic or metal (a coil, spiral, loop, etc.) that is inserted by a physician into a woman's uterus and left there. How it prevents pregnancy, no one knows.

With oral contraceptives, however, there are no doubts. The pill prevents conception by tricking the body into believing it is already pregnant. The pill accomplishes this with its two chemical ingredients that mimic the action of the female sex hormones–estrogen and progestogen.

One pill–the sequential type–consists of a synthetic estrogen tablet taken daily for two weeks, followed for one week by a daily tablet containing both synthetic hormones. The other–the combination type–contains both hormones in a single tablet that is taken daily for three weeks.

As each menstrual cycle rolls around, the pills' cumulative ef-

continued

Since 1956, Dr. Tyler has played a major role in developing and testing the pill. An associate clinical professor of obstetrics and gynecology at UCLA, he is also medical director of the Family Planning Centers of Greater Los Angeles.

BY EDWARD T. TYLER, M.D.,
WITH ROLAND H. BERG

LOOK 6-30-70 65

Popular Photography combined three same-size pictures and one big one, all in a square format, with some column rules for an opening spread in the back of the magazine. The main picture is cropped to lead the reader down the teeter-totter to the beginning of the article's title. Art director George N. Soppelsa was able to retain formally balanced sections (the title and the right-hand page) in an informally balanced context.

Playground seesaw becomes moving platform from which to shoot action scene of person on the other end.

The ups and downs of camera movements

... ON SEESAWS, SWINGS, AND SLIDES

BY BOB DUNCAN

PHOTOGRAPHS BY HARVEY V. FONDILLER

Mention camera movements to the man who has just lovingly unpacked and is in the process of loading his sleek new super 8, and chances are he'll react as he would to a word-association test. "Green" equals grass. "Fat" signifies mother-in-law. And "camera movement" implies panning. If he has given the instruction book or a how-do-to-it article a superficial going-over, he'll probably snarl at the very thought. Only a fathead, not in the know, would jeopardize precious footage by panning.

The other extreme is, sad to say, less far-fetched. Possibly our amateur film maker has never heard that the pan, like strychnine for the heart, is a valuable aid when used in moderation, but certain death if used to excess. That, or he simply cannot resist the temptation. So off he goes, as though armed with a flamethrower, never dreaming how it can backfire. Maybe he has had basic training with an enamel spray can, and is a master of the long, sweeping stroke. But if he has a strain of mercy in his makeup (and his self-preservation instinct is in good working order), he'll lay in a supply of tranquilizers prior to screening time.

Who—or which—is right? Obviously neither, and not only in the flat rejection or warm embrace of the pan shot, for camera movement is by no means synonymous with, nor restricted to, panning. Let's look into some of the other methods of putting the motion picture camera into motion, any of which can enhance your movies if, like the pan, they are used with some degree of discretion.

Before making a few observations on the pan, here is a significant statistic: an overwhelming percentage (maybe up to 95 percent) of home movie footage is shot from eye level. This makes for monotony, no matter how ingenious your variation of long, medium, and close shots, and no matter which of the camera movement devices suggested below you decide to experiment with.

If pan you must (and there are times when this is called for, especially when following a moving object), try a low level. Let's say you are filming running or toddling feet as your youngster moves across the lawn. Since it is feet that you want on film, lower the tripod and camera to their level, and see what a dramatic difference this take makes when cut in with other shots of the action. Now that you've gone low, try going high. Position yourself on a ladder with the tripod legs together and braced between your feet, or lashed to the ladder. Or, shoot from the porch roof or a second-floor window. Keep your pan short, first holding it on the subject for about three seconds before the action starts, then framing just ahead, allowing face room. Then end and hold as your subject moves off the movie screen.

Surrounded by tall buildings or tall trees? Here is another camera motion "additive," again in the panning department. First, select your shooting location. The most effective one quite likely will be somewhere near dead center. Set up and tilt up, scanning through the viewfinder for the most effective angle. Do a 360-degree dry run, revolving the camera slowly. One building or a treetop may be a bit taller than its neighbors, and depending upon how much sky area your framing calls for, adjust the tilt accordingly. Then shoot at a happy medium between a dizzying revolution and a leisurely, overlong pan. (N.B.: A fast, "dizzying" pan might just possibly prove useful as a special effect intending to convey exactly that sensation and might come in handy if it fits into your present or a future movie script.)

How to be a real swinger: grip camera firmly while swinging back and forth, thus producing a point-of-view shot.

So far, so good. You have already simulated two kinds of effects presumably reserved for Hollywood sets and enormously expensive gizmos such as the crane. But you have been limited to the pan. What about the so-called tracking shot, in which the camera moves parallel with the moving subject, and the dolly shot, in which the camera moves in upon or retreats from the target? Let's investigate the latter, which is more familiar, since in all probability you have used an apparent equivalent—a zoom lens. Well, it is and it isn't equivalent. True, the camera appears to move in and out when you zoom in and out. But there is a basic difference between zooming and dollying. At the beginning of a zoom-in, the lens shows about a forty-degree background area ... but when it's in telephoto position, it covers no more than about ten degrees. In dolly shots, the angle covered remains the same—a factor that is often highly desirable, especially if you want to retain, not diminish, a significant background.

How to get that dolly effect without liquidating your next year's film budget? You guessed it—use a caster-equipped platform dolly, which can be either bought or built. If you can handle a screwdriver, you're in business. Put a slab of ¾" plywood on a set of casters, or wheels from a baby carriage, or old roller skate, and your dolly is practically a reality. And for that matter, you may well ask yourself, why not use a baby buggy or a roller skate? No reason why not, though as in the case of whatever improvised dolly you may decide upon, you'll need some form of camera mount. If it's a flat-platform furniture dolly, a low tripod or an angle-iron will do the trick. With the baby buggy, use a tripod or straps. The latter will work if you use a roller skate. Guide the skate with an attached pole such as a broomstick. Or, as in the case with the furniture dolly (provided you haven't rigged it up with a rigid pushing-type handle) get a couple of assistants who can haul it with ropes or wires stretched at such an angle that they won't get in the way of the lens.

The supermarket buggy, the Red Racer rubber-tire wagon, borrowed, rented, or just plain expropriated from Junior or the Little Woman, will provide you with an efficient tracking or in-and-out dolly. And that's only the beginning, really. Try using the family car, with tires slightly deflated to minimize bumps, and the camera hand-held (the body serves as a shock-absorber). In fact, almost anything on wheels, even a wheelbarrow, can serve the purpose. Needless to say, pitted terrain or a pot-holed road should be avoided, even as a sway-backed beach. Bumpy sidewalks, especially the single-slab variety which have a grievous tendency to tilt askew, are a hazard. And a neighbor of ours, who gave no heed to his wife's protests over the molehills in their lawn, became a reformed character when he experimented with a kid-wagon dolly and realized they were indeed, *(continued on page 113)*

Poised for descent at top of slide (left), the cameraman starts the shot, which continues while he slides (right). A fast camera speed, such as 36 fps, will produce a slow-motion effect.

110

111

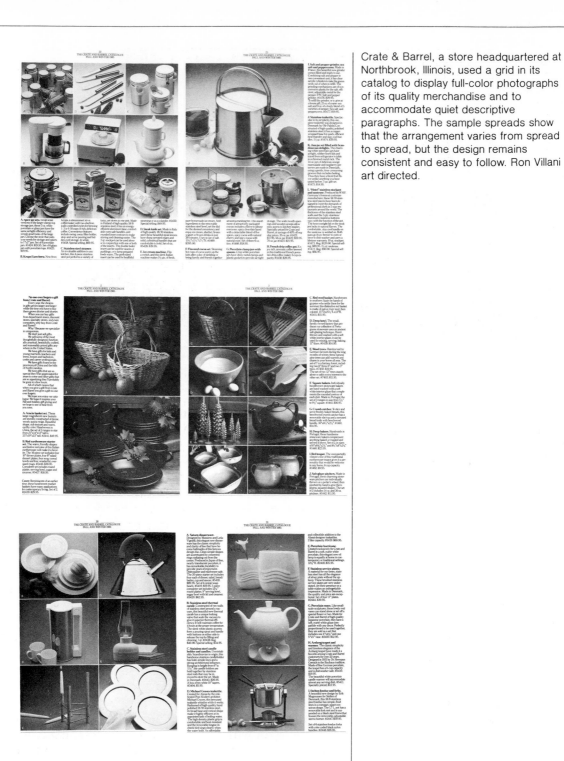

Crate & Barrel, a store headquartered at Northbrook, Illinois, used a grid in its catalog to display full-color photographs of its quality merchandise and to accommodate quiet descriptive paragraphs. The sample spreads show that the arrangement varies from spread to spread, but the design remains consistent and easy to follow. Ron Villani art directed.

The orderly approach

A publication with the orderly approach might make use of a single typeface for all its major titles. It might use ruled lines to set off some of the type, but otherwise it would avoid typographic frills. Such a publication might frame pictures in white and center them. Certainly it would avoid crowding. The look would be one of quiet luxury.

Don't be misled by the simplicity of the look. The subtle relationship of spaces is not easy to duplicate. Still, of the two basic approaches the

By Michele Cohen

LIFE IN THE ALUMINUM CITY

No taxes, no solicitors, no police, no crime — and maybe no future. Welcome to the City of Ocean Breeze Park, Fla.

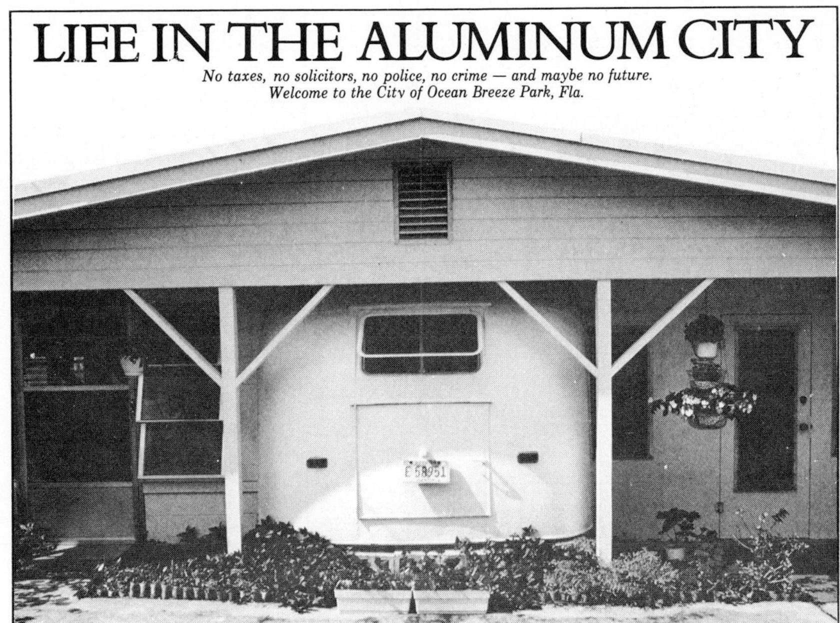

Photos by Jay Paris

From the moment you arrive, it's clear that the town is a strange one.

A map from a nearby real estate agency omits Ocean Breeze Park altogether, though a shopping center down the road is plainly marked. Hundreds of quaint, white trailers line a picturesque section of the Indian River in Martin County, as if a convoy of mobile homes nad screeched to a halt and stayed put for 40 years.

Inside the town, retirees clip hedges or sip coffee on tiny porches. The days pass, but there is little noticeable change. All smiles. No conflict. And a population almost a generation older than the age of retirement. All it needs is Rod Serling intoning "... and their destination is ... *The Twilight Zone.*"

For this sleepy town, Ocean Breeze Park, aside from being a veritable Rip Van Winkle, is also a modern-day fiefdom, a one-man show.

The one man is Mayor Carl Eugene (Gene) Hoke, a 68-year-old businessman whose father, Harry, founded the town. Gene is also the owner, manager, finance director and just about everything else. He probably would be the police chief, if the town needed one.

The 90-odd acres of Ocean Breeze Park have made Hoke a millionaire. His trailer, perched on the riverbank, houses a sauna, a hot tub and a pool room.

But wealth suits Hoke like an oversized coat. He has moved away from his town only once since he arrived in 1937, and that was for a four-year stint in the Army. He was stationed in France and England but what can Eutope offer compared to the splendor of a trailer park, the quiet life of good fishing and shuffleboard?

Hoke's tenants, who seem to view him as a benevolent uncle, would agree. Profusely. They are probably the only Floridians who have nothing bad to say about their city.

Perhaps the best illustration of what attracts them can be found in the brochure that promises Ocean Breezers *The Time of Your Life for the Rest of Your Life (Everything for Your Health and Happiness)*:

"There are no strangers here," the brochure reads. "Everybody greets you with a cheerful smile. If he doesn't, be assured he is not one of us. . . .Here beside the Indian River and just below the coconut line, in a semi-tropical climate, is everything we desire . . ."

Author Clyde Redinger, a rambling world traveler and free-lance writer, came to Ocean Breeze Park in 1955 with a life sentence of three months. He had fallen off the roof of his ranch home in Eugene, Oregon. His doctor warned that subsequent nerve and muscle spasms could trigger a years-old heart condition. Now, nearly 30 years later, he is alive and well at age 87. His right arm, once incapacitated, was reactivated by incessant shuffleboard-playing, for which he has garnered 38 trophies. Forget Rod Serling; what this place needs is Ronald Colman, eyes awestruck at finding Shangri-la.

"We seem to be in a little pocket here where all the hurricanes go around us and all the world goes past us," Redinger remarks.

A walk through the trailer park tells a tale of the town. On each home, a smartly painted sign gives the tenants' names, first and last, and the date they arrived. The sign allows for a friendly hello to newcomers. And visitors need not seek a street address before knocking on a trailer door.

For Bill and Elsie Folk, the paint on their sign is still fresh. They settled in just a few months ago, after nine years of sharing their retirement between Pennsylvania and Florida. Not enamored with the country-club life, the Folks opted for Ocean Breeze Park, "mainly because of the people and because of the Hokes."

Shortly after the move, Mrs. Folk discovered a beauty parlor in Jensen Beach, a mile or so away. Her stylist scarcely knew of the park and was surprised to learn it was a town. "She didn't know we had a mayor," says a bemused Mrs. Folk, still not accustomed to living amid obscurity. "You'd think after all these years that it would be well known."

As governments go, Ocean Breeze's doesn't go far. The way the city handles its business is, to put it mildly, informal. Even the mayor needs to be reminded when the next council meeting is due.

Most important, retirees escape the bothersome matter of taxes, budgets and bureaucrats, because Ocean Breeze Park has none. State and federal money flows in at a faster rate than the tiny town can spend it. The town savings account is five times larger than its annual expenses — a healthy $450,000.

Ocean Breeze Park's "comprehensive plan," required by the state, paints a future virtually identical to the past and present. A few hundred happy folks living out their Golden Years, until they finally drift away to a place that they probably believe to be a lot like Ocean Breeze Park itself.

But even Shangri-la had its naysayers, and Ocean Breeze Park is no exception.

County politicians clearly resent their lack of control over this prime riverfront spot, one of only four municipalities in Martin County. But

Art director Greg Paul used a large, close-up, head-on photograph along with title and blurb to span the gutter of this *Sunshine* spread. The formal pattern of the photograph calls for formal balance in design, with full columns of copy on each side. The credit line matches the byline (other photos follow). *Sunshine* is published by the Fort Lauderdale *News/Sun-Sentinel.*

ordered approach is the one that should be used by the editor-without-an-art-director. Ideally that editor should call in a consulting art director to set up a format, choose the types, and draw up a set of instructions and diagrams on how to handle special features and standing departments. Then the editor or staff art director takes over.

Two long-established magazines stand out as unique examples of the ordered approach. *The New Republic* from 1959 to 1967 was about as ordered as any magazine could be, and handsome for it. Noel Martin, brought in as a consultant for a complete format redesign, chose a roman typeface, Palatino, designed in 1950 by Hermann Zapf. Looking very contemporary, Palatino nevertheless draws its inspiration from the early Venetian types. It suggests a happy blend of tradition and progress. Martin used it not only for main titles but for subtitles, credit lines, body copy, the logo—everything. He permitted typographic variety only through varying the sizes and combining uprights with italics. The editors never varied Martin's simple two-column pattern until someone there, unfortunately, decided to jazz up the magazine with boldface versions of the type (most type designs lose their beauty when their strokes are thickened) and with an angular script that for some column headings occasionally ran on a diagonal. The magazine made some rather substantial changes again with the September 9, 1981, issue, getting rid of the two rectangular blocks that used to flank the logo, changing the logo to outline letters, and making other adjustments but staying with the Palatino type.

The New Yorker's design is so ordered as to be nonexistent. A cartoonist back in the early 1920s, when it was founded, designed its display face, and the magazine has never changed it. It uses a few spot drawings and, of course, those celebrated gag cartoons to provide occasional graphic oases, but otherwise its "designer" simply pours the editorial material into the holes left over by the advertising. There is no opening display for any of the articles or stories. The advertisers love it, because it makes their insertions, always well designed anyway, striking by comparison.

You can also list *Smithsonian, Audubon, Scientific American, Sports*

THE NEW AGE INTERVIEW

Lily Tomlin and friends are back with a new Broadway show and more insights about how things really are.

By Leonie Caldicott

Whose Reality Is It, Anyway?

THE GREAT American Music Hall in San Francisco is packed. Waiters and waitresses maneuver with difficulty among a tangle of tables in the spacious auditorium with its muted Victorian decor. The show is fifteen minutes late starting, and the crowd—from blue-rinse ladies to casually dressed juveniles—starts the good-humored chant: "Li-ly! Li-ly! LI-LY! LI-LY!" Suddenly a nimble form springs from the wings and is caught by the spotlight, provoking a thunderous welcome from the floor. Smiling and bowing with a studied grace that already touches on self-parody, Lily Tomlin, with sparse use of costumes and props and no accompanying cast, proceeds to deliver three hours of brilliant comedy. This is *Works in Process*, Lily Tomlin's new stage show, which just opened on Broadway under the new title *The Search for Signs of Intelligent Life in the Universe*. Written by Jane Wagner, who also wrote the Tony Award–winning *Appearing Nitely* in 1977, the show features a series of monologues by diverse characters—incisive commentaries on the current state of civilization.

Best known for her television appearances in the late '60s and early '70s on "Laugh-In," Tomlin has also received rave reviews for her roles in movies such as *Nashville, The Late Show, Nine to Five, The Incredible Shrinking Woman*, and most recently *All of Me*. But she has to be seen in live performance for her full genius to be appreciated. She has an extraordinary physical presence, a malleability of expression, voice, and movement that makes the transitions from one character to another utterly credible. At one point in the second half of the show, she comes on with a script in her hand. "This is new material, and I haven't learned it properly yet," she says, with an irresistible grin, her eyes suddenly creased into a warm, sparkling expression that conveys the sense of fun and tenderness with which she approaches the world. "But you seem like the sort of audi-

Leonie Caldecott is the author of Women of Our Century *(BBC Publications). Her interview with Liv Ullmann appeared in the July* New Age.

PHOTOGRAPH: MARK HANAUER

28 NEW AGE OCTOBER 1985 29

With his emphasis on geometric shapes and tilts, art director Greg Paul for this *New Age* spread used the "new wave" approach to magazine design.

Illustrated, and *Omni* among the magazines with an orderly look. But don't confuse *orderly* with *stilted.* These magazines still carry visual excitement on their pages. Often the excitement comes from the nature and subject matter of the art.

Amy Seissler, art director of *Omni,* certainly doesn't feel intimidated by what she calls the magazine's "heavily formatted" look. "Good design comes from being able to play off a well-established format, but still giving yourself an opportunity to break the rules."[4]

The lively approach

Whereas the orderly approach virtually guarantees reasonably good design, even for magazines with limited resources, the lively approach works only when directed by a professional designer. Its success depends to a considerable extent on violations of traditional principles of design.

In the lively approach the designer may arrange elements to create a large void on one side of a page, purposely disturbing the reader in order to focus attention on an article that deals, let's say, with student unrest. Out goes balance.

The "Entertainment" section in *Palm Springs Life Desert Guide* takes more than two pages an issue, but these two pages are representative of the design approach: plenty of white space with both rectangle-finish and silhouette photographs. The photographs are irregularly clustered to make a single unit. Like many publications of the late 1980s, this one makes use of short, heavy, horizontal bars as visual markers or starting places. Katie Richardson is art director of the *Guide;* Bill Russom is design director of Desert Publications, Inc.

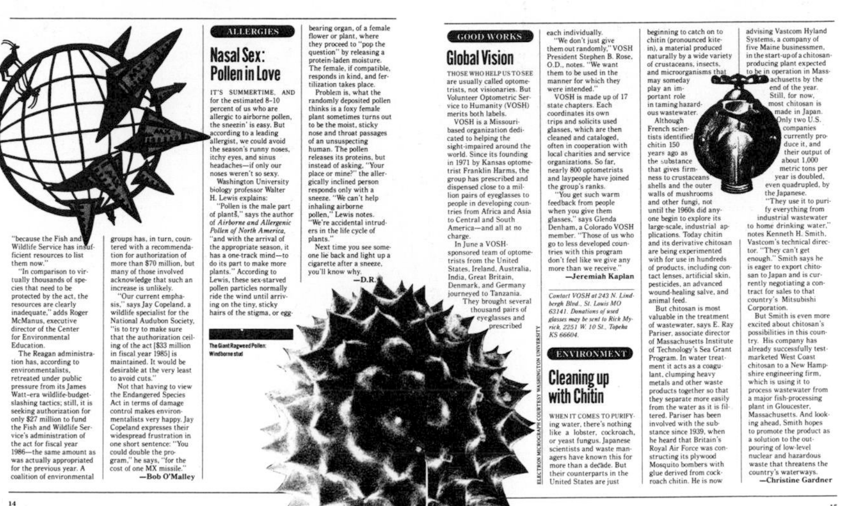

UPFRONT

ALLERGIES

Nasal Sex: Pollen in Love

GOOD WORKS

Global Vision

ENVIRONMENT

Cleaning up with Chitin

The sink remains the same on the several pages of an "Upfront" feature in *New Age,* to unite the pages. Each short item gets a kicker, with reverse type in a rounded-corner bar, and a condensed sans serif heading. In this spread, for the sake of unity, three different pieces of art take a circular shape. Chris Frame designed the spread, Mark Andresen did the drawings, and Greg Paul art directed.

Or the designer uses square- rather than rectangular-shaped photographs. The reasoning may be that for this particular set of photographs, cropping to squares brings out the best composition. Or the designer chooses a permanent square-page format, as Herb Lubalin did for *Avant Garde,* to make the magazine stand out from all others. Out goes standard proportion.

Or the designer doesn't care in which direction the reader goes. The designer scrambles the picture because there is no correct order. The effect need not be cumulative for the article: it is no how-to-do-it. Out goes sequence.

Or the designer wants to show the complicated strategy of a single football play, as *Esquire* did in one of its issues. Samuel Antupit ran a chart showing all players on both sides, officials and coaches, fans in the stands, the press corps, the stadium and scoreboard, with labels and captions and directional lines and boxes fighting for attention with the article itself and its title. Out goes simplicity.

Or the designer is dealing with an article that makes five or six main points, equally important. No one item should stand out. This calls for a series of equal-size pictures. Out goes contrast.

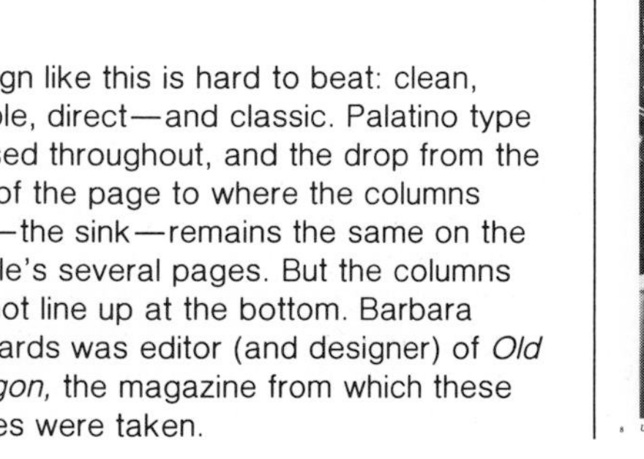

Collecting The Right Stuff

Nancy Woolum

Ed Kemp is bent on building a valid collection representing conservatism as an enduring political philosophy.

Design like this is hard to beat: clean, simple, direct—and classic. Palatino type is used throughout, and the drop from the top of the page to where the columns are—the sink—remains the same on the article's several pages. But the columns do not line up at the bottom. Barbara Edwards was editor (and designer) of *Old Oregon,* the magazine from which these pages were taken.

In a Gestalt experiment for a visual communications class at Chico State University, Chico, California, Terry Laks saw how many variations of a dragon fly she could come up with—realistic, cartoonlike, and abstract. Here are some of them. She ended up with a logo at the far right. Gregg Berryman was her instructor.

And yet in each case the designer maintains a semblance of each of the design principles. The concentration of white space is itself heavy and tends to counterbalance the dark elements on the other side of the page. Square-shaped photographs appear on a rectangular page. Scrambled pictures precede a column of type that moves in the conventional way from top to bottom. Visual confusion is confined only to the display types. One cluttered article fits into an issue filled otherwise with pages stark and clean. Even-size pictures, no one of them standing out from the others, form one large mass that overpowers a smaller copy block, providing contrast to the page after all.

It would be more accurate to say that the designer using the lively approach does not so much ignore design principles as emphasize one over the others.

The lively approach is the experimental approach. And experiment is best conducted by those who are grounded in the fundamentals.

Two of the most honored practitioners of the lively approach were Allen Hurlburt of *Look* and Otto Storch of *McCall's*. *Look's* imaginative handling of photographs in sequence caused *Life* to revitalize its appearance. *McCall's* brought new life to women's magazines.

Some observers feel the lively approach makes things difficult for the reader. But "it is more interesting for the reader if the visual pace of the magazine varies," Storch said. "Some pages can be quiet and others bold, some restful and others exciting, some with pictures dominating the layout and others with no pictures at all."

Magazines using basically the lively approach include *Life, Psychology Today, Seventeen, Rolling Stone,* and *American Health.* The lively approach works best for large-format publications. The *Digest* size of some magazines tends to cramp the style of the freewheeling designer.

In the mid-1980s a popular lively style involved extreme letterspacing of all-caps titles, heavy leading, and a sprinkling of geometric shapes arranged on unrelated diagonals to create the appearance that they were floating in space. These abstract shapes appeared to have no meaning, nor were they related to the articles' contents. Pastel colors were also popular. Some observers called this design "new wave." The design also was known as "Memphis," a name attached to a collection of incongruous furniture coming out of Italy in the early 1980s.[5] The name apparently was inspired by Bob Dylan's "Stuck Outside Mobile with the Memphis Blues Again."

The willingness to experiment

Conducting experiments is nothing new to the arts. Each of the art movements of the past had its mavericks, who broke away to form new movements. A primary goal of many artists—and graphic designers, too—is to shock. Henri Matisse, for example, put a green stripe down the front

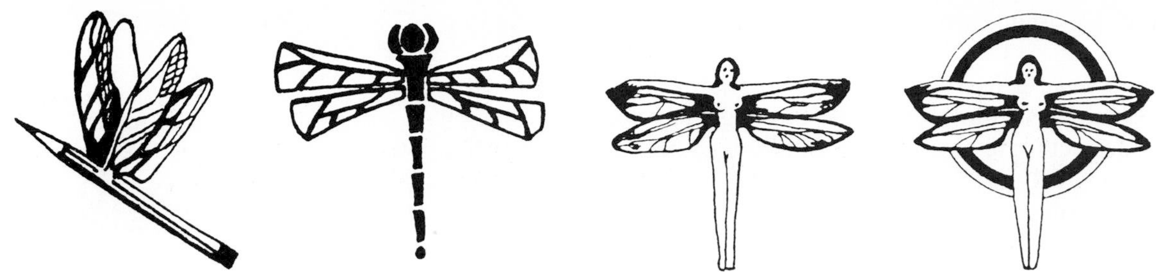

of the portrait he was painting of his wife—a portrait that was to become famous—and caused a stir in the art community.

Magazine designers—some of them—are like that. They like to push the limits of a page to its outer boundaries. At the least, they like to experiment within their given formats.

Brian Noyes, when he was art director of *Saturday Review,* was such an experimenter. His assignment was to change the magazine's traditional look to a more splashy one. A *Saturday Review* cover, for instance, was not a lot different from a *People* cover. Sometimes his experiments worked. Sometimes they didn't. "You think . . . [a spread] is going to look great, and then you're surprised at how bad it looks," he said of his work. "It's like building a house. You know exactly what you want. But then when company comes, you want to go and hang up new wallpaper."[6]

The need to simplify

Using either an orderly or a lively approach to design, you want to make things easy for your readers. They simply do not have the time to browse or hunt. But "to work to make something look simple is just as hard as making it look as though there is a whole lot of design going into it," says Nigel Holmes, executive art director of *Time.*[7]

One way to simplify is to give the reader as few elements per page or spread as you can. Instead of many small pictures—two or three large ones. Instead of three columns to the page—two or one. Instead of a mul-

Home & Garden

Home on the ridge

Clockwise from top left: A staircase leads to all three levels; the indoor pool sports a waterfall and tropical landscaping; the house faces downtown Los Gatos below; the elegant living room includes a 37-light chandelier; a well-kept putting green, flanked by a gazebo that seats 32 people, sharpens golfing skills; and spectacular views of the valley are evident everywhere.

Los Gatos Weekly, a tabloid paper published in Los Altos, California, allows photographs to radiate from the center of a spread, creating one irregular photographic shape. Notice how the steps in the top left photograph lead to the swimming pool edge, which leads to the photograph at the top right. The feature starts on the left-hand page, but the headline and caption material appear on the right. The line across the top and the picture spread unite the two pages. White space keeps to the outside, further uniting the pages. Art director, Tony Kasovich. Photographer, Dan Honda.

tidecked heading—a single title. Instead of a three-line title—a title in a single line.

Even when you have a half dozen or more photographs to work into the design, organize them into one mass, butting them together so they make either a true rectangle or a square. Some designers organize all the elements so that they will form three basic areas of unequal size separated from each other by unequal distances.

Thick and thin lines (or rules) gained popularity in the 1980s as design accessories. In magazines thick lines often ran horizontally, thin lines vertically to separate columns of copy. Many—perhaps too many—designers butted short thick lines against longer thin lines as attention getters.

Visualization

As a designer taking on a magazine assignment, you would first make a decision on format (see chapter 6). Then you would decide which of the two basic design approaches to take: the orderly or the lively.

Already you have placed some limitations on yourself. Additional limitations may come from the editor. You get a manuscript of, say, 2,500 words, a title, and four photographs, and you have five pages in the magazine where you can put them. You make of this what you can, deciding which photograph to play up, how far down on the page to start the article, where subheads will go, how much white space to allow. Other articles will follow. And similar restrictions will accompany them.

In this case you are not much more than a layout artist. You get some satisfaction out of fitting these things together, but clearly, you are not fully engaged in graphic design.

Far better is the arrangement whereby you plan the issue with the editor, helping decide subject areas for articles and stories. Occasionally you may plan the art and lay out the pages before the article is written; the article then is tailored to fit.

Most important in the visualization process is the setting of the mood. You decide: photographs or drawings or no art at all? color? sans serif or roman type for the title? two-column or three-column pages? initial letters or subheads? Realism may be better served through photography. Clarity may be better served through drawings. Color has psychological effects. Sans serif typefaces may say "now"; roman typefaces may say "yesterday." Wide columns may suggest urgency, but narrow columns may be more immediate. Initial letters can be decorated to suggest the period of the piece.

You consider all of this, keeping in mind, always, production problems likely to result. Color adds to costs. Wide columns take more space because type has to be set larger.

Designers faced a difficult assignment in the mid-1960s with the "Death of God" debate. Nearly every magazine dealt with the matter; the question was how to illustrate it. Designers could run mug shots of the theologians quoted, but these would not make very good opening spreads. And photographs of God himself were hard to come by. Most designers took this way out: beautiful display of the article titles in old roman type. This seemed appropriate to the mood. *Time* (April 8, 1966), doing a major story on the debate, settled, for the first time in its history, on an all-type cover.

Whether art follows copy or copy follows art, the two must work in harmony. An article on the hippies of the 1960s features psychedelic lettering and art. One of the navy appears under a title done in stencil letters. An article on the population explosion swells out to the edge of a crowded page.

The art accompanying the article should say the same thing the title

The second two pages of an article on packaging used silhouetted parts of packages at the outside edges to form a frame for the copy. From *nbeye,* Dana Lee Wood, editor. Design by Johnson & Simpson Graphic Designers.

says. For an article on "The Hectic Life of a College President," for instance, you would not select a routine shot of a well-dressed executive, hands folded, behind a cleared-off desk. For fiction you would use a drawing or painting for the opening spread; for nonfiction, photography. For fiction you can reach deep into the story for a scene to illustrate. The scene need not be thematic. For nonfiction the main piece of art should summarize what's in type.

As a designer you normally would read the manuscript before it is set in type to decide what kind of typographic and illustrative treatment it should have. You may have a copy made for the illustrator, who can then decide on which illustration technique to use.

Having some idea of what the picture or pictures will be and knowing how much space the manuscript will take, you begin with a series of thumbnail sketches of the pages, toying with space divisions. When you have thumbnails that show promise, you redraw them in actual size so that you can begin figuring exact dimensions.

Mike Salisbury, when he was art director of *West,* told how he did it: "I don't rework any layouts. The first ideas I sketch out are usually the ones produced. I work very loose and spontaneously, trying to keep a good

The last two pages of a four-page "Commentary" article in *Bell Telephone Magazine* use the folio line at the top to remind readers of the title "On Regulation." The folio line and the two initial letters are in red, forming a triangle of color. The spread features both initial letters and a blurb, plus a photograph, to keep the design active. The initial letters take scattered placement: one is low on its page, the other one is high; one is in a middle column, the other is in a left-hand column. Each of the pages in the article is surrounded by a thin-line box, and each of the columns is fenced in by the same thin lines. The heavier bars, used above and below the blurb, take their thickness from the black box that signals the article's end. The top bar lines up with the top of the photograph, helping to unify the two elements.

ON REGULATION

Confronted with public dissatisfaction in certain areas, the trend of regulation has been toward increasingly detailed and affirmative requirements. Uninsured driver coverage, compulsory coverage, and no-fault insurance coverage, for example, are some of the responses. While new regulations have often met with opposition, deregulation—and in particular the withdrawal of the regulators from the overseeing of rates and terms—has not been seriously proposed.

On the other hand, it seems to me that there has been general satisfaction with the regulated banking and telephone industries. (The regulated electric and gas utilities have had a mixed picture; general satisfaction with performance has been clouded in recent years by occasional power shortages and rapid rate escalation in some cases.)

• In the case of banking, the Justice Department and others have proposed some "deregulation," taking the form of federal requirements restraining state regulation (e.g., by relaxing the restraints on branch banking) and compelling open access of competitors to cooperative clearing and processing arrangements.

• In the field of electric power, the Justice Department has won antitrust court decisions requiring the involuntary sale and "wheeling" of power to neighboring companies in some cases. This is a variation of the deregulation theme that overrides, to some degree, the state and federal regulatory function of determining the scope of the monopoly.

There seems to be little public impetus behind these efforts, and they do not seem to relate to any considerable public complaints. They do, indeed, displace some state regulations, but it's done by putting a federal policeman in place of state jurisdiction.

The organization of the telephone industry, I believe, successfully exemplifies a unified and integrated arrangement, along with end-to-end service responsibility, toward which the ConRail and other rail consolidation plans aspire. The public has been fairly satisfied with telephone service. The FCC, however, has adopted regulatory changes that move in the opposite direction by licensing competing private line networks on major trunk telephone routes, the routes most attractive to competitors. (The traffic of competitors is handed by them to telepone company facilities for local delivery.)

In my opinion, although the reduced, even minimal, regulatory review of the service offerings and rates of the *new competitors* does move toward deregulation, the regulation of the competing rates and services of the *telephone companies*—and the terms of required interconnection of the competitors—has moved toward greater stringency.

This has required an enlarged regulatory staff. Thus, while the rail industry is moving toward imitation of the successful telephone industry, the FCC, it seems to me, is ironically moving toward the pattern of parallel routes and the interexchange of competing traffic—instead of end-to-end service—of the ailing railroads. (Telephone company inter-exchange of traffic, of course, has been a partnership service, rather than competitive offerings.)

The distinction between industries characterized by regulated competitors and those with a pattern of exclusive geographic franchise is another distinction that the deregulation publicity generally fails to mention. These groupings bear an intriguing similarity to the grouping by performance.

The transportation industry, for example, has had continuous regulator involvement (as the deciding voice) in an almost unending series of forensic battles between competitors. These decisions, and the competition they ruled over, seem to have been critical factors in shaping the rail industry towards its present unsatisfactory state.

On the other hand, regulators of the electric power and telephone industries have, until recent years, concentrated on setting rates and conditions of service, somewhat as a substitute for competition. For the most part, there have not been competitors, and, thus, no preoccupation of the hearing room with intercompetitor legal battles. Within these industries, there has been general satisfaction regarding service, although some dissatisfaction with rate increases. But there hasn't been any significant movement from the general public to deregulate or inject competition.

Thus, some service enterprises with area monopolies, such as electric power and telephone, enjoy public satisfaction with service, while some service enterprises in the rail passenger, mass transit, and auto insurance fields suffer service dissatisfaction despite the so-called spur of strong competition.

Certainly, the Penn Central and other bankrupt eastern railroads were unsatisfactory, in part because of—and not merely in spite of—competition. They could not pull out of losing regulated operations, while revenues from profitable operations were lost to competition. Eventually, they were unable to pay their bills or provide good service.

In contrast, U.S. phone service has been generally regarded as satisfactory even though there is no telephone competition. End-to-end service responsibility is exercised by an entity singly or with its partners, and good service in all parts spurs the revenues on which the whole depends.

Of course, no service is entirely without competition. Telegram and mail service "compete." But when phone service had already improved so much that such competitive impact was negligible, phone service nevertheless continued to improve. Over a long period, it would seem that good and improving service *can* be provided by enterprises that have a service responsibility and no close competition.

We often take for granted the provision of service without external competition in the case of municipal utility services, such as water supply and electricity. Some communities enjoy better services than others, but we do not force the explanation of these differences into a theory about competitive motivation.

It seems to me that the dynamics of *cooperation* and *mutuality of goals* are just as important—and perhaps just as complex and mysterious as those contained in a contest—in spurring good performance, whether it be from a boiler tender, lineman, or gandy dancer.

Even this cursory consideration of several regulated industries may show that we are dealing with complex, greatly varying factual situations. The problems will not all yield to some *a priori* concept or principle; the aims and capabilities of regulation must be assessed against performance in each situation.

Here are three nutshell examples:

• In the franchising of liquor stores in some states, one goal is to keep them an appropriate distance from certain other amenities, such as schools and churches, and an appropriate distance from each other.

• In the franchising of broadcasting stations, one goal is to divide up the use of the available frequencies so there is no interference among stations.

• In the oil fields of the South and Southwest, one goal is to keep producers from pumping out crude at such a rate that there is an underground adverse effect on the whole field. Because of this concern, production of all competitors is restricted to a "maximum efficient rate" that will not damage ultimate crude recovery.

While the rail industry is moving toward imitation of the successful telephone industry, the FCC is ironically moving toward some aspects of the ailing railroads.

In these cases, for policy, technical, or conservation reasons, the state imposes a cartel; the goals can be achieved neither by competition nor by deregulation if the law prohibits a private cartel.

A goal stated in the Federal Communications Act of 1934 is "to make available so far as possible, to all the people of the United States, a rapid, efficient, nationwide, and worldwide wire and radio communication service with adequate facilities at reasonable charges . . ."

The progress—some would say success—in reaching this goal is, in good measure, attributable to the close concert among noncompeting telephone companies, each having responsibility for a geographic area or a function. We must ask if here, too, there are aims which cannot be attained by committing the participants to seek opposing goals.

The transportation industry is undergoing some legislative rethinking, and the communications industry also appears to be on the agenda for a look at goals and means. Just how many other regulatory industries will receive a looking-over is speculative. But what about the more than 1,000 federal programs, the 60,000 pages of regulations published in 1975, the several score new federal agencies begun in the last year or two, the regulations at which I have suggested public resentment is really aimed? I, for one, do not expect any drastic cutbacks.

The sentiment of Congressman John Moss (D.-Calif.), testifying last May at a Senate Government Operations Committee hearing on the administration's and other regulatory reform proposals, is representative of most lawmakers:

"Undeniably, a number of older regulatory programs are candidates for thoroughgoing review and reform. However, the focus of our efforts, with respect to health and safety regulation in particular, must be to make these programs more effective, and not to cripple them . . ."

I believe that "more effective" may mean better, but will not translate to less regulation. The rubric "health and safety" would apply to the fields of occupational safety, medical programs, air, water, and noise pollution controls, along with other environmental endeavors, product safety, vehicle and highway safety, and so on.

Even though there will be discussion of new terms, such as "zero base budgeting," and cutbacks in some federal economic controls, I am persuaded that under the banner of "health and safety" (and irrespective of who sits in the White House), we should anticipate more federal policing, not less. ■

16

17

pacing of layout styles throughout the book. The less attention I give a layout's styling the better it will look. I spend more time getting the proper photos, illustrations, and research material organized. The layout is usually secondary in importance to the material used in the layout."[8]

In some cases you would do your designing with galley proofs and photostats of the art, cutting and pasting and moving items around until they give the fit and look you desire. This rough pasteup acts as a guide for the finished pasteup.

Terry Laks on assignment for this book did a diagram to illustrate many of the design clichés described on this page.

Stimulating creativity

"The most conspicuous quality of creative people is curiosity," the designer George Nelson said in the Charles Eames Memorial Lecture at the University of Michigan in March 1984. "Small children have a large supply of it. Where does it vanish when the kids grow up? And why?"

Nelson says we must all continue our education beyond school. "However, self-education is . . . not easy. It doesn't work unless there is curiosity and a desire to learn—*a very strong desire to learn*." Nelson says his own antidote for mental laziness, which we all have to some degree, is to focus on heroes, "individuals alive or dead whose thinking and writing . . . [we] admire and would like to emulate." One of his heroes is the writer Ortega y Gassett. "He has an extraordinary talent for saying exactly what he means."

Nelson admits that looking for heroes is out of style, but being out of style is part of being creative. People who want to be more creative should try "the interesting experience of being out of style or maybe just getting out of step once in a while."

Avoiding design clichés

In what may be misguided enthusiasm for one or the other of the design principles, or because of their lack of knowledge of what good design is, beginning designers make a number of mistakes, and make them consistently. Perhaps these designers have seen design solutions, liked them, and used them in new situations even when they didn't fit. The solutions have been used too often.

Writers have their tired-but-happys and last-but-not-leasts; designers have the following:

1. *Picture cutouts.* Beginning designers seem to think that pictures displayed in regular rectangular or square shapes bore the reader. They may—but only because the pictures themselves are boring. Cutting them into circles or triangles or stars or whatever will not make them better pictures. If the pictures are good to begin with, such cutting will stunt their impact, ruin their composition, and demoralize the photographer who took them.
2. *Tilts.* Closely related to the first cliché is the practice of putting a picture or a headline on a diagonal. Presumably, the designer feels this will make it stand out from others. It will, but at the expense of causing the reader irritation.

   The introduction of the diagonal suggests movement. The picture is falling. The reader gets caught up in this phenomenon and cannot give full attention to what the picture actually says. Readability suffers.

More defensible is the practice of putting the entire contents of the spread on a single or on parallel diagonals. But the designer should have a good reason for doing this—a reason better than "to be different."

3. *Vertical typography.* The designer has a deep vertical space left over and a title to fit in and therefore runs it with the letters on top of each other in succession down the page. The title is unreadable; and the designer has probably run it in type larger than necessary.

   The designer would save white space and make the title more readable—make it stand out better—by decreasing its size and running it in usual left-to-right form in a strategic spot near the article's beginning.
4. *Mortises.* Seeing an expanse of picture that is all sky or all foreground, some designers, prompted perhaps by a lack of space elsewhere, cut out a block and put type there. The block may be completely surrounded by photograph, or it may be at an edge or corner. Wherever the mortise is located, it usually hurts the composition of the picture and cheapens the page.

   The mortise is slightly more defensible when another photograph rather than type is placed into the cutout portion of the original photograph, providing a picture within a picture. *Look* used this technique effectively.
5. *Overlaps.* The designer runs type for a heading partly in the white space next to a photograph and partly in the photograph itself. As it passes from white space to photograph, the type can remain black (surprint). Or, as it makes the crossing, it can change to white letters (reverse printing).

   The designer resorts to this cliché for two reasons: (1) to save space (perhaps the heading is too wide for the space allotted to it) and (2) to draw type and picture together (the principle of unity). But the space saving comes at the expense of a visual interruption where the type crosses over. And the unification of type and photo comes at the expense of photo clarity and beauty.

The list of clichés could be expanded. For instance, it would be easy to make a case against all reverses and surprints. Designers too often resort to these—at some expense to readability.

Occasionally, a venturesome designer goes slumming among the clichés, picks one out, and lends some dignity to it. In goods hands, even a cliché can please.

Exposed-pipes-and-ducts design

You sometimes hear speakers at journalism conventions say that editors should let readers know more about their publications and even about the editors themselves. That may not be good advice; other editors and writers may be interested in the problems and people of editing, but ordinary readers have more important matters to consider. And frankly, the more mysterious editing processes appear to be, the better off editors probably are.

But in the design of publications, it is not a bad idea, once in a while, to turn to the infrastructure of the business for some visual relief. Readers may not understand the legitimacy of what goes on in design and production, but they can appreciate the patterns that emerge. Just as fancy restaurants and boutiques show off a building's pipes and ducts instead of hiding them, editors and art directors can display pieces and edges instead of cropping them. A model for this kind of design is that landmark of architecture, the Georges Pompidou Center in Paris, with its brightly colored exposed construction.

A common example of this kind of design in print can be found in full-color photographs run with the notched outlines found on original transparencies. Some designers even include small pieces of tape, as though the transparencies were fastened to a light table for inspection. (The tape would suggest that the transparencies are still in their transparent envelopes.)

Another example of this design can be found on pages that show the gridded paper used for the pasteup sheet. Sometimes a publication takes ordinary typewritten words and, for titles or blurbs, blows them up to a giant size so that their ribbon imperfections show up.

Rules, bars, boxes, and other design delights

Sorting through typical newspapers, you can pretty much tell the modern from the old-fashioned by the lack of column rules. Get rid of column rules, editors figure, go to all-lowercase heads, and change the nameplate from Old English to, say, Bodoni; or, if you are really daring, go to Helvetica, and you put your newspaper among the avant-garde.

What the newspaper throws away, the magazine picks up. Or, one medium's garbage is another medium's treasure.

Column rules are big in magazine design now. And when rules are not enough, there are bars. Nice, thick bars. Some magazines combine thick bars with thin rules. The bars can be used, for instance, as horizontal underlines or overlines, the thin rules as column or story separators.

When he was art director of *New York,* Milton Glaser brought the Scotch rule back into general use. A Scotch rule consists of a thick line sandwiched between two thin lines. Many magazines copied the look.

And for many editors and art directors, the box is a staple of design, especially when several vaguely related items appear on a page or spread.

This two-spread, four-page article from *Old Oregon,* an alumni magazine, is held together by a single photograph, full bleed on all pages. The editor/designer, Stan Bettis, who took the picture, used part of it for one spread, part for another. He ran the photo in a light tone so he could surprint the title and body copy. Note how the runner and the title move the reader to the initial letter that begins the article. The horizon line in the photo carries the reader from the first spread to the second.

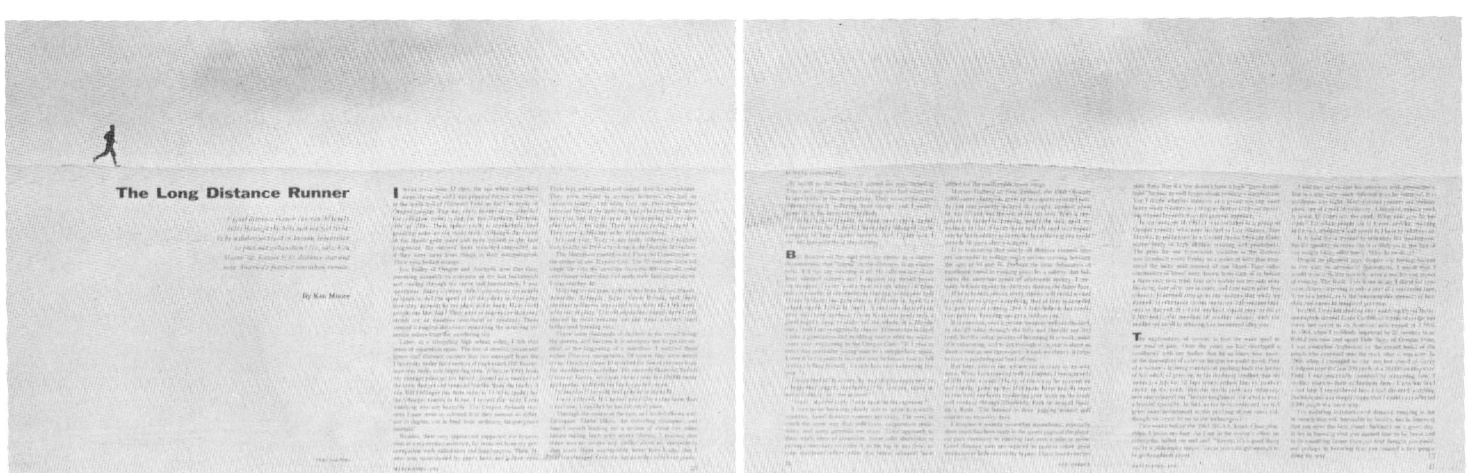

The Long Distance Runner

By Ken Moore

FUTURESCOPE

TV GOES TUBE-LESS

Come Fly With Me

Pressroom Wizard

FOR SALE: RECYCLED HOUSE

A set of boxes sometimes can best organize a page of miscellaneous items. In "Futurescope," a full-color page from *Johns-Manville Future,* the designer used different typefaces for each feature and where necessary wrapped copy around the art. The all-the-way-across-the-page heading, the black border, and the same-style drawings help unify the page that otherwise might have been a hodgepodge.

Boxes may be built from single-width lines, decorative lines, or sets of parallel lines (like Scotch rules). You can also get a box by running a tint block in gray or color under a unit of type.

Lines, bars, boxes, and other typographic gimmicks can help sort things out for the reader. But they can become clichés. One day, perhaps, magazine editors and art directors will grow tired of them and toss them aside, where young newspaper art directors (or makeup people) will rediscover them, and a new trend will come to newspaper design. In fact, looking at the handsome special sections of the New York *Times* and other important newspapers, you get the impression the trend has already begun. The ruled lines in this reincarnation run horizontally rather than vertically.

The swipe file

A cartoonist copies the cross-hatched, carefully controlled lines of David Levine, and his colleagues, if not his readers, will spot the plagiarism. An illustrator copies the delicate line, the flat colors, and the decorative look of Milton Glaser, and fellow painters will see at once the influence of the master. In practice the appropriation of another person's style or technique seldom results in work that is the equal of the original.

In the area of graphic design, lifting ideas comes more easily and with less stigma attached, although a few designers are beginning to copyright their work. The copyright law, which has long protected original writing and art, has recently been interpreted more broadly to include design. Joan Stoliar is thought to be the first designer to copyright a book design (*Illusions* by Richard Bach, Delacorte Press/Eleanor Fried, 1977). The design, such as it was, for *Paul McCartney: Composer/Artist* (Simon & Schuster, 1981) was copyrighted. But the U.S. Copyright Office, after a two-year study, decided it would not give protection to graphic design.

Anyway, it is difficult to successfully trace design to its source. It is the rare designer who is not influenced—and not just subconsciously—by the work of other designers. Nor is this bad. The innovators—Allen Hurlburt, Dugald Stermer, Henry Wolf, Peter Palazzo, Paul Rand, and the others—have doubtless had great influence on the look of magazines other than those they've designed, and they must be pleased to have played a role in upgrading the general level of graphic design. They did not have exclusive interest in any one solution, anyway; their great satisfaction lay in moving on to unexplored design plateaus.

Even designers like these maintain swipe files—printed portfolios of prize-winning work, if not the more obvious folders of clippings. All designers and editors should build up their own collections of designs that please, inspire, and, most important, communicate clearly.

There is such a thing as creative copying. As a beginning designer you can't get much satisfaction out of lifting a spread, whole, out of one publication and putting it down in your own magazine with a mere substitution of pictures and wording. You will try to change facings and picture sizes, adjust title length and placement, and so on, not solely to disguise the fact that you have lifted the design, but to try to improve on it. You should use another's design primarily as a starting point. And you should remember that good design is tailored to the needs of a specific article or story.

You will draw inspiration not only from other graphic designs but from architectural structures, oil paintings, and, of course, nature's landscapes.

You may find some stimulus from that classic set of ready-made de-

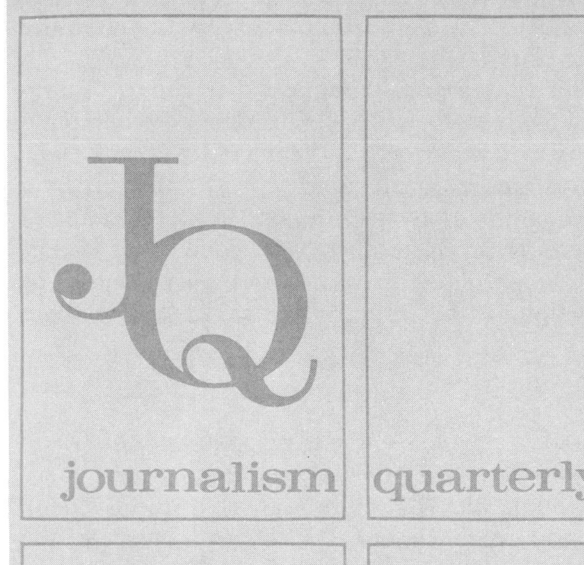

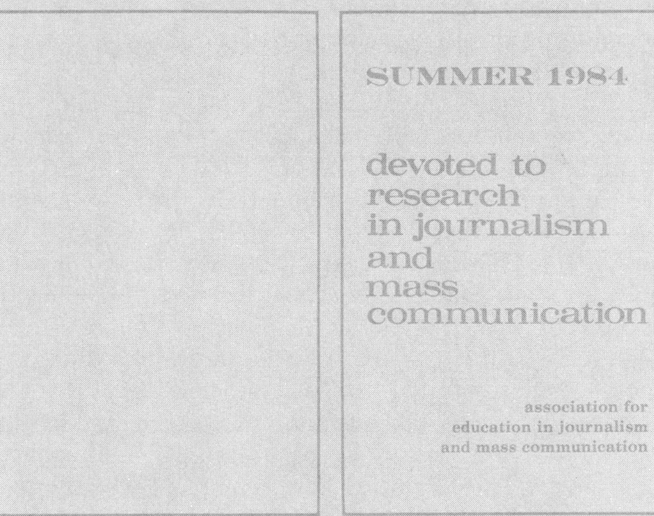

Professor William Korbus of the University of Texas got the job of redesigning the publications of the Association for Education in Journalism and Mass Communication. The old cover for *Journalism Quarterly* appears at the left, Korbus's suggested new cover format at the right. The organization decided it would run type in the area Korbus had given over to the photograph.

signs—the alphabet. An *L* or a *U* or an *A* or an *R*, or a number, or one of the letters turned sideways or upside-down might suggest a pattern for a page or spread. Of course the reader will not see the letter or figure. As a designer you will not be bound by it. You will merely use it as a beginning.

Obviously, much of publication design springs from advertising design. Advertising designers, probably more than publication designers, take chances with graphics. As a publication designer who borrows from advertisers, you will be keeping abreast of graphic design trends. You should remember, though, that many of these trends will turn out to be short-lived fads.

Redesign

When editors think redesign, they should think beyond typefaces and uses of art. They should start with basic size and format. They should reexamine their typesetting systems, their printing processes, their paper stock. They should even rethink their publications' purposes.

One major reason for rethinking design for a consumer magazine is to better attract potential advertisers. When a major magazine goes through redesign, it checks prototypes with advertising agencies to get their reactions. Agencies are concerned about the "editorial environment" for the ads they create. When the design of a magazine becomes unacceptable, an agency may buy space in a different magazine.

The major newsmagazines did some redesigning in the late 1970s to give themselves more of a contemporary look. *Time* hired Walter Bernard, former art director for *New York,* who chose a slightly different typeface for headlines, introduced secondary headlines, and made wider use of thin rules. The magazine said it was after "a simpler, cleaner-looking environment" for its full-color pictures, by then widely used on its pages. The new look started with the August 15, 1977, issue. You might want to examine this and compare it to the previous issue.

Prompted by *Time, Newsweek* brought in outside help and redesigned itself in 1979, using several new typefaces. Sections started with an elbowlike arrangement, with "NEWSWEEK" running up the side. Small boldface initial letters appeared frequently in the magazine. But the look was gimmicky, and *Newsweek* went back to a look closer to what it had had.

In late 1985 both *Newsweek* and *U.S. News & World Report* redesigned themselves, each taking on a bolder, more colorful look to better compete with *Time,* which retained its orderly look. *U.S. News & World Report,* especially, needed to reach out for younger readers.

The editor and art director may find, on getting into a change in format, that the old way of doing things wasn't so bad after all. A case in point is *Advertising Age.* In 1966 it called in John Peter to consider changing its looks. At first, Peter offered a multitude of suggestions for changes. "But the more he and our editors discussed the matter, the more they all agreed that only a minimum of change should be made—that basically, the typographic dress we've been using for 15 years or more was still pretty sound," the magazine said in a 1967 statement. A weekly, the magazine is really a news magazine; and so it wants a newspaper look.

Peter did do these things: He eliminated column rules. He modernized the logo, using a condensed Clarendon, a better looking slab serif type than the more standard slab serif the magazine had been using. He modernized (read that "simplified") the standing heads.

In 1971 *Advertising Age* made another modest change by substituting a modern sans serif for the slab serif it had been using for its heads. It has made a few other changes, but it still has its original look.

Christianity and Crisis is another magazine that thought it needed a complete change and then decided against it. The magazine gave full freedom to two designers to make major changes. The changes they recommended were trivial. They came up with a new logo and a new masthead, and that was about all. One of the designers, Robert Newman, said, "While all avenues were open, we decided not to change it very much. We concluded that the magazine is what it seems to be, which is rare and a virtue in typographic design."

A redesign job, when it is attempted, usually takes a period of several months while the designer learns all about the editorial processes of the publication (every publication develops its own routines) and finds out about the typesetting and the printing facilities available. Decisions must be made to cover every contingency, guidelines laid down to be followed more or less permanently by persons who may not have had a hand in the

Part of Korbus's job for AEJMC consisted of redesigning logos for the various publications. He did the pasteups himself, using a Chartpak press-on alphabet called Benguiat Medium. He created his own *CA* and *CT* ligatures by careful placement and touch-up. The oversize ending letters had to be blown up photographically before being put into place.

Sometimes an editor flirts with the idea of changing basic design, looks over suggested changes, then decides to stick with what has worked well enough in the past. A logo change is especially agonizing because of the investment of time it represents and its recognition value. The editor of *Update,* a tabloid for employees of Pacific Telephone, asked to see some logo ideas from this author/designer, and decided, finally, to stay with the original logo (the first example shown) because it seemed to fit the format best after all.

setting of the design. Henry Wolf reported in 1978 that he had "a two-year engagement to redo *House Beautiful.*"

The time to redesign is when a publication is still successful but is not looking the part. Waiting until their publications are slipping, editors wait too long. Beautiful new design can't hide a lack of editorial vitality.

It is better, probably, for editors to change their publications' looks gradually as the times change. Too abrupt and far-reaching changes could lose some loyal followers. Readers tend to be conservative in matters of design. They like the familiar.

The secret is to hold on to old readers with familiar typographic landmarks while luring new readers with innovation.

Looking back on the demise of the original *Saturday Evening Post* just after its radical design changes, James W. O'Bryan, art director of *National Review,* said, "I . . . believe that . . . [most] magazines become familiar habits to readers, and when you radically change the book you really upset the reader and cause in some special type magazines—actual resentment. Perhaps *T.S.E.P.,* was old fashioned, but, by God, it was what the reader enjoyed."

He added, "Here at *N.R.* we've made many changes since I first became A.D., but I try never to make a *drastic* change, one that will upset anyone, and yet even the subtle, almost imperceptible occasional changes do cause the letters of protest to come our way."[9]

Noting how *Motor Trend* and *Popular Science* had changed their looks, a reader of *Car and Driver* wrote to the editor in 1984 to ask him to keep things as they were. Of the other magazines the reader complained, "It is now hard to tell their ads from their articles." The editor, agreeing with his reader, answered, "If you don't fall asleep, it's an ad."[10]

Redesign sometimes leads to re-redesign. *Esquire* modernized its look in the 1970s with new management, then in 1980 changed its mind with still newer management. The magazine resurrected its distinctive script logo, causing Alfred Zelcer, art director of *TWA Ambassador,* to observe: "To revert to [the old logo] from a 'contemporary' face-lift is truly courageous. . . . In a business that becomes more bottom-line oriented every year, it gives me a sense of well-being to know that integrity and primal love of magazines is not a thing of more civilized, past times."[11]

Notes

1. Edward Gottschall, "But Is It Appropriate?" *U&lc.*, August 1985, p. 3.
2. Harold T. P. Hayes, "The Push Pin Conspiracy," *The New York Times Magazine*, March 6, 1977, pp. 19–22.
3. G. K. Chesterton in *All Is Grist*, reprinted in *As I Was Saying* by Robert Knille, ed., William B. Eerdmans Publishing Company, Grand Rapids, Michigan, 1985, p. 78.
4. Quoted by Richard Edel, "Magazines' Graphic Design Sets Style," *Advertising Age Thursday*, October 3, 1985, p. 19.
5. See Richard Horn's *Memphis: Objects, Furniture, and Patterns*, A Quarto Book, Running Press, Philadelphia, 1985.
6. Quoted by Daryl H. Miller in "Fullerton Grad Is Giving Sparkle, Color to *Saturday Review*," *The Orange County Register*, October 23, 1985, p. E 11.
7. Quoted by Richard Edel, "Designer Nigel Holmes Shows Simple Sells," *Advertising Age Thursday*, October 3, 1985, p. 56.
8. Letter to the author from Mike Salisbury, November 27, 1970.
9. Letter to the author from James W. O'Bryan, June 10, 1981.
10. Letter and editor's answer in *Car and Driver*, December 1984, p. 19.
11. Letter to the editor of *Esquire*, May 1980, p. 6.

Suggested further reading

Arnold, Edmund C., *Arnold's Ancient Axioms*, Ragan Report Press, Chicago, 1978.

Berryman, Gregg, *Notes on Graphic Design and Visual Communication*, William Kaufmann, Los Altos, California, 1979.

Booth-Clibborn, Eduard, and Daniele Baroni, *The Language of Graphics*, Harry N. Abrams, New York, 1980.

Conover, Theodore E., *Graphic Communications Today*, West Publishing Company, St. Paul, 1985.

De Sausmarez, Maurice, *Basic Design*, Van Nostrand Reinhold Company, New York, 1983.

Donahue, Bud, *The Language of Layout*, Prentice-Hall, Englewood Cliffs, New Jersey, 1978.

Garchik, Morton, *Creative Visual Thinking*, Art Direction Book Company, New York, 1982.

Gill, Bob, *Forget All the Rules You Ever Learned About Graphic Design, Including the Ones in This Book*, Watson-Guptill Publications, New York, 1981.

Goodchild, Jon, and Bill Henkin, *By Design: A Graphics Sourcebook of Materials, Equipment and Services*, Quick Fox, New York, 1980.

Hanks, Kurt, et al., *Design Yourself!*, William Kaufmann, Los Altos, California, 1977.

Hartmann, Robert, *Graphics for Designers*, Iowa State University Press, Ames, Iowa, 1979.

How: The Magazine of Ideas & Technique in Graphic Design, Bethesda, Maryland. (Bimonthly.)

Hurlburt, Allen F., *Publication Design*, 2d ed., Van Nostrand Reinhold Company, New York, 1976.

———, *Layout: The Design of the Printed Page*, Watson-Guptill Publications, New York, 1977.

———, *The Grid: A Modular System for the Design and Production of Newspapers, Magazines, and Books*, Van Nostrand Reinhold Company, New York, 1978.

———, *The Design Concept*, Watson-Guptill Publications, New York, 1981.

———, *Photo/Graphic Design*, Watson-Guptill Publications, New York, 1983.

Kince, Eli, *Visual Puns in Design*, Watson-Guptill Publications, New York, 1982.

Laing, John, ed., *Do-It-Yourself Graphic Design*, Facts on File, New York, 1984.

Magazine Design & Production, Overland Park, Kansas. (Monthly.)

Maier, Manfred, *Basic Principles of Design*, Van Nostrand Reinhold Company, New York, 1977. (Four volumes based on the program at the School of Design in Basel, Switzerland.)

Marquand, Ed, *How to Prepare and Present Roughs, Comps and Mock-ups,* Art Direction Book Company, New York, 1985.

Muller-Brockmann, Josef, *Grid Systems in Graphic Design,* Hastings House Publishers, New York, 1981.

———, *The Graphic Designer and His Design Problems,* rev. ed., Hastings House Publishers, New York, 1984.

Newcomb, John, *The Book of Graphic Problem-Solving,* R. R. Bowker Company, New York, 1984.

Print Casebooks 4, Print Magazine, Washington, D.C., 1980–81. (Six volumes.)

Rand, Paul, *Thoughts on Design,* 2d ed., Van Nostrand Reinhold Company, New York, 1971.

Resnick, Elizabeth, *Graphic Design: A Problem-Solving Approach to Visual Communication,* Prentice-Hall, Englewood Cliffs, New Jersey, 1984.

Silver, Gerald A., *Graphic Layout and Design,* Delmar Publications, Albany, New York, 1981.

Smith, Robert Charles, *Basic Graphic Design,* Prentice-Hall, Englewood Cliffs, New Jersey, 1985.

Step-by-Step Graphics, Peoria, Illinois. (Bimonthly.)

White, Jan V., *Graphic Idea Notebook,* Watson-Guptill Publications, New York, 1980.

———, *On Graphics: Tips for Editors,* Lawrence Ragan Communications, Chicago, 1982.

MOTHER JONES

"We Are Sandinistas"

CONVERSATIONS WITH NICARAGUA'S EMBATTLED LEADERS

Every time you see the phenomenon of nationalism in Latin America, and the recovery of a nation's own natural resources, it has provoked confrontations with the United States," said Daniel Ortega, the Sandinista leader who became Nicaragua's president after last year's elections, when I interviewed him in April in a former country club now turned into a government retreat in Managua. "Ronald Reagan is nothing more than heir to the historical relationship of the United States with Nicaragua, except that he uses the Soviet Union as a justification."

It would be absurd to believe that the Sandinistas' 1979 revolt against the dictator Anastasio Somoza was Soviet-inspired, continued Ortega. "Here it was almost like an instinctive struggle. There was resistance to North American occupation. We fought for our sovereignty. And so Sandinismo arises as a third force, the force of those Nicaraguans who want the right to self-determination."

Are the Sandinistas committed to human and civil rights and democratic freedoms? Or are they left-wing dictators who will eventually eliminate all dissent, political opposition, and religious freedom? Are the Sandinistas Marxist-Leninists? Is Nicaragua on the way to becoming another Cuba?

To these questions Ortega replies, "You can judge for yourself." This answer is in part, his invitation to the world to come to Nicaragua, to travel without restriction, and to fully investigate the government's behavior. But Ortega's answer also seems to imply that Nicaragua's situation is too complex for easy yes-or-no answers.

Nicaragua's leaders are a group of relatively young, well-educated men and women whose success at working together surpasses their ability to offer precise ideological compass points. They know one another well and seem to value their shared history and a kind of improvisational pragmatism, more than any labels.

I found that the leaders I met in Nicaragua often liked to respond to questions about the political definition of their revolution with a basic restatement, at once evasive and stubborn: "We are *Sandinistas.*" In other words, we do not fit your preconceptions. We are building something new.

What, then, *is* "Sandinismo"? Americans, whose government treats it as an enemy ideology, should know how Nicaragua's leaders describe it in their own words. To find out, a number of visiting Americans conversed at length with Bayardo Arce, coordinator of party affairs for the Sandinista National Liberation Front (FSLN):

"If you find a political project such as ours where 70 percent of the economy is in private hands, where you have 12 legally existing political parties, where all religion is freely operating, where you have radios and newspapers that freely operate pro and con; but simultaneously has still been able to diminish illiteracy, multiply by two our student population, and distribute land among the campesinos," said Arce—"that is Sandinismo, and that type of project certainly does not attract communists! Not in Cuba or the Soviet Union will you find 12 political parties, will you find private property, will you find opposition papers."

Next to him sat Rosario Murillo, the wife of President Ortega, pregnant with her eighth child. Just as though they were entertaining in a fashionable villa in any Latin country, the Sandinistas presented their guests with a succession of chilled drinks and cups of rich Nicaraguan coffee and servers passed platters of elaborate appetizers.

"During the time of Somoza it was only we who were courageous enough to call ourselves Sandinistas," said Arce, "and to say you were a Sandinista was to put your life in jeopardy, . . . and

BY DEIRDRE ENGLISH

Photography By Susan Meiselas / Magnum

AUG./SEPT. 1985
22

MOTHER JONES

BAYARDO ARCE, EX-GUERRILLA, IS ONE OF THE NINE DIRECTORS OF THE FSLN.

we fought. But then, after the revolution triumphed, everybody wanted to call themselves a Sandinista and we couldn't stop that. . . . But for us, to be a Sandinista means that you are able to renounce everything for social justice, and that means you are also willing to give your life." Said Murillo: "We need a cessation of hostilities with the United States so that we can follow through on the social ideals of the Sandinista revolution."

The North American visitors, who had arrived on one of the last Aeronica flights the Reagan administration allowed to depart from U.S. soil, had come motivated by concern over United States policy toward Nicaragua. Yet they seemed equally anxious not to fall into an uncritical enthusiasm for the Sandinistas, which might fade in the harsh light of reality. Their two hours with Bayardo Arce was therefore spent peppering him with skeptical questions, which he answered with apparent candor, wit, and detail.

"What is Sandinismo today? It is a synthesis of all of this here in Nicaragua. So I guess you could say that Sandinismo is Marxist-Leninism applied in Nicaragua. But I would also say that Sandinismo is Christianity applied in Nicaragua. And I can also tell you that it is liberalism applied in Nicaragua. . . . Reagan says we are Marxist-Leninists because with that he means to scare everybody. I have asked people who are afraid of that if they know what Marxist-Leninism is. And I have come to realize that usually they don't know. All that they know is that it must be something quite awful, something you would not want on your skin. It is a little bit difficult to explain to people who don't even know what Marxist-Leninism is anyway.

PRESIDENT DANIEL ORTEGA AND THE OMNIPRESENT IMAGE OF AUGUSTO SANDINO.

"So I ask them, do you think we're going to be like the Soviets? . . . We will not be. . . . We aren't going to be like the Cubans or the Czechoslovakians or the Vietnamese. Nor like the U.S. citizens or the French or the Spanish. Nor even the Mexicans. We are going to be what we are, learning from everything. For example, I would like to include the methods of the U.S. electoral system the next time we have elections. It's a good system."

It is the visual image of guerrilla leader Augusto César Sandino that is most in evidence on Managua's omnipresent billboards and supergraphics, not Daniel Ortega or other members of the current FSLN leadership. There are also the faces of the founders and fallen combatants of the FSLN, and occasionally the world-famous stencil of Che

AUG./SEPT. 1985
23

Article title, subtitle, and two pieces of art combine to form the visual thrust of this strongly designed opening spread for a *Mother Jones* article. The initial *E* and the byline and artist's credit line become subsidiary visual elements and help create a sort of triangle for the spread. The art pieces, put at the outside edges of the text matter, embrace it, holding the spread together. The main piece of art combines photography and drawing. Louise Kellenbaum art directed; Dian-Aziza Ooka designed; Susan Meiselas of Magnum took the pictures.

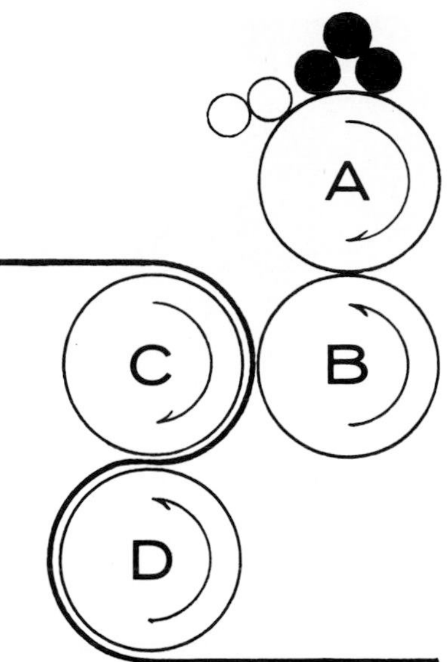

This diagram shows how offset lithography works. The thin, flexible plate wraps around cylinder A and picks up ink and the dampening agent from the rollers above. The plate transfers its image to the rubber blanket on cylinder B, which in turn transfers it to the web of paper delivered by cylinder C. Cylinder D delivers the paper from the press.

Production

"You don't simply read *Aspen*" said one of its promotion pieces, ". . . you hear it, hang it, feel it, fly it, sniff it, play with it." *Aspen* was "the magazine in a box," a collection of odds and ends that threatened the end to magazines as we had known them—the simple, flat, two-dimensional storehouses of printed information, opinion, entertainment, and advertisements. Like many interesting ventures in the publishing world, *Aspen* died young. Other unusual publishing ventures have come along to challenge magazines, and a number of people, including Marshall McLuhan, have predicted the end of traditional print media, including magazines. But standard-format media have adjusted with the times, and they continue to serve a vast audience, even if it is more segmented than before. The ways in which these publications are put togther has changed, too.

This chapter deals with putting publications together after stories are written and edited and design decisions are made. We call this postwriting, postediting, postdesign activity *production,* and at one time it was clearly delineated from other publishing activities. Today, with all the advances in technology, it is difficult to tell where production really starts on a publication. For instance, the newspaper reporter working at a terminal is really initiating the typesetting phase. No longer is it common for an editorial person to hand over typewriter-produced material to someone in the back shop who operates a Linotype machine.

Art directors need a knowledge of production in order to (1) get the effects they want and (2) cut down on costs. Most publications have a production director or production editor who acts as a sort of middle-man between the art director and the printer. The main consideration in production is printing.

Gutenberg and before

Johann Gutenberg in Germany did not invent printing; the Chinese beat him to it. He did not invent movable type; the Koreans beat him to that. But, unaware of what the Koreans had done, Gutenberg worked out his own system and introduced it to the Western world. He designed his types, taking as his model the black, close-fitting, angular calligraphy of the lowlands; carved them; punched them into metal to make molds; and cast them. The characters could be stored in individual compartments and used over and over again. Until then, printing had been done with wood blocks into which characters had been carved, in relief. Once used, the characters served no further purpose.

Before printing of any kind there were the scribes, working alone, who copied manuscripts by hand. When many copies were needed, a group of scribes would sit together in a semicircle around a reader. The scribes wrote while the reader dictated. This process produced several copies of a manuscript at a time—Middle Ages mass production.

Before the turn of the century, the process of engraving for reproduction in magazines involved enough hand work—enough artistry—to merit two signatures or credit lines: one for the illustrator, one for the engraver. This illustration appeared in *Frank Leslie's Popular Monthly Magazine.*

Printing processes

The printing process Gutenberg used is still around. We call it *letterpress:* printing from a raised surface. A few newspapers and magazines use the process, but most have switched to *offset lithography:* printing from a flat surface. A few magazines have switched to *gravure:* printing from tiny wells incised in a metal plate.

"For most printing jobs in the nation, the shift to offset lithography began the true growth of U.S. graphic design," observes the designer and design historian Byron Ferris. "Production of 'camera-ready art' . . . placed control of the whole job in the hands of the designer. . . . During the '50s, with design possibilities in place, graphic design in the U.S. grew into a profession."[1]

In the days of letterpress, printers followed the instructions given on a "dummy" sheet and moved metal type and cuts around in the shop as part of the production process. When offset lithography arrived, art directors and designers did much of this work in the studio, using proofs (printings) of type instead of the type itself. "Camera ready copy," rather than rough dummies, went to the printer. People who specialized in this kind of work became known as *pasteup artists.*

That designers were more in control of things was only one of offset's advantages. Another was that cheaper methods of typesetting could be utilized. Still another was that art could be reproduced more easily and, in some cases, with more fidelity. One reason for this was that the image transferred itself to a rubber-covered drum before impressing itself onto the paper (see the accompanying diagram). Other processes printed from hard, unyielding metal.

Flexography, a relatively new printing process related to letterpress, uses rubber plates or, more recently, photopolymer plates. The process has been used mostly for cheap paperback books. Newspaper publishers have been considering flexography and water-based inks as a way of eliminating complaints that the ink from newspapers printed by traditional letterpress or offset processes rubs off onto readers' hands.

Some magazines use more than one printing process for a single issue. The cover may be printed, say, by offset; the inside pages, by letterpress or gravure. Or an offset magazine may carry one signature (set of pages) printed by letterpress on a different stock and bound into the magazine with the offset pages. *Fortune,* when it was first published in the early 1930s, used sheetfed gravure for the halftones throughout and letterpress for the type.

Sheetfed printing presses, whatever the printing process, produce quality work but in short runs. Most publications use webfed presses—presses that make use of rolls of paper. Some presses print in one color at a time; others print in several colors, with each color coming from a separate unit

This drawing, shown actual size, comes from the stock-art file of IBM's Drawing Assistant software program. The tone in the dress was added, using a mouse and one of several patterns available. It is possible to move art around in this program and, of course, to do original drawing. Reducing art like this in printing can minimize the jagged outlines.

of the press. A *perfecting* press is one that prints on both sides of the paper as it passes through.

A book publisher producing a paperback might use a webfed press for the interior pages and a sheetfed press for the cover. Many magazines use more than one webfed printing process for a single issue. If you want to know what printing process a magazine uses, look it up in *Consumer Magazine and Farm Publication Rates and Data* or *Business Publication Rates and Data,* monthly publications of Standard Rate & Data Service, Inc. Under Entry 15 for each magazine you will find mechanical requirements and printing processes listed.

Daily newspapers and many weekly newspapers do their own printing. Most magazines and book publishers farm out their printing. Often the printing is done in cities far removed from the editorial offices. Magazines enter into long-term contracts with printers. Book publishers may dicker with printers for each book published.

An exception to all of this is the Review and Herald Publishing Association in Hagerstown, Maryland, an arm of the Seventh-Day Adventist Church. One of 50 publishing institutions operated by this church, the Review and Herald Publishing Association publishes 42 different periodicals and about 35 new books each year along with many textbooks for denominational schools. With 300 employees the association not only prints these publications; it also sets the type, edits and designs the publications, and circulates them.[2]

The revolution in production

Some editors foresee the day when their magazines will custom build each copy to fit the special needs of each subscriber: what a subscriber wants will be recorded on electronic tape, and a computerized bindery will pick up only materials that interest him.

Less dramatic changes in format have taken place already. Printing and typesetting technology has brought great fidelity to the printed page, better color, more flexibility. Some of the newest magazines are coming out in a square rather than in the usual rectangular format. Gatefold covers and center foldouts and booklets bound within magazines are commonplace. *Venture* used three-dimensional color photographs on its covers. *Aspen,* you remember, put itself in a box. *American Heritage* wrapped itself in hard covers. Some publishers have flirted with the idea of "video magazines" to take advantage of the video cassette and cartridge markets.

R. R. Donnelley & Sons Company, one of the big printers of magazines, now has available a selectivity service that magazines can offer their advertisers. Parts of ads can be addressed to subscribers by name.

The big revolution in production involves the computer and the technology it encourages. This technology includes systems that allow the combination of text and art on a video screen; scanners that convert continuous-tone art to digital halftones; digital typesetters; and laser printers. For instance, the Quadex Q6000 Graphics System produces whole pages with text matter and art (line and halftone) in place, eliminating the need for pasteup and stripping. The art director uses a mouse device to reposition elements on a high-resolution screen.

By the mid-1960s many U.S. dailies already had gone to computer composition. Computers produced tape that was fed into linecasting machines, quadrupling the speed of setting.

And computer editing was at hand. That was a system whereby copy was first typed into a computer, which hyphenated it, justified it, and fitted it into a layout. The layout was presented to the editor as a TV image. The editor used an electronic pointer and a keyboard to rewrite and rearrange the material.

The system moved to actual type after the editing was done, thereby eliminating any resetting. And if offset lithography was the printing process, hot-type composition was eliminated altogether. Pages could be transmitted instantaneously via facsimile to regional printing plants.

By 1970 *Life* was using an Editorial Layout Display System (ELDS).[3] ELDS was a 7,000-pound electromechanical optical system with a screen, a tabletop instrument panel, and some powerful transistorized equipment. Using projectors and computers, it edited, recorded, and printed layouts on demand.[4] It gave the art director immediate visualization of various layout ideas, in full color and in actual size.

It worked this way: The art director mounted all elements in the layout on 35 mm slides and slipped them into the machine. The machine held ninety-nine of them, plus a basic library of typefaces and a layout grid. Using the instrument panel, the art director could call any combination of elements into position, enlarge any of them, crop any of them—and work anywhere on the spread. Operators could be trained to use the machine in about two hours.

In 1977 *Reader's Digest* went to a computerized system that had the magazine's staff perform some functions normally associated with a typesetting house. *Digest* personnel put text material on computer tapes in binary coding suitable for driving the phototypesetters at York Graphic Services, where the type was set and typeset page negatives made.

Meanwhile, newspapers all over the country switched from letterpress to offset, to cold-type composition, and to computer technology.

The Pasadena *Star-News* in 1981 announced its plans for the installation of a pagination system (set up by Information International, Inc.) to handle halftones and line art as well as headlines and text matter. Pages were to be made up on video display terminals by operators in the news and advertising departments. In this system a scanner digitized photos and line art and stored them in disk memory while the system accepted and stored data from a text editing system. Any of this material could be displayed on the terminal, and the operator could then jump stories, rehyphenate, rejustify, edit, expand, cut, tighten, space out, etc. The system then allowed for the transmission of completed page layouts to a unit that made the film for platemaking.[5]

Another newspaper, *The Wall Street Journal,* began composing each edition with pagination equipment and sending completed pages by satellite to its several printing plants.

At the start of the 1980s it was possible, through the new technology, for a publication to create full-color art with a keyboard and a cathode-ray tube, using 128 colors. The future promised, among other wonders, programmed formats. The choices for art directors appeared to be endless. Everything could be done quicker and, on balance, more economically. Of course it all meant greater pressures on art directors. In many instances they had to make decisions in a hurry and stick by them. "Speed is becoming an element of talent," *U&lc.* observed in its "Vision '80" issue.[6]

Perry E. Jeffe, president of Jeffe Corporation, which offers computer-aided publication services, describes what we're going through right now in production as a "turmoil in graphics." Not only is there a revolution in typesetting and printing equipment but also in design itself. The new

When *Northwest,* magazine section of *The Oregonian,* was a letterpress operation, the editor, Joe Blanco, had to settle for bold, flat colors and a poster format. This example shows that the poster approach to covers can result in excellent design. The artist, E. Bruce Dauner.

design must accommodate itself to the new technology. "Design controls graphics," Jeffe writes. "You wouldn't think it to hear the talks at equipment conferences . . . , during which design is never mentioned. But you and I know that nothing is printed that a designer hasn't put there, except for aberrations of the production process."[7]

Unfortunately, as the new technology advances, people not trained in design involve themselves in setting type, creating art, and laying out pages. But gradually typographers, art directors, and designers are taking over. Designers insisting on traditional approaches—designers who avoid the new machinery—will be at a disadvantage compared to more adventurous designers who welcome the changes.

One big problem with the new technology is that it changes so fast. A printing establishment or a type house that installs new equipment finds it outdated in just a few years.

A bewildering assortment of computer equipment faces today's editor and art director. All of it promises that, once mastered, it will make things easier and faster in the workplace. Most users say that rather than stifling creativity, computer equipment enhances it. Magazines reporting on developments—and they are at an avalanche stage—include *Computer Graphics World, Graphic Arts Monthly, Technical Communication, Magazine Design & Production, TypeWorld,* and *U&lc.* Books on the new technology go out of date almost upon publication.

Desktop publishing

Media people are becoming familiar with all this equipment, of course, but so are people not usually associated with the media. Most big companies do a lot of publishing as part of their business. Many do their own typesetting and printing now. They set up what is called "desktop publishing" systems. Although setting up such a system is expensive, one industry expert estimates that capital expenditure can be recovered in as few as two years.[8] At least one magazine, *Desktop Publishing,* devotes itself exclusively to this activity.

Editors and art directors going into desktop publishing (or simply choosing computer equipment) need to pick their systems with great care. Often the type produced by these systems is inferior to real type or even to strike-on composition. "When a vendor claims that the fonts on a system are 'pretty good' or 'close enough' or 'almost correspondence quality,' this is the same as saying that the fonts are less than optimum and that the vendor has short-changed the reader on legibility," says Professor Charles Bigelow of Stanford.[9]

Aldus offers PageMaker; Boston Software Publishers, Inc. offers MacPublisher I and II; Manhattan Graphic offers ReadySetGo; and Microsoft offers Typographer desktop publishers. All of these run on the Apple Macintosh and allow users to mix text and graphics with what-you-see-is-what-you-get (WYSIWYG) display. Ventura Software, Inc. in Carmel, California, entered the desktop publishing field in 1986 by marketing a program designed for the IBM PC. The company advertised "total integration of text and graphics on the screen." Aldus also announced a PageMaker program for the IBM.

What you put up on the screen is one thing; the quality of the printout is another. The best printout quality for desktop publishers comes from laser printers. And "computers are still . . . at least several years away from helping with the more aesthetic aspects of design," says Steve Ro-

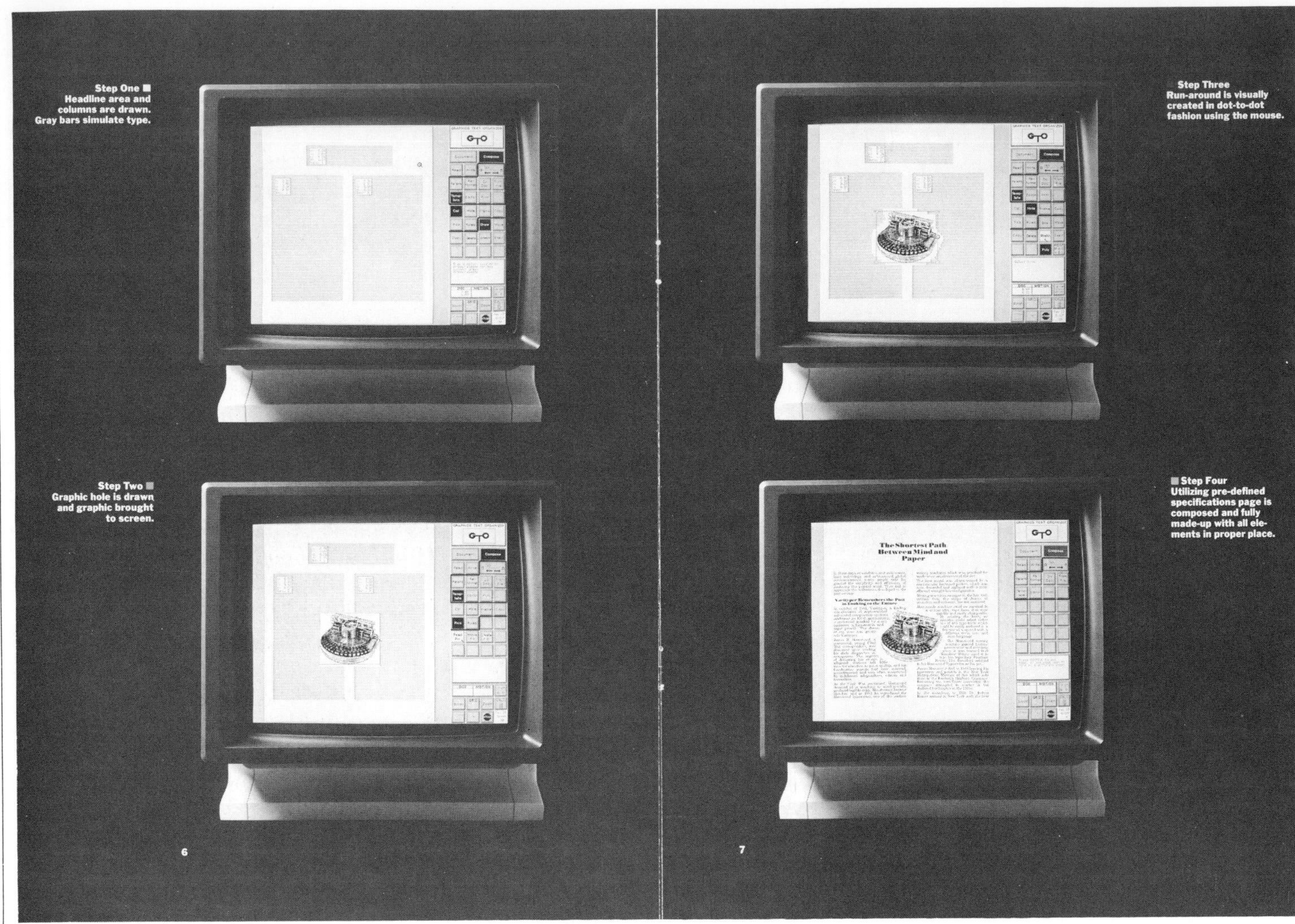

Varityper's Graphic Text Organizer (GTO) offers page makeup capability and text and art merging without the need for pasteup. The system uses a mouse to move units into place. This two-page spread from one of Varityper's booklets illustrates the process. Jan Allan Nowak art directed the spread.

senthal, contributing editor of *Desktop Publishing.* "While the computer can help with the mechanics it's still up to us [users] to provide the direction."[10]

Typesetting

The types of the early printers were set by hand. Today we still set some types this way. But, following Ottmar Mergenthaler's invention of the Linotype machine in 1884 and some follow-up inventions in both the United States and Great Britain, most types are set now by machine.

The type used in letterpress printing is set by one of the "hot type" composition systems: foundry (the system Gutenberg used), Ludlow (used primarily for headlines), Linotype and Intertype systems (used for body copy), and Monotype (used for high-quality letterpress printing). All of these systems can be used for offset too, after a first "printing" is made (or after a repro proof is pulled); but offset has the additional advantage over letterpress of being able to use any of the "cold type" composition systems besides: hand lettering, hand "setting" of paper type, strike-on composition, photolettering, phototypesetting, and systems made possible by the new technology. Before cold-type composition can be used in letterpress, it must first be converted to a photoengraving.

Cold-type systems cut typesetting costs in some cases to one-fourth of what they were with hot-type systems; they have broadened considerably the art director's choice of faces and have given everyone great flexibility in designing pages. Frank Romano, associate publisher of *TypeWorld,* estimates that the word processor "increases the efficiency of most editorial people by at least 40 percent."[11]

Printers and typesetters do not agree on the meanings of the various terms used in cold-type composition. But here are some generally accepted definitions.

Cold type refers to any method of type composition other than hot type. The type is cold because hot lead is not involved anywhere in the process.

Photocomposition as a term covers much but not all cold-type composition. It includes phototypesetting and photolettering, both of which require photographic paper. *Phototypesetting* refers to systems that set line after line of text matter. A computer often is involved. *Photolettering* refers to systems that set only display type, often in single lines or strips.

Strike-on composition refers to text matter produced by typewriter-like machines (and typewriters themselves). No photograph is involved at this early stage in the production process.

Unfortunately, some of the cold-type composition systems, especially strike-on systems, have resulted in inferior typography. The problem is especially noticeable in narrow-width columns of copy where justification of the right-hand margin is involved. Uneven spacing between words is something to watch for and eliminate. Some typewriter-composers produce letters designed to fit a single width or, at best, three or four widths, whereas in their ideal state letters occupy a great variety of widths.

Computer typesetting

When type was set only by hand, a speed of one character per second was possible. Mechanical typesetters increased the speed to five characters per second. Photographic typesetters after World War II brought it up to five hundred characters per second. By the end of the 1960s electronic-computer typesetting reached a speed of 10,000 characters per second.[12]

The new typesetters relate to computers that take care of justification and its necessary hyphenation. The new typesetters also offer kerning (fitting letters together so that their spaces overlap or, as one typographer describes it, "nesting . . . letters to avoid typographers gaposis"), hung punctuation (punctuation placed outside the edges of a copy block), and minus leading (less than normal spacing between lines). Of course they also offer the features standard typesetters have always offered—like letterspacing and regular leading.

And we have seen that newspapers and magazines now own typesetters that compose not just by columns but by pages and combine type with art electronically. Some newspapers use OCR (optical character reader) scanners that can read typed manuscripts and feed what they read directly into typesetting equipment.

Digital typesetting is one of the latest typographic wonders. Digital type consists of a series of tiny dots that combine to form letters. Photographic negatives are not involved. The master in this form of typesetting is a computerized matrix of dots. The operator of this typesetting equipment can manipulate the matrix to slant the letters, expand them, and condense them. At *Milwaukee Magazine* editors enter copy into four Digital Deckmate word processing terminals, edit it, then send it to an outside typesetter through a modem. Pasteup in 1985 was still being done manually, although the magazine planned to go to pagination.

Designers and typographers working with digital typefaces look forward to the time when such type, instead of imitating type produced by earlier means, develops its own character and takes full advantage of the flexibility computers offer.

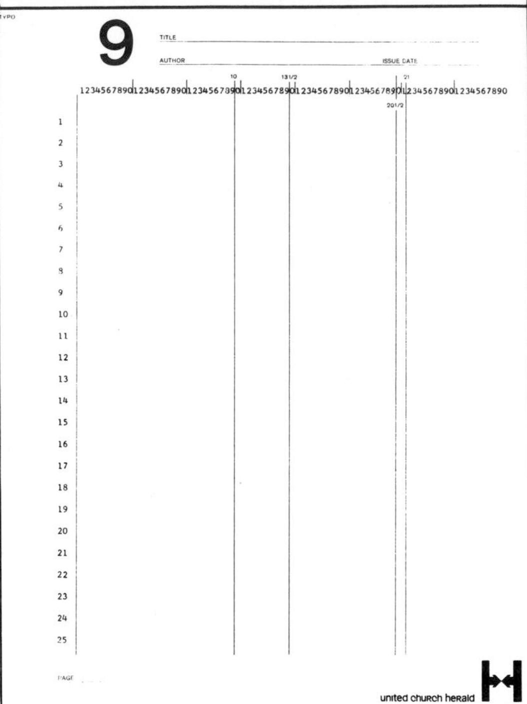

In-house typesetting

Most newspapers set their own type. They always have. First they set type by hand, using foundry type. Then came Linotype machines. The Linotype machines gave way to various cold-type systems with the coming of offset lithography. Magazines, which used to have all their type set by outside houses, are now using their own typesetting systems. A *Folio* survey of 559 magazines in 1980 showed that, even then, half of them were setting type in-house. Book publishing houses, too, are doing much of their own typesetting now.

TypeWorld reported in late 1985 that many people in the typesetting industry were beginning to wonder whether typesetting companies were doomed with so many publishers doing their typesetting in-house, using personal computers and laser printers. "We won't start to worry . . . [about this] until we see IBM produce its annual report in-house using their own typesetting equipment or until we see Apple produce its annual report on their Laser-writer," the editors commented in an editorial.[13]

Where publications do not set body copy in-house, they often set their own headlines and titles on photolettering machines. Some art directors and designers use press-on or dry-transfer letters, the kind you can buy in sheets at art-supply stores.

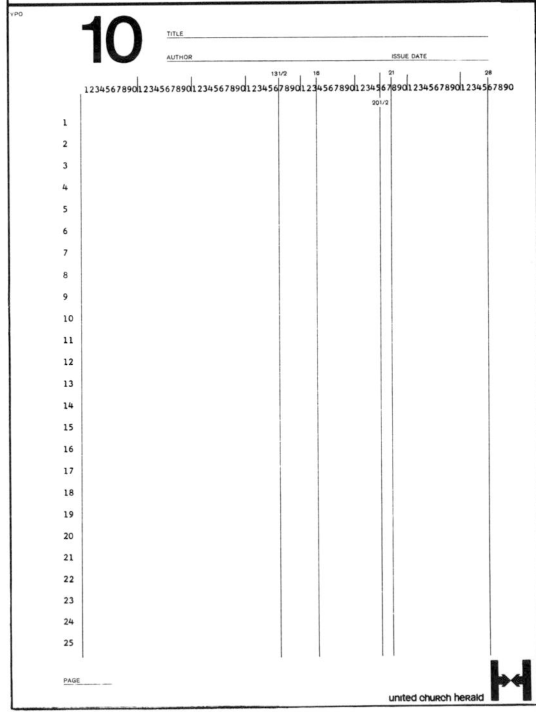

Copyfitting

Editors and art directors often find it necessary to determine, before body copy is set in type, how much space it will take in the publication. This is copyfitting. Essentially, copyfitting involves these five steps:

1. Decide on the width of the columns in print.
2. Consult a character-count chart (available from your type house) to find the number of characters you can get in that line width in the typeface you want to use.
3. Set the typewriter margins for that number of characters.
4. Type your copy, going only slightly under or over that count for each line.
5. Count the lines in your typed manuscript. You will know from previous settings how many printed lines you can get in a column.

On most publications there is considerable adjusting of copy during the layout or makeup stage. Lines are added or deleted, art is enlarged or reduced—all as part of the copyfitting process. One of the pleasant outcomes of the current practice of allowing columns to run to uneven lengths on pages in magazines and even in books is that copyfitting becomes less of a problem.

These are typical typing sheets used by a magazine in preparing its copy for the typesetter when a computer does not do the copyfitting. One sheet is for copy that will be set in 9-point type, the other for copy that will be set in 10-point. The typist chooses the vertical line at the right that represents the correct column width and ends each line of typing as close to that line as possible. The numbers going down the side at the left quickly show the editor how many lines the copy will take when it is set in type.

A typical magazine layout sheet or grid presents two facing pages in actual size. Each page can accommodate either a three- or four-column format. The tiny marks at the bottom left and right are for page numbers. The white lines in the grayed area are the edges for bleed pictures. This sheet can be used for both the rough layout and the pasteup. Some magazines design their layout sheets to show number of lines per column.

Copyfitting for titles and headlines becomes less a problem of counting and more a problem of tracing letters from existing alphabets and estimating space to be occupied. Increasingly, editors and art directors are asking typesetters to set to fit in the typeface chosen.

As in other aspects of publications work, the computer has come to the rescue, here serving those who don't like counting and fitting. Editors and art directors of computerized publications have a running account of how much copy is set and how much space it will occupy.

Whatever copyfitting system is used, the system of measurement remains the same. Publications people do not ordinarily speak in terms of inches; they speak, instead, in terms of points and picas. *Points* measure type sizes, *picas* column widths. There are 72 points to an inch. There are 12 points to a pica, hence 6 picas to an inch.

The point system is not universal. The U.S. and England use it; the countries on the Continent do not. There the Didot system prevails (points are slightly bigger).

Reproducing the art

Art meant for reproduction falls into two categories: *line* and *continuous tone.* Art drawn with black lines on white paper, with areas of solid black and even with areas produced through mechanical shading devices, qualifies as line art. Comic strips and most charts fall into this category. Continuous-tone art includes photographs, paintings, pencil sketches, and any other art that does not carry strong black and white contrasts.

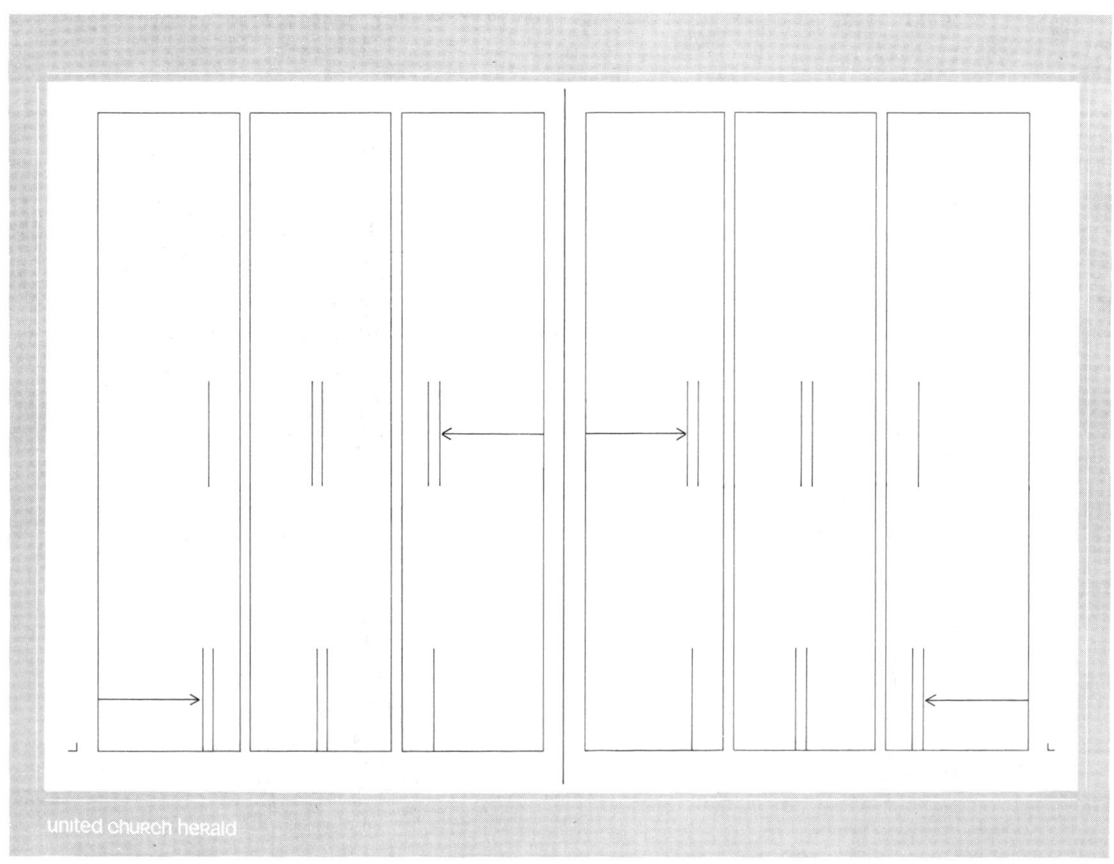

Line art requires line reproduction. Continuous-tone art requires halftone reproduction, which puts a screen between the camera lens and the film as the art is being photographed in the platemaking process. It is possible to introduce some pure white areas into a halftone through what is known as the *highlight* or *dropout* process. It is also possible to make a halftone take some shape other than the traditional square or rectangle. For instance, a halftone can appear in a publication as a silhouette, with the subject standing out against a pure white background.

In working with line art, you should see to it that all the pieces for a single article in a publication take the same reduction. This is desirable not only to save costs but also to keep consistent the strength of the artist's line. It is not a good idea to use both fine-line art and thick-line art in the same article. This means that you must decide where you want big art and where you want small art before giving out your assignments.

Line-art—halftone art, too—generally turns out best when reduced to about two-thirds of original size. The slight imperfections or irregularities are thus minimized. For a change of pace, however, you ought to try enlarging, or blowing up, your line artwork. This adds greatly to its strength and sometimes gives the art a refreshing crude, bold look that it doesn't have in its original state.

One of the advantages of line art over halftone art is that line art, at least when its run actual size, always comes out as the art director expects. With a halftone, you can never be quite sure.

Art directors soon learn that a photograph that has the necessary qualities to hang in an art gallery is not always the photograph that reproduces well. Some art directors feel that a photograph a little on the gray side reproduces better than one a little on the black side. Sometimes the photoengraver or offset camera operator can bring out a gray photograph by overexposing it; there is not much anyone can do with an already-overexposed print. You must choose your photographs not so much on the basis of how well they look in hand as on the basis of how well they will reproduce. Only long experience with photographs can really teach you this.

In the days of letterpress newspapers, printers used coarse screen halftones—made with 65-line screens—in order to get impressions on newsprint stock. Offset lithography allows the use of much finer screens, even when rough paper is used; and this means better fidelity in the reproduction. No longer can you get away with crude retouching on a photograph. Nor is it necessary. With the use of 35 mm cameras, editors and art directors now have plenty of prints to choose from.

Polaroid has made it possible for photographers working for offset publications to produce their own prescreened halftones, ready for pasteup as line art. It makes available a camera that houses its own screen in any coarseness, from 45 to 133 lines. The Polaroid camera is not an ideal camera for newspaper or magazine work—it is bulkier than a 35 mm, does not have the accessories, and produces pictures that are sometimes flatter than those made with other cameras—but for small weekly newspapers, especially, the prescreen feature may more than compensate for these disadvantages.

Although the usual halftone for both letterpress and offset appears in a dot pattern, newer developments in both photo preparation and photo reproduction make possible halftones in various line patterns and textures. When *Newsweek* did a cover story entitled "Does TV Tell It Straight?" it ran photographs of four TV newsmen—all in ruled-line

THE EVOLUTION OF AMERICAN CENSUS-TAKING 831

the exterior of the President's house, and to construct and to furnish the interior of the building in architectural harmony with the exterior.

Between the central columns of the entrance hall, one stone of the floor bears an ellipse of forty-five gilt stars inscribing the dates 1792–1902, which mark the years of construction and reconstruction. It will not be questioned seriously that the character of the work of reconstruction is such as to entitle the architects of to-day to stand with the original designers of the White House. As President Roosevelt says in his recent message: "Through a wise provision of the Congress at its last session, the White House, which had become disfigured by incongruous additions and changes, has now been restored to what it was planned to be by Washington. . . . The stately simplicity of its architecture is an expression of the character of the period in which it was built. It is a good thing to preserve such buildings as historic monuments which keep alive our sense of continuity with the nation's past."

THE EVOLUTION OF AMERICAN CENSUS-TAKING

BY THE HON. W. R. MERRIAM

Director of the Census

FIFTY years of intense activity along every line of human endeavor have developed the keenest competition for commercial supremacy among the trading nations of the earth. The trend of modern thought is toward commercial success, the upbuilding of vast enterprises, and the aggregation of capital. In all history this is the period when the people of the civilized world are living best, are educated best, and enjoy most of the comforts of life. One natural result of such conditions has been a demand for definite facts and figures; these have now become a necessity.

The merchant, the banker, the shipper, and the manufacturer, in order to carry on their business affairs successfully, must have daily information regarding the condition of growing crops, the shipments of wheat and cotton, the output of iron, the increase in the world's supply of gold and silver, and many other items of a similar character. The activity in statistical research thus created is one of the characteristics of the present period of the world's history, being, in a sense, its fruitage. Indeed, as Sir Robert Giffin recently declared, the century just closed could be called the "statistical century *par excellence*."

At the beginning of the nineteenth century the United States was the only nation which had made provision for a periodic census of its population. The collection of statistics relating to agriculture, manufactures, and mortality had not been attempted. Before the close of the century all civilized countries were making more or less extended investigation into population and into the most important facts of national life and progress.

It is the purpose of this article to trace briefly the conspicuous part which has been played by the United States in the evolution of census-taking.

The Constitution requires an enumeration once in ten years as a basis for the apportionment of representatives in Congress. The modern American census, which collects statistics relating to every important feature of national development, is

By the turn of the century, magazines were able to reproduce both line and halftone art, but real flair in design had not yet taken hold. This page from the April 1903 issue of *The Century Magazine* was typical. The look is more that of a book than a magazine. One article ends on this right-hand page, and another begins. The only art is an ending decoration and an embellished initial letter.

halftones. Because the photos were cut to a shape resembling a TV screen, the pattern related the halftones even more meaningfully to the subject.

Considering the print to be reproduced, you should remember that the closer it is to the original, the better. If you must turn in a copy, turn in a first copy. A copy of a copy is never as good as a copy, and a copy is never as good as the original. Have photographs made from original negatives; don't make copy prints from photographs unless you don't have access to original negatives.

Once in a while you may have to use an already-printed halftone, clipped from a newspaper, magazine, or book. You can treat such art as line art, because the screening has already been done. Sometimes you can improve a coarse-screen, already-printed halftone by reducing it, thereby making the screen finer. If the screen is already fine or the print indecisive, the printer may have to rescreen the halftone print.

In rescreening, the platemaker must avoid a moire pattern—a sort of swirl—in the final print. Sometimes you get a moire pattern even when working with an original photograph, as when a figure in that photograph wears a suit or dress with a pronounced pattern. The platemaker may be able to eliminate the moire in a second shooting by adjusting the angle of the screen.

Art directors have a number of ways to turn an ordinary photograph into something that looks like the work of an illustrator or painter. The most common practice—it has almost become a cliché—is to make a line reproduction from the photograph, rather than a halftone reproduction. The platemaker simply handles the photograph as if it were a line drawing, avoiding the use of a screen. What happens is that all the middle tones of gray drop out. You get a high-contrast print—stark, dramatic, bold. And sections of it, if desired, can easily be painted out or retouched. A

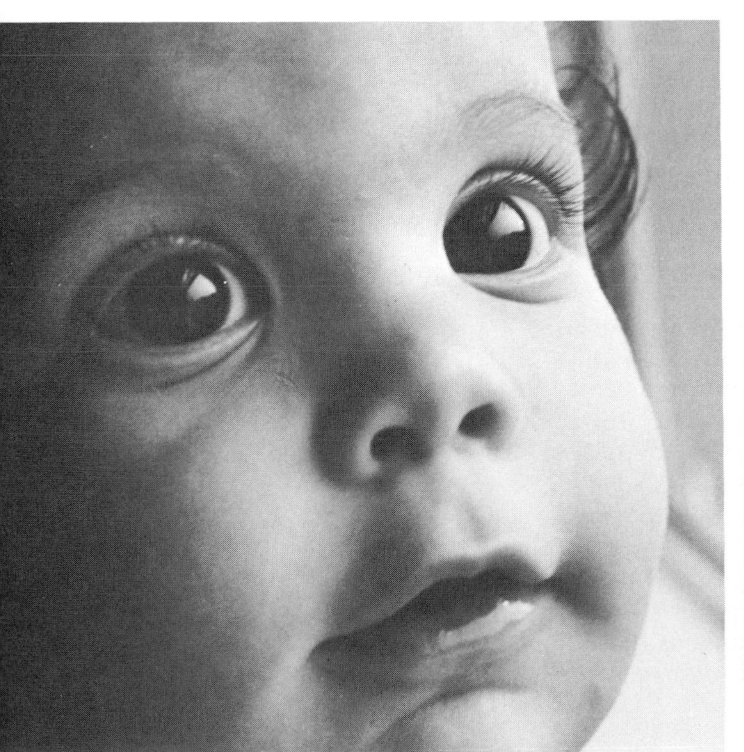

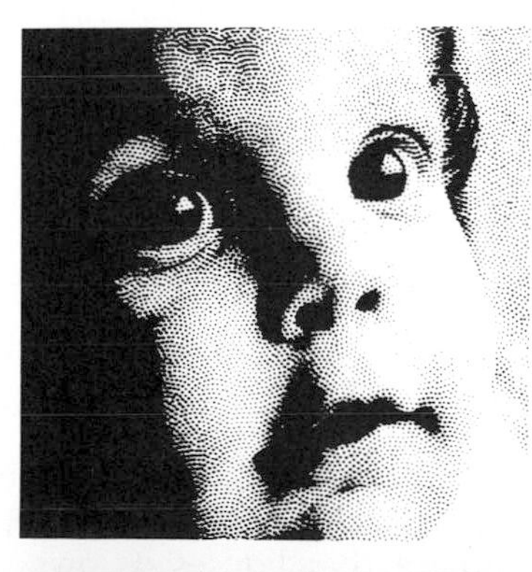

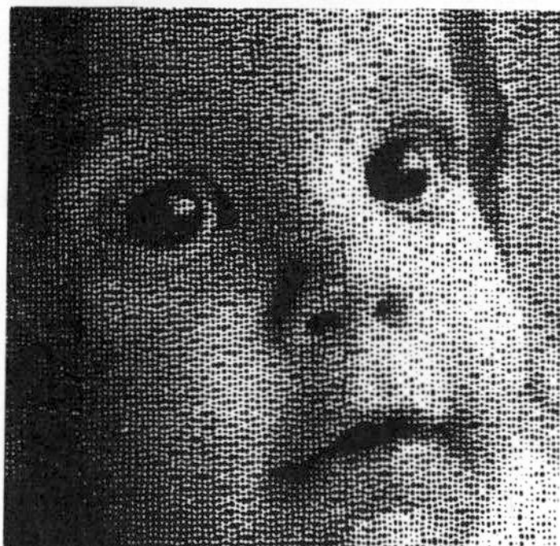

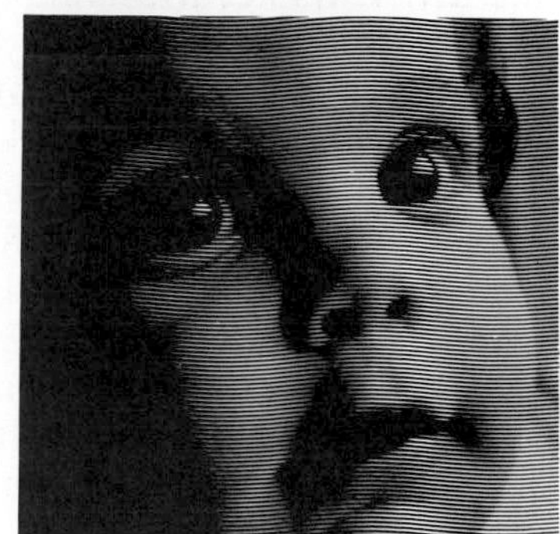

The original photograph was printed as a normal-screen halftone and, in a smaller size, four line art conversions: random dot (top left), spiral (top right), mesh (bottom left), and wavy line (bottom right). (Courtesy of Line Art Unlimited, Princeton, New Jersey.)

variation is to take the bold line art and screen it to, say, 60 percent of black or combine it with a block of solid second color.

You can get an unusual effect, too, by ordering this halftone in a jumbo size screen, so that the dots are much larger than normal. From a distance, the art looks like a photograph. Up close, it looks like a piece of pop art.

For his books on photography and cartooning for Prentice-Hall, the author/photographer/cartoonist Ken Muse turns in camera-ready copy. This saves the publisher typesetting costs and the author the possibility of a copyreader mercilessly wielding a blue pencil. It's just too much trouble for the publisher to make a lot of changes. Muse's excellent all-caps hand lettering is especially appropriate for a book to be read by cartoonists, most of whom do similar hand lettering as part of their jobs. This example is from *The Secrets of Professional Cartooning.* (© 1981 by Prentice-Hall.)

Working with the printer

Understanding the printing processes will keep the art director from asking the impossible of the printer. It will also open the art director's eyes to printing's possibilities. Alfred Lowry, art director of *Newsweek International,* thinks there is such a thing as knowing too much about printing. If you think an effect can't be had, you won't ask for it.

Every art director should know at least enough about printing and production to be able to converse intelligently with the printer. On any publication the printer and art director must reconcile differences resulting from a pragmatic approach to the job on the one hand and a visionary's approach on the other. Frequent consultation is necessary.

If the printer and the editor and staff members sit down and reason with each other, explain to each other their needs and limitations, and talk frankly about costs and if each side is willing to compromise, the relationship between editor and printer can be pleasant enough. Too many editors (and art directors) arrive at some arbitrary effect or size and hold out for it, despite the fact that with slight modification, the time involved in production (and hence the cost) could be greatly reduced.

Ideally, printing offices and editorial offices should be in the same city, but for reasons of economy, publications tend to let out contracts to printers in other parts of the country. For instance, many of the magazines edited on both the East and West Coasts are printed in the Midwest.

In seeking out a printer, it is important to find one interested in innovation. Settling for the printer who comes in with the lowest bid may not be the most economical way of publishing.

Every printer has certain strengths, certain idiosyncrasies. Every printer has a preferred way for the editor to mark and prepare copy. An unhurried discussion at the start and frequent conferrals with the printer along the way will do much to ease production problems on a publication.

Choosing paper

Working for a newspaper, you lose little sleep in your choice of a paper stock. You pick a newsprint sheet, pick it once, and then worry only about its skyrocketing costs.

Working for a magazine, you face a much wider choice of stocks. But again, you make a choice and, at least for a while, stick with it.

Working for a book publisher or a publisher of direct-mail pieces, your paper-choosing duties multiply. You face a bewildering selection of papers, and each job cries out for special attention.

Up to half of a general-circulation magazine's production costs and about a third of a trade magazine's production costs go to paper stock. Some big-circulation magazines, to eliminate printer's markup, buy their own paper. But this can result in problems, including storage, damage to the rolls, and lack of fit of the paper to the printer's presses.

Paper stock comes in a variety of finishes, including rough and hard, rough and soft, smooth and hard, and smooth and soft. It also comes in a variety of textures, colors, and weights.

You choose paper partly by its stated *basis weight.* This weight—34-pound, 40-pound, or whatever—comes from weighing 500 standard-size sheets. Standard-size sheets vary according to paper classes. The standard size for book paper, for instance, which is used for most magazines and books, is 25″×38″. The standard size for cover stock is 20″×26″.

A 40-pound basis weight book paper, therefore, will have a different real weight from a 40-pound basis weight cover stock. And two different 40-pound book papers may have different thicknesses. One of the papers may have been "bulked." Some magazines and books with few pages use bulked paper to make themselves look thicker.

Some magazines use more than one weight of paper in a single issue. And, of course, many magazines use a heavier stock for the cover than they use for inside pages. *Milwaukee Magazine,* to cite one example, uses a 60-pound coated cover stock and a 45-pound coated body stock. Big-circulation magazines use lighter stocks than these.

If the publication is a direct-mail piece coming off a sheetfed rather than a webfed press, it uses a heavier paper stock than most magazines use. A too-limp sheet can't be handled effectively.

A magazine with a lot of full-color photography is likely to choose a bright-white coated stock. The cheapest of the coated stocks is No. 5 Publication Coated, used by many consumer magazines in a 34-pound basis weight. A light-weight paper cuts down on mailing costs but, unfortunately, costs more to manufacture than heavier-weight paper.[14]

Four considerations should guide the editor and art director in their choice of paper stock.

1. *The look of the paper.* How do its brightness, color, and texture match the mood of the publication? Offset papers as chosen by editors of magazines are usually washday white, but they don't have to be. An off-white or even a light cream-colored stock has a richer appearance.

   If the publication contains mostly photographs, whiteness of the paper *is* important. You want as much contrast as possible between the ink and the paper.

Cuban Writers In Exile

By Charles Greenfield

For more than two decades now, Cuba, that exasperating, complicated social laboratory 90 miles from Key West, has clung to America's heel like some tenacious crab unwilling to let go.

On a much smaller scale, its relationship with its own writers has been equally turbulent. In the honeymoon days of the '60s, most Cuban writers, flushed with memories of recent revolutionary success and fervent to the point of overlooking the messy purges and blatant propaganda, were reluctant to rock the boat. By the '70s, serious writing had come virtually to a halt: trials of "reactionary" or "CIA sponsored" intellectuals, hollow confessions full of contrition and *mea culpa,* increased censorship often self-imposed, prison and solitary confinement, silence, brutality and sometimes death.

Today the intimidation continues. More than ever *El Exilio* seems the only choice left open to artists who — from the days of the poet and father of Cuban independence at the end of the last century, Jose Marti, to newly arrived Mariel refugee and poet-novelist Reynaldo Arenas — seek a voice for their anguish.

LYDIA CABRERA

"When Jicotea (the turtle) began to grow up, his mother asked him wisely:

— Son, you've got a good head on your shoulders and it's getting time to learn a trade. What do you want to be: a cook? a baker? a confectioner?

— No, mother . . .

— A locksmith? A barber?

— No, mother.

— A general?

— No, mother.

Then the old mother said very seriously:

— Son, do you want to be a rascal?

— Oh yes, mother dear!

The mother and son then smiled at each other. 'Thank God! a chip off the old block,' she said to herself."

— "Ayapa: Stories of Jicotea," Lydia Cabrera

Through the window the usual harsh Florida sun is beginning to weaken and Cuba's matriarch of let-

CONTINUED

ILLUSTRATION © 1981 BRAD HOLLAND

Brad Holland's line art, a crosshatch drawing done in pen and ink, surrounds the title and copy for this "Cuban Writers in Exile" article by Charles Greenfield, appearing in *The Plain Dealer Magazine.* The pointing finger here becomes a pen to better tell the story. Greg Paul art directed.

For special issues or for special sections, a colored stock can be arresting. It is cheaper than using a second color in printing, but with pure white gone, the art director faces a problem in giving photographs their best display.

As for texture, coated glossy or smooth papers best display photographs; coarse paper best displays type. But a typeface like Bodoni works best on coated stock because of the fine detail of the thin strokes and serifs.

Some editors like a paper stock with a noticeable pattern in it—like a stipple. Those editors should remember that the texture stays constant as the size of the sheet increases or decreases. The pattern may look innocuous enough on a large-size sheet, but when the sheet is cut down to page size, it may be too intrusive. Such a pattern would be better in a *Life*-size magazine than in a *Reader's Digest*-size magazine. Better to avoid it altogether.

2. *The feel of the paper.* Does the editor want a rough feel or a smooth one, a soft feel or a hard one, a thick sheet or a thin one?

   An interesting fact about roughness: it can carry the feel of cheapness, as in the paper that was used by the old pulp magazines, or the feel of quality, as in an Alfred A. Knopf book printed on antique paper. The feel of the paper does tell the reader something about quality.

   Most people like the feel of coated or polished stock, and that may be reason enough for editors to choose it—if they can afford it.

3. *The suitability of the paper.* Is the paper heavy enough to stand the strain of continued use?

   Is the paper permanent? A newspaper, quickly discarded, can go with newsprint. A scholarly quarterly, which will be bound and used for years by researchers, needs a longer-lasting stock.

   Is the paper suitable for the printing process? Papers manufactured for letterpress equipment will not work for offset. Offset needs a paper stock that can adapt to the dampness of the process and will not cause lint problems. Letterpress needs a paper stock that isn't too crisp. The various textures, smooth and rough, are available in both letterpress and offset stock.

   What typefaces should be used? Old style romans call for an antique stock, modern romans a glossy or polished stock. But most papers offered for magazine printing are versatile enough so that, within reason, any type can be used.

   Does the editor need a paper with high opacity? Or can the paper be more transparent? If photographs are a consideration or if masses of dark inks will be used, the editor will have to have an opaque paper. For good reproduction of photographs editors of magazines should use at least a 40-pound stock, but to fight rising costs, some have gone to lighter papers.

   Some publications use Bible paper, presumably to cut postage costs but perhaps for prestige reasons, too. A daily newspaper in Italy, *Giornale di Pavia,* printed bright color photographs on polyethylene. You could read this paper in the pouring rain, and when you were through, you could shake it out, fold it up like a handkerchief, and put it in your pocket. You could also use the paper as a makeshift raincoat.

   It is possible that as an editor you would want your paper stock

This carryover spread from *Go,* the Goodyear tire dealers' magazine, shows how photographs can be clustered to form one irregularly shaped unit, with copy wrapped around. The art shape for the spread is interesting without detracting from the photographs. And bringing the photographs together eliminates clutter and gives the small photographs bigger impact than they would have as scattered units. Larry Miller, editor. Robert R. Wise, art director.

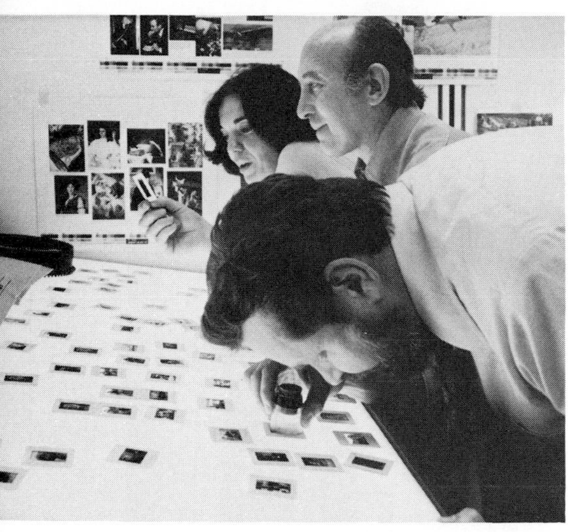

The way to check transparencies is to put them out on a light table and look at them through a magnifying glass. (Photo by Seldon Dix. Courtesy of *Time* magazine.)

to look inexpensive. If your publication goes to members of an organization or to the public supporting you through taxes, you might not want to convey the feel of quality and expense.

4. *The cost of the paper.* Paper stock represents a major production cost to all publications. The cost of the paper itself is only part of it. The cost of mailing comes into the picture, too. The heavier the paper, the more it will cost to mail copies of the magazine. A slight reduction in paper weight can mean thousands of dollars' difference in mailing costs over a period of a year. An editor choosing between two papers should have the printer make up dummies of each to take to the post office for a consultation.

   A magazine doesn't have to use high-quality paper to look well designed. The early *Rolling Stone* proved that, followed by *Rags* (no longer published). Using newsprint, *Rags* in 1970 was able to print and mail copies at less than ten cents each.

   The Progressive of Madison, Wisconsin, a national opinion journal of 50,000 circulation that operates on a shoestring, uses relatively inexpensive groundwood stock. A lively looking publication for its genre, the magazine finds that on such stock line art reproduces better than halftone art. Fortunately, line art fits the magazine's format.

Turning to color

From the time it was available, color in printing has played an important role in the growth of many general-circulation and specialized magazines. American Business Press, the organization of trade journals, found in a study conducted in 1980 that 90 percent of its members used color on their editorial (nonadvertising) pages. The magazine world's interest in color was spurred in the 1960s with the coming of color to television and in the late 1950s with the coming of Hi-Fi and later SpectaColor to advertisements in newspapers. Then newspapers began using color photography in their news coverage. But with better paper stock and less hurried production deadlines, magazines clearly had the color advantage over newspapers.

There seems little doubt that color can increase a publication's audience. The *National Star,* right after going to full color in 1975, experienced a 12 percent rise in newstand sales. *Us* magazine, which, since its founding in 1977, has always run a distant second to *People,* remade itself in 1985 into a full-color publication (*People* was in black and white) with better quality paper. The placement of the art director's name, Robert Priest, in the No. 2 position on the masthead, indicated the role that design was playing in the magazine's fight to catch up with *People.*

But cost is always a factor. A second color throughout can increase the printing bill for a publication by 25 percent. Full-color can double that.

Because of costs, color in some magazines has been more the tool of the advertising than the editorial department. The hue and placement of color may be dependent on decisions made by the advertising department in response to insertion order specifications from advertisers. The editorial department gets a free ride, provided it uses color only on pages in signatures carrying color advertisements. The bigger magazines, including the newsmagazines—*Time, Newsweek,* and *U.S. News & World Report*—all use R-O-P (run-of-paper) color.

Magazines that cannot afford color on a regular basis can use it occasionally, as when they put out special issues or special sections. The use of color then helps say "unique."

Not that editors and art directors are wholly sold on color. Some feel that the additional money spent on plates and color printing could be better spent on additional black-and-white pages. Nor are all artists sold on color. Henri Cartier-Bresson, a founder of the Magnum photographic agency, told *Time,* "I don't like color. By the time it goes through the printer, the inks, and the paper, it has nothing to do with the emotion you had when you shot it. Black and white is a transcription of that emotion, an abstraction of it." Irving Penn, another great photographer, said, "I don't think I have ever seen a really great color photograph." Penn's reservations about color stem from his belief in photography as an art form. He thinks that photography in its purest form must deviate from realism. And color is realism.

In the words of Vincent van Gogh, "Color expresses something by itself."[15] It also affects people psychologically. In an essay on color in *Audubon,* Peter Steinhart reported that factory workers lifting black boxes complained more about their weight than when the boxes were blue.

Steinhart reminds us that red excites us, arouses our passion, makes us hungry. No wonder restaurants paint their interiors red! Yellow is a warning color, possibly because insects and snakes tell us they're poisonous with their bright yellow colors, Steinhart says. Blue has a coolness and authority about it. "That is why we dress policemen in blue and why most banks use it in their corporate emblems," Steinhart observes.[16] He points out that green is reassuring, but it also symbolizes envy and jealousy.

One thing you should remember about color in printing: when you see it in isolation, it looks one way; when you see it next to another color, it takes on a different look. Another thing: it looks one way on antique or uncoated stock, another way on coated stock.

The biggest mistake editors and art directors make with color is that they don't plan their issues around it. When color becomes available in one of the signatures, the art director hastily finds some way to use it. Color is added to a page or merely substituted for black. It is not integrated as part of the design. Hence the many titles in color, blurbs in color blocks, photos in duotone. In some instances, line artwork is added to a page simply to make use of the color. John Peter of John Peter Associates, Inc., a magazine consulting firm, calls this the "we-got-it-why-not-use-it" approach to color, an approach that leads to results "that are usually regretted by the time the issue is off the press." He advises, "When in doubt about using color, stay with black and white."[17]

Matching the colors used in printing is easy enough with the availability of the Pantone Matching System (PMS), which offers papers in 505 colors, various swatch books of colors and tints printed on various papers, and other useful tools for designers. Letraset makes markers to match the Pantone colors. Using them, designers can produce layouts that give an accurate picture of what the colors will look like when printed.

Spot Color

A single solid color put down on a page somewhere as a bright spot or as an area of visual relief or as a focus of attention is known as *spot color* (or *flat color*). Some call it a "second color" because it runs as a complement to black.

Spring zoo attendance

	APRIL	MAY	JUNE
1984	50002	95073	104677
1985	82021	115391	119104

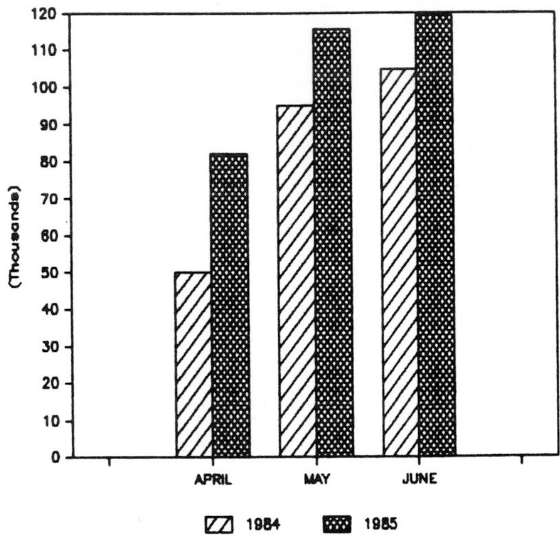

Here's one way the computer has speeded things up in newsrooms and art departments of daily newspapers. First, the data for spring attendance at the local zoo is entered into a personal computer. The P.C. then produces a bar chart. Total time involved: two minutes.

The computer-generated chart goes to the artist (Bill Morrow of *The Oregonian*) who converts the simple chart to something more interesting. The measuring has already been done, so the artist can concentrate on drawing and, in this case, preparing overlays, because the art is to be run in color.

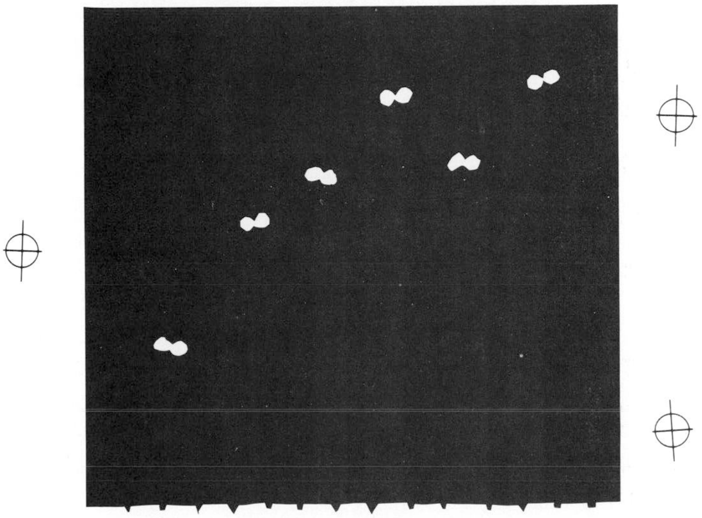

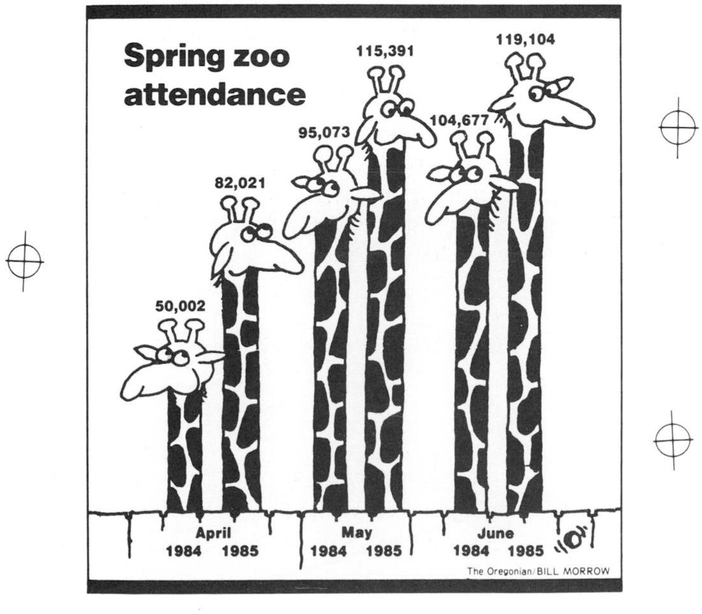

You see here Morrow's original black-and-white art with type pasted into place and an amberlith overlay he prepared for a 50% red and one for a 100% yellow. In the final printing the giraffes appeared in orange because of the printing of the red over the yellow. Only their eyes remained white. Note the register marks on each of the three pieces.

It does not have to be a solid color. It can be a screened version of a solid color. Often a spot color runs in both solid and screened versions on a page to create the illusion of several colors. Sometimes the art director combines the screened color with a screening of black to produce still another "color."

Some ways the art director can use a second color are identified here.

1. *For type.* Color is better for display sizes than for body sizes. When used for type, the color should be on the dark side. A bright red is all right. Yellow does not work. Sometimes it is a good idea to run only one word in a title in color to give it emphasis.

   If you reverse a title (run it in white) in a dark area, say in a black part of a photograph, you can run color in the reversed area, in which case the color can be light color, like yellow.
2. *For photographs.* The best way to print a black-and-white photograph is in black ink on white paper. When you print such a photograph in a color, say green, you diminish the tonal scale; the lighter the color, the less scale you have, and the less detailed your photograph will be. If you must print your photograph in a color, you should choose one that is close to black, like dark brown, dark blue, or dark green. If you want the photograph merely as a decorative element or as a backdrop for copy printed over it, then you can print it in a light color.

   If you want the complete tonal value plus the mood of color, you can print the black-and-white photograph twice, once in the color and once in black. This requires two plates printed so that the dots of the black plate register just to the side of the dots in the color plate. We call this kind of halftone a *duotone.* (Example: you might want to use a brown duotone when you have an old-time photograph to reproduce.) Yu can also run a black-and-white wash drawing as a duotone. And you can apply the color used in the duotone as ordinary spot color elsewhere on the page or signature.

   It is possible to take an ordinary black-and-white photo and *posterize* it for a run in black and one or more spot colors. The printer shoots it for line reproduction, dropping out the middle tones. He gives it more exposure for the color plate, less for black. In the printing the black covers only some of the area printed in color.

   It is also possible to print part of a photograph in black, part in

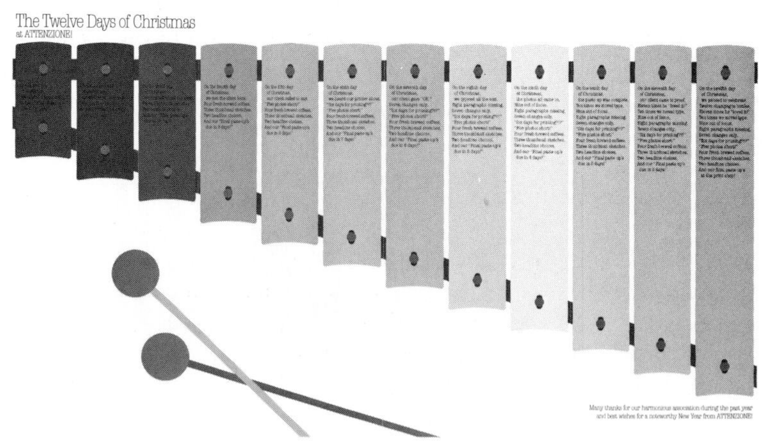

Attenzione!, a Corvallis, Oregon, advertising agency, did a takeoff on a popular Christmas song for its colorful Christmas card-folder. The text celebrates thumbnail sketches, final pasteups, and other realities of production. The all-on-one-side 19 × 11½ card went out to all the agency's clients. Linda Ahlers, copywriter; Deborah Kadas, art director; John Subert, production artist and illustrator.

a spot color. If you have a mug shot, for instance, you can run it as a silhouette, dropping out the background; and in that white area you can print your spot color, making a regular rectangle of the photograph. You can also reverse a circle, arrow, or number on a photograph, if one of these is needed, and fill it in with color.

3. *For line art.* A drawing can be printed in a spot color, or it can be printed in black with the spot color used to fill in certain areas.

   Spot color has special value in charts, graphs, maps, and tables. The color clarifies and emphasizes.

4. *For lines, boxes, and blocks.* Lines in black or in color, horizontal or vertical, help organize and departmentalize a page. Putting a box around a word in a title, or a section of an article, makes it stand out. Or you can use a box to completely surround an article or story.

   One excellent use of spot color is as a solid-color or tint block to serve as a backdrop for line artwork. Allen Hutt made good use of spot color—a light yellow—in his book, *The Changing Newspaper* (Gordon Fraser, London, 1973). The newspaper pages he showed were all on faded yellow. The color made the examples stand out from the white pages without the use of boxes. And the faded yellow look seemed appropriate to the look of newsprint.

   Over a block of color you can run titles, body copy, or even photographs. If the block is dark enough, you can reverse type in it. A photograph with a tint block is different from a duotone in that the dot pattern in the former is even and consistent. The photograph with a tint block doesn't have as much contrast as the duotone; it looks as if it were printed on a colored paper stock.

Spot color can involve more than a single color. It can involve all the colors, as in the Sunday comic sections of newspapers. What's needed then are separate pieces of art for each of the primary colors plus black, separate plates, and multiple printings. The art in two-, three-, or four-color spot color work requires line reproduction in most cases.

Process color

A much more expensive form of color is *process color,* necessary when the magazine has full-color paintings or full-color photographs to reproduce. In four-color spot color the magazine supplies separate art (called *overlays*) for each of the four plates. In process color it supplies only the one piece of art; the printer (or photoengraver) must separate the colors photographically, through the use of filters, and painstakingly reconstruct them for the four negatives used to make the four plates. In printing, the four plates can produce all the colors necessary to duplicate the original art or photograph.

You have three basic color separation systems to consider: conventional, direct, and scan.

In the conventional system a process color camera copies the original color art or photograph and makes four exposures—for printing in magenta, cyan blue, yellow, and black inks. The continuous-tone negatives can be reworked by highly skilled artists to correct the color. Then they are screened before being used to make the plates. A little more correction can be done after the screening through a process known as dot etching.

Direct-screen separations call for halftone screens being placed over each piece of film in the photocopying of the art. This takes less time, but you lose some quality. You can dot-etch only then, and dot etching is more limited than reworking continuous-tone negatives.

The third system, color-scanner separations, involves laser beams. The art is wrapped around a scanning drum. A light-sensing stylus travels the length of the drum while it rotates. Each of the primary colors is sensed and the information fed to a computer, which sends it to another stylus that emits light to expose a film. That light is screened, so you get already-screened film, as in the direct-screen process.

Of the three processes color scanning, so far as the editor is concerned, is the least expensive. But it has some limitations. The original art cannot exceed a certain size, and it can't be done on illustration board or anything that can't be wrapped around a cylinder. But "generally speaking, you can get high quality separations using any of the three systems. . . . The results depend, of course, on the skill of the camera or scanner operators and the amount of corrections you need performed, a *Folio* writer reports."[18]

For best printing results for color photographs (and you should refer to them as *color* photographs rather than *colored* photographs; the latter suggests that color is added after the picture is taken, as in the tinting of photographs) you should supply your printer with transparencies. The printer shouldn't use color prints unless they are all you have. They do not reproduce as well, and the printer charges more to handle them.

In working with transparencies, you should use the same kind of transparency viewer at every step of the reproduction process. It is necessary that everyone who makes a judgment about the transparency make it using the same kind of viewer. To expand this advice a little: you should inspect transparencies, color prints, artwork, proofs, and press sheets under identical lighting conditions in order to maintain control of the work, especially color quality. (Printers urge that one person—preferably a production chief—have full authority on production quality control for both the editorial and the advertising sides. Printers find it frustrating to get instructions from one person and final ok's from another. One person often does not agree with the other.)

You should not ask your printer to enlarge more than five times the original negative. A 2¼ × 2¼ camera is better for color than a 35 mm, so far as picture reproduction is concerned. A 4 × 5 or an 8 × 10 is best,

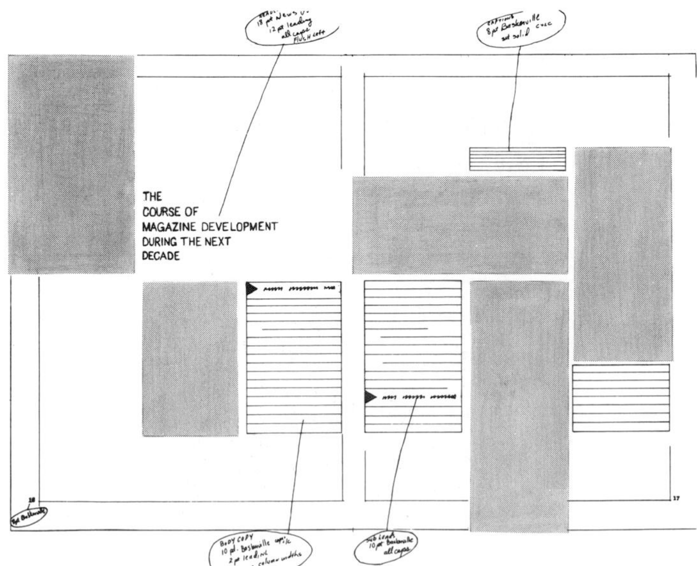

Early in the term of his Publication Design and Production course at the University of Illinois, Professor Glenn Hanson distributes copies of manuscripts and asks students to copyfit them and incorporate them into page design. This is a first effort by student Ralph Sullivan: a spread involving five photos. The student wrote notes in the margins to indicate his preferences in type styles and sizes. This is a rough layout. For a more comprehensive layout, he would be expected to omit the black outlines around the copy blocks and, using the drawing tools available to him, make the rectangles of gray actually look like photographs.

but of course such cameras are too cumbersome for most publications work.

Coated, or at least a calendered, stock is best for reproducing color photos and probably black-and-white photos, too, especially if the printing process used is letterpress. If the publication's process is offset, the smoothness of the stock is not so important a factor in photo reproduction.

Laying out the pages

Whether you provide camera-ready copy or merely rough layouts of dummies to your printer, you will have to work out the arrangement of articles, stories, and features on the various pages of your magazine, issue after issue. We call this arrangement the *dummy*. In the preceding chapter we went into design considerations for the dummy; in this chapter we will consider the mechanics.

The problem, of course, is to fit all the items, editorial and advertising, together so they will look good and read easily. It is impossible to tell someone who has not done it before exactly how to do it; fitting a magazine together is something one does by instinct or feeling. No two persons do it exactly the same way. There is a good deal of trial and error to the procedure, even for professionals. As a designer you will try one thing, discard it, and try another. When you see the proofs, you still will not be satisfied, and you'll probably adjust them, even at that late date.

Almost every magazine has a two-page layout sheet, or grid, on which to arrange layouts. Newspapers use single pasteup sheets. These sheets and grids can be used for both the rough dummy and the finished pasteup.

You can either draw in, roughly, the titles and art, or you can paste into place, also roughly, the galleys and photoprints of the art. If you use galleys, they will be a second set, marked with numbers to show the printer from what galley forms the various articles and stories were taken. The first set is used for proofreading.

The ads are already blocked in. What's left is what a newspaper person would call the "news hole," what a magazine person might call the "editorial hole." The hole consists of a number of beautifully blank spreads ready for your artistry.

In magazine layout the main chore lies with the several major items

Here is Roger Waterman's full-color comprehensive rough layout of a spread for *Chevron USA* along with the two pages as they actually appeared in the magazine. The typed note pasted down at an angle on the right-hand page is a reminder to the designer to make some adjustments: *HAWAII* is to be smaller and in heavier type. And *Motorambling in* is to be bigger. The reproduction does not show it clearly, but the smaller photo is marked to be recropped and lifted slightly on the page. Most magazines do not require so high a degree of finish for rough layouts.

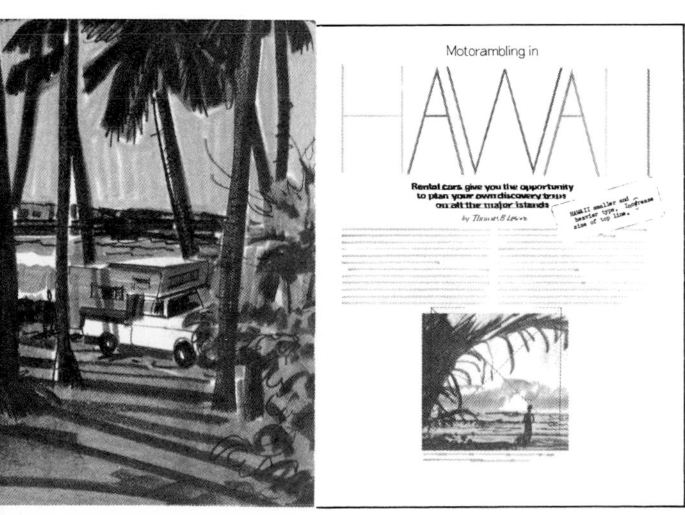

Motorambling In

HAWAII

Rental cars give you the opportunity to plan your own discovery trips on all the major islands

by Thomas B. Lesure

For the essence of the real Hawaii that often escapes first-time visitors, allow some of your vacation time for side trips by car. And plan your trips in a motorambling *hoomanawanui* style.

In Hawaiian, that means "take it easy," and there's no better way to enjoy the Islands.

Fortunately, Hawaii is a land of rental cars, and "U-drives" cover the island roads in astounding numbers, sizes and shapes (more information on page 43). With your own rental car, you can set your own pace.

Pull up beneath a rugged, green-clothed *pali* and marvel at the majestic, steep-walled beauty. Wander into little villages where yesteryears are a breath away. Walk down peaceful trails to shimmering waterfalls, rain forests or odd lava tree "woodlands."

Listen to the trade winds whisper through the undulating sugar cane fields. Pause at surf-caressed beaches — black, gold or gleaming white — where there'll be nobody but you to say *aloha* to the crashing waves. Picnic, swim, fish, go boating or indulge in any number of fresh-air sports as you go along.

Oahu

The so-called Oahu Circle from Honolulu over to the windward side of the island and back has become

Tropical sunrise tinges clear waters off the black sand at Kaimu Beach on the big island of Hawaii.

Fall 1970 — *Chevron USA* 41

that start in the front half of the book. A certain number of pages have already been set aside for each item. By previous decision, some items will occupy several pages; some will occupy one or two. Some items are to begin on a right-hand page, and some on a left-hand page. You often start with this already decided. You have a choice of three basic approaches.

An assignment in a magazine design class was to take a given title for an article and play around with the letters, to give the title more visual impact than it would have with ordinary type. This is Sherry Lee Bastion's solution.

1. *Start from the front.* You figure out where you want your opening art, and how big, and where you want your title and blurb, and then take what space you need for such display, and trail the article through the remaining space column by column. If you run over, you ask the editor to cut. If you're under, you increase the size of the art in front or add art to the body.
2. *Start from the back.* Assuming the publication does not use fillers, you start with the tail end of an article and work forward, allowing for subheads, if that is the magazine's style. The design at first is only tentative; if galleys are used, they are fastened down with small dabs of rubber cement. The amount of space between where the feature is supposed to begin and where the first paragraph happens to land is the amount of space available for title, blurb, and art. If it's not very much, you may use it all right there at the opening. If it is considerable, you will move part of the article forward and put additional art into the space thus opened up.
3. *Work backward and forward from the middle.* This results in a better designed feature usually, and requires, more than the other two approaches, coordination between editor and designer. The designer is as concerned with the looks of the back half of the article as with the opening spread. Some designers run their big art near the middle rather than at the beginning.

You can best estimate how much space the title type will take by actually lettering it. You indicate body copy with boxes or with a series of parallel lines. How do you know exactly how many lines of type the article will take? You use one of several copyfitting systems[19] or, better, you ask your editor to have all manuscripts typed at preset widths on calibrated copy paper. On most magazines a little editing at the proof stage is necessary for a perfect fit.

Company magazines designed by advertising agencies or design studios and some other magazines require much more finished dummies or layouts—"comprehensive roughs" or "comps," in the language of advertising. The designers treat their editors as though they were clients. A comp leaves little to the imagination; design that doesn't work can be corrected before type is set and pictures are taken. But comps take time, and designers who do them command high fees. Comps are out of reach of most magazine editors.

The tools of layout

Tools used by designers range from ordinary writing pencils to felt- and nylon-tip pens and markers used on anything from newsprint to illustration board. Starting out with thumbnail sketches, you may want to use a ballpoint or nylon-tip pen or a Rapidograph on sheets of cheap typing paper. Moving to actual-size roughs, you may want to work on sheets in a layout pad or tracing pad.

Another assignment was to build a spread around the title. Paul Thompson's solution was to adapt Piet Mondrian's painting style to the printed page, using various sizes of rectangles to help organize things and to approximate the real bars of punishment.

The crime of punishment

by Paul Thompson

You probably would want to draw small rectangles for all the pages of your publication to plan content in sequence. Then you'd do more careful, actual-size rough layouts that deal with design aspects.

To indicate copy, you'd draw or scribble a pattern of parallel lines. To indicate titles and headlines, you'd rough in the letters by size and weight, if not by their actual design. In indicating art, you would try to distinguish, through the choice of tools you use, between line drawings and continuous-tone art (photographs and paintings).

Markers, which come in warm and cool grays as well as colors, are particularly useful for indicating photographs and paintings. Some markers on some surfaces bleed or spread and seep through to the other side. It is a good idea to test them on extra sheets before using them on your layouts. You can spray a fixative onto your sheets before laying on a color and respray between color applications. This prevents bleeds, keeps the colors from fading, and gives your paper a good surface to receive the color.

Doing the pasteup

If the publication is printed by offset or gravure, the layout goes to its highest level—the pasteup. Using rubber cement or a waxing process, the designer—or a pasteup artist—fastens everything into place: reproduction proofs of titles and text and any actual-size line art.

What an offset publication turns over to the printer is what the printer prints, exactly—crooked lines and columns, uneven impressions on the repros, smudges, and all. It is safe to say that the editor of an offset publication has more production headaches than the editor of a letterpress publication.

Line art that is to be reduced along with photographs and paintings are submitted to the printer separately.

Photographs can be handled in either of two ways. They can be prescreened as Velox prints and pasted down with the type as though they were pieces of line art, or they can be shot separately as halftone negatives and "stripped in" by the printer. You get better fidelity, using the stripped-in process, but sometimes, as when you have many small photographs on a page, the use of Veloxes is practical. You can also easily retouch a Velox, bringing out highlights.

So far as copy is concerned, pasteup offers the desirable restriction of no last-minute partial leading between lines to even out a column. It is a lot of trouble for a pasteup artist to cut lines apart and respace them. (By contrast, it is a simple matter to extend a story set in hot type; your printer simply puts leads between lines.) Because with cold type you can't lead at the last minute, you won't have unequally leaded stories side-by-side in the publication, and that makes for consistency of pattern—a good thing in design.

In doing a pasteup, you trim pieces of copy to within a quarter or, better, an eighth of an inch of the print. You can use a single-edge razor blade or an X-acto knife on a self-healing plastic cutting board. Moving the pieces to position, you may want to use tweezers rather than your fingers. This will prevent smudges. To save wear and tear on artwork that may go through several hands, and perhaps also to protect the pasteups themselves, you may want to do flaps. These are overlays fastened down at the backs of the pieces and folded over to cover the working surfaces.

Some pasteup artists like to work at light tables, with light coming from below frosted glass to aid in the lining up process. Others prefer ordinary drawing tables with T-squares and triangles. Doing pasteup work, you should be particularly concerned about exact and even spacing. You will find a pair of dividers almost indispensable. Where you want to repeat a measurement, you set it once against an original measurement, and the sharp points help you mark it off elsewhere.

It is not a good idea, usually, to do your design thinking while you do the pasteup. You should do a rough sketch or comprehensive first or, at least, a rough pasteup. Then, after you have moved things around to your satisfaction, you turn to the final pieces. You want to handle them as infrequently as possible.

Patching on the final pasteup may result in shadows cast that will be picked up by the camera. These must be opaqued by the printer on the negative. You will see where the printer overlooked a printed shadow on

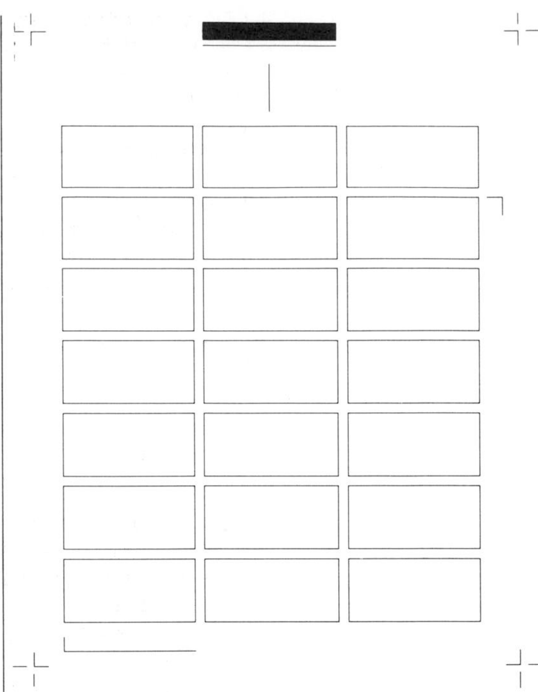

These are the left-hand and right-hand page forms for pasting up *Communication World,* the association journal for the International Association of Business Communicators. Note trim marks and page-corner marks. The black bar at the top trims off to a thinner one in the printing; the bar is part of the magazine's basic design.

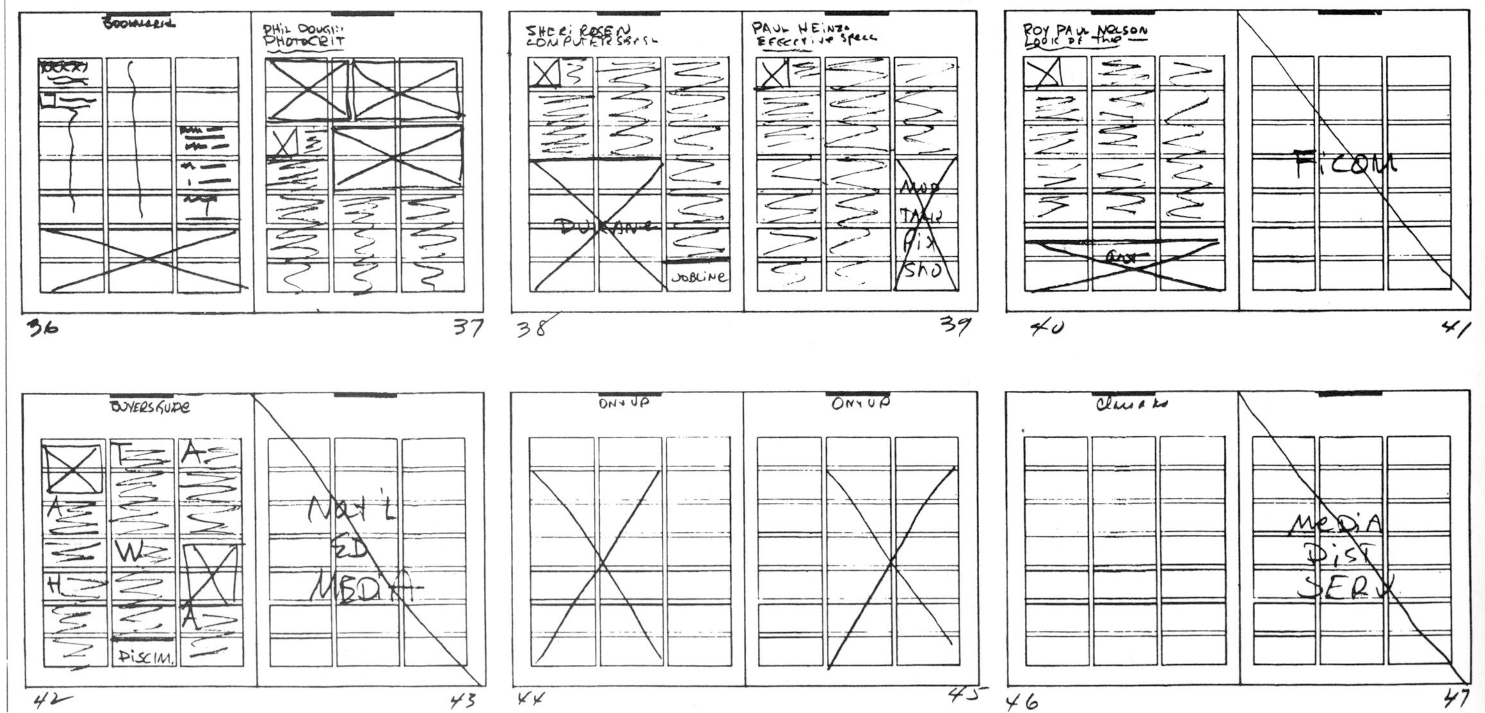

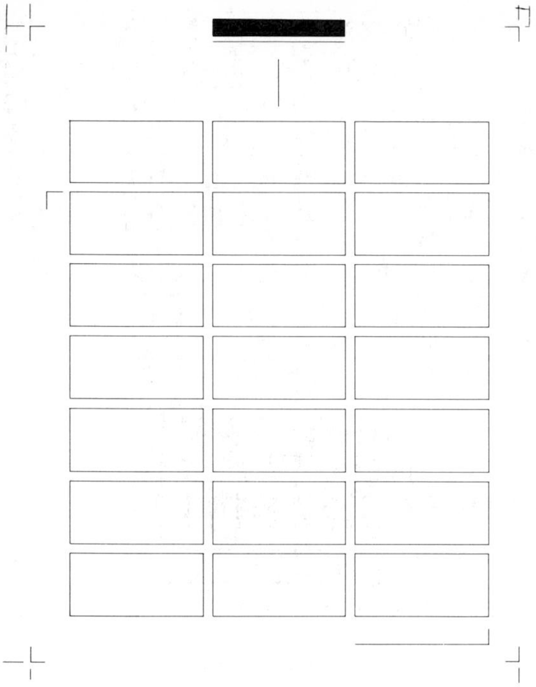

the blueline proofs, and you will circle the error for correction. Rubber cement residue can cause these unwanted marks, too.

Careful pasteup artists pasting down thick copy sheets like to shave the edges with a knife or emery board to eliminate the shadows. Some pasteup artists outline edges of thick copy sheets with a buildup of white opaque paint after the sheets are in place.

Some magazines leave the pasteups to their printers. The printers get rough or finished layouts or dummies to use as guides.

To many in the industry now, all this talk about pasteup is more historical than advisory. The new technology in some shops has made pasteup unnecessary. Pagination, discussed earlier in this book, makes possible the laying out of pages on video screens.

Binding it and wrapping it up

The production phase, after printing, continues with the binding of pages and ends with the readying of the product for distribution to the reader.

To save costs, newspapers avoid binding. The large-size pages probably don't need it. But some of the fatter tabloids or those printed on slick paper would be easier for the reader to handle if they were bound.

(Opposite page)
A magazine starts out innocently enough with scratched notes—thumbnails—like this, with the editor, often in consultation with the art director, planning things page-by-page and spread-by-spread. Boxes with *X*s in them are good enough at this stage to indicate art and ads. These thumbnails are for some interior pages of *Communication World*.

Even before the thumbnail stage, the editor may plan or diagram intended content on a form like this. The single page at the top represents the cover.

Sometimes a publication outgrows its binding style and moves on to another. After thirty-two years as a saddle-stitched magazine, *Playboy* in 1985 became a perfect-bound magazine and had to find a new way to present its centerfold feature.

Saddle (or saddle-wire) stitching is cheaper than adhesive (perfect) binding, but a magazine can grow too thick to take the cheaper binding. In saddle stitching, signatures of folded pages fit into each other on a V-shaped saddle. The stitches go in through the back and fold at the center spread. In adhesive binding, signatures fit on top of each other. Perfect-bound magazines have spines. They don't stay open and lie flat as saddle-stitched magazines do.

A publication distributed to the reader via the mails often goes in a wrapper of some kind: a paper sleeve, an envelope, even a box.

A sleeve may fully cover the face of the publication, as for a thick magazine, or it may cover only a part of the publication, as for a thin one that is folded vertically down the middle before the sleeve is fitted on. Some magazines, mailed flat, go out in transparent full wrappers that protect copies from rain and also allow subscribers to recognize their magazines at once when they arrive. A few magazines wrap themselves in extra covers, perhaps of kraft paper, which are saddle-stitched on as four-page extra signatures. They carry the address label, and they can be torn off when the magazines arrive to allow subscribers to fully appreciate well-designed front covers unmarred by stickers or rough handling in the mails.

Too often the wrapper is overlooked in planning. The art director should be as concerned about its design—about its form and typography—as about the magazine itself. The wrapper is the reader's first contact with each issue as it arrives.

Keeping costs down

To keep printing and production costs down, Roger V. Dickeson, president of Printing Efficiency Management Corporation, offers these suggestions:

1. Cut the publication's trim size, if only slightly. The trimming can save both paper and postage costs.
2. Decrease the paper weight.
3. Come to an understanding with your printer as to exactly what quality you expect and are willing to pay for. Dickeson says that many editors unknowingly add about 10 percent to their printing costs through "extended press makereadies, press running waste, 'make goods,' unnecessary time spent in endless argument and discussion, sending representatives to the printing plant to 'approve' press forms." Dickeson says requirements for paper, film, and ink—all three—should be worked out ahead of time.
4. Follow the schedules set up with the printer. The editor who doesn't "must pay a premium for any delay time he causes."

   Dickeson points out that dailies and weeklies work more efficiently with printers than monthlies do. There appears to be a law in operation here: "production inefficiency expands in direct relationship to the time interval between publication dates." What happens is that the rhythm is lost.[20]

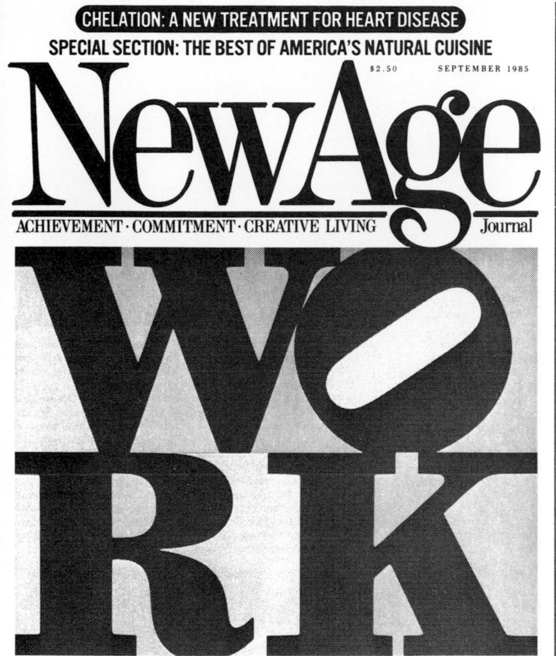

Greg Paul, art director of *New Age,* did a takeoff of Robert Indiana's famous "Love" design to create this "Work" cover.

Notes

1. Byron Ferris, "Annals of Design (3): Boom Years: 1948–1973," *Communication Arts,* May/June 1985, p. 32.
2. "Behind the Scenes," *Magazine Design & Production,* December 1985, p. 53.
3. "Art Direction Enters New Age as LIFE Begins Layout by Machine," *Publishers' Weekly,* July 6, 1970, pp. 28, 29.
4. Ibid., p. 28.
5. "Pasadena Star-News Buys $2 Million Pagination System," *TypeWorld,* June 26, 1981, p. 13.
6. *U&lc.,* June 1980, p. 39.
7. Perry E. Jeffe, "Computer Graphic Arts," *U&lc.,* August 1985, p. 26.
8. C. J. Wallis, "What's New in Desk-Top Publishing?" *Communication World,* January 1986, p. 32.
9. Charles Bigelow, "Font Design for Personal Workstations," *Byte,* January 1985, p. 255.
10. Steve Rosenthal, "Starting from Page One: The Fundamentals of Layout and Design (Part I)," *Desktop Publishing,* October 1985, p. 35.
11. Frank Romano, "Editing with Computers," *Magazine Design & Production,* November 1985, p. 36.
12. Gerald O. Walter, "Typesetting," *Scientific American,* May 1969, p. 61.
13. Editorial in *TypeWorld,* October 4, 1985, p. 2.
14. David Saltman, "The Colorful Side of Paper," *Magazine Design & Production,* October 1985, p. 31.
15. Quoted by Peter Steinhart, "Color and Culture," *Audubon,* September 1985, p. 10.
16. Peter Steinhart, "Color and Culture," *Audubon,* September 1985, pp. 8–9.
17. John Peter, "Second Color," *Better Editing,* Spring 1968, pp. 9, 10.
18. Jeffery R. Parnau, "The Basic Guide to Color Separation," *Folio,* August 1981, p. 82. See his complete article, pp. 81–93.
19. Like Glenn Hanson's *How to Take the Fits Out of Copyfitting,* The Mul-T-Rul Company, Fort Morgan, Colorado, 1967.
20. Roger V. Dickeson, "You Can Reduce Print Costs," *Folio,* August 1981, pp. 68 ff. Dickeson offers additional suggestions in this article, including the publisher's supplying of paper to the printer and better money management.

Suggested further reading

Arnold, Edmund C., *Ink on Paper 2,* Harper & Row Publishers, New York, 1972.

Bann, David, *The Print Production Handbook,* North Light Publishers, Cincinnati, Ohio, 1985.

Beach, Mark, Steve Shepro, and Ken Russon, *Getting It Printed,* Coast to Coast Books, Portland, Oreg., 1986.

Benevento, Frank S., et al., *Art and Copy Preparation, with an Introduction to Phototypesetting,* Graphic Arts Technical Foundation, Pittsburgh, 1976.

Berg, N. Edward, *Electronic Composition: A Guide to the Revolution in Typesetting.* Graphic Arts Technical Foundation, Pittsburgh, 1976.

Borowsky, Irvin J., *Handbook for Color Printing,* rev. ed., North American Publishing Company, Philadelphia, 1977. (Charts showing combinations in two-color printing.)

Brownstone, David, and Irene Franck, *The Dictionary of Publishing,* Van Nostrand Reinhold Company, New York, 1982.

Cardamone, Tom, *Mechanical Color Separation Skills for the Commercial Artist,* Van Nostrand Reinhold Company, New York, 1979.

———, *Advertising Agency and Studio Skills: A Guide to the Preparation of Art and Mechanicals for Reproduction,* rev. ed., Watson-Guptill Publications, New York, 1970.

Clements, Ben, and David Rosenfield, *Photographic Composition,* Prentice-Hall, Englewood Cliffs, New Jersey, 1974.

Cogoli, John, *Everything to Know About Photo-Offset,* North American Publishing Company, Philadelphia, 1973.

Cooke, Donald E., *Dramatic Color by Overprinting,* North American Publishing Company, Philadelphia, 1974.

Craig, James, *Production for the Graphic Designer,* Watson-Guptill Publications, New York, 1974.

Crow, Wendell C., *Communications Graphics,* Prentice-Hall, Englewood Cliffs, New Jersey, 1986.

Demuney, Jerry, and Susan E. Meyer, *Pasteups and Mechanicals,* Watson-Guptill Publications, New York, 1982.

Favre, Jean-Paul, and Andre November, *Color and Communication,* Hastings House, Publishers, New York, 1980.

Field, Janet N., ed., *Graphic Arts Manual,* Arno Press, New York, 1980.

Gottschall, Edward, *Graphic Communications '80s,* Prentice-Hall, Englewood Cliffs, New Jersey, 1981.

Graham, Walter B., *Complete Guide to Pasteup,* North American Publishing Company, Philadelphia, 1975.

Graphics Master 2, Dean Lem Associates, P.O. Box 25920, Los Angeles, California, 90025, 1977. (Expensive all-purpose reference book on production, printing, color, typesetting, copyfitting.)

Gross, Edmund J., *How to Do Your Own Pasteup for Printing,* Halls of Ivy Press, North Hollywood, California, 1979.

Halftone Reproduction Guide, Halftone Reproduction Guide, P.O. Box 212, Great Neck, New York 11022, 1975. (More than 1,200 different effects using two-color printing.)

Jauneau, Roger, *Small Printing Houses and Modern Technology,* The Unesco Press, Paris, 1981.

Kleper, Michael L., *Understanding Phototypesetting,* North American Publishing Company, Philadelphia, 1976.

Labuz, Ronald, *How to Typeset from a Word Processor,* R. R. Bowker, New York, 1984.

Levitan, Eli L., *Electronic Imaging Techniques,* Van Nostrand Reinhold Company, New York, 1977.

Lewis, John, *The Anatomy of Printing: The Influence of Art and History on its Design,* Watson-Guptill Publications, New York, 1970.

Memme, Susan, *Teach Yourself to Fit Copy,* Sunrise Communications, Box 1452, Brea, California 92621, 1980.

Mintz, Patricia Barns, *A Dictionary of Graphic Arts Terms,* Van Nostrand Reinhold Company, New York, 1981.

Moran, James, *Printing in the Twentieth Century: A Penrose Anthology,* Hastings House Publishers, New York, 1974.

Munce, Howard, *Graphics Handbook: A Beginner's Guide to Design, Copy Fitting and Printing Procedures,* North Light Publishers, Cincinnati, Ohio, 1982.

Murray, Ray, *How to Brief Designers and Buy Print,* Business Books, Brookfield Publishing, Brookfield, Vermont, 1984.

Paste-up Guide, Portage, P.O. Box 5500, Akron, Ohio, 1976.

Pickins, Judy, *The Copy-to-Press Handbook,* John Wiley and Sons, New York, 1985.

Pocket Pal: A Graphic Arts Digest for Printers and Advertising Production Managers, International Paper Company, New York.

Quick, John, *Artists' and Illustrators' Encyclopedia,* 2d ed., McGraw-Hill Book Company, New York, 1977.

Rasberry, Leslie, *Computer Age Copyfitting: A Method of Using the Small Electronic Calculator,* Art Direction Book Company, New York, 1977.

Sanders, Norman, and William Bevington, *Graphic Designer's Production Handbook,* Hastings House Publishers, New York, 1982.

Seybold, John W., *Fundamentals of Modern Composition,* Seybold Publications, Box 44, Media, Pennsylvania 19063, 1977.

Sidelinger, Stephen J., *The Color Manual,* Prentice-Hall, Englewood Cliffs, New Jersey, 1985.

Silver, Gerald A., *Modern Graphics Arts Paste-up,* 2d ed., Van Nostrand Reinhold Company, New York, 1983.

Simon, Herbert, *Introduction to Printing,* Faber & Faber, Salem, New Hampshire, 1980.

Simon, Hilda, *Color in Reproduction: Theory and Techniques for Artists and Designers,* Viking Press, New York, 1980.

Stevenson, George A., *Graphic Arts Encyclopedia,* 2d ed., McGraw-Hill Book Company, New York, 1979.

Stockton, James, *Designer's Guide to Color,* Chronicle Books, 1984. (Two volumes.)

Turnbull, Arthur T., Russell N. Baird, and Duncan McDonald, *The Graphics of Communication,* 5th ed., Holt, Rinehart and Winston, New York, 1987.

Van Deusen, Edmund, *Computer Videographics: Color, Design, Typography,* CCC Exchange, Box 1251, Laguna Beach, California 92652, 1981.

van Uchelen, Rod, *Paste-up: Production Techniques and New Applications,* Van Nostrand Reinhold Company, New York, 1976.

White, Jan, *Mastering Graphics: Design and Production Made Easy,* R. R. Bowker Company, New York, 1983.

White, William, *Laser Printing,* Carnegie Press, Madison, New Jersey, 1983.

4

GREECE
JAMAICA
Ceylon
China
MEXICO
Tahiti
Canada
Ireland
Scotland
Denmark
Japan
PORTUGAL
BRITAIN

Here are some attempts by art directors to find typefaces or letterforms appropriate to specific countries or places. Do they work? Well, if they do, they work in some cases because art directors have used them in the past to do similar jobs. In a few cases you could say the types are appropriate because of how they evolved. For instance, the *GREECE* imitates early Greek letters, scratched with a stylus on a wax tablet; the *China* has a Chinese calligraphy look; the *Ireland* stems from Irish calligraphy (semiuncials); the *Denmark* comes in the text or blackletter that developed out of the European lowlands.

Typography

The overriding consideration in typography is readability. If it's not readable, it's not good typography. Type arranged in tricky formation may work for an occasional heading; but for most headings and for long columns of text matter, the traditional types, traditionally spaced, work best. The reader's reaction should be "What an interesting article!" not "What interesting typography!"

Some typographers make a point of distinguishing between *readability* and *legibility*. *Legibility* has to do with the ease with which the reader distinguishes one letter from another. *Readability,* a broader term, has to do with the ease with which the reader takes in a column or page of type. Readability also has to do with the way the story or article is written.

Readability, from a typographic standpoint, is affected by these factors:

1. *The style of the typeface.* Familiar styles are usually the most readable.
2. *The size of the typeface.* Within reason, the larger the face, the better.
3. *The length of the line.* Comfortably narrow columns are better than wide columns.
4. *The amount of leading (pronounced "ledding") between lines.* Most body sizes can use at least one and probably two points.
5. *The pattern of the column of type.* It should be even-toned.
6. *The contrast between the darkness of the type and the lightness of the paper.* The more contrast the better.
7. *The texture of the paper.* It shouldn't be intrusive.
8. *The relationship of the type to other elements on the page.* The relationship should be obvious.
9. *The suitability of type to content.* The art director should exploit the "personality" of types.

Type development

The early types were designed to approximate the handwriting—the calligraphy—of the countries in which they developed. The first German types of Gutenberg and his followers in the fifteenth century were harsh, black, and closefitting—the German blackletter we today mistakenly refer to as

Old English. (A more accurate term for these types is *text,* taken from the "texture" of the page, with its heavy, woven look.)

In Italy the faces were lighter, more delicate, after the humanistic hand of Petrarch. These types were the forerunners of what we today call roman (small *r*) types.

During the first two centuries of printing in Europe (1450–1650) these two faces—blackletter and roman—were used extensively. One other took its place beside them. It was italic, a slanting type introduced by Aldus Manutius in 1501. The advantage of italic, as Manutius designed it, was that it was close-fitting. That meant you could get more type per page, and that was important because paper was expensive. And italic looked more like handwriting, which added to its desirability.

The design of new typefaces continues. The new technology makes the introduction of typefaces easier than ever. A new typeface appears on the market almost every week. And where type, new or not so new, is being set, a lens or computer can give it a wide range of variants, making choices for editors and art directors almost endless. Photo-Lettering, Inc., a New York typesetting and type-design firm, offers more than ten thousand display faces and more than seven hundred body faces.

Many of the new typefaces come from the producers of press-on (or dry-transfer) letters and from manufacturers of phototypesetting, digital, and other systems. Others come from special type-design houses. The most ubiquitous of these is the International Typeface Corporation (ITC) in New York. Many producers of press-on letters and manufacturers of phototypesetting equipment subscribe to ITC services. *U&lc.,* a widely circulated house organ (200,000 subscribers), helps sell ITC faces. Editors and art directors can get the magazine free. Among ITC's faces are Avant Garde Gothic, Souvenir, Zapf Book, Eras, and updated versions of standard romans like Garamond, Caslon, and Baskerville. ITC typefaces tend to have large x-heights and are designed for close fitting.[1]

Successful faces inspire imitators, and correctly identifying faces these days becomes almost impossible. For instance, Palatino, produced by Mergenthaler Linotype and by Berthold, comes from other firms as Paladium, Andover, Elegante, Malibu, Patina, and Pontiac. These faces differ very slightly from Palatino. Times Roman comes also as Times New Roman, Press Roman, London Roman, English, English Times, and Pegasus. Helvetica comes also as Helios, Newton, Vega, Claro, Corvus, Geneva, and Megaron. TypeSpecta's Souvenir Gothic is a lot like ITC's Souvenir but with the serifs eliminated.[2]

The copyright laws do not protect the designers of typefaces, except in their ways of presenting their typefaces in their brochures and advertising to clients. The alphabet itself is in the public domain, of course, and perhaps Congress feels that any restrictions on its use would hinder press freedom. Moreover, cataloging the distinctions among all the typefaces in order to protect them would be a monumental task.

Type sometimes goes from exclusive to general use. Avant Garde Gothic, for instance, started out as the logo typeface for a magazine with that name. Frutiger, another modern sans serif, served first as signage for the Charles de Gaulle Airport in Paris.

Some industry experts see the end of the process of marking copy for the typesetter, getting proofs, marking *them,* and finally getting reproduction proofs to paste up. "Now type is sprayed on paper from ink-jets, painted on electrostatic drums by laser beams, and written by electrons on high-resolution CRTs," says a writer in *U&lc.* "Type (as a physical

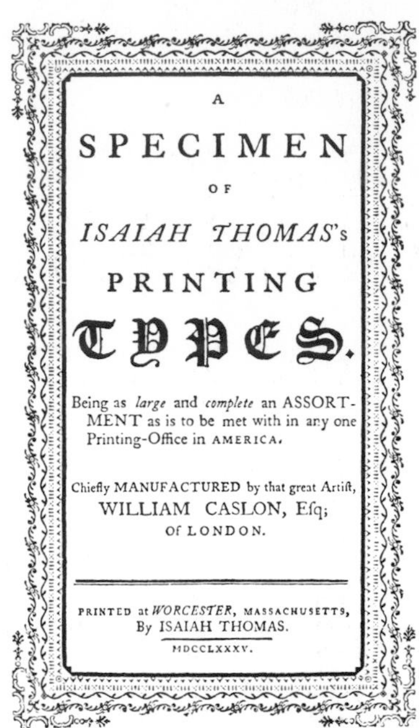

A

SPECIMEN

OF

ISAIAH THOMAS's

PRINTING

TYPES.

Being as *large* and *complete* an ASSORTMENT as is to be met with in any one Printing-Office in AMERICA.

Chiefly MANUFACTURED by that great Artift, WILLIAM CASLON, Efq; Of LONDON.

PRINTED at *WORCESTER,* MASSACHUSETTS, By ISAIAH THOMAS.

MDCCLXXXV.

A printer or typesetting house offers customers a type specimen book to use, with available types shown in complete alphabets and in a variety of sizes. One house in New York, Photo-Lettering, Inc., shows samples of more than 10,000 faces. Typesetting houses of an earlier era, when type was all foundry type, had fewer faces to show, but those houses put out books, too. This is the title page of the book offered by Isaiah Thomas, printer in Worcester, Massachusetts. The year was 1785.

This display shows many of the typefaces discussed in the opening pages of this chapter—and a few others. Most of these names are family names: the families come in various series. For instance, the family Eras, a sans serif offered by ITC, comes in light, book, demibold, bold, ultrabold, outline, and contour in addition to what is shown here.

CLARENDON
BASKERVILLE
Caslon Bold
Times Roman
Eras Medium
Stymie Black
Cooper Black Italic
Cheltenham Bold Condensed
Palatino
Bookman Italic
Optima
Helvetica Light
TIMES ROMAN ITALIC
Ultra Bodoni Italic
Palatino Semi-Bold
Bodoni Bold
Century Schoolbook Italic
Old English
Garamond
Futura Medium
BROADWAY
Helvetica Regular
SOUVENIR
Helvetica Bold

thing) no longer exists. It is a series of mathematical splines stored in memory, waiting to be called and filled in, shadowed, cross-hatched, condensed, obliqued or expanded."[3]

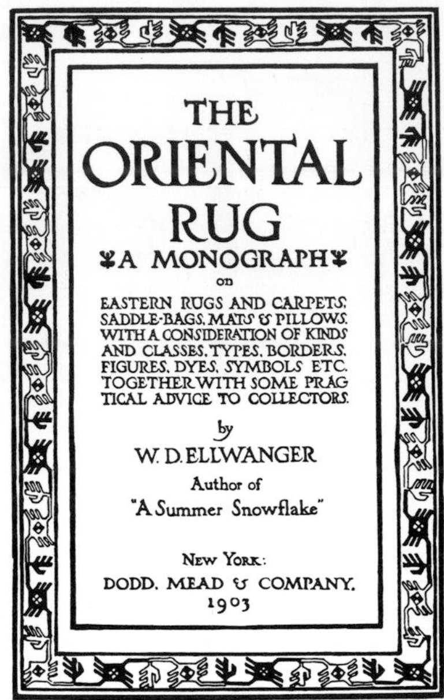
THE
ORIENTAL
RUG
A MONOGRAPH
on
EASTERN RUGS AND CARPETS. SADDLE-BAGS. MATS & PILLOWS. WITH A CONSIDERATION OF KINDS AND CLASSES. TYPES. BORDERS. FIGURES. DYES. SYMBOLS ETC. TOGETHER WITH SOME PRAGTICAL ADVICE TO COLLECTORS.
by
W. D. ELLWANGER
Author of
"A Summer Snowflake"
NEW YORK:
DODD. MEAD & COMPANY.
1903

Hand lettering put inside a border that looks like the border of a fine rug makes this exquisite title page from 1903 say "rug" twice, verbally and visually.

Type revivals

What may be good for one period of time in typography may not be good in another. Type preferences change. Types come and go—and come back again.

A case in point is Bookman, rediscovered in the mid-1960s as a display face. Bookman is a face adapted from an old-style antique face of the 1860s. It is like Clarendon, but it has more roundness.

At the turn of the century it had become so popular that a reaction set in against it. Designers began to consider it monotonous. It was kept alive by offset and gravure, because its strong lines and serifs stood up well in that kind of printing. (The old *Collier's* magazine used it.) As these processes became more sophisticated and better able to handle more fragile types, Bookman died out.

In revival it gives display matter a solid, strong look. In its italic version, with swash caps, it has a charm that has captivated some of our leading designers (see the *New York* logo in chapter 7).

In the 1970s, ITC's Souvenir, a bowlegged roman type, came on strong, both as display and body copy. Other types that have made a comeback in magazine design include Cooper Black, Cheltenham, Futura, and even Broadway.

Eventually, you will develop strong prejudices against many typefaces, strong preferences for others. You may conclude that only a few fit your publication. And you will change your mind from time to time as to which ones those are.

Categories of type

There are many ways to classify types. If you were to classify them from a historical standpoint, you would do it one way. If you were to classify them from a utilitarian standpoint, you would do it another.

Type in a small size (up to 14 points) is *body type*. Type in larger sizes (14 points or more) is *display type*.

Although many faces come in both body and display sizes, some come only as body types, and others come only as display types. In a face designed for both categories you can detect subtle changes as it moves from the large to the small. For instance, the interior area of the loop of the *e* has to be proportionately larger in the smaller sizes of a face. Otherwise it would fill in with ink.

The body faces are divided into *book* faces (the most common faces and the ones used for texts of magazines) and *news* faces. News faces have been especially designed for fast, relatively inexpensive printing in small sizes on newsprint. They are bold faces, essentially, with large x-heights.[4] They do not come in display sizes.

We can break down typefaces, body and display, into several broad categories, sometimes called "races."

1. *Roman.* These faces have two distinguishing characteristics: (1) thick and thin strokes and (2) serifs at the stroke terminals. Where the differences in the strokes are minimal and where serifs

In this two-page-spread article opener, it is hard to tell which came first: the art or the title type, which is obviously hand drawn, an example of calligraphy at work in magazines. The spike-like structure of the letters matches the comb of the rooster, painted magnificently by Alan E. Cober. The publication: *The Plain Dealer Magazine,* published by the Cleveland *Plain Dealer.* Art director: Greg Paul.

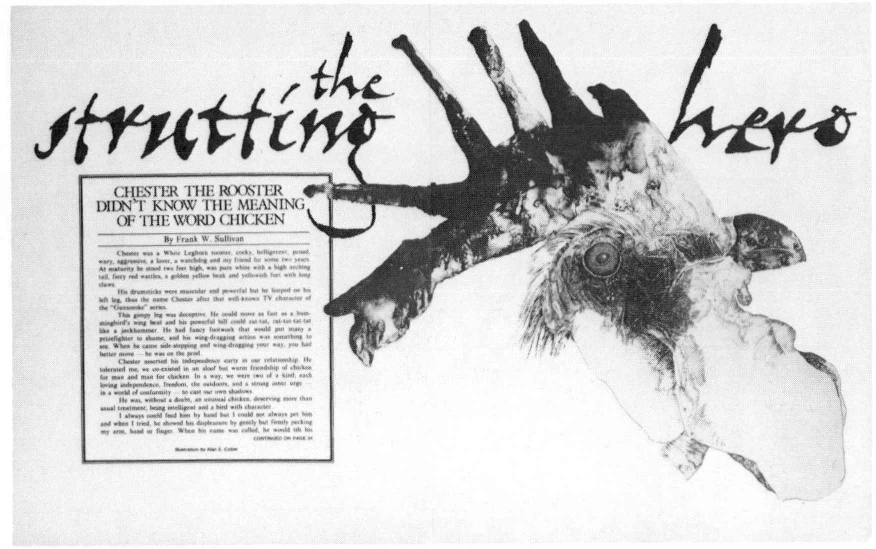

the strutting hero

CHESTER THE ROOSTER DIDN'T KNOW THE MEANING OF THE WORD CHICKEN

By Frank W. Sullivan

Chester was a White Leghorn rooster, cocky, belligerent, proud, wary, aggressive, a lover, a watchdog and my friend for some two years. At maturity he stood two feet high, was pure white with a high arching tail, fiery red wattles, a golden yellow beak and yellowish feet with long claws.

His drumsticks were muscular and powerful but he limped on his left leg, thus the name Chester after that well-known TV character of the "Gunsmoke" series.

This gimpy leg was deceptive. He could move as fast as a hummingbird's wing beat and his powerful bill could rat-tat, rat-tat-tat-tat like a jackhammer. He had fancy footwork that would put many a prizefighter to shame, and his wing-dragging action was something to see. When he came side-stepping and wing-dragging your way, you had better move — he was on the prod.

Chester asserted his independence early in our relationship. He tolerated me; we co-existed in an aloof but warm friendship of chicken for man and man for chicken. In a way, we were two of a kind; each loving independence, freedom, the outdoors, and a strong inner urge — in a world of conformity — to cast our own shadows.

He was, without a doubt, an unusual chicken, deserving more than usual treatment; being intelligent and a bird with character.

I always could feed him by hand but I could not always pet him and when I tried, he showed his displeasure by gently but firmly pecking my arm, hand or finger. When his name was called, he would tilt his

CONTINUED ON PAGE 34

Illustration by Alan E. Cober

blend into the letters, the romans are "old style"; where the differences are pronounced and where the serifs appear almost tacked on as an afterthought, the romans are "modern." In-between styles are "transitional."[5] You are reading a roman type right now.

2. *Sans serif.* Sans serif types came along first in the early 1800s and were revived by the Bauhaus in the 1920s. Their strokes are essentially of the same thickness. There are no serifs at the terminals. More recent sans serifs, with slight differences in stroke thickness and with a slightly squared look, are called "gothics" or "grotesques."[6] The captions used in this book are set in a sans serif face.
3. *Slab serif.* Slab or square serif types have even-thickness strokes as on the sans serif types, and serifs as on the roman types. The most beautiful of the slab serifs, because they lean toward the romans, are the Clarendons. Slab serifs were developed in England at a time when the country was fascinated by Egyptian culture, and the term *Egyptian,* for no particular reason, was applied to them. Many of the slab serif faces are named after Egyptian cities. These faces have also been referred to as "antiques."
4. *Ornamental.* Typefaces that don't belong in any of the first three categories can be lumped in this category. There are the text or black letters (Old English), the scripts (which are intended to look

Goudy Old Style Roman, designed by Frederic W. Goudy in the late 1920s, has a classic look that appeals to many designers. The face has grace and character. It is shown here in a 36-pt. size. Note the diamond-shape periods and dots.

ABCDEFGHIJKLMNOPQRSTU
VWXYZ
abcdefghijklmnopqrstuvwxyz
1234567891O.,?;:""'"!

Avant Garde Gothic, designed by Herb Lubalin and Tom Carnase, offers a great variety of ligatures and alternate characters. It has a large x-height and comes in five weights. Shown here is medium. (© 1970 by International Typeface Corporation. Reprinted by permission of International Typeface Corporation.)

like handwriting), and the gimmick letters (made to look like logs, pieces of furniture, etc.).

In each of the major categories are hundreds of subcategories, sometimes called "families." For instance, the sans serif category includes such families as Franklin Gothic, Futura, Helvetica, News Gothic, Record Gothic, Spartan, Tempo, Trade Gothic, Standard, and Univers. [7] You order types by family names such as these. Each of the types represented by these names usually comes in several varieties.

Not only will you find it difficult to distinguish among the various families (exactly how does Granjon differ from Janson?), you also will have difficulty distinguishing among variations within the family. One company's Garamond is likely to differ from another's.

Most families of type come in more than one weight (light, regular, bold, ultrabold) and more than one width (regular, expanded, condensed).

The italics

Although from a historical standpoint italics deserve their own category, typographers do not consider them as a category, major or otherwise. The reason is that italics have become more a style variation than a type in their own right. Almost every face has its italics version.

For some types the italics are exactly like the uprights, but slanted. For other types the italics are quite different—so different, in fact, that they

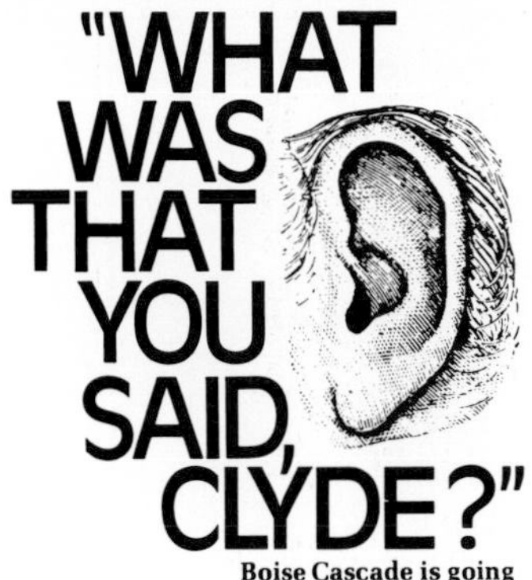
"WHAT
WAS
THAT
YOU
SAID,
CLYDE?"

Boise Cascade is going all out to reduce noise pollution at its pulp and paper mills.

By Linda Miller

Sometimes an art director incorporates a piece of art with the article's title. Art director Joe Erceg does it here for *Paper Times,* using some public-domain art. The title type wraps around the ear, and the blurb takes its place just below. A little extra space separates the byline from the title-blurb unit. Ragged-right and -left setting work for both title and blurb.

appear to be of a different design. Many art directors prefer italics different in design from their uprights because they are more useful as contrast types.

Ronald Labuz, columnist for *Magazine Design & Production,* warns editors that when specifying italics, they should insist on true italics, not "pseudo italics" of the kind coming from manipulation of digital typesetting equipment to slant roman faces. True italics, he reminds editors, are specially designed to go with roman faces; they are not simply slanted versions of those faces.[8]

Italics, as conceived by Manutius, were narrower than the uprights, but in some faces today they are actually wider. In Linotype and Intertype faces they are equal in width to their uprights. That's because both the upright and the italic version of each letter are on the same mat, one underneath the other.

Because they are designed on a diagonal, italics tend to project a mood of restlessness or haste. Italics are not quite as easy to read as uprights. Art directors find italics useful for captions, for emphasis in body copy, for foreign phraseology, and for names of publications, plays, ships, and works of art. Used column after column, solid italics can be fatiguing. Nor does the reader appreciate them as occasional paragraphs in body copy; when readers move back into the uprights, they get the optical illusion of reading type that bends over to the left.

When you underline a word in a manuscript, you are telling the typesetter to set the word in italics. You should make sure italics are available in that face; if not, the printer may set the word in boldface. It is a mistake to set names of publications in boldface. It makes them stand out unnecessarily from other words. If no italics are available, names of publications should be set in ordinary uprights.

Some magazines run the names of publications in italics but run their own names, when they're mentioned in the copy, in caps and small caps—like this: PUBLICATION DESIGN. Only as tall as the x-height of the letters, small caps are also useful for jobs ordinarily assigned to full-size caps: for instance, headlines quoted from newspapers and telegrams from letters-

For a class in calligraphy, Joanne Hasegawa created an experimental design with old style roman letters in various sizes. A feel for letterform should be part of the training of every potential art director.

to-the-editor writers. In many type designs small caps differ from ordinary caps in a given font not only in size but also in their squared-off appearance and slightly different weight distribution.

Character in types

Some types are versatile enough to be appropriate for almost any job. Others are more limited in what they can do. But all have some special qualities that set them apart. Art directors are not in agreement about these qualities, but here are a few familiar faces (subcategories or families, if you prefer), along with descriptions of the moods they seem to convey.

1. *Baskerville*—beauty, quality, urbanity
2. *Bodoni*—formality, aristocracy, modernity
3. *Caslon*—dignity, character, maturity
4. *Century*—elegance, clarity
5. *Cheltenham*—honesty, reliability, awkwardness
6. *Franklin Gothic*—urgency, bluntness
7. *Futura*—severity, utility
8. *Garamond*—grace, worth, fragility
9. *Standard*—order, newness
10. *Stymie*—precision, solidarity
11. *Times Roman*—tradition, efficiency

These qualities, if they come across to readers, come across only vaguely. Furthermore, a single face can have qualities that tend to cancel out each other. (Can a type be both tradition-oriented and efficient?) Even though you should be conscious of these qualities and make whatever use you can of them, you should not feel bound to any one type because of a mood you want to convey.

Baskerville
Bodoni
Caslon
Century
Cheltenham
Franklin Gothic
Futura
Garamond
Standard
Stymie
Times Roman

These are some familiar typefaces whose moods are described in the text on this page.

Assume that you are designing a radical, militant political magazine. Baskerville seems an unlikely choice for the title face. And yet Dugald Stermer used it successfully at *Ramparts* while Kenneth Stuart was using it, also successfully, at *Reader's Digest,* a magazine near the opposite end of the political spectrum.

Sometimes the best answer to the question of which type to use in title display is to go with a stately, readable type—like Baskerville—and rely upon the *words* in the title to express the mood of the piece.

This illustration comes from a whimisical ad sponsored by Quad Typographers, New York. The company has matched typefaces with illustration styles. These characters supposedly attended the typesetting company's "posh Fifth Anniversary Party." From left: European industrialist Claude Graphique, society columnist Lightline Gothic, impresario Futura Black, Baroness Excelsior Script, health faddist 20th Century Ultrabold, unidentified maid (her face is the company insignia), Texas tycoon Windsor Elongated, underground film star Prisma, Italian futurist designer Signor Modern Roman No. 20, former channel swimmer Samantha Smoke, and her escort, Seventh Avenue mogul Max Balloon. Concept and design by Peter Rauch and Herb Levitt; Illustration by Tim Lewis.

Which type to use

Personal preference and even bigotry have influenced choices of typefaces. Adolf Hitler didn't like Old English (known then as "Gothic Script"). He traced it to early Jews in Germany who had become printers. M. Bormann circulated a directive in 1941 saying that "the Fuehrer has decided that Roman type from now on shall be designated as the normal type."[9]

The history of a typeface, its aesthetics, the personality of the face, the mood of the article, the age level and station of the audience, the taste of the art director—all these can affect the choice. For those who choose, research holds some clues.

"Objective research has produced few dramatic results," said Herbert Spencer, "but it has provided a wealth of information about factors of typography which contribute to greater reader efficiency, and it has confirmed the validity of many established typographic conventions, but not of all."[10]

Among findings verified by research are these:

1. All-caps slows reading speed and also occupies up to 50 percent more space.

2. Italics are harder to read than uprights.
3. Very short lines—and very long lines—are hard to read.
4. Unjustified lines do *not* hurt readability, especially now that we are getting used to them.

Most art directors decide on a body type and stick with it, issue after issue. Occasionally an art director runs a special article in a different face or uses one face for articles and another for standing features like columns and departments.

In making your original choice for body type or types, you will take paper stock into consideration. For instance, old style romans work better on rough paper stock; modern romans reproduce best on smooth or coated stocks.

The choice of typeface should also be influenced by the printing process to be used. Some of the Bodoni faces, because of their hairline serifs, do not show up well in offset. Typefaces in gravure tend to darken; hence, for a text face you might not want to start out with a type already boldface. Because everything in gravure is screened, including the type, you might want to use a face without frills.

Once you make your choice of types for body copy, you live with it for a period of several years, perhaps even for the duration of the publication. Choosing type for titles, on the other hand, represents a continuing problem. You may well choose a different type to match the mood of each article.

That the display type does not match the body type shouldn't bother you. But you should see to it that the various display types for a spread come from the same family. The display types should be obviously related and perfectly matched. If that's not possible, then they should be *clearly* unrelated. You should not put display types together that are *almost* related. Almost-related types create the illusion that a mistake was made in setting.

You could combine an old style roman with a sans serif very nicely, but you would almost never combine an old style roman with a modern roman.

You-can't-go-wrong typefaces

Every art director has a favorite typeface, and one art director's favorite may differ radically from another's. Most art directors, however, could agree on a half dozen or so faces that form the standards against which other types are measured. A Basic Seven, so far as this author is concerned, would include these:

1. *Baskerville.* This face ranks as one of the most beautiful ever designed. It comes now in many versions, but it was originally designed by John Baskerville, a British calligrapher, around 1760. Considered a threat to Caslon when it was introduced, Baskerville represented a break with the past, a move to a more modern look. It is a transitional face, more precise than the old style romans but not so precise as Bodoni.

   A "wide set" type, it needs some leading. It looks best on smooth paper.

   A quirk in the design results in a lowercase *g* with an incomplete bottom loop.
2. *Bodoni.* Italian designer Giambattista Bodoni drew some inspi-

ABCDEFGHIJKL
MNOPQRSTUV
WXYZ
abcdefghijklmnopq
rstuvwxyz
1234567890

ABCDEFGHIJ
KLMNOPQRS
TUVWXYZ
abcdefghijklmno
pqrstuvwxyz
1234567890

ABCDEFGHIJ
KLMNOPQR
STUVWXYZ
abcdefghijklmn
opqrstuvwxyz
1234567890

ABCDEFGH
IJKLMNOP
QRSTUVW
XYZ
abcdefghijkl
mnopqrstuv
wxyz
1234567890

ABCDEFGHIJKL
MNOPQRSTUV
WXYZ
abcdefghijklmnop
qrstuvwxyz
1234567890

ABCDEFGHIJK
LMNOPQRSTU
VWXYZ
abcdefghijklmno
pqrstuvwxyz
1234567890

ABCDEFGHIJ
KLMNOPQRS
TUVWXYZ
abcdefghijklmno
pqrstuvwxyz
1234567890

These two pages show complete alphabets in 18-point sizes of what may be the most useful typefaces available. Opposite page, from the top: Baskerville, Bodoni, Caslon, and Craw Clarendon. This page, from the top: Garamond, Helvetica, and Times Roman.

ration from Baskerville as he created Bodoni, a beautifully balanced, if severe, face with marked differences in the thicks and thins of the strokes and with clean, harsh serifs.

The face looks best on slick paper and must be properly inked and printed. It is a little difficult to read in large doses. Like most faces its beauty is lost in its bold and ultrabold versions.

3. *Caslon.* To most printers over the years, Caslon, designed in the eighteenth century by the Englishman William Caslon, served as the No. 1 typeface. The rule was "When in doubt, use Caslon."

   The most familiar example of old style roman, this face still enjoys wide use. It has been described variously as "honest," "unobtrusive," and "classical."

   Its caps, when you study them, are surprisingly wide, and its cap *A* seems to have a chip cut out of its top. The bottom loop on the lowercase *g* seems small. Otherwise, the face has no eccentricities.

4. *Craw Clarendon.* Clarendon faces are a cross between slab serifs and old style romans. The serifs, heavy as in slab serif letters, are bracketed, as in roman. They merge into the main strokes.

   The first Clarendons appeared in England in the middle of the nineteenth century. Two recent versions are Hermann Eidenbenz's (1952) and Freeman Craw's (1954), the most popular.

5. *Garamond.* This face was named after a sixteenth-century French typefounder, Claude Garamond, but it was probably designed by Jean Jannon. Equipped with unpredictable serifs, it is, nonetheless, beautiful and readable. It is a rather narrow face with a small x-height. It can be set solid.

6. *Helvetica.* Three great gothic faces came out of Europe in 1957: Univers, from France, designed by Adrian Frutiger; Folio, from Germany, designed by Konrad Bauer and Walter Baum; and Helvetica, from Switzerland, designed by Max Miedinger and Edovard Hoffman. Clean and crisp, they look very much alike.

   Helvetica, introduced in America in 1963 in body and display sizes, is perhaps the most available of the three. Unlike Univers, it is a close-fitting type, even on the Linotype. Like all the newer gothics, its rounds are slightly squared, and its strokes vary just a bit in thickness. The terminals on letters such as *e* and *s* are cut on the horizontal, aiding in readability; in all a handsome, modern face.

   It comes in light, regular, regular italic, medium, bold, bold compact italic, regular extended, bold extended, extra bold extended, regular condensed, bold condensed, and extra bold condensed. The example shown here is Helvetica Regular.

7. *Times Roman.* Sometimes called *New Times Roman* or *Times New Roman,* this is the face designed by Stanley Morison for *The Times* of London in 1931. It is very much a twentieth-century type, not a revival, good for all kinds of jobs, although it is more of a body than a display face. Essentially an old style roman, it could, with its sharp-cut serifs, be classified as a transitional face. A peculiarity is the rounded bottom of the *b.*

   Its large x-height makes some leading necessary. With its bold look, it was first a newspaper face, becoming popular later as a magazine and book face, particularly in the U.S.

   Allen Hutt says Times Roman is not always a good body face for newspapers because it requires good press work.[11] In 1975 *The*

Times discontinued its use of Times Roman as a text face.
You are now reading Times Roman.

All of these faces came along before the cold-type revolution, when it was easy enough to tell one face from another because there were only a couple of hundred to choose from. But these faces are as useful—and up to date—as they ever were, and they are available in cold type as well as hot type, in a much greater variety of sizes and weights than before. You may find, however, that some of the newer types designed for cold-type setting have characteristics of these types with flourishes to make them even more useful or to give them late-twentieth century distinction. They will carry names quite different from the names here, of course.

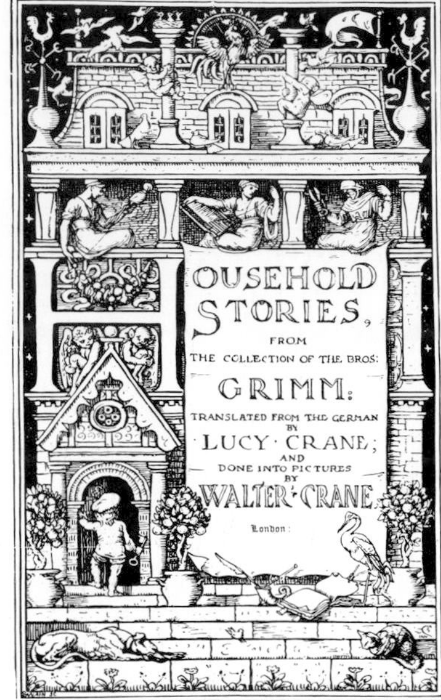

In every age designers have played with type to make illustrative art of it. In this example, from the year 1886, Walter Crane took the first letter of the book title he was working with and made it a unit in his drawing of a house.

What to tell the typesetter

Sending copy to the typesetter or printer, you would in most cases specify the following:

1. point size
2. name of the typeface
3. weight of the typeface, if other than regular (light, book, medium, bold, demibold, ultrabold, black)
4. style, if other than upright (italic, condensed, expanded; it could be both italic *and* condensed or expanded)
5. amount of leading between lines (the art director should specify "set solid" if no leading is desired)
6. width of column (in picas)
7. amount of letterspacing, if any
8. any special instructions on paragraph indentions and margins (flush left? flush right?)

Copyediting marks will take care of such matters as occasional use of italics, small caps, etc.

To save space, this book will not reproduce the various copyreading and proofreading marks used to communicate with the typesetter and printer. These marks, basically standardized, are shown in most good dictionaries, style books, editing books, and type specimen books.

Copyediting marks are made right on the original copy, which has been double-spaced—triple-spaced if for a newspaper—to provide the neces-

IRELAND'S CLEOPATRA

Complete on two pages, an article in *Aramco World Magazine* investigating an Irish legend uses a modernized version of Irish calligraphy for title type and italics for body copy. Ruled lines and carefully placed same-size photographs help unify the two pages. The color of the art under the title is, of course, green.

sary write-in area. Proofreading marks are made in the margins of galley or page proofs. Both copyreading and proofreading marks should be made with a soft pencil to facilitate erasures. The copyreader or proofreader sometimes has second thoughts about changes made.

Title and headline display

Titles for magazine articles differ from newspaper headlines in that their shape and placement are not dictated by a headline schedule. Only the designer's lack of imagination limits what may be done.

Many art directors fail to take advantage of the greater flexibility of magazines. The trade magazines, especially, seem wedded to old newspaper ideas about titles or headlines. They use the same old flush-left, multiline settings. Even the jargon of the headlines is the same. On the other hand, some magazines resort to so much typographic and design trickery that their readers become bewildered. And that isn't good either.

Only rarely should you make a title curve, dip, slant, overlap, pile on, or turn sideways. It should remain on the horizontal. A good starting point could be to design a title that occupies a single line of type in a size only slightly larger than the body copy. Perhaps it would be set in the same face as the body copy. The reader, then, finds it possible to take the title in as a single unit, not having to jump from one line to another. The title

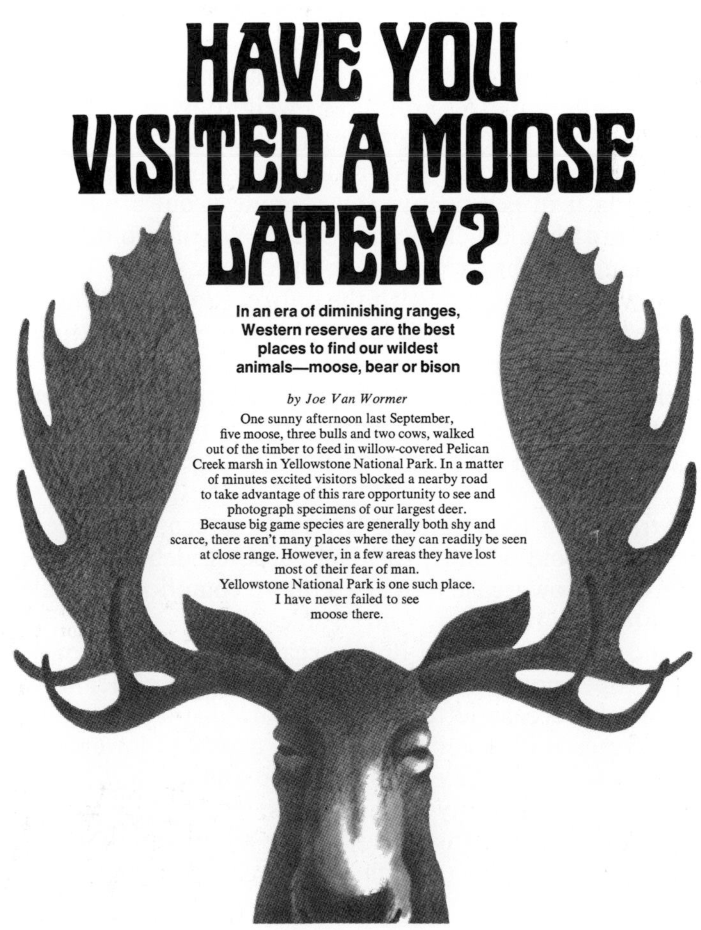

HAVE YOU VISITED A MOOSE LATELY?

In an era of diminishing ranges, Western reserves are the best places to find our wildest animals—moose, bear or bison

by Joe Van Wormer

One sunny afternoon last September, five moose, three bulls and two cows, walked out of the timber to feed in willow-covered Pelican Creek marsh in Yellowstone National Park. In a matter of minutes excited visitors blocked a nearby road to take advantage of this rare opportunity to see and photograph specimens of our largest deer.

Because big game species are generally both shy and scarce, there aren't many places where they can readily be seen at close range. However, in a few areas they have lost most of their fear of man.

Yellowstone National Park is one such place. I have never failed to see moose there.

Chevron USA's art director, Roger Waterman, for this righthand page opener, was able to come up with a typeface that perfectly matched his drawing of a moose. Or maybe it was the other way around: he drew his moose to take on the look of the type.

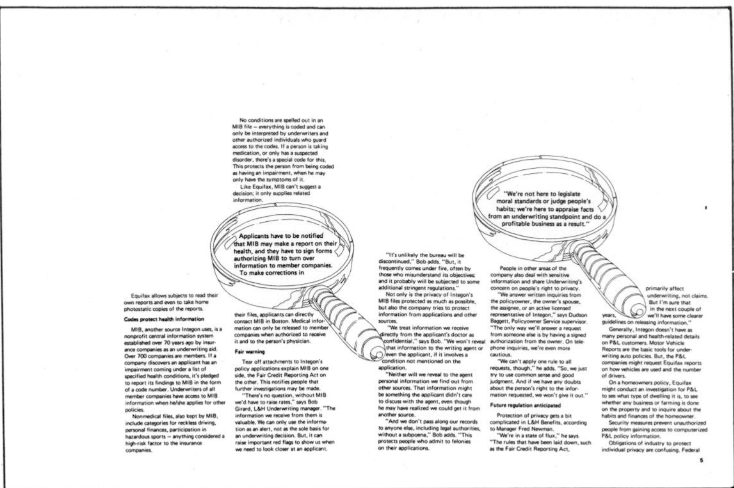

Equifax allows subjects to read their own reports and even to take home photostatic copies of the reports.

Codes protect health information

MIB, another source Integon uses, is a nonprofit central information system established over 70 years ago by insurance companies as an underwriting aid. Over 700 companies are members. If a company discovers an applicant has an impairment coming under a list of specified health conditions, it's pledged to report its findings to MIB in the form of a code number. Underwriters of all member companies have access to MIB information when he/she applies for other policies.

Nonmedical files, also kept by MIB, include categories for reckless driving, personal finances, participation in hazardous sports – anything considered a high-risk factor to the insurance companies.

No conditions are spelled out in an MIB file – everything is coded and can only be interpreted by underwriters and other authorized individuals who guard access to the codes. If a person is taking medication, or only has a suspected disorder, there's a special code for this. This protects the person from being coded as having an impairment, when he may only have the symptoms of it.

Like Equifax, MIB can't suggest a decision; it only supplies related information.

Applicants have to be notified that MIB may make a report on their health, and they have to sign forms authorizing MIB to turn over information to member companies. To make corrections in

their files, applicants can directly contact MIB in Boston. Medical information can only be released to member companies when authorized to receive it and to the person's physician.

Fair warning

Tear off attachments to Integon's policy applications explain MIB on one side, the Fair Credit Reporting Act on the other. This notifies people that further investigations may be made.

"There's no question, without MIB we'd have to raise rates," says Bob Girard, L&H Underwriting manager. "The information we receive from them is valuable. We can only use the information as an alert, not as the sole basis for an underwriting decision. But, it can raise important red flags to show us when we need to look closer at an applicant.

"It's unlikely the bureau will be discontinued," Bob adds. "But, it frequently comes under fire, often by those who misunderstand its objectives: and it probably will be subjected to some additional stringent regulations."

Not only is the privacy of Integon's MIB files protected as much as possible, but also the company tries to protect information from applications and other sources.

"We treat information we receive directly from the applicant's doctor as confidential," says Bob. "We won't reveal that information to the writing agent or even the applicant, if it involves a condition not mentioned on the application.

"Neither will we reveal to the agent personal information we find out from other sources. That information might be something the applicant didn't care to discuss with the agent, even though he may have realized we could get it from another source.

"And we don't pass along our records to anyone else, including legal authorities, without a subpoena," Bob adds. "This protects people who admit to felonies on their applications.

"We're not here to legislate moral standards or judge people's habits; we're here to appraise facts from an underwriting standpoint and do a profitable business as a result."

People in other areas of the company also deal with sensitive information and share Underwriting's concern on people's right to privacy.

"We answer written inquiries from the policyowner, the owner's spouse, the assignee, or an active licensed representative of Integon," says Dudson Baggett, Policyowner Service supervisor. "The only way we'll answer a request from someone else is by having a signed authorization from the owner. On telephone inquiries, we're even more cautious.

"We can't apply one rule to all requests, though," he adds. "So, we just try to use common sense and good judgment. And if we have any doubts about the person's right to the information requested, we won't give it out."

Future regulation anticipated

Protection of privacy gets a bit complicated in L&H Benefits, according to Manager Fred Newman.

"We're in a state of flux," he says. "The rules that have been laid down, such as the Fair Credit Reporting Act, primarily affect underwriting, not claims. But I'm sure that in the next couple of years, we'll have some clearer guidelines on releasing information."

Generally, Integon doesn't have as many personal and health-related details on P&L customers. Motor Vehicle Reports are the basic tools for underwriting auto policies. But, the P&L companies might request Equifax reports on how vehicles are used and the number of drivers.

On a homeowners policy, Equifax might conduct an investigation for P&L to see what type of dwelling it is, to see whether any business or farming is done on the property and to inquire about the habits and finances of the homeowner.

Security measures prevent unauthorized people from gaining access to computerized P&L policy information.

Obligations of industry to protect individual privacy are confusing. Federal

5

Here is an unusual way to dramatize interior blurbs within a spread. Actually, they aren't blurbs so much as parts of the article run large. The magnifying-glass motif is set up in the opening spread (on the previous two pages), where a detective is shown, page high, inspecting the title of the article, using his glass. The title is "Right to Privacy—at What Price?" Notice the generous amount of white space on this spread and the building of the columns from the bottom. Notice, too, that this continuation does not begin immediately in the left-hand column. It waits a column. The spread is from *Integon Listener,* a bimonthly published by Integon Corporation, Winston-Salem, North Carolina.

would be like a sentence taken from the copy and made larger for easy access.

For some magazines this style works very well, page after page. For other magazines a more lively arrangement is necessary. Not only might titles be broken up into two or more lines; they also might be in type considerably larger than and different from the body copy.

The mood of the article can dictate the choice of title typeface, and that choice may vary greatly from article to article in a single issue.

Sometimes you may choose to vary the typeface—or at least the size—*within* the title. Let's say one word in the title should stand out from the others. You can bring out its importance in many ways: by setting it in a different face, a different size, a different weight; by printing it in color; by putting a box around it or underlining it; by reversing it in a black box or a color block; by separating it from the other words with a small piece of art; by showing it in perspective; by running it out of alignment. But only that one word should get the treatment. When two different words are made to stand out, they cancel each other out.

Should you want to innovate with the entire title, you could try setting it in giant letters; building it with letters cut from a photographic background; surprinting or reversing it in a photograph or tint block; wrapping it around a photograph; arranging the lines in a piggyback fashion; nesting the lines partially inside other lines; fitting them inside the text; alternating the letters in black and color; superimposing them—the list is endless.

When *Sunset* sets a title in giant letters, it screens the letters to gray to keep them from looking cheap or loud. Another idea is to set giant-size titles in lowercase. Lowercase letters are more complicated in design and hence more interesting to view in large sizes.

Titles should ordinarily be set in lowercase anyway, with only the first word and all proper nouns capitalized. Lowercase is easier to read than all-caps because lowercase letters are easier to distinguish from one another. Also, lowercase is easier to read than caps and lowercase because caps and lowercase cause the eye to move up and down, like the springs on a car moving along a bumpy road. Besides, writing caps-and-lowercase titles takes longer than writing all-lowercase titles; the title writer faces a complicated set of rules on which words to capitalize, which ones to leave lowercase.

These all-cap titles or headlines show spacing possibilities. The first uses letterspacing. The second uses normal spacing between letters. The third uses tight spacing between letters, which in most magazines these days is normal spacing. Note the tight spacing between words, too.

P E O P L E

DON'T BE A STATISTIC

THEY'RE IN BUSINESS

HOW SHOULD WE THEN LIVE?

A designer can get too tricky with type, making things difficult rather than easy for the reader. The problem here is compounded by a playful if unpleasant typeface. The overlapping only adds to the confusion.

When you have a multiline title to deal with, you can show it flush left, flush right, or centered. It is not a good idea to run it flush left-flush right. To make it come out even on both sides usually takes some fancy and unnatural spacing. The most intriguing multiline titles are those set in a staggered pattern to form an irregular silhouette. The lines should be kept close enough together so the title reads as a unit.

In multiline titles it is almost never desirable to single out one word for emphasis. Asking the reader to jump from line to line is interruption enough. Asking acceptance of a change in type style in the middle of it is asking too much. If you *must* have one word in a multiline title stand out, you can put it on a line by itself, without changing the typeface. To make it stand out more, in a flush-left title you can run it a little to the left of the axis.

In planning a multiline title, you should pay more attention to the logic of the arrangement than its looks. It is desirable, of course, that lines be reasonably equal in length, but it is more important by far that they be easily read.

When the title comes as two sentences, you cannot very well separate them with a period (unless the publication's style is to end titles with periods), so you have to resort to some other device. You can use a semicolon, if you are designing for a newspaper; you can use a typographic dingbat at the beginning of each sentence; you can use some extra white space; you can change to another typeface or size for the second sentence; you can change to color; you can change the position.

Newspapers standardize their headlines, consistently using the same typeface and line arrangements, but once in a while in a spirit of playfulness they doctor the type or go with a different face. The staid *Wall Street Journal,* for a feature on the return of calligraphy in the United States, used real calligraphy for its headline and byline.

A matter of spacing

Good typography is largely a matter of spacing. Although it has been widely critized, the trend to close-fitting letters probably has resulted in increased readability.[12] Now instead of seeing only letters, readers see words and phrases. But close fitting can be overdone. Get the letters too close together, and they merge, making ligatures that are not graceful but are, instead, hard to read. And, of course, the pattern of the headline becomes spotty.

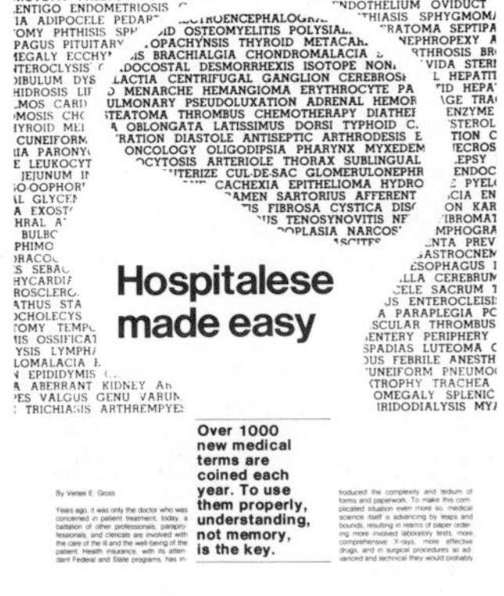

Hospitalese made easy

Over 1000 new medical terms are coined each year. To use them properly, understanding, not memory, is the key.

Inadequate grasp of terminology basics is often the weak spot in an otherwise well-rounded education.

In-Service Training and Education, now *Health Care Education,* uses type only to create the art that starts off this article on "hospitalese." Everything here, including body copy, is in sans serif type. The deep blurbs on each page help unite the pages.

In close fitting as in regular fitting, you have to make some allowance for optical illusions that occur as certain letters take their places next to others. You need to add a little space here, take away a little space there. The spacing becomes optical, not mechanical.

The spacing between the *lines* of a headline should also be consistent. But again, it may have to be optical rather than mechanical. A line with several ascending strokes, or descending strokes, may create an optical illusion in spacing. As a designer, you have to compensate for such illusions, making necessary adjustments between lines to please the eye.

Space between words and between lines in *body copy* should remain constant, too. Narrow columns that are justified (set so that lines form a straight line at the right as well as at the left) often end up with wide spaces in some lines and crowded spaces in others. And sometimes space considerations discourage art directors from giving body copy the proper amount of leading.

DROUGHT!

You can take a standard type and doctor it, coming up with a title like this one used by *Pacific Powerland,* a publication of Pacific Power & Light Company, Portland. "More dramatically than words," went the lead of the article underneath, "the parched mudflat pictured on the cover tells the story of an unprecedented six-month drought in much of the region served by Pacific Power." The texture in the letters duplicated the texture in the picture.

Playing around with type

Good typography calls for standard or classic typefaces evenly and consistently spaced with the message coming through quickly and easily without any visual interruption. Good typography is not self-conscious. It does not call attention to itself.

Still, there is something to be said for playing around with type occasionally, if only as a change of pace. The playfulness should be rare and appropriate, and it need not involve a whole title or headline. Punctuation can be involved along with the letters.

Quote
THAT'S
RIGHT.
people
EGGS
GROWTH
Audiovisual
Aides
ENERGY

These examples of nontraditional typography are explained in the section on "Playing Around with Type."

Note what *Re:cap,* a newsletter published by Mobil Corporation, did with its "Quote" heading for a column that reprints quotations of special interest to readers (see nearby art). The first "letter" does double duty as a single quotation mark and a *Q*.

In one of its ad headlines, Photo-Lettering, Inc. uses a *T* that sheds its right arm to make room for a double-duty apostrophe (see "THAT'S RIGHT").

The rules of good typography change from time to time, but gradually. The past couple of decades have seen a move to close-fitting letters, not necessarily to save space, although that is a factor, but to make display type readable in longer units. *Sask Tel News,* published by Saskatchewan Tellecommunications, carries the set-tight rule to an extreme by butting letters together in a "people" column heading. Readability is not hurt. The fortunate combination of rounds in this thin-line sans serif face, together with the several vertical strokes, makes this typeset unit almost a piece of art.

An ad for Fletcher's, a children's and maternity store, carries such playfulness a step further by actually overlapping letters (see "EGGS"). Booz, Allen & Hamilton, Inc., a management consulting firm, gathers some light-to-boldface sans serif letters to dramatize a one-word headline in a newspaper ad (see "GROWTH"). Visual Graphics Corporation takes away the space between two capitalized words and then drops each cap below the baseline to help frame the word in the second line and better unite it in the arrangement. The typeface here features lowercase letters that are really a mixture of caps and lowercase (see "Audio Visual Aides").

Typographical playfulness can come from the letters themselves as well as from their arrangement. *Sohio* magazine, published by Standard Oil of Ohio, puts an "ENERGY" title into letters that are almost abstract. The letters also have a stencil feel, adding an informality but still carrying the feeling of precision. The *ER* looks almost as if it were a ligature. Eliminating chunks of some of the vertical strokes, always at the same spot down from the top and up from the bottom, makes the letters strongly related. It is hard to tell whether a typeface like this was drawn to order or taken from among the thousands of typefaces now available from printers, typesetting houses, and dealers of press-on-letters.

A study of *U&lc.* shows that experimentation works even for body copy. You can change the face, size, and column width as you move from one page to the next. Of course, *U&lc.* is a magazine of typography that encourages experimentation. In the wrong hands such changing might result in a real problem for readers trying to keep up with the flow of the article.

Attached to letters used in column headings, the arrow has become a typographic cliché.

Title and headline clichés

Using a dollar sign for an *S* in a headline of a story on spending, putting hyphens between the letters in *STRETCH,* causing a headline to cross over into a photograph, there to be lost in a busy pattern of tones—these are typographic clichés.

Kickers are also something of a cliché. Kickers are small, short, second-thought headlines that appear just above main headlines. When kickers are used to categorize pieces—to tell the reader, for instance, that what follows is "An Editorial"—they probably serve a useful function. But when they are there simply to give readers more display type to look at before reading the stories, they only add clutter to the pages.

Arranging the lines of a headline on a diagonal or as a "step down" has also become a tired practice. You may have seen those old newspaper head schedules (or "hed" schedules) that showed all kinds of geometric contortions headlines could fit into. And in those days the typical newspaper headline consisted of several "decks," each with its own shape. They took up a lot of space.

Many of today's editors seem moved by diagonal axes. They understand that a diagonal thrust means action, as opposed to static vertical and horizontal thrusts. But is that kind of action necessary in a headline? There is a dated look to such a headline. The standard flush-left or each-line-centered arrangement works just as well while also looking contemporary.

‽

This interabang (see the section on "Punctuation Up Close") was made by combining a press-on question mark and an exclamation point.

Punctuation up close

You may find it easier to make a punctuation mistake in a title or headline than in the body of an article. Punctuation may seem unimportant as you write a heading to fit a layout and pick the appropriate typeface, but a wrong or omitted mark can completely alter your meaning.

Columbia Journalism Review found an interesting example from a newspaper for its "The Lower case" column:

Garden Grove Resident
Naive, Foolish Judge Says

Just as common as the missing comma is the missing question mark at the end of a question title or headline. "Listen. Can't You Hear the Ocean." That was a headline in an ad in *The New Yorker,* but you can find examples on nonadvertising pages in publications, too.

You can trace many punctuation errors in headings and copy to carelessness and haste. And you can trace some to ignorance. When you get right down to it, punctuation is mostly a matter of common sense and rhythm.

Punctuation errors occur both in the choice of marks and in the way they are displayed. Part of the problem comes from the way punctuation marks are designed.

We tend to think of the comma as a mere period with a tail, but it is a much more unpredictable character than that, as the sampling on this

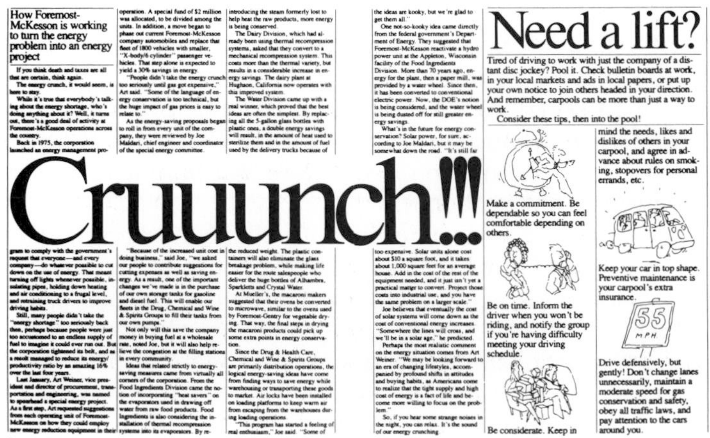

How Foremost-McKesson is working to turn the energy problem into an energy project

If you think death and taxes are all that are certain, think again.

The energy crunch, it would seem, is here to stay.

While it's true that everybody's talking about the energy shortage, who's doing anything about it? Well, it turns out, there's a good deal of activity at Foremost-McKesson operations across the country.

Back in 1975, the corporation launched an energy management pro-

Cruuunch!!!

Need a lift?

Tired of driving to work with just the company of a distant disc jockey? Pool it. Check bulletin boards at work, in your local markets and ads in local papers, or put up your own notice to join others headed in your direction. And remember, carpools can be more than just a way to work.

Consider these tips, then into the pool!

Make a commitment. Be dependable so you can feel comfortable depending on others.

Be on time. Inform the driver when you won't be riding, and notify the group if you're having difficulty meeting your driving schedule.

Be considerate. Keep in mind the needs, likes and dislikes of others in your carpool, and agree in advance about rules on smoking, stopovers for personal errands, etc.

Keep your car in top shape. Preventive maintenance is your carpool's extra insurance.

Drive defensively, but gently! Don't change lanes unnecessarily, maintain a moderate speed for gas conservation and safety, obey all traffic laws, and pay attention to the cars around you.

Direction, a magazine for employees of Foremost-McKesson, Inc., San Francisco, runs a one-word title across the gutter in this spread and stops it suddenly at an illustrated sidebar that tells how to participate in a carpool. The blurb at the top left, the article title, and the sidebar title are all in a second color—blue. The sidebar uses bigger body copy than the article itself uses.

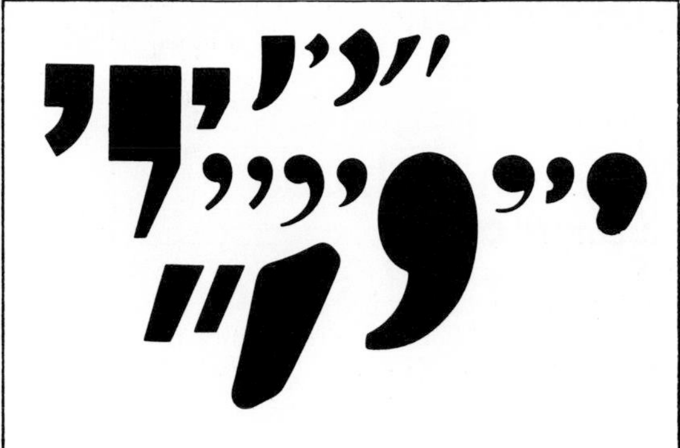

As you move from typeface to typeface you find a great variety of shapes in the characters, even in the commas.

page shows. The shape varies from typeface to typeface. Even for a single classification of type, like the slab serifs, where the dot is changed to a square, there are differences. The first three commas (all from slab serif faces) show a curved tail, a pointed tail, and a constant-width tail. Two of the "periods" are square; one is rectangular. (It is possible to create a houndstooth pattern out of slab serif commas, running them close together, line after line.)

One of the commas here looks like a *J*, another like an upside-down tear drop. Four of the commas are sliced at an angle at the top.

Some sans serif commas turn out to be mere wedges. This complicates in-house typesetting where press-on or dry-transfer letters ae used. A Bodoni comma is easy enough to handle: the dot part goes right on the base line. But where, exactly, do you put a Palatino comma?

The type specimen books do not help us solve our comma-placing problems because most of them do not show punctuation marks with their alphabets. So we miss the chance to really study the comma and other punctuation marks, which could help us identify typefaces. We fail to learn that an apostrophe or single quotation mark is not always just a comma raised up from the base line; these marks are not always interchangeable.

Colons should have their lower unit line up at the base line, their upper unit at the top of the x-height of the letters. In some faces, though, where the x-height is deep, the upper unit may be lowered. You don't want a lot of space separating the two units. Some designers working with big display type take the liberty of raising the entire colon above the base line to make it work visually a little more like a hyphen or dash.

Headlines and titles can use double or, to save space, single quotation marks. Interestingly, some faces give you the dot above and the tail below whereas other faces give you *6*-shaped mark, with the dot below.

The period and comma always go inside the ending quotation marks. In body copy sizes the quotation marks immediately follow the punctuation mark. In display type you can pile the quotation marks on top of the period.

If the title consists of several flush-left lines, you may elect to put the quotation marks outside the line of the axis. This is called "hung punctuation," and it results in margins that appear more straightly cut. It works for body copy, too, and includes all marks of punctuation that occur at the edges of copy blocks, but not many magazines and certainly few newspapers can afford the luxury of that kind of setting.

As art director you must be careful to put in apostrophes where they're called for. The word is *it's* when *it* and *is* are contracted. Only the possessive is *its*. The possessive for *men* is *men's,* never *mens.* An apostrophe always faces the same way, whether used at the begining, middle, or end of a word.

Sometimes you can take liberties with a hyphen, as in *nonstop*. The designer here decided that a slablike hyphen would not fit the character of the very round, thick-and-thin letters.

non•stop

Finally—the dash and hyphen. Both these marks should fit rather tightly against the words they follow and precede. The dash is considerably longer, at least as wide as the capital *N* or, better, the capital *M*. The dash is also thinner than the hyphen. Both should be placed somewhere below the top of the x-height of the letters.

The late Carl Dair made an interesting contribution to the typography of punctuation. He introduced for body copy an upright, straight line, the height of the x-height, set off with extra white space, to help readers make a distinction between a broken word (broken because it wouldn't fit at the end of the line) and a compound word (like *right-handed*). He used the ordinary hyphen for compound words only.[13]

Another punctuation contribution came from American Type Founders Company, which introduced the interabang, special punctuation combining both the question mark and the exclamation point (for use in such sentences as "Are you kidding?").

Body copy

In choosing a typeface for body copy, you are not quite so concerned with the beauty of the face as when you choose display type. Your primary concern should be: Is the type readable column after column? Further: What kind of pattern does the type make over a large area? The pattern should be even-textured, not spotty.

You see how important consistent spacing is when your typesetter puts a little too much space between the *e* and *r* in *therapist* or brings the *n* and the *i* too close together in "the pen is. . . ."

In newspapers, at least, the trend has been to wider columns and consequently slightly larger typeface. In a 1976 comparison of narrow to wide settings, Professor Lloyd R. Bostian of the University of Wisconsin found that on an 8½ × 11 page, a single wide column, provided it had some white space to set it off, could be as readable as two narrow columns.[14]

Professor Sandra Ernst Moriarty of the University of Colorado found in a mid-1980s study that, contrary to long-held views by typographers, people can read reasonably long lines faster than short lines. And, after studying various recommendations for optimum lengths for lines of type, Moriarty concluded that "there is not much agreement among . . . experts as to the ideal range or optimum line length. One expert's minimum is another expert's optimum or perhaps even maximum."[15]

Moriarity suggests that "longer lines are less of a problem to . . . [readability] than previously assumed" and that "12 pt. type size . . . appears to be easier to read than . . . [commonly used] 10 pt. type."[16]

A wider column produces shorter paragraphs, and this in itself may aid readability.

Most art directors prefer roman to sans serif faces for body copy simply because readers are used to them. Novelty hurts readability. But as sans serif finds increasing acceptance among readers of avant-garde magazines, it will find increasing acceptance among readers of all magazines. As a matter of fact, sans serif has in recent years become almost commonplace as body copy for many company magazines and some general-circulation and specialized magazines.

One objection to sans serif used to be that it was too "vertical"; it did not have serifs to help move the reader horizontally across the line. But the newer sans serifs feature terminals that are sliced horizontally, and this tends to do the job serifs do. Also, the strokes of the newer sans serifs vary slightly in thickness, just as roman strokes do; sans serif type now is less monotonous in large doses.

Sans serifs, because of their solid character, are especially recommended where printing quality is inferior. Types with intricate serifs need superior printing in order to reproduce well.

Art directors have also changed their minds about unjustified lines. More and more magazines and a few newspapers use them. Advertisers in their copy often get away with unjustified left-hand margins. In editorial matter, though, the lack of justification occurs only on the right. In long blocks of copy, readers need a constant margin at the left to which they can return, line after line.

Dog 'n pony
CASH N' CARRY
HEAT n EAT
rhythm 'n' blues
Cook'N' Clean
Sugar 'n' spice

Which of these abbreviated *and* units is correct? Only the last one. The first example leaves out the second apostrophe (you need two, because both the *a* and the *d* are missing). The second example leaves off the first apostrophe. The third example doesn't carry any. The fourth example uses single quotation marks rather than apostrophes. (The first mark, you can see, turns inward; that means it's not an apostrophe.) The fifth example capitalizes the *n*. It should not be capitalized. "Sugar 'n' spice" wins. But why not use an honest *and* and be done with all the apostrophes?

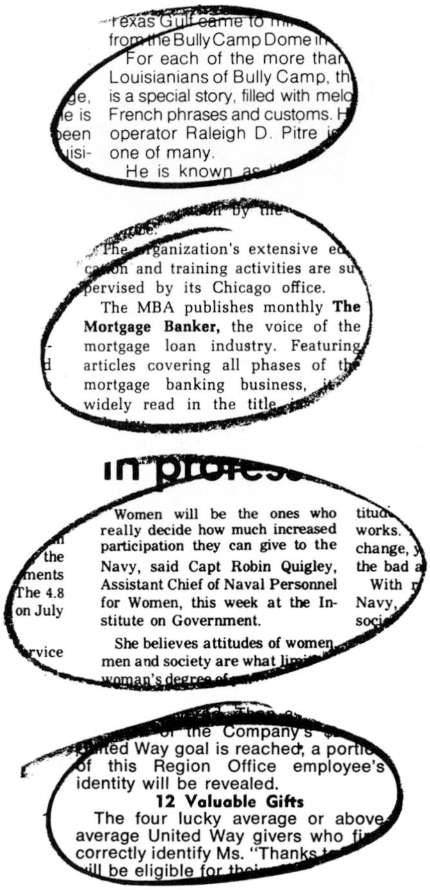

Can you spot the problems with these body-copy excerpts from various publications? The first example shows uneven spacing between letters. Compare *Bully* with *filled.* The pattern of the setting is faulty. The second example shows a publication name in boldface type. The machine setting this type, apparently, does not have italics available. The editor underlines the name of a publication on the manuscript and gets not italics but the only alternate characters available—boldface. Should the name of a publication jump out from the page? Not unless you run a column about the media. When italics are not available, you should treat names of publications as you would ordinary proper names. This excerpt also shows too much space between words. The third example shows unequal spacing between two of the lines. The makeup artist needs to measure accurately the distance between lines when patching copy. The fourth example shows a subhead with too little space above and below. The subhead doesn't stand out enough. It is lost between the paragraphs, even though it's in boldface.

Some types need more space between words than others. Expanded types need more space between words than condensed types. Types with large x-heights need more space between words than those with small x-heights. The spacing between words should never exceed the space between lines.

Copy needs extra spacing between lines when (1) the type has a large x-height; (2) the type has a pronounced vertical stress, as with Bodoni and with most of the sans serifs; and (3) the line length is longer than usual.

If copy is set in a single width, leading should be consistent throughout. It is best to specify the amount of leading before copy is set, as "Set 10 on 12" (which means, "Set it in 10-point type on a 12-point slug.") Adding leading between lines afterwards costs more in traditional typesetting systems.

If you want a highly contemporary, crowded look, you might consider the possibility of *minus*-leading. This means setting a point size (say 10-point) on a smaller body (say 9-point). You would do this only when you had a face with a large x-height (with short descenders). And you would do it for a minimum amount of copy because minus-leading is hard to read.

Many art directors no longer consider a widow—a less than full-length line at the top of a column in a multicolumn spread—as the typographic monstrosity it was thought to be. But when a widow consists of a single word or syllable, the leftover space is great enough to spoil the horizontal axis at the top of the columns. The art director then should do some rearranging of lines to get rid of the widow.

Readers do appreciate an occasional oasis deep into long columns of copy. Art directors supply it with subheadings or—better still—just a little extra white space. Sometimes an initial letter helps.

Article starts

Sometimes the design of a magazine page confuses readers, making it difficult for them to know where to start the article. For instance, the title may be off to the right. Do readers start right under the title, then, or do they move over to the left and start there?

If titles fit immediately above the first column of copy, no special typographic treatment is needed. The first paragraph can be set indented to look like the other paragraphs.

But in other cases, the readers need help. One solution is to use a large initial letter. Even if the spread has several such letters, readers will pick up first the initial letter at the far-left point. Another solution is to line up the column evenly across the top. Readers will see that the columns are related and start with the one at the extreme left. Still another solution, less often tried, is to put a small piece of art near the start, to sort of point to the beginning.

For many magazines the best way of saying, "Here is where the article starts," is to set the first paragraph without an indentation. The "indenting," which is nothing more than an arresting of reader attention anyway, has already been done by the title, these editors feel.

If as art director you have reason to doubt that readers will begin articles where they should, you should redesign the page. Getting readers started is a chief function of page design.

Initial letters

An oversize letter used at the beginning of an article or story and at each of its breaks can help get readers started and rekindle their interest as the story progresses. When using initial letters, you should go to the face of your title, not the face of your body copy.

The letter is called a two-, three-, four-, or five-line initial, depending upon how deep in lines it is. It can be bigger than the title type size. You may find it desirable to help readers make the step down from the initial to the body copy by giving them the remainder of the first word and maybe another word or two in all-caps or small caps. And you will probably want your body copy to fit snugly around the initial. Sometimes this takes some fancy work by the composing room.

You might want to consider using initial letters that project out or up from the body copy rather than fit down into it, in which case you can move the letters toward the centers of the columns. You may also want to use initial words instead of initial letters. *Go,* the Goodyear tire-dealer magazine, doesn't use initial letters but does start its articles off with one complete line of boldface type in sans serif, where the remainder of the body copy is in roman in a size slightly smaller than the boldface lead in.

Initials really become interesting when you contract to have them drawn to fit the mood of an article. For instance, you might ask an artist to construct the initials out of cartoon figures and props, perhaps adding a second color. One of the charms of Hendrick Willem van Loon's illustrated histories published in the 1920s and 1930s were the initial letters he drew for chapter openings.

For an article entitled "It's a Dirty Job . . . But Somebody's Gotta Do It," *Not Just Jazz* separated sections, not with initial letters or subheads, but with finger prints and smudges. *New York* used blocks of the kind babies play with for initial letters in an article on babies born to older couples.

It would be foolhardy to pick one style as being superior to others, or to argue that using initial letters in the first place is preferable to bypassing them. It comes down to one person's taste matched against another's.

One thing is certain: Initial letters poorly planned look a lot worse than standard openings and white-space interior rests. And it probably is true that to work well, initial letters should work boldly. Some designers use giant initials that dominate opening pages. *Parade* often does this.

When used in two or three places on a spread as interior rests, initials should be spaced so that distances between them vary. And ordinarily, they should not line up horizontally. They should succeed in dividing the columns of a spread into unequal portions.

You don't have to confine initials to body copy. Editors and designers have used them in headlines and titles, blurbs, and even captions.

Having settled on the kind and placement of initial letters, you had better sit back and give the spread some study. Do the letters by any chance

An initial letter can be more than a mere piece of type set large. This one is drawn, and it is as much a gag cartoon as an initial letter. Now as an editor all you would have to do to use this is make sure your article on sleep starts out with a word beginning with *Z*.

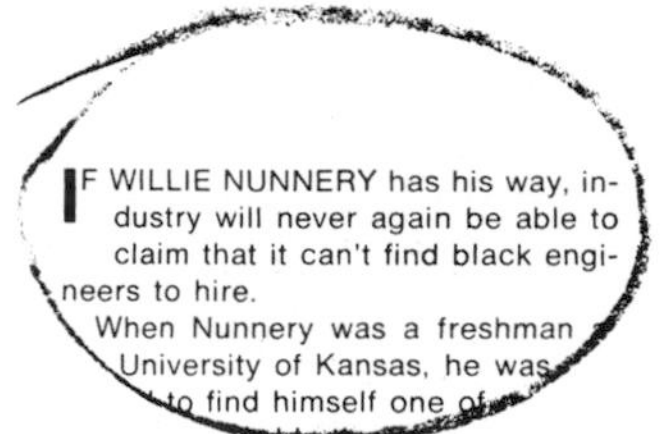
IF WILLIE NUNNERY has his way, industry will never again be able to claim that it can't find black engineers to hire.

When Nunnery was a freshman University of Kansas, he was to find himself one

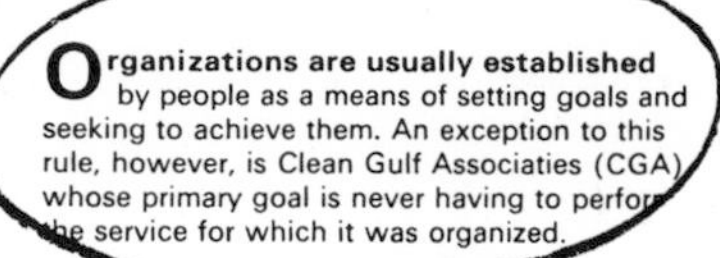
Organizations are usually established by people as a means of setting goals and seeking to achieve them. An exception to this rule, however, is Clean Gulf Associaties (CGA) whose primary goal is never having to perfo the service for which it was organized.

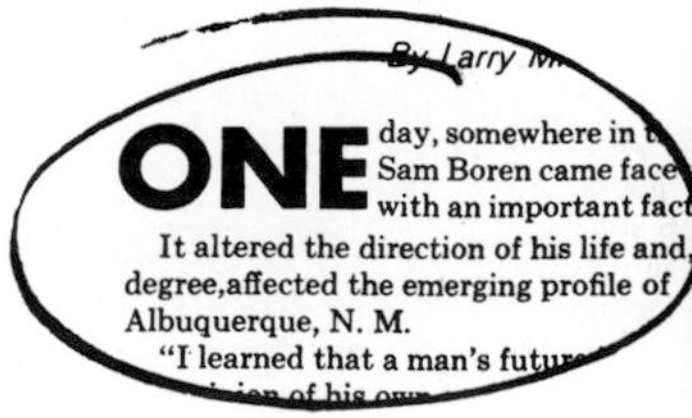
ONE day, somewhere in Sam Boren came face with an important fact. It altered the direction of his life and, degree,affected the emerging profile of Albuquerque, N. M.

"I learned that a man's fu

Here are some of the ways magazines handle initial letters, both at the beginnings and in the interiors of articles. The first is a two-line initial in a three-line setting. Several words in caps ease the reader from the initial into the text. The second uses boldface type to make the bridge and carries the boldfacing all the way across the first line. The third uses an initial word. Not a bad idea, unless you happen to begin an article with a word like *Paleontography*. The fourth, an interior initial, does not ask for any extra space between itself and the previous paragraph. Note that the copy fits around the initial. The fifth, also an interior initial, juts up from the line. The sixth illustrates what to do when you start out with a direct quote. You use quotation marks in the initial size, not in the body-copy size. Some designers leave off the beginning quotation marks in a situation like this. That works, too.

Some of the initial letters used in books and magazines early in this century incorporated art that almost overshadowed the letters. This *N*, drawn by C. J. Taylor, was used to start off an opening word (*Now*) in an essay on "Horse Sense vs. Science."

spell out some word your readers may find offensive? You may have to make some last minute changes, just as you would if, on looking over the final page proofs, you saw an ad placed right next to editorial matter that made a contradictory point.

Subheads

Subheads—small headlines within the columns of copy—give readers a place to catch their breath. Subheads make the copy look less foreboding. They divide it into easier—shorter—segments.

Subheads take the form usually of independent labels or sentences, summarizing what is to follow or teasing the reader to carry on. To set them apart from the body copy, you would put extra space above and below, especially above, and you would set them in boldface type, possibly in the same face and size as the body copy. Or you might set them in all-caps, small caps, or italics. You could center them or run them flush left. In a book you might choose to put them in the margins.

Book publishers, in contrast to magazine editors, set up a couple of levels of subheads, the more important ones appearing in a bolder type or being centered in the column. The book you are now reading, however, uses a single level of subheads.

Some newspapers have adopted a style of subheads that puts the first few words of a paragraph in all-caps, boldface type. The subhead is not a separate line. A little extra space separates the subhead from the paragraph above. The advantage of this system is that you don't have to write the subhead. It is already written. The disadvantage is that you find it harder to eliminate or add subheads after the copy is set.

Whatever style you choose, you should place subheads at several places in your article, not just in one place. A single subhead suggests too much of a break. The reader may get the impression that you are announcing a new article. If your article appears to be too short to carry more than one subhead, don't use any.

Editors who do not have a news-oriented content tend to avoid subheads. In place of subheads these editors use initial letters, blurbs or readouts in larger or bolder type, or merely units of white space. Some editors feel that small photographs or art pieces strategically placed serve as subheads.

Captions

In some quarters the caption has fallen from favor. The advertising-design look so prevalent in company magazines, for instance, tends to regard the caption as nothing more than visual clutter. So art directors—some of them—talk their editors out of captions. In the classroom the caption often disappears simply because the student, preoccupied with title and picture placement, forgets to plan for it.

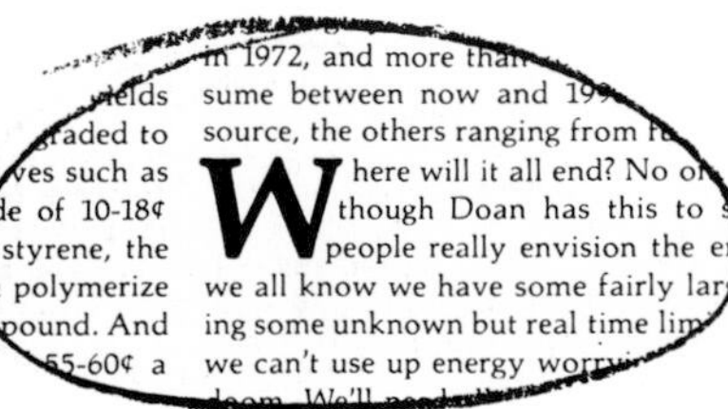

Where will it all end? No o... though Doan has this to ... people really envision the e... we all know we have some fairly lar... ing some unknown but real time li... we can't use up energy wo...

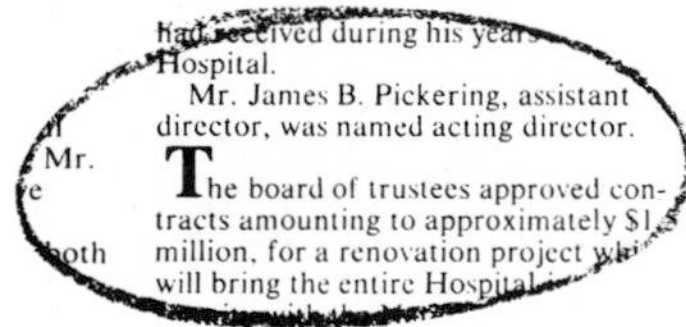

Mr. James B. Pickering, assistant director, was named acting director.

The board of trustees approved contracts amounting to approximately $1... million, for a renovation project wh... will bring the entire Hospital ...

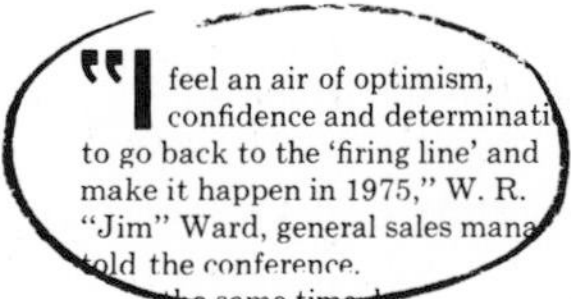

"I feel an air of optimism, confidence and determinati... to go back to the 'firing line' and make it happen in 1975," W. R. "Jim" Ward, general sales man... ...ld the conference.

Some photographers applaud the no-caption practice. They argue that captions are redundant. Considering what editors make some captions say, maybe the photographers are right.

Still, looking at the matter from a reader's standpoint, the caption is necessary for a full understanding of a photograph except in those cases—rare in news-oriented publications—where the photograph's purpose is merely to establish a mood. An operating rule ought to be that the editor should include a caption unless there is a compelling reason to leave it out.

Captions give photographs an additional dimension. They can tell what happened before the picture was taken. Or what happened afterwards. If the photograph itself is something of a mystery, a caption can clear things up.

Mug shots almost always need captions. When a publication runs a mug shot with a standing column, the reader can't tell whether the picture is of the columnist or the person being written about unless the shot carries a name.

Caption designing takes two basic approaches: either the captions appear adjacent to the pictures they describe, or they gather themselves together in a group and key themselves to the various pictures in the spread. You do not necessarily have to use numbers to key the captions; you can key through description. In one issue *Integon Listener,* published by the Integon Corporation in Winston-Salem, North Carolina, showed photographs of a business executive alone at his desk talking into a phone, the executive shaking hands with visitors, and the executive playing shuffleboard with his family. The caption off to the side read: "Despite his busy schedule, Ed Collette believes in making time for people, whether it's a customer or employee on the phone, a group of new fieldman like these from Provident Life, or his own family. . . ."

Haste in caption writing can lead to embarrassments. *National Review* spotted this correction in *Community Life:* "Mai Thai Finn is one of the students in the program and was in the center of the photo. We incorrectly listed her as one of the items on the menu."[17].

Art directors like the cluster-caption idea because it allows them to butt pictures against each other, bleed them, and in other ways better display them. Using a cluster caption, you don't have to plan for just the right space between the pictures to accommodate the various captions; you bring the captions together in a block.

But where names are involved, readers no doubt prefer captions right next to each picture for ready reference.

If your caption seems to be off to one side and not obviously connected to the photograph, your solution is *not* to include an arrow that points the reader in the right direction. Your solution is to redesign the page.

Captions right above or below photographs should appear in the same widths as the photographs—or narrower. You would not want to run them wider. Some art directors like to run captions at a standard width regardless of how wide the photographs are. This does help simplify the design and speed up the typesetting. You always know how wide to set your captions.

Photographs that stand by themselves—photographs not there to illustrate stories or features—need not only captions but also their own headlines, however small.

Some editors seem to feel that caption writers should even out the last line each time so that it is fully filled and flush with the other lines. This

THE ROAD BACK TO THE APOLLO

THE PATHS OF TEMPTATIONS LEGENDS EDDIE KENDRICK AND DAVID RUFFIN, AND MODERN POPSTERS DARYL HALL AND JOHN OATES, CROSSED OVER FIFTEEN YEARS AGO. NOW, IN 1985's HOTTEST COMEBACK CAPER, THEY CROSS AGAIN, SETTLING AN OLD AND VERY IMPORTANT DEBT.

LEMME TELL YOU, LIV… WAS A LONG WAY FR… DAYS OF GETTING OUT A… ON SOME DARK SOUTH… BACK ROAD IN THE EA… AND PUSHING THOSE O… KEN-DOWN WORLD WA… COMPANY CHARTERS … THOSE MOTOR TOWN R… TOURS. PHEW!"

BY TIMOTHY W…

Musician art director Gary Koepke uses all-caps sans serifs for the title, subtitle, blurb, and byline of this opening spread. Body copy is in sans serifs, too. Four-column, three-column, and two-column pages are all used in this Billboard Publications magazine.

Promotions & Transfers

Retirements

Anniversaries

Running a heading up the side works in this case because the *E* seen this way really looks like the "STEPS" of the heading. Just below the heading you see some subheads (out of context) that also are a bit playful, combining art with type. In actual use, of course, each of the subheads would have a number of short items underneath them. These examples are from *Seafirst News* published by Seattle First National Bank.

is folly. The time spent counting characters and rewriting to make that last line fit can be spent better on other editorial matters.

Publications like to run captions in a type different from body-copy type. As one exception, *Smithsonian* uses body-copy type for captions but with plenty of white space separating the captions from the body copy.

Bylines and credit lines

The New Yorker places bylines at the ends of articles or stories, apparently in the belief that readers should get into editorial material without regard for who wrote it. Most magazines, if they use bylines, place them at the beginnings. Some magazines run bylines well removed from the titles of articles and right next to the articles' beginnings.

Bylines are set in type smaller than that used for article or story titles but larger, usually, than type used for body copy.

Some magazines combine bylines with legends or blurbs about the author. For example, "Mathew S. Ogawa shows how after-midnight broadcasts are reaching Japanese youth." In this kind of arrangement the author's name is set in italics, boldface, all-caps, or even underlined to make it stand out. Other magazines run legends about the authors in small type at the bottoms of article openings, sort of as footnotes. Still others run separate columns combining information about all the contributors.

Where bylines honor writers, credit lines honor artists and photographers.

Some magazines run credit lines in a box on the table of contents page or somewhere else in the magazine. It is surprising that companies granting permission to reprint photographs or other illustrations settle for that kind of credit. Few readers study such a box to find out who took what picture. The more common practice is to run credit lines right next to the photographs, whether they be original or borrowed. Credit-line type is usually smaller than caption type to keep the two entirely separate; often a sans serif type is used. Some magazines run credit lines up the sides of pictures to keep the lines from interfering with captions.

Credit lines can also be reversed or surprinted inside the photographs at their bottom edges. If a magazine does not want to be bothered with separate settings for credit lines, it can run them as last lines of captions, set off by parentheses.

When one photographer takes all the pictures or one illustrator does all the sketches for a feature, a single byline rather than credit lines may be called for. The photographer's or illustrator's byline may be slightly smaller than the author's and placed away from the story's opening.

It may be that credit lines are getting out of hand. *Communication Arts* under a photograph of Kinuko Y. Craft, a magazine illustrator, ran this one: "Photograph by Bryon Ferris, print by Rob Reynolds." Now all we have to know is who wrapped the package to mail it to the editor.

Typographic endings

Like a good cup of coffee after a meal, a writer has said—that's what an article's ending should be. The reader should feel the end of the article or story and then move away inspired, shocked, amused, instructed, perhaps even intent on some course of action.

Many editors feel that the writing alone may not be enough to signal that the encounter between the writer and reader is over. Some typo-

ABCDEFGHIJ
KLMNOPQRS
TUVWXYZ&

ABCDEFGHIJ
KLMNOPQRS
TUVWXYZ&

John Graham used his video camera to record this P. T. Barnum-like alphabet (the face is Belgian, offered to the trade in 1870), then his Macintosh MacPaint computer program to digitize the alphabet and give it its texture.

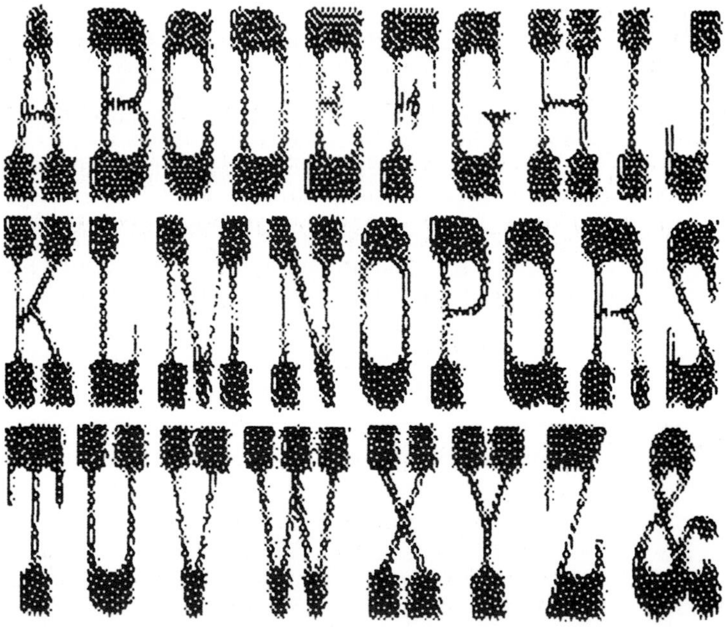

Biemann Classic, a typeface designed by Photo-Lettering, Inc., shows why type classification is so difficult. This is essentially a sans serif, but if you look closely at the stroke terminals, you'll see just a hint of serifs. Furthermore, you'll notice a slight difference in thickness in the main strokes. And even in the sans serif types there are affectations setting one family apart from another. Note the *b*, *d*, and *a* with loops that don't quite close. Both light and bold versions of the type are shown here.

TASTEFUL
bold face

This display shows some out-of-the-ordinary versions of typefaces that, like most typefaces, come in solid black. Neuland, popular these days with calligraphers who like to draw the letters with single pen strokes, is shown here in *inline* form—that is, with a thin white line running down the centers of the strokes. Eras is shown in *contour* form. The strokes are outlined. Windsor, the typeface with the strange *W,* is shown in *outline* form, with no black inside.

graphic accessory should announce, in effect, that this is The End. This is especially true now that so few magazines provide a cushion of fillers at the ends of articles. Articles end at the bottoms of pages.

The standard typographic device is the small, square box, available on any linecasting machine. Some magazines design their own end device and see that it is made available to the typesetter. The ending device may be a tiny version of the logo or, simply, the word *End.*

A book needs none of these devices to end a chapter. A little leftover space does the job.

Notes

1. L. W. Wallis, "Type Designs 1970–1985," TypeWorld, August 2, 1985, p. 4.
2. Ibid., p. 13.
3. Perry Jeffe, "Computer Graphic Arts," *U&lc.,* November 1985, p. 23.
4. The x-height is the height of the lowercase *x.*
5. The term *roman* is used by some printers to designate all upright types (as opposed to italic—or slanted—types).
6. The word *gothic* has been applied to many new—and hence controversial—types, including the type we know as Old English.
7. One of the interesting features of Univers is that the designer of the face, instead of giving the various versions descriptive names like "light" and "heavy" and "expanded," gave them numbers. He reserved odd numbers in Univers for upright letters, even numbers for italics.
8. Ronald Labuz, "Typespeak," *Magazine Design & Production,* August 1985, p. 22.
9. Hellmut Lehmann-Haupt, *Art Under a Dictatorship,* Oxford University Press, New York, 1954, p. 172. Reprinted in 1973 by Octagon.
10. Herbert Spencer, *The Visible Word,* Hastings House Publishers, New York, 1969, p. 6.
11. Allen Hutt, "Times Roman: A Reassessment," *The Journal of Typographic Research,* Summer 1970, pp. 259–70.
12. Sandra Ernst Moriarty and Edward C. Scheiner, "A Study of Close-Set Text Type," *Journal of Applied Psychology," vol. 69, no. 4, 1984, p. 702.*
13. See how the system works in his book, *Design with Type,* University of Toronto Press, Toronto, Canada, 1967.
14. See Lloyd R. Bostian, "Effect of Line Width on Reading Speed and Comprehension," *Journalism Quarterly,* Summer 1976, pp. 328–330.
15. Sandra Ernst Moriarty, *A Search for the Optimum Line Length,* paper prepared at the School of Journalism and Mass Communications, University of Colorado, Boulder, n.d., p. 2.
16. Ibid., p. 7.
17. "The Week," *National Review,* July 24, 1981, p. 818.

Suggested further reading

Biegeleisen, J. I., *Art Directors' Book of Type Faces,* rev. and enl. ed., Arco Publishing Company, New York, 1976.

Biggs, John R., *Letter-forms & Lettering,* Pentalic Corporation, New York, 1977.

Chadbourne, Bill N., *What Every Editor Should Know About Layout and Typography,* National Composition Association, 1730 N. Lynn St., Arlington, Virginia 22209, n.d.

Cirillo, Bob, and Kevin Ahearn, *Dry Faces,* Art Direction Book Company, New York, 1978. (Shows 1000 faces available from manufacturers of dry-transfer letters.)

Craig, James, *Phototypesetting: A Design Manual,* Watson-Guptill Publications, New York, 1978.

———, *Designing with Type,* rev. ed., Watson-Guptill Publications, New York, 1980.

Digital Typeface Library, Art Direction Book Company, New York, 1985. (Shows 1,350 digital typefaces; expensive.)

Ernst, Sandra B., *The ABC's of Typography,* rev. ed., Art Direction Book Company, New York, 1984.

Haley, Allen, *Phototypography: A Guide to In-house Typography and Design,* Charles Scribner's Sons, New York, 1980.

Hess, Stanley, *The Modification of Letterforms,* rev. ed., Art Direction Book Company, New York, 1985.

Hopkins, Richard L., *Origin of the American Point System for Pinters' Type Measurement,* Hill & Dale Press, Terra Alta, West Virginia, 1976.

King, Jean Callan, and Tony Esposito, *The Designers's Guide to Text Type,* Van Nostrand Reinhold, New York, 1980.
Lawson, Alexander, *Printing Types,* Beacon Press, Boston, 1971.
———, and Archie Provan, *Typography for Composition,* National Composition Association, 1730 N. Lynn St., Arlington, Virginia 22209, 1976.
LeWinter, Renee, (compiler), *Directory of Evocative Typography,* GAMA Communications, P.O. Box 597, Salem, New Hampshire 03079, 1980.
Lewis, John, *Typography: Design and Practice,* rev. ed., Taplinger, New York, 1978.
Morison, Stanley, *A Tally of Types,* Cambridge University Press, New York, 1973, (Covering types designed by Morison.)
———, *Selected Essays,* Cambridge University Press, New York, 1982. (Two volumes; expensive.)
Ogg, Oscar, *The 26 Letters,* rev. ed., Thomas Y. Crowell Company, New York, 1983.
Rehe, Rolf F., *Typography: How to Make It More Legible,* Design Research Publications, Indianapolis, 1974.
Rosen, Ben, *Type and Typography: The Designer's Notebook,* rev. ed., Van Nostrand Reinhold Company, New York, 1976.
Ruder, Emil, *Typography: A Manual of Design,* Hastings House Publishers, New York, 1980.
Solomon, Martin, *The Art of Typography: An Introduction to Typo-icon-ography,* Watson-Guptill Publications, New York, 1985.
Soppeland, Mark, *Words,* William Kaufman, Los Altos, California, 1980. (Unusual drawings of 110 words.)
Spencer, Herbert, *Pioneers of Modern Typography,* MIT Press, Cambridge, Massachusetts, 1983. (Paperback edition of 1969 book.)
The Type Specimen Book, Van Nostrand Reinhold Company, New York, 1974. (544 faces, 3,000 sizes.)
U&l.c., New York. (Quarterly.)
Updike, Daniel Berkeley, *Printing Types: Their History, Forms and Use,* Dover Publications, New York, 1980. (Reprint of the Harvard University Press classic.)
Zapf, Hermann, *About Alphabets: Some Marginal Notes on Type Design,* MIT Press, Cambridge, Massachusetts, 1970.

Stevie Wonder

Illustrator Marianne Clancy occasionally turns from traditional art mediums to her Macintosh and its MacPaint program in order to force herself into a cruder or more sophisticated style. She took about half an hour, using a mouse, to draw this portrait of Little Stevie Wonder at age 14. You see her drawing in actual size printed with a dot-matrix printer.

THINK
SUMMER

Computer enthusiasts sometimes are too willing to accept type from inferior dot-matrix printers for their printing. This headline, shown actual size, appeared on a poster advertising summer classes at a university. The square-dot pattern works all right for straight lines but not for rounds and diagonals. The dot resolution for a dot-matrix printer is from 30 to 100 per inch. A laser printer offers 300 dots per inch and much better resolution.

6

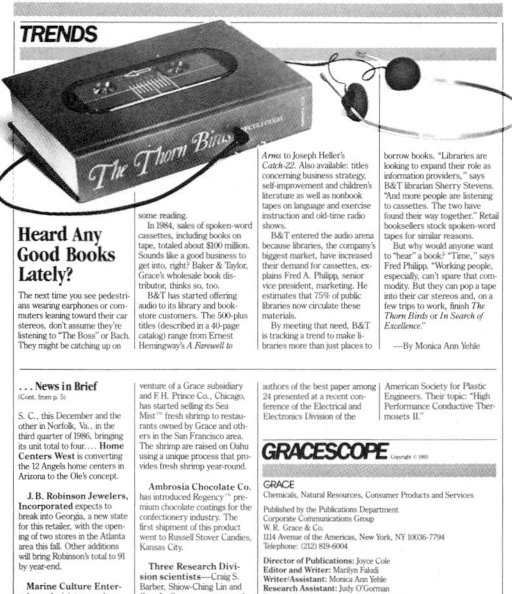

TRENDS

Heard Any Good Books Lately?

The next time you see pedestrians wearing earphones or commuters leaning toward their car stereos, don't assume they're listening to "The Boss" or Bach. They might be catching up on some reading.

In 1984, sales of spoken-word cassettes, including books on tape, totaled about $100 million. Sounds like a good business to get into, right? Baker & Taylor, Grace's wholesale book distributor, thinks so, too.

B&T has started offering audio to its library and bookstore customers. The 500-plus titles (described in a 40-page catalog) range from Ernest Hemingway's *A Farewell to Arms* to Joseph Heller's *Catch-22*. Also available: titles concerning business strategy, self-improvement and children's literature as well as nonbook tapes on language and exercise instruction and old-time radio shows.

B&T entered the audio arena because libraries, the company's biggest market, have increased their demand for cassettes, explains Fred A. Philipp, senior vice president, marketing. He estimates that 75% of public libraries now circulate these materials.

By meeting that need, B&T is tracking a trend to make libraries more than just places to borrow books. "Libraries are looking to expand their role as information providers," says B&T librarian Sherry Stevens. "And more people are listening to cassettes. The two have found their way together." Retail booksellers stock spoken-word tapes for similar reasons.

But why would anyone want to "hear" a book? "Time," says Fred Philipp. "Working people, especially, can't spare that commodity. But they can pop a tape into their car stereos and, on a few trips to work, finish *The Thorn Birds* or *In Search of Excellence*."

—By Monica Ann Yehle

. . . News in Brief
(Cont. from p. 5)

S. C., this December and the other in Norfolk, Va., in the third quarter of 1986, bringing its unit total to four. . . . **Home Centers West** is converting the 12 Angels home centers in Arizona to the Ole's concept.

J. B. Robinson Jewelers, Incorporated expects to break into Georgia, a new state for this retailer, with the opening of two stores in the Atlanta area this fall. Other additions will bring Robinson's total to 91 by year-end.

Marine Culture Enterprises, the joint aquaculture venture of a Grace subsidiary and F. H. Prince Co., Chicago, has started selling its Sea Mist™ fresh shrimp to restaurants owned by Grace and others in the San Francisco area. The shrimp are raised on Oahu using a unique process that provides fresh shrimp year-round.

Ambrosia Chocolate Co. has introduced Regency™ premium chocolate coatings for the confectionery industry. The first shipment of this product went to Russell Stover Candies, Kansas City.

Three Research Division scientists—Craig S. Barber, Shiow-Ching Lin and Gary L. Causer—were voted authors of the best paper among 24 presented at a recent conference of the Electrical and Electronics Division of the American Society for Plastic Engineers. Their topic: "High Performance Conductive Thermosets II."

GRACESCOPE

GRACE
Chemicals, Natural Resources, Consumer Products and Services

Published by the Publications Department
Corporate Communications Group
W. R. Grace & Co.
1114 Avenue of the Americas, New York, NY 10036-7794
Telephone: (212) 819-6004

Director of Publications: Joyce Cole
Editor and Writer: Marilyn Faludi
Writer/Assistant: Monica Ann Yehle
Research Assistant: Judy O'Gorman
Design: Bernhardt Fudyma Design Group

The sixth and final page of an issue of *Gracescope,* a newsletter published by W. R. Grace & Company, New York, uses an art oxymoron—a book that is also a tape recorder. This doctored photograph illustrates a story on spoken-word cassettes, a $100 million industry. Art director, Craig Bernhardt.

5

Art

Art in a publication can either stand by itself as a separate feature, with or without a caption, or work with text matter as an illustration. Art that stands by itself often originates outside the editorial offices. It may be submitted as something of a surprise to the editor or art director. Illustrative art, on the other hand, is commissioned by the editor or art director, who wants it for one or more of these reasons:

1. to create a mood for a cover or feature
2. to merely decorate a cover or feature
3. to amplify or explain what's in a title or headline or what's in the text
4. to fill space when words fall short

It is not a good idea, usually, to allow the art to add a new dimension to the title or article or to follow a different line of thought. This could confuse the readers. It could result in the art's *competing* with the text. Art—and we are talking about illustrative art here—should make a story or concept more vivid, not more complex.

Art directors cannot agree on whether photographs or art pieces do the better job. Nor can they agree on matters of style and technique. They cannot agree on whether art should be realistic or abstract. But they can agree on this: *The illustration should be well designed.* The principles of design that govern the arrangement of type and illustration on a page or spread also govern the placement of figures, props, and background within an illustration. Every illustration, from the crudest cartoon to the finest photograph or painting, should be well designed.

The art of photography

The halftone process of reproducing photographs was developed in the 1880s. *National Geographic* was one of the first magazines to use halftones regularly, beginning in 1903. But *Life's* contribution to the development of photography in magazines was undoubtedly greater than *National Geographic's.* Started in 1936 as a sort of illustrated *Time, Life* gradually changed from a newsmagazine to a magazine of special features. More than any other publication it developed the idea of photojournalism: great photographs taken on the spot, where and when important things were happening. Sometimes the photographs merely reported, sometimes they expressed a form of opinion. Often their greatness was accidental.

For many years the photograph, like the painting or drawing, was used merely to illustrate an article or story. It still is used that way. But in the 1930s some editors, especially those at *Life,* worked out an additional use for photographs, putting them into a spread or a series of spreads and

A hill-tribe woman on her way to fish in northeastern Thailand waters. Native dress like hers with its bright colors and shoulder designs served as inspiration in the West for fashionable evening coats in the 1980s. Photographer Steven R. Lorton, an editor at *Sunset,* decided a head-on pose would best show off his subject. The short depth of field puts detail where it should be in the photograph.

Pattern often is enough to make a photograph interesting. Peter Haley took this shot for the Salem (Oregon.) *Statesman-Journal* to illustrate a feature on high interest rates and their effect in stacking up inventories for the forest products industries.

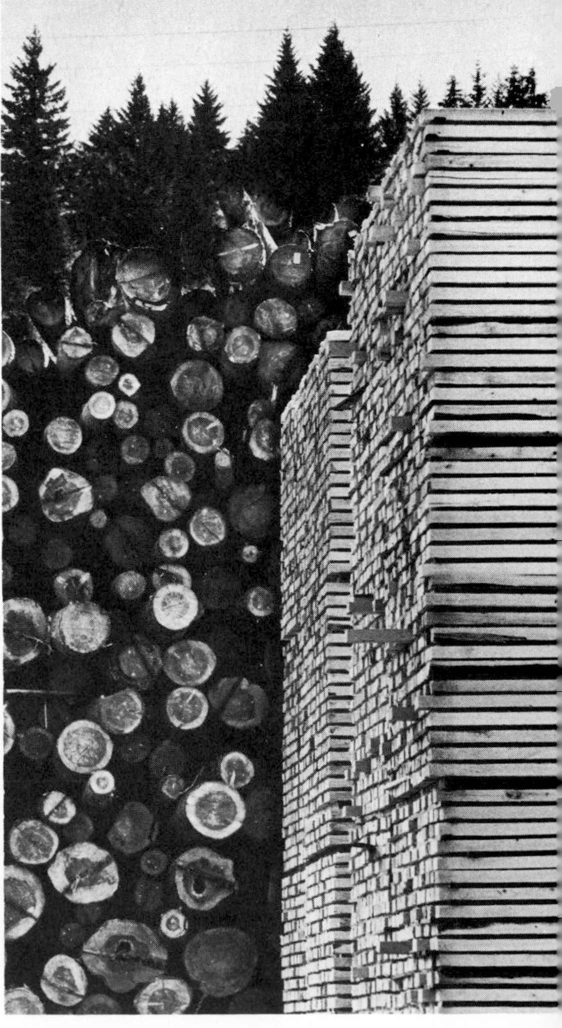

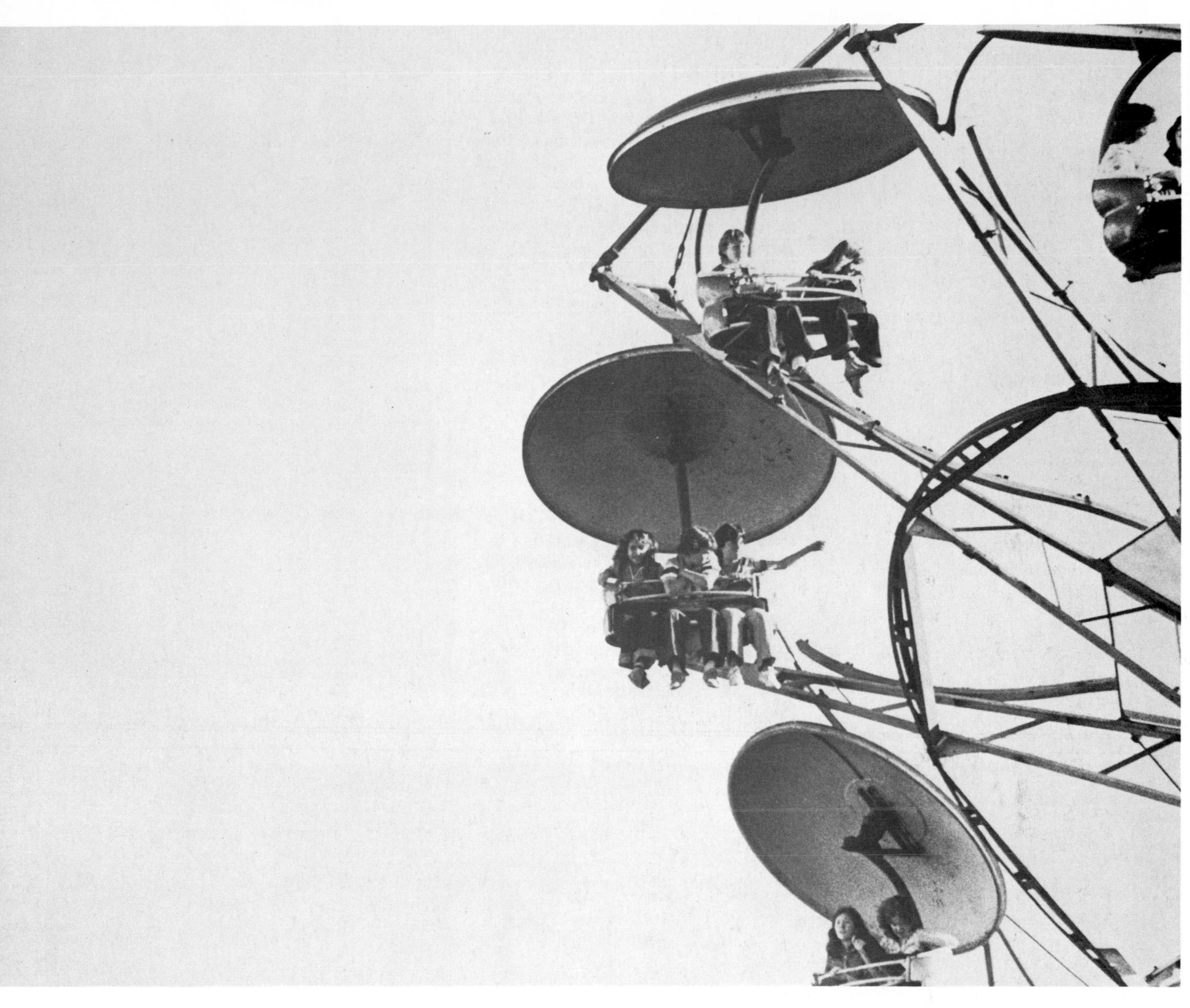

This photo is an editor's delight because the photographer (Chris Craft) has purposely left a lot of white sky onto which columns of type can be superimposed. The photograph could be run as a full-page bleed, with the rounded art at the bottom of the page serving as a silhouette, providing a nice contrast to the straight columns of type.

letting them tell their own story, sometimes without captions. The photo essay was born.

Like a piece of prose, a photo essay has a story to tell or a point to make. The pictures all revolve around a central theme. They may be uniform in size, or they may vary greatly in both size and shape. There is always a key photograph for the series, but there may be a sub key photograph for each spread, too. It is up to the art director to unify the photographs.

Any combination of pictures is likely to say something different from what each picture says by itself. The sum is different from its parts. As an art director you must share with the photographer the responsibility for developing the theme of an essay. The order of presentation and the juxtaposition of one picture with another greatly affect what the essay says.

The new photographic equipment available makes all kinds of effects

Photographer Chris Craft had to take off her shoes and get up on a counter to take this bird's-eye shot of the then governor of Oregon, Vic Atiyeh, cutting a ribbon at a bank opening. She used a wide-angle lens to bring in the background. Too often routine shots like this, necessary to a publication, are made from usual vantage points with no attempt to really compose them. The bold-shapes and darkness in the foreground add dimension to this picture.

In a confrontation shot like this one, much depends upon the expressions a photographer is able to capture. People here are objecting to herbicide spraying. That's a Bureau of Land Management official at the left who is weathering the protests. Peter Haley of *Daily Tidings* of Ashland, Oregon, took the picture.

Peter Haley used a fish-eye lens to make this routine shot memorable.

possible. "There's an embarrassment of riches as far as lenses are concerned," says Jean-Claude Suares. "What you see now is a lack of discipline in the use of lenses, to the point that photographers are getting everything in one picture. . . ." Such pictures seem "right," but there are too many of them. For contrast, Suares looks for "wrong" pictures, just as among illustrations he looks for "crazy stuff" instead of slick drawings.[1]

Robert N. Essman, art director of *People,* notes a deterioration in photography submitted to magazines. Photographs to him these days seem too precious, as though they were taken for museum display rather than for publication. And often when the pictures are good, the focus is bad.

The magazines' infatuation with blurred photographs in the early 1970s became the subject of some satire in *Saturday Review.* "What has happened," wrote Dereck Williamson, ". . . is that the improperly exposed and badly focused photograph has become Art. The bad picture is now good, and the good picture is bad. For amateur 35-millimeter photographers like myself, this is distressing news. For years I've been culling my slides and throwing away Art. Many of my mistakes would now be worth big money in the modern magazine market place."

He cites a number of his culls, including "One Tennis Shoe, with Kneecap," "Child Unrolling Agfachrome at High Noon," and "Daughter's Birthday Party with Failing Flashcube." His "Giant Redwoods and Finger," had it been sent to a magazine, would probably have been accepted and captioned: "A personal statement of the photographer concerning man's ruthless attitude toward his environment."[2]

There are still plenty of art directors who insist on sharply focused, well-lighted photographs. Editors and art directors like them because they say things that need to be said. And they are readily available. Although only a few persons can turn out usable drawings or paintings, almost anyone can turn out publishable photographs, not the kind that would delight the heart of a Harry Benson, perhaps, but publishable nevertheless. To many, photography represents "instant art"; and everyone can participate. Out of thousands upon thousands of routine photographs, there just have to be some that, if they don't qualify as works of art, at least have enough clarity or meaning to justify reproduction in some publication.

More and more publications these days expect their editors or writers to take their own pictures. "We can't afford to hire a freelance photographer when the writer is on location in the boondocks," says Joe Ruskin, photography director at McGraw-Hill Publications Company. "It's too expensive to hire a photographer just to take one picture a day." At *Construction Equipment Maintenance,* a Cahners Publishing Company magazine, one of the first questions editorial job applicants face is "Can you take pictures?"[3]

It was natural that art directors, working closely with photographers, should begin to do their own shooting. Perhaps the photographer missed

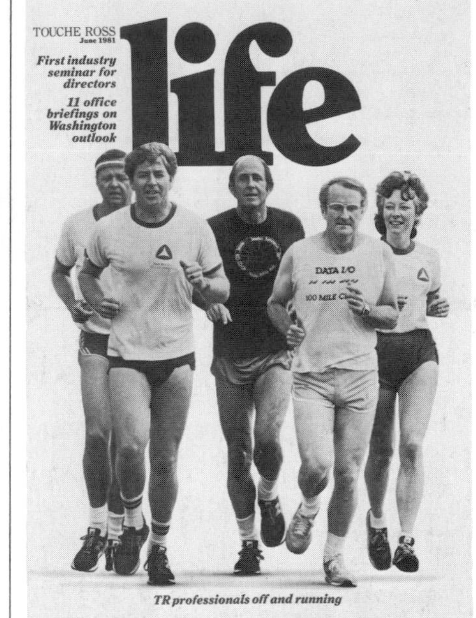

This 12 × 6 magapaper uses a silhouetted photograph for one of its covers, allowing a couple of the heads of the runners to overlap the big logo, which is printed in a second color. (From *Touche Ross Life,* June 1981, published by Touche Ross & Co. Reprinted by permission of Touch Ross & Co.)

GUILT

AMERICAN STYLE

BY JOSEPH N BELL

Steve Hill's full-color photograph of a man covering his face with a hat nicely illustrates the "Guilt" in the title of an article in *Sunshine,* the Sunday magazine of the Fort Lauderdale *News/Sun-Sentinel.* Art director, Greg Paul. The title and byline unit is designed to parallel the trunk of the figure, the man's left hand pointing the reader back to the title. The article starts out with a line of capital letters, not an initial. An initial would detract from the one-two nature of title and art.

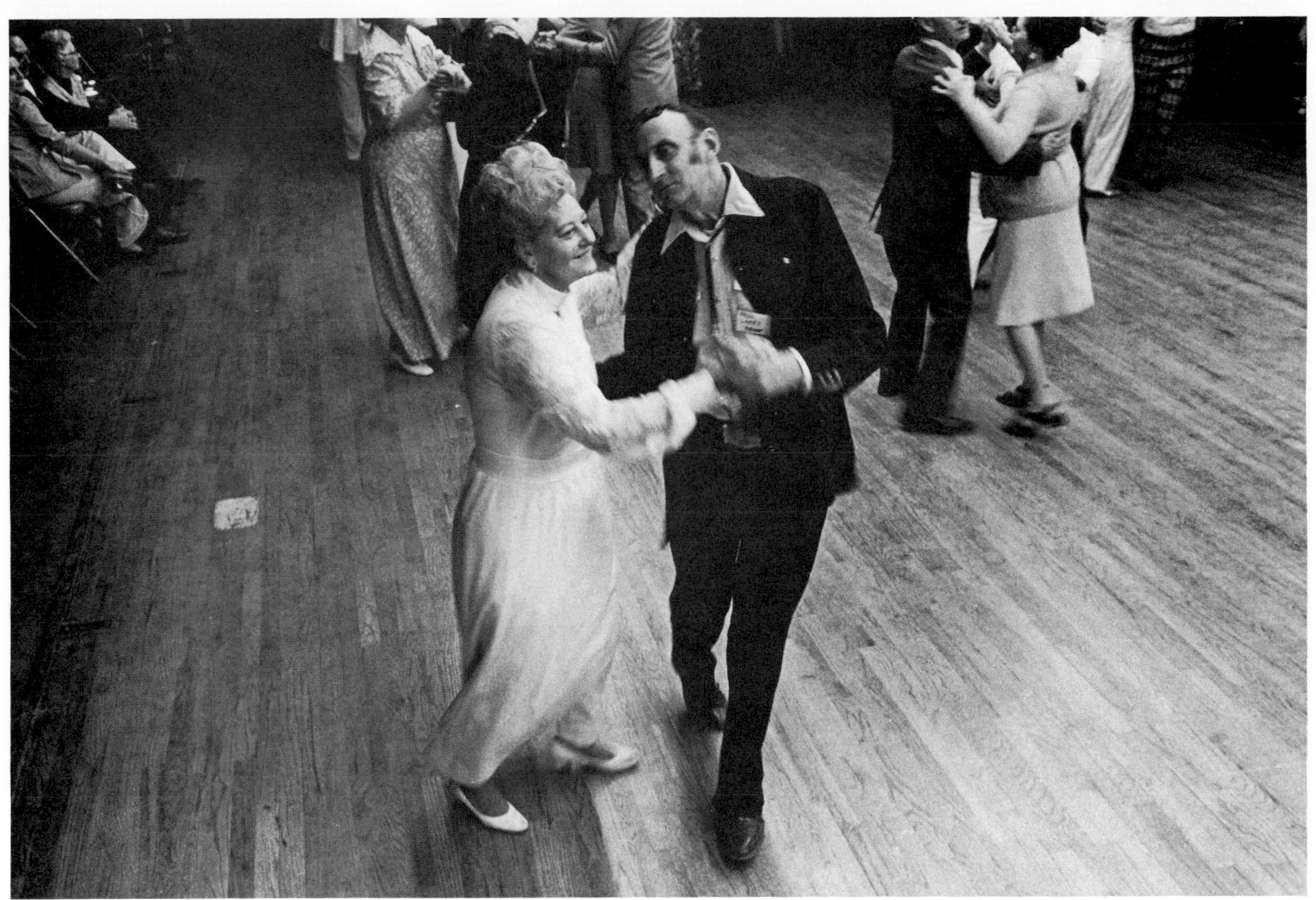

To make one dancing couple stand out at a fiddlers' association dance, John Bauguess shot from above and arranged things into a sort of *T* formation, showing only parts of the dancing couples in the background. Effective silhouetting of the centered couples and subtle expressions add to the readability and enjoyment of this exceptional piece of art. (© by John Bauguess.)

a deadline. Perhaps the art director had a better feel for proportion than the photographer had. Otto Storch became so intrigued with the camera that he gave up his job at *McCall's* to go into film work. And a number of cover and interior shots for magazines like *Harper's* have been taken by the sometimes-magazine-art-director Henry Wolf.

Among the most popular courses offered on college campuses these days—and in the high schools, too—are the courses in photography. Moholy-Nagy once said, prophetically, "The illiterate of the future will be the man who does not know how to take a photograph."

Deciding on photographs

You should make sure the photographer fully understands any assignment and knows how the pictures will be used, whether for illustration or essay purposes.

If you want to emphasize height, you should direct the photographer to take the picture from a worm's-eye angle. If you want to show an item in context with its surroundings, you may ask for a bird's-eye view.

Often a photograph does not tell the complete story unless scale is included. A photograph of a tree seedling may not mean much unless a knife or shovel or some other item whose size is understood is included in the picture. When *Posh,* the quarterly published by P & O Lines, Inc., ran an article on sculptures in miniature, the art director saw to it that photographs showed the various pieces held in hands. Closeup shots were made from different angles to heighten interest.

As art director you should insist on a wide selection of prints. Contact sheets are good enough. You can study the prints with an 8-power magnifier. You should ask for more blowups than you can use—three or four times as many—because no matter how well you read the prints, you'll see new things when they're bigger. You should have some choices at that level, too.

On some publications you can't afford the luxury of choice. Small publications often settle for the single picture or two that are available. As art director you might have to use a picture you know is inferior; but it may be the only one that is available to you. A way to minimize the poor quality is to run it small.

Sometimes you have two or three excellent shots, but there is not much difference among them in camera angle, camera distance, or subject matter. You should resist the impulse to use them all. Redundancy spoils good photography.

There is some merit, however, in using a series of similar shots of an individual who is the subject of an interview. A series of photographs tells the reader more about the interviewee than a single photograph can. Besides, the several similar pictures give the reader a feeling of visual continuity.

When you need a mug shot to go with an article or story and you have several to choose from, you should select the one that has an expression appropriate to the mood of the article. The reader can't help being puzzled to see the victim of a tragedy wearing a silly grin. At the least the caption should explain that the picture was taken on some earlier occasion.

For certain kinds of magazines—those dealing with exquisite scenery and luxurious travel, for instance—full-color photography is a must. But full color is expensive.

Another problem with full-color photography is that it makes *everything* look beautiful. By focusing close, the photographer makes the pattern and the splash of color more important than the content of the picture. Ugly things, like filth washing up on a river bank, become works of art to be admired. For this reason, even when you can afford color, you may choose to stay with black and white for some of your features.

A variation of full-color photography involves hand tinting black-and-white photographs and then, in reproduction, treating them as regular color prints. This creates a dated, even funky look.

Many less expensive uses of color also get editors' consideration. One is to run a black-and-white photograph as a duotone. The printer makes two halftones from one photograph and prints one in black, the other in a color. Another is to print a halftone in black over a tint block of color.

Still another is to print the black-and-white photograph in a colored ink. This technique is used only when you want a photograph to produce a mood or act as a symbol; it lacks the definition of a photograph printed in black with the tonal range black offers. Some publications use so light a color that they can print type over the photograph without hurting the type's readability. Of course, they don't exactly make a prize winner out of the printed photograph.

It is also possible to print a spot of color on one part of a black-and-white photograph to exaggerate one of the photo's qualities. For instance,

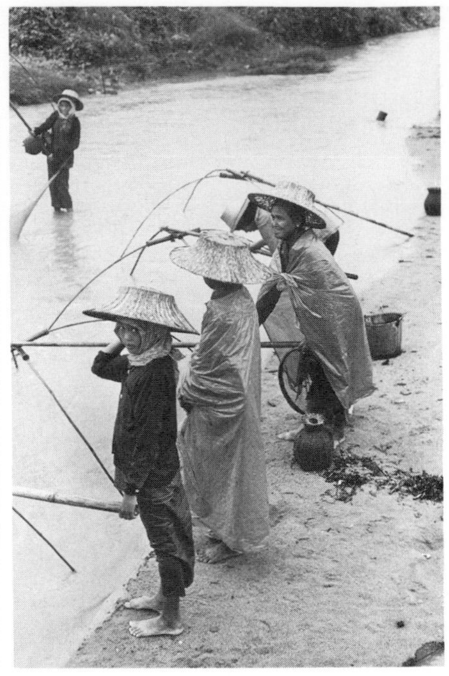

In this shot of country women fishing in central Thailand, Steve Lorton put a participant with a winsome look in the foreground and concentrated on her.

For this shot Lorton stepped farther back to put his subjects into better context with the landscape and to better show off the fishing gear. Note the strong diagonal thrust running from upper left to lower right.

The accepting-the-award picture will, unfortunately, always be with us, and in many cases it will be in a form no less awkward than this.

a green tint over a face could indicate sickness. This almost makes a cartoon out of the photograph.

Photographic clichés

Even though any pose, from any angle, with any focus can find a place in today's publications, certain poses, at least in ordinary usage, should be avoided if for no other reason than that they have been used too often. The following poses qualify as clichés:

1. people shaking hands during award ceremonies
2. public officials signing proclamations and other papers
3. people studying documents
4. people pointing to maps, to trees, to anything
5. committees at work
6. public speakers at the rostrum

But even the photographic cliché has its place in well-designed publications. The fact that a picture is "camp" may be reason enough to run it. Or maybe the nature of the article calls for a photograph that, under other circumstances, would be considered too stilted to use. Art directors seem more willing than they have been in the past to run group shots, with subjects looking straight ahead into the lens of the camera. In a publicity stunt the Western Art Directors Club got away with a photographic cliché when it sent out a formal group shot of newly elected officers. All persons but one were looking straight ahead into the camera, painfully serious. That one, in the middle of the front row, had his back facing the camera. He was the outgoing president.

William H. Neubeck, editor of the New Jersey *Herald,* a small daily, makes a case for the familiar and discredited group shot. Neubeck is tired of the outside expert—someone, say, from a 200,000-circulation paper—holding up such a picture as a horrible example. Such experts "may know a lot about photography or graphics, but few, it seems, know very much about community newspapers." Readers of community papers like to see pictures—even group pictures—of people they know. "I suppose we could arrange the [fire department] chief, deputy chief, et al., around one of the fire engines or sliding down a fire pole (if we could find a firehouse that still has a fire pole). But after doing that once or twice, wouldn't the novelty have worn off?"[4]

You can keep track of your cropping by drawing a four-unit box like this and putting down three already-determined measurements while you work out the fourth (represented by *X*). The arrows at the top represent widths and depths. The words at the left represent "original size" and "to-be-printed" size. For example, 9½ is to 4 as 6 is to *X*. This system works for inches or picas.

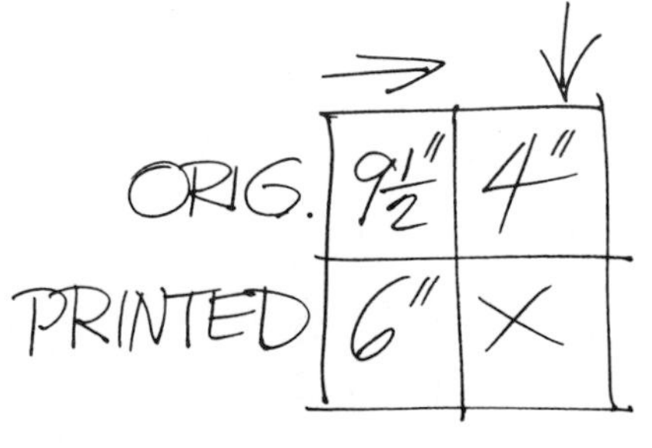

Handling photographs

When finally laying out the pages, you work with 8 × 10 prints. Using a grease crayon, you make your crop marks in the margin. You do not write on the backs of photos for fear of denting the front surfaces. Dents, bends, and folds show up in the final printing.

You should be particularly careful in your handling of transparencies. When a black-and-white print is lost, a new one can be made easily. But when a transparency is lost, all is lost.

In indicating sizes to the photographer or printer, you always give width first, then depth. (In Great Britain you would do just the opposite.) You can make sure there is no misunderstanding when you write down a size by marking a short horizontal line above the width and a short vertical line above the depth.

Cropping

It has taken editors—especially newspaper editors—a long time to appreciate the value of neutral area in a photograph. The tendency has been to crop away "unimportant" parts of a photograph to move in close on the subject. Sometimes such cropping does improve a photograph. Sometimes, to help a story better make its point, the cropping is necessary.

But often neutral area is necessary to better display the subject. The neutral area provides context and contrast. Besides, the photographer probably planned the neutral area for better composition.

No wonder photographers complain when their work is cropped. To avoid conflict, editors should explain to photographers how photographs will be used on a page or spread. Photographs then can be taken to accommodate unusual handling.

For instance, the editor may want to run photographs within photographs. Smaller but related photographs may go into neutral areas, surrounded by thin white lines so they aren't confused with the main photographs. Or the editor may want mortises in the photographs to carry the captions. Maybe that would not be the magazine's usual style, but it

The toned area represents a photograph. Assuming you want only part of the photograph, this is the way you would mark it for cropping. You would mark the size wanted in the space between crop marks at the bottom.

A single photo yields several quite different emphases, as this photo, cropped in several ways, shows.

To illustrate an article on how to "deal" with customers swarming the marketplace "after a long winter's sleep," *Go,* the Goodyear magazine for tire dealers, came up with this photograph taken by Don Landstrom, an amateur magician. The article "Goodyear Cuts the Deck and Deals" discussed a nationwide promotion. Because few magicians or even gamblers are able to shuffle cards like this, Landstrom drilled a hole through the center of the cards and threaded them with a string to "enable the cards to follow a predetermined path from the top hand to the bottom," according to the editor Larry Miller.

might be the style for all the photographs in a single article to make it stand out from the others in that issue. Color could be involved in either the inset photographs or the mortises.

A mortise or even an inset often does violence to the main photograph, even when planned. The technique belongs more to new wave than to traditional design. More commonly, editors and art directors reverse type (run it in white) or surprint it (run it in black) in neutral areas or nontextured areas of photographs. The technique works best with full-page bleed photographs, but like all such techniques it deserves only limited use.

Neutral space in a photograph is like white space on a page or a pause or a rest in a musical composition. It serves a useful purpose.

One place where cropping may be necessary is on a page of same-size mug shots. The photographs, let's say, come in from different sources and with faces in different sizes. Camera distances vary. Your job then may be to crop each so that the faces line up in printing, with the same amount of bust showing for each person.

In cropping a mug shot, you would ordinarily leave a little space above the head and a bit of the chest showing. The rough sketch below shows a wrong—an uncomfortable—cropping. It is never a good idea to crop exactly at the neck for a mug shot or at the ankles for a full-figure shot. And on a full figure, you should leave a little foreground for the feet.

Doctoring photographs

Inexperienced art directors often cut photographs into odd shapes because squares and rectangles are "monotonous." These art directors make the mistake of thinking that readers are more interested in shape than in content.

Nothing—nothing—beats the rectangle or square as a shape for a photograph. A circle, a triangle, a star, a free form—these may have occasional impact; but as a general rule, they should be avoided. If you want some added impact, you can crop your photographs into extremely wide or tall rectangles.

A silhouette halftone—the reproduction of a photograph in which a figure is outlined against a white background—provides an effective change of pace for the art director. The silhouette is much preferred to the photograph with doctored edges because it does not represent shape for the sake of shape; it emphasizes content. A single silhouette can be used for contrast on a spread of photographs that are rectangles and squares.

If you feel that one element in a picture should "walk out" from the rest of the picture, you can put that element—or part of it—into a silhouette and square off the rest of the picture. You can also box in the white area of the photograph.

When silhouetting (also referred to as outlining) a photograph, you may find it necessary to do your own cutting or opaquing. You should be sure the figure or object in the photograph is large enough to take the silhouetting. You should avoid intricate silhouettes, such as a woman with windblown hair.

The silhouette in photography often comes naturally, without any need for doctoring. It starts with the photographer taking the picture so that the subject—say it's a businesswoman hailing a taxi—is mostly in dark tones against a light background. There are few in-between tones.

Silhouette photographs, provided you don't overuse them, can dress up a publication. They work especially well as covers or introductions. As an art director you would try to select silhouette photographs with low vantage points. Such photographs better display the subject against, say, the sky. One way for a photographer to take a silhouette photograph is to get the subject to block out the sun, thus allowing light to fill in all around her.

The doctoring of a photograph can also mean changing what the photograph says—after the fact. The latest twist in this art involves the digitizing of photographs.

Whole Earth Review for July 1985 ran as a cover story "The End of Photography as Evidence of Anything." The authors pointed out that a number of magazines are using the "new capability" that "comes from the merging of laser technology, used to scan the original photographs and convert them into digital data, and computer technology, whose increasing power at decreasing cost allows sophisticated manipulation of the no-longer-photographic image." For one of its covers, for instance, *National Geographic* "moved one of the pyramids of Giza to suit their cover design. *Popular Science* put an airplane from one photo onto the background of another photo on one of its covers. . . ."[5] To illustrate the technique, *Whole Earth Review* itself ran a "photograph" of flying saucers landing in San Francisco.

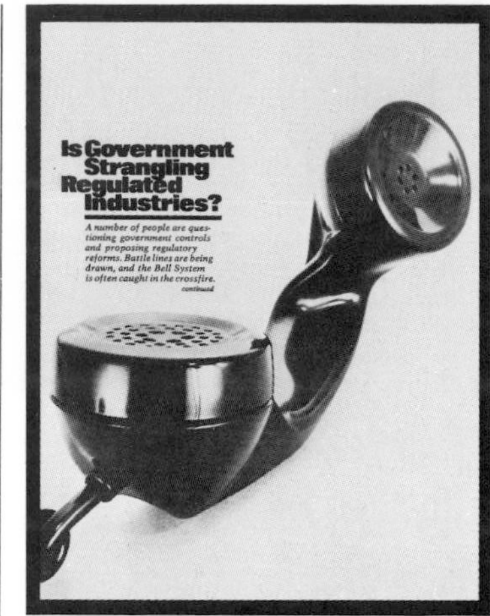

A right-hand page opener for an article in *Bell Telephone Magazine* on government regulation. The black border is appropriate in view of the word *Strangling* in the title. Further dramatizing the concept of strangling is the twisted shape of the phone, accomplished by heating it in an oven and working it over before taking the photograph. To tell readers that the article really starts on the next page, the editor runs the word *continued* after the italicized blurb.

John Graham created this portrait of Benjamin Franklin by taking a video-camera picture of a public-domain etching and using Macintosh's MacVision program to digitize the image.

To create this art, David K. Brunn, a photographer and computer expert, brought together three different scenes—color slides—and digitized them into a Macintosh computer, using the MacVision program. Then he manipulated the images, using the MacPaint program. The picture of the house too close to the sea, then, beautifully composed and executed, is a composite.

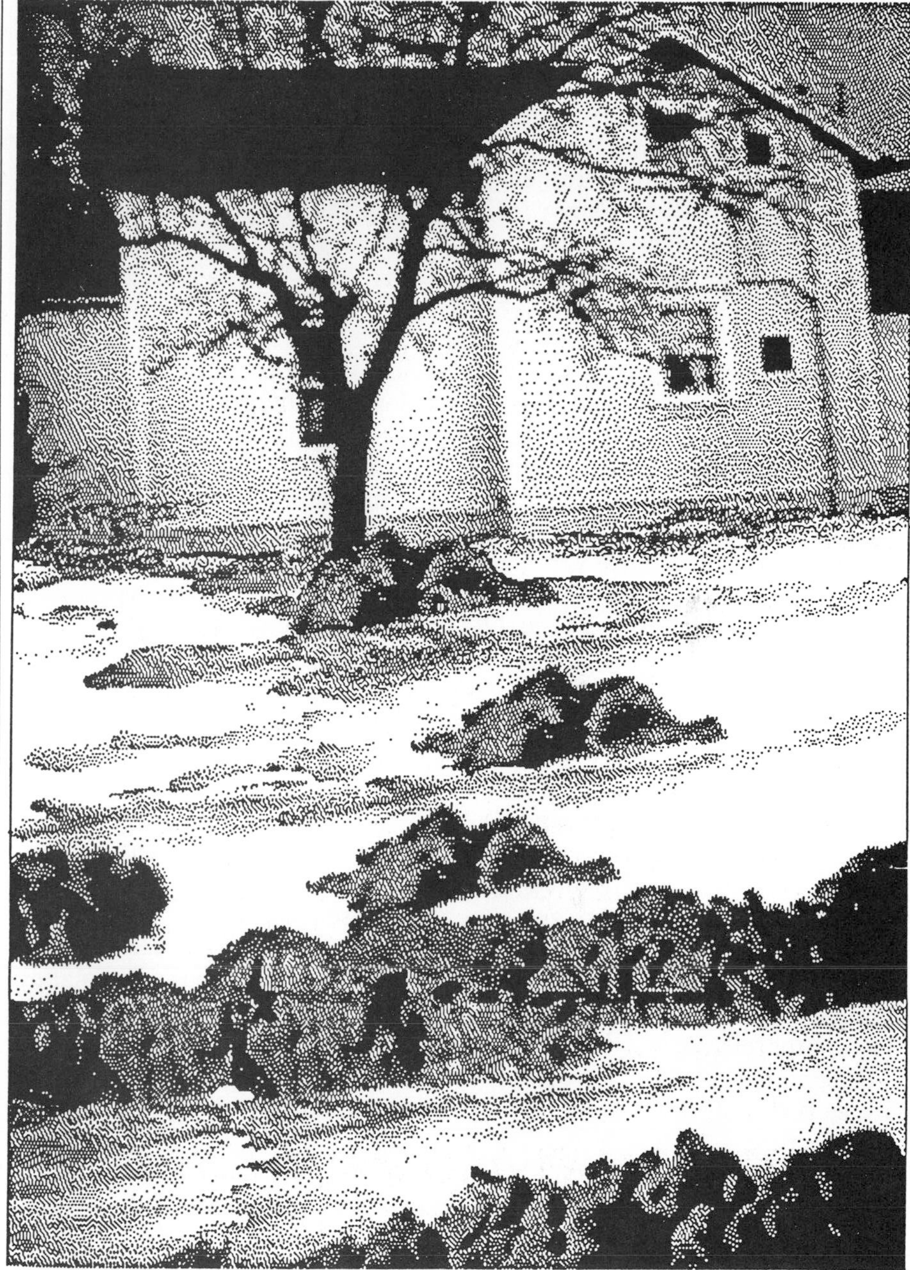

The process is far advanced over the old retouch-with-paint process, used by early newspapers for coarse-screen halftones, and later airbrush retouching.

Bleeding photographs

Art directors do not agree on whether it's best to bleed photographs (let them run off the pages) or surround them with margins of white. Bleeding tends to expand photos and, some say, to give the magazine a contemporary look. Leaving white margins tends to give a page more of a classical look.

Generally speaking, only large photographs should be bled. It is never advisable to bleed small mug shots. Nor is it necessary, when you use bleeds, to bleed consistently throughout the magazine. Sometimes a combination of bleed and nonbleed pictures is best.

It is not a good idea to bleed photographs that are outlined with thin black lines. When you bleed such a photograph, you lose some of the outlines and introduce some inconsistency.

You must order your halftones with an extra one-eighth to one-quarter inch strip (final halftone size) for each edge that bleeds. Because extra trimming may be involved and an oversize sheet must be used, the printer may charge more for bleed pages.

In this set of nine faces, used on the cover of a college catalog, the designer Jim Bodoh of the University of Oregon was careful to pick faces to represent all classes of students. The faces started out as regular photographs, but the reproduction called for was line. On his prints Bodoh did some retouching to dramatize some of the shapes. And of course he gave careful attention to cropping in every case.

Flopping photographs

You may be tempted occasionally to flop a photograph—change its facing—if it seems to point off a page. But this is tricky business.

Flop a portrait, and the part in the hair is on the wrong side. The suit is buttoned on the wrong side. If a sign is included in the picture, it will read from right to left.

Scholastic Editor once ran a photograph of the cover of *Onondagan,* the yearbook of Syracuse University. On the yearbook's cover was a picture of a light switch turned on. The *ON* in caps showed plainly (*On* is a shortened version of the yearbook's name). But for the sake of a facing, the editor of *Scholastic Editor* flopped the photograph. And the *ON* came out reading *NO.*

Arranging photos on the page

It might be useful here to consider the design principles of chapter 2 as they apply to the use of photographs.

To bring order to your pages, you should use fewer pictures—perhaps fewer than you would consider desirable—and you should use them in large sizes. A large photograph is many times more effective than a smaller one. The impact does not increase arithmetically; it increases by geometric progression.

Big photographs also save money. It costs as much to take a small picture as it does to take a big one. As much thinking and effort go into a small picture.

For the sake of unity, you should bring related photographs together in your layout. Organization for content is more important than organization based on the way photographs happen to face.

Company magazines, especially, like to use several photos in a sequence, as when an executive changes expressions during an interview or gestures while making a speech. The several close-up shots shown usually come from the same distance and camera angle. This brings unity to the series. There is a danger here, though, photographer Philip N. Douglis points out in his column in *Communication World:* "the concept of pacing is ignored." Each image should add a new phase that helps accumulate meaning, he says. There must be some recognizable differences among the shots. A sequence should offer variety instead of redundancy.[6]

When you use several photographs per page or spread, you should consider placing the close-ups at the bottom because this conforms more naturally to the way we see things in perspective. You should keep your photographs all the same size—or you should make them obviously different in size. You want to avoid making them almost—but not quite—equal. In most cases you would have some large, some middle-size, some

Captions under or right next to photographs make things easy for the reader, but it is sometimes necessary, from a design standpoint, to run photographs together as a unit, uninterrupted by type. These beautiful full-color photographs form one bleed unit on the right-hand page of a two-page spread; only a thin white line separates them from each other. The one caption for the pictures appears on the left-hand page, about in the middle of the third column, in a slightly smaller, different type, printed in blue ink. It was not necessary to number the photographs so that the caption could point to them. The caption starts out this way: "Clockwise from upper left." The pages, part of a six-page article are from *Exxon USA,* published by the Exxon Company, U.S.A., Houston, Downs Matthews, editor; Richard Payne, art director.

small photographs; and you would combine squares with rectangles, and among your rectangles you would have some horizontals and some verticals.

It is not a good idea to run full-page pictures on both left- and right-hand pages, especially if they bleed on three sides and run into the gutter. The two then appear to be a single, massive photograph. A small band of white should separate them at the gutter.

You can draw on a number of techniques for combining several photographs on a page, unifying them and yet allowing them to stand separately.

1. *Run a small band of white between them.* The band may vary in width, or it can stay the same throughout the spread. Art directors used to prefer separations of no more than an eighth of an inch, but now they seem to prefer a wider band—a quarter of an inch or more.
2. *Butt the photos up against each other.* This works well if the photos are of different sizes; some of the photo edges will be printed against a field of white. Some art directors like to run a thin black line where the photographs join.
3. *Overlap the photos.* This means cutting mortises into photos and slipping portions of other photos into the holes. The overlap can fit snugly. Or it can have a small white line around it to help separate one photo from the other.

   Overlapping is not always desirable because it calls attention to shape rather than content. When you overlap, you get photos that are *L*- or *U*-shaped. This spoils the composition of the photos, even when what is mortised out appears to be unimportant foreground or sky.

   The usual overlap allows only one of the photographs to print in the shared area. For an unusual effect you can print one photograph in black, one in color, without bothering to mortise; you can let them both show. Or you can print one photograph in one color, one in another, and you will get a third color where they overlap.
4. *Fit one photo inside the other.* You can do this when the center of

interest of the base photograph is concentrated in one area. Your base photograph would be one you would otherwise crop. The smaller photo would fit into an internal mortise. Again it could fit snugly, or it could carry a thin white outline.

Photographs or illustrations?
In a review of *America's Great Illustrators,* Tom Wolfe points out that "the period 1880 to 1930 was the half-century in which the magazine industry grew up and boomed, and magazines became the dominant form of popular entertainment. Magazine illustration idealized and reshaped popular taste in a way that film and, to some extent, comic strips would after 1920."

The early magazine illustrators worked without the stigma of being "mere illustrators." The split between fine art and commercial art had not yet occurred. "So much of the prestigious painting of the 19th century was itself illustration. . . . As late as 1900 artists moved back and forth from easel painting to commercial illustration without any real sense of crossing a boundary line," Wolfe adds.[7]

Early in this century magazine illustrators became important persons in building circulations for magazines. People became much more familiar with art in magazines than in museums. The most popular magazine artist of all, of course, was Norman Rockwell, who did a total of 317 covers for *The Saturday Evening Post.* One estimate had it that each of his covers was seen by four million persons.

Illustrators whose work appeared *inside* the magazines became popular, too. Charles Dana Gibson, who drew for *Life, Collier's,* and *Harper's Weekly,* set the standard for the beautiful girl in America. The Gibson Girl was the American ideal from the early 1890s to World War I.

Newspapers employed illustrators, too, but, facing tight deadline schedules, relied on their own staffs rather than on freelancers. Big newspapers employed teams of artists, some of them cartoonists.

Illustrators enjoyed a golden age in the 1930s, 1940s, and early 1950s. But in the mid-1950s their magazine market shriveled. Magazines were hard hit by that new medium, television, and in their search for a new identity they turned to the camera. Fiction was no longer a major part of magazines; nonfiction seemed better served by photographs. Illustrators, if they got magazine assignments at all, had to offer something the camera could not. One illustrator, Mark English, remarked that "the camera has

LAUGHING MATTERS

CLEVELAND'S COMEDY SCENE

The man who calls himself a comic is standing with a death grip on the microphone, sweating, even as the audience is calmly sitting and waiting.

He already has run through a bundle of tasteless and aging party jokes.

A nervous, uncomfortable rustling stirs the crowd, like a stiff wind moving through aspen trees. You couldn't call it laughter.

He decides to go for his killer material.

"My wife," he says, "is so big that when she sits around the house..." — No, it can't be — "... she really sits around the house."

Except for a fat man in a leisure suit seated next to me, a man who clearly thinks this clown is the hottest thing since Uncle Miltie in drag, the audience seems stunned, submissive and helpless. The silence is punctuated by thunking sounds that turn out to be foreheads crashing against table tops in simulation of unconsciousness.

The comic, who really is old enough to know better than to pass off months-old party jokes and Henny Youngman rejects as an act, gets the same look in his eyes that you see in those of small animals as they're reflected in onrushing headlights. What to do? Stall.

"You're a great audience," he tells the ominously quiet crowd. "Give yourself a hand." He lunges for a water pitcher on the side of the stage as the aspen trees whisper.

The only thing missing, this night in the comedy club, was laughter.

It's not like there are a lot of honest good times and laughs to be had in Cleveland. Oh, if you're gregarious by nature, you can go to bars and risk contracting a lethal mixture of sexually transmitted disease and loneliness, or go slightly higher on the ladder and hit some nightclubs, where you can watch computer programmers dance to what is unquestionably the world's worst music.

Idle moments in front of the tube can lead one to speculate on the luxuriousness of the anchorman's toupee, or the kind of demented minds that could foist this garbage on an unsuspecting populace.

But the problem is that these things are all funny/peculiar, not funny/ha-ha, guilty pleasures for the bored, restless mind. Intentional humor in Cleveland largely has been limited to touring Vegas schlock or disc jockey sniggering.

Even as Cleveland humor has remained fixated somewhere in the early 1960s, laughter across the country has been making quantum leaps past the Jackie-Shecky-Joey axis around which it had revolved since the best of the vaudeville talents

BY SCOTT EYMAN

CONTINUED ON PAGE 18

James McMullan, a distinguished illustrator, did the full-color illustration for "Laughing Matters," an article in *The Plain Dealer Magazine* covering Cleveland's comedy scene. "International humor in Cleveland largely has been limited to touring Vegas schlock or disc jockey sniggering," reported the writer, Scott Eyman. Design director for this strong spread, Greg Paul.

A line drawing allows patching pieces together, and the patching does not show in reproduction. For an illustration in *Humorous Illustration and Cartooning* (Prentice-Hall, 1984) this author, using a brush, drew an unlikely lady sitting and smoking carelessly in an eighteenth century French rococo chair. It was easy to trim the edges of the lady with an X-acto knife and paste her into the highly patterned chair, which came from public-domain art.

helped the artist see the direction he shouldn't be going in." Newspapers already had abandoned their large art staffs for teams of photographers.

No doubt about it, the camera put many illustrators out of work. Art directors preferred photographers because they were more realistic, when realism was important; and they were more readily available and less expensive. Furthermore, the photographer gave the art director a choice of many poses and scenes.

But illustration has made a comeback. Fiction did not return to magazines, but think pieces multiplied, and illustrations seem better suited to these than photographs. "Although concept photography can be employed it's usually easier to draw symbols than to photograph them," says designer John Peter. Peter observes that the new illustrations devote themselves to spirit or mood. The old illustrations dealt only with narrative or incident.

Illustration has become especially popular with the newly launched magazines, many of which need special identity.

And many different styles find favor with art directors these days. Some styles are merely revivals; others appear to be innovative, even shrill. Magazines and books, especially, hold many visual surprises for readers. Illustrators now are willing to experiment.

In his days on *Look,* Allen Hurlburt preferred photographs to illustrations, but *Look,* like *Life,* was essentially a photographic magazine. Even on *Look* Hurlburt saw situations where illustrations were called for. For instance, carrying a camera sometimes can be dangerous or even illegal, or sometimes it is difficult or impossible to gain model releases. An example of Hurlburt's imaginative approach to illustration was his commissioning of Norman Rockwell to do a series of paintings on integration. Hurlburt reasoned that because Rockwell had so long been trusted and admired by the middle class as an upholder of traditional American values, his work in this area would be all the more effective.

Realism or abstraction?

The penchant for realism in art goes back a long way. The closer a piece of art was to real life, the better. *Time* tells the story of Zeuxis, a Greek artist in the fifth century B.C., competing with another artist to see who could paint the most realistic picture. When his painting of grapes was unveiled, birds flew down and pecked at them. Surely he had won. But when the judges started to unveil the other painting, they were stunned.

THERE'S NO PLACE LIKE HOME... NOT ANYMORE

By Mike Mahoney

Harry Miller, once upon a time, felt he had everything he wanted in life in the palm of his hand. Today, he sits in a bare-bones back-room office in a Lake County foreign car dealership and wonders how it all slipped through his fingers. And he wonders, too, whether he will ever get the chance to build his dreams again.

Facing foreclosure isn't one of life's finest moments, and Harry made sure his real name wouldn't hit the paper. He doesn't need to remind his friends, neighbors and customers he lost a house.

Harry wonders whether he'll really see the fruits of his work again. It takes a long time to work your way out of $400,000 in debt, even when you're making $60,000 a year. You can read in Harry's eyes the realism of a gambler who risked too much at the big table — and lost.

Harry pulled in more than $1,000 a week before the bottom dropped out of the car market five years ago. He owned a $65,000 house in Mentor, and was building a $120,000 house in a plush part of Concord Township in Lake County. Payments on a nice boat, a Porsche and a Cadillac never seemed to strain the family budget. And, after all, he reasoned, he was a top-flight sales manager for one of the most successful auto dealerships in Cleveland.

That was before his dealership's sales fell from 150 cars a month to 45, and before mechanics at the dealership went on strike, warning folks away from the showroom. The owner cut his pay and lowered sales commissions for his best people, but when Harry protested he found himself cut out of the action completely.

On the street, job hunting looked discouraging. At home it was worse, with creditors monopolizing his family's life. He tried to pay off or sell off assets, working for another dealer at about half his former salary, but still he fell behind.

"So I went Chapter 13," Harry recalls, alluding to bankruptcy court. "But I defaulted. And I filed another Chapter 13 plan and defaulted on that.

"In the middle of the night my cars were gone. The bank took possession of my boat. Both my first and second houses were put into foreclosure proceedings."

The consequences for Miller's family have been steep. Four years later, Harry has lost the house he was building, none of his four children made it to college, and he faces at least another year of climbing out of old debts.

Two builders in Harry's wife's family, including the one who built the Concord home, went bankrupt. Two of the three real estate agencies he hired to sell the Concord house are out of business. He has access to only a fraction of his salary, since most goes to arrearages on his house payments, the IRS and other creditors he must repay.

"I had been in the business 17 years," he said. "I was at the head of one dealership, and I had always been an outstanding salesman. But they were putting pressure on me like I was a rookie, and the rookies were getting blown out the door.

"I had attained a status to the point where I thought I was secure. But there is no security."

In the '50s and '60s, foreclosure was something that happened in the Great Depression, a tragedy that played upon the stage long ago and far away. But maybe the speculative house fever of the 1970s — when anyone who invested in real estate made a profit — has caught up with the speculators like an avenging angel. The new reality of foreclosure is upon us. One in 20 homeowners are behind in their payments, mostly because nearly 1 in 10 workers are unemployed.

This kind of atmosphere breeds a sort of slavery, a new wave of feudalism that ties workers to present jobs for fear of abandoning security for a new one. It's keeping all but the most daring from moving to better opportunities, especially if it means entering the harsh world of real estate markets in another state, another city or even just an unfamiliar suburb. CONTINUED ON PAGE 28

"It's the American dream gone sour, the idea of ownership of the home. It was once considered the right of people. In 1950, seven out of ten Americans could afford to own a home, and in 1978 seven out of ten couldn't."

An article in *The Plain Dealer Magazine* making the point that few people can afford to own houses anymore got an appropriate Brad Holland illustration, a full-color painting showing a house going out of sight. Greg Paul art directed.

The veil was the painting. Zeuxis had fooled the birds, but his opponent had fooled the judges.

The coming of photography in the 1800s brought into question the idea that art was imitation. The camera was an instrument that could do the job better. Many artists then assumed a new role. Art became more than imitation; it became something with a value of its own.

Abstraction followed. Not that artists had not worked in abstractions before. But now abstraction became a dominant movement in art. Eventually, almost anything could pass for art: pieces of junk, objects that moved, combinations of common artifacts.

Not everyone was impressed. A writer in *True* told the story of a man who told Pablo Picasso that he didn't like modern paintings because they weren't realistic. When the man later showed Picasso a snapshot of his girl friend, Picasso asked, "My word, is she really as small as all that?"

With the Armory Show in 1913, when modern art made its debut in America, artists staying with realism as an art form lost favor with the critics. But the average person continued to admire the Norman Rockwell kind of artist. Late in his career, perhaps because Americans then enjoyed what *Newsweek* called the "vogue for the old," partly because Andrew Wyeth had made realism respectable again, Rockwell staged a comeback in the magazines. Several books came out offering his collected works. Even the critics reassessed the man.

Art as it has appeared in magazines has been slow to give up realism. Only in recent years have magazines made the move toward abstraction. But now the leaders among them and the smaller, specialized magazines, too, seem willing to experiment with unconventional art forms.

Rubbery buildings make this *St. Nicholas Magazine* illustration a visual oxymoron.

Visual oxymora

An oxymoron is a combination of opposing words, as in "loud silence" or "happy pessimist." Parting, it has been said, is such "sweet sorrow."

Novelist Peter DeVries used an oxymoron when he wrote, "Deep down he's shallow." The expression "He cried all the way to the bank" is a sort of oxymoron. (Writers who use "laughed all the way to the bank" miss the intended irony or paradox.) "New classic" is an oxymoron, although advertising copywriters do not seem to be aware of it.

Patrick Hughes deals with oxymorons and other oddments of speech in his *More on Oxymorons* (Penguin Books, New York, 1983). Among his quotations is one from Oscar Wilde: "He hadn't a single redeeming vice." Hughes also quotes a graffito that reads, "I'd give my right arm to be ambidextrous."

Oxymora are not confined to the verbal. They can occur in the visual as well. Some of the best art in magazines turns out to be oxymora.

Hughes says that in a visual oxymoron "the material of which a thing is made (or appears to be made) takes the place of the adjective, and the thing itself (or thing represented) takes the place of the noun." He offers as one example a photograph of a hedge trimmed to look like an ocean liner. The thing itself (the noun) is the liner; the hedge (the adjective) is the material from which the liner is made. He also describes a scene from a Buster Keaton movie, *The Boat,* in which an anchor thrown overboard floats rather than sinks. "In Keaton's anchor scene, part of the fun lies in the play between appearance and reality—the anchor looks like an anchor but it performs like a lifeboat."[8]

Early in the century the cartoonist Art Young "respectfully suggested" that some of the Carnegie libraries should be built to represent white elephants. Here is his drawing—an oxymoron—to go along with his suggestion.

Visual oxymora often involve raw material that doesn't behave in a normal way. Softness turns out to be stiff, and vice versa. The rubbery buildings shown nearby, taken from an early-in-the-century *St. Nicholas Magazine,* remind us that visual oxymora are nothing new. Perhaps the best-known oxymoronic painting is Salvador Dali's *The Persistence of Memory* with its melting watches.

Oxymora extend to shadows in drawings of figures, the shadows forming unexpected shapes or taking on a life of their own. For instance, a business person carrying a briefcase casts a shadow in the form of a dollar sign. David Suter, whose abstract, woodcut style makes him one of the nation's hottest magazine and newspaper illustrators, often relies on shadows to create his oxymora. The optical illusions he creates are in a class with the work of M. C. Escher, the late Dutch graphic artist.

Guy Billout is another popular magazine illustrator producing oxymora. His are usually in full color and in large sizes, their tight rendering contrasting with one small visual surprise somewhere in the composition, almost like the editorial cartoonist Pat Oliphant's Punk the Penguin.

Some of the best visual oxymora have appeared on magazine covers. Many students of magazines remember fondly Geo Lois's *Esquire* covers of the 1960s and the early *New York* covers.

To illustrate a cover blurb, "Home Is Where the Computer Is," *Newsweek* some time ago showed a painting of Whistler's mother; but the old woman, facing to the left as expected, sat at a computer keyboard and terminal. To illustrate an essay on daydreams, J. C. Suares for *Time* showed a short-haired, middle-aged man looking into the mirror to do a self-portrait. The mirror reflected the man's plainness, but the painting showed him as a virile, adventurous (he was carrying a gun), and even sinister.

A magazine like *Alaska* or *Sunset* or *National Geographic* would not resort to oxymora. Photographs, maps, and diagrams, good as they are in these magazines, play it safe. Nor would oxymora fit their editorial formulas.

But for many magazines visual oxymora—offbeat drawings, paintings, or photographs—are almost a necessity. They can both bemuse and amuse a magazine's readers. They are a good way to get readers involved in a magazine's contents, if only to find out what's going on in the art.

Sources of illustrations

One of the notable advantages of offset lithography is that almost anything from almost any source can be reproduced with little or no additional expense. In fact the flexibility and adaptability of offset has tempted editors of marginal publications to steal printed photographs and artwork from more affluent publications. The only reason these editors are not prosecuted is that their publications attract virtually no attention outside their own limited audiences. But clearly they are violating the law if the material they appropriate is copyrighted, and usually it is.

There are enough low-cost art and photographic services around to make such illegal activity unnecessary, even for the most mendicant of editors.

Up until 1978 any art published in books or magazines that were fifty-six years old or older could be clipped and used with or without credit at no cost to the user. After fifty-six years the original copyright (granted for a twenty-eight-year period) and the second and final copyright (granted for another twenty-eight-year period if it was applied for) had expired. The art had fallen into the public domain.

Now, because Congress changed the copyright law to make it conform to the law in other countries, things are more complicated. Editors and art directors are still free to lift material from publications whose copyrights expired before 1978. But material whose copyright periods extend beyond January 1978 and material copyrighted since then come under a different ruling: the copyrights last for the lifetime of the holders and for fifty years beyond that.

Still, plenty of material remains in the public domain. And if it is not yet there, you can always contact the owner and get permission to use it, possibly paying a small fee for the privilege. Also in the public domain are most government publications.

Although the price is right for public-domain art, the dated look of much of the material may be a problem.

If you can't find what you want from public-domain sources, you can turn to any of the hundreds of picture agencies and stock-art houses, to government agencies, to chambers of commerce, to trade and professional organizations, to businesses, to libraries, to historical societies, to other publications that sell or loan prints, or to publishers who make clipbooks available.[9]

Dover Publications (180 Varick Street, New York, New York 10014), remains a leader in this field, with its Pictorial Archives Series of inexpensive collections, mostly of public-domain art. Dover also puts out a Clip-Art Series of contemporary stock art. Hart Publishing Company, Inc.

Popular in literary and book-review magazines and in newspaper "forum" sections or on op-ed pages is line art with scratchy shading and barely defined features. Such art carries the feel of sophistication. This example by Sovetskii Khudozhnik comes from *Album: Fifty Years of Soviet Art: Graphic Arts,* Moscow, n.d.

Let's say your subject is love, and you need an illustration. You could use a piece of public-domain art like this. It appeared originally in *Werbezeichen: An Album,* Munich, n.d.

(15 West 4th Street, New York, New York 10012), has entered the stock-art field with some first-rate collections centering on, for instance, chairs, weather, dining and drinking, trades and professions, and animals.

Art Direction Book Company (19 West 44th Street, New York, New York 10036), publisher of *Art Direction* magazine, publishes and distributes a number of clipbooks of public-domain art.

Print magazine (6400 Goldsboro Road, Bethesda, Maryland 20817) offers *Creativ Collection* (with a missing "e"), a six-volume set of books containing ten thousand copyright-free illustrations, many from Europe. The collection is supplemented bimonthly on a subscription basis.

Among organizations offering a regularly issued clipboard service are Volk Studios (Pleasantville, New Jersey 08232) and Dynamics Graphics, Inc. (6707 N. Sheridan Road, Peoria, Illinois 61614). The work from these and similar organizations is contemporary, executed by a variety of artists in a kind of house style—adequate, slick, and not particularly exciting.

One of the newer stock-art services, Editor's Choice (Box 539, Kitty Hawk, North Carolina 27949), specializes in illustrations and headings for newsletters and company magazines. It started out as an art supplier for hospital magazines.

In addition to stock-art organizations you have hundreds of stock-photo organizations and agencies at your call. Some specialize; others offer a great variety of photographs. A stock-art house differs from a stock-photo house in that once you purchase the clipbook or service from a stock-art house, you are free to use it in any way that you wish and as often as you wish. A stock-photo house ordinarily grants you one-time use.

A problem with both of these sources, of course, is that ordinarily you would not get exclusive use. You face the chance that some other publication will show the same material.

An advantage of using stock photographs is that you can show scenes from all over the world without incurring travel costs. You also avoid seasonal changes, which could interfere with on-assignment shots.

Stock photographs come not only from stock-photo houses (more than 100 of these operate in the United States) but also from photographers who work from their own files to sell one-time rights. Some photographers make a career of shooting stock rather than on-assignment photographs. "For many years, shooting stock was considered the 'art of imaging the cliche,' thus stock came to have the reputation of being on the same visual aesthetic level as 'sitcoms' on . . . TV," notes Michal Heron, who cochairs the American Society of Magazine Photographers Stock Photography Committee. But that has changed. Heron points to "a new breed of stock photographers whose work consists of artful and imaginative photographs."[10]

Mario Micossi of Italy, whose works form part of the permanent collection of at least a dozen museums in Europe and the United States, frequently does his scratchboard drawings for American magazines, especially *The New Yorker.* This one appeared originally in *The Reporter,* no longer published.

Working from a catalog, you can order a selection of photographs by phone from a stock-photo house. For an extra fee the house will search for photographs that meet your needs.

(Opposite page)
Illustrators tend to specialize. Art directors pick from those who are available depending upon the style that is wanted and the subject to be illustrated. Some illustrators, like Mark Andresen, are versatile. They are at home in any number of styles. Here are a few random selections of his work from *New Age*.

Art from within

Accessible as it is, public-domain or stock art does not often exactly fit your needs. So when possible—when you can afford it—you order art to fit. Or you go to a staff artist or photographer.

If you have a staff artist or photographer, you make assignments as you would with a freelancer. The chief advantage is that the staffer will be readily available at a comparatively modest cost. But there has to be a continuous flow of work to make such an arrangement pay off.

You may want to go out on shoots with your photographer, to actually direct things or maybe just to act as an assistant. For a studio or set-up shot, you might want the photographer to take a Polaroid shot first, as a sort of test. This can save you later disappointment when contact prints and transparencies tell the awful story that you didn't get what you were after.

Working with artists and photographers, you are likely to face some tensions. An artist or photographer is not likely to be as awed by deadlines as you are. Nor will the artist take kindly to changes in submitted work, however necessary they may be from an editorial standpoint. As far as the artist is concerned, an art director always wants the work yesterday and decides what's really needed only after the final art is in.

As an art director you need not only sales skills to convince the editor that the decisions made are the right ones but also public relations and personnel management skills to see things from the artist's viewpoint. You may find that the artist has much more to offer than an ability to follow directions. A good artist may have ideas for illustrating the story or article that you didn't think of. You should be willing to listen to suggestions and consider alternative sketches or photos. A photographer may find new illustrative possibilities at the scene that weren't discussed when the two of you worked out the plans for photographic coverage.

You owe it to your artist to explain the nature of the story or article being illustrated, the reasons for the art, the intended use and placement of the art, and the nature of other art for that issue. Often you provide the artist with a rough layout of the planned pages and a copy of the manuscript to read.

Art from freelancers

Freelancers are everywhere. Once the word gets out that your publication is in the market, you will face a steady stream of them—illustrators and photographers nervously clutching their portfolios of examples. ("Sorry—what's the name again?—we really don't have many assignments that call for charcoal renderings of nudes.") In case you don't find the freelancer you want, you can turn to several directories now available.

One way to arrange for photographs in a faraway section of the country is to line up a member of the American Society of Magazine Photographers—easy enough to do if you refer to the *ASMP Book,* an annual that lists the organization's members. (ASMP's address is 205 Lexington Avenue, New York 10016.)

It is one thing to select prints or drawings from among those submitted

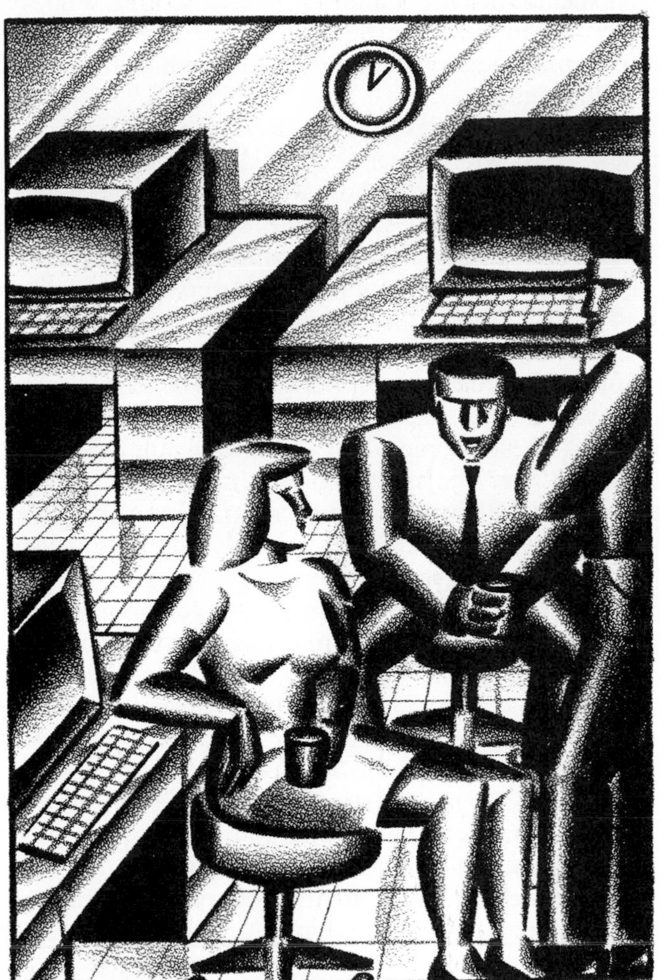

VANILLA
CHOC.
STRAW.
ICE
CREAM
15¢

on speculation. It is another to choose a photographer or illustrator from among those available and send that person off on an assignment. A portfolio may not be representative of what an artist can do under adverse conditions.

Another problem has to do with deadlines. You can't be sure that a new artist will deliver the work on time. So you tend to stick to a small stable of freelancers whose work and working habits you are familiar with.

Samuel Antupit says art directors have been negligent in developing new talent. They should be willing to try the work of the lesser-knowns, he argues. Only the small specialized magazines seem willing to heed his advice, if for no other reason than that they can't afford the big names.

The big magazines have shown some interest in using name artists in unfamiliar roles. Herb Bleiweiss, when he was art director for *Ladies' Home Journal,* used photographers on assignments they had not tried before. "These people when working in a new area approach problems with a fresh eye," he said. When *LHJ* ran Truman Capote's "A Christmas Memory," Bleiweiss used a painting by Andrew Wyeth to illustrate it.

Magazine art directors not only line up fine artists to do illustrations; they also encourage commercial artists to use fine-arts pieces as inspiration for illustrations. Sometimes the fine-arts-inspired pieces parody the originals, like those numerous takeoffs on Grant Wood's *American Gothic.* Sometimes the new pieces simply borrow the original artist's idea. Cover art for "No Exit: The Tragedy of Juvenile Court," an article featured in *Tropic,* the Sunday magazine of the Miami *Herald,* relied on an adaptation of an M. C. Escher optical illusion showing a stairway with no ending. In *Tropic*'s version the steps were crowded with juveniles on their way to nowhere. There was no attempt here to hide the source. If the readers recognized the art underlying the new illustration, their enjoyment increased. A publication carrying art like this should acknowledge the original art in a caption or a credit line, even though the adaptation involves art in the public domain.

Each story calls for its own individual technique," says Robert Quackenbush, who did the illustration for this right-hand opener for *Clipper.* "For this reason, I experiment with many mediums and tools to find the 'right' technique for a story." Note how well the art here is integrated with the display types; each has a bold, hand-carved look. (From *Clipper* Magazine, published and copyrighted by Pan American World Airways. Reproduced by permission.)

Settling on rates

Most newspapers employ photographers and artists full-time. Some magazines do, too. But many magazines and most book publishers buy art from freelancers. Some magazines and book publishers even buy their design from outside. What they pay for such services varies widely.

The Graphic Artists Guild suggests that a freelance designer charge from $250 to $850 for a spread, depending on the magazine's circulation and purpose and any color involvement. These prices would include tissues or rough layouts and a comp but not the pasteup. A cover would cost as much as $2000 for a large-circulation magazine with color. Again, the price would not include the pasteup.

Illustration prices would be added to these figures. Cover illustrators, using Graphic Artists Guild guidelines, ask from $1,000 to $2,500 for full-color cover art for company magazines. The rates for color cover art for consumer magazines go up to $3,500. Book jacket illustrations range from $450 to $3,000.[11]

A study of *Artist's Market,* published annually by Writer's Digest Books in Cincinnati, shows that many publishers using freelancers pay far less than the guild recommends. Clarkson N. Potter, a New York book publisher, pays $300 to $400 for a jacket design, $450 for text design, and $50 for a full-page illustration. *Yankee Magazine* pays from $200 to $750 for a color cover and from $100 to $550 for a black-and-white illustration inside.

Magazines that buy a lot of work from outside often adopt standard rates, upping them gradually for regular contributors, although the contributors may have to nudge the magazines occasionally. In other cases editors or art directors and freelancers or their reps negotiate rates. Every job is different. Some artists set their own rates—take them or leave them. Artists usually are willing to work for less for magazines than for advertising clients.

Because it is an association magazine serving editors of company magazines, *Communication World* is a showcase for artists and so is able to get work at modest fees. Of course its relatively low circulation helps, too. (Artists expect to be paid according to circulation.) A full-page full-color piece of art, commissioned by the magazine, brings the artist $250. Spot art in color brings $150; spot art in black and white brings $100. Small spots and second-rights art bring less. The usual procedure for this magazine is to ask for rough sketches first, then a finish. Sometimes the editor asks the artist to incorporate the best parts of two different sketches.[12]

The American Society of Magazine Photographers publishes a price guide for photographs. Prices asked by photographers also vary widely.

Photographers, more than illustrators, face high materials and equipment costs, which must be reflected in their rates. A professional photographer on assignment for a magazine is likely to charge $250 a day plus materials and expenses. Rates are negotiable, of course, with small magazines paying less than big magazines. Some magazines pay flat rates for photographs and as little as $25 per print or transparency.

Studio photography is often more expensive than on-location photography. Payment usually doubles if for some reason the magazine wants to retain the negatives.

Editors and art directors should know whether they are buying first-runs. If a picture was sold earlier to a magazine, the picture should cost less. If exclusivity is not a factor, going to a stock-photo house may be an even cheaper answer to photo acquisition.

A local photographer is likely to charge more for color than for black and white even though black and white these days is a little more expensive for the photographer to produce.

One continuing problem centers on the ownership of negatives. Does the buyer own them? Or does the photographer? What happens when the editor needs another print or wants to reuse the photograph in another issue or another publication? Freelancers like to hold onto negatives and get paid for each additional use, of course; but some editors manage to buy all rights to photos and negatives. Walter F. Giersbach, manager of international communications for the Dun & Bradstreet Corporation in New York, operates this way: "I have stopped short of having each still photographer sign over all rights to our company, but there is a clear verbal understanding that we own negatives and prints, can reorder prints for internal non-commercial use at a fair market price, and that negatives will be filed by the photographer or a laboratory that meets with our approval."[13]

Editors and art directors face a constant stream of art school graduates and established professionals showing off their portfolios and asking for assignments. These individuals try all kinds of approaches to get noticed. One San Francisco photographer adopted the name f. Stop Fitzgerald.

The newer freelancers are usually willing to work for minimum prices just to get started and build their portfolios.

The names of the best artists, photographers, and designers go into a file along with samples of their work. Calls go out later, and sometimes the freelancer lives up to promise.

Positioning your art

Ordinarily art, in a large size, would start out an article or feature. Smaller pieces might be scattered throughout the piece. Sometimes it is a good idea to let pieces of art evolve as the article progresses. In a magazine, for instance, each right-hand page might show the subject in a progressively more advanced stage.

Sometimes you might want to hold off your impact art until the reader turns the opening page; then you hit hard. Or you might want to sandwich the article between impressive opening and closing art, perhaps art that holds a one-two punch.

To cut down on units on a page, you might want to incorporate the title with the art, making a single visual unit.

Where space is a problem and one big illustration does not seem appropriate, you can order small drawings made, all the same size, to be used as inserts. Each of these drawings might occupy half-column squares or rectangles with the copy wrapping around them.

When three photographs, say, go on a spread, they work best when one is large, probably spanning the gutter, one is medium size, and one is small. But sometimes a series of same-size photographs works best, as when comparisons are to be made or when the subject of the article is to be shown with several expressions.

A large photograph that dominates a page doesn't have to be the busiest or most complicated of the batch; it could be a closeup of, say, a face. The largeness combines with the closeness to make the photograph all the more dramatic.

A thin white line or a thicker margin usually separates photographs shown together on a spread. But the art director can also butt them together, making them appear more as a unit. Butted-together photographs work best when they have different textures, subject matters, or camera

PERSONNEL

TAPPING MUNICIPAL EMPLOYEES' CREATIVE TALENTS

WILLIAM V. DONALDSON

■ OUR PRESENT national concern over cities and their problems has often focused on the shortage of qualified and imaginative public employees. The complexity of urban life and the quality of the new breed of elected officials have exposed the inadequacy and inflexibility of city government in general and the triumph of the "Peter Principle" in city staffing.

Attempts to use some of the new technologies to assist cities in solving some of the more critical problems have been ineffective because there are so few people who understand both cities and these new technologies. Proposals to improve the quality of city staffing have usually involved either ways of attracting bright young men and women to local government and improving the training they receive, as well as advanced training for existing public employees.

The critics of city government have done a much better job of identifying the problems of city staffing than they have done in suggesting workable solutions. By and large their best ideas have to do with doing more of what has been so unproductive in the past and overlooking some rather obvious and simple steps that most cities could take to help themselves.

It may be that the problems of our cities seem so large, complex, and unresolvable that we have overlooked the simple fact that we are not utilizing the human resources that are already on our payroll. A short visit with almost any city employee, whether he be in the refuse division, the police department, or on the planning staff, will prove my point. The creativity and imagination that is part of every man's nature is not being used as part of his job, but is being released in hobbies and non-employment-connected avocations. It is almost as if city government told the employee to keep his best qualities at home and bring to work only a slavish "follow-the-leader" dedication to "this is how we have always done it." This has produced frustrated and disgruntled employees whose actions are often unresponsive to the needs

Continued on page 13

NATION'S CITIES · AUGUST 1970 11

PERSONNEL

Continued from page 11

of citizens they are supposed to be serving. Decisions and rules are made at some level which is remote from the government's interaction with people and often reflect an attitude based on a remote idealization of the past and not on the needs of today.

While we lament what we perceive to be resistance to change on the part of public employees, the true situation may really only reflect a resistance to change which employees are not a part of or which they correctly know to be inappropriate. If we change our attitude and organization to allow employees to bring to bear their imagination and ideas on our problems, we might find an almost miraculous change in our ability to deal with municipal problems.

The city council of Scottsdale, Ariz., has encouraged a sense of participation on the part of city employees which is beginning to pay off with a new attitude of "why not?" rather than the old "it can't be done." To encourage employees to participate in decision-making, the city used the services of a psychiatrist to re-examine its system of evaluating employees. The upshot was we let employees evaluate the job and the city, as well as their own performance. The employee was encouraged to identify the areas where he felt he needed training or where he felt the organization could be changed to increase his efficiency or where in the city staff he felt he could be most useful.

We were surprised to find that an equipment operator wanted to be a renewal representative; a police lieutenant wanted to be finance director; a police captain wanted to run the data processing system; and a permit clerk wanted to be a planner. With a minimum of training, all of these people are now doing the jobs they identified better than they were doing before, and all of the city employees have been encouraged to look at the total city operation and the part they might play in it.

By asking employees about their interests, ideas, and concerns, we found that they were often able to make valuable suggestions in areas outside their normal jobs. To take advantage of these ideas we restructured the city organization to use teams when dealing with particular problems. A new program to deal with juvenile delinquency was devised by a team composed of the municipal judge, a police captain, the parks and recreation director, an administrative assistant, and a high school principal. The team developed its own staff, its own budget, and is operating its own program which cuts across departmental lines and is even involved in other jurisdictions such as the schools, which are not a part of our city government.

We also found that employees were anxious to expand their experiences and try other jobs. The public works department and parks and recreation department both started a program of rotating division heads. For six months an engineer would act as a building department chief, then serve six months as operating superintendent. This process was repeated with most of the professional employees in those two departments. This procedure resulted in the introduction of a number of new ideas and outlooks which have led to the reorganization of both departments.

We have found that employees are willing to reorganize their own work in order to take on new and different responsibilities. The mechanics in the equipment maintenance division were able to organize their work in such a way as to be available to work with four young men who are on juvenile court probation. At the end of 18 months, the men will graduate with General Educational Development (GED) certificates, mechanic's helpers certificates, and the feeling that someone cared enough about them to invest time and effort in their future. The mechanics who did the training designed the program and put it into operation with a minimum of help and an almost complete lack of supervision. Members of the fire department developed a program for Neighborhood Youth Corps members which has resulted in the employment of a number of them as permanent firemen, both in Scottsdale and in surrounding cities. The program was their idea and they carried it out.

The idea of involving everyone in the city in solving our problems seems to have the same virulent qualities as Asian flu—everybody gets it! We now have refuse workers trained as auxiliary firemen; street employees trained as special traffic officers; finance department employees working as juvenile counsellors, and Urban Corps students developing plans for a museum.

We opened our municipal intern program to any city employee who has completed college. Members of the fire, police, and parks and recreation departments have all completed six months of work in the city manager's office and have carried back to their departments a new appreciation for the total role that the city plays.

I am sure that many of the things we have done in Scottsdale may not be appropriate in other cities, but the idea of unlocking our employees' talents and creativity will work anywhere and produce the same total commitment to solving problems and responding to the changes in our cities. ■

WILLIAM V. DONALDSON *is City Manager of Scottsdale, Arizona.*

NATION'S CITIES · AUGUST 1970 13

Nation's Cities used a piece of line art to supply visual interest to a right-hand opener, and then, where the article continued, reused part of the art to help the reader adjust to the new page. Actually, the magazine reused two parts of the art—the bottom five figures and two more figures ahead of them in the line. Art directors are Louise Levine and Evelyn Sanford.

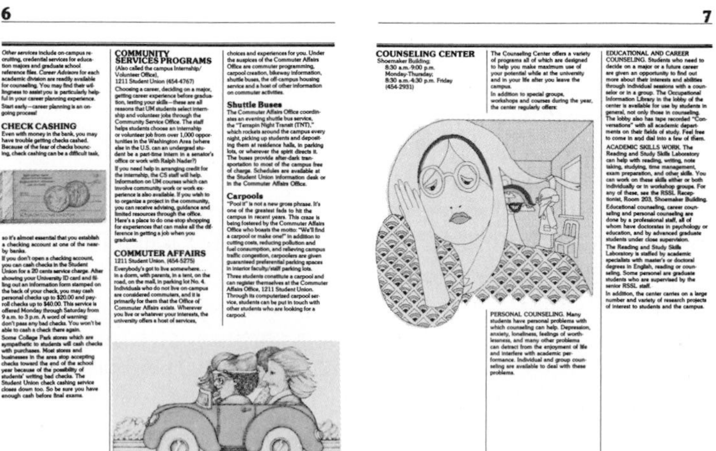

6

Other services include on-campus recruiting, credential services for education majors and graduate school reference files. *Career Advisors* for each academic division are readily available for counseling. You may find their willingness to assist you is particularly helpful in your career planning experience. Start early—career planning is an ongoing process!

CHECK CASHING

Even with money in the bank, you may have trouble getting checks cashed. Because of the fear of checks bouncing, check cashing can be a difficult task, so it's almost essential that you establish a checking account at one of the nearby banks.

If you don't open a checking account, you can cash checks in the Student Union for a 20 cents service charge. After showing your University ID card and filing out an information form stamped on the back of your check, you may cash personal checks up to $20.00 and payroll checks up to $40.00. This service is offered Monday through Saturday from 9 a.m. to 3 p.m. A word of warning: don't pass any bad checks. You won't be able to cash a check there again.

Some College Park stores which are sympathetic to students will cash checks with purchases. Most stores and businesses in the area stop accepting checks toward the end of the school year because of the possibility of students' writing bad checks. The Student Union check cashing service closes down too. So be sure you have enough cash before final exams.

COMMUNITY SERVICES PROGRAMS

(Also called the campus Internship/Volunteer Office),
1211 Student Union (454-4767)

Choosing a career, deciding on a major, getting career experience before graduation, testing your skills—these are all reasons that UM students select internship and volunteer jobs through the Community Service Office. The staff helps students choose an internship or volunteer job from over 1,000 opportunities in the Washington Area (where else in the U.S. can an undergrad student be a part-time intern in a senator's office or work with Ralph Nader?)

If you need help in arranging credit for the internship, the CS staff will help. Information on UM courses which can involve community work or work experience is also available. If you wish to to organize a project in the community, you can receive advising, guidance and limited resources through the office. Here's a place to do one-stop shopping for experiences that can make all the difference in getting a job when you graduate.

COMMUTER AFFAIRS

1211 Student Union, (454-5275)

Everybody's got to live somewhere . . . in a dorm, with parents, in a tent, on the road, on the mall, in parking lot No. 4. Individuals who do not live on-campus are considered commuters, and it is primarily for them that the Office of Commuter Affairs exists. Wherever you live or whatever your interests, the university offers a host of services, choices and experiences for you. Under the auspices of the Commuter Affairs Office are commuter programming, carpool creation, bikeway information, shuttle buses, the off-campus housing service and a host of other information on commuter activities.

Shuttle Buses

The Commuter Affairs Office coordinates an evening shuttle bus service, the "Terrapin Night Transit (TNT)," which rockets around the campus every night, picking up students and depositing them at residence halls, in parking lots, or wherever the spirit directs it. The buses provide after-dark transportation to most of the campus free of charge. Schedules are available at the Student Union information desk or in the Commuter Affairs Office.

Carpools

"Pool it" is not a new gross phrase. It's one of the greatest fads to hit the campus in recent years. This craze is being fostered by the Commuter Affairs Office who boasts the motto: "We'll find a carpool or make one!" In addition to cutting costs, reducing pollution and fuel consumption, and relieving campus traffic congestion, carpoolers are given guaranteed preferential parking spaces in interior faculty/staff parking lots.

Three students constitute a carpool and can register themselves at the Commuter Affairs Office, 1211 Student Union. Through its computerized carpool service, students can be put in touch with other students who are looking for a carpool.

7

COUNSELING CENTER

Shoemaker Building;
8:30 a.m.-9:00 p.m. Monday-Thursday;
8:30 a.m.-4:30 p.m. Friday
(454-2931)

The Counseling Center offers a variety of programs all of which are designed to help you make maximum use of your potential while at the university and in your life after you leave the campus.

In addition to special groups, workshops and courses during the year, the center regularly offers:

PERSONAL COUNSELING. Many students have personal problems with which counseling can help. Depression, anxiety, loneliness, feelings of worthlessness, and many other problems can detract from the enjoyment of life and interfere with academic performance. Individual and group counseling are available to deal with these problems.

EDUCATIONAL AND CAREER COUNSELING. Students who need to decide on a major or a future career are given an opportunity to find out more about their interests and abilities through individual sessions with a counselor or in a group. The Occupational Information Library in the lobby of the center is available for use by students in general, not only those in counseling. The lobby also has tape recorded "Conversations" with all academic departments on their fields of study. Feel free to come in and dial into a few of them.

ACADEMIC SKILLS WORK. The Reading and Study Skills Laboratory can help with reading, writing, note taking, studying, time management, exam preparation, and other skills. You can work on these skills either or both individually or in workshop groups. For any of these, see the RSSL Receptionist, Room 203, Shoemaker Building.

Educational counseling, career counseling and personal counseling are done by a professional staff, all of whom have doctorates in psychology or education, and by advanced graduate students under close supervision.

The Reading and Study Skills Laboratory is staffed by academic specialists with master's or doctoral degrees in English, reading or counseling. Some personal are graduate students who are supervised by the senior RSSL staff.

In addition, the center carries on a large number and variety of research projects of interest to students and the campus.

A University of Maryland student handbook uses the ideal number of art pieces (three) for one of its spreads, with one piece dominating the others. The pieces also take different shapes. The art could be classed as funky. Roz Hiebert edited this 54-page book; Heidi Kingsley designed it.

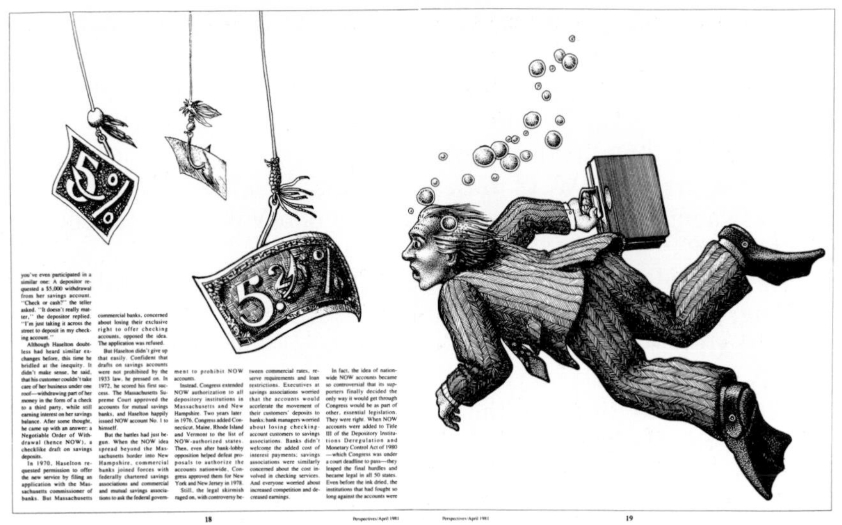

you've even participated in a similar one: A depositor requested a $5,000 withdrawal from her savings account. "Check or cash?" the teller asked. "It doesn't really matter," the depositor replied. "I'm just taking it across the street to deposit in my checking account."

Although Haselton doubtless had heard similar exchanges before, this time he bridled at the inequity. It didn't make sense, he said, that his customer couldn't take care of her business under one roof—withdrawing part of her money in the form of a check to a third party, while still earning interest on her savings balance. After some thought, he came up with an answer: a Negotiable Order of Withdrawal (hence NOW), a checklike draft on savings deposits.

In 1970, Haselton requested permission to offer the new service by filing an application with the Massachusetts commissioner of banks. But Massachusetts commercial banks, concerned about losing their exclusive right to offer checking accounts, opposed the idea. The application was refused.

But Haselton didn't give up that easily. Confident that drafts on savings accounts were not prohibited by the 1933 law, he pressed on. In 1972, he scored his first success. The Massachusetts Supreme Court approved the accounts for mutual savings banks, and Haselton happily issued NOW account No. 1 to himself.

But the battles had just begun. When the NOW idea spread beyond the Massachusetts border into New Hampshire, commercial banks joined forces with federally chartered savings associations and commercial and mutual savings associations to ask the federal government to prohibit NOW accounts.

Instead, Congress extended NOW authorization to all depository institutions in Massachusetts and New Hampshire. Two years later in 1976, Congress added Connecticut, Maine, Rhode Island and Vermont to the list of NOW-authorized states. Then, even after bank-lobby opposition helped defeat proposals to authorize the accounts nationwide, Congress approved them for New York and New Jersey in 1978.

Still, the legal skirmish raged on, with controversy between commercial rates, reserve requirements and loan restrictions. Executives at savings associations worried that the accounts would accelerate the movement of their customers' deposits to banks; bank managers worried about losing checking-account customers to savings associations. Banks didn't welcome the added cost of interest payments; savings associations were similarly concerned about the cost involved in checking services. And everyone worried about increased competition and decreased earnings.

In fact, the idea of nationwide NOW accounts became so controversial that its supporters finally decided the only way it would get through Congress would be as part of other, essential legislation. They were right. When NOW accounts were added to Title III of the Depository Institutions Deregulation and Monetary Control Act of 1980—which Congress was under a court deadline to pass—they leaped the final hurdles and became legal in all 50 states. Even before the ink dried, the institutions that had fought so long against the accounts were

18 Perspectives/April 1981 Perspectives/April 1981 19

Pennzoil Perspectives, an 11 × 13 monthly, lets art dominate these two pages, part of a seven-page article on the interest-bearing NOW checking accounts offered by banks. This all-in-line drawing by R. Edwards helps the copy make the point that the NOW accounts lure people as bait lures fish. (© 1981 by the Pennzoil Company, Houston. Reprinted by permission.)

angles. Then they don't lose their identity. They don't become a montage.

Photographers sometimes take their pictures from nature's nooks, allowing foliage and rock formations, dark and out of focus, to frame something more important. A magazine designer can do the same thing, using artwork so that there is room inside for an article title and some columns of copy. The beauty of framing a page or spread is that the elements in the design hold together, as though cupped in the hands made famous by Allstate. There is something cozy about frame layout. The art does not have to completely surround the copy. It can form a cul-de-sac into which the type is placed. Or the art can go all the way across a spread and bleed to four sides, with the type then surprinted or reversed in a neutral area.

Some company magazines pick out an employee at random for each issue and run that employee's picture near the masthead or maybe on the back page with this kind of caption: "Published bimonthly for employees like Charles B. Rogers. . . ." It is a good way to give some attention to an employee who otherwise would not get any, but the practice may strike some readers as condescending or mere spacefilling.

Using art imaginatively

What the art director tries to do is come up with the one visualization that will tell the story immediately and forcefully. One indication of Otto Storch's genius was the illustration he commissioned for a *McCall's* article on infidelity: a big red apple with a couple of bites taken out of it. Nothing else. To illustrate an article entitled "Are the Arts Endangered in Our Schools?" *Better Homes & Gardens* showed a realistic violin with its neck tied into a knot.

When Herb Bleiweiss of *Ladies' Home Journal* had the job of illustrating a feature on women's nightgowns, he didn't show the women in typical poses; he caught them in action, including one woman being rescued from a burning building.

For a feature on the builds of athletes, *Esquire* showed actual-size photos of the biceps of Arnold Schwarzenegger, the neck of Mean Joe

Greene, the forearm of Rod Laver, the hand of Robyn C. Smith, and the thigh of Pele.

For an article entitled "What To Do in Case of Armed Robbery," *Go,* Goodyear's dealer magazine, showed a frightening close-up of a gun pointing straight out at the reader.

For a feature on "9 Ways to Beat Winter," *Small World,* the magazine for Volkswagen owners, showed a drawing of a VW, head on, enclosed in giant earmuffs.

For a feature on "Values & Violence in Sports: The Morality of Bone Crushing," *Psychology Today* showed a retouched close-up photograph of a football player, with a halo over his head and horns growing out of his curly hair.

As cover art to illustrate the blurb "Gumps: Will Its Next Owner Be the Bull in the China Shop?" *California Living,* the magazine of the San Francisco *Sunday Examiner & Chronicle,* showed a real bull in this famous San Francisco carriage-trade store. The effect was achieved by a San Francisco photography studio, Murealism, which put together a collage of three black-and-white shots of the store's interior and one of a Texas longhorn—with horns. Each print was hand tinted. Taking some artistic license, Bennett Hall of Murealism photographically rearranged the store, but the interior was easily recognized as Gumps by San Francisco readers. The big problem for Murealism involved finding a bull with horns. (They're bred these days without horns so that they won't gouge each other in the feedlots.) Hall finally found one on a ranch in nearby Half Moon Bay.

To illustrate the title "Aging is Coming of Age: Society Scraps a Stereotype," Polly Pattison, designer for *Soundings,* published by Pacific Mutual, came up with a rocking chair crammed into a garbage can. It was the second part of a one-two visual; the cover showed a rocking chair in a more traditional lace-curtain setting.

To go with a feature on privacy (and the lack of it), Ted Thai for *Time* posed the chairman of a government privacy commission so that he could be photographed through a keyhole. The portrait, then, when it ran in the magazine was framed with a keyhole-shaped black border.

To promote an article recognizing the emergence of a "hardline culture" at the beginning of the 1980s, *Esquire* ran a picture of John Wayne, with wings, waste deep in clouds. The blurb read, "Somewhere the Duke is Smiling."

When *Parade* ran Jane Fonda on its cover, it showed her angry, her fists clenched. And rightly so, for the cover blurb read, "Jane Fonda: Why Is She Hollywood's Angry Woman?" Loring Eutemy's illustration for an article in *Ladies' Home Journal,* " 'My Husband Thinks He's My Father,' " showed a wife in a baby carriage and a husband looking proud and tickling her under her chin.

The usual procedure on a magazine is to accept or assign an article and later go looking for the art. In this visual age an argument can be made for doing it the other way around: dream up some great art and then have someone write to fit it.

The art for a piece can be nothing more than texture. If the subject is forests, you can make a rubbing or painting from a piece of bark and use it as a piece of line art. If the subject is accidents, you can make a rubbing or printing from a piece of bandage cloth.

The style of technique of illustration doesn't have to have an obvious connection with the subject matter. Art Young, the socialist cartoonist,

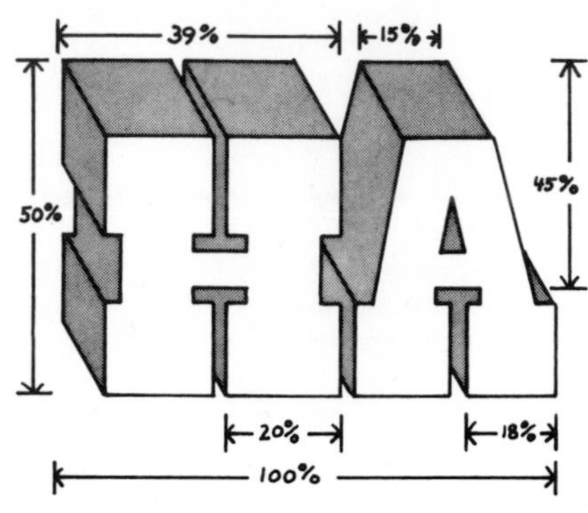

John Simon in one of his theater columns in *New York* makes the point that critics should not feel obligated to report on the length or loudness of the laughter of the audience for any given play. "For that you could install laugh-and-applause meters in the theaters and publish graphs instead of reviews." To illustrate the column, Beth Charney lettered a laugh complete with some imaginary measurements.

used an outdated drawing style, not unlike that of a crude woodcut, to fight capitalism and social injustice. Young considered the matter later in one of his autobiographies. "Here I was, a man commonly thought to be 'ahead of the procession' in ideas, who was for progress and change, and with little reverence for tradition, and yet my style was 'archaic,' reminiscent of the ancient past."[14]

Nor does the artist have to use traditional media. Art directors recently have encouraged their illustrators to experiment. The collage has lately become popular: the pasting together of fragments of art, already-printed art, or papers and textiles. These can be used to form an abstraction or something that, viewed from a distance, looks quite representational. Some art directors are even using photographs of pieces of sculpture done especially for their magazines. For a cover on "Suburbia: A Myth Challenged," *Time* used a color photo of a needlepoint picture.

What kind of art you settle for depends upon what you want your art to do. Do you want it to be informative? Then you ask for realism, either in photographs or illustrations. Do you want it to supply mood for the article or story? Then you ask for abstraction, something as simple, say, as a black border to symbolize death. Do you want it simply to decorate your page? Then you ask for ornament.

The motive may be to keep art costs down, or it may be to help unify pages; whichever, some publications take a single piece of art and use it—or parts of it—several times in an issue. The piece, uncropped, may appear full-size at the beginning of the article and then in sections on the table of contents page and on later pages in the article. *The New Yorker* often reuses the spot illustrations that decorate some of its pages.

Using cartoons

The cartoon continues to play an important role—sometimes diversionary, sometimes propagandistic—for many publications. Newspapers run *editorial cartoons* on their editorial pages to bring current events into sharp, if distorted, focus. And they give over most of a page daily to a selection of *comic strips* purchased from feature syndicates.

Gag cartoons are largely the province of magazines. Whereas editorial cartoons and comic strips are done on a salary or contract basis, gag cartoons are done on speculation by freelancers. The cartoon editors on magazines buy them occasionally, paying from $10 to $200 or more for each one, and keep them ready to drop into holes in the back of the book. These

You can put Zipatone shading on a line drawing and still reproduce the drawing in line. When you use gray markers instead (far right), your drawing has to be reproduced as a highlight (or dropout) halftone.

cartoons are used primarily as fillers. But *The New Yorker,* the magazine that really developed this art form in America, continues to use gag cartoons as a principal element of editorial display.

A fourth kind of cartoon is the *humorous illustration,* used as any illustration might be used for stories, articles, or features deserving of a light touch.

Cartoons have a universal appeal. They fit all kinds of publications, from the lowbrow *National Enquirer* to sophisticated magazines like *The Economist.* A serious-minded but spritely British weekly with a U.S. edition, *The Economist* sprinkles anonymously drawn cartoon illustrations throughout its pages to bring visual touches to its stories and articles.

Some publications that do not originate their own cartoons reprint them from other magazines—for a fee or maybe, in some cases, for just a credit line. Of course permissions need to be arranged. The New York *Times,* which doesn't have its own editorial cartoonist, reprints editorial cartoons from other newspapers in its Sunday "The Week in Review" section. Weekly newsmagazines like *Time, Newsweek,* and *U.S. News & World Report* republish editorial cartoons from newspapers and the syndicates. Cartoonists appreciate the extra exposure.

When they run editorial cartoons from newspapers, the newsmagazines often add color, something easy enough to do. A staff artist makes an overlay for each color desired. The newsmagazines also occasionally break an editorial cartoon into two parts and run the parts at opposite ends of a page.

Some editors are all-too-willing to tamper with a cartoonist's caption—to omit it even when it may be necessary to the meaning or to change its wording. It is one thing to change a few words of a manuscript without consulting the author; it is another to change a word or two in a four- or five-word caption. A "minor" caption change may represent a 25 or even 50 percent change in the cartoonist's "manuscript."

There are two kinds of captions for editorial cartoons: those that represent further comment of the cartoonist and those that represent conversation coming from someone within the cartoon—from the character with his mouth open. Only in the latter case should quotation marks be used.

In gag cartoons—as distinguished from editorial cartoons—the caption (or gagline) always carries quotation marks. Captions without quotation marks—descriptive captions—belong above a cartoon. Captions in quotes go below.

Other suggestions to consider in using cartoons are these:

1. *Avoid cropping a cartoon.* If it is well drawn—and why buy it if it is not?—it has been deliberately composed for a square or vertical or horizontal showing. An expanse of "unused" foreground in a farm scene, for instance, should not be an open invitation to change a vertical into a horizontal.
2. *Do not reduce the cartoon to a size where the reader has to strain to get its message or enjoy its hilarity.* The move to miniatures has reduced the effectiveness of comic strips in our newspapers. In magazines it is better to run one or two generous-size gag cartoons than a half dozen the size of postage stamps. *World Press Review* does its readers a service by reprinting editorial cartoons from all over to amplify the text matter, but they are so small that you can't always make them out. To make matters worse, the cartoons some-

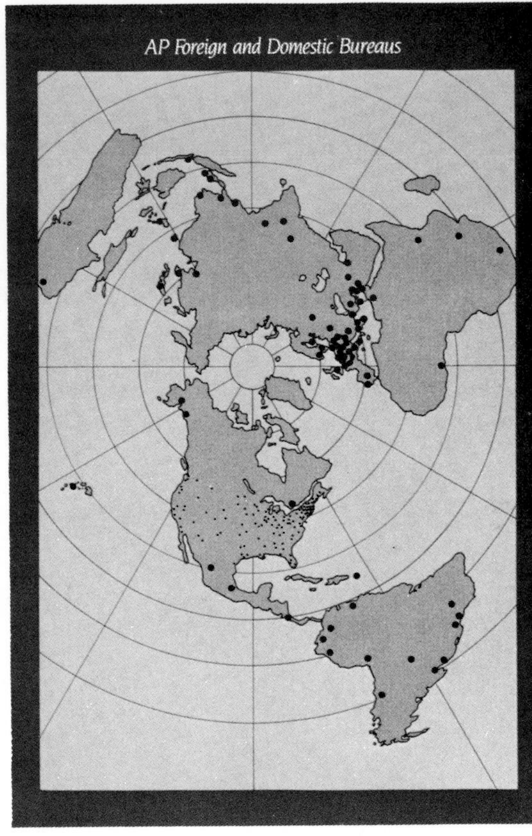

Sheila Norman-Culp, editor of *AP World,* sent a list of AP bureaus to an outside designer with instructions to spot them on a world map. Unfortunately, the designer did not know much about geography and placed dots nowhere near where some of the bureaus are located. Because of an impending deadline, Norman-Culp, with no art background, had to do the spotting herself. She bought some Lettraset dots and spent four hours putting them into place. She had to make the domestic bureaus with smaller dots because she ran out of big dots. Still, the map turned out to be a useful quick guide to all the places AP operates. (From the booklet *Associated Press: Reporting the World.)*

times appear in tint blocks, which reduce contrast and therefore readability.

3. *Don't consider the cartoon as simply a change of page texture, a visual oasis in a landscape of body copy.* Treat it as you would any other feature in your publication. Subject it to the same rigid test of usefulness to the reader that you would employ with a piece of copy. Thanks to paper patches and white paint, a cartoon can be corrected by its originator as easily as a piece of copy can be corrected by a writer.
4. *Guard against too big a dose of cartoons in a single issue.* The magazine that brings a half dozen gag cartoons together on a single spread or the newspaper that crowds several editorial cartoons onto the editorial page is not giving any of the cartoons much chance to make a point.

Charts, graphs, tables, maps, and diagrams

When the text matter deals with statistics, you can amplify, clarify, or summarize them with charts, graphs, or tables. Purely abstract thoughts and information already simple enough to understand do not lend themselves to charts, graphs, or tables, but almost everything else does. What you need to look for is what Matthew P. Murgio in his *Communications Graphics* has described as a "visual handle."

Chocolatier, a magazine that runs recipes, uses tiny Hershey kisses in silhouette to indicate the degree of difficulty. One kiss indicates that the recipe is foolproof. Anyone can handle it. Two kisses indicate that the recipe is "fairly simple." Three indicate that the recipe requires skill and advance preparation.

You can use a *flow chart* to show how machinery works, an *organization chart* to show how a company functions, a *line graph* or *bar chart* to show growth in numbers over a given period of time, or a *pie chart* to show percentages of a whole.

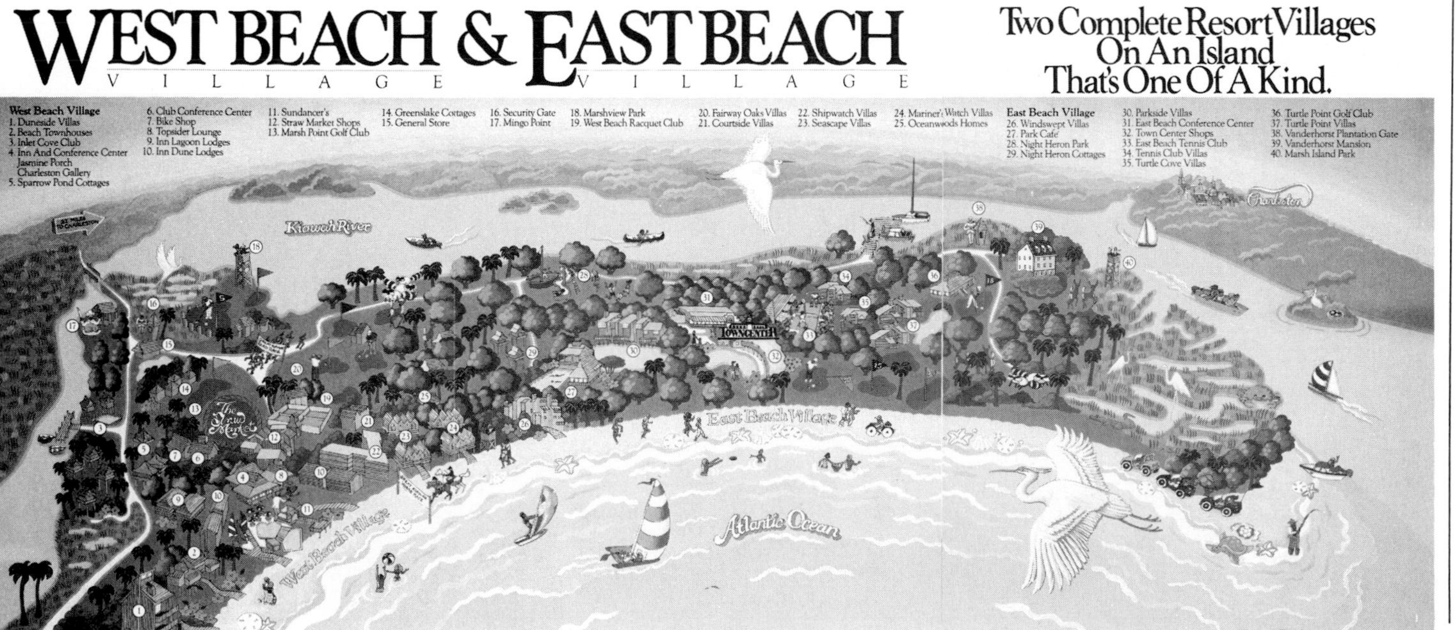

Kiawah, a magazine published to promote Kiawah Island Resort, located twenty-one miles south of historic Charleston on the South Carolina coast, used a gatefold cover for one of its issues that opens up to a full-color three-page bird's-eye-view map of the resort's two villages. A listing, across the top, of attractions and accommodations is keyed to the drawings included in the map. Brenda Losey is the illustrator; Christopher Connerly of Austin Kelley Advertising, Inc., the art director.

Plant Locations: Worldwide

● Consumer Products Group
▲ Chemical Products Group

With the acquisition of the Stauffer Chemical Co., Chesebrough-Pond's Inc. now has a total of 94 domestic and 50 international manufacturing plants. In addition, the company uses the facilities of manufacturing and selling representatives in many other important markets throughout the world.

Hendrik Hertzberg built an entire book around a single graph—page after page of dots, one million of them. "This book is a yardstick, a ruler divided into a million parts instead of a dozen," he said in his introduction. "The chief value of the book is as an aid to comprehension, and to contemplation. By riffling slowly through its pages, the reader may discover precisely what is meant by one million." At various intervals the reader finds a blank spot where a dot is supposed to be; a line runs from that blank spot out into the margin, and there the dot is reproduced with a caption. Dot No. 2, for instance, represents the "population of the Garden of Eden," Dot No. 46,399 the "number of times the word 'and' appears in the King James Bible," Dot No. 407,316 the number of "U.S. soldiers killed in World War II."[15]

Ordinary charts and graphs are clear enough, but an artist can heighten their impact by changing them to what *U.S. News & World Report* calls pictographs: drawings in which lines, bars, or circles have been converted to representational art shown in perspective. For instance, people can be shown in place of bars or a silver dollar in place of a pie chart. But when using pictographs, you must make certain the scale is not distorted.[16]

With the acquisition of Stauffer Chemical Company, Chesebrough-Pond's, Inc. in its *Chesebrough-Pond's World* ran a map showing the worldwide locations of its many plants. The map, printed in a solid blue, is really an abstraction, with straight edges identifying the various continents. Such handling makes the dots and triangles—plant locations—stand out better than they would in ordinary map handling. Corporate Annual Reports, Inc., New York, designed the map.

A bar chart with its caption in the first column lines up with a box at the bottom of the fourth column to bring unity to this spread from *The Aging Ear,* one of a series of six booklets based on *The Hurt That Does Not Show,* a print supplement to the PBS series on difficulties in hearing conversation. Design by Ellen Shapiro; art by Steven Guarnaccia. The booklets were made possible by a grant from the Grace Foundation, Inc.

West High School, Iowa City, Iowa, found it possible in an issue of its newsmagazine to fully identify all its seniors shown in a large and rather informal group shot by including a tracing with the printed photograph. A long caption referred to the numbers in the faces. The artist gave the line drawing a photographic look by using Zipatone to imitate the tones of the photographs. The line drawing ran slightly smaller and just below the photograph.

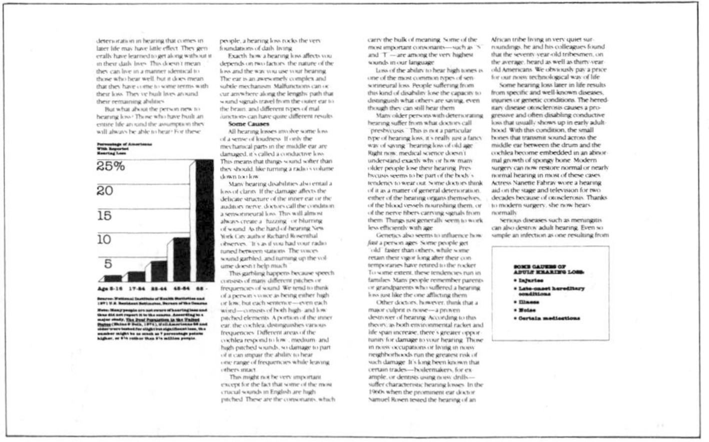

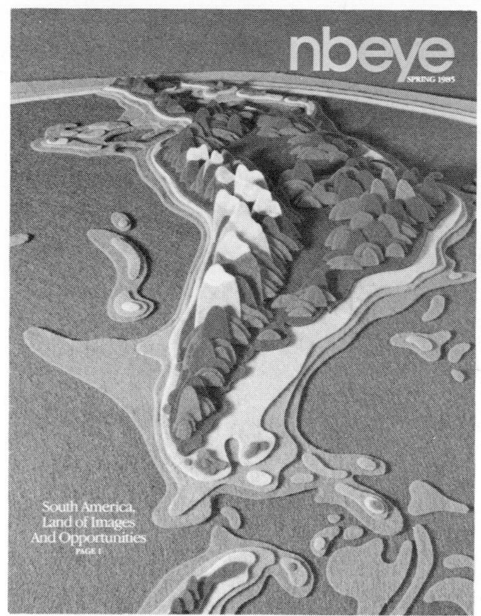

Ray Ameijide, for this cover art, constructed a map of South America from flannel cloth. The three-dimensional map with its exaggerated mountains and coast lines was then photographed in full color. *nbeye* is a company magazine published by Nabisco Brands, Inc., East Hanover, New Jersey. The back cover is given over to a table of contents and masthead, with space at the bottom for a mailing label.

You can make a *table* more useful by careful organization of material and skillful use of color, tint blocks, and rules. You can add drama to a *map* by showing it in perspective, by showing its topography as well as its outline, or by simplifying and stylizing its outline. It may even be desirable to distort a map to make a point (provided the reader understands), as an airline did in its advertising to dramatize the fact that its fast planes had brought Europe and North America close together.

One of the occasional features of *Los Angeles Times Magazine,* which began in 1985, has been the bird's-eye-view maps of Southern California communities. They are colorful, close up, and almost cartoonlike; and they help put the towns and communities into context with the area. A back-cover gatefold gives them the room they need. Paul Shaffer of Westwood is the artist.

You can change the shape of a map to make it better fit its assigned space by viewing it from an unusual angle. And the change does not have to affect its accuracy. *USA Today* on its weather page likes to show a large map of the United States, but it doesn't want the map to go too far down the page. So it bends it back to give the reader a sort of worm's-eye view. You can also "condense" a map by turning it to the left or right, giving the reader a three-quarters view. You might want to do that if you have to show a U.S. map, basically a horizontal, in a vertical space.

You can also present statistical and other information through *diagrams.* To illustrate "What a Way to Make a Living," an article about the injuries suffered by the running backs in professional football, *Sports Illustrated* ran a drawing of a player, standing, facing the front. The various injuries to the players were listed at the side. Ruled lines connected the various listings to the various parts of the body, allowing readers to see at a glance where the concentration of injuries was.

It is possible to make a chart out of an ordinary photograph. Suppose you want to illustrate an article on high school dropouts. You can take an ordinary shot of students walking in a school hallway, and white-out a scattered portion of them in proportion to real dropout numbers.

Style in art

On his deathbed in 1898, Aubrey Beardsley, only 25, asked his friends to "burn all the indecent poems and drawings."[17] Fortunately his plea went unheeded, and today publishers continue to bring out collections of Beardsley's work.

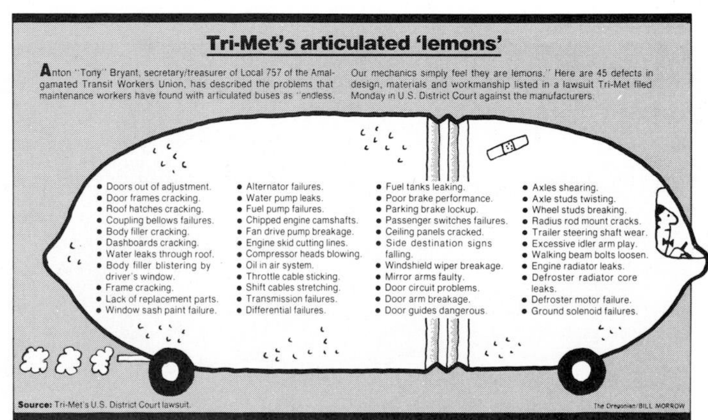

Portland's Tri-Met transportation system had some trouble with its new "articulated" buses—long buses that bend in the middle to make turns. Mechanics saw the buses as lemons, so Bill Morrow drew one that way to use as a chart listing the various problems. He did an amberlith overlay and marked it for a 15% screen of the tone area. He could have used Zipatone, but he finds this system easier. (Courtesy of *The Oregonian.*)

Beardsley had shocked Victorian England with erotic drawings that, by today's standards, seem tame enough. Influenced by Japanese prints, by artists like James Abbott McNeill Whistler, and by what came to be known as the Arts and Crafts Movement, Beardsley brought out his own collections and supplied illustrations for books by Oscar Wilde, among other writers. He also served as art editor of *The Yellow Book,* an avant-garde magazine published in London.

Along with artists like Edvard Munch, Henri de Toulouse-Lautrec, and Paul Gauguin, Beardsley became part of the Art Nouveau movement with its decorative, curving lines and patterns taken from nature. "Cigarette-smoke art," some critics called it. Flowers, peacocks, and nymphs, at least for Beardsley, became favorite subjects.

An example of Art Nouveau from *The Studio.*

During his short life Beardsley made countless black-and-white line drawings, many for publication. His drawings were as remarkable for their fine design as for their quality of line and draftsmanship. Art Nouveau, as practiced by Beardsley, served as a good example of coordination of art and design in publications.

Art Nouveau, which originated around 1870, died out at the beginning of World War I, but it came back again, as art styles and art movements do, in the 1960s. Art Nouveau was big with the hippies, who added a psychedelic touch. Many of the underground papers of the 1960s and early 1970s and some of the alternative papers of today have an Art Nouveau feel.

Art Deco was a style popular from about 1910 to 1940, with revivals of interest since. It affected architects as well as graphic and industrial designers. You can see it in the Chrysler Building and Radio City Music Hall in New York. It made wide use of geometric forms. Some people refer to it as "modernistic" or "skyscraper modern." It was a stern reaction to what some considered the excesses of Art Nouveau.

In the 1920s the Bauhaus made its influence felt; the look was orderly, geometric, functional. The Bauhaus look never did die out. It took a slightly more elegant turn in the 1950s with the introduction of Swiss design; the magazine page was still tightly organized, but some of the stiffness was gone.

Art Nouveau made a comeback in the 1960s, as did almost every art style. The 1960s were a decade of revival and experimentation. Among the new styles were op art, with its illusions in color and shape; pop art, with its attachment to the comic strip and high-camp packaging; and the psychedelic look, with its sliding blobs of color in weird combinations, its illegible typefaces expanded, condensed, and contorted to fit curved spaces.

To execute this small-town winter scene, Professor Glenn Hanson of the University of Illinois Department of Journalism used nylon-tip pens and, finally, some Zipatone at the top for the sky. Hanson's composition leads you right into the center of the picture. He used a low horizon line to give you almost a worm's-eye-view. He provided three distinct textures: the Zipatone dot-pattern, the tree-top lace-pattern, and the horizontal-line pattern for the shading on the buildings and the shadows in the snow.

More recently "new wave" and "punk" styles have made themselves felt, especially in fashion magazines. With so much freedom in art and design these days it is hard to separate one style from another. We have lived through a lot of crossover.

Some art pieces are clearly Art Nouveau or Art Deco or pop art or new wave. Other pieces don't fall so neatly into categories. They are an amalgamation of styles, or they represent a one-of-a-kind style. The work of some artists is immediately recognizable. Milt Glaser is one such artist. So is Guy Billout. You can easily tell a Guy Billout illustration by its tight architectural quality, its bigness contrasted with smallness, and its touch of irony. You've seen his covers on *Time, New York, Vogue, Fortune,* and other magazines. Chapter 7 reproduces one of his covers.

Art techniques

Preferences in art styles change. So do preferences in techniques. Brush painting, pallet knife painting, wash drawing, line drawing, scratchboard drawing, pencil drawing, felt- and nylon-tip drawing—they all go in and out of favor with artists and art directors. Some techniques require tight handling, some a loose flair. Every imaginable tool is used on every kind of surface. In the 1960s, for instance, many illustrators were working in washes on glossy paper not meant to take washes. This resulted in tones that seemed to shrivel, like water on an oily surface.

Print expressed concern that illustrators are preoccupied with techniques—at the expense of content. Maybe so. But illustrators need to constantly experiment with their styles and techniques, and art directors should encourage them to do so.

Now, of course, everyone is interested in techniques that involve the computer. Some marvelous pieces of art are being created, and we are getting away from simply showing off what the new medium can do. We are finding that the medium not only saves time; it opens new techniques and even styles to us.

The InterCAD 2040, one piece of equipment, "lets the illustrator concentrate on concept and design while it provides the automated drawing tools to enhance productivity." It becomes an "original art library. Illustrations can be easily retrieved for modification and used in new illustrations by electronic cut and paste. . . . The illustrator doesn't need computer expertise, just illustrating talent."[18]

One way an artist can get tone into a line drawing is by doing the art in ink on textured paper and then using a grease crayon for shading. This detail from a Horace Greeley drawing by the author shows the texture offered by Glarco No. 12 paper.

Artists working for publications make use of two kinds of computer graphics systems. One is a paint system that manipulates dots (or pixels); the other is a draw system, refined to a point now where lines do not have to look jagged, as they did at first.

One of the computer painting techniques results in an airbrush look. The computer artist touches one part of an image and calls for a dark color, then touches another part and calls for a light color. The computer mixes the colors to a gradation between.

Some computer art systems make use of a hand-held "mouse" to position a cursor on a screen. Others allow you to draw on a screen by using a stylus interface on a digitizing tablet.

The resulting images are digital images that, displayed on the screen, can be reconstructed in many ways. "The power to create and—more importantly—to modify visual images makes digital image-processing machines important tools for magazine publishers who need to turn out good-looking charts and graphs and hard hitting illustrations on a tight schedule and limited budgets," says Jack Powers, who teaches at Pratt's Center for Computer Graphics in Design in New York.[19]

A photographer has to move in close and get just the right lighting to show that someone is wearing a contact lens. That is what Jim Bambenek did for this *Rochester Methodist Hospital News* cover photo. Editor-designer Bev Parker bleeds the photo all around and finds just the right place to reverse the title and blurb.

Planning the art's reproduction

Photographers who consider themselves fine artists and look down their noses at photojournalists often turn out prints that, although beautiful, may not be suitable for reproduction. For instance, a soft-focus shot may create an excellent mood, but the offset camera has trouble picking up the subtleties, and printing on a web press further reduces fidelity.

You can seldom improve a photograph through reproduction. You must pick out a quality photograph to begin with—one in focus with a wide tonal range. Some editors make the mistake of trying to salvage a poor photograph by using a novel reproduction technique. If you must go to press with a poor quality photograph, the best thing to do is run it small.

It is not a good idea to put photographs of varying quality—some light, some dark—on the same page or spread. Looking over the photographs when they come in, you should, if possible, design the spreads to keep photographs of similar quality together. For instance, all the underexposed photos should go on one spread. Skillful camera work at the offset plant and careful inking can bring out some good qualities in these photographs. But they should be kept together.

Newspapers, especially, like to put thin rules at the edges of their halftones to better define their rectangular shapes. Sometimes magazines, to make one article look different from others in an issue, outline photographs for that one article.

Is art necessary?

Not every article and story needs art in the traditional sense. Carefully selected display typography, tastefully arranged with generous amounts of white space, can be art enough.

Some subjects simply do not lend themselves to art. A subject can be too momentous, too tragic, too lofty to picture. In this case art would be at best redundant, at worst anticlimactic.

And when as art director you can't afford art or you find only mediocre photography for a feature, you should be willing to design your pages without art. A quiet, even stilted spread is preferable to an amateurish one.

Creating art with words

There is a kind of art, too, that comes through to the reader in the words on the page—what they say and how they say it.

Caroline Green, a freelance writer, sees the writer as someone working out of a giant crayon box. As a child she received a box of seventy-two crayons with a built-in sharpener. Of the many colors available to her, she remembers especially and fondly midnight blue. She could do wonders with midnight blue. If you couldn't create remarkable pictures with a set like the one she had, she says, you were hopeless as an artist.

Green sees the English language as the ultimate crayon box: "There is a word to describe every shade or meaning." She adds, "It's sad that in our writing most of us use only the primary colors—the same words over and over again."[20]

The correct way to put a contact lens in your eye: how would you show it? Artist Sarah Qualey for *Rochester Methodist Hospital News* used pure line, and chose a side view. She also moved in close. A line drawing like this can be more explicit than a photograph.

Nobody painted word pictures better than P. G. Wodehouse. For example, "She looked as if she had been poured into her clothes and had forgotten to say 'when.' " Or, if you want a Wodehouse picture in motion, "The butler entered the room, a solemn procession of one."

In his *Tap City,* the new novelist Ron Abell used this sentence with a lean, slouching character: "He stood up, and the effect was like the slow unfolding of a carpenter's rule."

A piece of writing can do some drawing right before the reader's eyes. Of a character in his novel *Small World,* David Lodge wrote, "Beneath the large, balding, bespectacled head is a pale, pear-shaped torso, with skinny limbs attached like afterthoughts in a child's drawing." Finis Farr described Henry Wallace, with his strain of mysticism, as a person who "lacked crispness of outline."

Nowhere does drawing with words work better than in capturing faces. The columnist Mary McGrory described Senator Howell Helfin from Alabama as a person with "a man-in-the-moon profile." (What often results from facial descriptions may be insulting and so may not have a place in organizational publications.) *Time* described Howard Jarvis, the man behind Proposition 13, as having a face that "looks a bit like a California mudslide. . . ." More recently, M. G. Lord in a book review referred to Ronald Reagan as Old Iguana Neck. Lord, one of the nation's few women editorial cartoonists, is in the business of noticing physical as well as political deformity, and age is no excuse for those persecuted by cartoonists—at the board or in front of a typewriter.

Drawing with words goes beyond faces themselves, of course. To describe a facial expression, Ring Lardner offered, "He looked at me as if I was a side dish he hadn't ordered." (Don't worry about the *was* instead of *were;* Lardner was Lardner.)

Reviews offer an excellent opportunity to draw pictures or even diagrams. Stephen Holder in a review in the New York *Times* said that Emmylou Harris's singing "suggests three parts silk and lace to one part steel," which was something of a tribute. Whitney Balliett dismissed a fellow writer by pointing out that his prose was "knotty pine at best."

The effectiveness of visual writing often lies in its exaggeration. The art is cartoonlike. Art Spander, columnist for the San Francisco *Examiner,* quoted the sportswriter Jim Murray as saying of the Los Angeles Dodgers' fielding, "Nobody seems to be able to pick up a rolling ball. At least not before it stops."

Words that become pictures often take the form of similes. "He is like a gigantic firefly who emits just enough light to call attention to himself, but not enough to illumine the subject," said Joseph Sobran of writer Garry Wills. Homer Croy said of Westbrook Pegler that "his sense of humor runs through him like a wick through a candle."

James Wolcott in a recent *Vanity Fair* described the *Village Voice* like this: "Viewed through glass, the *Village Voice* resembles an ant farm for the funky. A sandy plantation of tunnels and leaf-toting caravans and workers wiggling their antennae. Copy is born like prize crumbs to the lairs of red bwana ants, who coat the material with their own ideological secretions before shutting it back down the line." Later, talking about the magazine's early militant stands, he wrote, "Its angry black print came off in your hands like gunpowder."

Or the writing becomes a metaphor. Of a rapturous ex-writer for the *Voice,* Wolcott said, "Prose is her vibrator."

Art-oriented language doesn't belong only to the print media. *Country*

This textured landscape comes from using Macintosh's MacPaint program. The art takes line reproduction. John Graham is the artist.

Crossroads, a national Baptist radio program, offers to send listeners booklets that are written in "plain, shirtsleeve language."

Word pictures lead naturally to anecdotes, important to writing everywhere. Alec Wilkinson's subject for a recent *New Yorker* profile was Garland Bunting, who hunts moonshiners and who admits to a "sweet-potato shape." Bunting told Wilkinson that he walked into a men's store once to buy a suit, opened his jacket to show off his expansive belly, and said, "I'd like to see something to fit this." The salesman replied, "I would, too."

Notes

1. Kurt Wilner, "Too Much Isn't Enough: J. C. Saures," *Art Direction,* May 1979, p. 87.
2. Dereck Williamson, "Shutter Shudders," Phoenix Nest column of *Saturday Review,* December 5, 1970, p. 4.
3. "More Editors Trained to Take Photos," *Folio,* January 1981, p. 19.
4. William H. Neubeck, "Would You Use This Photo?" *The Bulletin of the Society of Newspaper Editors,* February 1981, p. 52.
5. Stewart Brand, Kevin Kelly, and Jay Kinney, "Digital Retouching: The End of Photography as Evidence of Anything," *Whole Earth Review,* July 1985, p. 42.
6. Philip N. Douglis, "Photo Critique," *Communication World,* December 1985, p. 40.
7. Tom Wolfe, "Golden Age," *The New York Times Book Review,* June 4, 1978, p. 45.
8. Patrick Hughes, *More on Oxymoron,* Penguin Books, New York, 1983, p. 60.
9. See listings in *Literary Market Place, Writer's Market,* and *Photographer's Market.*
10. Michal Heron, "Imagination Unlimited Through Photographs in Stock," *Public Relations Journal,* April 1985, p. 34.
11. *Graphic Artists Guild Handbook: Pricing and Ethical Guidelines,* 5th ed., Robert Silver Associates, New York, 1984.
12. Interview with Gloria Gordon, San Francisco, September 3, 1985.
13. Walter F. Giersbach in a letter to the editor, *IABC News,* May 1981, p. 23.

Art teacher Marilyn McKenzie Chaffee showed how to make a realistic portrait by pasting down pieces of black paper where she wanted deep shadows and pieces of printed body copy where she wanted lighter shadows. The printed-body-copy technique is appropriate for this portrait: it is of Graham Greene, the writer.

Walt Whirl, magazine and advertising illustrator, used an ordinary pencil to make this sensitive line drawing. He combined a fine outline with areas of texture, letting the edges of the textured areas define some of the outline of the figure. He distorted the perspective in order to create tension in the drawing.

14. Art Young, *On My Way,* Horace Liveright, New York, 1928, p. 193.
15. See Hendrik Hertzberg's *One Million,* Simon & Schuster, New York, 1970.
16. See Darrell Huff's *How to Lie with Statistics,* W. W. Norton & Company, New York, 1954.
17. Quoted by Jonathan Green in *Famous Last Words,* Quick Fox, New York, 1979, p. 97.
18. From an ad in *In-Plant Reproductions,* October 1985, p. 14.
19. Jack Powers, "Computer Art," *Magazine Design & Production,* October 1985, p. 30.
20. Interview with Caroline Green, Eugene, Oregon, October 23, 1985.

Suggested further reading

Art Books, 1950–1979, R. R. Bowker Company, New York, 1979. (Listing of 37,000 books on fine and applied arts, including design.)

Benson, Harry, and Gigi Benson, *Harry Benson on Photojournalism,* Harmony Books (Crown Publishers), New York, 1982.

Borgman, Harry, *Art & Illustration Techniques,* Watson-Guptill Publications, New York, 1979.
Brackman, Henrietta, *The Perfect Portfolio: Professional Techniques for Presenting Yourself and Your Photographs,* Amphoto, New York, 1985.
Cardamone, Tom, *Chart and Graph Preparation Skills,* Van Nostrand Reinhold Company, New York, 1981.
Cherry, David, *Preparing Artwork for Reproduction,* Crown Publishers, New York, 1976. (From the standpoint of a British artist.)
Corbett, Ruth, *Art as a Living,* Art Direction Book Company, New York, 1985.
Crawford, Tad, *Legal Guide for the Visual Artist,* Hawthorn Books, New York, 1977.
Croy, O. R., *Croy's Camera Trickery,* Hastings House Publishers, New York, 1977.
Curl, David H., *Photocommunication,* Macmillan Publishing Company, New York, 1978.
Curtis, Seng-Gye Tombs, and Christopher Hunt, *The Airbrush Book,* Van Nostrand Reinhold Company, New York, 1980.
Dalley, Terence, *The Complete Guide to Illustration and Design: Techniques and Materials,* Chartwell Books, 110 Enterprise Ave., Secaucus, New Jersey 07094, 1980.
Davis, Phil, *Photography,* 4th ed., Wm. C. Brown Company Publishers, Dubuque, Iowa, 1981.
Douglis, Phil, *Communicating with Pictures,* Lawrence Ragan Communications, Chicago, 1979.
Editors of Eastman Kodak Company, *The Joy of Photography,* Addison-Wesley, Reading, Massachusetts, 1980.
———, *More Joy of Photography,* Addison-Wesley, Reading, Massachusetts, 1981.
Edom, Clifton C., *Photojournalism,* 2d ed., Wm. C. Brown Company Publishers, Dubuque, Iowa, 1980.
Evans, Harold, *Pictures on a Page: Photojournalism and Picture Editing,* Wadsworth Publishing Company, Belmont, California, 1979.
Evans, Hilary, *The Art of Picture Research,* David & Charles, London, 1980.
Fincher, Terry, *Creative Techniques in Photojournalism,* Lippincott & Crowell Publishers, New York, 1980.
Frankel, Annabel, and Rocky Morton, *Creative Computer Graphics,* Cambridge University Press, New York, 1985.
Geraci, Philip C., *Photojournalism: Making Pictures for Publication,* 2d ed., Kendall/Hunt Publishing Company, Dubuque, Iowa, 1978.
Gray, Bill, *More Studio Tips for Artists and Graphic Designers,* Van Nostrand Reinhold Company, New York, 1978.
Grode, Susan, *The Visual Artists Manual,* Doubleday, New York, 1984.
Herdeg, Walter, *Graphis/Diagrams: The Graphic Visualization of Abstract Data,* new ed., Hastings House Publishers, New York, 1982.
Holden, Donald, *Art Career Guide,* Watson-Guptill Publications, New York, 1983. (Fourth Edition.)
Holmes, Nigel, *Designer's Guide to Creating Charts and Diagrams,* Watson-Guptill Publications, New York, 1985.
Kerns, Robert L., *Photojournalism: Photography with a Purpose,* Prentice-Hall, Englewood Cliffs, New Jersey, 1980.
Kobre, Kenneth, *Photojournalism: The Professionals' Approach,* Van Nostrand Reinhold Company, New York, 1980.
Marcus, Aaron, *Managing Facts and Concepts: Computer Graphics and Information Graphics from a Graphic Designer's Perspective,* National Endowment for the Arts, Washington, D.C., 1983.
McDarrah, Fred W., ed., *Stock Photo and Assignment Source Book,* R. R. Bowker Company, New York, 1977. (Guide to photos available from 6,000 sources.)
McMullan, James, *Revealing Illustrations,* Watson-Guptill Publications, New York, 1981.
Melot, Michel, *The Art of Illustration,* Skira/Rizzoli, New York, 1984.
Nelson, Roy Paul, *Cartooning,* Henry Regnery Company Publishers, Chicago, 1975.
———, *Comic Art and Caricature,* Contemporary Books, Chicago, 1978.
———, *Humorous Illustration and Cartooning: A Guide for Editors, Advertisers and Artists,* Prentice-Hall, Englewood Cliffs, New Jersey, 1984.
Newcomb, John, *The Book of Graphic Problem-Solving: How to Get Visual Ideas When You Need Them,* R. R. Bowker Company, New York, 1984.
Philippe, Robert, *Political Graphics: Art as a Weapon,* Abbeville Press, New York, 1982.
Photo/Design, Minneapolis. (Bimonthly.)
Pollack, Peter, *The Picture History of Photography,* rev. ed., Harry N. Abrams, New York, 1970.

Porter, Tom, and Bob Greenstreet, *Manual of Graphic Techniques for Architects, Graphic Designers, and Artists,* Charles Scribner's Sons, New York, 1980.

Professional Business Practices in Photography, American Society of Magazine Photographers, New York, 1981.

Rhode, Robert B., and Floyd H. McCall, *Introduction to Photography,* 3d ed., Macmillan Company, New York, 1976.

Rodewald, Fred C., and Edward Gottschall, *Commercial Art as a Business,* 2d rev. ed., Viking Press, New York, 1970.

Rosen, Marvin J., *Introduction to Photography,* 2d ed., Houghton Mifflin, Boston, 1982.

Rothstein, Arthur, *Photojournalism,* 4th ed., Amphoto, Garden City, New York, 1979.

Sanders, Norman, *Photographing for Publication,* R. R. Bowker Company, New York, 1983.

Sontag, Susan, *On Photography,* Farrar Straus and Giroux, New York, 1976.

Strong, William, *The Copyright Book,* MIT Press, Cambridge, Massachusetts, 1984.

Swedlund, Charles, *Photography: A Handbook of History, Materials and Processes,* Holt, Rinehart and Winston, New York, 1981.

Thompson, Philip, and Peter Davenport, *The Dictionary of Graphic Images,* St. Martin's Press, New York, 1980.

Tufte, Edward R., *The Visual Display of Quantitative Information,* Graphics Press, Cheshire, Connecticut, 1984.

van Uchelen, Rod, *Say It with Pictures,* Van Nostrand Reinhold Company, New York, 1979.

Wakerman, Elyce, *Air Powered: The Art of the Airbrush,* Random House, New York, 1980.

White, Jan V., *Using Charts and Graphs* R. R. Bowker Company, New York, 1984.

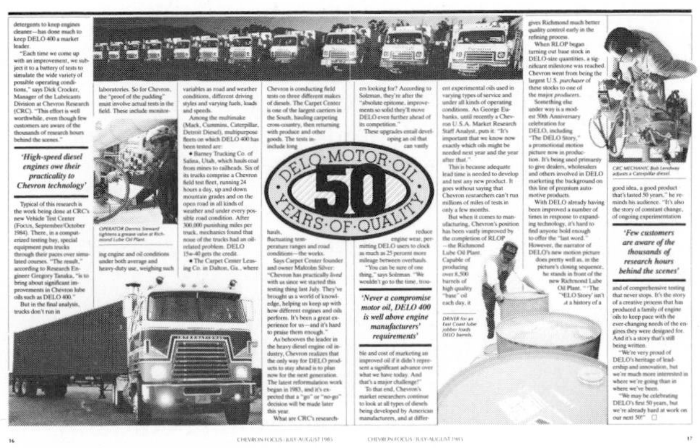

Chevron Focus's article on "Delco: What Makes It the Best-Selling Universal Engine Oil in the United States?" takes four pages and eleven pieces of art, most of it in full color. The copy is overprinted on a tint block. A margin of white surrounds the pages. This is the second of the two spreads. Note the variety of approaches the art director, Stephen F. Spoja, uses for the art, some of it silhouetted. Blurbs in red add to the liveliness of the pages, and lines and bars aid the composition.

Magazine formula and format

What *Publication Design* has observed and advised so far applies generally to all the print media. Now in this chapter and in the two chapters to follow, the book concentrates on magazines. Later chapters deal specifically with newspapers, books, and miscellaneous publications.

It is becoming increasingly difficult to separate the various media. Newspapers are looking more like magazines. Magazines are picking up some of the old newspaper design practices, modernizing them, and incorporating them into their pages. Magazines have gone into book publishing; and of course, book publishers publish magazines. Both book publishers and magazines publish calendars.

Sally Jessy Rafael refers to her radio talk show as an "advice column." TV shows like "60 Minutes" and "20–20" become known as "magazine programs" or "TV newsmagazines."[1] With flagging interest in documentaries, the networks turn to "docudramas," hybrids of editorial material and entertainment. Recording companies talk about "publishing" their records. And those that can be ordered by music lovers are said to be "in print."

Among print media, magazines have been the innovators in design. Magazine editors and designers have more time to plan issues than newspaper people have. At the same time, magazines can absorb design exaggerations and mistakes more easily than books can because magazines, although they are more permanent than newspapers, are not so permanent as books. Understandably, book designers tend to be more conservative than magazine art directors.

Magazine art directors tend to come from the ranks of advertising agency art directors. They move into magazine work effortlessly. On small magazines art directors may even find themselves assigned the job of designing ads for small firms that don't have their ads prepared by or placed through advertising agencies.

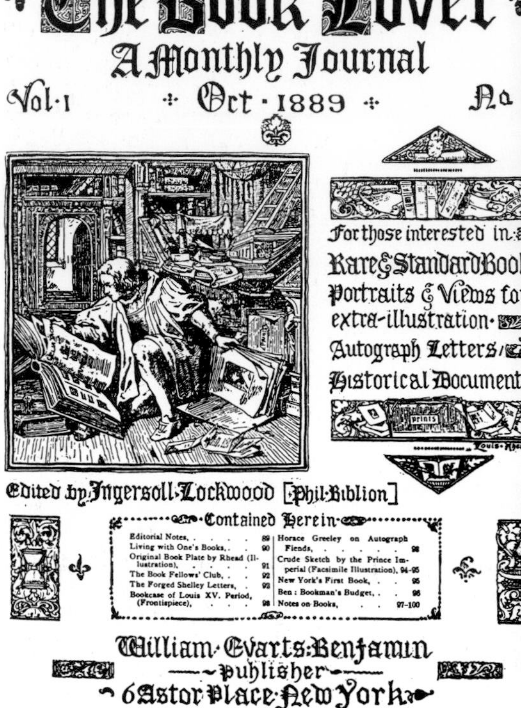

This cover for a nineteenth century magazine has a charm about it despite the clutter. *The Book Lover* was "for those interested in Rare & Standard Books, Portraits & Views for Extra-Illustration, Autograph Letters and Historical Documents."

The magazine's formula

Every magazine has its unique mixture of articles and stories. We call this its *formula*. Editors may not put their formulas down on paper, but they and their staff members have a general understanding of what it is.

After an informal study of alumni magazine publishing, Anthony A.

This 11 × 17 newsprint publication, *Clinton St. Quarterly,* has a reputation for strong, effective covers as well as provocative contents. A free publication financed by its advertising, it must catch the attention of hurried downtowners, and so its covers are always posterlike and in color. This one features a linocut (a print from a linoleum block) by Tim Braun. Art director Jim Blashfield found a place at the left to place three blurbs as well as some black-and-white art, done in a very different style, that appears inside. (Reprinted by permission of Out of the Ashes Press, P.O. Box 3588, Portland, Oregon 97208.)

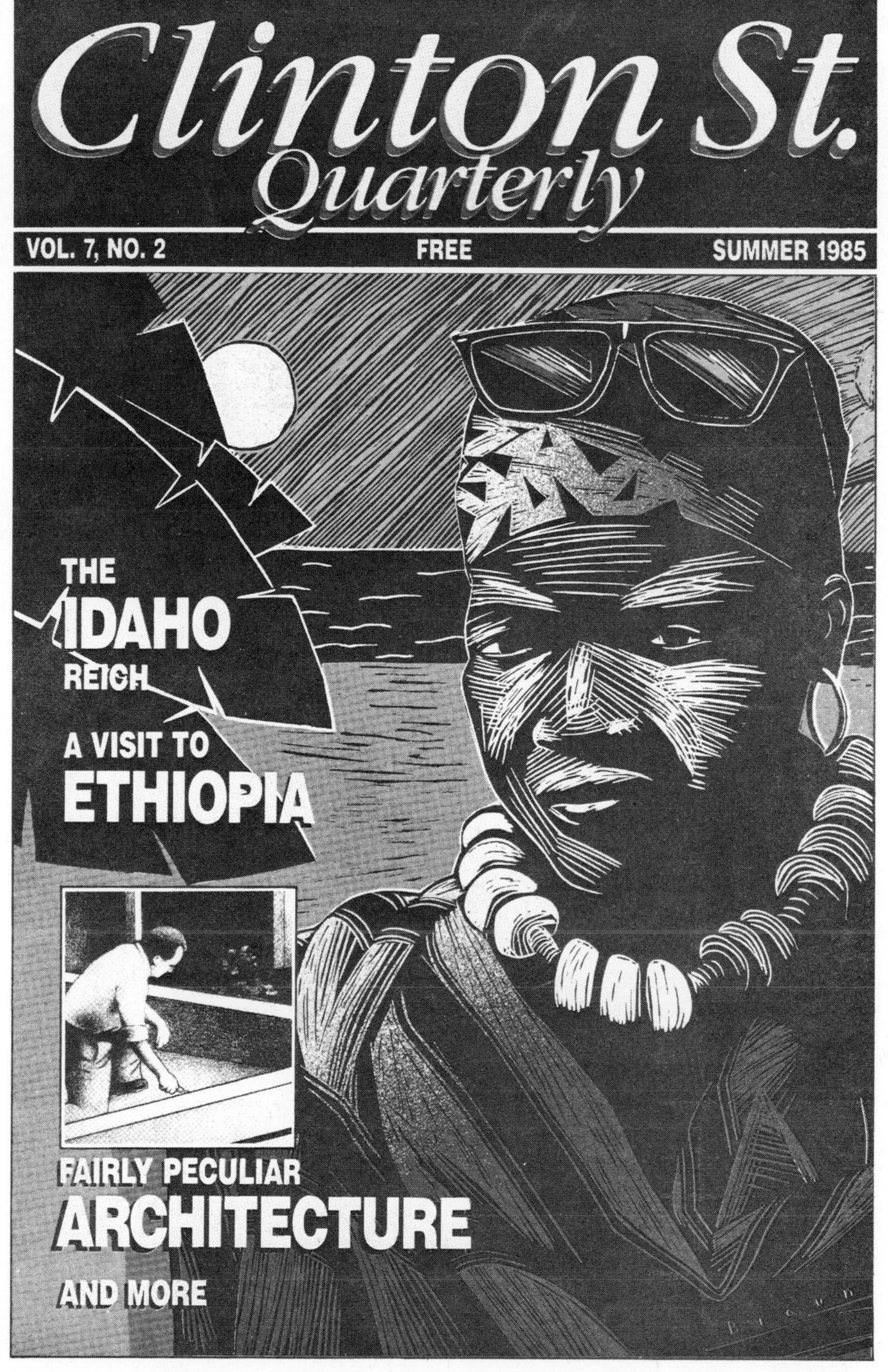

Lyle, editor of the *Pennsylvania Gazette,* an alumni magazine itself, found some interesting goals expressed by the editors. One said, "We strive for a delicate balance of predictability and surprise. . . ." Another said, "As the only University publication which consistently reaches alumni, it is also used to help maintain the integrity of alumni address files."[2]

A prime consideration is, What is the purpose of the magazine? Does the magazine, like *Ladies' Home Journal* or *Iron Age,* exist to make money? Does it, like *The New Republic* or *National Review,* exist to spread ideas? Does it, like *JD Journal* (published by John Deere) or *Menninger*

BEAUTY IN BUILDINGS AND SOME THINGS THAT LEAD TO IT BY BARRY PARKER

I PUT the word buildings instead of architecture in my title,—I had architecture at first,—because if I had used the latter word many would not have attached to it just the meaning I wished. We all have preconceived notions of the ideas which this word is used to convey, but we may not all have the same notions. To some it suggests the study of styles and periods; the history of the art of building; the archaeologist's point of view, in fact. To these my using the word would have conveyed the impression that I was going to talk about the development of one style from another; that I would show some of the chief characteristics by which one can tell at what time in the world's history, or to what style, a building, or some part of a building, belongs. To the minds of others, the use of the word "architecture" would have suggested those "finishing touches," those architectural features, those evidences of a knowledge of a vague intangible science of proportion which is supposed by some to be the business of an architect to add to a building. These are among the impressions I should have conveyed, and which I did not wish to convey. Therefore, I used the word "buildings," instead of the word "architecture."

For to regard architecture as something which may be separated from the art of building is to take a false position, and one which will set us on the wrong tack at the very outset. Also, the study of the history of architecture, fascinating as it is, is apart from my present purpose. My intention is to try to formulate a few fundamental principles and guiding instincts which have led to beautiful results, and the neglect of which, on the other hand, has led to failure, in all styles, and at all times, throughout the history of the art. Hence the second part of my title, "some things which lead to it." This I feel has been far too seldom attempted, in spite of the fact that there is, as is often said, "too much talk about art nowadays." Do we ever hear anyone trying to show us, when something beautiful is before us, or be-

The Craftsman magazine looked more like a book than a conventional magazine. This right-hand page from a 1902 issue followed a four-page glossy-paper signature showing halftone photographs. The regular stock for the magazine was of the antique category: rough finish but high quality. And the paper was deckle-edged. Note the understated display of the article title and byline and the wider-than-usual paragraph indentation.

RAIDERS OF THE LOST AVIATRIX

BY MICHAEL HOWARD

It began in South Florida. In the last week of May, 1937, Amelia Earhart arrived in Miami on the initial leg of the first attempted equatorial flight around the world.

She had flown in from Oakland, Calif., by way of Tucson and New Orleans. With her was her navigator, Fred Noonan, a former pilot for Miami-based Pan American, who had been down on his luck of late. Earhart had decided to give a second chance to Noonan, even though he was known to have a problem with the bottle.

ILLUSTRATION BY DENNIS ZIEMIENSKI

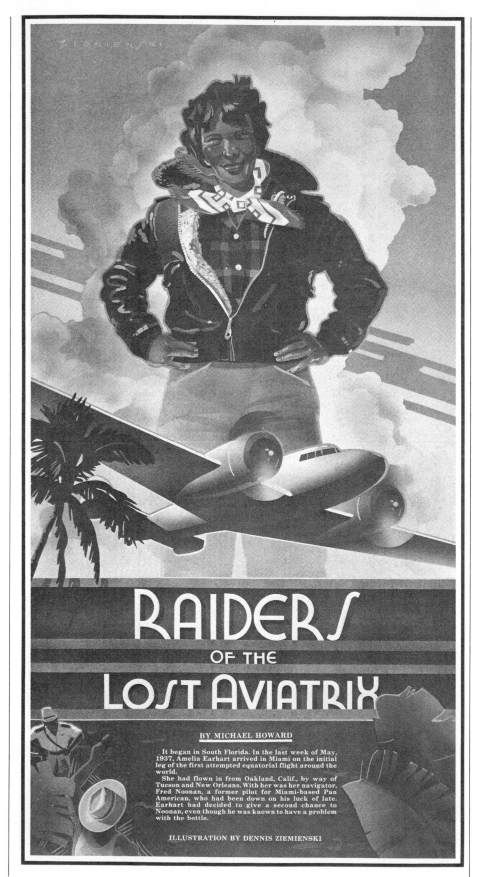

For a center-spread article opening in *Sunshine,* the Sunday magazine of the Fort Lauderdale *News/Sun-Sentinel,* the art director, Greg Paul, turned his design on its side to give it deep impact. Michael Howard's "Raiders of the Lost Aviatrix" deals with Amelia Earhart, who stopped off in Miami on her attempted equatorial flight around the world. The design purposely takes the look of 1937. Illustrations by Dennis Ziemienski.

Spectra

SEPTEMBER/OCTOBER 1985

"It's just a job," John tried to tell himself, looking at his family photo hidden behind a stack of claim files.

One of his favorite clients had just pulled out of a retraining program – another injury, after weeks of learning the new job. And he'd been doing so well. Back to time loss ...

"I can't worry about it now," he thought, reaching for a stack of investigation reports.

That afternoon, John leaves early.

But the next morning, he doesn't come in. Before, he used to work Saturdays.

Job Burnout.

This malady knows no age, rank or occupation boundaries. And it takes a smoldering toll in lost productivity, employee turn-over and family problems.

Experts say burnout has increased largely due to the growing shift from the traditional work ethic to the "worth" ethic. People expect more personal fulfillment from their jobs.

According to Craig Van, who offers training to cope with job burnout through Chemeketa Community College, employees in the helping professions such as workers' compensation are easy prey. Van is also Support Services Manager for Hillcrest School. He's trained about 300 state employees, including Hillcrest staff.

"To put it simply, burnout is disillusionment, emotional exhaustion. It happens when career rewards fall short of your efforts, after a prolonged time – normally a few years," Van said.

People often enter the helping professions to save the world, so to speak. They have high expectations for change and rewards. "After beating your head against 'the system,' these ambitions gradually erode," Van said. "Eventually, and often without even knowing it, you withdraw. It's very subtle."

It's also very normal – and curable. Most people feel it at least once in their professional lives, with some suffering at depressingly regular intervals. Van noted a study of Fortune 500 executives, where 6 out of 10 had burnout.

Although closely related, don't confuse burnout with stress. Stress is a physiological reaction, based on mental and physical events. Burnout is a prolonged set of circumstances and more importantly, your beliefs about them.

Great expectations

Good candidates for burnout tend to be the high achievers with little patience, Van said. The perfectionists, those who feel a strong need to control the situation ... those who look for simple solutions to every problem ... Those with high expectations of success, appreciation and status ... Those who expect people to be as motivated as they are.

"These qualities, by themselves, are good," Van said. "We just need to corral them in the right perspective. The key is to recognize what you can change and what you can't. Then, creatively work within the system, and accept certain givens, which may include your company policies, state laws and rules."

Cont. on next page

3 SAIF on safari 4 SMT comments on Ozwer 6 Meanwhile, back at the branch ... 7 Chop talk with Katrina Pruett

Spectra, an eight-page bimonthly magapaper published by SAIF Corporation, Salem, Oregon, replaced a four-page newsletter in 1985, giving employees more and longer articles to read. The new format also opened up the design. This front page, with its burnt-match art, starts off an article on job burnout. A different kind of table of contents (some would call it an index) stretches across the bottom. Michael Satern is the designer.

Perspective (published by the Menninger Foundation), exist to do a public relations job? Does it, like *The Rotarian* or *The Elks Magazine,* exist to serve members of an organization?

Or does it exist merely to act as an outlet for someone's creative urges or to spread the word about someone's consuming interest? Fanzines are magazines published usually by lone individuals and distributed to a selected list of persons who publish similar magazines. Some of the publishers, forming a sort of network, simply trade copies with each other. Often the magazines revolve around art and science fiction. Others provide inside information about comic books and seek to build paid circulations. Still another group evolves from fan clubs for musicians, actors, and other celebrities. Some of these are rather elaborate publications, like real magazines; others are cheaply produced newsletters for a mere one or two hundred subscribers. Some are produced on office copying machines.

Keeping the purpose in mind, the editor of any magazine works out a formula that best serves the intended audience or perpetuates the editor's strong convictions.

Since the advent of television, magazines by and large have given up the idea of serving large, general audiences and have moved into areas of specialization. It is hard to think of any interest area that is not served by a magazine or a set of magazines. David Z. Orlow, in a satire in *Folio* on the trend to put together magazines to appeal to ever more specialized audiences, suggests *Death,* "the magazine of the inevitable." As a character in Orlow's story explains it, it would be a picture magazine "featuring the most dramatic aspects of the subject—obscure diseases, dramatic accidents, berserk assassins, disasters, wars, and things like that." The magazine would be "absolutely lurid with respect to photography while at the same time absolutely nonemotional with respect to copy." It would be a magazine to appeal to a generation brought up on media violence. "True enough, the reader time per copy may be only three minutes due to reaction to some of the better pictures, but word-of-mouth will make it the best pass-along book since the advent of beauty parlor magazines."[3]

In one of the "M*A*S*H" episodes, Hawkeye, to satirize the narrow focus in magazines, brought up the possibility of *Toilet & Garden. National Lampoon* dreamed up *Guns and Sandwiches* and *Negligent Mother,* among others. A number of years ago *Life* brought up *Beautiful Spot: A Magazine of Parking.* Erma Bombeck talked about *Bleeding Gums Journal* and Bob and Ray about *Wasting Time Magazine.*

But it is hard to upstage real life, which in this age of specialization has given us magazines nearly as exotic as these for every conceivable activity or condition. The general-circulation magazines got in on the trend early with their regional editions for advertisers. City magazines proliferated to serve local causes. But even cities turned out to be territories too diverse. Soon there were specialized magazines in the cities to cover just their businesses, their entertainment, their urban survival possibilities, and their alternative lifestyles.

Even magazines in the same field have subtle and not-so-subtle differences. Religious magazines, for instance, range from left of the liberal *Christian Century* to right of the conservative *Christian Herald.* Magazines for ethnic groups vary widely, too. One of the most successful of such magazines is *Ebony,* which says in its advertising to media buyers that "we give Black Americans a pure, positive view of their life and times.

General media? They give a watered-down, diluted and sometimes biased view of the black experience." *Ebony* is far from being alone among black-oriented magazines. For instance, *Jet* is sort of a black version of *People. The Crisis* serves politically aware black readers. *Black College Sports Review* reaches young black athletes. *Essence* reaches fashion-conscious black women. *MBM* (for *m*odern *b*lack *m*en) reaches ambitious middle-class black males.

There are magazines for writers, like *Writer's Digest* and *The Writer,* but there are even more specialized magazines here, too. *The Christian Writer* is one. Editors in each of the media categories have their own magazines. And these publications are becoming more specialized. For instance, members of the American Association of Sunday and Feature Editors have a magazine—*Style.*

Magazines make changes in their formulas when new editors take over. Under the direction of Helen Gurley Brown, *Cosmopolitan,* a foundering general-interest magazine, became a sort of woman's *Playboy* in 1965 with the introduction of the worldly *Cosmo* girl ("Yes, we're still calling her a girl," Brown admits). It was a sudden, dramatic shift, and the magazine picked up a brand new audience. An *Advertising Age* writer calls it one of "the industry's most successful makeovers."[4] *Playgirl* came along later to appeal to an even less inhibited audience, not all of them women, and the mainline women's magazines became more sexually explicit than they had been in the past.

To stay alive, magazines must change with the times. When rock music lost some of its fascination, *Rolling Stone,* its bible, began concentrating more on articles dealing with politics, culture, and life-styles. It also sought to erase its earlier antiestablishment image. "We have never been an underground publication," the editor, Jann S. Wenner, is quoted as having said. "We have always said we wanted to make money." *Mother Jones* in 1986 began changing its emphasis from exposés to sophisticated analyses because it wanted a less radical image. It also wanted to appeal more to advertisers, who tend to shy away from persistently leftist publications. To reach a better spending audience, *Sports Afield* went from a magazine appealing only to hunters to one appealing to general outdoor types, especially those with money to spend. Its slick-paper pages took on a classic look.

Magazines—or rather their advertisers—like the young, but not necessarily the very young. Establishing a college readership, for instance, doesn't make much sense because college is only a temporary station. But beyond-college magazines like *Time* or *Newsweek* make an effort to introduce themselves to readers still in school with the idea of establishing a habit and future loyalty.

Some magazines change because they cannot overtake the leader in the field. Being No. 2, even a close No. 2, can be disastrous. Advertisers are likely to feel that, with space rates almost the same, they should buy space from No. 1. Their budgets may not allow space in both No. 1 and No. 2.

The No. 2 magazine in any field is the one most likely to change its formula. When *Playboy* outstripped *Esquire* in the mid- to late-fifties, *Esquire* dropped the nudes and turned to more serious matters. When the women's magazines were locked in a death struggle in the mid-1950s, *McCall's,* second to *Ladies' Home Journal,* tried to spread out to include the entire family, calling itself a magazine of "togetherness." The formula didn't work, and today *McCall's* and *Ladies' Home Journal* are very close again in formula.

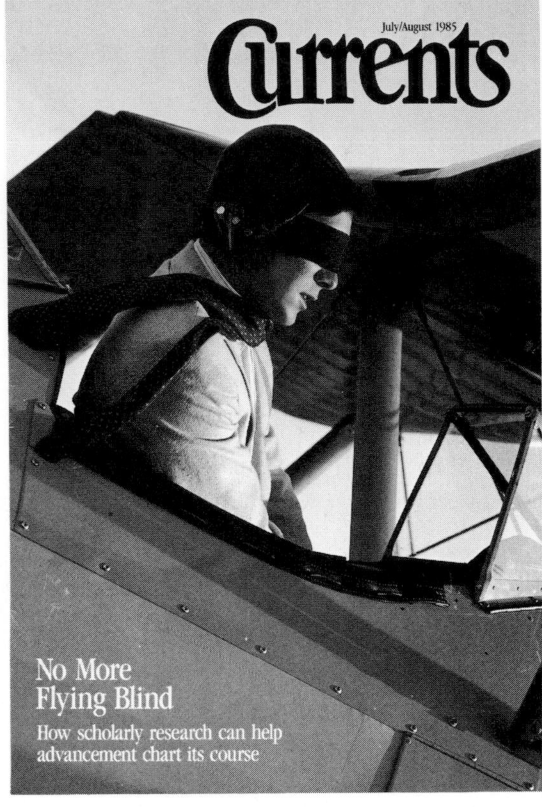

Currents, a magazine published by the Council for Advancement and Support of Education, took its 8 × 12 size when it was founded in 1975 because it wanted to include tips for members and notices of trends at the tops of pages. So an inch was added to the depth. Tim Girvin designed the tight-fitting logo with its unusual *ts* ligature.

The New Yorker continues to operate with a formula that offers humor mixed with social consciousness; great reporting done in a casual and sometimes rambling style; stories that have no endings; and, of course, the best gag cartoons anywhere. *New York,* a newer magazine some people may confuse with *The New Yorker,* has quite a different formula: a merging of the so-called "new journalism" with helpful advice on how to survive in Manhattan.

Reader's Digest is another magazine with a unique formula: dogmatism, conservatism, optimism—and, some would say, simplistic solutions to complicated problems. It is among the most consistent of magazines. Its formula has not changed basically since it was started in the early 1920s; nor, with one of the largest circulations of any magazine, is it likely to.

Art director Suren Ermoyan used the oversize pages of newly redesigned *Madison Avenue* to good advantage by going to a five-column-per-page format for "Words of Mouth," one of the magazine's regular features. The top of the title lines up with the tops of the columns on these and a following page. This axis, along with the two rows of art work, unite the pages. The wash drawings at the top are by J. B. Handelsman, a *New Yorker* cartoonist. The boldface captions for the drawings are in various colors. Most of the art at the bottom is in full color.

The magazine's format

When a magazine changes its formula, it also usually changes its *format.* The format is the look of the publication: its size, its shape, its arrangement of copy and pictures on the page. Format includes design. Sometimes a magazine changes its format, or at least its design, without changing its formula.

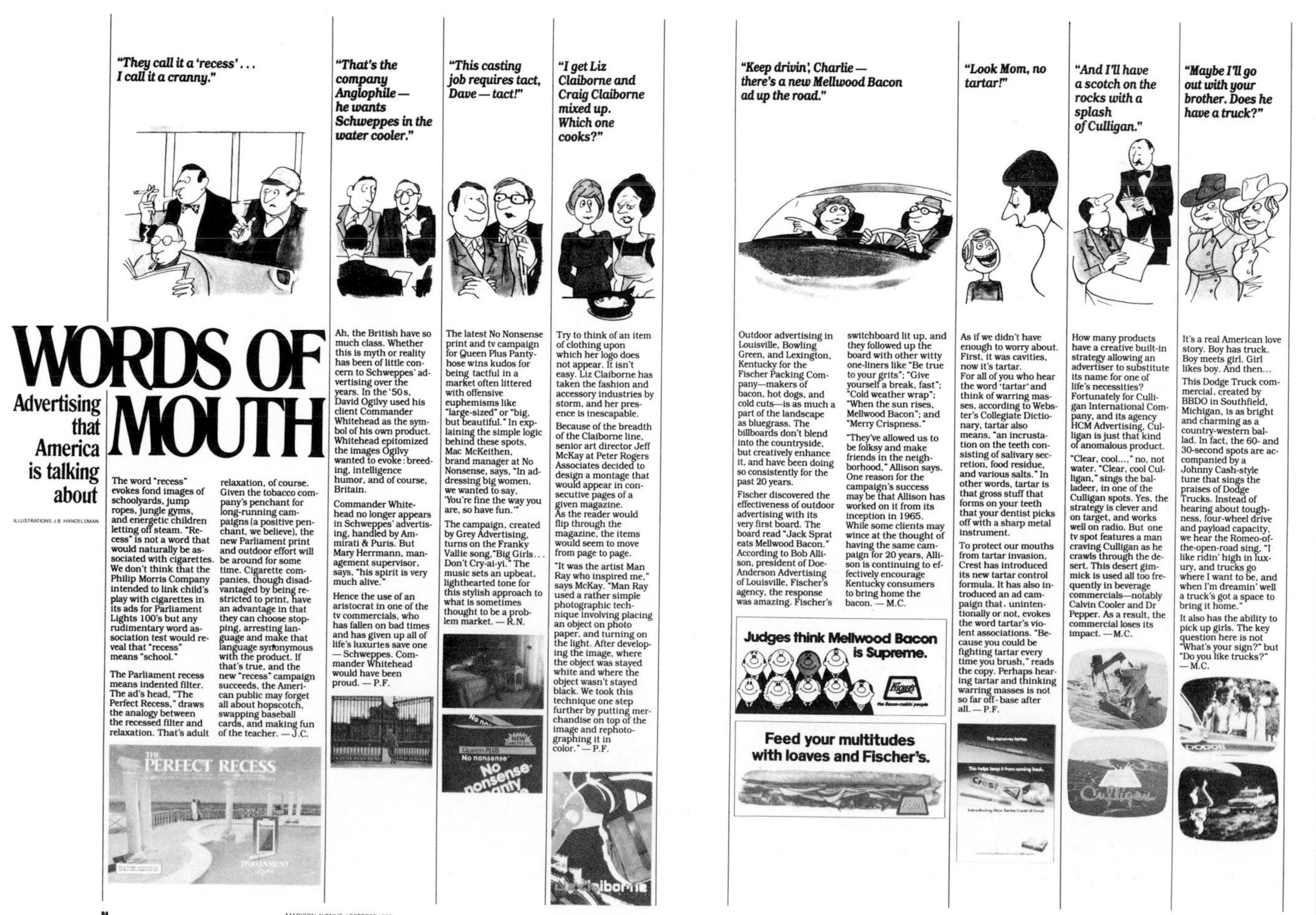

WORDS OF MOUTH

Advertising that America is talking about

ILLUSTRATIONS J.B. HANDELSMAN

The word "recess" evokes fond images of schoolyards, jump ropes, jungle gyms, and energetic children letting off steam. "Recess" is not a word that would naturally be associated with cigarettes. We don't think that the Philip Morris Company intended to link child's play with cigarettes in its ads for Parliament Lights 100's but any rudimentary word association test would reveal that "recess" means "school."

The Parliament recess means indented filter. The ad's head, "The Perfect Recess," draws the analogy between the recessed filter and relaxation. That's adult relaxation, of course. Given the tobacco company's penchant for long-running campaigns (a positive penchant, we believe), the new Parliament print and outdoor effort will be around for some time. Cigarette companies, though disadvantaged by being restricted to print, have an advantage in that they can choose stopping, arresting language and make that language synonymous with the product. If that's true, and the new "recess" campaign succeeds, the American public may forget all about hopscotch, swapping baseball cards, and making fun of the teacher. — J.C.

Ah, the British have so much class. Whether this is myth or reality has been of little concern to Schweppes' advertising over the years. In the '50s, David Ogilvy used his client Commander Whitehead as the symbol of his own product. Whitehead epitomized the images Ogilvy wanted to evoke: breeding, intelligence humor, and of course, Britain.

Commander Whitehead no longer appears in Schweppes' advertising, handled by Ammirati & Puris. But Mary Herrmann, management supervisor, says, "his spirit is very much alive."

Hence the use of an aristocrat in one of the tv commercials, who has fallen on bad times and has given up all of life's luxuries save one — Schweppes. Commander Whitehead would have been proud. — P.F.

The latest No Nonsense print and tv campaign for Queen Plus Pantyhose wins kudos for being tactful in a market often littered with offensive euphemisms like "large-sized" or "big, but beautiful." In explaining the simple logic behind these spots, Mac McKeithen, brand manager at No Nonsense, says, "In addressing big women, we wanted to say, 'You're fine the way you are, so have fun.'"

The campaign, created by Grey Advertising, turns on the Franky Vallie song, "Big Girls... Don't Cry-ai-yi." The music sets an upbeat, lighthearted tone for this stylish approach to what is sometimes thought to be a problem market. — R.N.

Try to think of an item of clothing upon which her logo does not appear. It isn't easy. Liz Claiborne has taken the fashion and accessory industries by storm, and her presence is inescapable.

Because of the breadth of the Claiborne line, senior art director Jeff McKay at Peter Rogers Associates decided to design a montage that would appear in consecutive pages of a given magazine. As the reader would flip through the magazine, the items would seem to move from page to page.

"It was the artist Man Ray who inspired me," says McKay. "Man Ray used a rather simple photographic technique involving placing an object on photo paper, and turning on the light. After developing the image, where the object was stayed white and where the object wasn't stayed black. We took this technique one step further by putting merchandise on top of the image and rephotographing it in color." — P.F.

Outdoor advertising in Louisville, Bowling Green, and Lexington, Kentucky for the Fischer Packing Company—makers of bacon, hot dogs, and cold cuts—is as much a part of the landscape as bluegrass. The billboards don't blend into the countryside, but creatively enhance it, and have been doing so consistently for the past 20 years.

Fischer discovered the effectiveness of outdoor advertising with its very first board. The board read "Jack Sprat eats Mellwood Bacon." According to Bob Allison, president of Doe-Anderson Advertising of Louisville, Fischer's agency, the response was amazing. Fischer's switchboard lit up, and they followed up the board with other witty one-liners like "Be true to your grits"; "Give yourself a break, fast"; "Cold weather wrap"; "When the sun rises, Mellwood Bacon"; and "Merry Crispness."

"They've allowed us to be folksy and make friends in the neighborhood," Allison says. One reason for the campaign's success may be that Allison has worked on it from its inception in 1965. While some clients may wince at the thought of having the same campaign for 20 years, Allison is continuing to effectively encourage Kentucky consumers to bring home the bacon. — M.C.

As if we didn't have enough to worry about. First, it was cavities, now it's tartar. For all of you who hear the word 'tartar' and think of warring masses, according to Webster's Collegiate Dictionary, tartar also means, "an incrustation on the teeth consisting of salivary secretion, food residue, and various salts." In other words, tartar is that gross stuff that forms on your teeth that your dentist picks off with a sharp metal instrument.

To protect our mouths from tartar invasion, Crest has introduced its new tartar control formula. It has also introduced an ad campaign that, unintentionally or not, evokes the word tartar's violent associations. "Because you could be fighting tartar every time you brush," reads the copy. Perhaps hearing tartar and thinking warring masses is not so far off-base after all. — P.F.

How many products have a creative built-in strategy allowing an advertiser to substitute its name for one of life's necessities? Fortunately for Culligan International Company, and its agency HCM Advertising, Culligan is just that kind of anomalous product.

"Clear, cool...," no, not water. "Clear, cool Culligan," sings the balladeer, in one of the Culligan spots. Yes, the strategy is clever and on target, and works well on radio. But one tv spot features a man craving Culligan as he crawls through the desert. This desert gimmick is used all too frequently in beverage commercials—notably Calvin Cooler and Dr Pepper. As a result, the commercial loses its impact. —M.C.

It's a real American love story. Boy has truck. Boy meets girl. Girl likes boy. And then...

This Dodge Truck commercial, created by BBDO in Southfield, Michigan, is as bright and charming as a country-western ballad. In fact, the 60- and 30-second spots are accompanied by a Johnny Cash-style tune that sings the praises of Dodge Trucks. Instead of hearing about toughness, four-wheel drive and payload capacity, we hear the Romeo-of-the-open-road sing, "I like ridin' high in luxury, and trucks go where I want to be, and when I'm dreamin' well a truck's got a space to bring it home."

It also has the ability to pick up girls. The key question here is not "What's your sign?" but "Do you like trucks?" — M.C.

84 MADISON AVENUE / OCTOBER 1985

OCTOBER 1985 / MADISON AVENUE 85

Some magazines are best suited to visual excitement and novelty. Others are best suited to visual order. The first thing an editor and art director must decide, then, is, What kind of look are we after?

The purpose of the magazine should have something to do with the kind of look they settle for. A magazine published to make a profit must lure and hold the reader with visually exciting pages. A magazine published to disseminate ideas can exist with a more austere format as, for example, one finds in *Foreign Affairs*. Its readers already believe; they don't have to be pampered. Such magazines generally will settle for a coarse, sometimes cheap paper stock and pages unrelieved by illustrations.

A magazine published to do a public relations job needs a glossy appearance if it is to go to outsiders; if it is an internal publication, it can be more homey. A magazine published to serve members of an organization must watch closely what it spends. If the members of the organization pay fees to belong and the members are cost-conscious, they are not likely to appreciate getting a pretentious publication.

But purpose is only one factor in deciding format. Policy is another. Two magazines may have as their policy the spreading of ideas: the one is leftist and activist; the other is moderately Republican. Will the same format serve both? Possibly. But if the tone of the articles is different, it seems reasonable to expect a difference, too, in the setting in which these articles are presented. Are there angry, vitriolic typefaces available for headlines? There are. And what about artwork—are some drawing styles more militant than others? See the work that appeared in the 1930s in *New Masses*.[5]

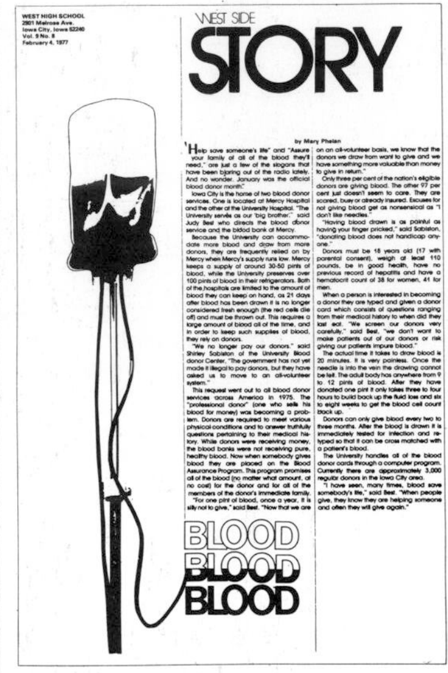

The front page of a newsmagazine tabloid published by West High School, Iowa City, Iowa, puts the logo in the upper right, with the dateline and other information in the upper left. The article's title is below, hooked up with the art. The uncluttered look continues inside.

Five basic formats

Although opinion research may dictate in part a magazine's formula, it has little to do with deciding a magazine's format. Format is still largely a matter of personal preference, taste, and intuition; and that's what makes it so challenging a topic.

Publications appear in a variety of formats, the most common of which are described here.

1. *Magazines* consist of a series of bound pages that have been printed in multiples of four, eight, sixteen, or thirty-two (these are called signatures), then folded down to size and trimmed.

   Phil Douglis, photographer and columnist, thinks the magazine format's chief advantage over the newspaper, newsletter, and magapaper format is "the ability to relate pictures to each other as a sequence over a series of pages, alternately withholding them from our view and then revealing them, carrying the reader through a visual process not unlike the frame-by-frame and scene-by-scene method of cinema."[6]
2. *Newspapers* consist of a series of oversize sheets folded down the middle to make four pages. Each set of four pages loosely houses another, which loosely houses still another, etc. An occasional loose sheet is included. A newspaper that is bulky enough divides its sets of pages into sections. The pages are so large that, for delivery, the entire newspaper has to be folded once and then opened up when the reader gets to it.

   Some magazines take on a newspaper format. The fashion publication *W* stands as an example.

WEST HIGH SCHOOL
2901 Melrose Ave.
Iowa City, Iowa 52240
Vol. 9 No. 11
April 15, 1977

WEST SIDE
STORY

Suicide

by Tracy Summerwill

A lonely high school student, a girl who argues constantly with her family, a depressed teenage boy. A common solution to these problems? Suicide. Teenage suicide is now the third most common cause of death, preceded only by homicides and accidents. The rate of suicide in the teens has nearly doubled during the seventies and the percentage of suicides in Iowa City has risen sharply.

In response to the high percentage, the Iowa City Crisis Center developed a suicide line in November, 1976. Since then there has been over 100 suicide related calls; 66 percent of them made by females, 34 percent made by males. Alan Zaback, Assistant Director of the Crisis Center, does not feel that this is unusual. "Girls are far more likely to call and confide in someone about their problems and intentions than guys are, who will just go out and take their lives with out letting anyone know about it."

The main intention of the suicide line is basically to provide a means of communication between a suicidal person and someone who cares. Depression, interpersonal, financial, and family problems, loneliness, alcohol and drugs were among the biggest problems that accompanied suicidal intentions in the contacts made with the crises center.

Attempted suicide is considered as big a problem as suicide is. Nine times as many people attempt to take their lives than the number of people who actually kill themselves. Alternatives for help in attempted suicide are limited and the most common aid is a psychiatrist. Child psychiatrist Dr. Mark Stewart, says, "With teenagers, the main reasons for suicide are attention and blackmail. For example, a boy who doesn't want his girlfriend to break up with him will tell the girl that if she leaves him he'll kill himself."

Dr. Stewart handles many suicide cases and says they are quite common. Many psychiatrists believe that attempted suicide is a cry for help. This is especially true of teenagers whose methods of suicide lean towards alcohol and drugs. "If a teenager takes an overdose, it usually is a very small one, with a good chance of someone being around to rescue them," said Stewart.

Parental reactions to their child's attempted suicide vary with the type of family. "Most parents can recognize the fact that their child needs help but others will not accept it or get mad at their child for what he did to them," commented Stewart.

Reasons for suicide attempts vary from the weather to the position of the moon, and on the surface they may even seem trivial. A broken date, a family argument or a bad day at school could be enough to send a suicidal person to his death. Beneath the surface, the reasons are far more complex. "Suicide generally occurs when something had been building up in a person for such a long time that a very small incident triggered it," said Stewart.

Broken and unstable homes are considered breeding grounds for suicidal tendancies in children. Rejection and a low self-image in an individual also produce suicidal characteristics.

Because suicide has always been hushed, myths about it developed. Most common of these myths is the fact that people who talk about suicide are doing it solely to gain attention. People who talk of suicide are seriously considering it and need help. Myth number two: most suicides occur at night. False. Most suicides take place during the day where the possibility of someone seeing and stopping them is greater than at night when friends and family members are asleep.

Myth number three: that suicidal tendancies can be inherited. Genetic inheritance has nothing to do with suicide but psychological reasons might lead to more than one suicide in a family.

Myth number four: after a person attempts to take his life, he won't try again. This, too, is definitely not the case. People who have already attempted to take their lives find it easier to try again. Four of five people who have committed suicide made previous attempts on their lives.

Suicide is not limited to one race, religion, age group, social class, or sex; and it is still a forbidden topic in our society today, consequently its reasons and motives are left unknown.

Another front page for *West Side Story,* three issues later. The style remains, but this time reverse type on a black page with rules and plenty of "black space" are art enough. The black is appropriate to the subject.

3. *Tabloids* consist of a series of unbound oversize pages that are about half the size of regular newspaper pages. The New York *Daily News* is a tabloid. So is the magazine *TypeWorld.*
4. *Magapapers* combine qualities of both newspapers and magazines and look a bit like tabloids, but slightly smaller and printed usually on quality stock. Often they consist of only four pages. This format has become a favorite with editors of company publications for employees.
5. *Newsletters* consist often, but not always, of 8½ × 11 sheets printed inexpensively and stapled at the top or side. Related to this format are all the formats that have been developed over the years by direct-mail advertisers. Chapter 11 describes these miscellaneous formats.

Anything goes

Conditions beyond the control of the designer may dictate the choice of format. When a strike in 1964 made a regular magazine impossible for Vail-Ballou Press, Inc., a printing and manufacturing firm in Binghamton, New York, for the book trade, it brought out its house organ in galley proof form as an emergency measure. The "publication" was 5 × 21, single column. The format seemed particularly appropriate for this particular company. The circulation, after all, was only six hundred. Editor L. Jeanette Clarke said at the time, "No company should feel that if it can't have a breath-taking, expensive magazine, newsletter or tabloid it should have none at all. To a large extent employees are captive readers." She said that because her readers were by nature curious, they didn't have to be lured by fancy trimmings.

Another strange format was introduced by *Datebook,* a teenyboppers' magazine now defunct. To create the effect of two magazines in one, *Datebook* carried a front cover at both ends. The teenage reader worked her way through half the magazine, came to an upside-down page, closed the magazine and turned to the other cover, and worked her way through that half.

Foreign Policy uses a tall, slim format—4½ inches wide by 10⅛ inches deep. That means, of course, one column per page. Why that size? "We wanted a distinctive magazine that was easy to read and put in a pocket," answers the editor, Bill Manyes.[7]

Art directors of Canadian magazines often have to design side-by-side pages or columns to show articles in both English and French. Places in the United States where a second language is prominent sometimes offer publications that incorporate parallel pages or sections in each language.

Some magazines run magazines within magazines, a sort of extension of the newsletter idea. Sometimes the additions are on the same stock, sometimes on another. *Cyclist* runs *The Compleat Cyclist: Your Guide to Riding Better, Faster and Farther.* The items are shorter than those in the regular magazine and are illustrated with line drawings and diagrams.

Fast Folk, which calls itself a "musical magazine," includes a 12-inch LP of folk songs with each issue.

Raw, published semiannually, calls itself "The Torn-Again Graphix Magazine." A 1985 issue had the top right corner of the cover torn off deliberately and taped onto the table of contents page. It is a sort of oversize, grown-up comic magazine with bound-in smaller magazines. Cover price: $6.

Format innovation was one of the selling points of *Flair* when it was being published in the early 1950s. The editors constantly titillated readers with die-cut covers, inserts of sizes different from the page size, sections inside the magazine printed on unusual paper stocks, and so on. These practices will continue to intrigue art directors, but those who resort to them are advised to check first with the post office, where regulations change frequently on what is allowed under second-class and bulk-rate mailing permits.

Page sizes

Magazines come in three basic sizes:

1. *Life*-size, roughly 10½ × 13. *Life* popularized the size with its founding in 1936, and many other magazines went to that size before paper prices and postage rates forced their scaling down. *Ebony* used the size until early 1982, when it dropped down to *Time*-size. (At that time it also went from letterpress to offset lithography.)

   Madison Avenue moved in an opposite direction in late 1985 when it changed from an 8½ x 11 magazine to an 11 x 14¾ magazine, giving its pages an impact they didn't have before and better serving advertisers who also appeared in the large-size *Advertising Age*. "You've done a glorious job re-thinking, re-making and re-designing the magazine," said Edward H. Meyer, chairman of the board of Grey Advertising in New York. *"Madison Avenue,* with its new format, is absolutely *ravishing* and riveting," said Helen Gurley Brown, editor of *Cosmopolitan*.[8] You can see an example of a *Madison Avenue* spread on page 161.
2. *Time*-size, roughly 8½ × 11—by far the most popular size for magazines. In 1985 the Los Angeles *Times* and the San Francisco *Examiner & Chronicle* brought out 8½ × 11 magazines for inclusion in their Sunday issues. Other big-city newspapers were considering moving from tabloid Sunday magazines to standard-size ones, too—part of the industry's answer to the independently published city magazines that have flourished everywhere.
3. *Reader's Digest*-size, roughly 5½ × 7½. Other magazines using this size are *TV Guide* and *Prevention*.

February 28, 1977 / Volume 11 / Number 3

THE VISITING FIREMAN

Captain Lee Clearwater, marine surveyor for Fireman's Fund, watches company-insured cargo being loaded aboard ship at San Francisco's Embarcadero. See page 3.

THE VISITING FIREMAN

New posts for Benedict, Sellick, Kirchen

At presstime

Barton, Boyd, Talarico named assistant vice president

FFA Life launches IRA program

The Visiting Fireman, published biweekly by Fireman's Fund Insurance Companies, San Francisco, uses the one-extra-fold tabloid format. You see here the 7½ × 11 front page along with the 11 × 15 second front page. The first one acts more like a magazine cover, the second more like a newspaper front page. As you unfold to the second front page, of course, you turn the publication ninety degrees. The original comes in black plus a second color. Note the thin lines that separate each line of the headlines. Ken Borger, a freelancer, is the designer.

The square—or near-square—format is popular with some editors. Here's a beautifully simple brown-and-yellow cover for square-format magazine *Lines,* published by Reliance Insurance Companies. A note inside the front cover explains: "The inflationary 'dragon' is still lurking nearby—preying upon the homes and businesses of underinsured policy-holders. The story on page 2 explains what Reliance is doing to help its agents 'slay the dragon.' "

The Illuminator, published monthly for employees of Appalachian Power Company and Kingsport Power Company, comes in a tabloid format, but with a difference: its main pages consist of three unequal-width columns. The body type runs with unjustified right-hand margins. The nameplate, designed in letters that suggest a neon sign, and the center story both appear in wine-colored ink. Heavy bars underline the last lines of the all-cap headlines. This is a device seen on all the pages, helping to unite them.

THE ILLUMINATOR

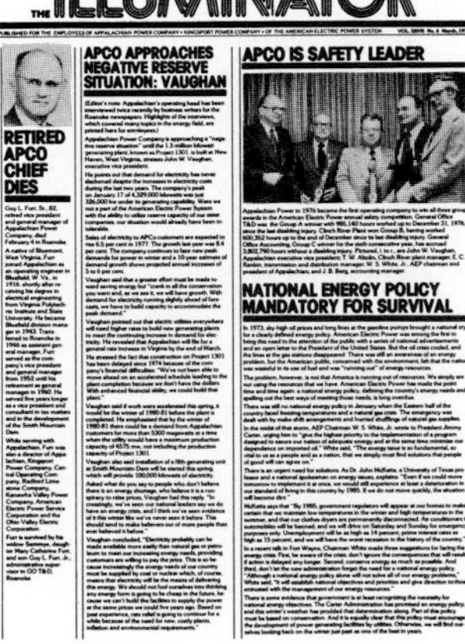
APCO APPROACHES NEGATIVE RESERVE SITUATION: VAUGHAN

APCO IS SAFETY LEADER

RETIRED APCO CHIEF DIES

NATIONAL ENERGY POLICY MANDATORY FOR SURVIVAL

These three sizes aren't the only ones. A company magazine might come in a 6 × 9, 7½ × 9½, 7 × 10, 8½ × 13, or a 9 × 12 size. The size depends upon the equipment the printer uses and the availability of paper stock. *Interview,* Andy Warhol's chic monthly, is almost 11 × 17, a saddle-stitched magazine with avant-garde design printed on near-newsprint stock.

Ries Cappiello Colwell, an advertising agency, conducted a study of magazines in 1978 and found nine different sizes. Not one magazine actually used an 8½ × 11 size: "8½ × 11" magazines turned out to be 8⅛ × 10⅞, 8¼ × 11¾, 8 3/16 × 10⅞, or some other similar size.

Magazine pages are almost always vertical. A magazine not dependent upon advertising should consider the novelty and even the design advantages of an 11 × 8½ page. Opened out, the magazine would be unusually horizontal.

A few magazines in recent years, along with some books—particularly art books—have gone for a square format. *Avant Garde,* an 11 × 11 publication, was one. But a square format can mean paper waste. If a magazine is big enough, it can special order paper to size. If not, it can do what *Avant Garde* did: use the paper waste—the odd-cut sheets—for direct-mail advertising campaigns.

Some editors like the square-format look because they think it says "now." You can achieve the square look in an 8½ × 11 magazine by adopting a consistent deep sink on the pages. That means making the "live area" of the pages—the part inside the margins—start low on the page. Instead of a one-inch sink, for instance, your magazine could carry a two- or three-inch sink. That does not keep you from printing anything above the sink. An occasional title may fit in that space, or a piece of art may jut into it. Even a caption might appear there. But body copy would always be confined to the square or near-square grid that you have adopted.

Whatever size page a magazine adopts, if it contains advertising, it should provide column widths and lengths that are compatible with other magazines in the field. An advertising agency doesn't like to custom design each ad for every magazine scheduled to run it.

Lithopinion, the defunct graphic arts and public affairs quarterly of Local One, Amalgamated Lithographers of America, used to change its format from issue to issue to "illuminate the versatility of lithography by example." On the other hand, about the only thing that remained the same for *Kaiser News* was the page size: 8½ × 11. It constantly changed design, frequency of publication, and printers. "What we are striving for is continuity through change," said the editor, Don Fabun.[9]

The page size, of course, seriously affects the design. Most art directors feel that a *Life*-size book is easier to design than a *Time*-size book. Certainly a *Life* or *Time* page is easier to design than a *Reader's Digest* page. Ralph Hudgins, art director of *Westward* (5½ × 7½), found his pages rather difficult to work with, but he said that he derived satisfaction from coming up with effective layouts within the limitations of the format. His pages were sometimes crammed, but there was an excitement about them.

An advantage of the *Digest* size is that it is close to book format, and readers have more of a tendency to save the magazine. Portability, too, is an important consideration. The *Digest* size was originally adopted by magazines to fit the pocket.

16 NOT JUST JAZZ — *The Uncommon Denominator* — Volume 1, Number 7

INNERVIEW

Who Ever Heard Of An 1,100 Pound Calling Card?

by Jack Feuer

Illustration by David Brier

***NJJ** sent freelance writer Jack Feuer to find out why **PRO PIANO** has such a great reputation for providing instruments and service to some of the most creative musical artists—classical, jazz, pop and rock—in the world. Jack interviewed owner Ricard De La Rosa at the New York showroom.*

Q. *I spoke to your manager in San Francisco yesterday, and he said, among other things, that your company was unique, that nobody does what you do.*

A. That's not to say that nobody rents instruments, but I don't think anybody rents the caliber instrument we do. And certainly nobody rents to the artistic quality we strive to please—everybody from Linda Ronstadt, right on through the world's most gifted pianists.

Q. *And they all autograph your pianos!*

A. Yeah, that's my only sign of being starstruck. I'm not, really, but that is one thing I'll allow myself. Our clients all sign our pianos.

Q. *How did you get into this business?*

A. I started as a piano tuner, and the first client I had was Crosby, Stills and Nash in San Francisco in 1972. I had been tuning pianos for them in studios throughout the West Coast so Graham Nash's office called me and said "Ricard, where can we get an excellent piano?" So we called around and got them the piano. I'll never forget, I said to Danta, my partner and my girlfriend of the last 18 years, "Wow, this is it!" We were dancing around because we were so happy. We'd found something that clicked, you see. And that was the beginning.

We began from there, through the grapevine, picking up clients. We tapped into the Joni Mitchell circuit, Neil Young, that kind of thing. Gradually, as our pianos became more noteworthy, we began to be noticed by artists in other areas, like Herbie Hancock, Chick Corea, Keith Jarrett. That was kind of our second tier. And we've run the gamut—America, ELO, Jefferson Starship, The Grateful Dead.

Q. *So you started with one piano in San Francisco.*

A. Right, as a piano-purveying firm. We had already been in business as a piano-service company. I'm proud of the fact that I'm an excellent piano tuner.

Q. *And not a bad businessman.*

A. Well, yes, but it isn't so much that as being attuned to the slavery aspect; viewing myself as a slave to art, so to speak. That makes the whole difference, that makes it work. Because we have that sensitivity, there are no obstacles for us. It's because I've never abused the artist's psyche, the artist's will. So it flows to me.

Q. *When did you open in Los Angeles?*

A. L.A. is basically only a WATS-line to the San Francisco office and we choose the jobs we want. We do intend to open a regular shop there in the near future, though. We'll have a full-sized showroom there just as we do now in New York.

Q. *And the New York showroom?*

A. We've been in New York since September of 1979. It was obvious to me, and I think to Danta too—certainly to some of our bankers—that New York is the center of it all. Once the classical pianists found out that we had these Hamburg-Steinways, which is our real calling card as we are the only people who maintain an inventory of them, we began to gain a following.

Q. *No one else rents Hamburg-Steinways?*

A. No. They're prohibitively expensive, the maintenance factor is cost-prohibitive and highly skill-intensive. You simply have to maintain those pianos, their quality demands so much care.

Q. *So you don't merely deliver an instrument, you maintain it, accompany it on tours, etc.?*

A. Oh yes. No one touches our pianos but us. It's almost an unspoken rule. In fact, we've probably lost a couple of jobs because of it. People have a lot of good reasons for being loyal to their piano tuners, whether subjective or objective reasons. Once in a while you'll get a recording engineer who won't do a session without his piano tuner, so that's it. It's us and the piano or the tuner. Most of them choose the piano. It's not that I'm better or they're better, but, you know, it's my piano; I've done everything to it, whether it's good, bad or indifferent. I know it and I'm not going to make a mistake again. The next guy may blow something that I blew six months ago; he may do it again.

Q. *That's a good point. What kind of problems do you encounter—on the road, for example?*

A. We've never lost a piano, but we've had some *almost* disasters, which is natural on the road. We've had lighting equipment fall on the instrument. I remember the Jefferson Starship used a piano once in Germany and Grace Slick couldn't perform. The crowd, being a rock and roll crowd and pretty, well, you know, didn't take the news well when it was announced. They got angered and stormed the stage, threw all the instruments, including the piano, over the hill. Tried to set fire to it. Those are the kinds of things we encounter.

Q. *What happened to the piano?*

A. We repaired it. That's part of the job.

Q. *Is there a difference in what you do for a rock pianist and a classical pianist?*

A. I think everything you try to do is based on one standard, whatever standard you set for yourself. Most pianists, no matter what they play, assume you're a professional and let you do the tuning. I mean, this is just one of maybe 20,000 pianos they'll play in their lifetime, so they don't put a lot of attention on it. That's your job as the technician.

Q. *Aren't there any perfectionists out there?*

A. There are a few that from the word "go" you know are going to be real nit-picky, so you make extra sure you're absolutely perfect for them. Christie McVie of Fleetwood Mac is a perfectionist.

Q. *What is your current inventory?*

A. We have in the area of sixty pianos. Of the Hamburgs, there are six *D*s, a *B* and an *O*, and another *B* I just acquired, and three more *D*s coming in. The rest run the gamut, Yamahas, Steinways, Baldwins. Right now, I'm having a beautiful old piano, from about 1858, restored. That isn't going to be rented, of course. It's a Steinway, very rare, almost a prototype of a modern piano.

Q. *You use your showrooms as rehearsal areas as well, don't you?*

A. Oh yes. There's someone here almost every day. Ilana Vered is, you could say, our artist in residence. She has a rehearsal stall here that's her space.

Q. *What about the ratio of clients, rock to classical?*

A. On the West Coast it's pretty even. Here in New York I'd say the majority of our clientele is classical. For classical pianists, New York is where they want to perform because the reviewers of influence are here. In San Francisco, they'll rely on their promoter to call us or someone else. But in New York they'll invariably come into the showroom and choose a piano themselves.

Q. *Is there an average price for rental?*

A. It depends on where the instrument is going. Are there stairs, is it a day tour, etc. For the bulk of the business, which is one-day rentals, it can average $50 to $500, depending on the instrument. A Hamburg *D* will be at the top and a Wurlitzer electric at the other end of the scale. Also, there are other factors, like how often do they want it tuned, etc. It's all relative.

Q. *What's the longest period of time anyone has rented a Pro Piano?*

A. Barry Manilow and Keith Emerson have taken pianos for six months at a time. A lot of recording studios will also lease pianos from us for two or three years.

Q. *Which are your favorite performing halls?*

A. Carnegie Hall of course. The Boston Symphony Hall, Philadelphia and Cinncinnatti have beautiful halls. I'm also really beginning to like Fisher Hall and Tully Hall as well. San Francisco has a great new hall, Davies Hall.

Carnegie Hall for us is a tough one. First off, there are 15 stairs straight up; you have to maneuver through some close situations. There are a lot of regulations, too, and rightly so—it's a national landmark.

Q. *How many people work for you now?*

A. We have about seven or eight. Everybody that works with us should be a piano tuner. There's no reason why that shouldn't be so. People sometimes have a hard time with that, but it's just better for us that we have people who view the whole process, so that they take responsibility for the whole thing. People don't realize that just the way the piano is moved can make the piano tuning that much more, well, proper. So you definitely need that extra dimension.

Q. *Does your protection of the piano ever conflict with the hall's moving regulations?*

continued on 21

David Brier, art/design director of *Not Just Jazz,* a tabloid, used horizontal bars and his own abstract, silhouette illustration to top the first page of an "Innerview" with the owner of a musical instrument company. The title wraps around the piano to make one unit of the bars, title, and art.

The role of design

The history of journalism records the names of a number of editors who were able to build and hold audiences for publications that, from a design standpoint, had the grace of a row of neon signs or, at best, the monotonous, unadorned look of a telephone directory. One remembers Lyle Stuart's *Expose* and *Independent,* George Seldes's *In Fact,* and I. F. Stone's newsletter. Publications like these are often radical sheets, yet their editors hold design views that can be considered only ultraconservative.

The late Professor Curtis D. MacDougall of Northwestern University, who could identify with many of the causes of these publications, said that "strong editorial material can overcome bad design. On the other hand, bad design can't kill good contents." But why give editorial matter the additional burden of bad design? The job of communicating is already difficult enough.

Good design, by itself, can't make a publication useful or important; but combined with well-conceived, well-reasoned, and well-written content, it can make the printed page a joy rather than a chore.

And what is good design?

The answer is important. *Good design is design that is readable.* The key word is *readable*—not unique, not compelling, not even beautiful, although all these qualities can play a part, but readable.

Some editors look upon design as a magic ingredient to be applied to an ailing publication, and presto! the publication's problems are solved.

"A . . . reason for the confusion about design is the prevailing notion that it is a kind of frosting, an aesthetic overlay that makes humdrum objects more appetizing," says the eminent designer George Nelson. "No responsible designer believes this." Nelson adds that design models from nature "never show decoration that isn't functional, never show the slightest concern for aesthetics, and always try to match the organism with its environment so that it will survive."[10]

"Some publications work backwards, tailoring the editorial content to fit the graphics, but they won't live very long," comments the design consultant Jan V. White. "They may make a big splash when they first appear because they are undoubtedly interesting to *look* at, but being nice to look at is not enough; if the shallowness of the content leads to reader dissatisfaction (as it must, when it becomes obvious) then the publication is on the road to oblivion."[11]

Design and personality

Every magazine develops a personality. Even the city and regional magazines develop differences. James Warren, writing for the Chicago Tribune News Service, calls *New York* "maniacally trendy," *Los Angeles* "fluffy and wry," *Chicago* "fat and humdrum," and *Texas Monthly* "down-home sophisticated."

Some magazines take on the look of other magazines but operate in a different context. *Southern Accents,* published in Atlanta, does for the South what *Architectural Digest* does nationally.[12]

The politics of a magazine do not necessarily dictate its looks. *Radical History Review,* for instance, despite its somewhat playful logo, looks like

'All Business And No Play' Is Corrected By D&B-Israel

Tennis competition among execs who are listed in DunsGuide Israel is closely watched by public and the press

Dun & Bradstreet-Israel has added a social dimension to the business services it provides by sponsoring the first annual Dun & Bradstreet executive tennis tournament for managers listed in its *DunsGuide Israel Business Directory.*

"We wanted to encourage businessmen to indulge in more sports activities," says Marc Gueron, general manager of D&B-Israel and initiator of the tournament. Joseph Heksch, a hotel manager and a tennis partner of Gueron, volunteered the Dan Accadia Hotel Courts, located on the Mediterranean beach north of Tel Aviv, as the tournament site.

"The clubhouse took on the air of a business party," reports Gueron. Many contacts and relationships were established among the 64 participants from such multinationals as IBM, General Electric, Baxter Travenol, and Avis, as well as major Israeli companies.

But, tennis was serious business. The tournament had attracted a high level of veteran tennis players ranging in age from 32 to 72, and included a number of well-known native-born players. The winner, 34-year-old advertising executive Oded Shai, was a former Davis Cup competitor for Israel. Gabriel Dubitsky, another former Davis Cup contender, won the second place D&B Cup. Gueron, knocked out in the first round, made the presentations of the Cups and respective bonuses of a weekend for two and dinner for four at Dan Caessarea Hotels.

The Dun & Bradstreet Cup was a popular event that was closely followed by the business community and the press. For the two-week tournament period, Gueron reports there was good coverage in both the business and sports pages. And it was no surprise that the finals played to a packed audience.

Plans are underway for next year's tournament. And if the number of requests reaching Dun & Bradstreet from Israel's executives are any indication, the second annual event may well include close to 200 participants.

In the first D&B-Israel tennis cup winner's circle is Oded Shai (far left), advertising executive, receiving first-place cup. Having a hand in the presentation are (left to right) Jack Monsell, coach — Israel National Soccer Team; Joseph Heksch, manager — Dan Hotels; Marc Gueron, general manager, D&B-Israel; and Tal Brody, former Tel Aviv basketball star.

National CSS Is Joined by Software Developer

Program Products Incorporated will add new dimensions

Program Products Incorporated of Montvale, New Jersey, became a member of National CSS October 2, and will operate as part of NCSS' Software Products Group.

Program Products Incorporated specializes in the development and sale of computer software products that facilitate the retrieval and reporting of computerized data. The firm was founded in 1971 and presently employs 53 people in Montvale and at branch offices in Chicago, Atlanta, Dallas, Boston and Los Angeles. Its products are also distributed in most European countries, Israel, South America and Southeast Asia.

The company's software products include the Data Analyzer, a general purpose report generator, and the Audit Analyzer, a specialized program designed for use in accounting and auditing. Project Monitor, another product introduced in late 1979, is an automated project control system.

The purchase of Program Products Incorporated is part of National CSS' strategy to build a significant position in the software products marketplace.

Rolling 'Beetle Boards' Push the 'Walking Fingers'

Volkswagen autos serve as mobile billboards for C&P Telephone campaign prompting RHD contest

Reuben H. Donnelley's client, Chesapeake & Potomac Telephone, is getting extra mileage from a new line of Volkswagens. Some of the cars resemble a Yellow Pages directory, while other "beetleboards" carry an energy-saving reminder, "Go by the Book." The custom "Yellow Pages" can be seen at county fairs and in and around Williamsburg, Virginia. The "beetleboards" are privately-owned showpieces rented at a rate of $25 per month by C&P Telephone for the advertising campaign.

"We're supporting the campaign in our region because any client push of the Yellow Pages is good for us," says Donnelley Sales Promotion Manager Ken Stuart of RHD's C&P Region. The support is in the form of a contest for C&P employees who can win $5 for spotting any one of the 125 VWs in the Baltimore, Norfolk, Richmond and Washington areas.

4

IR-100 Awards Recognize Significant Scientific Entries

Unique applied science award focuses on technological advances made in the past year

A portable dialysis machine, a pocket radiation warning device, an energy-saving fluorescent lamp controller, and a single-chip microcomputer all have one thing in common. *Industrial Research & Development (IR&D),* a Technical Publishing publication, presented I-R 100 Awards to the inventors of these and 96 other significant innovations of 1979.

In conjunction with the I-R 100 Awards, a Scientist of the Year Award was presented to Jacob Rabinow, retired Chief Engineer of the National Bureau of Standards. The 15th scientist so honored, Rabinow, an inventor since the age of 11, has introduced a wide range of mechanical and electrical devices including an automatically-regulated clock, a letter-sorting device for post offices and a magnetic clutch.

More than 500 people representing business, government agencies, research organizations, and universities attended the 18th annual presentation at Chicago's Museum of Science and Industry the evening of September 18.

"No one else offers any such award for applied science," says Robert R. Jones, chairman of I-R 100 and editor of *Industrial Research & Development.* "As the leading publication in our field—reaching more than 103,000 scientists, engineers, and technical managers engaged in applied research and development—it was logical for us to have this program to recognize and honor the leading edge of science," says Jones. This represents the "creative genius that has made it possible to continually improve the standard of living throughout the world."

In addition, the I-R 100 Awards and a month-long exhibit at the Museum of Science and Industry focus public attention on the technological community and the results of its work, says Tim Burkholder, publisher of the publication. Since 1963 more than 4,000 frontier scientists in the U.S. and abroad have been given recognition as I-R 100 winners.

Categories for the awards are not fixed, but the products, materials and processes submitted for the 1980 competition represent 16 categories in such fields as medicine, electricity, plastics, chemistry, energy, and computer science. An independent Advisory Board of scientists and engineers and IR&D's editorial staff judge the entries on the basis of significance and uniqueness.

"These are not laboratory curiosities," says Jones, "The products, materials or processes have been marketed, or are available on order in the case of 'big ticket' items."

Entries have rapidly increased since the mid-1970s. This is due, in part, to more media coverage and public interest as gauged by attendance at the Museum where more than 400,000 visited the I-R 100 exhibit last year. Also, there is widespread recognition that a product gains significant prestige when companies advertise in annual reports and on displays that it is an I-R 100 winner.

The General Electric Company leads the field of I-R 100 winners with 130 awards, including six this year. Other companies honored this year include Westinghouse Electric Company, Union Carbide Corporation, NASA's Lewis Research Center, and the National Bureau of Standards.

Producing an I-R 100 winner is, on the average, a long and costly process. In 1979, an investment of 28,000 man-hours (over a period of 43 months) and $907,800 went into producing one product which would sell for an average of $68,654.

"In the past, many of the products recognized by IR&D have established themselves as major elements in our everyday lives," says Burkholder. "The flash cube, the Speak and Spell computer learning system, and Polaroid instant color film were all once new products honored in the I-R 100."

"Invention means sweat and blood," Jacob Rabinow (left) can say authoritatively, who holds some 300 U.S. and foreign patents. Robert Jones, editor, is presenting the IR&D Scientist of the Year Award.

These Monsanto representatives will receive an award for a gas separation process and device which can increase separation efficiency by 20 percent or more.

Representatives of Westinghouse and the U.S. Navy Civil Engineering Laboratory receive an I-R 100 plaque for a hydraulic motor that is a boon to divers.

5

Management Update, a monthly 11 × 16 magapaper published by the Dun & Bradstreet Corporation, uses two-deck flush-right headlines at the sides of stories, as this spread shows. The publication combines rectangular photographs with silhouetted photographs to bring variety to its pages. On the right-hand page, the photographs partially overlap.

Sesame shrimp stir-fry offers juicy Gulf shrimp with crisp-tender vegetables such as snow peas and cauliflower coated with a light oriental sauce. Toasted sesame seeds are sprinkled over the top. The calorie count: 340.

HOULIHAN'S SEES THE LIGHT AND CUTS THE CALORIES

Customers savor low-fat, low-salt foods on this restaurant chain's menu.

Scarlett O'Hara would have wilted in Atlanta's Fourth of July 1983 heat.

At 8:15 a.m., the rising mercury stood at 77 degrees and the humidity, a steam-kettle 87 percent. But 28,000 runners thundered 6.2 miles down Peachtree Street, a former Indian path, for the 14th annual Peachtree Road Race. Later, many returned to their cars sardined in front of Houlihan's restaurant. And hundreds swarmed into this Grace-owned eatery to celebrate finishing (more than 40 didn't; they had collapsed from heat exhaustion). One successful macadam-pounder, decked out in a canary-yellow "1983 Peachtree Road Race" T-shirt, told a server he loved the restaurant's fried potato skins with sour cream. But couldn't it offer lighter choices, too? Good-tasting food fit for the fit?

His idea proved as upwardly mobile as Houlihan's 25- to 45-year-old clientele. It soared through the ranks to the chain's executive suite and brought all the cooks into Houlihan's test kitchen in Kansas City, Missouri.

"John Bettin, our director of culinary and a very talented guy, went through hell shaving off calories while still preserving the quality and generous servings," recalls Frederick R. Hipp, president, Houlihan's/Casual Dining Division, part of Grace's Gilbert/Robinson, Inc., in Kansas City. "Customers judge value by the portions on their plates. They want to say there was so much there they could hardly eat it all."

On June 6, 1984, Houlihan's pulled off a first among U.S. restaurant chains. It rolled out an alternative light menu of 24 calorie-counted drinks, appetizers, salads, entrées and desserts.

2

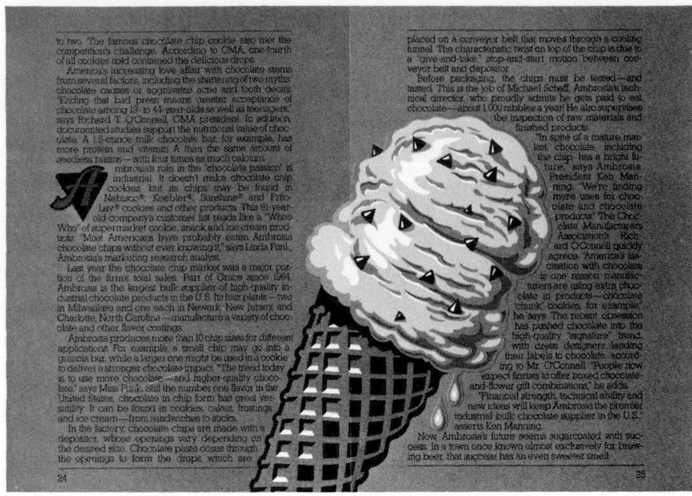

to two. The famous chocolate chip cookie also met the competition's challenge. According to CMA, one-fourth of all cookies sold contained the delicious drops.

America's increasing love affair with chocolate stems from several factors, including the shattering of two myths: chocolate causes or aggravates acne and tooth decay. "Ending that bad press means greater acceptance of chocolate among 13- to 44-year-olds as well as teenagers," says Richard T. O'Connell, CMA president. In addition, documented studies support the nutritional value of chocolate. A 1.5-ounce milk chocolate bar, for example, has more protein and vitamin A than the same amount of seedless raisins—with four times as much calcium.

Ambrosia's role in the "chocolate passion" is industrial. It doesn't make chocolate chip cookies, but its chips may be found in Nabisco®, Keebler®, Sunshine® and Frito-Lay® cookies and other products. This 91-year-old company's customer list reads like a "Who's Who" of supermarket cookie, snack and ice cream products. "Most Americans have probably eaten Ambrosia chocolate chips without ever knowing it," says Linda Funk, Ambrosia's marketing research analyst.

Last year the chocolate chip market was a major portion of the firm's total sales. Part of Grace since 1964, Ambrosia is the largest bulk supplier of high-quality industrial chocolate products in the U.S. Its four plants—two in Milwaukee and one each in Newark, New Jersey, and Charlotte, North Carolina—manufacture a variety of chocolate and other flavor coatings.

Ambrosia produces more than 10 chip sizes for different applications. For example, a small chip may go into a granola bar, while a larger one might be used in a cookie to deliver a stronger chocolate impact. "The trend today is to use more chocolate—and higher-quality chocolate," says Miss Funk. Still the number one flavor in the United States, chocolate in chip form has great versatility. It can be found in cookies, cakes, frostings and ice cream—from sandwiches to sticks.

In the factory, chocolate chips are made with a depositor, whose openings vary depending on the desired size. Chocolate paste oozes through the openings to form the drops, which are

24

placed on a conveyor belt that moves through a cooling tunnel. The characteristic twist on top of the chip is due to a "give-and-take," stop-and-start motion between conveyor belt and depositor.

Before packaging, the chips must be tested—and tasted. This is the job of Michael Schaff, Ambrosia's technical director, who proudly admits he gets paid to eat chocolate—about 1,000 nibbles a year! He also supervises the inspection of raw materials and finished products.

"In spite of a mature market, chocolate, including the chip, has a bright future," says Ambrosia President Ken Manning. "We're finding more uses for chocolate and chocolate products." The Chocolate Manufacturers Association's Richard O'Connell quickly agrees. "America's fascination with chocolate is one reason manufacturers are using extra chocolate in products—chocolate 'chunk' cookies, for example," he says. The recent obsession has pushed chocolate into the high-quality "signature" trend, with dress designers lending their labels to chocolate, according to Mr. O'Connell. "People now expect florists to offer boxed chocolate-and-flower gift combinations," he adds.

"Financial strength, technical ability and new ideas will keep Ambrosia the premier industrial bulk chocolate supplier in the U.S.," asserts Ken Manning.

Now, Ambrosia's future seems sugarcoated with success. In a town once known almost exclusively for brewing beer, that success has an even sweeter smell.

25

the typical quarterly inside: small, centered roman (Palatino) titles and justified roman body copy (also Palatino) set as one-column pages.

One of the liveliest of the liberal to left journals of opinion, at least from a design standpoint, is *The Progressive.* Its full-color covers are crowded and experimental, its inside pages bold, with plenty of art and lots of black bars, initials, and heavy contemporary sans serif titles. But *progressive* in design? Some art directors would say the look is dated.

How a publication looks should not be dictated by taste alone but by a knowledge of the personalities of typefaces and an understanding of how they affect the mood and "color" of the page when they are combined with the other elements on the page.

Here are some moods an editor might want and some suggestions on how an art director might achieve them.

1. *Dignity.* Use old roman typefaces, centered headings and art, generous amounts of white space, medium-size photos or paintings, or drawings made to resemble woodcuts.
2. *Power.* Use bold sans serif typefaces, boldface body copy, flush-left headings, large black photos or drawings made with lithographic crayons.
3. *Grace.* Use italic with swash caps or script types, light-face body copy with unjustified (ragged edge) right-hand margins, carefully composed photographs or wash drawings, an uncrowded look.
4. *Excitement.* Use a mixture of typefaces, color, close cropping of pictures, an unbalanced and crowded page.
5. *Precision.* Use the newer sans serifs or a slab serif for headings and body copy, sharp-focus photos or tight line drawings, horizontal or vertical ruled lines, highly organized design based on a grid system.

These are only suggestions, timidly advanced. Obviously they may not always work; and as a designer you will discover other ways of creating similar moods on the page. For instance, you may develop a way of taking an old roman face, with its built-in dignity and grace, and enlist it to establish a mood of excitement or even power. What is being said in a headline or copy is always more important than the type chosen to deliver it or the art chosen to amplify or surround it.

The lead article in an issue of *Grace Digest*—a classy, colorful semi-annual pocketbook-size magazine published by W. R. Grace & Company, New York, for shareholders and employees—dealt with Houlihan's, a chain of restaurants owned by the company. The restaurant specializes in low-calorie dishes, and so the art, as this opening spread shows, focused on appropriate dishes and, by showing scales, suggested calorie counting. Note that even the initial-letter art is being measured. Art direction by Bernhardt Fudyma Design Group.

A later spread in the same magazine, part of a "Cashing in on Chips" article about the Ambrosia Chocolate Company, Milwaukee, shows an entirely different design approach. The single column of copy printed over an orange tint block wraps around the pop art. The initial letter picks up the pattern of both the chips and the cone.

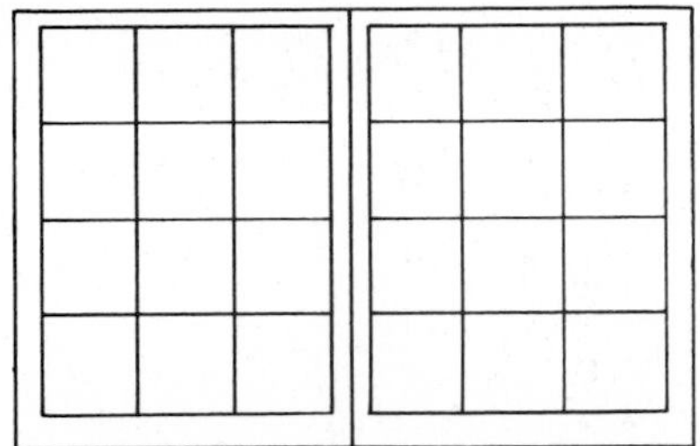

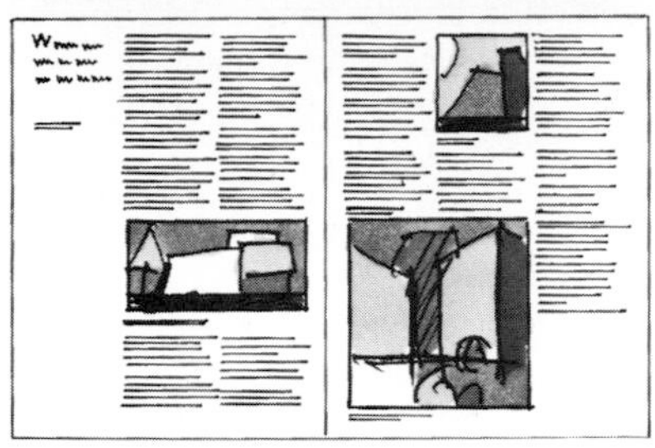

A grid consists of squares or rectangles that mark off areas for type and art. The three spreads shown in the rough sketches evolved from the grid shown at the top. There are hundreds of other possibilities from this one grid pattern. And there are many other patterns, of course. A grid can be made from rectangles as well as squares, and the rectangles need not be the same size.

The grid

For any kind of format some kind of grid is almost mandatory. A grid, made up of vertical and horizontal lines, sets the limits of printing areas. It is usually a printed two-page spread with lines ruled in to show the edges of the pages, edges on the outside of the pages to indicate bleeds, the place for folios, and columns for body copy. The columns are often prepared with a series of ruled lines, one for the bottom of each line of type.

One grid system involves the dividing of pages into squares, which in the design can be gathered into quarters, thirds, or halves of pages. Under this system all headings rest on a line in the grid, and all photos and columns of copy occupy one or more squares.

The art director draws up a master grid in India ink, and the printer runs enough of them, in a light blue or gray ink, to last a year or two. The printed grids can be used for both rough layouts and finished pasteups.

For a more formal looking publication, with highly organized pages, a more detailed grid is called for. It is calibrated not only in columns and lines for copy, but also in areas for pictures and headings.

Many art directors enjoy working with a fully developed grid that establishes boundaries for every possibility. Within the restrictions of such a grid lie all kinds of challenges, and the possibilities for variety in type and picture arrangements are still endless. The grid no more spoils creativity than a net spoils the pleasure of a tennis game.

Width of the columns

How wide should a column of type be? Well, any width, really. But the wider the column, the bigger the type should be.

An oft-stated rule for length of line is 1½ alphabets of lowercase letters, or 39 characters. The rule is too restrictive. George A. Stevenson in *Graphic Arts Encyclopedia* (McGraw-Hill, 1968) advanced the 39-character rule in a column of type that was itself more than 60 characters wide!

A column can be a little less than 39 characters wide, as in a newspaper, or even more than 60, as in some books. It depends to some extent on the age of the reader. It depends also on the mood the magazine is trying to create.

The fewer columns per page, the more bookish the look. A one- or two-column page looks more formal than a three-column page. A four-or-more-column page begins to look like a newspaper page.

The look you want determines the number of columns per page. There is no reason why a magazine can't have some narrow-column pages and some wide-column pages. A *Time*-size magazine, for instance, can run two columns per page for part of the magazine and three columns per page for the remainder. Nor is there any reason an article can't start out at one width and, on another page, narrow down to another.

Lineup of the pages

The magazine designer arranges articles and stories as a baseball manager arranges a batting lineup. In baseball the lineup has traditionally started off with a player who gets singles consistently. The second one up is a good bunter; the third one, another consistent hitter, but one who more often gets extra-base hits; the fourth one, a home run hitter; and so on.

The lead-off article in a magazine may not be the blockbuster; it may be a more routine kind of article. The second piece may be entertaining. The third piece may be cerebral. And so on. The editor—and art director—strive for change of pace from feature to feature.

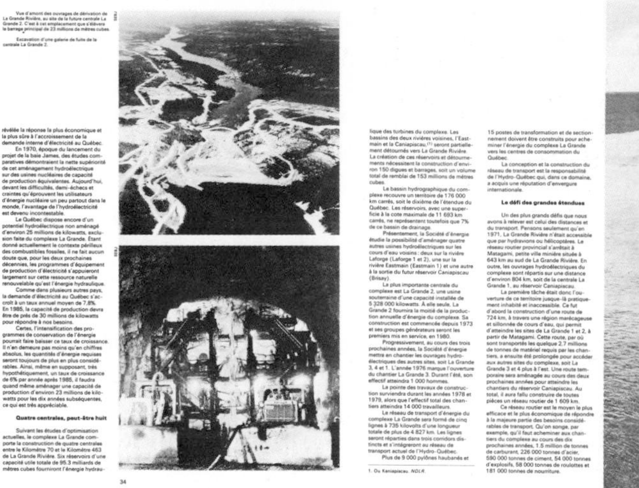

Here are the second two pages of an eight-page article in *Forces,* Montreal, Quebec, Canada. The 3¼″ sink remains constant throughout the 9 × 12 magazine, with an occasional jutting of photos, titles, and copy blocks. The beautifully designed and printed magazine obviously follows a carefully worked out grid.

Two pages from another article, same issue, where the sink is ignored, but the basic three-column format holds steady. This spread, although it occurs after an opening spread, starts with a column of white space to set off the one column of art. A deep vertical piece of art contrasts with a wide horizontal piece. The horizontal photograph is airbrushed at the top to make a vignette out of it. The boldface subhead consists of three lines, the first one indented.

One more variation of the *Forces* grid comes from inside another article. The two photographs reestablish the sink. The photos also share a common bottom axis. The copy in *Forces,* set in an unjustified sans serif type, occasionally extends up into the sink area.

A regular feature on "Design/Architecture" in *The Plain Dealer Magazine,* published by the Cleveland *Plain Dealer,* uses the same heading each time, the same title type, and similar well-composed photographs. The basically preset, crowded format does not prevent the art director, Gerard Sealy, from coming up with a different look each time.

ARCHITECTURE DESIGN BY WILMA SALISBURY

So, what's new and different on old E. 9th St.?

A downtown building does not exist in a vacuum. A tower that makes a statement on the skyline, a parking garage that clings to the earth, a landmark that preserves history — all are part of the fabric that gives a city its architectural character.

For years, Erieview Tower stood isolated on a windswept plaza. Designed in 1964 by Harrison and Abramovitz of New York, it was intended to be the centerpiece of the Erieview urban renewal plan. Because the plan was not completed as conceived, however, the 40-story green glass giant had nothing of comparable scale nearby to relate to.

With the building of One Cleveland Center and Ohio Bell around the edges of Erieview Plaza, the tower has become part of a neighborhood of tall buildings that includes the Federal Building, Bond Court and Cuyahoga Savings. In addition, the construction of North Point to the north of the plaza is strengthening the urban design of E. 9th St. as a tower-lined corridor leading to the heart of downtown Cleveland.

North Point was designed by architect Gerald J. Payto of Dalton, Dalton, Newport to be a good neighbor. As the economical low-rise complex takes shape, its neighborly qualities are beginning to emerge. A pair of modest five-story buildings joined by a glass-covered atrium, Phase I of North Point bows low to the monumentality of Ohio Bell and tips its peaked atrium hat to the angular shape of One Cleveland Center.

With its neat wrapping of green ribbon glass and beige patterned tile, the building is properly dressed for its appearance with City Hall to the west. When its courtyard is landscaped, it will supplement the attractive green space of Willard Park across the street. Because of its low profile, North Point does not obstruct views of Lake Erie from high-rise buildings along E. 9th St.

Ohio Bell, designed by Norman Perttula of Dalton, Dalton, Newport, also shows concern for context. The sweeping curve of the north facade extends a dramatic welcome to motorists coming off the shoreway. The sharp cut-away corner and angled reflective glass on its south facade provide a neat sense of closure for Erieview Plaza. The green glass and gray granite of its surface complements the silver aluminum and green glass skin of One Cleveland Center. The building's spacious lobby of granite, glass, chrome and stainless steel brings the outside indoors to a cold public space that is warmed by

St. John's Cathedral, above, is the only sacred architecture in the tower-lined E. 9th St. corridor. Opposite page, Erieview Plaza, top, has developed into a neighborhood of tall buildings including, from left: Ohio Bell, One Cleveland Center and the Federal Building. The crown jewels of E. 9th St., below, are Huntington Bank and AmeriTrust.

THE PLAIN DEALER MAGAZINE 44

bright textiles suspended from the ceilings. Heavy and grand, Ohio Bell looks best at night when interior lighting alters the proportion of opaque and transparent horizontal bands of granite and glass on the north facade. By day, the building is a monumental mass that solidly anchors the corner of E. 9th St. and Lakeside Ave.

In contrast to the weightiness of Ohio Bell, One Cleveland Center soars to the sky with aerodynamic sleekness. Known as the silver chisel (because of its shape) or the silver elephant (because of its leasing problems), the 30-story tower designed by Hugh Stubbins of Cambridge, Mass., turns at an angle toward Erieview Plaza. A shedlike five-story atrium at street level, an undulating blue auditorium at the rear and a lumpy gray attached garage are less elegant than the slender tower. However, One Cleveland Center's peaked roof and glowing reflective skin make it the most distinctive addition to the downtown skyline since Terminal Tower was built in the 1920s.

If a model of the Federal Building had been tested in a wind tunnel as One Cleveland Center was, the design might have been revised.

Wrapped in a smooth curtain wall of stainless steel and gray glass and set back from the street on a landscaped plaza, the 31-story box looks inviting on a calm summer day. When the wind blows off Lake Erie, however, the plaza becomes a no-man's land, negotiable only by sturdy pedestrians with a good sense of balance and a keen eye for the handrailings and wind shelters that have been installed for safety's sake.

Completing the west edge of Erieview Plaza are the 20-story Bond Court Building, completed in 1971, and the 15-story Cuyahoga Savings Building, completed in 1965. International-style boxes, these buildings get what personality they have from the color and texture of their curtain walls. Bronzed aluminum and bronze-tone glass give a sophisticated look to Bond Court, designed by Bruce Graham of Skidmore, Owings and Merrill of Chicago. Pre-cast concrete slabs give a more mundane appearance to Cuyahoga Savings, designed by Schafer, Flynn and van Dijk.

South of Erieveiw Plaza stands St. John's Cathedral, an ecclesiastical oasis in a sea of commercial office buildings. Although not nearly so magnificent as it was before its drastic re-

THE PLAIN DEALER MAGAZINE 45

ARCHITECTURE DESIGN BY WILMA SALISBURY

National Park Service gives an old town new life

Jaite is an old company town in rural Brecksville. Located in the Cuyahoga Valley National Recreation Area, it was built between 1905 and 1924 to house workers at the Jaite paper mill. Although the town was never incorporated, it once had a post office, jail and general store as well as four single-family homes, five duplexes, a shower house, carriage barn, public privy and several railroad buildings.

The Jaite family owned the mill and the town until the 1950s, and the mill continued in operation until last year. Now, however, the entire complex is owned by the National Park Service, which is restoring the town to its original look and adapting the buildings to a new use as headquarters for the park administration.

Jaite is listed on the National Register of Historic Places, not because of the architectural quality of the buildings, but because the collection of small structures clearly represents a well-preserved company town typical of the time.

In the early 20th century, pioneering industrialists attracted workers to rural areas such as the Cuyahoga Valley by providing modest living quarters. The houses built by Charles Jaite, a German immigrant who worked with the Cleveland-Akron Paper Co. before starting his own business, were occupied by managers in his mill. As many as 80 workers slept in shifts in a small dormitory over the general store. Other workers commuted by train or wagon from Peninsula, Boston and other nearby communities. At one time, more than 200 people (one-third of them women) were employed in the mill.

The four single-family homes remaining in Jaite stand in a neat row next to the general store at the intersection of Riverview and Vaughn roads. Identical in size, setback and floor plan, each cozy bungalow is designed in an eclectic style with Dutch colonial gambrel roof, pedimented porch and classical columns. Each has clapboard siding and an asphalt shingle roof. Each has a front door with two keyholes: one for the renter's key and the other for the landlord's master key. Built in 1919, the houses had no inside bathrooms until the 1960s, when small square additions were tacked onto the back.

The four single-family houses remaining in Jaite are identical in size, setback and floor plan. Built in 1919, they had no inside bathrooms until the 1960s, when small additions were tacked onto the back.

Although the houses are uniform in design, each facade has a touch of individuality. An off-center front door, a Palladian window, a sunburst decoration, shingles on the second story and other decorative details relieve the standardized look.

When the National Park Service acquired the houses in 1980, each was painted a different candystick color. Under the direction of historic architect Edward Adelman, the houses were restored to their original color: yellow with dark green doors and window sash and light yellow porch columns and trim.

Simple and functional, the company houses were probably not designed by an architect. Since catalog houses were popular at the time, it is likely that the four residences were built from kits ordered from Sears Roebuck.

In adapting the houses for use as offices, Adelman and the National Park Service staff made only minor modifications inside the houses.

PHOTO BY ED ADELMAN

In adapting the houses for use as offices, only minor modifications were made inside.

The general store, a classic revival style building, has undergone a more drastic renovation. Adelman and his staff did extensive research before replacing a two-story front porch, linking the shower house and carriage barn to the store with a cleverly designed connector and rebuilding the two-door privy as a station for electric meters.

Painted yellow like the houses, the store looks like part of the old company town on the exterior. The interior, however, has been significantly altered to suit its new use as a conference center and office building.

Restoration work is still in progress on the two duplexes across Riverview Road from the store. Large Victorian houses with clapboard siding, sawn cedar shingles and two-story bay windows, the duplexes are more elaborate than the bungalows and probably did not come from a catalog. In 1906, five double houses were built, but three burned down. The surviving two will be painted light yellow with darker yellow trim and dark green doors and window sash.

Clustered between the railroad tracks and Riverview Road, the houses and store have a unified look that is enhanced by the National Park Service landscaping. Although rustic yard rails, cement sidewalks and asphalt driveways are not true to the history of the company town, they tie the complex of buildings into the landscape design of the Cuyahoga Valley National Recreational Area.

Across the river about a mile east of the town stands the Jaite Mill. A sprawling industrial complex built of large concrete blocks manufactured on the site in 1905, the mill contains 180,000 square feet of open space. Initially, the mill manufactured paper bags for flour and cement. Processed with pure water from a deep artesian well on the site, the Jaite paper was said to be stronger than paper made from ordinary water. In its prime, the mill manufactured eight tons of paper daily.

Today, most of the huge mill stands empty. The Cuyahoga Valley Line leases office space in the building. Adelman said the National Park Service is considering a number of alternative uses for the mill. It could become an interpretive center housing exhibitions relating to industrial themes of the valley. It could be developed into recreational facilities, a lodge, meeting rooms or retail stores.

Because the National Park Service is in the business of preserving historic buildings, the mill will not be torn down. Like the town of Jaite, it has outlived its original function. But, like the company town, it will eventually be recycled to a new identity.

Restoration work is in progress on the two duplexes across Riverview Road from the store.

THE PLAIN DEALER MAGAZINE 18

THE PLAIN DEALER MAGAZINE 19

A person mentioned in *National Review* gets this decorative 3 × 9 card with the notation "You are mentioned on page 00 of the attached issue of . . . NATIONAL REVIEW. Cordially, the EDITORS." James W. O'Bryan was the designer.

When magazine articles and stories are not arranged by kind in the magazine proper, the arranging is usually done in the table of contents at the front of the book. There all the articles are grouped together, all the short stories, all the regular departments or columns. Some magazines even carry a separate table of contents of advertisements listed alphabetically at the back of the book.

Most readers read magazines front to back, but others—especially the browsers—read them from back to front. As far as advertisers are concerned, the best display impact is found in the first part of the magazine on right-hand pages; the best impact for the last part of the magazine, especially if it is side-stitched, is found on the left-hand pages. Most advertisers consider the first part of the magazine more important than the last half, and right-hand pages for them are highly desirable. They often accompany their insertion orders with the note "Up-front, right-hand placement urgently requested."

Convinced that many readers work through the magazine from back to front, some editors start editorials or articles on a back page and continue them on preceding pages. *U.S. News & World Report,* when it ran its long editorials by David Lawrence, did this. *Esquire* followed a maddening practice of starting articles or stories in the middle or back part of the magazine and continuing them on pages near the front. Some of *The New Yorker*'s best articles start in the last half of the magazine.

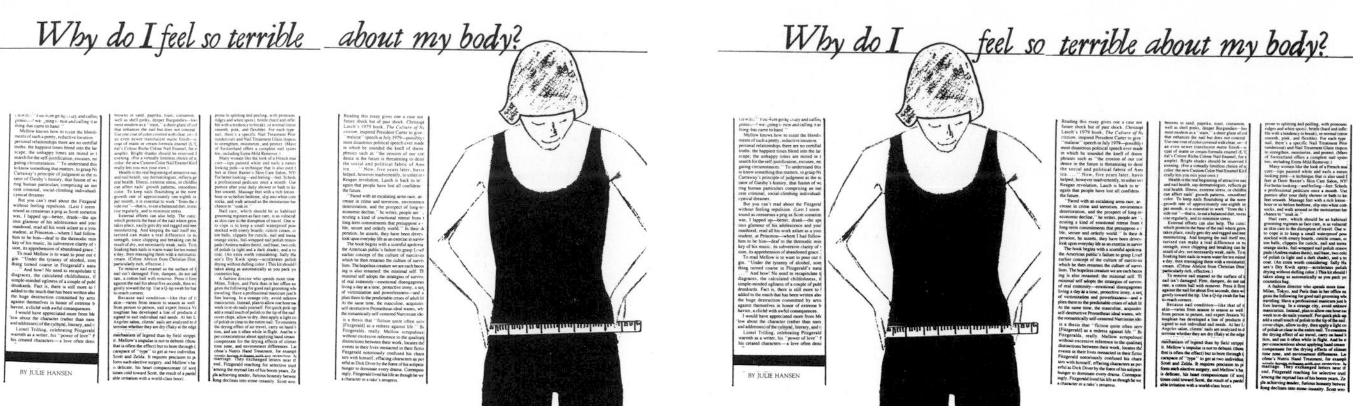

Why do I feel so terrible about my body?
BY JULIE HANSEN
Why do I feel so terrible about my body?
BY JULIE HANSEN

Virtue, a magazine for Christian women, asked students in a magazine design class to create opening spreads for an article scheduled for publication. The title was already written. This was Cindy Kent's rough layout solution.

Page numbering

The reader will thank the art director for leaving room on every page for page numbers. The art director will make exceptions only for full-page bleed photos or advertisements. Even then, the reader would prefer the numbers. Right-hand pages are always odd-numbered, of course; left-hand pages are even-numbered.

An art director with a last-minute signature to insert into a magazine whose other pages are already printed with numbers can number the insert pages with letters. For instance, if the last numbered page in the signature before the new one is 48, the first page of the new signature would be 48a, the next 48b, and so on. You see this numbering system used in the slicks with their regional editions.

Some magazines, embarrassed because of the thinness of the issues and not wanting the readers to realize they are reading only twenty-four- or thirty-six- or forty-eight-page publications, start numbering the pages in the first issue of the year and carry through the numbering until the last issue of the year. The reader can pick up an issue in July, for instance, and find the issue beginning with, say, page 173. Some of the opinion magazines use this system. They might argue that they do it because the issues are part of a volume, and such numbering is an aid to the researcher.

Page numbering for some magazines starts on the cover and for other magazines on the first right-hand page after the cover. It is the embarrassingly thin magazine that considers its cover page 1.

A magazine's thickness

Most magazines let the amount of advertising dictate the number of pages of any particular issue. The more ads the magazine gets, the more pages it runs. Its thickest issues are in late fall, before Christmas. Its thinnest issues are right after the first of the year and in the middle of the summer. The ratio of ad space to editorial space, ideally, runs 70:30. For some magazines it runs closer to 50:50 or even 40:60. When the ratio gets that low, the magazine is in trouble.

A few magazines offer readers the same amount of editorial matter issue after issue. Only the amount of advertising changes. A magazine that is highly departmentalized almost has to operate like that.

Magazines that do not contain advertising often run the same number of pages issue after issue. Company magazines fall into this category. And, because they contain so little advertising, so do opinion magazines.

The newsletter is the simplest and least expensive of publication formats. No photos or drawings are needed to make it inviting, provided the designer uses enough white space and carefully plans the placing of the headings. The front page sets the style. Note that for this one the news items are blocked off into two-column rectangular units. The format works for either a printed or a duplicated piece. Designed by the author.

School of Journalism, University of Oregon | December 1967

ALUMNI NEWSLETTER

The numbers game

And on through the summer

A $62,500 grant for the school

The number of pages for most magazines runs to thirty-two—two sixteen-page signatures. After the printing the sheet is folded down to page size and trimmed. Signatures come in multiples of four or eight or sixteen, depending upon the size of the page and the size of the press used to print the magazine.

If a magazine has a cover on a heavier stock—a separate cover—that's another four-page signature. Wrap it around two sixteen-page signatures, and you have a thirty-six-page magazine.

Magazine bindings

Magazines face a choice of three basic bindings: saddle stapling (or saddle stitching), side stapling (or side stitching), and perfect (glued) binding.

The big advantage of saddle stapling is that the magazine opens up easily and lies flat on the table or desk. Readers can tear out pages they want to save.

And a saddle-stapled magazine may be easier to design. For instance, you can more easily run pictures and type across the gutter. When *Harper's* went from side stapling to saddle stapling, it said in its announcement that it was doing it for design reasons. *The Atlantic* soon followed with a saddle-stapled format. Saddle stapling also allows for an uninterrupted center spread.

Side stapling, on the other hand, makes for a more permanent binding. It suggests to the reader that this magazine ought to be kept. Editors wanting to make it easy for readers to tear out articles can have the pages perforated. Side stapling is especially recommended for magazines of many pages.

After World War II *Reader's Digest* experimented with perfect binding—side binding without staples—and today the *Digest* and many other major magazines, including women's fashion magazines, are bound in this way. Such magazines end up with spines, like books, on which their names can be printed. In 1978 the East/West Network, publishers of several in-flight magazines, went to perfect binding. The Network said that such binding made things more flexible. For instance, it could easily insert ad supplements in any size anywhere in the magazines.

Many magazines choose a heavier stock for their covers than for their inside pages and have their covers printed separately, to be bound around

Ordinarily content dicates design, but sometimes you have to do designing first. Here is one of several spreads designed by the author to help the editor of a new Crown Zellerbach magazine decide on a format before material for his first issue was completed. This article was to be about a fish hatchery, but the title and blurb were not yet written, and photographs were not yet available. Placement, margins, and sizes could be indicated, and a few strokes from a felt marker, if nothing else, could show where photos (one square, one widely horizontal) would go. The extra space between the first two columns of copy represents the gutter. Because the letters in "HATCHERY" were to be so large, the designer lined up the tail of the *Y*—not the *Y* itself—with the right-hand margin of the far-right column.

the inside pages. This works for side-bound as well as saddle-bound publications.

American Heritage originally came out as a hardbound publication, but in 1981 it offered subscribers a choice of bindings—hard or soft.

Notes

1. See Edwin Diamond, "The Great Magazine Race," *New York,* August 26, 1985, pp. 34–40.
2. Anthony A. Lyle, "It Was Written," *Pennsylvania Gazette,* June 1978, p. 2.
3. David Z. Orlow, "The Magazine of the Inevitable," *Folio,* January 1977, pp. 22, 23.
4. Stuart J. Elliott, "*Cosmo* Celebrates That Girl's 20th," *Advertising Age,* July 22, 1985, p. 3.
5. A source is Joseph North, ed., *New Masses: An Anthology of the Rebel Thirties,* International Publishers, New York, 1969.
6. Phil Douglis, "How Magazine Pages Help Sequence Pictures," *IABC News,* October 1976, p. 3.
7. Quoted by John Peter, "The Leading Edge," *Folio,* September 1980, p. 146.
8. Letters to the editor, *Madison Avenue,* October 1985, p. 6.
9. Don Fabun, "Dedicated to Human Questions," *DA: The Paper Quarterly for the Graphic Arts,* Second Quarter, 1970, p. 8.
10. George Nelson, "We Are Here by Design," *Harper's,* April 1975, p. 3.
11. Jan V. White, *Designing for Magazines,* R. R. Bowker Company, New York, 1976, p. x.
12. James Warren in a Chicago Tribune News Service feature, "Magazine Pays Tribute to Southern Elegance," *The Oregonian,* October 6, 1985, p. 12.

Suggested further reading

Click, J. W., and Russell N. Baird, *Magazine Editing and Production,* 4th ed., Wm. C. Brown Company Publishers, Dubuque, Iowa, 1986.

Darrow, Ralph C., *House Journal Editing,* Interstate Printers & Publishers, Danville, Illinois, 1974.

Editors of Folio, *Magazine Publishing Management,* Folio Magazine Publishing Corporation, New Canaan, Connecticut, 1977.

Ferguson, Rowena, *Editing the Small Magazine,* 2d ed. Columbia University Press, New York, 1976.

Hubbard, J. T. W., *Magazine Editing: How to Acquire the Skills You Need to Win a Job and Succeed in the Magazine Business,* Prentice-Hall, Englewood Cliffs, New Jersey, 1982.

Lattimore, Dan L., and John W. Windhauser, *The Editorial Process,* Morton Publishing Company, Denver, Colorado, 1977. (A workbook.)

Magazine Profiles: Studies of Magazines Today, Medill School of Journalism, Northwestern University, Evanston, Illinois, 1974.

Making Magazines, American Society of Magazine Editors, New York, 1978.

Mann, Jim, *Solving Publishing's Toughest Problems,* Folio Magazine Publishing Corporation, New Canaan, Connecticut, 1981.

Mayes, Herbert R., *The Magazine Maze: A Prejudiced Perspective,* Doubleday, Garden City, New York, 1980.

Mogel, Leonard, *The Magazine: Everything You Need to Know to Make It in the Magazine Business,* Prentice-Hall, Englewood Cliffs, New Jersey, 1979.

Rice, Don, *How to Publish Your Own Magazine,* David McKay, New York, 1978.

Williams, W. P., and Joseph Van Zandt, *How to Start Your Own Magazine,* Contemporary Books, Chicago, 1978.

The magazine cover

BYU Today, the bimonthly alumni magazine of Brigham Young University, uses Mark Philbrick's full-color, full-page photograph of the statue of Karl G. Maeser, which now stands in front of the remodeled Maeser Building. Four carefully placed horizontal bars help make the cover blurb stand out. Randall M. Moore art directed. The cover story inside deals with several buildings on the Provo, Utah, campus.

The ultimate goal for some people, it seems, is to make the cover of a national magazine. Dr. Hook and the Medicine Show did a song about getting on the cover of *Rolling Stone,* and a few weeks after the song hit the Top 40, Dr. Hook made it. A few weeks after that, Dr. Hook walked into the magazine's San Francisco office (it has since moved to New York) and bought five copies for his mother, as the song suggested he would do.

The most prestigious cover spot, probably, is on the front of *Time.* Malcolm Muggeridge contemptuously called the *Time* cover spot "post-Christendom's most notable stained-glass window." At the end of each year *Time's* editors and letter-to-the-editor writers engage in a navel-contemplation maneuver as the decision is made about the "Man of the Year."

A low point in magazine covers came in 1977 with the publication and national distribution of *Assassin.* The cover of the first issue showed a picture of President Carter with the crosshairs of a telescopic sight superimposed on his face. The blurb said, "How Would You Do It: See Special Entry Page." Inside the magazine also was information on how to blow up a car using a homemade bomb and how to build an atomic bomb.

What the cover does

No feature is as important to a magazine as its cover, no matter how the magazine is circulated.

A magazine cover does these things:

1. *It identifies the magazine.* The art director tries to come up with something in the cover design to set the magazine apart from all others.
2. *It attracts attention.* The art director must allure readers somehow—and then get them inside. Milton Glaser says a magazine cover can capture attention "by creating a tension between clarity and novelty."[2]
3. *It creates a suitable mood for the reader.*

And if the magazine is displayed on newsstands, the cover has one more function:

SOHIO

spring '81

BOO! HISS! BUSINESS PLAYS THE VILLAIN

WALL STREE

1981 Dow Jones & Company, Inc

WEDNESDAY, FEBRUARY

News

Also featuring:

Murray Weidenbaum on the economy

Give your child the gift of music

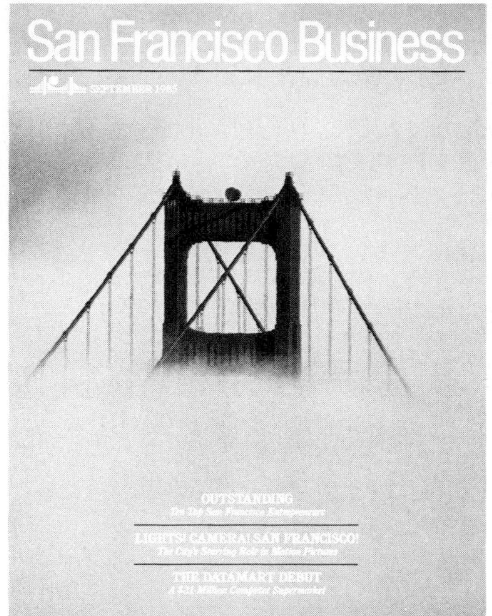

Company magazines and many association magazines enjoy the luxury of wraparound covers. Ads do not have to go on the back. For this issue of *San Francisco Business,* published by the San Francisco Chamber of Commerce, Mark E. Gibson's full-color photograph of the fog-shrouded Golden Gate Bridge provides an ideal background for the reversed logo and cover lines on the front cover and nicely unites front and back. Patricia Doherty art directed.

Designer Janusz Einhorn of Herbick & Held used a number of symbols to illustrate a blurb on a full-color *Sohio* magazine cover, a blurb that suggests how Hollywood deals with business people, who are always villains. The symbols are a tough-looking businessman in a striped suit, *The Wall Street Journal,* and a piece of movie film. In reverse letters in the film are two blurbs for other articles in the issue. *Sohio* is published quarterly by the Standard Oil Company of Ohio.

4. *It sells the magazine.*

In 1976, for the first time, the top general-circulation or consumer magazines—those with circulations of 300,000 or more—sold more copies on newsstands than they circulated through the mails. With postal rates so high, magazines were making a concerted effort to sell single copies. *TV Guide* set its subscription rate higher than a year's worth of single copies would cost.

What goes on the cover acquires added importance when a magazine depends mostly on newsstand sales. A magazine's circulation then rests on impulse buying. What is shown on the cover and how the blurbs are worded become vital editorial decisions.

But covers are important for nonnewsstand magazines, too. Howard Paine, chief of editorial layout for *National Geographic,* says, "We may not have to compete on the newsstand but we do have to compete on the coffee table."[3]

Covers are so important to *Der Spiegel* in Germany that a department of four people there works on nothing but covers.

What goes on the cover

At first, magazines adopted permanent cover designs, usually without art. Will Bradley in the late 1800s talked *The Inland Printer* into changing covers each month, setting the trend for other magazines. *The Inland Printer* even changed its logo and moved it around from issue to issue.

Covers require both a permanent decision on basic format and an issue-by-issue decision on art and typography.

For your basic format you must answer the following questions:

1. Should the cover be of the same stock as the remainder of the magazine? Or should it be of a heavier stock?
2. What process should be used to print the cover? The same as for the remainder of the magazine or some other?
3. What kind of logo does the magazine need? Where should it go on the cover? Need it stay in the same place issue after issue?
4. Does the cover need art? Photograph or illustration? Must the art be tied to an inside feature? Or can it stand on its own, like the old Norman Rockwell covers for *The Saturday Evening Post?*
5. Does the cover need color? Spot color or process color?
6. Are titles or blurbs necessary? Where should they go on the cover?
7. Will a regular cover do? Or is a gatefold called for? Or maybe an oversize cover, like those on the pulp magazines of the 1930s?

The typical magazine cover carries a logo, date of the issue and price per copy, art, and titles of major features along with names of authors.

Major display on covers takes any of these forms:

1. *A photograph or illustration tied to a feature inside.* "Is Inflation Out of Control?" asked *Newsweek* on one of its 1980 covers. To illustrate the blurb, the magazine showed a full-color photograph of a dollar bill, larger than life-size, on fire, the flame reaching up to and under the logo.
2. *Abstract art or a photograph or illustration that stands by itself.* The art director may want to keep such art free of all type, in-

REGIONAL MAGAZINE OF THE YEAR
APRIL 1985/$1.50
OHIO
Who's To Blame for Acid Rain? Guilty or No, Ohio's Going To Pay
Be It Ever So Humble, There's No Place Like the Town of Linndale
Hear That Lonesome Whistle Call
The Cuyahoga Valley Line Rides Again
7TH ANNIVERSARY ISSUE

Ohio Magazine changed its logo in 1985 from a spread-out Bodoni-like set of letters to a narrower unit of classic romans with more white space not only around the logo but also around the art, for a more sophisticated look. This is the first cover in the new series—and the cover for the seventh anniversary issue. Bird's-eye-view photograph by Mike Steinberg and Tom Simon. Design by Thomas E. Hawley. (From *Ohio Magazine,* April 1985. Reprinted by permission.)

cluding the logo, so that it will be suitable for framing. An explanation of the art can be carried in a caption on the title page.

The cover of the *Bulletin of the Atomic Scientists* accommodates a "doomsday" clock. The hands occasionally move back and forth as world conditions change. The hands, of course, are always close to midnight.

3. *Type only.* The type can be in the form of a title or two from articles inside, as in the case of most of the opinion magazines; or as a table of contents, a form *Reader's Digest* was instrumental in popularizing.
4. *The beginning of an article or editorial that continues inside. The New Republic* has used an occcasional cover for this purpose. Some magazines—*Advertising Age* and *Billboard,* for example—run several articles or stories on the cover, newspaper-style.
5. *An advertisement. Editor & Publisher* uses its cover for this purpose. A cover ad brings premium rates.

Communication World manages to find a spot for its logo and another spot for its cover blurbs without hurting the excellent full-color art by Guy Billout. The crowded-type look contrasts nicely with Billout's depiction of space. This black-and-white reproduction does not show that among the endless rows of red flowers there is, near the prostrate figure, one yellow one. Gloria Gordon, the magazine's managing editor, art directed.

COMMUNICATION WORLD

THE NEWSMAGAZINE
FOR COMMUNICATION
AND PUBLIC RELATIONS
PROFESSIONALS
SEPTEMBER 1985

INTERNATIONAL ASSOCIATION OF BUSINESS COMMUNICATORS

The New Yorker runs covers with no type except for the logo and the accompanying date and price. No blurbs (also called "cover lines") show up over or near the art to detract from it.

Not many newsstand magazines enjoy this luxury. Blurbs become a necessity for magazines fighting each other for attention on the newsstands. The blurbs tell browsers and readers what to expect inside. Sometimes the blurbs dominate the cover.

Editors and art directors try to put blurbs in neutral or nonpattern areas of the art in a typeface heavy enough to show through or in areas outside the art if it does not bleed. If two or more blurbs are involved, they are separated so that they don't read as a single multiline headline.

The cover art should amplify the main blurb. It may be the best of the art pieces submitted with the lead article. Or it may be a piece arranged for independently. Sometimes the nature of the art dictates the wording of the cover blurb.

When a cover carries several blurbs, you can separate them by (1) adding space or rules between them, (2) running one in a larger type than the others, (3) ending each with a period, (4) putting one—say the one in the center—in color, or (5) running them across from each other as multiline units instead of under each other. It is not necessary to include a page number after a cover blurb, especially if the magazine is a thin one. It *is* necessary, a lot of readers would argue, to word the blurb to conform with the wording of the article title inside.

Fortunately for editors of company magazines, cover blurbs are not a necessity, because there is no immediate competition to worry about. Certainly no price has to be carried on the cover and no Universal Product Code. A few innovative company editors glorying in simplification even leave off the dates of their issues, allowing the art to announce the month or season—if either of these has to be announced. (The masthead inside carries the month and year, of course, along with other vital statistics.)

The best covers for magazines in any category contain an element of surprise—something that maybe isn't picked up at first glance. One of the beauties of a gatefold is that the surprise can come after the cover is unfolded, as a surprise comes in a studio greeting card when you get inside. George Lois's covers for *Esquire* in the 1960s often carried visual surprises.

National Review, even though some of its circulation comes from newsstand sales, changes back and forth from a full logo to an initials logo with the full name in small type below. James W. O'Bryan, when he was art director, usually used full color, but for this cover a black-and-white photo seemed appropriate to illustrate William F. Buckley, Jr.'s review of *Scoundrel Time* inside. The photo is from a full-page ad for a fur coat that the author of *Scoundrel Time,* Lillian Hellman, had recently posed for.

Newsstand considerations

A magazine sold on the newsstands, in contrast to one delivered only by mail, needs to (1) sell itself to the impulse buyer and (2) identify itself for the regular buyer. Whereas a through-the-mail magazine can run its logo anywhere on the cover and in different typefaces from issue to issue, the newsstand magazine needs a standard logo in a standard position.

Most newsstand magazines are displayed in an upright position, often with only the left side showing. This is why many newsstand magazines have their logos crowded in the upper left. If the magazine is *Life*-size, it lies on its back, in stacks, often low in the stands.

What art and blurbs the art director puts on the cover seriously affect sales. "Trends in cover art change rapidly," said Norman P. Schoenfeld, when he was art director at *True*. "We have to keep close tabs on how a given cover sells on the newsstand. . . . Naturally, our circulation department takes a keen interest in our cover selection." A cover can affect newsstand sales by as much as 20 percent.[4]

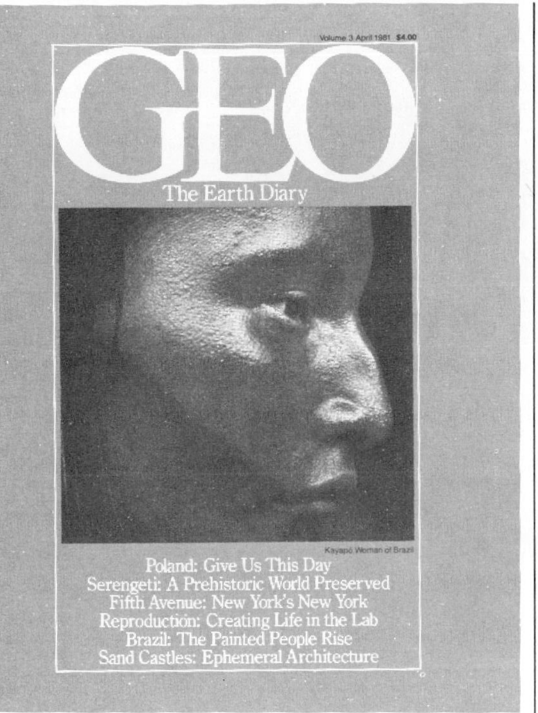

Geo, a handsome, slick-paper magazine, keeps full-color art a nominal size for its covers, surrounding it with a box reversed in a field of green. The shortness of the name allows it to be shown in large, classic capital letters. The blurbs, all with colons, are centered. Photograph by Maureen Bisilliat. (© 1981 by *Geo.*)

Bob Ciano, art director of the reborn *Life,* finds that his bestselling covers often break all the rules he learned at school. Even a mediocre photograph on a cover can work better than a photograph that might better please an art director. The subject matter makes a big difference.

Ciano told an American Society of Magazine Editors seminar in 1981 that no one has been able to identify a design pattern for the cover that will, automatically, boost sales. "I think we worry too much about what our readers want and don't want," Ciano said. "I think we all bring years of experience to magazines and don't often enough go with that experience and gut reaction." John Volger, art director for *Business Week,* told the same seminar that for his magazine a black-and-white cover with just one color often does better than a full-color cover. A black-and-white cover can stand out on a newstand aflood with color.[5]

Who is featured on the cover is important, of course. *Paris Match* reports that singers do more for circulation than politicians do. *People* reports the same findings. And at *People,* TV subjects are better than music subjects. *People* does a lot of cover research, but Richard B. Stolley, managing editor, admits that "every time we think we know something, . . . things change. We find we don't really know much at all."[6]

Timing

A magazine that features people in the news on its covers may be deeply embarrassed as news changes while the magazine is being printed and delivered.

An embarrassment on the cover is much more serious than an embarrassment inside. When choosing cover art, you must give some thought to what a sudden turn of events might do to the message your cover art conveys. Perhaps the wording of the blurb can be adjusted to make it more flexible.

Another problem involves duplication. Editors (and art directors) come from similar backgrounds and hence tend to think alike. Often, then, they arrive at similar ideas for covers. Competing magazines like *Time* and *Newsweek* can't help appearing often with the same cover themes. It is not a matter of editorial leaks—one magazine does not want to copy the other. Nor can it be prevented by taking precautions to avoid the duplication. If a story is there, it gets the coverage. It is a matter of staying abreast of the times.

Jeff MacNelly in the comic strip *Shoe* shows the ultimate *Time-Newsweek* cover duplication. One character is reading a copy of *Newsweek* with a *Time* cover and logo printed on it; the other is reading *Time,* which carries a *Newsweek* cover and logo.

When you see a magazine for one week moving away from serious cover art to, say, art showing a well-endowed female entertainer, you can rightly suspect it is that time of year when the magazine is attempting to step up newsstand sales to impress advertisers or make a good showing in a circulation audit.

What's in a name?

After one hundred years of publication *Your Life and Health* was dying when Ralph Blodgett took over as editor in 1984. After a year of revamping, Blodgett managed to turn things around, making it one of the nation's fastest-growing Christian magazines (it's published by the Re-

This *Sunshine* cover uses colorful high-tech art to portray someone who made a lot of money quickly and lived a fast life. Illustration by Mark Chickinelli. Art direction by Greg Paul. Published by the Fort Lauderdale *News/Sun-Sentinel.*

view and Herald Publishing Association). One of the changes involved the name; the magazine became *Vibrant Life.*

The name change was necessary to erase a negative image the magazine had developed and to reflect a new direction. Going from a four-word to a two-word name followed Blodgett's own newsstand survey, which showed that out of five hundred magazines only 1 percent had four-word names and 2 percent had three-word names. All others had one- or two-word names.

Blodgett and an advisory committee settled on two names: *Vitality* and *Vibrant Life.* But a search of registered magazine names at the U.S. Patent Office in Arlington, Virginia, always necessary when naming a magazine, showed that another organization already had pinned down *Vitality.* That left *Vibrant Life.* "A Christian Guide for Total Health" was added to attract the right audience.[7]

Picking a name for a magazine can be the single most important step a publisher or editor makes. Once decided upon, the name sticks, even when the formula for the magazine changes. That's why editors are well advised not to include publication frequency in the name. Put *Quarterly* into the title, and what do you do when the publication becomes successful enough to go bimonthly or monthly? What is the significance now of the *Saturday* in *Saturday Review* and *Saturday Evening Post?*

Your emphasis may seem permanent at the start, but in a few years, as times change, you may want your magazine to change. How can anyone take seriously a magazine that still goes by the name of *Playboy?*

You want to be clever in your name choice but appropriate, too. So how does *The Avant Gardener* strike you? Or *Statutory Rap,* a publication of the University of Dayton Law School? Or *Rider's Digest,* a publication of the Metropolitan Atlanta Rapid Transit Authority? Or *The Eggsaminer,* once published for egg producers?

In *Annie Hall* Woody Allen came up with a name for the merger of *Dissent* with *Commentary:* the name was *Dissentary. Atlas,* a digest of foreign press news, features, and comment, was named after the Titan who held up the heavens. "Our own more modest purpose," said the ed-

Emergency Medicine for this issue allowed part of the art to partially cover the logo. The doll put up on the shelf to be mended is a full-color painting (by Donald Hedin) rather than a photograph. Tom Lennon designed this cover; Ira Silberlicht art directed.

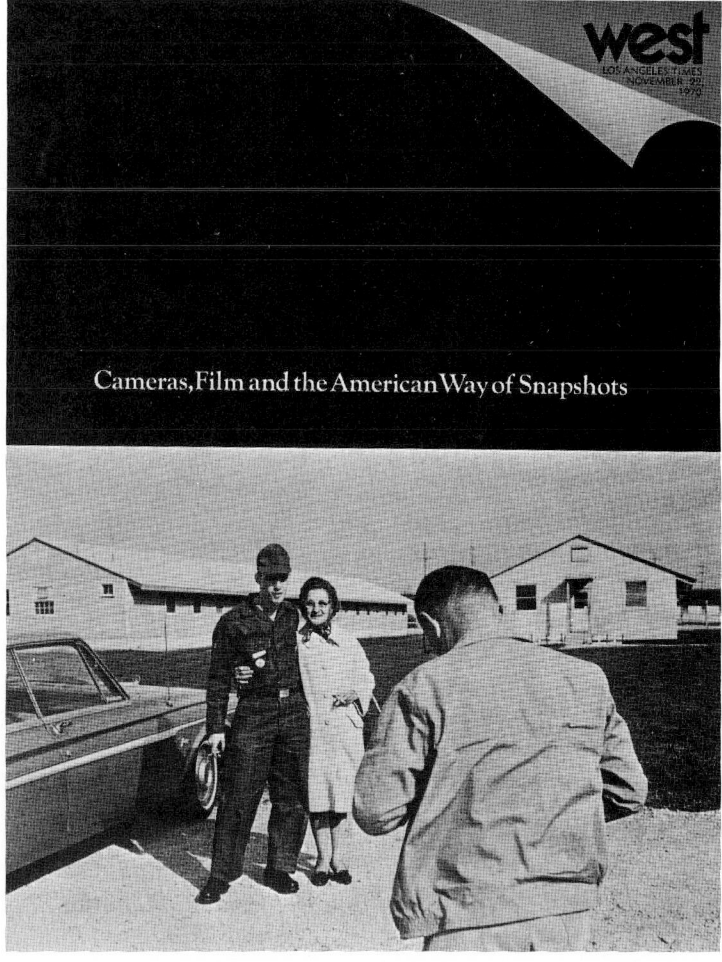

West was not afraid to change the size of the logo from issue to issue or to move it around on the cover. For this cover, promoting an article on photography as "everyman's art form," the art director, Mike Salisbury, put his logo into a setting that approximates the Kodak logo. (This was before *Time* turned down the corner on its covers.) Photographer Ron Mesaros used a Polaroid camera to take this picture of someone taking a picture.

itors, "is to hold the world up to our readers." But *Atlas* changed to *World Press Review* in March of 1980 because, its editors decided, *Atlas* suggested to would-be readers a book of maps or tables.

Many magazines incorporate apostrophes in their names. The *Reader's Digest* name suggests that the magazine is for a single reader. *Publishers' Auxiliary* suggests that the publication is for many or all publishers. *Publishers Weekly* uses its *Publishers* as an adjective rather than a possessive, hence no apostrophe. At one time the magazine did include an apostrophe in its name.

Some magazines like a *The* in their names. And some use names on their covers that differ slightly from the names on the mastheads inside, causing scholars some confusion when citing sources.

Magazines with long names can make references to themselves less cumbersome by going to initials. Hence, the Journal of the American Medical Association becomes *JAMA* and the Journal of the Association of Operating Room Nurses becomes the *AORN Journal. CA* was lucky enough in its initials that when it wanted to erase the commercial art image (it was originally called *Commercial Art*), it found its initials also stood for *Communication Arts,* the name by which it is now known. *National Review* sometimes features a big *NR* on its cover rather than its full name. *FMR,* which calls itself "the most beautiful magazine in the world," gets its name from the initials of its founder, Franco Maria Ricci.

Self Help for Hard of Hearing People, Inc. in Bethesda, Maryland, takes the first four important initials of its name, makes an acronym of it, and uses it as the name of its bimonthly magazine, *Shhh,* with the last three letters of the name in lowercase. It is a strange name for a magazine devoted to people who don't hear well. "Shhh" is not a command we usually associate with them.

A magazine with a long name can run part of the name in smaller type. *The New York Review of Books* runs *of Books* centered below the main part of the title, in much smaller type but in the same slab serif face. Another book review magazine years ago dropped *of Literature* from its name and carried on, sometimes sporadically, as *Saturday Review,* with a broader base than that of a mere book review publication.

Bruce Jenner's Better Health & Living magazine has one of the longest names around, but the words *Health & Living* are considerably larger than any of the other words in the logo.

Some of the older magazines also carry their founders' names: *McCall's, Forbes, Hoard's Dairyman, Best's Insurance News.* Sometimes this causes confusion. *Moody Monthly* is not a magazine for depressed persons; it is a religious magazine named after the evangelist Dwight L. Moody and a Bible institute.

A modifier seems useful to some editors, who put a *Modern* or *Today's* in front of the title or an *Age* or *World* behind it; but often a single, straightforward word does the job—*Banking* or *Eternity.* Of course, a single name can be jarring to someone outside the magazine's readership. The student senate of the University of Louisville School of Dentistry publishes the perfectly serious *Abscess.*

Because it appears in the West, one important consumer magazine calls itself *Sunset.*

Often it is hard to find a name because all the possibilities seem to be taken. *Esquire* editors worked with *Trend, Stag,* and *Beaut* before getting a letter addressed with the quaint *Esq.* after the recipient's name, and decided to try that word spelled out.

An earlier chapter shows a silhouetted photograph cover for *Touche Ross Life.* The monthly magapaper uses a variety of art forms for its covers. This one, in red and black, features abstract, Art Deco line art. (From *Touche Ross Life,* May 1981. Published by Touche Ross & Co. Reprinted by permission.)

(Right)
Long Lines starts an article on the cover for this issue. The large-type lead continues on page 1 inside the magazine, then narrows down to regular-size columns. In the original the logo appears in black, the lead in green, the silhouette art in full color. A thin line in red tops the story beginning. *Long Lines* is a slick-paper magazine for the employees of the Long Lines Department of the American Telephone & Telegraph Company.

(Below)
Mark Andresen adopted futurist and German expressionist styles to create the art for this "Cleveland's Leftists" cover for *The Plain Dealer Magazine*. The style had been popular in Bolshevik posters during the Russian Revolution. Greg Paul art directed.

Prison publications have shown a feel for the ironic with such title choices as these: *Time & Tied, The Stretch, Bars & Stripes, Detour, The New Leaf, The Key,* and (are you ready for this?) *The Prism.*

Company magazines have shown imagination in their choices of names, too. The company that makes Heath bars publishes *Sweet Talk,* Blue Chip Stamps publishes *Chip Chat,* Gulf Oil Corporation publishes *Gulf Oilmanac,* Wisconsin Electric Power publishes *The Outlet,* and Public Service Indiana puts out *Watts Cookin'.*

The job of the art director is to come up with the right typeface to help say visually what the title says in words. But that does not mean that *Sweet Talk* should be dripping in chocolate or that *The Outlet* has to be in a script made from an electric cord.

The logo

The logo, a typographic rendering of the magazine's name, is much like a company trademark. Its adoption is a serious matter. Once selected, it settles in for many years of service. Its value increases to the point where its owner feels reluctant to abandon it even when its design becomes outmoded.

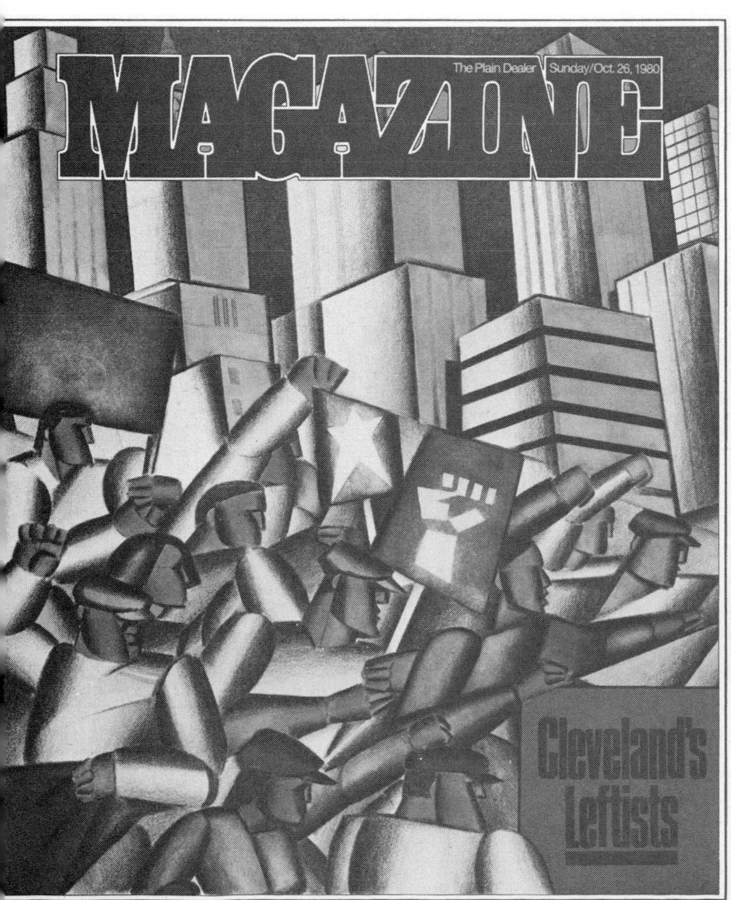

Long Lines
AUGUST / SEPTEMBER 1975

Before his day is over, he will make 25 phone calls, answer 15 others, travel 200 miles and read scores of reports and technical materials. He'll write a dozen memos (some of them to himself) and talk with his boss five times. He'll answer a hundred questions and ask twice as many. At microwave facilities, he'll make note of weeds that need uprooting and scratch his head about a sniper who's been taking potshots at a tower beacon, youths who are jumping a fence...

(continued on page 1)

HARPER'S

The *Harper's* logo, designed by Samuel Antupit in consultation with the editor, Lewis H. Lapham, uses classic roman caps, tightly spaced to form ligatures. The thin, vertical, short line that acts as an apostrophe, a "wrong font" in the hands of a nonprofessional, gives the beautifully simple logo character and something of a contemporary feel.

In designing a logo, then, you avoid types or letterforms that soon will be out of date. Yet you choose type that is distinctive. More important, you select type that is appropriate. You might decide on a typeface for the letters actually used, not for the beauty of the face as a whole. How a single letter looks might well influence your decision.

The Sporting News is an example of a magazine with an inappropriate logo face: Old English. The editors would argue that their weekly publication is newspaperlike in its approach, and Old English has been used, historically, for newspaper logos. But Old English has an ecclesiastical feel; it is far removed from the roughness and vitality of the sports world.

Whatever face you choose, you have to decide whether you want all caps, caps and small caps, caps and lowercase, an initial cap and lowercase, all lowercase, upright and italics, solid or outline letters.

You may want to rough out the idea for your logo, but because of its specialized nature, its importance, and its permanence, you should call in a professional calligrapher or letterform artist to complete the job. You should not allow your logo to be hand-lettered by just anyone who knows how to draw. Illustrators as a rule are unfamiliar with type and letterform, and many of them do a poor job of lettering.

Settling for a regularly set typeface instead of hand lettering is the best solution when professional lettering help is not available or affordable. Without much ability as a lettering artist, you can do some innovating with type yourself. You can order reproduction proofs of the type and then cut the letters apart and respace them to bring to your logo a flair ordinary typography can't supply. Because logos involve only one or two words and because readers have a chance to study them issue after issue, you can do things with spacing that you wouldn't do when working on article and story titles. For instance, you can move two capitalized words together, with no space between.

LikeThis

You can doctor some of the letters, too, so that they would be unrecognizable were they not seen in context. *Dare,* a magazine once published for barbershops, ran its logo in mirror reverse, so that it read from right to left. It was in keeping with the nature of the magazine; it "dared" to be different.

STATE OF OREGON
Public Employes
Retirement System
Official Bimonthly Newsletter
PERSPECTIVES

The organization publishing this bimonthly newsletter is Public Employees Retirement System, or PERS. So "Perspective" was a natural as a name. The editor, Bernerd Fred Park, and the graphic artist, Arnold Albertson, got together and worked out this logo that emphasizes the *PERS* initials. The small type at the top lines up with the *S* in *PERS*, and the State of Oregon seal is placed to act as a sort of dot for the *I*.

NewTimes

THE FEATURE NEWS MAGAZINE

Family Circle

Steve Phillips, art director of the magazine, designed the *New Times* logo using tightly spaced sans serifs and bringing the two words together by allowing the *T* to overlap the *w*. The *T* picks up the slant of the *w* for its left cross-bar; the right cross-bar does extra duty as the dot for the *i*. *New Times* is no longer published.

This logo, designed by Herb Lubalin for *Family Circle,* was one of the first of the "nestled" logos, with letters from one line fitting snugly against letters from another. The *C* actually overlaps the *m*. *Circle* is so placed that a couple of vertical axes are formed, one with the two *i*'s, the other with the *l* and *r*. The tail of the *y* is clipped to fit the tail of the *r*. And of course the letters are unusually close-fitting horizontally.

The logo for *New York Life News,* a magapaper, incorporates an unusual amount of art, but the art—the New York skyline—is highly abstract and decorative. The final *S* becomes a cap to make it match the height of the *N* in *News* and to provide a well for "New York Life." The caps for "New York Life" are in a boldface version of the slab serif type to relate them to the boldness of the type used for *News*. The logo is pushed to one side of a band of white running across the page, so it doesn't take as much room as its deepness might indicate. The designer was Joe Lombardo.

Punch, the British humor weekly, makes a laughing half-moon clown out of the *c* in its name. The other letters are normal, with thick and thin strokes and slight serifs.

Tennis's script logo, with its rounded stroke terminals, looks as though it were done by carefully dipping a tennis ball in white paint and moving it across the surface from its lowercase *t* beginning to its *s* ending. The dot over the *i* is an abstract tennis ball. And article endings have a small black tennis ball instead of the small box used by many other magazines.

For its logo *Popular Photography* found it necessary to separate the word *Photography.* (The *Popular* in the title is run small and up the side, an inconspicuous part of the logo.) The dictionary separates *photography* between the *g* and the *r*. But that doesn't read right. The magazine wanted *Photo* to stand out. So it went ahead and separated the word as *Photo-graphy,* even though the separation technically is wrong.

The logo can tolerate some tampering from issue to issue without hurting a magazine's identity. At the least, it can frequently change color. Many

art directors move their logos around each time and change its size. Or they allow cover photographs to intrude a bit, hiding some of the type.

There comes a time in a magazine's growth when it must—it just must—change its logo. Some magazines change suddenly, some gradually. Perhaps the rule should be, If the logo is salvageable, change it gradually, in order to retain what recognition value the logo holds for the reader. If the resistance to change has gone on too long and the logo is hopelessly outdated, go ahead and make a clean break. When redesign involves the entire magazine, the logo usually changes dramatically.

The liberties a designer takes with a logo should not affect the way a writer or researcher uses the name of the magazine in an article or report. Some logos appear in all caps; or they use only lowercase letters without starting caps. A writer should stick to standard usage in referring to such publications. *LIFE* and *TIME*, for instance, appear in copy as *Life* and *Time,* and in italics, of course.

Art on the cover

Art directors of newsstand magazines think of their covers as posters to be seen from thirty feet away. They look for close-up art with a strong silhouette—art not dissimilar from the art on billboards.

Whether you should use photographs or illustrations depends again on the nature of the magazine and its audience. A journalistic magazine would normally use photographs, a literary magazine illustrations. It is probably not a good idea to switch back and forth.

Photographs have virtually replaced illustrations as cover art on magazines because photographs are more readily available on short notice and, in most cases, cheaper. Close-ups of people usually work well as covers, and the people don't have to be young and flawless women. Dorn Communications, a Midwest publisher of business magazines, has found that mug shots of mid-life male executives on covers help newsstand circulation.

When working out your cover format, you are wise to select a square rather than a rectangular hole for the photograph. In choosing a rectangle, you commit yourself to all horizontal or all vertical shots for your cover. By deciding on a square, you can, with judicious cropping, accommodate both horizontals and verticals, and of course you can run photographs from 2¼ × 2¼ negatives without any cropping. Whatever shape you choose, the photograph should dominate the page, perhaps even bleeding all around.

If you use art that ties in with something inside, you'll want to run a blurb on the cover pointing to that tie. If the art is independent, you'll have to separate the cover blurbs, if any, from the art to prevent the reader from making a wrong—and sometimes incongruous—connection.

Even though abstraction in cover art—both in photography and in illustration—is making gains, realism still works best for certain magazines. Petersen Publications, publishers of magazines for car buffs, gun lovers, and hot rodders, experimented with arty covers but found they did not sell as well as covers crowded with type and illustrated with no-nonsense, sleeves-rolled-up paintings. Good design for Petersen audiences is not necessarily what good design might be for other audiences.

In spite of the serious nature of its contents, *Medical Economics* isn't afraid to use humor on its cover. The covers for this magazine often feature visual puns. And the editor and art director make sure that the cover

Print

Close-fitting sans serif letters make up the logo for *Print.* It is always run small and to the side at the top of the cover. Note that the *r* and *t* are designed to pick up the shape of the *n.* And note that the cross-bar on the *t* is elongated to give the letter better balance in context with the other letters.

almamater

For its logo *Alma Mater,* a publication for alumni directors, overlaps the two words of its name. The overlapping *ma* takes on the character of letters both at the left and at the right. The result is a logo made up of three kinds of letters. Yet the designer succeeds in making it all look like one tightly ordered unit.

"The Magazine of Winter" almost buries its logo in snow. But enough of the type shows so that the name stays readable.

For its logo *Reach,* published by the Church of God, Anderson, Indiana, uses some trick typography to capture the spirit of the magazine.

bird

For his magazine called *Bird,* created for a magazine editing class, a student, William Lingle, produced an all-lowercase logo with press-on Helvetica bold letters. To make the logo appropriate to the subject matter of his magazine, he substituted for the dot of an *i* a bird drawn in silhouette. It had to be a fat, squatting bird so it wouldn't be too different from the expected dot.

Change forms its logo from a set of ligatures (the *Ch* and the *an*). This handsome type is based on a photolettering face that the magazine uses for titles inside.

NEW YORK

New York's logo is adopted from an earlier one used by *New York* when it was part of the *Herald Tribune.* The original was in Casion swash. Now, in a bolder version, it combines elements of both Casion and Bookman. Designer, Tom Carnase. Art director, Walter Bernard.

blurb fits the art. A French psychology journal once used a painting by a mental patient as cover art. The readers could study it for its psychological implications.

The use of offbeat art can unsettle the reader not accustomed to it. When *Time* for one of its covers ran a photograph of a papier-mâché bust of Kenneth Gailbraith by Gerald Scarfe, one reader wrote in, "My five-year-old son looked at the cover picture and said: 'Well, I guess they did the best they could.' "

National Geographic has used holograms on its covers: three-dimensional laser images like those found now on some credit cards to discourage counterfeiting. Zebra Books, publishers of romance novels, has also used cover holograms.

Cover blurbs

Blurbs, or cover lines, are meant to lure the reader inside. Some magazines devote their entire cover to them. Others combine them with art. Obviously, the simpler the cover, the better. If blurbs must be included, they should be held down to just a few words in two or three lines at the most.

With several blurbs on the cover, one right after the other, the reader may not see, immediately, where one stops and another begins. Four one-line blurbs may look like one four-line blurb. To solve this problem, you can set the blurbs in different sizes or in different faces. But this might hurt the consistency of your design.

A better answer might be to use punctuation—a period—after each blurb, as advertisers use periods after lines of a headline. Or, if you have a second color available, you can run every other blurb in a color ink. That nicely separates them. With no second color, you can set every other blurb in italics.

Or you can set one of the blurbs in a "slash." A slash is a diagonal stripe at a top corner of the magazine usually printed in a color. The slash suggests immediacy. Or it says that the item in question is so important it has to be added, even though it clutters the design. *Time* uses a variation of the slash with its "turned down" corner. That gimmick—a flat, almost abstract design—has been widely copied by other publications, especially by college and company magazines.

The beauty of the typeface and its arrangement on the cover are not nearly so important as the wording. The trouble with some blurbs is that people read them two ways. "Outlaw Pitchers" reads a blurb on the cover of *Inside Sports.* Is that a command? Does it mean pitchers should not be used in baseball? Or is the phrase simply a description of some pitchers now at work on mounds in the major leagues—pitchers who use spitballs or who attempt to bean the batters?

Color on the cover

Editors who don't use color anywhere else seem to feel they must use it at least on the cover. The possibilities include process color, spot color, and one-color printing. If the cover is printed separately from the magazine itself, color on the cover is within the budget of most magazines even when they can't afford color throughout.

Small magazines usually go the second-color route, using a bright color that will contrast with the black-and-white photography. Often the seond color consists of a band or block into which the logo or blurbs have been surprinted or reversed.

When only a second color is available, you are unlikely to come up with a more useful and powerful color than a red that is light enough to contrast with black but dark enough to carry reverse letters. Even when you have full color available, you want to have one color predominate. Colors tend to convey certain moods; and often the subject of the cover will dictate what color you want to stand out.

Editors and art directors—and circulation managers, too—have some rather firm ideas as to which colors work best for their magazines. *House & Garden,* for instance, found that for its covers blue sold best, followed by green, then red.

Some magazines adopt a color and stay with it issue after issue, sort of as a trademark. *Time* uses a special red border. *National Geographic* similarly uses yellow. In the 1930s *Redbook* used the color red as a backdrop for each piece of cover art, usually a close-up of a woman's face.

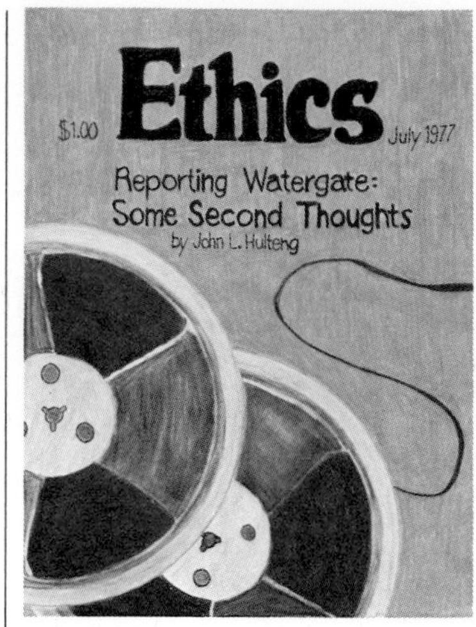

The assignment was to do a cover, including logo, for *Ethics,* a simulated new magazine with some newsstand distribution. (There is a real quarterly called *Ethics* published by the University of Chicago.) The cover was to feature an article on "Reporting Watergate: Some Second Thoughts" by John L. Hulteng. Full-color was available, and the basic design was to be able to be utilized in follow-up issues. Here is one student's solution. Robin Andrea Teter centered her bold logo, put the blurb immediately below, and offered large art symbolic of the article. The colors are mostly green and brown. The strength of her design lies in the proportions.

Production and promotional considerations

Production involves the coordinating of all these elements for printing. It may involve the bringing together of covers from one printer, inside pages from another.

Small-circulation magazines unable to afford original art and the printing of full-color covers can turn to a house that mass produces them for local imprinting. Editors and art directors simply choose from among a series of nicely produced, if mundane, scenes and order enough sheets to wrap around each of the copies of the magazines. Each cover acts as an extra four-page signature. The inside front cover, inside back cover, and back cover are blank. The editor works out copy for these and has the local printer run the sheets through a press to print appropriate material on the blank pages and the magazine's name over part of the full-color cover art. Monthly Cover Service (400 North Michigan Avenue, Chicago, Illinois 60601) supplies stock covers.

If a cover is a gatefold, the art director may have to make arrangements to adjust the design of the first right-hand page after the cover, to leave a blank area or a solid color area running down the extreme right side. Gatefold pages are often slightly narrower than regular cover sizes to make it easy for the reader to do the necessary unfolding.

In the end the art director puts a disproportionate amount of time on the cover, agonizing over the art, worrying about the placement of the type, checking the color proofs—and checking them again. Finally, it all fits. Everything is perfect. The magazine is printed. The circulation department takes over.

And what happens? The subscriber gets the magazine, and plunked down right over the type and art is a mailing sticker.

A unique case involved a 1969 issue of *Time,* which featured a cover portrait of Vice-President Spiro T. Agnew right after his first attack on the news media. About 320,000 copies of the magazine (only part of the press run) went out with the label pasted across Agnew's mouth. A spokesman for the magazine said it was "a production error."

Sometimes the circulation department is not content with the cover as printed; it adds some promotional literature of its own. To sell copies or subscriptions or to urge renewals, circulation people attach slips of paper to the cover or bind or blow cards into the magazines. Readers not kept

Sometimes a magazine runs a cover within a cover. This is a cover designed by Gerard Sealy for a special section of "Interiors" for *The Plain Dealer Magazine*. Full-color illustrations by Terry Allen.

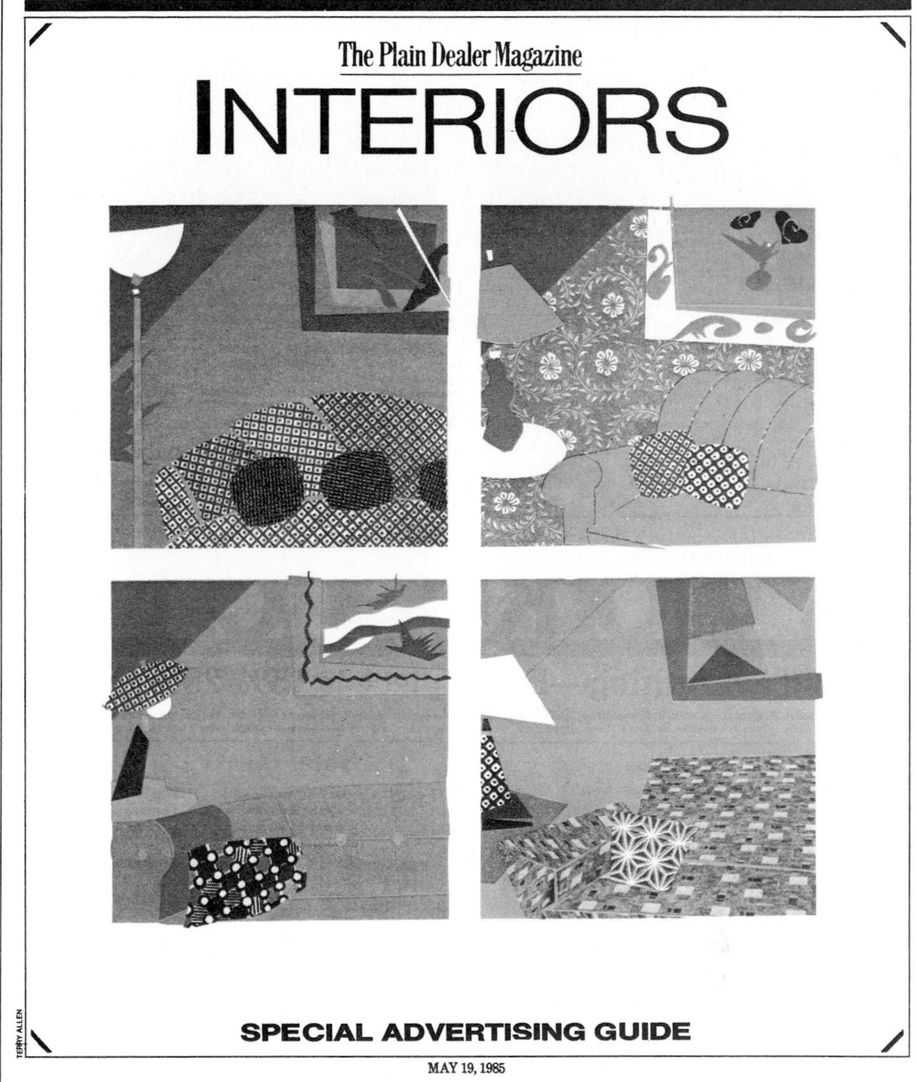

busy tearing out the cards to make pages easier to turn find themselves picking up cards that fall out as they open their magazines. Magazines believe in overkill with these cards. They are an annoyance but probably a necessity in a competitive media world.

Magazine art directors usually have nothing to do with the design of these cards. Many of them are ugly. They are advertising, not editorial, pieces. Perhaps it would be better if there was more design coordination between the magazine and the pieces that seem to be a part of them.

The cover stick-ons are often localized for newsstand display. They call attention to articles high in local interest. Even though the magazine puts out several regional editions, covers themselves stay the same.

However, for one of its issues *Esquire*'s editor decided he needed seven different covers, one for most of the country, six others for selected large cities featured in an article. It was an experiment not often to be duplicated.[8] *Sunset,* which publishes four regional editions, has used two different covers for an occasional issue, better to set the stage for material inside.

Chicago in its December 1981 issue put then Mayor Jane Byrne on its cover but used two different photographs. For half the copies the photograph showed the mayor smiling; for half, frowning. Newsstands had both versions. In the inner city a frowning mayor sold best. In the suburbs the opposite was true. *New York* did something similar for its December 28, 1981–January 4, 1982, issue dedicated to the "Single in the City." The cover showed an arm reaching out of the shower for a "MINE" towel. Half the copies had it as a female arm, half as a male. "If your cover doesn't match your preference," said a cover note inside, "you can swap it with a friend or neighbor. It might turn into something."

When a magazine offers reprints of an article, it wraps the reprint with the cover for that issue. An advertiser requesting reprints of an ad for direct-mail use expects the cover to accompany the reprint. A picture of the cover may also be included in advertising directed to media buyers in advertising agencies. For that reason the cover should be reproducible in a reduced size.

Covers to remember

Esquire's covers of the 1960s and early 1970s were among the industry's most memorable. They were the ideas of George Lois, the advertising executive and art director, with photography supplied by Carl Fischer—"the photographic magician," as Dugald Stermer called him. As "concept covers," they referred to lead articles inside the magazine. Lieutenant Calley posed with children looking very Vietnamese. Muhammed Ali posed with arrows stuck in his chest. Andy Warhol drowned in a can of Campbell's tomato soup. Many of the effects resulted from doctoring photographs, but some of them resulted from celebrities' willingness to pose.

Lois said that "nobody ever refused to do anything, no matter how outrageous. . . ." "So why do they put up with it?" Stermer asked Lois. "Pure ego seems to be the answer; . . . people, at least many people, suffer any indignity to have their face out there in public."[9]

Rivaling *Esquire* with the uniqueness of its covers was a younger magazine, *New York,* like *Esquire* an exponent of the "new journalism." For a cover promoting an article on ice cream, *New York* showed a nude woman holding out two ice cream cones, placed to look at first like a bra. The title, parodying a best-selling book at the time, was "Everything You Always Wanted to Know About Ice Cream But Were Too Fat to Ask."

Parade commissioned a piece of art for a cover, then used closeup details of it inside to decorate a spread. The thick, short bars inside that set off the pieces of art match the thick strokes of the typeface in the article's title. The vertical bars on each side of the title match the thin strokes of those letters. Ira Yoffe is director of design at *Parade.*

A renowned social scientist discovers a powerful trend among Americans

ARE YOU TAKING RISKS WITH YOUR LIFE ?

by Daniel Yankelovich

For its back cover *Soldiers*, not bothered by advertising, promotes one of its inside features. Under this arrangement both the front and back covers can be used to get the reader inside. Both covers for *Soldiers* appear in full color.

Even *The Atlantic* became more innovative in its covers. For one issue it ran a gatefold for the first time. That provided plenty of room to display a collage by Larry Rivers for a "Soldiers" feature. A title running across the bottom read, "The Army is the Only Damn Thing [and then you had to turn the flap] Holding this Country Together." To illustrate a "Trains in Trouble" blurb, another *Atlantic* cover showed a drawing of an old-fashioned train engine chained to photographed railroad tracks with a circular inset of a woman in period costume, agonizing, asking, "Will help arrive in time?"

National Lampoon came up with a much talked-about cover when it showed a dog with a gun pointed to its head. The blurb read, "If You Don't Buy This Magazine, We'll Kill This Dog."

Mad magazine spoofed the universal product code on the cover of its October 1979 issue with a drawing of its mascot running a lawn mower up to it. The code represented the high grass about to be mowed.

The gatefold cover gives art directors their best chance for drama. The folded extra sheet makes possible not only a cover with a one-two punch but also an inside cover ad that stretches over three facing pages. A classic gatefold was *The Saturday Evening Post*'s for April 28, 1962. It showed first a lineup of ball players looking pious while the "Star Spangled Banner" was being played, then a wild fight involving the players and umpires. Another classic gatefold was *Esquire*'s cover for November 1966. Hubert Humphrey, then vice-president, was shown saying, "I have known for 16 years his courage, his wisdom, his tact, his persuasion, his judgment, and his leadership." When you turned the page, you found Humphrey was really sitting on President Johnson's lap. He was a ventriloquist's puppet! Johnson is shown saying, "You tell 'em, Hubert."

It took a magazine like *Psychology Today* to give the gatefold its ultimate impact. For July 1971 the magazine ran a *six*-page gatefold cover, which featured a game readers could play and also made possible an ad that spread over four side-by-side pages inside.

Some of the most admired covers in the industry appear on *The New Yorker*. They are subtle, beautifully drawn or painted, and they have nothing to do with what is inside the magazine. People wallpaper rooms with them. Once each February *The New Yorker* reruns its first cover, designed in the early 1920s by the cartoonist Rea Irwin. It shows a foppish gentleman studying a butterfly. *The Saturday Evening Post* used to devote one cover each year to Benjamin Franklin, even after the historian Frank Luther Mott assessed the magazine's tie to Franklin as tenuous.

Many magazines like to tie their covers to the seasons of the year. *McCall's* has used the *M* and *C* of its name to spell out *Merry Christmas*.

The other covers

In a newsstand magazine the inside front cover (second cover), inside back cover (third cover), and back cover (fourth cover) are reserved for advertisers. These pages, especially the back cover, bring premium prices. These covers sometimes present a problem to the editors of company magazines, especially when the covers are of a heavier stock than the inside pages.

Some company magazines use inside and back covers for house ads, editorials, bleed photographs, or messages from the president. *Enterprise*, an association journal published by the National Association of Manufacturers, has printed them with solid colors. They act then as pleasant rest stops alongside busy pages, something like the end papers and back covers of books.

With a typical magazine the back cover ranks second only to the front cover in its impact on and its accessibility to the reader. If it is not to carry advertising, it deserves the art director's thoughtful attention.

Logic suggests that the back cover be appealing—but not too appealing. It should not overshadow the front cover. The editor wants to encourage readers to start at the beginning of the magazine. Too many readers already seem inclined to start at the back and flip forward.

Whether the magazine is a self-cover or whether it wraps itself in a separate, heavy-stock, four-page signature makes a difference in the plans. If the magazine is a self-cover, the back cover might serve as just another page, as in a tabloid. An article on previous pages could carry over onto the back cover. But if it is built of firmer stock, the back cover should be a self-contained unit or at least part of a unit that is separate from the interior of the magazine. Whether the magazine is a self-mailer with a part of the back cover reserved for addressing affects the plans, too.

Here are some ways in which magazines with separate-stock covers—and with self-covers, too—can solve their back-cover problems.

1. Choose horizontal art and wrap it around the spine. But make sure the art divides itself logically into two sections. The art on the back need not stretch all the way across the page.
2. Flop the front-cover art so that it reads right-to-left on the back.
3. Repeat the front-cover art, but without the logo. A variation of this has been tried by *Items,* published by the Federal Reserve Bank of Dallas. The back cover repeats the front-cover photo, slightly cropped and in a smaller size, and includes a caption for the photo.
4. If the waste doesn't disturb you, leave the back cover blank. Or pick up one of the front cover colors and spread it across the back page.
5. Use a different photo or piece of art on the back cover from what you use on the front cover. *Reader's Digest* carries this idea to the extreme of placing the *only* cover art on the back, reserving the front—or most of it—for a table of contents.
6. Put your table of contents on the back cover, as *Exxon USA* has done.
7. Use public-service material, as from the Advertising Council, National Safety Council, etc. There is enough of it around to give you plenty of variety.
8. Use a company ad designed originally for consumer magazines with a "this is how we're advertising" introduction.
9. Design ads specifically for your readers. Or use material the company might also use for plant posters.
10. Give the page over to cartoons, short humor pieces, poems, or other literary or art creations.
11. Use the page for a one-page feature that differs from features inside the book. A series of personality sketches of interesting employees has worked out well for some publications. The format should be somewhat standardized, but within that standardization is room for some variety: the title can go across the top or at the side; the art can be big or little, in a rectangular shape or in silhouette; sometimes you can go to two columns, sometimes three.

Published for the employees and friends of
Ralston Purina Company
Checkerboard Square
St. Louis, Missouri 63188

The festive mola on our cover is to Panama what plaid kilts are to Scotland and Madras is to India. Handcrafted by the Cuna Indians, these appliqued clothes capture the Panamanians' exuberance for life. To learn about Ralston's venture in this Central American country, see pages 1-9.

Number Two, 1981

George H. Kyd
Division Vice President and Director of Public Relations

Winston Gifford

Harriet Blickenstaff

Claudia Burris
Assistant Editor/Photographer

Mike Tripoli/PGAV
Art Director

No part of this publication may be reproduced in any form without express written permission from the editor.

©Ralston Purina Company, 1981

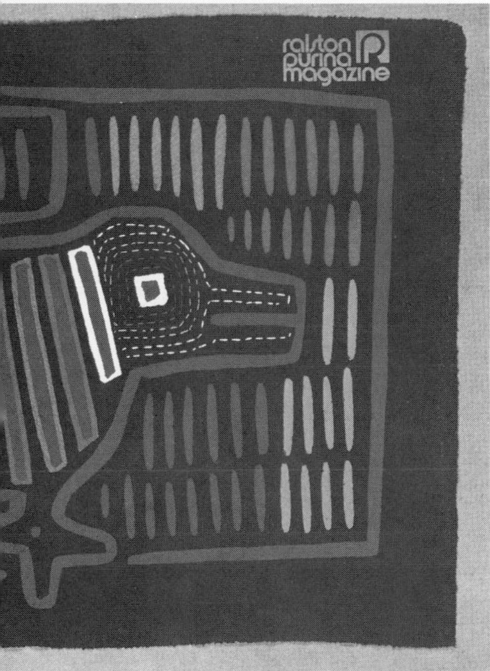

A general-circulation magazine editor doesn't have to worry about the back cover. That goes to an advertiser. But a company magazine editor does have to put something there. For one of its issues *Ralston Purina Magazine* used a wraparound, the art starting on the front cover (shown at the right in this spread) and carrying over to the back. Part of the back cover is given to masthead information. The art—an appliqued cloth—prepares the reader for a long piece on Panama.

But you would strive for consistency from issue to issue if only by retaining the same family of typefaces.

One of the interesting cover ideas of the past was developed by *Mad* in 1960. The day after the elections the newsstand browser was surprised to see a picture of John Kennedy, the newly elected President, and a congratulatory message. How could the magazine's production allow such planning? It was to be a close election. The answer was on the back cover. There the reader found a picture of Nixon, with the same congratulatory message. All the dealer needed to do, it turned out, was to make sure the right cover was facing up when the magazine went on display after the election.

Notes

1. Peter A. Janssen, "*Rolling Stone*'s Quest for Respectability," *Columbia Journalism Review,* January/February 1974, p. 59.
2. "The Importance of Being Rockwell," *Columbia Journalism Review,* November/December 1979, p. 40.
3. Quoted in *Folio,* March/April 1974, p. 58.
4. Patricia Frantz Kery, *Great Magazine Covers of the World,* Abbeville Press, New York, 1982, p. 45.
5. "Best Covers Often Defy the Rules of Good Graphics," *Folio,* July 1981, p. 6.
6. Quoted by Kery, *Great Magazine Covers of the World,* p. 46.
7. Ralph Blodgett, "Putting on a New Face," *Magazine Design & Production,* December 1985, p. 53.
8. It must have been a production and distribution nightmare. It was tried because a new editor didn't know any better. Reported the magazine, "So in the end it turned out to be easier to do than to make him understand why it couldn't be done."
9. Quoted by Dugald Stermer, "Carl Fischer," *Communication Arts,* May/June 1975, p. 30.

Suggested further reading

Buechner, Thomas, *Norman Rockwell: Artist and Illustrator,* Harry N. Abrams, New York, 1970. (All 317 *Saturday Evening Post* covers plus other illustrations are reproduced.)

Finch, Christopher, *Norman Rockwell's 332 Magazine Covers,* Abbeville Press/Random House, New York, 1979.

Kery, Patricia Frantz, *Great Magazine Covers of the World,* Abbeville Press, New York, 1982.

Lois, George, *The Art of Advertising,* Harry N. Abrams, New York, 1977. (Some of the 92 covers he did for *Esquire* are included.)

Packer, William, *The Art of Vogue Covers: 1909–1940,* Crown Publishers, New York, 1980.

Pattison, Polly, *How to Design a Nameplate,* Lawrence Ragan Communications, Chicago, 1982.

Inside pages

The reader opens up a magazine and sees a left- and right-hand page together. It is up to you as the designer to arrange these two pages to form a single unit. At the same time you must make each page readable in itself. You must create design within design.

And then you must come up with an arrangement that unites the spreads so that, one after the other, they look as though they belong together in the magazine.

Some magazines like to have all pages related. Others are content to unify only those pages used for a specific article; the collection of article units within a single issue can represent any number of design approaches.

As you unite your spreads, you may well think of yourself as performing a function similar to that of the motion picture art director. In fact a background in motion picture work would not be bad preparation for a magazine art director. Asger Jerrild got his experience at Warner Brothers before he took over as art director of *The Saturday Evening Post*.

You can achieve a continuity for each spread or series of spreads by staying with the same typefaces and the same kind of art and by positioning these elements consistently on the pages. You can also set up a series of visual axes and relate each spread to them.

Crossing the gutter

The gutter running between the pages of a spread, a psychological as well as a physical barrier, represents a major problem with inside pages. When left and right pages are complete in themselves, the gutter actually helps readers by acting as a separator; but for most spreads you must build some kind of graphic bridge to get the reader across.

You can be obvious about it, positioning a piece of art or a heading so that part is on one side of the gutter, part on the other. Or you can do it more subtly, repeating on the right-hand page a style of art, a pattern, or a color from the left-hand page to help the reader make a visual association.

If you choose to run art across the gutter, you should plan the crossing for a natural break. If a face or figure is involved, you should not let the

CREATIVE LIVING

Greensleeves

There are few sadder sights than a wad of wilted lettuce left to shrivel, neglected, in a corner of the refrigerator. One hears apocryphal stories of such abandoned heads simply vanishing into thin air—but surely your arugula deserves better. ***Woodchips Designers,*** a young silk-screen firm on Martha's Vineyard, has come up with a good-looking **Greens Keeper**—a large, gaily sprigged cotton envelope that, when moistened, will keep salad fixings crisp and fresh for days. Two smaller pouches complete the set: an **Herb Keeper** (also printed green on white) and the **Mushroom Keeper** (forest brown). Each sells for less than $5 at gourmet stores; write the company at P.O. Box 1746, Vineyard Haven MA 02568, for a wholesale catalog. Even if you end up serving all your salads fashionably warm or *fatigué*, these handsome keepers are healthful as well as handy.

Earth Tones

Making terra-cotta cookery is a human ac ity that harks back mi lennia, but Maine pott Montgomery Smith ha managed to improve o tradition. His oven-to- stoneware **baking dis** are high-fired sculptur that can stand up to e day abuse and even th modern affronts of a m wave or dishwasher. T tough, waterproof sur retains cooking juices

is easy to clean; over t it develops a lovely coppery patina. Smith' designs—mostly animis have interesting ances tors. The three-quart bit casserole, with ears folded back to form a l handle, derives from a eighth-century Chines incense burner. The chicken—a design lifte from an early America weather vane—looks aggrieved enough to squawk. Other motifs include ducks and can ists. ***Swan Island Designs*** ($45–$70) are view at more than thr hundred fine stores, o send for a color brochu and order directly: P.O Box 145, Richmond M 04357.

Bias Cut

At last—a knife that combines the heft of an Oriental cleaver with the finesse of a Sabatier! ***Brookstone***—the premier mail-order tool company—imports a Japanese **all-purpose knife** that's a pleasure to hold and behold. It's an eleven-inch sweep of vanadium stainless steel (dishwasher-safe and seemingly indestructible): your fingers fit through an opening diecut into the shank and grip a smooth rosewood handle riveted right over the blade. The control is incomparable: the knife feels like an extension of your hand, and you'll cut through the toughest stuff like Bruce Lee doing finger exercises. The knife is available for $18.40 postpaid from Brookstone, 653 Vose Farm Rd., Peterborough NH 03458.

PHOTOGRAPHS: FRANK RAPP

56

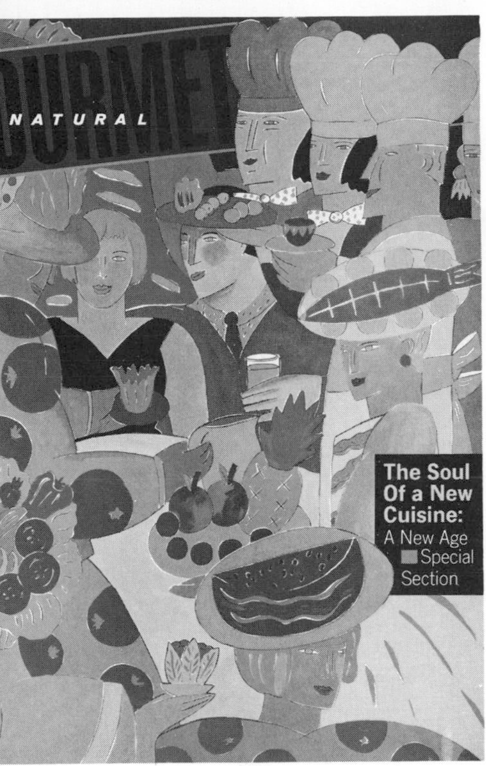

"Creative Living" at the left is the second page of a two-page *New Age* feature on kitchen furnishings. It was designed by Chris Frame. "Gourmet Natural" on the facing page begins a special section on "The Soul of a New Cuisine." The painting is by Karen Barbour. Greg Paul designed the page and art directed the spread.

gutter split it in two. You should not split any art exactly down the middle, unless you want it to stretch all the way across the spread and bleed left and right. In most cases more of the art should be put on one side of the gutter than on the other.

Unaware of production limitations, you may make the mistake of running art across the gutter at a spot on the signature, or between signatures, where perfect alignment is impossible. It is a good idea to check with the printer to determine where across-the-gutter placement will permit the best production.

When you use a line of display type to bridge the gutter, you should use it in a large size. You should not separate the line between letters; you should separate it between words. You should also leave a little extra space at the point of separation, especially if the magazine is side stapled.

The opening spread

You achieve your most dramatic display when you use an entire spread—a left- and right-hand page facing one another—to open an article or story.

Sometimes it is necessary to start an article on a right-hand page. If the left-hand page is an ad, you will have an easy enough time of making the opening look different from the advertisement so the two will not be read together. If the left-hand page is the ending of a previous article, you should keep art off that page so that it will not compete with the new opening page.

To induce the reader to turn the page, you should direct the thrust of the page to the right. You might want a slug saying *Continued* at the bottom of the page.

The two-openings spread

Sometimes it is necessary to run two article openers on one spread. The article on the left page is a one-pager. A new article begins on the right-hand page. Both articles contain illustrations. How do you keep them separated visually?

Here are some possibilities:

1. You run a wider-than-usual river of white between the two. You can, of course, separate them horizontally rather than vertically, running one across the top of the two pages, the other across the bottom.
2. If you separate the articles vertically, keeping one on the left-hand page and the other on the right-, you can hold the illustrations for the one on the right until later in the article.
3. You can make the heading of one article bigger than the other.
4. You can put one article in a box or run a tint block over it.
5. You can set the articles in different types or set one in two-column format, the other in three-column format.
6. You can establish an optical gap by using and positioning artwork that pulls the reader to the outside edges of both articles.

When one of the articles or openers is to occupy more space than the other, taking up more than one page, spilling over onto the next page, you will want to make a special effort to close the gap at the gutter and establish a new gap between the articles. In addition to the devices already

EDITED BY PATRICIA SHARP

TOUTS

THEY ALSO SERVE

Why not give thanks this Thanksgiving for platters, plates, and pots that raise function to a fine art?

1 Artist Sarah Frederick fashions corpulent ceramic teapots, airbrushes designs on them through a piece of lace or a stencil, and sands the surface to impart a velvety texture. Her signature lids are apples, gourds, or peaches, and she twists the cane-and-reed handles herself ($185, Culler Concepts, Irving).

2 Vegetarianism goes to the limit with Barbara Eigen's edible-motif serving pieces, including platters, tureens, and dishes that feature leeks, asparagus, and more ($110–$120, the Cadeau, Austin; Marshall Field's Galleria store, Macy's, Houston).

3 Take a geometry lesson from Michael Lambert's pedestal bowl—a cone poised over a triangle that sits on three tiers of rectangles. The seven-inch ceramic bowls come in peach, turquoise, black, white, wine, or gray, and the shape of each base is different, depending on its color ($42–$50, Cowgirls and Flowers, Austin; Ole Moon, Dallas; Homestead, San Antonio).

4 "It's a little like making an ice-cream cake roll," says Beth Forer of the technique called *nerikomi,* which she uses to produce her unusual salt and pepper shakers. To make them she stacks and slices black and white clay again and again; the resulting design forms a series of feathery patterns as different as snowflakes ($64 a pair, Graubart Rudy, Houston).

5 "Inverse inlay" is the term Claudia Reese has coined to describe her method of using clay as a pigment. This striking large earthenware platter from her Midnight series is one of a wide range of sizes, shapes, and designs ($336, Willingheart Gallery, Austin; Culler Concepts, Irving).

6 First cousin to silver and pewter, Nambé is both a metal alloy and a line of sophisticated serving pieces, each sand-cast and hand-polished. Amenable to heat and cold, Nambé goes from refrigerator or oven to table with equal aplomb ($92–$105, Scarbroughs, Austin; Bloomingdale's, Gumps, Marshall Field's, Dallas).

232 · NOVEMBER 1985

PHOTOGRAPHY BY JOHN SAXON. SELECTION BY KAT HUGHES AND MINDY JO ROVMAN

TEXAS MONTHLY

A "Touts" spread in *Texas Monthly* gives thanks for "platters, plates, and pots that raise function to a fine art." The design uses condensed letters in blocks, letterspacing, and six butted-together full-color photographs to form one art unit. Fred Woodward, art director; David Kampa, designer. (From *Texas Monthy,* November 1985. © 1985 by *Texas Monthly.* Reprinted by permission.)

described for separating articles, you can use a rule or bar to separate them.

When you have to display more than two articles on a spread, especially when they are illustrated, you might consider using boxes or ruled lines.

Designing for titles

The title of an article affects the article's design and the selection of type and art. What the title says should be reflected in the type used to set it and the art used to amplify it.

A single issue of a magazine should carry titles written with some variety. Not all titles should be phrased as questions, for instance. Some of the best titles are takeoffs on popular song, movie, or book titles or advertising slogans, or they use clichés and give them a surprising twist. One of the most-used titles is the one that begins, "Two Cheers for. . . ." The implication is that the article is pleased about something, but not overly pleased. "Where There's Smoke" has been a popular title for articles dealing with the smoking controversy. *Chatelaine,* a Canadian women's

In this "Creative Living" section in *New Age,* the designer, Chris Frame, arranges for two pieces of silhouette art to cross the gutter to unite the pages. The lively, inviting look comes from the variety of art pieces, all printed in full color. The narrow setting of the columns makes ragged-right setting a necessity. Justified, these columns would have erratic spacing between words. Greg Paul art directed.

CREATIVE LIVING

The Stuff of Dreams

What with all the down wafting about these days, most of us have our beds pretty well covered. But the undercover aspect can be just as crucial where coziness—as well as comfort—is concerned.

The **Woolrest** is an insulating underlay made of prime New Zealand fleece, thickly tufted like a flokati rug. In the two years the innovative mattress pad has been available in this country, it has brought sound sleep to multitudes—and set stateside competitors scheming into the night. But to date the Woolrest is still one of the few products of its kind that is 100 percent wool, including the backing (no pesky synthetics), and it comes with an irresistible, no-risk guarantee: try it for ninety nights and, if unsatisfied, you can send it back for a full refund. I bet you won't be. Ours turned a zwieback of a bed into a piece of cake—angel food, actually.

The Woolrest runs from $129 for a twin size to $289 for a king and can be ordered directly from ***Woolrest U.S.A.*** headquarters in Seattle: (800) 426-1213. It's also featured at the same price in several fine catalogs, such as ***Norm Thompson*** (P.O. Box 3999, Portland OR 97208). While browsing through Thompson's fall offerings, you might decide to round out your bed's winter wardrobe with some sky-blue Israeli **flannel sheets** sporting countable cloudlike sheep ($30–$60 per set) or an Irish **Lap Robe** handwoven in the valley of Avoca from heavenly shades of natural and blue new wool ($45)—airy and delicate, it's lovely enough to pass as a fiber-art shawl. And for those midnight dashes out to the woodpile: Velcro-fastened **Snow Trainers** jogging boots in lightweight gray suede ($39.50), pile-lined for warmth and ridge-soled for optimum traction.

Cool Weather Warmers

By Sandy MacDonald

Irish lap robe from Norm Thompson

J. Crow Company's mulling mixes

Creature Comforts

It's not easy keeping little children warm: no sooner do they sit up and start poking around than they figure out how to tear off their clothes. One answer is the **Suzo suit,** an animal costume made of snuggly velour that's interesting enough to keep on for a while. You can choose from a wide range of species—cat, mouse, rabbit, panda, penguin, bat, ladybug, and bee—in sizes for ages six months to eight years. Prices are in the $40 vicinity—not a bad investment, considering the built-in bonus at Halloween. For a catalog, contact ***Suzo*** at P.O. Box 55, Grafton VT 05146, (802) 875-3980 or toll-free (800) 451-4453.

PHOTOGRAPHS: FRANK RAPP

Panda suit by Suzo

Warmth Psychology

How is it that a hot toddy can warm the soul before you even put it to your lips? Pure suggestibility. You can fool an entire household into feeling toasty by setting some mulled wine or cider on to simmer. ***J. Crow Company*** (in real life, orchard keeper Jeff Krouk) makes terrific **mulling mixes,** along with assorted teas, herbs, and extracts to chase away chills. You might track them down at your local natural-foods store or small supermarket or request a list (several hundred items long) directly from J. Crow Company, P.O. Box 172, New Ipswich NH 03071.

A Geothermal Griddle

Soapstone bedwarmers have been helping New Englanders stoically weather winters for centuries. Another tradition, nearly forgotten now, is the **soapstone griddle,** which not only heats evenly but retains heat for hours. You can turn out perfect pancakes in the morning (right on the wood stove, if you like) and have enough grill power left over for a *croque-monsieur* come midday.

Winterset Designs of Harmonyville, Vermont, makes a beauty: blue-green soapstone ensconced in copper, in a thirteen-inch round (about $54 postpaid) or a twenty-inch-long oval ($75). Rural entrepreneurs Bill and Holly Cullen also offer heart-shaped bun warmers ($14.95 complete with a basket and calico napkin), mitten and boot warmers (fashioned, appropriately, as hands and feet: $9–$13 per pair), and a classic bed warmer cushioned in a flower-sprigged pouch ($18). The various items turn up from time to time, incognito, in countrified catalogs such as ***L. L. Bean's*** (free from Freeport ME 04033), or you may inquire of the industrious manufacturers at their outlet on Route 30, Harmonyville VT 05353.

Soapstone griddle by Winterset Designs

Shades for Show

Half your home's heat flies right out the window—unless you're among the clever few who have caught on to **Window Quilts,** five layers of space-age insulators ultrasonically bonded for zero leakage. The original, introduced in 1977, actually looks like a quilt, pulled taut along an airtight tracking system; it may still be just the right touch for certain rooms. However, a recent addition, the **Window Showcase,** allows more design latitude. You can cover it with any fabric you like, from Brunschwig et Fils to Keith Haring, and make a statement. For information on the Window Quilt line (it's carried by more than 2,300 dealers nationwide), contact the ***Appropriate Technology Corporation,*** P.O. Box 975, Brattleboro VT 05301, (802) 257-4501.

The Window Quilt: space-age insulation

76 NEW AGE OCTOBER 1985 77

magazine, let "puppy love" turn into "Yuppie Love" as the title for an article on Yuppie values.

A good title often appears to be controversial. Only when readers get into the piece do they see that the idea advanced in big type does make good sense.

Often a superlative is what's needed. The title promises that the article deals with something or someone who is biggest, smallest, fastest, strongest, best, oddest—whatever.

Another good title approach is to pit one word against its opposite: "The High Cost of Low ______," "Good News About Bad ______," "Tough Guys and Tender ______," "The Long Road to Short ______."

A bit of alliteration helps some titles. "Latins Are Lousy Lovers" was the title of a famous article in *Esquire.* But use alliteration only occasionally. Readers tire of it in title after title or with too much of it in a single title.

Every title benefits from rhythm. It is the designer's job to arrange the lines to take advantage of rhythm. The title becomes a kind of poem.

A right-hand page has already introduced this article in *Resource.* That's the opening paragraph of copy in the upper left. The article continues on another spread. This spread features one large across-the-gutter full-color photograph in contrast with two small ones. The large photograph carries its caption in one unbusy corner. Design by Sidjakov & Berman & Associates.

NAUTICAL QUARTERLY

design, *Regardless*, had won two races overall. Then the sea turned murderous, 15 racers died, six Holland boats lost carbon-fiber rudders, and Holland almost saw the bottom blow out of his life.

Holland's first office in Ireland was in a manor house on an ancient estate of several hundred acres, bordered on o River. The estate has become a compound for His right-hand man, Butch Dalrymple-Smit Drake's Pool, where Sir Francis hid from a purs

Below is the ancient house in Currabinny that Laurel Holland is rebuilding one room at a time. The office is but a few paces away. Said Holland about the priorities in his life, "I don't have a living room, but I have a damn nice office. That's the priority in my life." That may be true, but the living room is in better shape than when they bought the house; then there was a river running through it. That successfully dammed, there is now a set of killer drums, which the former drummer from Down Under beats to escape from the world constantly beating on his door. Left, two Irish drafts-men, Peter Sheehan and Pat Lynch, turn Holland's ideas into lines.

Nautical Quarterly with its square pages uses a unique approach to captions. The caption for the large, partially silhouetted photograph shown here starts with the large *B*. The caption for the smaller photograph starts low in the second column with "Left, two Irish draftsmen. . . ."

You may want to let available art—photographs submitted by the author, for instance—dictate the approach you take with the title.

Words in a title must be handled with precision. Pruning a title to make it fit can change its meaning. "Has Busing Worked?" suggests to the reader something quite different from "Has Busing Really Worked?"

When the title is accompanied by a subtitle, the subtitle should add a dimension; it should not merely restate the title at greater length. Subtitles can go above or below main titles in a face smaller than that used for main titles. They should be longer than titles—they can go on for several sentences—to provide some contrast. You can consider a subtitle a halfway step from the big type of the title to the small type of the body copy.

The table of contents page

For many years the table of contents was only an afterthought in American magazines. No longer. Now the table of contents—and the entire table of contents page—is a magazine showpiece.

What goes on that page varies from magazine to magazine, but in most magazines the page includes (1) the table of contents, (2) the listing of staff members, (3) the masthead, and (4) a caption for the cover picture along with a miniature version of the cover. There may also be some copy on the page—for example, an editorial, a preface to the issue, a statement from the publisher or editor, or an advertisement.

For some reason *The New Yorker,* along among major magazines, did not run a table of contents for many years. For that matter it did not—nor does it yet—run bylines, except at the ends of articles and stories. Nor do many of the opening spreads carry art. Perhaps the magazine expected readers to start at the beginning and read straight through. Perhaps it felt readers didn't have to be lured. Competition from *New York* and a general change in readers' attitudes changed *The New Yorker,* at least to the extent that in the late 1960s it began to carry a regular table of contents.

The table of contents for a magazine lists the titles of articles and stories, the names of authors, and the page numbers where the articles and stories start. If the table is extensive, the editor divides it into sections, like "Articles," "Stories," and "Departments."

Editors find it difficult to settle on categories that fully cover what goes into their magazines. Some features can fit into more than one category. The use of "Humor" as a category does not work well because humor might well be part of features with basically serious intentions. More important, the term does a disservice to the writer in that it telegraphs punches. Putting "Humor" over the title of an article inside a magazine is like having a speaker introduce a joke at the beginning of a speech by saying, "I am now going to tell you a joke."

For their tables of contents art directors increasingly are taking parts of illustrations inside their magazines and reproducing them with the tables of contents. On its table of contents page *Aramco World Magazine* shows the complete opening spread for each article listed, but in miniature size.

Saturday Review, which has died and risen again several times since its start in 1924 as *Saturday Review of Literature,* uses a two-page-spread table of contents. The spread includes a logo, a listing of staff members, a masthead of basic information, full-color photographs, and a listing of contents separated into "Articles" and "Features." Features include regular columns and departments. *American Solon,* a trade magazine, uses "Features" to refer to articles and "Departments" to refer to columns.

A magazine of fewer than sixteen pages probably doesn't need a table of contents. There isn't enough hunting around for the reader to do. Certainly for a small magazine you wouldn't want elaborate treatment or much space devoted to a table of contents.

The masthead

The masthead (not to be confused with the logo) may be too long or too involved to go on the table of contents page. It may go at the bottom or side of some other page (on the back cover of some company magazines). With the masthead often goes a list of staff members.

The listing of staff members should feature the members in the order of their rank and in parallel terminology. It should not, for instance, use *editor* for one staff member and *production* for another. Many magazines find it desirable to list principal staff members in one size type, lesser staff members in another. Editorial staff members are usually run separately from business staff members. On many magazines the three top editorial staffers are the editor, the managing editor, and the art director. The listing need not be in the form of a table; it can be "run in" to save space.

The New Yorker lists the full names of cartoonists appearing in each issue—a worthwhile service when you consider the unreadability of most cartoonists' signatures. The person who does the in-house typesetting needs to display a bit of artistry, and that person deserves some recognition. *Air Cal,* an in-flight magazine, lists its typesetter in the masthead right below the names of the editorial assistants.

The masthead should make it easy for the contributor and subscriber to find the correct addresses (editorial offices often have addresses different from circulation offices). It might be a good idea to introduce each address with a boldface line: "If you want to submit a manuscript" for one and "If you want to subscribe to the magazine" for the other. Perhaps

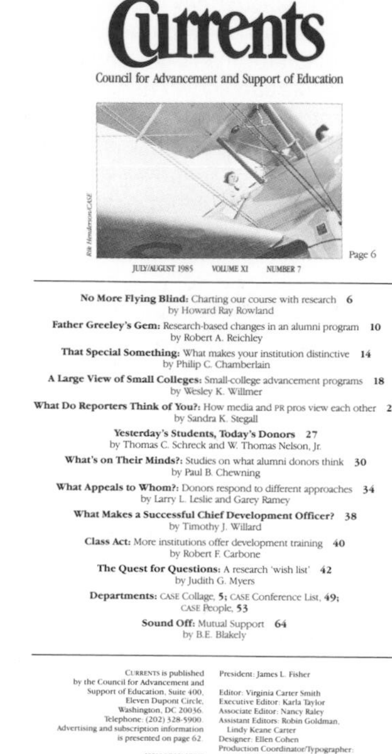

Currents

Council for Advancement and Support of Education

Rik Henderson/CASE

Page 6

JULY/AUGUST 1985 VOLUME XI NUMBER 7

No More Flying Blind: Charting our course with research **6**
by Howard Ray Rowland

Father Greeley's Gem: Research-based changes in an alumni program **10**
by Robert A. Reichley

That Special Something: What makes your institution distinctive **14**
by Philip C. Chamberlain

A Large View of Small Colleges: Small-college advancement programs **18**
by Wesley K. Willmer

What Do Reporters Think of You?: How media and PR pros view each other **22**
by Sandra K. Stegall

Yesterday's Students, Today's Donors 27
by Thomas C. Schreck and W. Thomas Nelson, Jr.

What's on Their Minds?: Studies on what alumni donors think **30**
by Paul B. Chewning

What Appeals to Whom?: Donors respond to different approaches **34**
by Larry L. Leslie and Garey Ramey

What Makes a Successful Chief Development Officer? 38
by Timothy J. Willard

Class Act: More institutions offer development training **40**
by Robert F. Carbone

The Quest for Questions: A research 'wish list' **42**
by Judith G. Myers

Departments: CASE Collage, **5;** CASE Conference List, **49;** CASE People, **53**

Sound Off: Mutual Support **64**
by B.E. Blakely

CURRENTS is published by the Council for Advancement and Support of Education, Suite 400, Eleven Dupont Circle, Washington, DC 20036. Telephone: (202) 328-5900. Advertising and subscription information is presented on page 62.

ISSN 0748-478X
© Copyright 1985 by the Council for Advancement and Support of Education
Printing by Sauls Lithograph Co., Inc.

President: James L. Fisher

Editor: Virginia Carter Smith
Executive Editor: Karla Taylor
Associate Editor: Nancy Raley
Assistant Editors: Robin Goldman, Lindy Keane Carter
Designer: Ellen Cohen
Production Coordinator/Typographer: Janet R. Wilson
Cover photo by Rik Henderson/CASE

Issue Editor: Nancy Raley

JULY/AUGUST 1985

Currents, published by the Council for Advancement and Support of Education, uses an all-centered approach for its table of contents. Art director is Ellen Cohen.

Chocolatier

THE MAGAZINE FOR GOURMET CHOCOLATE LOVERS

VOL. I, NO. 7
1985

FEATURES

26
TRAVELS WITH CHOCOLATIER
LONDON:
WHERE CHOCOLATE REIGNS SUPREME
By Lorna J. Sass

34
HARRODS:
SO MUCH MORE THAN THE AVERAGE STORE
By Janet Cook Wilmoth

42
A MENU FROM
ANDREWS RIVERSIDE

50
BROWNIES:
THE NEWEST, THE CHEWIEST, THE BEST!
By Jim Fobel

72
REMARKABLY
MODERN MOUSSES
By Michael McLaughlin

DEPARTMENTS

3
A WORD OF WELCOME
FROM THE EDITOR

6
LETTERS
AS YOU WRITE US

8
SWEET INSPIRATIONS
FAVORITE CHOCOLATE CREATIONS

12
AN INSIDER'S VIEW
FUDGE FOIBLES
By Bert Greene

16
RECIPE SHOWCASE
CHOCOLATE TEMPTATIONS

58
CHOCOLATIER COOKING CLASS
CHOCOLATE MOLDING MADE EASY
By Elaine Gonzalez

64
CITYSCENE
HAWAII:
CHOCOLATE ADVENTURES IN PARADISE
By Janice Wald Henderson

82
COOKBOOK REVIEW
CHOCOLATE GUIDEBOOKS:
A SWEET SEARCH
By Richard Sax

88
SPIRITED SUGGESTIONS
WONDERFUL WAYS WITH VODKA
By Emanuel & Madeline Greenberg

92
EDIBLY, INEDIBLY YOURS
POTPOURRI

97
THE LAST WORD
MOST FREQUENTLY ASKED QUESTIONS
By Judith Olney

MARKETPLACE
98 RECIPE INDEX
98 SHOPPING SOURCES

EDITOR-IN-CHIEF
JOAN STEUER
ASSOCIATE EDITOR
SUSAN SHAPIRO
CONTRIBUTING EDITOR
MARY GOODBODY
CORRESPONDING EDITOR
JANICE WALD HENDERSON
ART DIRECTOR
DENNIS ANDES
ASSOCIATE ART DIRECTORS
MICHELE BURGEVIN
LAURA DUNN
ILLUSTRATORS
SCOTT BENGE
DENNIS FALCON
JOSEPH TRAINOR
PRODUCTION
CHRISTOPHER CARTER
MARK KAMMERER
ADVISORY BOARD
IRENA CHALMERS
GARY GOLDBERG
BERT GREENE
MARTIN JOHNER
CAROLE LALLI
RICHARD SAX
PHILLIP SCHULZ
PUBLISHER
MICHAEL SCHNEIDER
MANAGING DIRECTOR
RICHARD STEVENS
BUSINESS MANAGER
MATTHEW STEVENS
CONTROLLER
DANIEL TUNICK
CIRCULATION DIRECTOR
W. CHARLES SQUIRES
DIRECTOR OF PROMOTION
JOYCE K. FUCHS
SUBSCRIBER SERVICES
SHIRLEY ROSANIA
TRADE SERVICES
BETH MORROW KAY
TRAVEL COORDINATOR
RITA JEAN MOSS
RESEARCH ASSISTANT
MELODIA SMITH WILSON
ADVERTISING DIRECTOR
LYNNE DOMINICK
ADVERTISING MANAGER
ELIZABETH HALL
ADVERTISING TRAFFIC MANAGER
ROBIN LEVINE

Advertising offices at 45 W. 34th St., Suite 407, NY, NY 10001, (212) 239-0855.

CHOCOLATIER is published quarterly by Haymarket Group Ltd, 45 West 34th Street, NY, NY 10001; Michael Schneider President. Application to mail at 2nd Class postage rates is pending at New York, NY and additional mailing offices. © Copyright 1984 by Haymarket Group Ltd. All rights reserved. © under Universal International and Pan American Copyright conventions. Subscriptions in U.S. and possessions, $10 for one year, $18 for two years. In Canada and elsewhere, payable in advance, $13.50 for one year, $24 for two years. Single copies: U.S. $3, Canada and elsewhere $3.50. Back issues $5. SUBSCRIBER SERVICES: Direct all address changes or matters concerning your subscription to Chocolatier, P.O. Box 333, Mt. Morris, IL 61054 or call (815) 734-4151. Eight weeks are required for change of address. Please give both new and old address as printed on last label. First copy of new subscription will be mailed within eight weeks after receipt of order. Postmaster, send address changes to Chocolatier, 45 West 34th Street, Suite 407, New York, NY 10001. Manuscripts, drawings and other material submitted must be accompanied by a stamped self-addressed envelope. Reproduction of editorial or pictorial content in any manner is prohibited. Chocolatier cannot be responsible for unsolicited material.

Chocolatier, a magazine for gourmet chocolate lovers, uses a two-page spread for its illustrated table of contents and, at the right, its masthead, printed over a tint block. The spread is unusual in that everything except bylines and a couple of paragraphs of vital statistics (lower right corner) is in all-caps. Dennis Andes is art director.

A table of contents page (inside front cover) for *Resource,* a monthly publication of Crown Zellerbach Corporation, San Francisco, uses gray all over and, for contrast, bright, full colors with white in the art. Thin lines and one thick line help organize the material. Some basic information at the top is centered, to give the page a formal look, and the columns of copy are staggered at the bottom, to give the page an informal look. This sophisticated design is the product of Sidjakov & Berman & Associates.

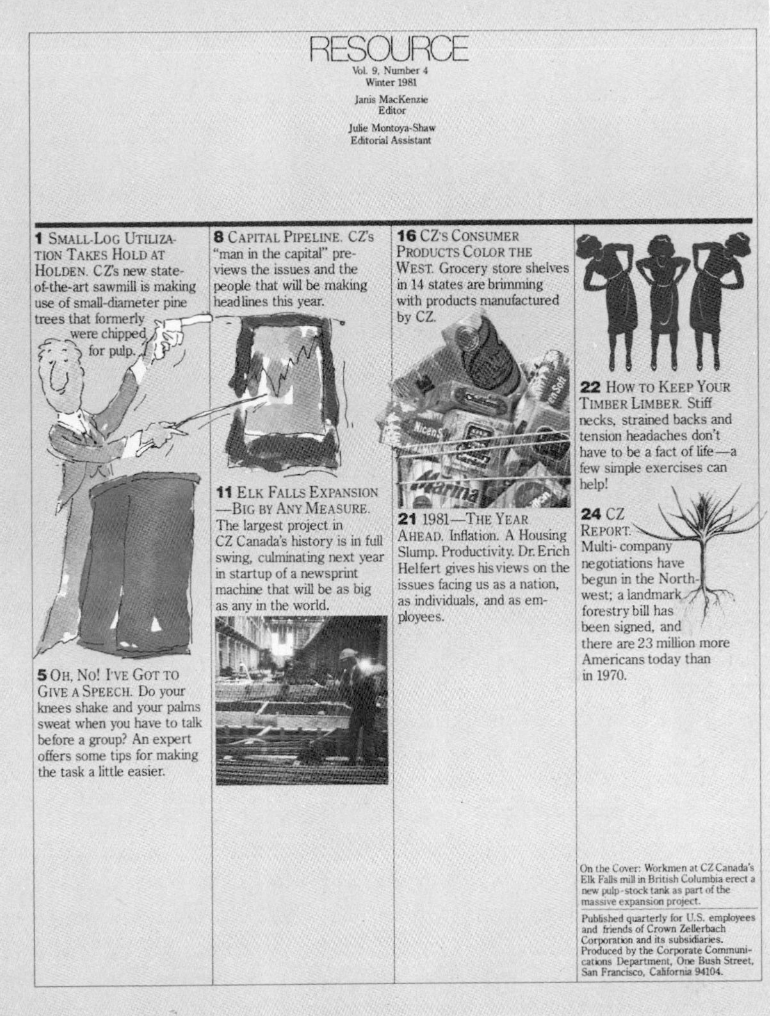

RESOURCE
Vol. 9, Number 4
Winter 1981
Janis MacKenzie
Editor
Julie Montoya-Shaw
Editorial Assistant

On the Cover: Workmen at CZ Canada's Elk Falls mill in British Columbia erect a new pulp-stock tank as part of the massive expansion project.

Published quarterly for U.S. employees and friends of Crown Zellerbach Corporation and its subsidiaries. Produced by the Corporate Communications Department, One Bush Street, San Francisco, California 94104.

Many magazines dress their contents pages with sections of art taken from inside the issue. *Ms.* magazine, for its contents page, organizes material under across-the-page headings: Features, Departments, Fiction & Poetry, Reading, and the *Ms.* Gazette. With this kind of arrangement, listings can vary in length. Columns do not line up at the bottom. (© 1981 by the Foundation for Education and Communication. Reprinted by permission.)

JULY/1981
VOLUME X, No. 1

Cover photograph of Gayle Barron by Jane Sobel (see page 50)

a third will be needed: "If you want to place an advertisement." Every editor should take time occasionally to rethink the masthead to better organize the material it contains.

The masthead carries basic information about the magazine: date of issue, volume number, frequency of publication, name of publishing firm, editorial and business addresses, information on submitting manuscripts, information on circulation, price per copy, and annual subscription rate. *Llewellyn's New Times,* published by "the Western Hemisphere's oldest publisher of astrology and new-age books" in St. Paul, Minnesota, says flatly in its masthead that the bimonthly "is sent without charge to all active mail order buyers of Llewellyn products. Subscriptions are otherwise available for $5.00 a year."

Set in agate or small type, masthead information is necessary for record-keeping and even legal reasons, but it doesn't have to be dull. It can briefly summarize a magazine's history and philosophy. The masthead for *Mother Jones* carries a photograph of the woman for whom the magazine was named and this inscription: " 'Sit down and read. Educate yourself for the coming conflicts.'—Mary Harris 'Mother' Jones (1830?–1930), orator, union organizer, and hell-raiser." *Mad* lists its attorney's name in the masthead.

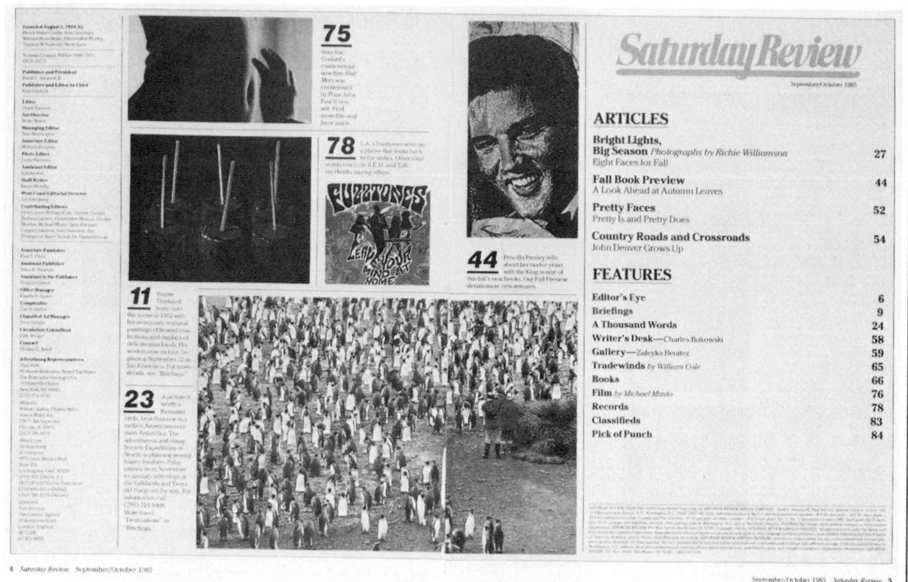

Saturday Review

September/October 1985

ARTICLES

FEATURES

Saturday Review

November/December 1985

ARTICLES

FEATURES

COLUMNS

Cover: Isabella Rossellini by Lynn Goldsmith/LGI; Marilyn Monroe by Wide World Photos.

Saturday Review combines a listing of staff members, representative art in full color from the issue, a standard table of contents (far right), and a paragraph of vital statistics (frequency of publication, addresses, etc.) on one single, useful spread. The combination of units is boxed, and at least one of the art pieces crosses the gutter—decisions that help unite the two pages. The art director is Brian Noyes.

Another *Saturday Review* table of contents allows a closeup photo, partly silhouetted, to dominate the spread. Art facings determine the order in which the large page numbers appear.

This comes from the masthead of the tabloid *Uncle Jam,* "the world's best free paper" published in Long Beach, California: "All rights reserved. No portion of *Uncle Jam,* the neat articles, the high quality photos, our handmade ads, nothing, may be reproduced in whole or in part without the written permission of the publishers. So please don't rip us off—we work too hard!"

And just below that: "*Uncle Jam* is published whenever we get enough people in the room to do it, usually TWICE a month by Fragments West. . . . *Uncle Jam* comes from the Sumerian 'Un Kell Jom,' meaning, you have just stepped on a toad. For advertising rates or a good time call. . . ."

The American Spectator in its masthead briefly traces its origins: "*The*

American Spectator was founded in 1924 by George Nathan and Truman Newberry over a cheap domestic ale in McSorley's Old Ale House. . . ." The name was changed to *The Alternative: An American Spectator* in 1967, "but by November 1977 the word 'alternative' had acquired such an esoteric fragrance that in order to discourage unsolicited manuscripts from florists, beauticians, and other creative types" the magazine took back its original name. The magazine does not even take seriously its house advertising. An ad inviting subscriptions "quotes" H. L. Mencken: "If I were alive today, *The American Spectator* would be my favorite magazine."

The case for departmentalizing

Routine stories—of deaths, job changes, etc.—should be gathered under collective headings. This makes the design job much easier. It also makes related items easy for the reader to identify.

An obit column with a single heading makes unnecessary an editor's hunt for synonyms for death. The subheadings over each item can simply name the person.

In the letters-to-the-editor column it is not necessary to start each letter with "Dear Editor" or "To the Editor." The salutation is understood. Letters should be grouped by subject. Nor does each letter need a subheading. A new subheading is necessary only when the subject changes. Usually a group of letters respond to a particular article, agreeing or arguing with it. Author response to the criticism can be run in italics after each group.

You can add interest to letters columns by supplying illustrative cartoons occasionally or by taking sample quotes from leters and playing them up in display type—one for each page or column of letters. The type for this display can be simulated typewriter type. You can also occasionally show a small reproduction of a letter as written, as when you receive a cute note from a semiliterate youngster.

You probably would want to run a box or legend at the end of the column giving the magazine's address and explaining the policy of editing and publishing letters.

At one or two spots inside the magazine you might want to run a smaller version of the cover logo: on the table of contents page and, if you have a number of advertising pages intervening before you get to your article section, at the head of the opening article. How well a cover logo will take reduction should be a consideration in its design.

Handling magazine editorials

We think of editorials as appearing only in newspapers. But magazines carry them, too. A magazine like *The New Republic* carries several of them at the beginning of each issue, before the articles. The general-circulation weeklies used to carry editorial pages about a third of the way into the publication.

A trade journal is likely to give an early page up front to an editorial and let the editor sign it. (Newspaper editorials are almost always unsigned.) A company magazine often carries as its "editorial" a letter from the president, along with a mug shot. The signing might better be done in type than in handwriting.

But the editorial, because it represents pure opinion, should be made

The assignment in a magazine design class was to take an existing magazine without an editorial page and give it one, picking up the basic design used by the magazine for its various departments. This is Karen Rathe's rough-layout solution—for *Vogue*.

EDITORIAL

BY MARIE SMITH

The ERA—Is it dead or just slumbering?

Ann-Margret, Linda Evans—Fantastic Bodies at any age and proof that regular exercise defies chronology—as well as Jamie Lee Curtis, Lisa Hartman, Mickey Rourke, Christopher Reeve, the list goes on . . . "If a client shows me a picture of what she/he wants to look like, I can estimate how long it will take to reshape her/his body."

It took two months to produce Travolta's muscled look . . . but now, in the movies as in real life, muscles are out, energy's in. "The world has seen enough muscle," says Isaacson. The new '80s goal: a body that looks fit, ready for anything.

To clients, Isaacson is The Great Motivator. His "secrets" are the sensible
Dan Isaacson—Hollywood's most in-demand trainer—has given new meaning to the words "House Calls": he sees clients at his private gym, adjacent to Burbank Studios, in their own home gyms (which Isaacson undoubtedly built), or on location. In a world of star treatment, crazy schedules, and sky-high expenses, Isaacson also builds gyms on movie sets, works out with clients at midnight, and flies to New York to check progress of East Coast clients.

Clients are devoted; female stars (*half* his clientele) say they're hooked. Since Isaacson reshaped John Travolta for *Staying Alive*, word of mouth built his business: Ann-Margret, Linda Evans—Fantastic Bodies at any age and proof that regular exercise defies chronology—as well as Jamie Lee Curtis, Lisa Hartman, Mickey Rourke, Christopher Reeve, the list goes on . . . "If a client shows me a picture of what she/he wants to look like, I can estimate how long it will take to reshape her/his body."

It took two months to produce Travolta's muscled look . . . but now, in the movies as in real life, muscles are out, energy's in. "The world has seen enough muscle," says Isaacson. The new '80s goal: a body that looks fit, ready for anything.

To clients, Isaacson is The Great Motivator. His "secrets" are the sensible basics, his "tools," his black books—training logs filled with photos, measurements, histories—details of each client's body. His expertise doesn't come cheap—stars, studios gratefully pay his price: $1500 a month.

But Isaacson is no Fitness Guru. "I'm realistic about time. It's a matter of priorities, and everyone's are different. Mine are God, family, work, workout—but I still find time to exercise a little every day."

Here, Isaacson talks with Vogue . . .

basics, his "tools," his black books—training logs filled with photos, measurements, histories—details of each client's body. His expertise doesn't come cheap—stars, studios gratefully pay his price: $1500 a month.

But Isaacson is no Fitness Guru. "I'm realistic about time. It's a matter of priorities, and everyone's are different. Mine are God, family, work, workout—but I still
mand trainer—has given new meaning to the words "House Calls": he sees clients at his private gym, adjacent to Burbank Studios, in their own home gyms (which Isaacson undoubtedly built), or on location. In a world of star treatment, crazy schedules, and sky-high expenses, Isaacson also builds gyms on movie sets, works out with clients at midnight, and flies to New York to check progress of East Coast clients.

Clients are devoted; female stars (*half* his clientele) say they're hooked. Since Isaacson reshaped John Travolta for *Staying Alive*, word of mouth built his business: Ann-Margret, Linda Evans—Fantastic Bodies at any age and proof that regular exercise defies chronology—as well as Jamie Lee Curtis, Lisa Hartman, Mickey Rourke, Christopher Reeve, the list goes on . . . "If a client shows me a picture of what she/he wants to look like, I can estimate how long it will take to reshape her/his body."

It took two months to produce Travolta's muscled look . . . but now, in the movies as in real life, muscles are out, energy's in. "The world has seen enough muscle," says Isaacson. The new '80s goal: a body that looks fit, ready for anything.

To clients, Isaacson is The Great Motivator. His "secrets" are the sensible basics, his "tools," his black books—training logs filled with photos, measurements, histories—details of each client's body. His expertise doesn't come cheap—stars, studios gratefully pay his price: $1500 a month.

But Isaacson is no Fitness Guru. "I'm realistic about time. It's a matter of priorities, and everyone's are different. Mine are God, family, work, workout—but I still

women lack both confidence and skills. They have a much harder time being physical then men do.

The modern demands on women's time/energy, coupled with a lack of understanding about fitness, contribute to inadequate exercise. Women who don't exercise are bewildered by what's out there; women who do exercise don't know if they're doing it correctly.
aren't any. You can't force exercise; it has to be an integral part of your life style. To achieve fitness, there are basics for everyone: get a doctor's okay; seek out a qualified nutritionist to assist in diet planning; find a personal trainer to be your guide for at least the first three months; then, you can move on to a good sports-medicine center, physical therapist, or athletic trainer who is knowledgeable about fitness and injury.

In addition, I ask clients to educate themselves. We all need accurate information about diet and exercise.

The best way to take control is to be intelligent about what you do. The problem today is there's so much "expertise" that it confuses the general public.

My fifth requirement is taking a personal inventory. Look at yourself; be realistic abut what *you* want to—and can—achieve. I discuss goals with every client. We discuss where/when to exercise. And establish healthful basics: sleep, relaxation time, consuming adequate liquids, sitting correctly, walking enough, eating regularly. I suggest clients know their metabolic rate, cholesterol level, calories expended on exercise, target heart rate.

The key to success—if there is one—is feeling confident to move ahead. Most women lack both confidence and skills. They have a much harder time being physical then men do.

The modern demands on women's time/energy, coupled with a lack of understanding about fitness, contribute to inadequate exercise. Women who don't exercise are bewildered by what's out there; women who do exercise don't know if they're doing it correctly.

20 VOGUE, November 1985

to look different from anything else in the magazine. One way to set it apart is to present it in one wide column, heavily leaded, with extra white space on either side. The format should allow for a different length each time. An editorial writer should not be made to write to fit.

There is no reason why a magazine can't dress up its editorial or editorial page with an editorial cartoon, either drawn especially for the magazine or selected as a reprint from a newspaper or syndicate.

Interior logos

One of the jobs of the art director is to segregate special departments and columns from articles and features. The special departments or columns appear either early or late in the publication, and standing heads mark them. Ideally, these heads share a design approach that ties them to the logo on the cover. We call them *interior logos*. Some magazines manage with type alone; others incorporate art. Like regular logos, interior logos work best with a flat, almost abstract look that over the months does not grow tiresome. They must be kept small—smaller, certainly, than the logo on the cover.

Interior logos often incorporate bylines and mug shots of the writers and a bit of art that tells what the writing deals with. You give your imagination a brisk workout as you try to come up with names for your standing columns. What you settle for is important when you consider that you will be using the names for months, maybe years.

Some magazines use no-nonsense names, like "Letters" for the letters-to-the-editor column, and that may be the safe course. But other magazines are more inventive. *Trans-action,* before it changes its own name, came up with "Feedback from Our Readers," which was appropriate for its social scientist readers. *Essence,* the high-fashion magazine for black women, for a time called its letters column "Write On!" *Campus Life* called its letters column "Assault & Flattery." Sears and Roebuck called its letters column in *Pacific Coaster* "Seariously Speaking."

JAMA, the Journal of the American Medical Association, used "AMAgrams" for its column of short news items: *AMA* for the American Medical Association and *gram*[*s*] from a Greek word meaning "written." The art put each letter in a block, and the blocks were slightly scattered to represent blocks used in the game of anagrams. *Fitness for Living* headed its column of short news items on fitness with "All the News That's Fit," a takeoff on the slogan of the New York *Times. Oak Leaves* in Oak Park, Illinois, called its birth announcement column "Hello World" (a good title, but it needed a comma after *Hello*).

National Review for years has put a *RIP* over its obit-editorials, and although the acronym is perfectly proper ("Rest in Peace"), it startles the reader somewhat because of a recent meaning *rip* has acquired.

Tennis uses "Your Serve" as the name of its letters column, "My Point" as the name of an editor's column, and "Funny Bounces" as the name of a page of cartoons.

Dealing with advertising

Although the bigger magazines have nothing to do with the design of the ads they run, they exercise the right to turn down ads that conflict with their editorial policies. *The New Yorker* has turned down ads because they conflicted with the editor's taste. In 1985 that magazine, under new

These are four of the many interior logos used by *Boys' Life* to mark special sections or columns in the magazine. These go above whatever title or byline the features carry for that month. The depth changes a bit, but the width and basic format remain the same. In each case a bigger rounded rectangle with illustration sits atop a smaller rounded rectangle with type. The stencil type duplicates the stencil-type logo on the cover. Larry Ortino is the designer. *Boys' Life* is published by the Boy Scouts of America.

NEWS NOTES

Any news? Send us a note.

One of the best-read sections of a company magazine is the section dealing with job changes and other personnel matters. Names appear frequently in boldface, so they will stand out, and mug shots decorate the page. It is a problem, sometimes, to gather the information. Some departments or plants cooperate with the editor, and some don't. One answer is running a special box on the page, although it does have the disadvantage of making people who appear on the page look like publicity seekers.

ownership, began accepting ads that would never have been accepted earlier. For instance, an Obsession Perfume ad showed a nude woman with four men. The magazine, under S. I. Newhouse ownership, was making changes to increase a long-standing 500,000 circulation and to appeal to a younger readership.

Sometimes a magazine's editorial side makes a special effort to cooperate with an advertiser. Fashion magazines in Italy let Ragnp, an underwear manufacturer, imitate cover photos in inside-cover ads, which used the same models but dressed them in only their underwear instead of the clothing that appeared on the covers. The magazines' logos became the manufacturer's name in the ads.

Some magazines offer advertisers space shapes other than rectangles, making life more complicated for the magazines' art directors. The ads may come into the magazines in stair-step or checkerboard arrangements. One part of an ad may be designed to appear on one side of a page, the other part to appear across the page.

Some magazines put together products pages, which are a sort of hybrid: part editorial matter, part advertising. The editor and art director work from press releases and photos supplied by manufacturers. For each item you have a headline, some description, and usually some art. Or maybe you have just a photograph and caption. A tag line invites the reader to circle a number on a Reader Service Card and send it in for further information.

One way to handle product pages is to run them with four or five columns instead of the usual three. You can get more on a page that way—narrow columns allow for smaller body type—and you don't have to run pictures so big.

Such services to advertisers put the magazine art director into collaboration with the magazine's advertising department, a position some art directors find uncomfortable. Ordinarily, magazine art directors (and editors) work with advertising departments only to the extent of making sure that an article with a strong theme does not appear next to advertising that makes an opposing point. For instance, an antismoking article

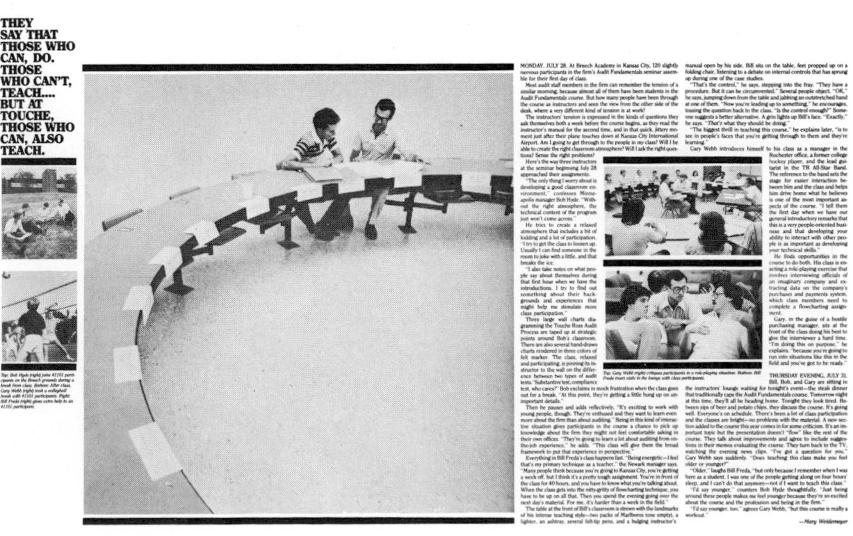
THEY SAY THAT THOSE WHO CAN, DO. THOSE WHO CAN'T, TEACH.... BUT AT TOUCHE, THOSE WHO CAN, ALSO TEACH.

Touche Ross Life, a magapaper, resisted the urge to crop the "unnecessary" area in a large photograph. The uncropped photograph provides a marvelous sweep from the title and small photographs at the left to the beginning of the article at the right. The second-color horizontal bars are in orange. (From *Touche Ross Life,* November 1980. Published by Touche Ross & Co. Reprinted by permission.)

Some magazines offer advertisers special sizes and shapes and wrap editorial matter around them. Such ads bring magazines premium rates.

should not be adjacent to a cigarette ad. It is true, though, that any magazine accepting advertising finds places for ads first and then asks the art director to weave articles and stories around them. Ad space is contracted for in advance; editorial material can more easily be manipulated at the last minute. In most cases the editorial space left for the art director is in blocks or full pages that can be designed independently of advertising.

Cortland Gray Smith, as editor of *Better Editing,* drew up a list of rules for separating editorial matter from advertising. Among them:

New Age illustrator Mark Andresen draws a couple of rings to act as links in a chain that underlines an article title, "The New Relationship." Art director Greg Paul gives the words of the title a cozy feeling and fits the body copy up against the strong diagonal that unites the two pages. He uses color everywhere except in a few places in the rings and chain links.

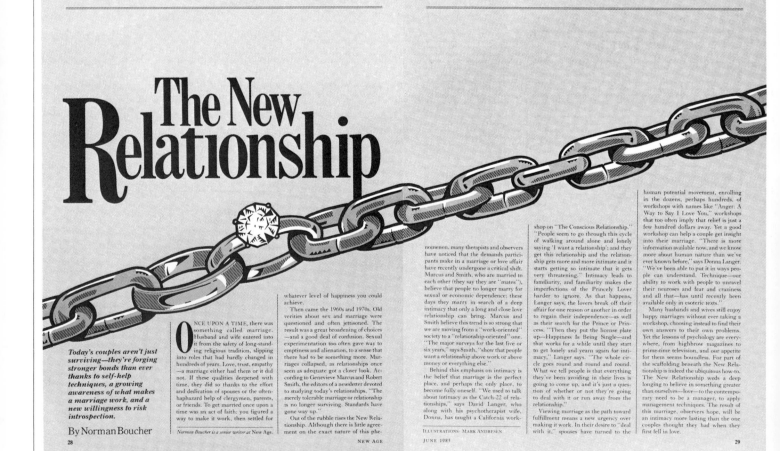

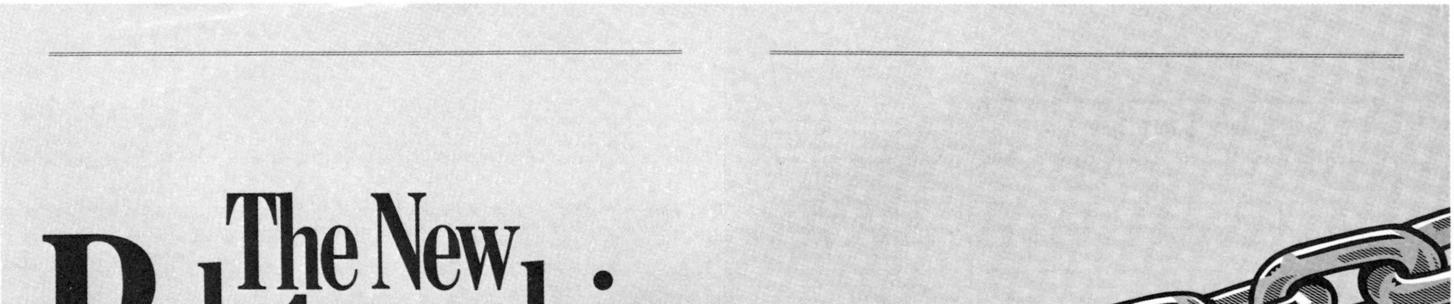

The New Relationship

Today's couples aren't just surviving—they're forging stronger bonds than ever thanks to self-help techniques, a growing awareness of what makes a marriage work, and a new willingness to risk introspection.

By Norman Boucher

ONCE UPON A TIME, there was something called marriage. Husband and wife entered into it from the safety of long-standing religious tradition, slipping into roles that had hardly changed in hundreds of years. Love, trust, empathy—a marriage either had them or it did not. If these qualities deepened with time, they did so thanks to the effort and dedication of spouses or the often-haphazard help of clergymen, parents, or friends. To get married once upon a time was an act of faith: you figured a way to make it work, then settled for whatever level of happiness you could achieve.

Then came the 1960s and 1970s. Old verities about sex and marriage were questioned and often jettisoned. The result was a great broadening of choices—and a good deal of confusion. Sexual experimentation too often gave way to emptiness and alienation, to a sense that there had to be something more. Marriages collapsed, as relationships once seen as adequate got a closer look. According to Genevieve Marcus and Robert Smith, the editors of a newsletter devoted to studying today's relationships, "The merely tolerable marriage or relationship is no longer surviving. Standards have gone way up."

Out of the rubble rises the New Relationship. Although there is little agreement on the exact nature of this phenomenon, many therapists and observers have noticed that the demands participants make in a marriage or love affair have recently undergone a critical shift. Marcus and Smith, who are married to each other (they say they are "mates"), believe that people no longer marry for sexual or economic dependence; these days they marry in search of a deep intimacy that only a long and close love relationship can bring. Marcus and Smith believe this trend is so strong that we are moving from a "work-oriented" society to a "relationship-oriented" one. "The major surveys for the last five or six years," says Smith, "show that people want a relationship above work or above money or everything else."

Behind this emphasis on intimacy is the belief that marriage is the perfect place, and perhaps the only place, to become fully oneself. "We used to talk about intimacy as the Catch-22 of relationships," says David Langer, who along with his psychotherapist wife, Donna, has taught a California workshop on "The Conscious Relationship." "People seem to go through this cycle of walking around alone and lonely saying 'I want a relationship'; and they get this relationship and the relationship gets more and more intimate and it starts getting so intimate that it gets very threatening." Intimacy leads to familiarity, and familiarity makes the imperfections of the Princely Lover harder to ignore. As that happens, Langer says, the lovers break off their affair for one reason or another in order to regain their independence—as well as their search for the Prince or Princess. "Then they put the license plate up—Happiness Is Being Single—and that works for a while until they start to get lonely and yearn again for intimacy," Langer says. "The whole circle goes round and round and round. What we tell people is that everything they've been avoiding in their lives is going to come up, and it's just a question of whether or not they're going to deal with it or run away from the relationship."

Viewing marriage as the path toward fulfillment means a new urgency over making it work. In their desire to "deal with it," spouses have turned to the human potential movement, enrolling in the dozens, perhaps hundreds, of workshops with names like "Anger: A Way to Say I Love You," workshops that too often imply that relief is just a few hundred dollars away. Yet a good workshop can help a couple get insight into their marriage. "There is more information available now, and we know more about human nature than we've ever known before," says Donna Langer. "We've been able to put it in ways people can understand. Technique—our ability to work with people to unravel their neuroses and fear and craziness and all that—has until recently been available only in esoteric texts."

Many husbands and wives still enjoy happy marriages without ever taking a workshop, choosing instead to find their own answers to their own problems. Yet the lessons of psychology are everywhere, from highbrow magazines to prime-time television, and our appetite for them seems boundless. For part of the scaffolding beneath the New Relationship is indeed the ubiquitous how-to. The New Relationship weds a deep longing to believe in something greater than ourselves—love—to the contemporary need to be a manager, to apply management techniques. The result of this marriage, observers hope, will be an intimacy more lasting than the one couples thought they had when they first fell in love.

Norman Boucher is a senior writer at New Age.

ILLUSTRATIONS: MARK ANDRESEN

28 NEW AGE

JUNE 1985 29

HARPER'S INDEX

Number of delegates to the 1984 Democratic National Convention not chosen in a primary or caucus : 873
Number of such delegates to the 1980 convention : 0 (see page 57)
Number of countries whose armed forces are combating a revolutionary or separatist insurgency : 30
Percentage of Americans who believe foreign relations is the most important problem facing the country today : 2
Amount of aid to El Salvador proposed by the Reagan Administration, per guerrilla : $30,000
Federal spending per American citizen : $3,878
Amount that a nuclear freeze would save the U.S. between now and the year 2000 : $400,000,000,000
Portion of Medicare funds that go to people with less than a year to live : 1/3
American lives lost by drowning in 1983 : 6,500
Number of emergency-room admissions for fireworks-related injuries in 1983 : 8,278
Number of these injuries that resulted in the loss of fingers : 126
Medals awarded by the U.S. Army for action in Grenada : 9,754
Medals awarded by Britain for action in the Falklands : 679
Flag "desecrations" recorded by the FBI in 1983 : 5
Percentage of Americans who believe that the accused are guilty until proven innocent : 50
Percentage of Americans who believe that files are being kept on them for unknown reasons : 67
Percentage who believed this in 1974 : 44
Number of days each year that TV broadcasting is prohibited in Iceland : 79
Rank of Iceland, among the nations of Europe, in the number of bookstores per capita : 1
Number of Rolls-Royces in the Soviet Union : 10 (see page 45)
Average speed of the winner in the men's mile at the 1896 Olympics, in miles per hour : 14.24
At the 1980 Olympics : 16.97
Percentage of Americans who think science and technology may destroy the human race : 74
Cost of planting the average 25-by-50-foot American vegetable garden : $25
Value of the average garden's yield of fruits and vegetables : $414
Percentage of American men earning less than $5,000 a year who say they cheat on their wives : 16
Percentage of men earning $60,000 or more who say they do : 70
Percentage of marital arguments that are about sex or adultery : 25
That are about money : 78
Earnings of the average U.S. female worker, expressed as a percentage of the average male's, in 1981 : 59.9
In 1955 : 63.9
Average number of times that a man cries in a month : 1.4
That a woman cries : 5.3
Body fluids lost by perspiration per hour of exercise in hot weather (in ounces) : 54
Percentage of the nation's electrical output that is used for cooling purposes : 15
Grains of sand on the surface of New York's Jones Beach : 2,230,000,000,000
Gallons of suntan lotion and oil used by Americans last year : 1,263,000
Ranking of Denmark, Italy, and the U.S. in the percentage of women who wear C- or D-cup bras : 1, 2, 3
Percentage of American women who consider themselves pretty : 13
Percentage of American men who consider themselves handsome : 28

Figures cited are the latest available from public documents and private sources as of May 1984.

HARPER'S INDEX 9

"Harper's Index," a unique front-of-the-book one-page feature, recites odd or obscure one-line facts involving numbers. For instance, "Average number of times that a man cries in a month: 1.4." *Harper's* art director, Samuel Antupit, and the editor, Lewis H. Lapham, decided on all-centered lines when the feature began in the magazine. Note the emphasis given the colons.

1. Make editorial matter look "as different as possible from the usual advertising pattern." Editorial material usually has a quieter look.
2. Adopt an editorial look or pattern that is consistent in its use of type styles and spacing. What Smith is saying, essentially, is that the formalized, highly ordered magazine has an easier time separating editorial copy from advertising than the more circuslike magazine.
3. Allow an extra measure of white space between editorial matter and advertising.
4. Concentrate ads *between* editorial features, not *within* them. He's asking here that the art director, representing the editorial department, work with the business and advertising department to establish a better lineup of page allocations.

Much has been written about how placement of an ad affects readership; and some advertisers pay premium rates for op-ed placement, up-front placement, and so on. Recent studies tend to show that placement has less effect than was originally supposed. Ads do not necessarily have to be next to "reading matter." Editors have been moving away from the practice of continuing articles and stories in the back of the book so they trail through ads. Perhaps eventually they will bunch the ads completely in one section of the magazine so that art directors can arrange editorial material into a unified whole.

Suggested further reading

Dorn, Raymond, *How to Design & Improve Magazine Layouts.* Brookwood Publications, P.O. Box 1229, Oakbrook, Illinois 60521, 1976.

Hill, Donald E., *Techniques of Magazine Layout and Design.* Donald E. Hill, Huntsville, Alabama, 1970.

McLean, Rauri, *Magazine Design,* Oxford University Press, New York, 1969.

Smith, Cortland Gray, *Magazine Layout: Principles, Patterns, Practices,* published by the author, Plandome, New York, 1973.

White, Jan V., *Editing by Design,* R. R. Bowker Company, 2d ed., New York, 1982.

———, *Designing for Magazines,* 2d ed., R. R. Bowker Company, New York, 1982.

CURRENTS 10

Welcome

New Employees

Continuing Education

INSIDE No. 1

Solar Committee

In Memoriam

CURRENTS 11

Speeches

New Arrivals

Do You Know...

Your Correspondent

"Currents," a collection of short items, appears in the back of the 10 × 14 *Inside,* the monthly magapaper for employees of Southern Company Services, Inc., Atlanta. The band running across both pages with the reverse title reminds readers what section they are dealing with (this spread is a carryover from a previous page). To further aid readers, the subheads are repeated at the tops of columns when appropriate, but in smaller type.

New York

New York Faces Future Shock

By Alvin Toffler

"... Future shock may turn out to be the most devastating urban disease of tomorrow, and millions of New Yorkers are first in line, as usual. The challenge: how to control change..."

This article, written especially for "New York," is based on "Future Shock," a new book by Mr. Toffler to be published by Random House next week. Copyright © 1970 by Alvin Toffler.

20 NEW YORK

To accommodate the new urban millions, we would have to build a duplicate city for each of the hundreds that already dot the globe. A new New York, Tokyo, London, a new Rome and Rangoon —all in 11 years.

NEW YORK 21

The lead time for adjustment to new discoveries is slashed. The lead time between introduction and peak production of the refrigerator was 34 years, for the electric fry pan eight years, for transistor radios even shorter.

22 NEW YORK

"... It is impossible to understand what is happening to human relationships in America unless we examine their duration ..."

NEW YORK 23

"... Instead of conversations, we send high-speed communiqués and search for all sorts of magic to accelerate friendship ..."

24 NEW YORK

Technology leads to physical objects that are cheaper to throw away than to repair, objects that pass into and out of our lives at a rapid clip. From birth on, our children are in a throwaway culture.

NEW YORK 25

"... Future shock strikes at our ability to make rational decisions—in government, in business, in our personal lives ..."

Even our ties with architecture, that part of the environment that has contributed most heavily to man's sense of permanence, are now more short-lived. We tear down neighborhoods at a mind-numbing rate.

New social forms erupt into being—urban communes, free universities, Black Panther-run day nurseries. New movements, each shorter-lived than the last, leap into headlines.

"...To depressurize the city—to moderate tensions between Hard Hat and student, black and white—we must avoid future shock..."

The main illustration develops right before the reader's eyes, spread after spread, in this ten-page *New York* article. An accompanying boldface blurb changes position on each two pages as the illustration changes, adding to the feeling of movement. The original is in full color. Like many magazines *New York* runs a small-size reproduction of its logo at the beginning of the main article in each issue to remind readers plowing through pages of advertising what magazine they are reading.

PULL

Newspaper design and layout

It is not exactly the kind of newspaper to gladden the hearts of sophisticated graphic designers, and even its content leaves some critics cold. It has been called the McPaper. When it first appeared, editors of established newspapers gave it an icy stare. The country already had a couple of national daily newspapers—*The Wall Street Journal* and *The Christian Science Monitor,* both highly respected, if somewhat specialized. Was there a market for another daily newspaper, especially one for the general reader?

There was. And that paper, despite the criticism, firmly established itself and, more than that, seriously affected the content and especially the look of other dailies with their local rather than national audiences.

The paper, of course, is *USA Today.* Geared toward an audience raised on TV, it offered short news items; lots of art, including maps and charts; excellent printing; and color. Lots of color. Even its preoccupation with weather news (a large part of its audience consists of airline travelers) seems to have affected other papers.

The look of the Herald Trib

The history of newspapers as well as magazines is replete with trendsetters: publications that get a hunch for what readers want and offer it first, even at the expense of negative reaction. In the past, when we had so many two-newspaper towns, the paper willing to experiment was Paper No. 2, which had less to lose and which even felt some desperation. Such a paper was the New York *Herald Tribune.*[1]

It would be nice to report that because it tried harder, the Avis of New York newspapers was able to catch up with the then-stodgy New York *Times.* Unfortunately, the *Herald Tribune* not only failed to catch up; it failed to survive. And yet, in its last days it was, by all odds, America's best-designed newspaper.

Once a near-equal to the *Times* in circulation in the New York morning field, the *Herald Tribune* by 1963 had fallen far behind. In desperation its management considered a number of design changes. Long a pacesetter in typographic excellence among newspapers, the *Herald Tribune* decided a radical change was in order.

The man management turned to was a stranger to newspapers: Peter

That's not a real person sitting reading a paper outside the office of *The Lapeer County Press,* "America's largest country weekly," published in Lapeer, Michigan. It's a statue—of the mythical Len Ganeway, who represents the "strength of the people, the importance of the land, the country's firm roots," according to Lynn Myers, editor of the paper. Sculptor Derek Wernher worked on the statue for about a year. Joe Bybee took this picture.

ROCHESTER, NEW YORK

TIMES-UNION

Monday Evening, December 16, 1985 | *Published by Gannett* | *35 Cents Newsstand*

METRO EDITION

INSIDE

People making a career out of being ill

Disorder described – 1B

Bridge	*5B*	*Money*	*9-11D*
Classified	*6C*	*Movies*	*4C*
Comics	*5B*	*Newswatch*	*2B*
Crossword	*5B*	*People*	*3A*
Dear Abby	*3C*	*Peter Taub*	*1B*
Deaths	*6C*	*Scoreboard*	*2D*
Editorial	*8A*	*State*	*3B*
Horoscope	*5B*	*Stocks*	*11D*
Letters	*9A*	*Television*	*2C*

Four news sections

THE WEATHER *Snow changing to flurries tonight. An inch or so possible. Low around 15. Cold with occasional flurries tomorrow. High 20 to 25. (Details on page 2A)*

METRO

FATAL CRASH *City man is charged – 1B*

SPORTS

ASSESSING MARIS *Does he belong in the Hall of Fame? – 1D*

BAD-LUCK BILLS *Freak play – 1D*

upfront

FUR THEMSELVES *Career women are setting a new pace for fur industry – 1C*

Face it, good looks give pupils a boost, study finds

The Associated Press

STATE COLLEGE, Pa. — Good-looking children do better at school and athletics and get along better with other children than ugly children, says a Pennsylvania State University study.

Richard M. Lerner, director of Penn State's Center for the Study of Child and Adolescent Development, said a child's self-concept, temperament, sexual development and other factors played much less of a role than did attractiveness.

Lerner and his wife, Jacqueline V. Lerner, assistant professor of human development, are studying 130 children from the beginning of sixth grade through the end of seventh grade.

"Teachers rated the attractive kids as more scholastically and socially capable, as more athletic, and as having fewer behavior problems than unattractive kids," Lerner said.

"Parents rated their attractive kids as less of a problem than did the parents of unattractive kids," he said, adding that attractive children also got along better with their friends.

The Lerners are assessing the children at the beginning, middle and end of each school year, and so far have gathered data from the sixth-grade year and the beginning of the seventh. They plan to collect more data next month.

To determine who is attractive and who isn't, the Lerners had 100 people who don't know the children look at snapshots. They also had teachers rate the children's attractiveness, and compared those responses to the children's opinions of themselves.

State finds four city schools need help

Charlotte, Franklin, Jefferson and Douglass to plan improvements

By SHARON APPELBAUM
Times-Union

The state Education Department has found that four Rochester schools are among about 512 New York state schools "most in need of assistance."

The Rochester schools — Douglass Junior High School and Charlotte, Franklin and Jefferson junior-senior high schools — were included in the list either because of their dropout rates or students' scores on standardized tests.

Acting Superintendent Peter J. McWalters said he sees the state report as an opportunity not just to focus on particular test scores but to address several of the schools' troubles.

"We could treat these indicators and fall off the (report) next year," he said. "But we would still be left with fundamental problems in secondary schools."

District officials will present the findings to the school board at a 7 p.m. meeting today at the district's Administrative Offices, 131 W. Broad St.

State officials said no other Monroe County schools, public or parochial, and no city elementary schools are among the low-performing schools. And no schools were cited in Orleans, Genesee, Livingston, Ontario or Wayne counties.

District and school officials have until April 30 to work with state officials and submit plans on how to improve performance. State officials will visit the district Thursday to begin the process.

The state's list is part of the Regents Action Plan, aimed to improve academic performance. The list was based on reports submitted by all school districts on about 6,000 private and public schools.

The reports, called Comprehensive Assessment Reports, included such information as demographics, attendance, test scores and dropout rates.

Please turn to back of section

Bell ringers draw fewer donations this year

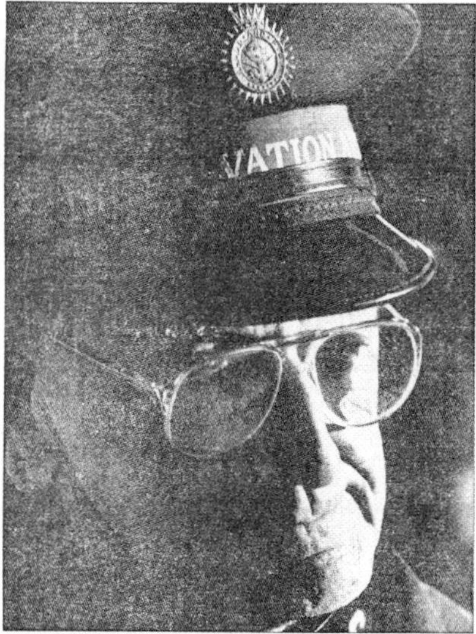

Dennis R. Floss/Times-Union

Salvation Army veteran bell ringer Roy Johnson, 79, during long day at Pittsford Plaza.

Salvation Army lowers goal as receipts dip 20%

By DIANNE CARRAWAY
Times-Union

After more than 60 years as a bell ringer for the Salvation Army, Roy Johnson sets the standards.

"We can often gauge how any day is going by Roy's kettle," Lt. Andrew Murray, the local Salvation Army Corps officer, said. "If Roy is low, then all the others are going to be real bad."

Johnson, 79, of 40 Rosedale St., was one of the first kettle workers for the Salvation Army when the kettles appeared on the streets of Rochester about 1920. He has stood at his present post outside the J.C. Penney store in Pittsford Plaza for 25 years.

Johnson has become such a fixture at J.C. Penney's during Christmas that when Murray called the store manager to ask if a kettle could be posted there this year, the manager's response was, "What would Christmas be without Roy?"

Johnson has seen his share of good years and bad ones. This year will be the worst in the last eight years, Murray said.

THE AMOUNT collected so far is about $10,000, or 20 percent, less than was collected last year at this time. As of Friday the Army had raised about $37,900. Last year's receipts at this time were at $48,000.

Murray said donations had been steadily increasing over the last seven or eight years. This year, however, "We've taken one big leap backwards."

"I'm really a little bit worried," Murray said.

As a result, he has lowered the goal this year from $80,000 to $70,000. Last year, $78,000 was collected.

KETTLE COLLECTIONS aren't the only contributions that are down, Murray said. Individual and group donations of food and toys also are down, he said.

This situation is not isolated to the Rochester area, he said. In fact, he added, Rochester is "less behind" than the average post.

Please turn to back of section

DICK DOUGHERTY

'Ol' Shop' ready to go for broke in season's final week

Now let's go down to the parking lot where Milt is talking to the legendary "Shop" Dougherty, the yuletide's leading ground gainer on the east side.

Thanks, Irv. "Shop," you're heading into this final week and despite your nimble work in the shopping malls you still haven't gone broke. Do you still think you can pull it off in the closing minutes?

Well, Milt, you have to look at it this way: If I can stay behind my blocker and she can make the holes for me, I can break out and maybe go all the way. I've piled up the yardage. The legs are holding up and I feel good. I just haven't scored enough times so I've still got some money left. But I think I can go all the way.

What happened, exactly, last week when they carried you off? It looked as if you took a pretty good shot.

Yeah, well, I was running a sweep around the fountain at Eastview and my blocker veered off. She headed toward Sears just as I made my cut. And then this wiry little lady got lucky. Came out of nowhere. She blindsided me. Right by the shoe store.

Regal?

Please turn to page 5A

The Associated Press

Casket and body transfer cases at Dover Air Force Base, Dover, Del., awaiting crash victims.

Gander residents pay respects to crash victims

Flight recorder gives more information but no cause, Canadian officials say

Los Angeles Times
and The Associated Press

GANDER, Newfoundland — They wanted to show the Americans that they cared, so they gathered in the spare wooden church at the center of this lonely, snow-swept town yesterday to pay their final respects.

There were the Mounties, resplendent in their red dress uniforms; the aging members of the Canadian Legion, bedecked with combat medals from World War II; the robed vestrymen and choir, standing stiffly at attention.

But most were ordinary townspeople, 600 men, women and children — everyone who could be squeezed inside — all raising their voices in the *Battle Hymn of the Republic* to pay homage to the 256

Please turn to back of section

Recession in '87 growing possibility

Economists say new balanced-budget law may rock the boat after '86 gain

The Associated Press

WASHINGTON — The United States should enjoy slightly better economic growth next year but a recession looms as a growing possibility in 1987 with a great likelihood the downturn will either be triggered or made worse by the new balanced-budget law, the nation's business economists said today.

The National Association of Business Economists said its latest poll of 300 of its members found an overwhelming 85 percent believe the country will be in a recession by the end of 1987.

Only 15 percent of those polled believed the current recovery, which is now entering its fourth year, would survive into 1988 or beyond.

The economists also expressed little confidence in the legislation Congress passed last week requiring a balanced budget by 1991.

A substantial majority, 59 percent, said they did not believe the balanced-budget bill would be an effective way to reduce soaring federal budget deficits, objecting in part to the automatic nature of the cuts.

The problem, as the economists see it, is that federal budget cuts will reduce the stimulus needed to drive the economy forward and that the alternative, raising taxes, also would retard economic growth.

Please turn to back of section

Lower interest rates ahead? – 10D

A typical front page of the Rochester, New York, *Times-Union* puts all stories in thin-rule boxes and makes room for several pieces of art. In the index at the top left, a silhouetted figure juts out of a box and partially covers the "Published by Gannett" line. The tight-fitting roman all-caps logo is in red.

Jack Barrett of the St. Petersburg *Times* ranks as one of the most accomplished newspaper artists in the nation. This charcoal pencil and gray pastel drawing was one of several he did to illustrate a feature—a diary by Virginia d'Albert-Lake—about Nazi prisoners during World War II. The woman, to the surprise of a fellow prisoner, is shown discovering a piece of meat in her soup. Barrett used a kneaded eraser to pick out some of the white highlights within the drawing. This kind of art requires highlight (or dropout) halftone reproduction.

Palazzo, an advertising and graphic designer. With no preconceived notions of what a newspaper should look like, Palazzo conducted a study and was surprised to find that newspapers—all newspapers—had scarcely changed at all in format over the years. The typical daily or weekly was not designed, really; its parts were merely fitted together. They were usually combined in such a way as to fill in all the available space—to the top, the sides, the bottom of the page—somewhat like a jigsaw puzzle.

It was a format that had not been seriously challenged in several cen-

turies and was not being challenged much in the 1960s, not even with all the technological changes going on. The late Bernard Kilgore, editor of *The Wall Street Journal,* represented the thinking of many newspaper people when he said, "The market wraps fish in paper. We wrap news in paper.The content is what counts, not the wrapper."

Convinced, however, that in competition with magazines, newspapers were running a poor second from the standpoint of quality, Palazzo recommended changes for the *Herald Tribune* in design and even editorial content. To improve itself, the paper would have to coordinate its editorial and design operations. And yet Palazzo asked for nothing revolutionary. He worried, rightly, about reader habits.

"One must be very careful about tampering with habits which have built up over a long period of time," he said. Perhaps he was thinking of the storm that followed the about-face made by *The Saturday Evening Post* in the early 1960s.

What Palazzo asked for and got, essentially, was a magazine look for the paper. He concentrated on the Sunday issue, especially the Sunday magazine section and the front pages of the other sections. He insisted that more thought be given to selection, editing, and placement of pictures. Cropping of pictures was often needed, he admitted, but he reminded his client that when you crop a picture you change what it says. Cropping does more than simply "move the reader in close."

For its headlines the *Herald Tribune* has been using Bodoni Bold, an "in" face then among the better-designed newspapers in the United States. Palazzo requested Caslon, which, as far as management was concerned, was a face for advertising and book typography. Anyway, did it have the quality Palazzo ascribed to it? To convince the skeptics, Palazzo lettered a four-letter word, first in Bodoni, then in Caslon. And, by golly, in Caslon the word looked almost respectable!

Print, the pretigious magazine of graphic design, applauded the new *Trib* look, saying the change had been "widely hailed as a milestone in newspaper design." But other papers, at least at first, were not willing to emulate it because it was, essentially, a magazine look. In their locally produced magazine sections, though, the look took hold quickly. Most ed-

ROCHESTER, NEW YORK
TIMES-UNION

October 1985

THE IROQUOIS
A PEOPLE APART

Rhonda Pierce, 12, junior princess at the Seneca Indian Fall Festival at the Cattaraugus Reservation south of Buffalo, in traditional dress made by her mother and grandmother.

SPECIAL REPORT

The front page of a Rochester, New York, *Times-Union* special report on the Iroquois features an almost full-page photograph of a junior princess for the Seneca Indian Fall Festival. Michael Schwarz is the photographer, Ray Stanczak the art director, Michael Brown the photo editor. The special section brings together material that appeared in the paper earlier, over a five-day period. Schwarz and the writer, Chis Lavin, spent several months on the project. They visited six Iroquois reservations.

LOS GATOS Weekly

VOLUME I, NUMBER 8 · An independent and locally owned newspaper · APRIL 28, 1982

THE DAY THE PHONES DIED

How it happened and why

A SPECIAL REPORT

by Dan Pulcrano

As Los Gatos and Monte Sereno slept, four technicians were working at the Montebello Way switching station with a computer program that would increase the capacity of the area's phone network.

At 3:18 am the entire system went down. Residents awoke that Wednesday to no dial tone. Emergency services could receive no calls. Many businesses were quieter than usual.

Around offices, normally unfunny lines like "It's for you," or "If anyone calls, take a message," became the running gags of the day.

The memory banks for the computer that routes calls to 9000 customers in the 354, 395 and 399 exchanges had been completely wiped out. Local personnel worked feverishly to reprogram the system but were having no luck.

General Telephone chartered a Lear jet, and a rapid deployment force of five experts was dispatched from the company's Santa Monica office to tackle the problem. They brought with them a tape of instructions needed to put $12 million in idle electronic gear back in action.

Meanwhile, General Telephone quickly installed special lines for the police department and Town Hall, and courtesy telephones were provided for the public at a table along Montebello Way. Some users took advantage of the opportunity to conduct business or make free long distance calls.

Continued on page 8

Has Los Gatos missed the hydro boat?

There are obvious advantages to a non-polluting power generated from a renewable resource that falls from the sky for free.

by Scott Knies

WHEREVER WATER FLOWS DOWNHILL, THE POTENTIAL for developing low-cost power exists. Since 1952, nowhere has the potential been more apparent than five miles south of Los Gatos.

All that water rushing out of Lexington Reservoir could easily crank a generator which in turn would provide electricity to Los Gatos residents at half of what PG&E charges.

Unfortunately, local residents may never benefit directly from this scenario because a hydroelectric system at Lexington is already being planned by another group, which would use the electricity to trim their own PG&E bills.

The Santa Clara Valley Water District, owner of Lexington and other major reservoirs in the county, gets first shot at developing local hydro power by virtue of filing a permit request with the Federal Energy Regulatory Commission last December.

The federal permit not only gives the SCVWD sole right to plan a low-head hydro system at Lexington, but also grants the agency two years to study the feasibility of such a project.

As SCVWD maintenance manager Dan Kriege put it: "We get to take the first crack at developing hydroelectric at our own reservoirs."

It actually did not matter that the SCVWD owned Lexington because the law gives no preference to ownership. Under a 1978 amendment to the Federal Energy Act, *anybody* is entitled to file a request for development of power from alternative technology — including private entrepreneurs or public entities, like town governments.

According to Planning Commissioner Richard Gaines, Los Gatos missed a golden opportunity to cheap hydro power from Lexington and, more importantly, a chance at partial energy autonomy from the ever-increasing rates of PG&E.

Continued on page 10

To illustrate the feature, "The Day the Phones Died," the Los Altos, California, *Weekly* on its front page showed a phone using its own cord to hang itself. The paper is a tabloid.

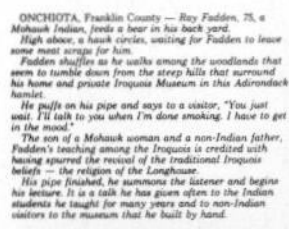

'We must remember our traditions, even if we work in the white man's world'

Mohawk Ray Fadden.

Ray Fadden, lifelong Mohawk teacher, now spends his days feeding animals at his retirement home in the Adirondacks.

The special report runs fourteen full-size newspaper pages. This page allows two photographs and a sidebar to separate the two main columns of body copy. A little more white space than is normal for newspapers aids in the display.

itors of these sections recognized *New York,* the Sunday magazine of the *Herald Tribune,* as the most beautiful in the industry. Some of these editors, moved by what they saw, shortly after the appearance of the new *Trib* began to make greater use of white space, heavy and light horizontal rules, old-style roman headline faces in lighter-than-usual weights, and even italic swash capitals where appropriate. *West,* the Sunday magazine of the Los Angeles *Times,* took on the look of the *Herald Trib.*

By the end of 1966 the New York *Herald Tribune,* its design already compromised through merger with other papers earlier in the year, gave up altogether. Good design—and some fine writing, especially in the magazine section—could not save the paper.

AN AMERICAN TRADITION CONTINUES: PIGSKIN PICK 'EM/D-4

Wednesday September 18, 1985

Morning final 25 cents

Vol. CXV No. 140 Copyright © 1985 Los Angeles Herald Examiner

IN MONEY: NOW DOCTORS X-RAY YOUR WALLET, TOO A-10

IN STYLE: DONAHUE FANS GET THEIR PHIL LIVE FROM L.A. C-1

IN SPORTS: STEVE HOWE AT POINT OF NO RETURN? D-1

Senate OKs 'visitor' laborers

Wilson plan would admit 350,000 for harvests

By Robert Pear
New York Times News Service

WASHINGTON — The Senate voted yesterday to establish a new government program under which farmers could bring up to 350,000 aliens into the United States to harvest perishable fruit and vegetables.

The proposal was adopted by a vote of 51-44 as an amendment to a comprehensive bill designed to curtail illegal immigration. The Senate last week rejected a similar amendment by a vote of 50-48.

The two proposals differed in one significant way: The amendment adopted yesterday set an explicit limit on the number of temporary foreign workers who could be admitted under the program at any one time.

Both amendments were offered by Sen. Pete Wilson, R-Calif., who said California produces nearly half of the nation's perishable fruit and vegetables. With the ceiling of 350,000 workers, Wilson said, the bill would not contain "an open-ended authorization for seasonal workers."

Nevertheless, Sen. Howard M. Metzenbaum, D-Ohio, opposing the Wilson amendment, said it would create "a massive migrant foreign worker program" and would take jobs away from Americans. The amendment, he said, was evidence of "the power of big agriculture."

Metzenbaum said that more than 350,000 foreign workers might come into the United States in the course of a year because the limit would apply to the number of visas that could be issued "at any given time." Some workers could return to their countries and others replace them over the course of a year.

However, Wilson said he did not expect many more workers in any 12-month period. The amendment provides that after three years' experience with the new program,

Immigration/A-9, Col. 3

Ramirez defense wins gag order on Stalker case

By Nancy Hill-Holtzman
Herald staff writer

In an effort to squelch pretrial publicity, a Municipal Court judge yesterday slapped a comprehensive gag order on the Night Stalker case, forbidding attorneys, police, witnesses and public officials from discussing what they know about accused killer Richard Ramirez.

The order was issued by Municipal Judge Elva Soper at the request of Ramirez's attorney, Deputy Public Defender Allen R. Adashek.

As Soper read the order, a jovial Ramirez smiled broadly

Stalker/A-9, Col. 1

President Reagan makes a point during his first formal news conference since June.

Reagan won't give up on Star Wars testing

Herald news services

WASHINGTON — President Reagan last night ruled out any summit agreement with the Soviet Union that would block testing and development of his "Star Wars" missile defense system.

But the president, answering questions at his first formal news conference in three months, said he would be willing to negotiate with Soviet leader Mikhail Gorbachev over the deployment of the multi-billion-dollar system if that would help "rid the world of the nuclear threat."

With the Reagan-Gorbachev summit set for Nov. 19-20 in Geneva, the president also defended the recent test of an American anti-satellite weapon as "catch-up." He said the Soviets have tested such a system, and added, "We couldn't stand by and allow them to have a monopoly on the ability to shoot down satellites."

Reagan said he was taking his prospective meeting with Gorbachev seriously and added, "This has got to be more than just get acquainted."

But he added, "I wasn't going to give him a friendship ring or anything.

"It isn't necessary that we love or even like each other," he said, but it is important for the two superpowers to negotiate.

Making his first prime-time television appearance since undergoing cancer surgery July 13, the 74-year-old president sported his usual ruddy cheeks and walked gracefully, showing no sign of the stiffness that was apparent in the days after the operation.

Although he spent less time than usual preparing for the session,

Reagan/A-6, Col. 2

President says he sympathizes with worries about AIDS

WASHINGTON (UPI) — President Reagan, asked whether he would send a young child of his to school with AIDS-stricken students, said yesterday he could understand the position of parents who have refused to do so.

"I'm glad I'm not faced with that problem today. And I can well understand the plight of the parents and how they feel about it," the president said during his nationally broadcast news conference.

Scientists have said that acquired immune deficiency syndrome cannot be spread by casual contact.

"It is true that some medical sources had said that this cannot be

AIDS/A-6, Col. 2

West German spy scandal grows as two more defect

By James M. Markham
New York Times News Service

BONN — A secretary in Chancellor Helmut Kohl's office was reported yesterday to have defected to East Germany with her husband, a senior official in a foundation close to one of West Germany's governing parties. Both are suspected of spying.

The defection to East Germany by the couple, Herbert Adolf Willner and Herta-Astrid Willner, was the latest in a chain of disappearances that has disclosed widespread penetration of Bonn's power centers by communist agents.

Germany/A-16, Col. 1

A move to add AIDS education in L.A. schools

By Joelle Cohen
Herald staff writer

A plan to have every Los Angeles high school student learn about AIDS and other venereal diseases this year is being prepared for consideration by the Los Angeles school board, possibly as a prelude to revamping the district's entire sex education program.

School board members Roberta Weintraub and Jackie Goldberg hope to introduce a motion next Monday that would add information about the deadly disease AIDS — acquired immune deficiency syndrome — to some class that every high schooler will take this year.

"Our teen-agers now are a relatively clean population," said Weintraub, referring to the fact that few victims of AIDS are in their teens.

★ President Reagan understands why parents are concerned about AIDS among children/Also on A-1.

★ Leading medical scientists give answers to commonly asked questions about AIDS/C-8.

"But they are very experimental, they do like the idea of spontaneity, and they have not been inculcated with a knowledge of the dangers," she said. "I would hope we could tell them about it before it spreads to the point where several million teenagers have the disease."

AIDS is caused by a virus which destroys the body's immune system. It is known to be spread through sexual intercourse, blood transfusions and contaminated needles.

No Los Angeles students are known to have the disease, officials said.

Sex/A-16, Col. 3

The suspect, Richard Rosenkrantz, and the alleged murder weapon, an Uzi rifle.

Calabasas teen-ager to stand trial in Uzi killing of boy, 17

By Milton McGriff
Herald staff writer

A Calabasas teen-ager, accused in the Uzi slaying of another Calabasas youngster, was ordered to stand trial in Los Angeles County Superior Court after a daylong preliminary hearing yesterday.

Defense attorneys failed in their effort to have special circumstance allegations dropped against Richard Rosenkrantz, 18, which means he could receive the death penalty if convicted.

Authorities say he allegedly gunned down Stephen Redman, 17, a close friend of Rosenkrantz's

Uzi/A-9, Col. 3

L.A.'S MORNING BRIEFING

Conviction No. 6 for MADD driver

SACRAMENTO — The man who inspired the formation of Mothers Against Drunk Driving to form was convicted yesterday of his sixth drunken driving charge.

Clarence Busch, 52, found guilty of drunken driving with bodily injury, faces up to four years in prison.

Busch was convicted in 1980 of vehicular manslaughter in the death of Cari Lightner, 13, whose mother, Candy, founded MADD.

Oregon police study Rajneesh's charges

RAJNEESHPURAM, Ore. — State law enforcement officials yesterday began studying allegations by guru Bhagwan Shree Rajneesh that his ousted top aides poisoned restaurant food, tapped phones and tried to murder his doctor and dentist.

Caterer keeps cool following assault

TEMPLETON — A 52-year-old man shot three times and then run over by his assailants' pickup truck closed up his catering van and drove himself home before seeking medical help. Les Hughant said he never feared for his life during the attack by two teen-agers.

— from staff and news service reports

NEWS FOCUS

Surgeon general puts new labels on old warning: Stop smoking

Health groups begin advertising blitz

By Don Kirkman
Scripps Howard News Service

WASHINGTON — Three national health organizations have launched a nationwide campaign to publicize the surgeon general's four new warnings against cigarette smoking.

Working together for the first time, the American Cancer Society, American Heart Association and American Lung Association announced yesterday they will conduct a multimedia blitz for the messages that begin appearing on cigarette packages Oct. 12.

The messages will say:

■ SURGEON GENERAL'S WARNING: Smoking Causes Lung Cancer, Heart Disease, Emphysema, And May Complicate Pregnancy.

■ SURGEON GENERAL'S WARNING: Smoking By Pregnant Women May Result in Fetal Injury, Premature Birth, And Low Birth Weight.

■ SURGEON GENERAL'S WARNING: Quitting Smoking Now Greatly Reduces Serious Risks to Your Health.

■ SURGEON GENERAL'S WARNING: Cigarette Smoke Contains Carbon Monoxide.

The new warnings, which were approved last year by Congress, replace the more general warning cigarette packages have carried since 1966.

"We believe the new warning labels will help educate the American public about the specific health hazards of smoking," said Walter Hatcher, president of the lung association.

Surgeon General C. Everett Koop lambasted cigarettes as "one of the most destructive substances in our society" and "the No. 1 cause of preventable deaths."

Cigarette manufacturers will print one of the four warnings on cigarette packages for three months, then switch to the second, third and fourth warnings every three months.

Together, the warnings cover the chief health hazards of cigarette smoking, particularly its links to heart disease, cancer, lung diseases and problem pregnancies.

The federal Office on Smoking

News Focus/A-9, Col. 1

INDEX

Weather Mostly cloudy today with a slight chance of showers. Cooler with highs in the lower 70s. Clearing tonight. Details: C-8

Editorial (213) 744-8000 · Display (213) 744-8233 · Classified (213) 744-8100 · Circulation (213) 744-1122

Badges of courage for 'bravest of the brave'

Nine police officers, one of them killed in the line of duty, were awarded LAPD's Medal of Valor yesterday. Calling the nine "the bravest of the brave," actor Cary Grant became emotional when presenting the posthumous award to Officer Duane Johnson's widow/A-8.

This front page of the Los Angeles *Herald Examiner* (the nameplate all but eliminates *Examiner*) shows the paper's interest in initial letters to start some stories (three initials on this page and many more inside), its use of thin rules to outline photographs, its use of both thick and thin rules as horizontal separators or as boxes, and its determination to achieve a contemporary feel. For headlines the paper uses both sans serifs and romans; and some of the headlines employ italics. The skyline material, incorporating the nameplate, uses red and blue ink as well as black. John Lindsay designed this page.

A True Life Story About MIAMI

By Teri Hein

Illustration by Fay Jones

18 Clinton St. Quarterly

Clinton St. Quarterly 19

Clinton St. Quarterly, a tabloid, offers visual surprises throughout, with a different art and design style for each article. Fay Jones produced the strong art for this spread, which was art directed by Jim Blashfield.

Following his experience with the *Herald Tribune,* Palazzo redesigned a number of other papers, including the Providence *Journal* and the Winnipeg (Menitoba) *Tribune.*

When the New York *Times* was making plans in 1975 to go from eight to six columns for page one, *New York* asked Peter Palazzo, as an exercise for that magazine, to redesign the *Times'* page one. You can see his solution in a two-page sequence in the April 1975 issue (pages 45 and 46).

One criticism Palazzo had for the eight-column paper was that it didn't tell readers clearly enough which stories were really important. "Why must page one be a do-it-yourself kit?" Another criticism centered on the use of pictures more to break up blocks of type than for the information the pictures themselves carry.

Palazzo argued against the concept of bylines. They are great ego boosters for reporters, he said; but they are a design nuisance. He suggested "tag lines" at the ends of stories instead. Palazzo also quarreled with the use of condensed, all-cap headlines, the overuse of decks for headlines (although he did not advocate doing away with them altogether), and the arbitrary appearance of an occasional all-italics headline.

His redesigned page had more of a horizontal look; with multicolumn rather than single-column headlines; photographs clustered rather than scattered; pictures and captions presented as self-contained units; a summary column of news that, with page numbers, served as a general table of contents for what was inside; better displayed stories but fewer of them; and consistent typographic devices to segregate "hard" and "soft" news.

Many of these practices became standard on American newspapers. Louis Silverstein, when he was assistant managing editor of the New York *Times* and design director of the paper, noted that generous amounts of white space became the goal of newspaper makeup people in the 1960s. Horizontal makeup became the goal in the 1970s. In the 1980s generous use of graphics was in vogue.[2]

A study by the Associated Press Managing Editors in 1985 showed that

In the same issue *Clinton St. Quarterly* came up with a more formal, quiet design, with sensitive line art by Elsa Warnick spanning the gutter to unite the two large black-and-white pages. Three wide, tinted bars further unite the pages. The article continues on another page. Jim Blashfield art directed.

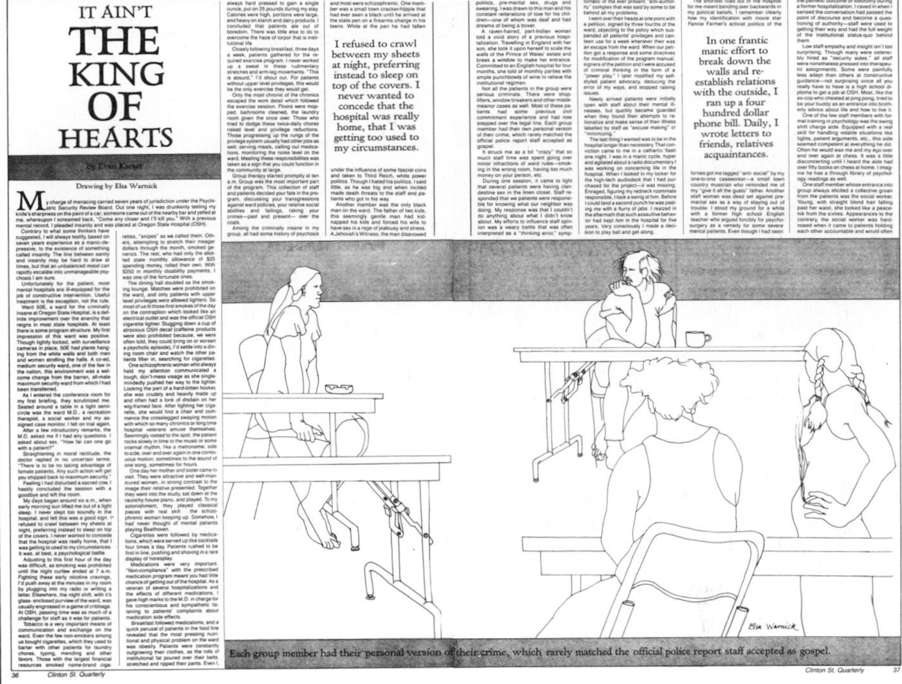

IT AIN'T THE KING OF HEARTS

by Evan Kaeser

Drawing by Elsa Warnick

I refused to crawl between my sheets at night, preferring instead to sleep on top of the covers. I never wanted to concede that the hospital was really home, that I was getting too used to my circumstances.

In one frantic manic effort to break down the walls and re-establish relations with the outside, I ran up a four hundred dollar phone bill. Daily, I wrote letters to friends, relatives acquaintances.

Each group member had their personal version of their crime, which rarely matched the official police report staff accepted as gospel.

36 Clinton St. Quarterly

Clinton St. Quarterly 37

Los Gatos Weekly, Los Gatos, California, crowds silhouettes of cars together with type to dramatize the parking problem discussed in a front-page feature. That the one-word headline does not hyphenate correctly helps point to the chaos. Art director, Tony Kasovich.

PA RKI N G

Town officials and business leaders are looking for an affordable way to solve the problem

by Ben Hawkins and Scott Shifrel

Dorothy Gibson returned to her Los Gatos real estate office one morning to find all the nearby parking spots filled. After circling the block several times, she double-parked and dashed in to pick up her messages.

A police officer wrote a ticket before she could dash back.

Gibson says she has no trouble parking when she comes in early in the morning. But sitting in an office is no way to make a living in real estate. So when she leaves to look at property or to show potential customers property, she gives up her parking space.

The town has been trying to solve the growing parking problem for years, but lately things have been heating up.

A March 7 meeting between town officials and 200 downtown business and property owners was only the first of many to come this year.

The problem and a possible solution were outlined by three of the town's staff members: Jim Van Houten, director of public works; Lee Bowman, planning director; and Dave Mora, town manager.

Mora, Van Houten and Bowman explained one possible solution suggested by a town-initiated parking committee that comprised residents, business owners, property owners and town officials.

"The purpose (of the meeting) was to provide information so you can ask questions," Mora told the crowd.

There was opposition, however. "I don't see how anybody in their right mind can agree to this," said former mayor Chuck DeFretias, one property owner who expressed doubt.

Altough DeFretias wasn't alone in his opposition, Mora still hopes the business and property owners can form a subcommittee that would work with the town to fine-tune the parking committee's plan.

The town's goal is to develop a plan acceptable to enough property owners to form a parking district by April 1985.

The agreement of those paying at least 60 percent of the assessed dollars in the proposed district is needed to begin the legal process.

Continued on Page 12

newspapers had made a number of changes on their front pages in the twenty previous years. The study found bigger photographs, more charts and diagrams, and more teaser art to get readers inside. It also found fewer stories, to make room for all the art. The average fell from thirteen to six.[3]

The look of the New York Times

In the 1970s and into the 1980s, the New York *Times* gradually improved its appearance so that today, besides being the nation's "newspaper of record," it is quietly handsome (if you discount the poor printing quality) and something of a trendsetter. It has made particular strides in the redesign of its special sections carried in the Sunday issues. The crisp typography there, the horizontal rules, the white space, and the imaginative art have inspired newspapers all over the country to reexamine their dress.

And on its news page the paper's use of photography has been outstanding. A writer in the *Columbia Journalism Review* noted that the "good, gray *Times*" publishes more pictures than the *Daily News,* which used to call itself New York's picture newspaper.

Like many other newspapers, the *Times* went to a six-column format, not so much to improve the looks of the front page as to save money. In changing from eight narrow to six wider columns, the paper was able to chop off a modest three-quarters of an inch from the page and save itself $4 million a year in newsprint costs.[4]

The newspaper art director

Newspaper art directors often come up through the ranks as photographers. They do a splendid job of assigning, selecting, and editing photographs and even supervising the work of people in the art department, but

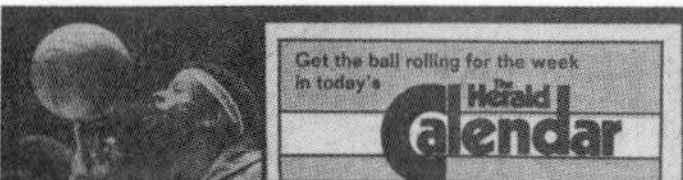

Ejected

After all the bumping and shoving, the Sonics had another win. Page 1C.

WEDNESDAY **The Herald** EVERETT AREA EDITION

February 10, 1982

90th Year No. 52 ©1982, The Daily Herald Co.

Jodi Walters leads a cheer at Valley High School (below). But before the game, she has to put on her artificial left leg (right) at home. "I go through false legs so fast you wouldn't believe it," she says.

AP photos

Her only worry is seeing her leg sail into stands

By THE ASSOCIATED PRESS

ABERDEEN — "You shouldn't be afraid to do what you want to do," says one-legged cheerleader Jodi Walters. "If you're afraid, you won't do anything."

The 19-year-old Raymond resident is a senior at Valley High School, one of four cheerleaders who jump, bounce, kick and twirl for high school sports fans.

She has worn an artificial left leg below the knee since she first started walking. Her present prosthesis is the 20th supplied by Shriners' Hospital in Portland at no charge to her family. Each artificial limb costs $1,600.

"The doctors didn't want me to do as much as I do, but it didn't stop me," she said. "But, I go through false legs so fast you wouldn't believe it."

Always active, she had doubts about becoming a cheerleader and putting herself in the spotlight.

"Sometimes, I'm afraid if I kick my leg too hard, it's going to go flying into the stands," she said. "It's happened before — I'd kick out, lose my leg and fall."

Walters was born with leg defects. Her left foot, a strip of tissue and skin, was amputated shortly after birth, her mother said. The right foot was sound but "completely turned backward." It has required reconstructive surgery and painful months in a cast.

"They've done pretty much everything they can for it," Walters said.

"Surgery didn't seem to bother Jodi," her mother said. "That's what amazed the doctors. She always looked forward, not backward."

When she was small she didn't realize she was different, her mother said. Growing up she enjoyed horseback riding and swimming, like other children. She won ribbons and trophies for riding in 4-H horse shows. For swimming, she kept a special leg she didn't mind getting wet.

Facing her handicap with a sense of humor has carried her through many uneasy situations. Once, when she was swimming, a boy asked her what happened to her leg.

"Jaws" got it, she said.

Another time she took apart her artificial ankle for a grade school show-and-tell.

But she had doubts about cheerleading.

"I almost didn't want to do this but my boyfriend talked me into it," she said. "He said to do it so I wouldn't be afraid of what people think."

Seen from the stands, her left leg looks more like she is wearing a knee brace than an artificial limb.

She still gets a few awkward looks. In particular, some referees "stare at me, and I hate it," she said.

"It's hard. A lot of times I say, 'Why me?' But like my mom says, it could have been worse."

Marine firm may move to Mukilteo

By JIM FULTON
Herald Economics Writer

Snohomish County's dwindling employment may get a needed boost, but not until 1983 and beyond.

Honeywell Inc. confirmed today it is negotiating to purchase a 40-acre site on part of the Daon Corp.'s Harbor Pointe development south of Mukilteo.

The company plans to move its 1,100-employee Marine Systems Operation from its present location in Seattle's Ballard area to the new site, where total employment could reach about 1,500 to 1,600 by 1990, said Jim Durand, manager of facilities planning for the Marine Systems Operation. Durand said Honeywell would not begin the move until late 1983.

But Michael Bonsignore, vice president and general manager of the division, said moving the entire facility is only one alternative. Another would be keeping the Ballard site, he said.

Honeywell hopes to wrap up purchase negotiations with Daon by the end of March, said Durand, who would not reveal a price tag.

The number of new jobs the move will bring to Snohomish County is undetermined, but it could be as many as 400 to 500 by 1990 if it moves its entire Ballard operation to Mukilteo. However, Durand said Honeywell might have increased its employment in Ballard from the present 1,100 workers by the time it begins the move to Mukilteo in late 1983, which could mean fewer new jobs to be filled in Snohomish County.

Plans call for a 350,000-square-foot building that would house both engineering offices and light manufacturing. The 130,000-square-foot first phase of construction could begin this fall, and 200 to 300 employees from Ballard would move to the site when the first phase is completed in late 1983, Durand said.

The 220,000-square-foot second phase could be completed in mid-1986, by which time the remainder of the Ballard employees would be moved here. A third phase of 50,000 to 100,000 square feet "probably" would be added in 1988, said Durand.

The company is moving because it is "outgrowing" its 10 acres in Ballard, Durand said. Honeywell's Marine Systems Operation designs and assembles electronic equipment for offshore oil drilling and other operations and for Navy contracts.

El Salvador torture not down, says group

By THE ASSOCIATED PRESS

NEW YORK — The U.S. branch of Amnesty International has rejected the State Department's contention that violence is on a "downward trend" in the Central American nation of El Salvador.

The organization sent a telegram to President Reagan asserting the "pattern or abduction, torture and murder" in El Salvador cited in the Amnesty International's 1981 report was unchanged.

In its telegram, Amnesty International said the State Department's findings were inconsistent with the volunteer group's information on human rights in El Salvador.

In its survey of human rights around the world presented to Congress last week, the State Department said the government of El Salvador is making a "concerted and significant effort to comply with internationally recognized human rights."

According to Amnesty International's findings, "Thousands of people detained without warrant have disappeared or been murdered by the security forces" in the year ending May, 1981.

An estimated 12,000 people were killed during the period, the group said.

The State Department report, on the other hand, said, "Human rights violations were frequent, but there was a downward trend in political violence" in 1981.

So send me to jail, Watt dares his foes

By THE ASSOCIATED PRESS

WASHINGTON — Interior Secretary James Watt predicted victory today in his battle over a possible contempt of Congress citation, but he said he would be willing to go to jail to uphold the principle of executive privilege.

Watt told reporters at an impromptu press conference he had been assured by Justice Department attorneys that the administration was on firm ground in refusing to turn over to a House committee documents relating to Canadian energy policy.

"This is a constitutional issue that has been looking for birth for many decades," Watt said. "At some time it will need to go to the Supreme Court for resolution."

Watt said he had tried to cooperate with the House energy and commerce subcommittee on investigations and had handed over 24 of the 31 documents sought by the panel.

But he said President Reagan made the decision that the remaining seven documents concerned questions of international relations covered by executive privilege and should not be turned over.

Watt said he was just a "pawn" in the dispute between the president and Congress because Reagan made the final decision on executive privilege.

But when asked what he would do if the full Congress and the courts ruled against him and in the unlikely event he was ordered to jail, Watt said: "I would like to think that I would be as brave as you in the press corps. Yes, I would go to jail."

The House subcommittee voted 11-6 on Tuesday to cite Watt for contempt for refusing to deliver the documents. It was Reagan's first claim of executive privilege before Congress, and the first contempt citation levied by a congressional panel against a Reagan Cabinet official.

The documents sought by the subcommittee deal with the administration's decision on whether Canada discriminates against U.S. citizens wanting to invest in Canadian energy companies. Watt said last week that Canada did not discriminate. Had he ruled otherwise, Canadian investors could have been barred from owning shares in companies holding mineral leases on federal lands in the United States.

The subcommittee has been seeking documents since last summer to find out details of the decision-making process.

AP photo

James Watt at today's news conference: "This is a constitutional issue."

Lawmakers shift Everett to 1st District

OLYMPIA — In a surprise move, the Legislature early this afternoon approved a redistricting plan shifting Everett residents to the Seattle-oriented, 1st Congressional District.

The plan was approved by both the House and Senate in a matter of minutes just before 1 p.m. and was sent on to the governor's desk to be signed into law.

Gov. John Spellman has indicated he will not veto the plan.

Everett, now the hub of Congressman Al Swift's 2nd Congressional District, would be placed in a new 1st District with south Snohomish County and the communities of Kirkland and Redmond. Congressman Joel Pritchard, a King County Republican, now represents voters in that district.

The redistricting proposal, known as Plan 10, had been languishing in a Senate committee after a move last week by Sen. Larry Vognild, D-Everett. Vognild, against the wishes of Senate Republican leaders, had successfully amended the plan to put Everett back in its home district.

Senate GOP leaders pulled that bill, as amended, from the Rules Committee this morning and won passage in a 35-11 vote. They then sent the proposal to the House.

House lawmakers, who had previously passed the bill without the pro-Everett amendment, refused to agree to the amended version. They asked the Senate to back off the amendment and the Senate did so, placing Everett in the new 1st District.

The proposal was then sent on to the governor.

Everett officials, who have vowed to file suit if the proposal is signed into law, were not immediately available for comment this afternoon.

Senators Sue Gould of Edmonds and Ellen Craswell of Bremerton were the only Republicans to vote against the proposal on Everett's behalf. But two Democrats voted with the Republicans, who have a 25-24 edge in the Senate, to approve the new congressional district boundaries.

Inside

Rain?

Increasing chance rain tonight and Thursday. Warmer tonight. Highs in 40s. Lows tonight in 30s. Details on Page 2G.

Index

Our phones

Information	
Everett	339-3000
Lynnwood	672-3000
Classified	
Everett	339-3100
Lynnwood	672-3003
Circulation	
Everett	339-3200
Lynnwood	672-3000

County Council hikes garbage rates by 75%

By ROBERT T. NELSON
Herald Staff Writer

The Snohomish County Council increased garbage rates by 75 percent Tuesday in a move that will cost residential customers at least an extra $1.30 each month by mid-April.

As a result of the unanimous council action, the actual rate to commercial haulers will leap from the present $20-a-ton charge to $35 per ton beginning April 11. The hikes mean that for the second straight year, rates have gone up by more than 25 percent.

The new fees affect residential and commercial garbage

See GARBAGE, Page 4A

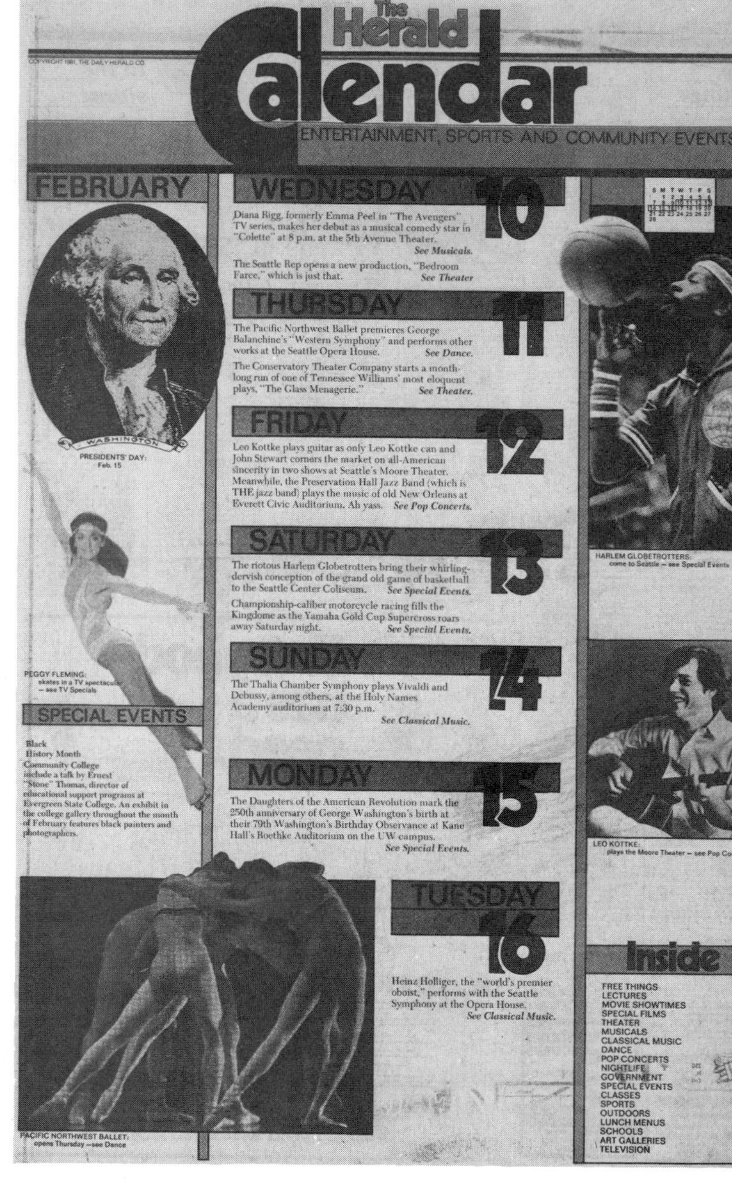

COPYRIGHT 1981, THE DAILY HERALD CO.

The Herald Calendar

ENTERTAINMENT, SPORTS AND COMMUNITY EVENTS

FEBRUARY

WASHINGTON

PRESIDENTS' DAY: Feb. 15

WEDNESDAY 10

Diana Rigg, formerly Emma Peel in "The Avengers" TV series, makes her debut as a musical comedy star in "Colette" at 8 p.m. at the 5th Avenue Theater. *See Musicals.*

The Seattle Rep opens a new production, "Bedroom Farce," which is just that. *See Theater*

THURSDAY 11

The Pacific Northwest Ballet premieres George Balanchine's "Western Symphony" and performs other works at the Seattle Opera House. *See Dance.*

The Conservatory Theater Company starts a month-long run of one of Tennessee Williams' most eloquent plays, "The Glass Menagerie." *See Theater.*

FRIDAY 12

Leo Kottke plays guitar as only Leo Kottke can and John Stewart corners the market on all-American sincerity in two shows at Seattle's Moore Theater. Meanwhile, the Preservation Hall Jazz Band (which is THE jazz band) plays the music of old New Orleans at Everett Civic Auditorium. Ah yass. *See Pop Concerts.*

SATURDAY 13

The riotous Harlem Globetrotters bring their whirling-dervish conception of the grand old game of basketball to the Seattle Center Coliseum. *See Special Events.*

Championship-caliber motorcycle racing fills the Kingdome as the Yamaha Gold Cup Supercross roars away Saturday night. *See Special Events.*

SUNDAY 14

The Thalia Chamber Symphony plays Vivaldi and Debussy, among others, at the Holy Names Academy auditorium at 7:30 p.m. *See Classical Music.*

MONDAY 15

The Daughters of the American Revolution mark the 250th anniversary of George Washington's birth at their 79th Washington's Birthday Observance at Kane Hall's Roethke Auditorium on the UW campus. *See Special Events.*

TUESDAY 16

Heinz Holliger, the "world's premier oboist," performs with the Seattle Symphony at the Opera House. *See Classical Music.*

PEGGY FLEMING: skates in a TV spectacular — see TV Specials

SPECIAL EVENTS

Black History Month ... Community College include a talk by Ernest "Stone" Thomas, director of educational support programs at Evergreen State College. An exhibit in the college gallery throughout the month of February features black painters and photographers.

PACIFIC NORTHWEST BALLET: opens Thursday — see Dance

HARLEM GLOBETROTTERS: come to Seattle — see Special Events

LEO KOTTKE: plays the Moore Theater — see Pop Concerts

Inside

FREE THINGS	2
LECTURES	2
MOVIE SHOWTIMES	3
SPECIAL FILMS	3
THEATER	3
MUSICALS	4
CLASSICAL MUSIC	4
DANCE	4
POP CONCERTS	4
NIGHTLIFE	4
GOVERNMENT	5
SPECIAL EVENTS	5
CLASSES	5
SPORTS	7
OUTDOORS	7
LUNCH MENUS	7
SCHOOLS	7
ART GALLERIES	8
TELEVISION	9

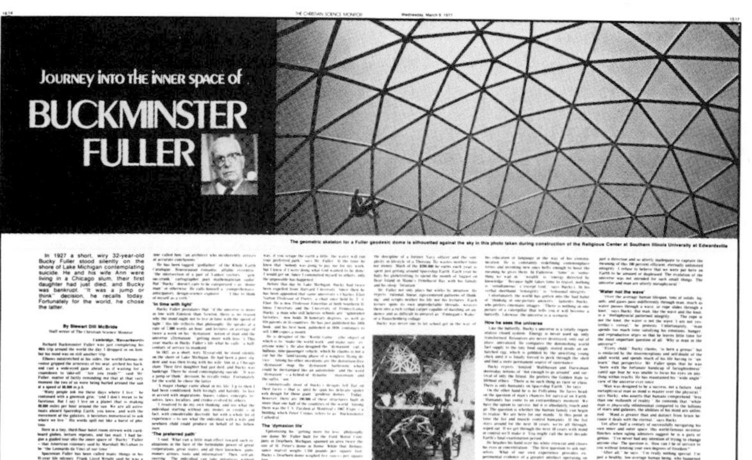

THE CHRISTIAN SCIENCE MONITOR

JOURNEY INTO THE INNER SPACE OF BUCKMINSTER FULLER

The geometric skeleton for a Fuller geodesic dome is silhouetted against the sky in this photo taken during construction of the Religious Center at Southern Illinois University at Edwardsville

In 1927 a short, wiry 32-year-old Bucky Fuller stood silently on the shore of Lake Michigan contemplating suicide. He and his wife Ann were living in a Chicago slum, their first daughter had just died, and Bucky was bankrupt. "It was a jump or think" decision, he recalls today. Fortunately for the world, he chose the latter.

By Stewart Dill McBride
Staff writer of The Christian Science Monitor

'In time with light'

'The preferred path'

The 'dymaxion life'

Fuller with dome components — late 1940s

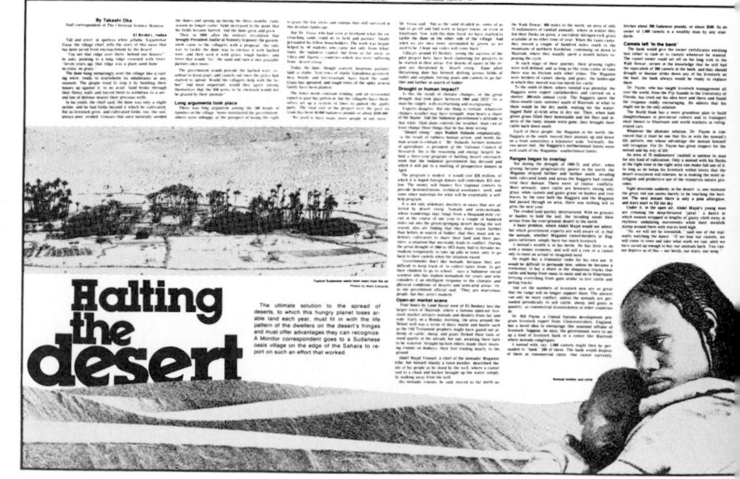

THE CHRISTIAN SCIENCE MONITOR

By Takashi Oka

Halting the desert

The ultimate solution to the spread of deserts, to which this hungry planet loses arable land each year, must fit in with the life pattern of the dwellers on the desert's fringes and must offer advantages they can recognize. A Monitor correspondent goes to a Sudanese oasis village on the edge of the Sahara to report on such an effort that worked

Open-air market scene

The Herald of Everett, Washington, uses both thick and thin horizontal rules on front and inside pages. It also outlines photographs with thick rules and sets off bylines with thin rules. The day of the week gets prominent display with the nameplate.

The Herald's "Calendar" section (run in Wednesday's paper) uses big numbers on the front page to make it serve as a table of contents. Art takes all kinds of shapes to bring plenty of display to the page. There is lots of color, too.

These are two examples of center spreads in *The Christian Science Monitor.* That two pages are on a sheet encourages the use of across-the-gutter art and headlines. The *Monitor* makes dramatic use of this space, varying the approach from issue to issue. The center spread almost always has a strong horizontal thrust. Note especially the handling of the "Halting the Desert" feature and the way the sifting sand partially covers the headline. For some of the photographs on these spreads the editors used a textured screen. (From *The Christian Science Monitor.* © 1977 by the Christian Science Publishing Society. All rights reserved. Reprinted by permission.)

sometimes they lack an understanding of typography. Some newspapers seek design help from outside.

Maureen Decker, assistant managing editor in charge of graphics at *The Morning Call* in Allentown, Pennsylvania, doesn't raid other newspapers for people to add to her design staff. People with established careers on newspapers "tend to think very traditionally," she says. She needs more adventurous people to design the *Call,* a paper recognized for its design innovation. Decker herself came to the paper from an advertising design background. Her graphics editor, Ken Raniere, came from a teaching and architectural studies background, "a perfect mix when it comes to creating informational graphics."

When looking at portfolios of job hunters, Decker hopes to find evidence that a potential designer—or illustrator—is "able to take a routine subject and turn it into an eye-catching idea." She wants people who can conceptualize and who can explain how they arrived at their design decisions.[5]

Still, art directors for newspapers have little to do with the day-to-day look of the front page. Because of late-breaking news and deadline pressures, editors usually lay out the front pages. Editors tend to feel that art directors don't have enough news judgment to handle front-page display.

The layout procedure

The talk about modernizing newspapers—making them more attractive and maybe more magazinelike—fails to take fully into account the problems of daily and even hourly deadlines, production limitations and challenges, quick news decisions, and word- rather than visual-oriented management. There is something to be said for the "newspaper look" that for so many years dominated newsroom operations. Traditional layout practices—even "makeup" practices, to go back to a term prevalent during the days of letterpress—can accomplish more than today's critics may be willing to acknowledge. Newspaper makeup helps the reader "go through the newspaper and find stories of interest or skip those with no appeal," writes Martin L. Gibson, a journalism professor at the University of Texas. "Proper makeup, in this sense, includes a big dose of what we used to call 'good editing.' It includes grouping by subject or geography, perhaps, and arranging the pages in some orderly progression from one kind of news to another."[6]

On the typical daily newspaper the city editor, in charge of local news produced by reporters, and the news editor, in charge of national and international news from the wire services, meet with the managing editor and whoever does the layout to discuss what should be played on the front page. These negotiations often go on near deadline time, which means that the actual laying out must be done in a matter of minutes. This scene differs from that in a magazine office, where deliberation between editor and art director can go on for hours.

On some papers it is the news editor who lays out the pages. On others, the managing editor. On still others, the copy chief, who also supervises the work of the copy editors. The idea of full-time art directors has taken hold only on the larger papers.

On a big daily the front page changes several times a day as each new edition is issued. The newsstand edition published to attract commuters on their way home from work, for instance, would have a more urgent look than the home delivered edition. As the laying out takes place, a new

Minneapolis **Tribune**

Friday June 12, 1981 — 1A Final — 4 Sections — 25¢

Begin: Iraq had secret A-bomb facility

Cancer-ravaged family loses another son

Quake hits Iran; thousands said dead

Jerry Haus of St. Paul gave his friend Walt Harris, 10, a piggyback ride Thursday during a picnic near Lake Harriet. It seemed like a good day for a picnic yesterday, until rain put a damper on things.

Kania asks 'new plan' to solve crisis

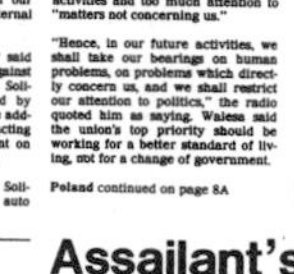

Council may impose sanctions on City Center developers

Larry Blackwell

Almanac

Assailant's bosses sued in rape case

Minneapolis Tribune

Friday, June 12, 1981

Reagan and the Namibian impasse

Letters from readers

Moderate rent control

DFL and sales tax

Traffic around stadium

Educating handicapped

School vacation

'Eating our seed corn'

Proper indictment

Parents fear for daughters' safety

Liberal Califano's way of thinking

Joseph Califano

lead for a story may come in, or a new story may break that cries out for prominent placement. Above all, a newspaper layout artist must be flexible.

Whoever lays out the page usually starts with a piece of paper on which is printed a grid of the page showing columns across and inches running down the sides. These sheets, called dummies, are sometimes a quarter of the actual size. Working in miniature speeds things up. What the layout artist creates is no work of art, merely a piece of visual shorthand clear enough to show the pasteup artist what to put where. On some papers editors roughly paste galley proofs onto full-size layout sheets. (The printer makes available simultaneously two sets of proofs: one to proofread, the other to clip and paste.) Using a pencil, the layout artist marks the number of the galley across the face of every story—perhaps every paragraph—

Here is a front page and an editorial page of the Minneapolis *Tribune*, a paper redesigned by British designer Frank Ariss back in 1971. With its precise, clean, contemporary look—appropriate for computer-assisted production—the *Tribune*, which recently merged with the Minneapolis *Star*, is one of the most attractive and readable newspapers in the United States. There are no column rules and no paragraph indentations. The nameplate and headline face are in Helvetica. The symbol of the open newspaper (or of the sheet of paper on a web press, depending upon how you look at it) appears on various pages.

Today's business

Briefcase

July nonfarm job rate falls with cutbacks

Utility to file Chapter 11

Rural real estate value dips

Airline adds Chicago run

Stress hits women more

In other business news

Information line

Landlords can't enter without notice

Robert F. Neuwoehner: Dubuque's on a roll

The Dubuque, Iowa, *Telegraph Herald* occasionally runs a drawing rather than a photograph of a business person on its "Today's Business" page and runs it large to give it adequate display. The drawing accompanies a feature about the person. Gary Olsen, editor of *Tracks,* a company magazine in the same city, does the drawings on a freelance basis.

and then with scissors or razor blade cuts away excess paper, making a unit out of each story.

The final pasteup, as distinguished from the rough pasteup or layout, involves careful placement of type and art on a full-size page so that it can be photographed for platemaking. Increasingly on newspapers the pasteup, both rough and finished, is being done on a video screen.

The horizontal look

Until recent years the vertical look predominated among newspapers. Single-column, multiple-deck headlines plunged deep into each page, while unbroken black lines fenced off each column from its neighbor. Today on an increasing percentage of papers, the horizontal look prevails.

The first break with the past came with the extension of headlines across one column and into the next. Not only were multicolumn heads better looking; they were also more readable. That headline writers had more space to work with meant they could avoid some of the headline clichés—those miserable three-, four-, and five-letter words that only a person on a copydesk could love.

Another break came with the elimination of column rules, which had made pages monotonously vertical. But it was impossible to eliminate column rules without adding extra white space. Without rules you needed as much as a full pica of space between columns. Otherwise, you sometimes had more space between words than you had between columns.

Where was the extra space to come from? Newspapers couldn't very well make their pages wider. Nor could they make their columns narrower. Columns were too narrow as it was. The standard column measured out at 11 or 12 picas, too narrow for good readability, even with copy set in small news type. Two Minnesota researchers showed that columns set in 7- or 8-point types, common then, would be more readable if the columns were 15 or even 18 picas wide. Yet at the close of World War II, publishers, facing rising newsprint costs, trimmed another pica from their narrow columns. (It was a painless way to raise advertising rates; a column inch was still a column inch, even when it took up less space.) To compound the felony against readability, they increased body-type size to 9 points.

The logical step was to cut down on the number of columns—from nine or eight columns to seven or six. Edmund Arnold saw value in the "7½"

News & Review Interview: The Compleat Bernard Richter

The Chico, California *News & Review,* a tabloid, devotes two full pages here to an interview, and shows that the piece is an interview by enclosing it in giant quotation marks. There is not much white space on this spread; but it concentrates itself in two or three places, giving itself more impact than it would have if it were scattered.

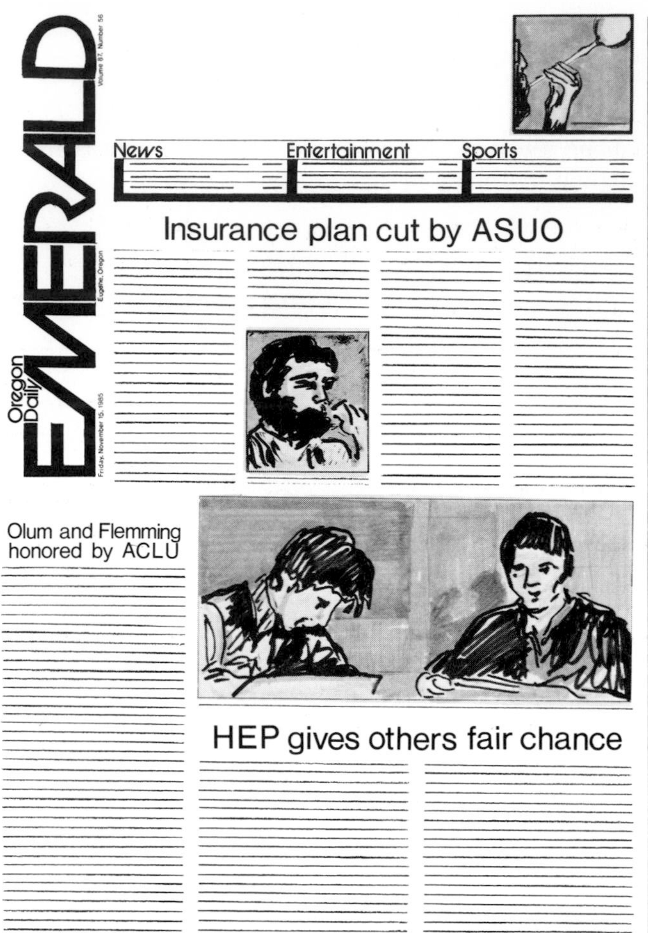
Oregon Daily EMERALD

News | Entertainment | Sports

Insurance plan cut by ASUO

Olum and Flemming honored by ACLU

HEP gives others fair chance

The classroom assignment was to take a traditionally designed newspaper and give it a more contemporary look. Terry Laks chose the *Oregon Daily Emerald* and, using press-on type and both black and gray markers, came up with this handsome front page with its running-up-the-side nameplate and its across-the-top table of contents.

format, in which one column was slightly wider than the other six. The slightly wider column could be used for a feature column or a news roundup. Eventually publishers accepted the idea of the wide column for newspapers. Today the six-column format is common.[7]

But it would be a mistake to write off the narrow column altogether. In some circumstances, in limited doses, the narrow column serves the

Peter Palazzo at a Louisville *Times* seminar offered several redesign possibilities for the paper. You see them here. Note especially his handling of the nameplate. Some of his pages make use of a three- rather than six-column format. The *Times* is a full-size newspaper.

The Louisville Times

COMMITTEE SUBPOENAS TAPES

Mitchell denies trying to fix Vesco case

Plea-Bargaining leaves rape targets victims

Court drops building-items price order

The calm after...

THE LOUISVILLE TIMES

Impeachment committee subpoenas Nixon tapes

Mitchell denies fixing Vesco case

Court drops building-items price order

Plea-Bargaining leaves rape targets twice victims

The calm after...

THE LOUISVILLE TIMES

Mitchell denies fixing Vesco case

Committee subpoenas Nixon tapes

Plea-Bargaining leaves rape targets twice victims

Court drops building-items price order

the louisville times

Mitchell denies trying to fix Vesco case

Court drops building-items price order

Committee subpoenas tapes

Plea-Bargaining leaves rape targets twice victims

The calm after...

LOUISVILLE TIMES

Mitchell denies trying to fix Vesco case

Court drops building-items price order

Committee subpoenas tapes

Plea-Bargaining leaves rape targets twice victims

The calm after...

A student, Brooks Dareff, tried his hand at modernizing the front page of Portland's big daily. *The Oregonian,* moving away from the traditional Old English for the nameplate, putting an across-the-page index under the nameplate, and allowing pieces of art to congregate in an uneven line at the bottom. He also combined silhouette art with regular rectangles and varied the widths (and type sizes) of the columns of body copy. The headlines form a tombstone, but at no expense to readability because the typefaces are different sizes. It is not a practical page because it does not crowd in enough stories in sufficient length, and it doesn't provide for cutlines; but it shows, anyway, one way to bring newspaper design up to date.

THE OREGONIAN

TUESDAY FEBRUARY 24 1981 / 20¢

NATIONAL LOCAL SPORTS SCENE

Doctor's lover convicted

Reagan cautious on El Salvador

Spanish rebels end coup bid

Charles to wed Lady Diana

Where to look

THE LOUISVILLE TIMES

COMMITTEE SUBPOENAS NIXON TAPES

Mitchell denies fixing Vesco case

Plea-Bargaining leaves rape victims targets

The calm after...

Court drops building-items price order

The Louisville Times

COMMITTEE SUBPOENAS NIXON TAPE

Mitchell denies fixing Vesco case.

Plea-Bargaining leaves rape victims targets

The calm after...

Court drops building-items price order

reader well, especially when it is set with an unjustified right edge. But when columns stretch from top of page to bottom, row on row, page after page, a narrow measure puts too much of a burden on readers.

A study conducted by Jack Nuchols, Jr., working under the direction of J. K. Hvistendahl, associate professor of journalism at South Dakota State University, showed that 9-point Imperial, a news face, could be read 4.1 percent faster in a 15-pica width than in an 11-pica width. Moreover, narrow columns take longer to set. Albert Leicht, also working under the direction of Professor Hvistendahl, found that Linotype operators, using the same face, could set matter with 15-pica lines 35 percent faster than matter with 11-pica lines. Wider columns mean fewer lines, less hyphenation at the ends of lines, and more consistent spacing between words.

Varying the look

Radio and television news programs present their stories with a sameness that makes it difficult for listeners and viewers to sort out the important from the unimportant. Newspapers allow readers to skip and choose, and when something is really important, newspapers can turn up the visual volume. A newspaper with a usually quiet, subdued front page especially serve its readers in times of crises. When crisis comes, an across-the-page banner announces it, and the readers understand. An always-screaming newspaper, on the other hand, has no typographic device to turn to.

Logic tells you that a front page on a normal or quiet news day should look quite different from a front page on an assassination-of-a-public-official day. A newspaper should not adopt a standard pattern to use regularly. News should not be fitted to a pattern. Instead, news should *dictate* the pattern.

Of course, a layout artist could work out a series of patterns to cover various conditions and call one into play as the news unfolds. For instance, one pattern could fit a day with two moderately important events to play up, another to fit a day with one big event and two smaller ones, etc. But the best procedure is to create design on the spot, taking into account the nature of each story and especially the quality and number of photographs.

You can do a lot in design when working with the front page of a newspaper and certain special pages inside, but much of your work involves pages cluttered with ads arranged by the ad staff. Your territory then is not only cramped but also nonrectangular. On such pages the best you can hope for is some visual order, a bit of graphic relief, an obvious separation of news-editorial matter from advertising.

Stoutenburgh retires in surprise move

Dr. William Stoutenburgh ... move ends controversy

ALLENTOWN AND LEHIGH COUNTY

THE MORNING CALL

LEHIGH VALLEY'S GREATEST NEWSPAPER

FRIDAY, SEPTEMBER 27, 1985 • 30¢

Over 200,000 flee Gloria

5 states declare emergencies; 'eye' passes over Cape Hatteras

FACTS ON GLORIA

HURRICANE: THE GREATEST STORM ON EARTH

PATH OF GLORIA

WHEN HURRICANES MOVE ASHORE

Pa. keeps wary eye on storm

INSIDE TODAY

Steel to close slag facilities

Salvadoran 'illegals' speak in Valley

Rostenkowski offers his tax reform plan

Senate overwhelmingly votes $7.5-billion 'Superfund' bill

$6 million included for radon problem

The Morning Call of Allentown, Pennsylvania, used maps and plenty of color on this front page covering a hurricane. The stories on the page break into short takes to make things easy for the reader. A "skyline" story runs above the nameplate with the three names on the nameplate stacked rather than running horizontally. The wide columns and other columns throughout the newspaper are unjustified. Those are small ads—four of them—running across the bottom of the page.

Broadsheets and tabloids

The newspaper editor has two basic page-size choices: the full-size broadsheet, approximately 15 inches wide by 23 inches deep, usually with 6 and sometimes 7 or 8 columns to the page; and the tabloid sheet, approximately 11 inches by 15 inches, with 4 or 5 columns to the page. The broadsheet was originally a tax dodge. Beginning in 1712 British papers were taxed by the page. Taxes eventually disappeared, but by then editors and readers had gotten used to the oversize page.

The tabloid, a half-size paper, was developed to serve the straphangers on mass transit systems. It became less popular with the demise of mass transit systems and because of its association with the discredited sensational press in some big cities. But interest in the tabloid format has revived in recent years.

The format has the advantage of making a small paper look thicker. A four-page broadsheet turns into an eight-page tabloid. It is also easier to departmentalize in a tabloid. You can give one full page over to business news, another to religious news, another to entertainment news, etc. You have a better chance, too, of creating ad-less pages. The smaller-size pages allow you to segregate ads on pages of their own without burying them.

One problem with a tabloid is that it doesn't easily break into separate sections so that, say, the sports section can be read apart from the remainder of the paper. Another problem is that you must limit the number of pages. A tabloid that is too thick becomes hard to handle. The small, unbound pages too easily slip out of place as you turn the pages.

COMMENT

THE MORNING CALL

Taxpayers lose in Bethlehem war

ANDREW J. GLASS

The real Latin American revolution

This tuition is too expensive

WILLIAM F. BUCKLEY JR.

Boren's plan for PACs

RUSSELL BAKER

The man has a problem with comets

COMMENT

LETTERS

Berry's World

ANOTHER VIEW

Accuracy in Academia violates the academic contract

MIKE ROYKO

Harry needs a federal subsidy

THE BEAUTIFUL LEHIGH VALLEY

CURRENT QUOTES

The Morning Call labels its editorial page and op-ed page "Comment." A thick horizontal bar with the name in reverse letters goes over each column. Ordinary boxes enclose each editorial. A thick-line, thin-line box encloses each blurb. Pat Oliphant's editorial cartoon gets more than the usual space so that it can really be appreciated. The letters to the editor congregate in one place (on the op-ed page) rather than in a couple of places, as in some other newspapers. Maureen E. Decker serves as assistant managing editor in charge of graphics for this well-designed newspaper. Jeff Lindenmuth is design editor.

Some two dozen dailies and many weeklies are now using the tabloid format. Two of the best are *The Christian Science Monitor* and Long Island's *Newsday.*

Kinds of front pages

"In theory, all front pages begin as blank paper," observed Clive Irving. "In fact, they all have a preordained basic structure: the vertical division imposed by the columns, and less visible horizontal boundaries which determine the placing of stories—in descending order of importance."[8]

Authors dealing with newspaper design and layout (or makeup) tend to categorize front pages under five headings:

1. *Symmetrical.* You'll be hard pressed to find examples of symmetrical newspaper pages today. Even the New York *Times* has abandoned them.
2. *Informal balance.* This is far more common and sensible; all the other kinds of layout are really nothing but variations. One variation goes by the name *quadrant,* where informal balance is achieved on a page cut into imaginary quarters; each quarter has some art and some heavy typography.
3. *Brace.* Liberal use is made of stories that start out with multi-column heads and leads, funneling down to single-column tails. One *L*-shaped story fits snugly into another; or a picture fits into the *L.* Stories look like braced wall shelves, hence the name. Brace layout is regarded by some critics as dated, although in Great Britain,

where it is widely used on tabloids, it results in some lively looking pages.

Edmund Arnold defends the use of *L*-shaped stories because of the variety and flexibility they bring to newspaper design. "Some editors are slavishly devoted to so-called 'modular makeup.' This requires every story to be in a square or rectangle. That imposes an unwanted and unnecessary handicap. . . ."[9]

4. *Circus*. Such layout is loudly informal and gimmick-ridden. Otto Storch gave it magazine respectability on the pages of *McCall's* in the late 1950s.
5. *Horizontal*. This informal layout has many multicolumn heads and pictures, with stories blocked off into horizontal rectangles several columns wide. Horizontal, but not vertical, column rules are used.

A newspaper tends to hold its front-page design to one of these categories, but it varies the approach each day to keep the look interesting. Above all, the design must be functional, putting emphasis where it belongs and helping readers pick their way through the various offerings on the page.

Whatever kind of layout you use, a crucial decision is whether to crowd as many stories as possible onto the front page or to limit the selection to just a few. Using many stories increases the chance that every reader will find *something* of interest on the page. A page with only a few stories, on the other hand, makes for less clutter, allows for more white space, and makes possible full development of the stories on that page. Fewer jumps to inside pages are needed.

Edgar T. Zelsmann, president of Carl J. Nelson Research Corporation in Chicago, says surveys show that half the readers are lost when a story jumps from one page to another. Furthermore, when readers follow a story to another page, they may not get back to the page where they started the story. For these reasons newspapers try to develop their stories as complete units on a page. They break a long story into two stories and put the second on an inside page.

Newspapers that jump stories should make finding them as easy as possible for readers. Carrying all jumps to a single page inside is one approach, giving that page a general "Continued" label. Repeating or partially repeating the original headlines helps, too. The repeated headline can be smaller or in a screened version of the type used for the original headline. Some papers make sure the last paragraphs of stories to be continued are complete. Readers, then, do not have to carry partial sentences with them. The new jump headlines may be based on what is contained in those last paragraphs on the front page.

When stories jump, they should jump to a page in the section they start in, ideally to the back page of that section. Then the reader can easily return to the front page.

You signal the reader that a jump is ahead with a "Continued on" or "Please turn to" line. When a story simply carries over to another column, you do not need such a line. In a magazine you don't need such a line when an article carries over to the next page or spread.

Whether using jumps or not, editors look for ways to make long stories appear to be shorter than they are. A one-column by fifteen-inch story, for instance, goes down easier as a three-column by five-inch story. And whether the story stays in one column or moves along to several, subheads can break it into more pleasant components. Some papers set occasional

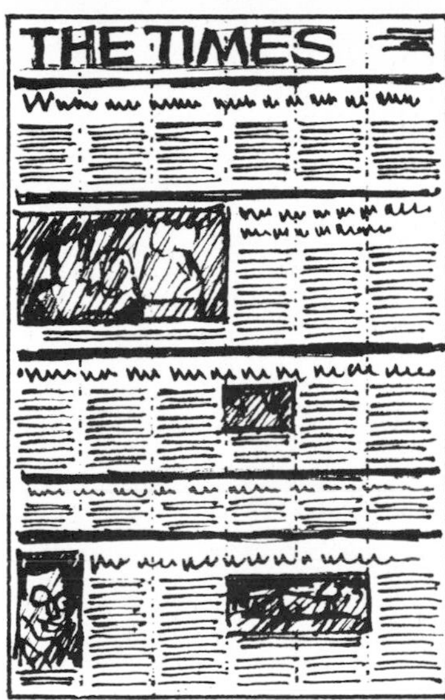

These rough sketches—thumbnails—show an example of each of five basic newspaper layout approaches: symmetrical, informal balance, brace, circus, and horizontal. *The Times* would pick one of these and vary it from issue to issue.

paragraphs in boldface type and maybe a narrower measure as a change of pace, but such paragraphs tend to cheapen a page and to give arbitrary emphasis to parts of stories.

The nameplate

From journalism's beginnings, editors have felt the names of their newspapers should stand out as copies were peddled and hawked on city streets. Originally, about the only dark type known or available was the black-letter, a face we know today as Old English. Even today, partly because of tradition, partly because of what editors consider the "dignity" of the face, many nameplates still appear in that same unlikely face. But most papers now have adopted faces for nameplates more in keeping with the times and with their headline and body types. Plenty of boldface types are available; and we know today that even small faces can stand out, provided they are displayed with a generous amount of white space.

If a paper can't bring itself to give up Old English for its nameplate, it can at least simplify the type. The New York *Times* did this, greatly improving the looks of the nameplate. Compare it to that of the Washington *Post,* also Old English but with double lines.

The typeface in a nameplate can be in strong contrast to the headline face, or it can be in the same face, say in all-caps where headlines are caps and lowercase.

Actually, a newspaper's nameplate is almost always drawn, and in the days of letterpress it was photoengraved—that's why it's called a name-*plate.* A nameplate is to a newspaper what a logo is to a magazine. The drawing often incorporates a line sketch of an insignia or some local scene. An effective nameplate can be made of reproduction proofs of type cut and repasted and retouched by an artist familiar with letterform.

Many newspapers use a single design in more than one size. The nameplate may "float" to any location from issue to issue.

The question of emphasis

Newspaper layout is largely a matter of assigning proper emphasis to stories. Usually, one story receives greater emphasis than any other. On some days, however, the front page may have two stories of equal significance. Maybe three.

It is a good idea to think of stories as falling into three general categories of importance—major stories, important stories, and fillers or change-of-pace material—and assign emphasis accordingly.

You can emphasize through placement. You can also emphasize through story length, headline size, body-copy size, art boldness, color.

Until recently, the No. 1 spot on the front page was always the top of the last column, because that was where the banner headline ended. With decreased emphasis on newsstand sales, the banner is less important and not often used; there is no reason, then, why the No. 1 story can't go at the top left of the page, where the eye normally first settles.

At one time all the emphasis was confined to the top half of a page. Now the entire page is considered; editors take specific steps to get some typographic display "below the fold." Edmund Arnold talks about "anchoring" all four corners of a page with something heavy. Run dark headlines, boxes, pictures, or other typographic weights to "define" each corner, he advises. One wonders, though, what's so important or mysterious about corners that they need defining?

Making things easy for the reader

Readers appreciate a news digest on the front page, boxed or otherwise set aside, perhaps over the nameplate, with a single paragraph devoted to each of the major stories. But the editor should be stingy with details here so as not to spoil the reader for the whole story. When page numbers follow each entry, the digest serves, too, as a special table of contents.

For large papers there should be a general table of contents pointing the reader to regular features. The thoughtful editor runs standing features and pages in the same position, issue after issue.

Obits should be gathered in one section of the paper under a consistent

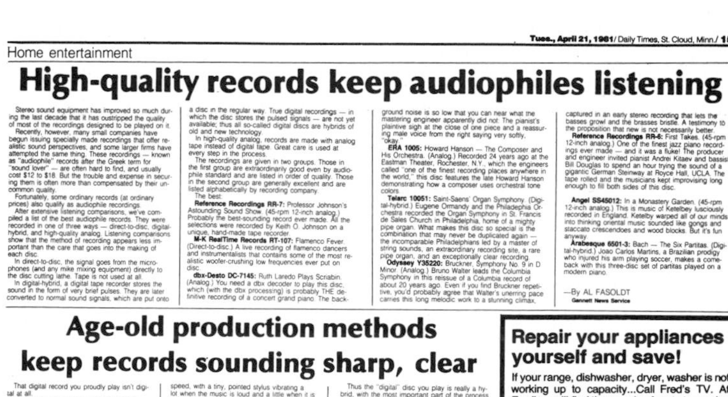

Tues., April 21, 1981/ Daily Times, St. Cloud, Minn./ **15E**

Home entertainment

High-quality records keep audiophiles listening

Stereo sound equipment has improved so much during the last decade that it has outstripped the quality of most of the recordings designed to be played on it.

Recently, however, many small companies have begun issuing specially made recordings that offer realistic sound perspectives, and some larger firms have attempted the same thing. These recordings — known as "audiophile" records after the Greek term for "sound lover" — are often hard to find, and usually cost $12 to $18. But the trouble and expense in securing them is often more than compensated by their uncommon quality.

Fortunately, some ordinary records (at ordinary prices) also qualify as audiophile recordings.

After extensive listening comparisons, we've compiled a list of the best audiophile records. They were recorded in one of three ways — direct-to-disc, digital-hybrid, and high-quality analog. Listening comparisons show that the method of recording appears less important than the care that goes into the making of each disc.

In direct-to-disc, the signal goes from the microphones (and any mike mixing equipment) directly to the disc cutting lathe. Tape is not used at all.

In digital-hybrid, a digital tape recorder stores the sound in the form of very brief pulses. They are later converted to normal sound signals, which are put onto a disc in the regular way. True digital recordings — in which the disc stores the pulsed signals — are not yet available; thus all so-called digital discs are hybrids of old and new technology.

In high-quality analog, records are made with analog tape instead of digital tape. Great care is used at every step in the process.

The recordings are given in two groups. Those in the first group are extraordinarily good even by audiophile standard and are listed in order of quality. Those in the second group are generally excellent and are listed alphabetically by recording company.

The best:

Reference Recordings RR-7: Professor Johnson's Astounding Sound Show. (45-rpm 12-inch analog.) Probably the best-sounding record ever made. All the selections were recorded by Keith O. Johnson on a unique, hand-made tape recorder.

M-K RealTime Records RT-107: Flamenco Fever. (Direct-to-disc.) A live recording of flamenco dancers and instrumentalists that contains some of the most realistic woofer-crushing low frequencies ever put on disc.

dbx-Desto DC-7145: Ruth Laredo Plays Scriabin. (Analog.) You need a dbx decoder to play this disc, which (with the dbx processing) is probably THE definitive recording of a concert grand piano. The background noise is so low that you can hear what the mastering engineer apparently did not: The pianist's plaintive sigh at the close of one piece and a reassuring male voice from the right saying very softly, "okay."

ERA 1005: Howard Hanson — The Composer and His Orchestra. (Analog.) Recorded 24 years ago at the Eastman Theater, Rochester, N.Y., which the engineers called "one of the finest recording places anywhere in the world," this disc features the late Howard Hanson demonstrating how a composer uses orchestral tone colors.

Telarc 10051: Saint-Saens' Organ Symphony. (Digital-hybrid.) Eugene Ormandy and the Philadephia Orchestra recorded the Organ Symphony in St. Francis de Sales Church in Philadelphia, home of a mighty pipe organ. What makes this disc so special is the combination that may never be duplicated again — the incomparable Philadelphians led by a master of string sounds, an extraordinary recording site, a rare pipe organ, and an exceptionally clear recording.

Odyssey Y35220: Bruckner, Symphony No. 9 in D Minor. (Analog.) Bruno Walter leads the Columbia Symphony in this reissue of a Columbia record of about 20 years ago. Even if you find Bruckner repetitive, you'd probably agree that Walter's unerring pace carries this long melodic work to a stunning climax, captured in an early stereo recording that lets the basses growl and the brasses bristle. A testimony to the proposition that new is not necessarily better.

Reference Recordings RR-6: First Takes. (45-rpm 12-inch analog.) One of the finest jazz piano recordings ever made — and it was a fluke! The producer and engineer invited pianist Andrei Kitaev and bassist Bill Douglas to spend an hour trying the sound of a gigantic German Steinway at Royce Hall, UCLA. The tape rolled and the musicians kept improvising long enough to fill both sides of this disc.

Angel SS45012: In a Monastery Garden. (45-rpm 12-inch analog.) This is music of Ketelbey lusciously recorded in England. Ketelby warped all of our minds into thinking oriental music sounded like gongs and staccato crescendoes and wood blocks. But it's fun anyway.

Arabesque 6501-3: Bach — The Six Partitas. (Digital-hybrid.) Joao Carlos Martins, a Brazilian prodigy who injured his arm playing soccer, makes a comeback with this three-disc set of partitas played on a modern piano.

—By AL FASOLDT
Gannett News Service

Age-old production methods keep records sounding sharp, clear

That digital record you proudly play isn't digital at all.

It's old-fashioned analog, just like the 78s grandmother used to play.

Just like the old Victrola shellacs, your new-fangled digital disc has a long, spiral groove that wiggles a needle (stylus, it's called these days), and those wiggles make up an analog of the actual sound.

("Analog" is engineer's talk for something that behaves in a fashion similar to something else. For example, if one thing got bigger, its analog would get bigger, too.)

And just like those old crank-'em-up Victrolas, your modern record player can't play anything but analog, grooved discs spun at a steady speed, with a tiny, pointed stylus vibrating a lot when the music is loud and a little when it is soft.

No digital allowed.

Then why do the record companies call those analog discs "digital"? Because they used a digital tape recorder in the recording chain.

Here are the stages of a typical "digital" recording: performers make music; microphones send out electrical signals that are analogs of the sound; those electrical analog signals are changed to pulses in a digital recorder; those digital pulses are changed back to analog electrical signals on playback, and those analog signals are sent to a disc recording lathe to make a record.

Thus the "digital" disc you play is really a hybrid, with the most important part of the process — the actual representation of the sound on the disc — still decidedly analog.

So don't be surprised if you don't hear much of a difference over regular records. If digital sound storage is superior to analog storage, as its backers claim, you'll have to wait till the day some years from now when you can put a real digital disc on your turntable. Working mod%ls are in the testing stages.

For now, it doesn't matter what the record jacket says; that flat piece of vinyl inside is analog just the same.

—By AL FASOLDT
Gannett News Service

Sound stereo advice

Here are some questions and answers on high-quality sound reproduction:

Question: Do I need an expensive stereo system to get the most from audiophile recordings?

Answer: No. You need a stereo system that meets basic standards, that's all.

Q: What kind of standards?

A: Mostly, reasonably flat frequency response and low distortion.

Your sound system should treat low, middle and high tones pretty much the same — not emphasizing one range at the expense of the others — and it shouldn't add any unpleasant edge to the sound.

Q: How can I tell if my system meets those requirements? It's a couple of years old. There must be something better on the market by now.

A: You've actually got two separate concerns. Let's consider the second one first, since it's the easiest to answer: With only one exception, the age of your stereo system has nothing to do with how good it sounds.

As for the exception, it's the phonograph stylus. It wears out and needs to be replaced every 1,000 hours or so.

Now to the first part of the question. The easiest way to check the quality of a sound system is to listen carefully while it reproduces familiar sounds.

One general sound everybody is used to is applause. It's full of sudden, sharp sounds that are hard to reproduce, and so makes a good test for a system — if you can find a record with enough hand-clapping on it.

Another familiar sound is a piano. Of all instruments, it is probably the most difficult to reproduce because it is both a string instrument, with sonorous vibrations, and a percussion instrument, with sharp hammerings.

Q: Suppose the piano sounds a little thin, as if the bottom notes aren't strong enough — does that mean I need new speakers?

A: Not necessarily. It might mean only that you should turn up your bass control a trifle.

Q: And if that doesn't do it?

A: If you're otherwise satisfied with the sound, you could learn to live with the thin low notes. Of all of music's frequencies, the lowest are the hardest to reproduce and the least missed.

Q: But if I miss them anyway?

A: Try a subwoofer — a single speaker that plays only the low notes.

Q: When I play music loud, it sounds pretty good, but the neighbors complain. When I play it soft, the neighbors are happy but the sound seems lifeless. Why?

A: Because the ear hears frequencies differently at varying loudness levels. Low frequencies, especially, are nearly inaudible unless they're fairly loud. So when you play your music softly, all the notes — high, middle and low — are reduced by the same amount, but to your ears it seems like the low notes have dropped right out.

If you want to listen to loud music try your headphones.

—By Al Fasholdt
Gannett News Service

Ads arranged in a half pyramid make difficult the designing of inside pages of a newspaper. How do you give the news-editorial material a look of its own? Often there is no room for art. Nor is art always a good thing. Editorial art may fight advertising art for attention. The St. Cloud, Minnesota, *Daily Times* solves the problem nicely on this page from "3rd Tuesday," a monthly full-newspaper-page magazine section. The three features, all sat in unjustified type with column rules, use same-size type for the headlines. You see three different body-copy widths.

It's OK to *disco*, you can fry it with *Crisco*, but don't call it **censored**

The City's 'salty' nickname takes a verbal beating

By Lynn Ludlow

In 1851, humorist Artemus Ward came here and called it **censored**, the name bestowed by English sailors on the port village of Yerba Buena.

Used also by Jack London, James M. Cain and tourists from all over, the term became The City's only cuss word. By 1943, incredibly, Mayor Angelo Rossi went to Hollywood to demand another name for "Hello, **censored**, Hello." At the movie's premiere here, as a sop to Rossi, the signs on the marquees said, "Hello, San Francisco, Hello."

The official pamphlet of the Convention and Visitors Bureau is entitled, "Don't Call It **censored**."

And after 132 years, the final humiliation was ordered yesterday by Municipal Judge Dorothy von Beroldingen, sitting as judge pro tem of the wholly unofficial Court of Historical Review and Appeals.

She said she had sifted the testimony and evidence during an hour-long hearing during lunch in a packed courtroom at City Hall. And her memorandum opinion, miraculously, was already typed up.

"Ordered, adjudged and decreed, that the City of St. Francis is henceforth and forever to be known only by its full and true name of 'San Francisco.'"

★ ★ ★

Don't expect dispassionate objectivity. I was a witness for the losing side, which asked the court to rehabilitate this affectionate nickname for a city where the usual response is a look of shock.

The winning side was represented by attorney Claire Pilcher, president of the city Public Utilities Commission, who couldn't bring herself to say "**censored**" without murmuring, "God forgive me."

During cross-examination, she asked: "Does your publisher know you're here?"

"Uh, no."

"I thought not. No further questions."

★ ★ ★

The unofficial court was the proper forum for unofficial laws against unofficial words, which are normally welcomed in a city known for its tolerance toward unofficial behavior. Words like "disco" and "Crisco" can be hurled about with impunity, but **censored** prompts stern measures.

Russell Joyner, executive director of the International Society for General Semantics, told the judge that the word, "a salty term," is part of the vocabulary of working people throughout America. At St. Anthony's Dining Room, for example, a new arrival might say something about coming to **censored** — and would be mystified at any corrections.

Pilcher asked: "You don't call it Tony's Diner, do you?"

★ ★ ★

Those who sought to reintroduce the fine old colloquialism were represented by Supervisor Quentin Kopp. When questioning school board member Jule Anderson, who produced a petition opposed to **censored**, he took the exhibit and said: "Would you read the last name on this petition for the record?"

ST. FRANCIS OF ASSISI, THE CITY'S PATRON SAINT
The other word may have come from 'el fresco,' the cool place

Anderson said: "Frank Newcomer."

"Just as I thought," said Kopp. "No further questions."

He told the court:

"It's been shown beyond doubt that **censored** should be restored for reasons that are sentimental, historical and practical."

★ ★ ★

... The new middle class gave authority to the dictionaries and grammarians in return for "correct usage" rules that helped solidify their social position."

—Dictionary of American Slang

Some say the word was a squeezing of San Francisco; others claim it is a misspelling of "el fresco," sometimes used by early Californians to describe "the cool place"; some others say that **censored** is a wrong nickname for The City's patron saint, Francis of Assisi (more likely nicknames would be Cisco or Pancho; in life he was known as Giovanni, or John.)

But among sailors, then and now, The City by the Golden Gate was known as **censored**. Peter Tamony, 77, who traces the history of slang words, said the term probably comes from "frith-soken," an archaic Middle English word for "place of refuge" or "safe harbor." Applied to the Bay of San Francisco when sailing ships came during the Gold Rush, the word probably stuck because of the other associations.

Joseph C. Tarantino, who grew up in North Beach, argued for restoration of the word.

"I'm sure that St. Francis would be tickled pink to have this city known as **censored**," he said.

It was a position disputed by Msgr. Richard Knapp, pastor of Mission Dolores Basilica.

"I don't think our holy father would welcome the word," he said.

Pilcher asked: "Is it, in fact, a sacrilege?"

"I would leave that," said the monsignor, "to Higher Authority."

★ ★ ★

San Francisco's only court-decreed bad word, if spoken, won't necessarily lead to arrest and jail.

Von Beroldingen, who was substituting for Superior Court Judge Harry Low, reaffirmed the First Amendment's right to freedom of expression "so long as in so doing the rights of others are not unreasonably impinged."

She added: "The court finds that it will not unreasonably restrict the rights of those who prefer the use of the name **censored**...

"The court further finds that it would be neither fitting nor proper to refer to the gentle St. Francis of Assisi by a nickname, and accordingly, in the interest of preserving the dignity of one whose high purposes we hope will always be emulated by the citizens of San Francisco, it is not appropriate to acknowledge a nickname for the city that bears his name."

The San Francisco *Examiner* used some typographic imagination in readying this feature for publication. It deals with the obliquity of calling San Francisco "Frisco." For each mention of the hated word, a "censored" mark appears. (Reprinted by permission.)

heading or between symbolic black bars. Obits need no individualized heads. How many ways can you say—would you want to say—that a person has died, anyway? The full name by itself is headline enough. Beside, you avoid awkward part-present tense, part-past tense heads like JOE SMITH DIES TUESDAY (sounds as if poor Joe is set to face a firing squad).

The Indianapolis *News* solves the problem of obit headlines by using subjects and predicates but putting them in the past tense. The past tense, contrasting with the present tense elsewhere in the paper, says "death" by implication: "Joe Blank Ran Car Agency" or "Carol Cook Taught at Jefferson." The Denver *Post* bunches its obits under a column heading that includes an abstract drawing of a sunset.

Similarly, engagements and weddings can be gathered together under standard headings and run with label, name-only heads.

Newspapers often organize news by subject and region. Like a number of other newspapers, the Miami *Herald* runs a column of short items under the heading "Around the Nation." The column divides itself into four parts—"East," "South," "Mid-America," and "West"—each having a map showing the states involved.

Readers appreciate an arrangement of material—possible only with large newspapers—that makes separate sections out of sports pages, financial pages, and other special pages. That way the whole family can enjoy the paper at the same time. Some papers have printed special sections, like sports sections, on a tinted stock.

Inside the paper

Most newspaper design concentrates on the front page. But, as Arnold tells his seminars on newspaper design, "We have to make sure there isn't an immediate and dramatic letdown in quality when a reader turns to Page Two."

In laying out inside pages, you might want to see them as front pages but with ads at the bottom and at the side. You can treat the ads as though they were unrelated photographs. Of course, if there are so many ads that the triangular-shaped newshole turns out to be only a small portion of the page, there is nothing you can do to make it attractive and precious little you can do to make it even readable.

The ads are already marked for placement when you receive an inside page to lay out. But chances are, you won't see them. Only boxes will be there. You won't know what kind of art or headline a story will be competing with. It is a good idea to run solid columns of copy next to ads, keeping your own art—editorial art—safely away from the ads. This gives both your art and the advertising better display. It also helps keep the lines drawn between news/editorial material and advertising.

OPINION

No More ECU

THE DISPATCH

L.A. MARTIN

October

LETTERS

Carter On Pride

BILL NOBLITT/TODAY IN NORTH CAROLINA

JACK ANDERSON

Bottling The Air Bill

Education For Offenders

PATRICK BUCHANAN

Last Of The New Frontiersmen

For its editorial page *The Dispatch* of Lexington, North Carolina, uses the nameplate type for "OPINION" with bold lines across the top, as on page 1. The neatly designed masthead (the box that names the top officers and gives other information) is centered in the area carrying the editorial (for this issue an editorial from another paper), with the Pat Oliphant editorial cartoon just below. Mug shots of columnists are cropped unusually close and made into horizontals instead of the usual verticals. Perhaps the design theme would be better served on this page if the double-ruled lines above the "Letters" column, the Jack Anderson column, and the Patrick Buchanan column and under the cartoon were filled in to make single lines as bold as the ones at the top of the page.

An editorial page of the Louisville *Courier-Journal* features Hugh Haynie's Ronald-Reagan-looking-like-Teddy-Roosevelt editoral cartoon at the upper left instead of the upper right, where most papers would put it, and a photograph to accompany the lead—or at least the top-of-the-page—editorial. That editorial is long enough for its third leg to get a subhead. The letters section gives one letter a multicolumn headline. (© by the *Courier-Journal.* Reprinted by permission.)

"Now, really . . . do I look like the sort who'd meddle in the affairs of El Salvador?"

OPINION

The Courier-Journal

BARRY BINGHAM JR. — Editor and Publisher

ROBERT T. BARNARD — Opinion Page Editor

THURSDAY, FEBRUARY 26, 1981. FOUNDED 1826.

Associate Editors: JOHN HART, BERT EMKE, JAMES EDDLEMAN; HUGH HAYNIE, Cartoonist

Regulators need more time before ruling on phone rates

Phone rates have lagged

SENATOR SOAPER says:

Election watchdog errs in taking Reader's Digest to task

Second thoughts on surgical 'second opinions'

READERS' VIEWS

People looking for heroes?

Never listened to Lennon . . .

. . . 'Subversive qualities'

. . . Acted irresponsibly?

Snyder's remarks 'tacky'

African-American schools?

Thanks from foster parents

Do we really want government run like a business?

Many newspapers prohibit advertisers from using in their ads the same typeface used in headlines for news stories.

To eliminate the confusion in ad sizes in newspapers, a problem advertising agencies had for many years, the newspaper industry adopted Standard Advertising Units. The program was designed to help newspaper makeup people as well as advertisers, especially national advertisers. Now, a national ad can be designed in a size that fits most newspapers.

Editorial and op-ed pages

The late William Loeb, the crusty, outspoken, ultraconservative publisher of Manchester New Hampshire *Union Leader,* ran some of his editorials on the front page of his paper in boldface type and all-caps to give them urgency. Loeb delighted in name calling: Democrats were "left-wing

TV TONIGHT

Chart compiled by Robin Tanner
✓ denotes recommended viewing

	8:00	8:30	9:00	9:30	10:00	10:30	11:00	11:30	12:00
2 CBS	**Stir Crazy**/(Premiere.) Based on the hit movie. Two men, convicted of a crime they didn't do, arrange a unique prison escape and then try to keep one step ahead of the authorities. Larry Riley and Joseph Guzaldo star.		**Charlie and Company**/(Premiere.) Charlie (Flip Wilson) has stage fright when he appears before his son's high school class.	**George Burns Comedy Week**/(Premiere.) A detective tries to help an institutionalized woman (Catherine O'Hara) reclaim her estate.	**Equalizer**/(Premiere.) Edward Woodward stars as Robert McCall, a former spy who comes out of retirement to balance the scales of justice on the streets of Manhattan. Tonight: a computer technician stumbles onto a government blackmailing scheme.		**News**/Tritia Toyota and John Schubeck.	**Movie: The Awakening of Candra**/(1981) Blanche Baker ("Sixteen Candles") stars as a teen bride abducted on her honeymoon by a crazed fisherman. Cliff de Young co-stars; based on a true story.	
4 NBC	**Highway to Heaven**/(Season premiere.) Jonathan and Mark become involved in the lives of three youngsters who are attending Camp Good Times, a facility for dying children.		**Hell Town**/Father Noah "Hardstep" Rivers tries to recover a goat that helped a young boy emerge from catatonia.		**St. Elsewhere**/(Season premiere.) Chandler contines to grieve over the loss of his brother in Vietnam; Auschander begins a search for Westphall's replacement; the new head (Alfre Woodard) of obstetrics and gynecology counsels a childless couple.		**News**/Nick Clooney and Kelly Lange.	**The Tonight Show**/Host: Johnny Carson. Rivers. Scheduled: Glynis Barber, Joe Garagiola.	
5	**Movie: Arabesque**/(1966) When an American professor in England is kidnapped, help comes in the form of a mysterious woman who is the mistress of an oil magnate. Gregory Peck and Sophia Loren star. ✓				**News**/Hal Fishman and Debby Davison.		**Taxi**/Zena announces her wedding plans. (R)	**Saturday Night**/Host: Charles Grodin. Guest: Paul Simon. (R)	
7 ABC	**ABC News Special: 45/85**/Former Presidents Richard Nixon, Gerald Ford and Jimmy Carter along with prominent personalities from the U.S. and abroad join co-anchors Peter Jennings and Ted Koppel for an overview of people, places and events from 1945 to 1985.						**News**/Paul Moyer and Terry Murphy.	**ABC Nightline**	**Eye on Hollywood**
9	**Joker's Wild**/Host: Bill Cullen.	**Tic Tac Dough**/Host: Wink Martindale.	**News**/Wendy Gordon and Tom Lawrence.		**Fantasy Island**/Roddy McDowell stars as the Devil. (R)		**Lou Grant**/Lou tries to go home again. (R)		**Gong Show**
11	**News**/Marcia Brandwynne and Jay Scott.	**PM Magazine**/Featured: Pia Zadora and Marine boot camp.	**Star Search**/Guest: Ann Jillian.		**News**/Marcia Brandwynne and Jay Scott.		**WKRP in Cincinnati**/A DJ is held up during a live broadcast. (R)	**Merv Griffin**	
13	**Movie: Rollerball**/(1975) In a rigidly controlled society of the future, the superstar of the number-one sport challenges the established order by refusing to retire from the game. James Caan, Maud Adams, John Houseman and Moses Gunn star.				**News 13**/Wendy Rutledge and Tim Malloy.	**Independent Network News**	**Barney Miller**/Harris goes undercover. (R)	**Hawaii Five-O** (R)	
28 PBS	**Abortion Battle**/The right to have an abortion is examined through documentaries and commentary illustrating pro-choice and pro-life viewpoints; included are clips from "Silent No More," "So Many Voices," "Conceived in Liberty" and "The Silent Scream." ✓						**Only When I Laugh**/Roy thinks one of the roommates is a goner when he overhears a doctor.	**Latenight America**	
34	**Bianca Vidal**		**Muy Especial: Brazil Musical**		**Dancin' Days**	**24 Horas**		**La Traicion**	**Movie: Al Fin a Solas**/Cesar Costa.
56	**Movie: Susanna Pass**/(1949) A game warden battles a gang of crooks trying to get at the oil deposits under a lake. Roy Rogers and Dale Evans star. (7:30)		**Bowling**		**Roller Stars** (R)		**Miller's Court**	**Paul Ryan**	**700 Club**/Religion.
A&E	**Man From Moscow** (7:30)		**Swindle: The Rise and Rise of Bernie Cornfeld**		**American Songwriter**			**Man From Moscow**	
C-SPAN	**Event of the Day**				**Viewer Call-In** (R)		**Event of the Day**		
DIS	**Still the Beaver**	**Mousterpiece Theater**	**Movie: Caesar and Cleopatra**/(1946) An Egyptian temptress dallies with an aging emperor. Vivien Leigh and Claude Rains star.				**DTV** (11:15)	**Mosby's Marauders**/(1967) Kurt Russell and James MacArthur star in this action adventure.	
ESPN	**Boxing** (6:00)	**SportsCenter**	**SportsLook**	**Outdoor Life**	**Track and Field '85 Review**		**Julius Erving's Sports Focus**	**SportsCenter**	**Australian Rules Football**/Semifinal from Victoria. (R)
HBO	**Movie: The Terminator**/(1984) A cyborg travels from the future to kill a woman marked by destiny. Arnold Schwarzenegger and Linda Hamilton star.				**Movie: Mussolini: The Decline and Fall of Il Duce**/(1985) As World War II sweeps across Italy, a personal war rages between members of Benito Mussolini's family. (Part 1 of 2.)				**UFOs: What's Going On?** (11:50)
MAX	**Movie: The Blues Brothers**/(1980) Dan Aykroyd and John Belushi star in this comedy about two musicians trying to raise money to save their orphanage. Cab Calloway and John Candy co-star.				**Eros International** (10:15)		**Movie: The Philadelphia Experiment**/(1984) Michael Pare stars as a soldier in World War II sent ahead in time to 1984.		
ON; SEL	**Movie: Cloak and Dagger**/(1984) A young boy sees a murder and tries to persuade his father to get involved. Henry Thomas and Dabney Coleman star. (7:00)		**Movie: Dreamscape**/(1984) Dennis Quaid stars in this sci-fi thriller about a device that allows one to invade the dreams of another.				**Adult Movie**		
SHO	**Brothers**	**Washingtoon**	**Movie: Popeye**/(1980) Robin Williams, Shelley Duvall and Ray Walston star in this musical based on the cartoons.				**Movie: Squeeze Play**/Adult entertainment.		
TMC	**Movie: Once Upon a Time in America**/(1984) Robert De Niro and James Woods star in this gangster movie.								**Movie: Never Say Never Again**/(1983) Sean Connery stars.
USA	**Gong Show**	**Make Me Laugh**	**Edge of Night**	**Heartlight City** (R)		**Japan Today**	**Wrestling**		
WTBS	**Movie: QB VII**/(1974) Anthony Hopkins stars as an accused Nazi war criminal in this adaptation of Leon Uris' novel. (Conclusion.) (7:20)					**Movie: Seven Days in May**/(1964) Burt Lancaster and Kirk Douglas star as two generals in this drama about the military takeover of the U.S. Frederic March co-stars; Rod Serling wrote the script. ✓			
Z	**Movie: Topper**/(1937) Two pesky ghosts haunt a portly businessman. Constance Bennett, Cary Grant, Roland Young and Billie Burke star. (7:00) ✓		**Movie: Teachers**/(1984) A burned-out high school teacher (Nick Nolte) misses class and gets drunk with his boss in this look at modern-day education. Judd Hirsch and JoBeth Williams co-star.				**Movie: A Week's Vacation**/(1981) Nathalie Baye and Phillippe Noiret star.		

Not all TV listings in newspapers are as easy to read as the one Robin Tanner compiles for the Los Angeles *Herald Examiner.* This one lets the reader see at a glance what's beginning on a given station at a given time and what's a carryover from a previous hour. Recommended programs get a check mark. An occasional mug shot offers graphic relief.

kooks," President Eisenhower was "a stinking hypocrite," President Kennedy was "the No. 1 liar in the United States."

Loeb dictated rather than wrote his editorials to give them a "plain talk" feel. And where better to alert his readers about the dangers to the republic than on the front page? Other powerful newspaper editors and publishers used their front pages for editorializing, too.

As far as most journalists are concerned, though, editorials belong on an inside page set aside for them. It is usually the next-to-the-last left-hand page in the first section. That page needs a design treatment to make it different from other pages in the paper. Because of its essentially serious nature, it is, as a rule, more subdued typographically. On some papers the headline face is a classic one—say Caslon or Garamond—to contrast with a sans serif head schedule elsewhere. Columns often are wider. The one illustration, usually, is a multicolumn editorial cartoon to the right of the column of editorials, which occupy the first columns.

Editorial cartoons in the past took a vertical format, but most of them today appear as horizontals, often done on a special kind of paper called Grafix, which allows for painted-on line shading. The bigger papers hire their own editorial cartoonists; both the bigger and the smaller papers subscribe to editorial cartoons offered by syndicates.

Cartoons can be expected to ridicule people. In fact, that is what they should do, especially those appearing on the editorial page. However, editorial cartoonists more and more are finding themselves and their newspapers involved in libel suits in a sue-happy age. As of this writing no cartoonist has been convicted, but defending against such suits is costly and time-consuming. Some editors and cartoonists feel threatened. Paul Szep, editorial cartoonist for the Boston *Globe,* who has been sued several times, says that a cartoonist's only defense may be to "turn around and sue the person for frivolous lawsuit."

One suit directed against Szep and the *Globe* was filed by a politician claiming he had been held up to ridicule. "My goodness," commented an editor, "a political cartoonist holding up a politician to ridicule. That's not libel, that's a job description."[10]

Still, editors and art directors have to keep the possibility of libel suits in mind as they choose art for their publications. That's why in 1985 some editors left out a "Doonesbury" episode satirizing Frank Sinatra; the editors found the content borderline. That was from a legal standpoint. That

6 Willamette Week For the Week Ending November 25, 1974

Calendar

For November 20 through 27

Theater

Music

Club Music

All Week

Lectures

Meetings

Cinema

Et cetera

Children

Dance

Visual Arts

TV best bets for November 20 through 27

Eddie Albert (left) portrays Benjamin Franklin and Gig Young plays the Count de Vergennes in The Ambassador, first in a series of four specials on the colonial statesman. (Thurs., 9 pm, Ch.6)

Sports

Here is an efficiently organized page of information about goings-on in Portland, Oregon, the area served by *Williamette Week,* a weekly alternative newspaper. The roman type for headlines remains constant, except for size changes. The combination of thick and thin rules nicely segregates the material. Outlined photographs combine with small line sketches to give the page some areas of visual relief.

Letters from readers

Ellen
Peck

Will Jones
after last night

Two versions of a heading for the letters column of the Minneapolis *Tribune,* are shown here actual size. When the column spreads over onto two pages, the paper runs one of these on the editorial page, the other on the op-ed page.

Headings for regular columns in the *Tribune* are look-alikes: each carries a line-conversion portrait, balanced at the right by a heavy bar that forms a near-box. Samples are shown here in actual size. Note that one heading only names the columnist; the other does that and carries a column title, too. Still, the headings clearly are related.

same year Universal Press Syndicate, which distributes the strip, canceled a sequence on abortion. That was a matter of choice.

An editorial cartoonist does not have to resort to action in a cartoon to subject a person to ridicule. The cartoonist can ridicule through caricature alone. The way a face is drawn tells you what a cartoonist thinks of someone in the news. Whenever Herblock of the Washington *Post* shows William Casey of the CIA, he shows him with a bag over his head. That's enough to tell readers that Herblock doesn't consider Casey very alert to what's going on. Pat Oliphant of Universal Press Syndicate always shows the postal service as a snail.

Sometimes a newspaper's editorial cartoonist takes a stand that is different from what the paper itself takes or goes beyond what the paper wants to say editorially. One answer to the conflict of points of view between the editorial writers and the cartoonist is to confine the cartoonist to the op-ed page, as the Los Angeles *Times* has done with Paul Conrad.

The more innovative editorial pages experiment with photographs or drawings as inserts in editorials. The syndicated columns may show art as part of their headings. The letters column may use cartoon illustrations.

Newspapers encourage a flow of letters to the editor, a column that ranks among the best-read features. In 1986 the Phoenix (Arizona) *Ga-*

The logo for *The Floridian,* a Sunday magazine published by the St. Petersburg *Times,* uses a second color for the filled-in *O* and allows the beginning and ending letters to drop below the baseline to partially enclose a couple of blurbs. Richard A. McCormick and Cliff Snuffin designed the logo.

zette began accepting letters to the editor typed on personal computers and sent to the paper via phone lines. The paper hoped to attract letters from younger readers that way.

As the world has become more complex and more in need of explaining, as syndicated columnists and cartoonists have multiplied, and as people have written more letters, newspapers have allowed the contents of their editorial pages to expand to the adjacent right-hand page, called the op-ed page.

Newspapers blessed with a flow of letters to the editor sometimes let them spill over onto the op-ed page, giving them a second heading there. It would be better to put all the letters under a single heading so that the two sections don't compete with each other.

Some newspapers are experimenting on their editorial pages by giving them a more horizontal thrust, running editorials across the top, for instance, rather than down the side. It is a good idea to make the format flexible enough so that the amount of space you give to editorials each day can vary. On some days there might not be much to editorialize about. You can then give over most of the space to columns and other syndicated features.

Whatever basic design is adopted, it must fit into the design of the paper as a whole. If the page uses a different type for headlines, for instance, at least the body type should remain the same, although it could go to a larger size. The interior logo on the page would use the same type the front-page logo uses, but the interior logo would be smaller.

Newspaper typography

The character of the publication, the kind of paper it's printed on, the amount of space available—these considerations affect the designer's choice of typefaces. That the typical newspaper is published for persons of varying backgrounds and ages suggests that body faces should be simple and familiar. That the paper stock used is cheap, absorbent newsprint suggests that these faces should be open and somewhat heavy. That space is at a premium suggests that they should be somewhat condensed with a large x-height.

A newspaper's narrow columns dictate a body-copy type size no larger than 9 or 10 points. Anything larger results in uneven spacing between words and letters. Another advantage of keeping type small is that it makes stories appear to be shorter. And you can get more on the page. When columns of type are not justified, you can go up a point or two in size.

For headline type, newspapers use sans serif, slab or square serif, or modern roman in display sizes. A few use old style or transitional romans, provided they are on the heavy side, like Cheltenham. Most editors prefer a condensed face so that they can get a better "count" for their headlines. Among the sans serifs, Spartan is popular; among the slab serifs, Stymie;

among the moderns, Bodoni Bold. Countless new romans and sans serifs are available to give newspapers a more contemporary look.

Edmund Arnold has recorded two important dates in the use of headlines: September 1, 1908, and December 4, 1928. On the first date the Minneapolis *Tribune* became what Arnold believes was the first newspaper to use caps-and-lowercase headlines. Until then, newspaper headlines had been all-caps; and for years afterward—on through most of the 1920s—most newspapers continued to use all-caps headlines. Unreadable though they are, they find favor with a few newspapers even today.

On that second date the *Morning Telegraph,* a specialized newspaper in New York, became the first newspaper to use flush-left headlines. Until then, newspaper headlines had been contorted into inverted pyramids, hanging indentions, and other stringent and crowded shapes. Today a few newspapers in the East continue to use hard-to-read and hard-to-write heads.

The argument now is over the adoption of all-lowercase heads. These are heads with only the first word and all proper nouns capitalized. Magazines have long since adopted such heads—or titles, as they are called in that medium; newspapers gradually are coming around. A newspaper headline contains a subject and predicate. It is a sentence picked out from among the first few paragraphs and enlarged. It follows, then, that it should *look* like a sentence. Capitalizing each word does not help.

The modern newspaper has dropped the idea, too, of the multiple-deck headline. Today, on most papers a headline consists of one or, at the most, two decks of two or three lines each. Headlines are not so deep as they were; but they are wider. They spread across several columns, adding to the horizontal look.

Columns

		Units per pica	1	2	3	4	5	6
14	R	1.794	24	50				
	I	1.704	23	47½				
18	R	1.395	18½	39	59	79½		
	I	1.326	18	37	56	75½		
24	R	1.046	13½	29	44	59½		
	I	.9945	13	27½	42	56½		
30	R	.8372	11	23	35½	47½	60	72
	I	.7856	10½	22	33	44½	56	67½
36	R	.6977	9½	19½	29½	39½	50	60
	I	.663	9	18½	28	37½	47½	57
42	R	.5978	8	16½	25	34	42½	51½
	I	.5755	7½	16	24	32	41	49½
48	R	.5233	7	14½	22	29½	37	45
	I	.4973	6½	14	21	28	35½	42½
60	R	.4186	5½	11½	17½	24	30	36
	I	.3978	5	11	17	22½	28½	34

The head chart worked out by Dave Emery for the Eugene, Oregon, *Register-Guard,* an offset daily newspaper, uses large numbers running down the side to represent type sizes for upright letters (the *R* is for *roman*) and italics. The uprights happen to be Cheltenham; the italics Goudy. The big numbers running across the top represent widths in columns (columns are 13½ picas wide). Hence, for a two-column head set in 18-point Cheltenham, the count would be 39. The units-per-pica column takes care of odd-width headings. Emery designed a lamp-shade-like box to hang down over the copy desk with the head chart reproduced on all four sides. The box is built to be bigger at the top so that the chart slants at an angle for easy reading. No head chart works all the time because the count is based on average widths of letters, but this one works 95 percent of the time.

The head schedule

A newspaper draws up a "head chart" or "head schedule," which reproduces sample heads in various sizes and arrangements, gives them numbers, and tells what the maximum count is per line. The count can only be approximate; it is based on a system that puts all letters, numbers, and punctuation marks into four width categories: ½, 1, 1½, and 2. With some exceptions punctuation marks are ½; lowercase letters *f, i, j, t,* and *l* usually count as ½, lowercase *m* and *w* as 1½, and other lowercase letters as 1; numbers and capital letters are 1½, but caps *I* and *J* are 1. The space between words can be ½ or 1 unit, but it should be consistently one or the other.

The advantage of a head chart is this: by referring to it, the copyreader can pick quickly a "stock" style and size appropriate to the story, scribble the code number at the top of the sheet, and shoot it over to the headline writer. The code tells the headline writer what style is wanted, how wide in columns the head is to be, how many decks are wanted, how many lines are wanted in each deck—and what the maximum count is. The headline can't exceed the maximum count, but it can stay under it. Some newspapers insist that each line take up at least two-thirds of the maximum count and that in a multiline headline the longest lines be kept at the top. The computer equipment now in use in newsrooms makes the counting less of a chore than before.

The few newspapers that remain faithful to the geometric-shaped heads of an earlier era—flush-left-and-right, cross-line, step-line, hanging indention, inverted pyramid—require an exact count. Fortunately, the flush-left heads now so universally used do not so seriously restrict the headline writer. The heads are more readable, and they are better looking, too.

Ideally, headlines should be written to be wholly appropriate to stories, not to fit assigned spaces. The lines in a headline should not be separated according to count; they should be separated according to sense. If that means a one- or two-word line followed by a six-word line, so be it. Whenever possible, the whole headline should go on a single line.

It should not be necessary to vary the weight of the headline according to the length of the story. A same-size headline face in several column widths is a variety enough. Additional variety can be achieved through picture sizes and shapes, placement of white space, and use of ruled lines.

Nor should headlines be subject to arbitrary editorial rules that say they must always have a subject and a predicate, be written in present tense, be free of words like *and* and *the.* Headlines should be given more flair than today's head schedules allow.

That's *ideally.* No doubt the exigencies of newspapering will keep headline writing and display pretty much as they have been.

The case for unjustified body-copy lines

People who went to small high schools that couldn't afford printed newspapers may remember the problems of getting stencils ready for mimeographed papers. The mark of a smart paper in those schools was the justification of the right-hand margins of body copy. The copy had to be typed twice, once to find how many extra spaces were needed to fill out each line and once to actually add the spaces. The result was some spotty copy, but to the young editors the paper somehow looked really printed.

The young editors could not accept the fact that ordinary typewriters are not flexible enough to produce natural-looking justified lines. Nor could they see that the 10- or 12-point typewriter typefaces (elite or pica) were too large for their narrow columns. They made a mistake all too common

Pasteup artists work on pages for *The Daily Transcript* and *The Middlesex News*, two papers belonging to the Hart-Hanks chain. Photo by Bill Edmunds, *The Middlesex News*, Framingham, Massachusetts.

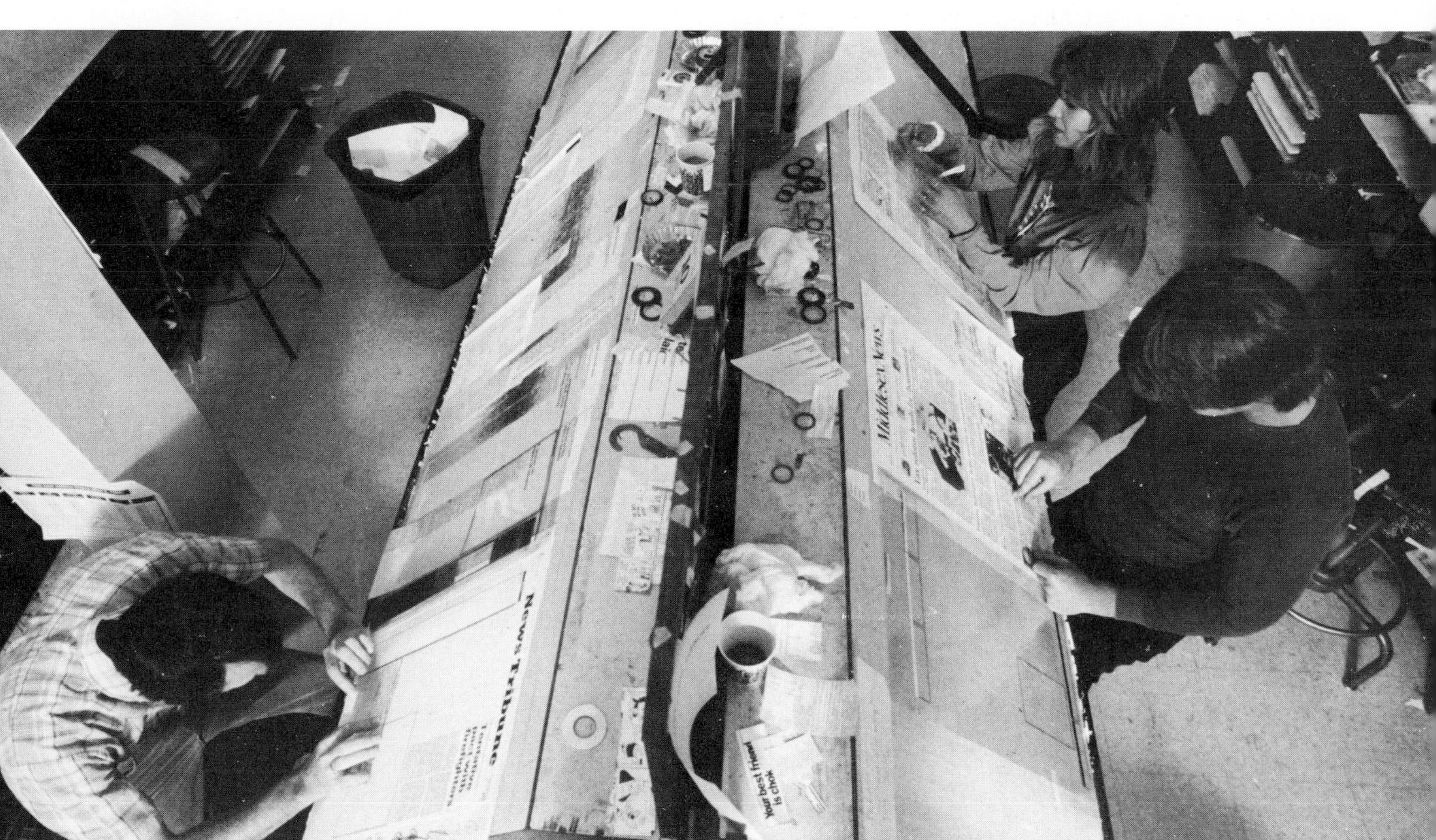

in the graphic arts: they tried to make one medium fit the mold of another. Young artists for letterpress papers made a similar mistake. In the days when linoleum blocks were used for line art (photoengraving was too expensive for some school-paper budgets), these artists did everything they could—including the heating of the linoleum to make cutting easier—to make the block look like a regular line engraving. They failed to realize that the inherent crude, strong, black look of a linoleum block could be the look of graphic art of a high order.

Ironically, while the young editors of mimeographed papers were trying to emulate regular printed newspapers by justifying their columns, regular printed newspapers were toying the the idea, already established in advertising, of ragged-right edges for their new columns.

The advantages of unjustified lines appear to be these: complete consistency of spacing between words, less need for hyphenation at ends of lines, less chance of readers losing their places as they move from line to line, and less expense in setting copy and making corrections.

Some newspapers use both justified and unjustified copy. The unjustified setting marks the feature stories, the bylined columns, and possibly the editorials, making them stand out from the hard news.

Newspaper photographs and illustrations

Phil Douglis has called the daily press "a photographic disaster area." What bothers Douglis and other critics is the preponderance of staged shots and meeting pictures that can interest only those persons who arrange for the shots or pose for them. Newspaper editors—some of them—put photographs in a role secondary to copy. Editors use pictures to fill holes.

A swearing-in ceremony does not offer much chance for innovative photography. And Eugene, Oregon *Register-Guard* photographer Paul Petersen would not place this shot among his best photographs. But compared to what an unimaginative photographer would do with an assignment like this, Petersen's photograph is a nicely designed piece of art.

This wash drawing was executed by the author in India ink. The ink was used in its original state for outlines and in a watered down version for tones. Such a drawing calls for highlight-halftone reproduction. The Eugene, Oregon, *Register-Guard* ran the drawing to illustrate a feature on too-talkative suspects.

And the cutlines that accompany the photographs strain credibility. J. C. Donahue, Jr., editor and publisher of *Suburban Trends,* in Butler, New Jersey, complained about the photographs that followed up the call-in show put on by CBS radio for President Carter shortly after he took office. "In paper aftr paper," Donahue said, "there appeared photos of people with telephones, ostensibly elated at being one of the elect to reach the President. It doesn't take much to figure there was no way of knowing in advance who was going to get through, in order to assign a photographer to record the moment. Yet not one cutline among those I saw identified the photo as a posed, after-the-fact set-up, or reenactment. In fact, they seemed designed to mislead."[11]

The constant search for novelty or irony or humor leads sometimes to embarrassments. A prestigious small daily, to accompany a news story about the state senate's passing a bill to allow terminally ill persons to direct the withdrawal of life-support systems, used a photograph of the bill's co-sponsor that happened to include an exit sign in the background. So the paper cropped the photograph into a dramatic deep vertical that showed only the state senator and the sign. The cutlines said that the senator "co-sponsored the bill passed by the Senate Wednesday that would allow Oregonians to exit with dignity." No doubt the cutline writer was happy with the visual pun.

Some dramatic changes have taken place on newspapers since editors have become more visually alert and more willing to take advantage of

Peter Haley for the San Francisco *Chronicle* captured the drama of fighting a three-alarm fire at Berkeley. The rainbow stream of water adds an artistic note to the urgency of the scene. It takes many frantic shots on location to come up with a photograph as effective as this one.

Some photographs lend themselves to severe horizontal or vertical cropping. Such odd rectangular shapes, shown large on the page, bring variety to newspaper makeup. In this example from a county commissioners' meeting, run in the *Daily Tidings* of Ashland, Oregon, the photographer Peter Haley was able to capture some interesting and perhaps revealing expressions as one commissioner was making a point.

Bill Kuykendall for the Worthington, Minnesota, *Daily Globe* captures Ralph Nader in a memorable photograph. The story accompanying the photo describes Nader on the platform: "As he speaks, his eyes lift up to meet the crowd, his back arches up, his voice gains in volume and authority. He does things with his hands. He folds them into prayer position. . . ."

offset lithography's ability to reproduce photographs. Photographers taking pictures for newspapers work on the *ideas* behind photographs now and pay more attention to composition. Editors run photographs large. Most editors agree with their photographers that the paper is best off with fewer but larger pictures.

As newspapers added photographers to their ranks, they reduced their staffs of illustrators. Before the turn of the century the typical daily newspaper employed a dozen or more staff artists, whose job it was to supply illustrations for feature stories, maps and charts for news stories, cartoons for columns, editorial cartoons, and other visual delights. When photography and the syndicates came along, the need for local staff artists shriveled.

An interest in nonphotographic art has resurfaced on newspapers, but much of the art comes from freelancers. One survey found that two-thirds of the dailies buy some illustrations from outside. Newspapers pay less than other publications for freelance work, the survey found.[12]

A paper today might employ one or two illustrators for the news/editorial department and a few more for the advertising department; but the art factories that once existed on newspapers have closed down. Artists employed by newspapers now are more likely doing pasteups. And nobody spends a lot of time retouching photographs anymore.

Newspapers have a wealth of syndicated material to draw from. Syndicated editorial cartoonists, for instance, supply caricatures along with their regular features. Editors can drop these into their stories and columns about public figures. There are also plenty of stock-art services, as chapter 5 points out. What editors must guard against is reaching over into the advertising stock-art services for editorial art. The art from there has an advertising look that the knowledgeable reader is able to spot.

Once in a while you run across a syndicate that serves weekly rather than daily newspapers. Such a syndicate is Mark Times Features, Inc., Lakewood, Colorado, whose big feature is Ace Reid's *Cowpokes,* going out weekly to some 500 publications, including some farm and ranch magazines. A cartoon panel, it stars Jake, shown above, and his wife and rural and cowboy friends. Calendars and books and "pre-sweat stained" cowboy hats are part of *Cowpokes'* sideline industry.

Syndicates

Wire services like AP and UPI sell news to any papers wanting to buy it, but feature syndicates offer exclusive rights to papers in their circulation areas.

A Newspaper Features Council meeting in San Francisco in later 1985 debated the practice of territorial exclusivity for syndicate offerings. The Los Angeles *Daily News* editor, Tim Kelly, called the practice "the newspaper version of apartheid." It "has overtones of restraint of trade and censorship." But David Hendin, editorial director of United Media, which owns United Feature Syndicate and Newspaper Enterprise Association, asked whether newspapers who don't like the idea of exclusivity would be willing to share their reporters with competing papers. He also reminded editors that there are more than ten or fifteen comic strips available.[13]

There are *many* more. Hundreds in fact. But most of the 1750 daily newspapers seem to want only the popular or trendy strips.

Newspaper editors don't often take dictation from outside, but a number of them did in 1984 when they redesigned their comic pages to meet the demands of Garry Trudeau and Universal Press Syndicate that the rejuvenated "Doonesbury" be run in larger-than-normal size. Trudeau had gone into retirement for twenty-one months to regroup his characters and adjust his story line. Playing a J. D. Salinger role, Trudeau, as usual, avoided giving interviews, but it turned out that he was not all that adverse to publicity. The fanfare on TV and in newspapers and magazines over the return of "Doonesbury" would make a good case history for PR textbooks.

The size agreement was a remarkable capitulation when you consider that "Doonesbury" is only one strip among the many. The *Editor & Publisher Syndicate Directory* each year lists between three and four hundred syndicates offering close to four hundred regular comic strips, two hundred cartoon panels, and two hundred Sunday comic strips that editors can choose from.

Neither the old nor the new "Doonesbury" quite reaches the one-thousand-newpaper mark in circulation (a half dozen other comic strips

Ed Sullivan runs his own syndicate—Avant Features in Salem, Ohio—to circulate his weekly gag cartoons to religious publications and the religion sections of newspapers.

CONAN
©1984 AVANT FEATURES
Sullivan
8/31
"I'M SURE CONAN THE BARBARIAN'S MOTHER MADE HIM SAY HIS PRAYERS, TOO."

do), but the feature has a strong enough following to cause editors who buy it to treat it reverently. It appeals to the audience newspapers want most to capture: the affluent young who prefer the electronic to the print media. And "Doonesbury" politics are one of a kind to appeal to many newspaper editors, if not their publishers.

You can't blame a cartoonist for wanting more space. The standard width for comic strips has shrunk over the years to a point where the drawing has to be close up and simplified and the words in the balloons held to a bare minimum. But should an editor run one strip larger than others on a page just because a cartoonist wants it? What happens then to the remainder of the page?

The editor of a newspaper should be able to decide where a syndicated comic strip goes and in what size. But everyone would agree that the editor does not have the right to change the art or wording in the strip. When a strip becomes offensive or controversial, the editor can omit it, of course, but that comes at the risk of angry phone calls and letters from the strip's fans.

Syndicates face shrinking news holes and a preference among editors now for local material. Some syndicates are trying to regionalize their materials. And some are moving into the video market. Nannette Wiser, editorial director and market manager for Copley News Service, sees an expanding area for syndicates in food and life-style sections.[14]

The Los Angeles Times Syndicate offers newspapers an "Op Art" weekly package of art for op-ed pages. The pieces, done by a variety of artists, illustrate events and concepts that are likely to be written about on op-ed pages. They are generic enough to fit a variety of themes. Universal Press Syndicate offers "The Mini Page" by Betty Debnam to newspapers wanting a special feature for children. The feature consists of puzzles, facts, recipes, and other items that can be cut apart and rearranged, if necessary. The heading has an amateur touch to suggest elementary school lettering and drawing.

Syndicates serve mostly daily newspapers. But a few weeklies and semiweeklies buy editorial cartoons and strips suited to small-newspaper audiences. Some syndicates think nondailies represent a growing market. Suburban Features Plus, in Mobile, Alabama, serves weeklies with editorial features and art for their advertising departments. Mark Time Features, Inc. in Lakewood, Colorado, offers weeklies a cartoon panel, "Cow Pokes," which, a syndicate executive says, is "designed for middle America, not California."[15]

The weeklies and the alternative papers

Weeklies far outnumber dailies in the United States, but of course their total circulation is smaller. Some go out to a mere one or two thousand subscribers.

Weeklies ignore national and international news and concentrate on what the nearby big dailies can't cover—local news. The wire services or press associations do not serve the weeklies, and few feature syndicates offer these papers anything they can use—or afford.

The National Newspaper Association, the weeklies' trade organization, in 1985 published Robert F. Karolevitz's history of weeklies, *From Quill to Computer*. Karolevitz includes reproductions of a number of pages from early and recent papers.

Weeklies doesn't quite describe these papers; some of them come out more often than weekly. They come out semiweekly and even three times a week. Some become dailies as their circulations grow.

Design of the weeklies varies from dreadful to sparkling and innovative. Because they had less to lose and less investment in letterpress, typesetting, and photoengraving equipment, they turned to offset printing before the dailies did. Some of the weeklies led the move to big photographs in newspaper journalism.

The term *weeklies* can be expanded to include the alternative papers that have sprung up in the cities to serve audiences that traditional weeklies—and dailies—overlook. Alternative papers vary from near-underground papers, of the kind that flourished in the 1960s, to serious-minded interpretive papers. They may come out less frequently than weekly. Some devote themselves to entertainment and the arts.

Clinton St. Quarterly, more sophisticated and eclectic than many of the alternative papers, circulates to fifty thousand in Oregon and Washington and wants to spread out. It is an outgrowth of a motion picture theater that once showed porn films but later featured films of interest to social activists. "I felt there was a hole for us to fill," says Lenny Dee, the *Quarterly*'s founder. The press in the area had been ignoring the subjects Dee thought were important. When the paper started in 1979, its editors laid it out on Dee's living room table. The first issue contained, among other articles, a tongue-in-cheek piece about sex as a cure for cancer. But most pieces were serious. Today the paper has its own offices, described by one writer, not disapprovingly, as looking "like the waiting room in some '60s free health clinic—scruffy, with a saggy old sofa and yellowing copies of the paper tacked on the walls." The same writer described the paper's graphics as "stunning."[16] You can see examples in this chapter.

THE CARRIER NEWS

TURN YOUR STOPS INTO STARTS

THE NEW FOOTBALL SECTION IS SALES DYNAMITE

YAHOOO

THE BEST DARNED VACATION YA EVER HEARD OF

Yahoo! Here's the trip you've been waiting for! And it's yours for only 125 points!

KEY TO APARTMENT SALES IS MANAGER

ILL WIND BLOWS MIKE SOME GOOD

ALL ROADS LEAD TO FUN AT CEDAR POINT

Newspapers, like magazines, get into subsidiary publications: publications for advertisers and for employees, for instance. Publications for employees or near-employees can become specialized, as this one for 13,000 carriers shows. It is a quarterly publication of the Detroit *News.* Coming in a 12-inch square format on newsprint, the 12-page publication presents its news of awards and circulation drives in a lively fashion. The front cover serves as an illustrated table of contents.

Newspaper color

Newspapers pride themselves these days on the quality of color they get from their offset presses compared to what they used to obtain in letterpress operations. They look for excuses to run fullcolor photographs on the front page. If there is no full color, then at least there is a ribbon of a single color somewhere, or perhaps a nameplate or banner headline in solid red or blue.

Indiscriminate use of color does nothing to improve communication. In fact, color can hurt rather than help. Why hold out for a washed-out, too-purple halftone when a less-costly-to-produce black-and-white halftone shows up more clearly? Nor does spot color necessarily improve communication. Type in a too-light color becomes hard to read. Halftones in a too-light color lose their detail. Spot color is best when laid out in reasonably large areas in solid or screened tones to contrast with nearby type or art.

Process color should be reserved for times when you have transparencies with plenty of close-up detail.

With so many newspapers running color photographs, some AP bureaus have gone to color-only photography. This eliminates duplication of effort with little or no sacrifice in quality, even when the color photographs are run in black and white by member newspapers. But color takes longer to process and transmit.

Some newspapers also shoot only in color now.

Newspaper magazines and special sections

Several nationally syndicated newspaper/magazines once went out to local newspapers for Sunday distribution. Does anyone remember *American Weekly* and *This Week?* Two big ones are left: *Parade,* with a circulation of around thirty million, the largest of any magazine, and *USA Weekend,* which took over *Family Weekly* in 1985. Some newspapers that had carried *Family Weekly* did not continue with *USA Weekend* because they felt its ties were too close to *USA Today* and the new logo looked too much like that of *USA Today.*[17]

In 1986 *Parade* was promoting its tandem program, in which it printed a newspaper's own magazine section and bound it into *Parade* for easy pullout. In that way both magazines could be printed in rotogravure. The Sunday Atlanta *Journal and Constitution* was one newspaper that used the system.

A number of papers include on Sundays one or the other of the syndicated magazines along with a locally produced magazine.

Locally produced newspaper magazines get the same kind of design thinking that regular magazines get. But the pages are bigger: the magazines are almost always tabloids. The designer has plenty of room to make an impact with art and type. The design of a locally produced magazine does not have to bear a relationship to the design of the newspaper itself. Nor does the magazine necessarily appeal to the average reader of the newspaper. With some newspapers the Sunday magazine serves mostly Yuppies, the same group that might be expected to buy the city magazine.

In 1985 two different newspapers in California, the Los Angeles *Times* and the San Francisco *Sunday Examiner & Chronicle,* began publication of newsstand-size magazines instead of the usual oversize magazines that other Sunday newspapers publish. Readers will "open their Sunday editions. . . . And a remarkable, new magazine will fall out in their laps," the *Examiner & Chronicle* said in an ad announcing the new publication.[18] Its magazine is *Image;* the *Times* magazine is *Los Angeles Times Magazine.*

The Los Angeles *Times* explained to advertisers, "This [new magazine size] means the ads you place in other magazines can be scheduled into Los Angeles Times Magazine with virtually no production costs."[19]

Locally produced Sunday magazines do not always receive the parent support editors would like to have. Often there is little contact between the regular reporters and the people who work on the magazine. The magazine editor may work more with freelancers than with staff writers. Getting enough advertisers for the magazine section can be a problem, too; one reason is that the magazine needs more lead time.

A paper needs a circulation of 150,000 or more to make a locally produced Sunday magazine pay off. One count in 1981 put the number of locally edited newspaper magazine sections at fifty. Few of the magazines now are printed by rotogravure. The printing process usually is offset lithography, as it is for the remainder of the paper. And pages, as in the regular paper, are unbound.

The fattest of the locally produced magazines is *The New York Times Magazine,* a rotogravure publication, saddle stapled, which some weeks expands to two hundred pages. Other newspaper magazines are as thin as sixteen pages.

Important big-city newspapers like the New York *Times,* the Washington *Post,* and the Chicago *Tribune* bring out book-review magazines in addition to their general-interest magazines. Other newspapers publish book-review pages. These magazines and pages represent a challenge to the art director who wants more than book covers/jackets or drawings from the books as art. One way to bring art to a book-review magazine is to do a feature on what celebrities are reading. The Washington *Post*'s *Book World,* for instance, in an end-of-year issue ran "The Most Memorable Books of the Year," which gave reports from well-known Washingtonians on books they had read and recommended. This gave the magazine an excuse to run photographs of Gary Hart, Art Buchwald, Judith Martin, and others.

Some newspapers publish special sections or tabloids in addition to or in place of locally edited magazines. Special sections lure advertisers who otherwise would stay away from the paper. The sections concentrate on recreation or the outdoors or entertainment or life-styles. Some special sections contain nothing but puffery to amplify the advertising. Others contain real features that treat material advertisers like to see accompanying their advertising, but they treat it in an objective way, perhaps even avoiding naming brands and stores.

The Cleveland *Plain Dealer* runs from fifty to one hundred special sections and "grand opening pages" a year, with Roy Adams in charge of most of them. Some of his tabloids run as long as fifty-two pages. They cover such subjects as travel, gardens, retirement plans, income taxes, careers, education, and health. Adams operates essentially as a one-person staff, but he can order help from freelance writers. He does the layout himself as well as the usual editing chores.

The *Plain Dealer,* he says, considers special sections "an extension of the feature sections, providing informative, mostly non-promotional, useful material on which a reader can chew and benefit thereby."[20] Adams notes that not all newspapers—or advertisers—are convinced that placing same-subject ads in a special section is a good idea.

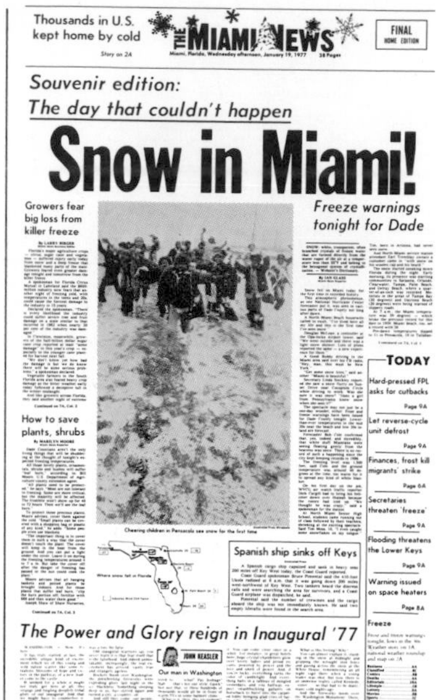

Thousands in U.S. kept home by cold
Story on 2A

THE MIAMI NEWS
Miami, Florida, Wednesday afternoon, January 19, 1977 · 38 Pages

FINAL
HOME EDITION

Souvenir edition:
The day that couldn't happen

Snow in Miami!

Growers fear big loss from killer freeze

Freeze warnings tonight for Dade

How to save plants, shrubs

Cheering children in Pensacola see snow for the first time

Where snow fell in Florida

Spanish ship sinks off Keys

TODAY

Hard-pressed FPL asks for cutbacks — Page 9A

Let reverse-cycle unit defrost — Page 9A

Finances, frost kill migrants' strike — Page 6A

Secretaries threaten 'freeze' — Page 9A

Flooding threatens the Lower Keys — Page 9A

Warning issued on space heaters — Page 8A

Freeze

The Power and Glory reign in Inaugural '77

JOHN KEASLER
Our man in Washington

When the weather takes an unusual turn, a newspaper may doctor its nameplate to make it appropriate. Here's a doctored nameplate and a front-page story you are not likely to see again coming out of Miami. The year was 1977. Note the snowflakes and the snow-covered tree in and around *The Miami News.*

A survey of readers convinced the Seattle *Times* in 1985 to bring out a special Saturday issue to better serve its readers—to help them plan their weekends. New sections included "Weekend," "Outdoors," "Sports," "Money," "Autos," "Home," "Editorial," and, of course, "News."

Some newspapers put out publications not included in regular editions. The New York *Times* publishes *Large Type Weekly,* with type about twice as large as that of the regular paper, for people with limited vision or those whose eyes tire easily. The thirty-two page *Weekly* prints material from the regular paper, including news, feature stories, and columns. The Washington *Times* puts out a newsmagazine called *Insight* to compete with newsmagazines such as *Time, Newsweek,* and *U.S. News & World Report*. The Washington *Post* publishes a calendar, with a special price to subscribers, that features the best photographs from the previous year's issues.

How research helps

After the Rapid City (South Dakota) *Journal* discovered, through research, that its readers wanted more information they could use in their daily lives, the paper in 1976 became more consistent in its placement of items, making them easy to find, and more willing to put national and international news on inside pages, devoting the front part of the paper mainly to local news. A "Life-style" section each day concentrated on a single subject. For instance, on Monday the subject was "Money."

Research can be useful in helping designers make up their minds about which course to take. And if the newspaper itself can't conduct the research, plenty of studies exist that can be consulted.

In the 1970s the American Newspaper Publishers Association in Washington, D.C., sponsored a series of News Research Bulletins on newspaper design and typography. One, by J. W. Click and Guido H. Stemple III, showed that readers, young and old, prefer newspapers with "modern" front pages. By "modern" the authors meant six-column instead of eight-column pages with a horizontal rather than a vertical emphasis. David K. Weaver, L. E. Mullins, and Maxwell E. McCombs found that there was a tendency in competing situations for the second newspaper to adopt a more modern format: no column rules, six rather than eight columns to the page, fewer stories on the front page, larger photographs and color photographs, smaller headlines. J. K. Hvistendahl and Mary R. Kahl found that newspaper readers prefer roman to sans serif body types. The Carl J. Nelson Research Corporation reported that headlines four or more columns wide attract twice as many readers as one-column headlines do.

Relying on research findings like these makes more sense than pushing ahead solely on the basis of personal preference.

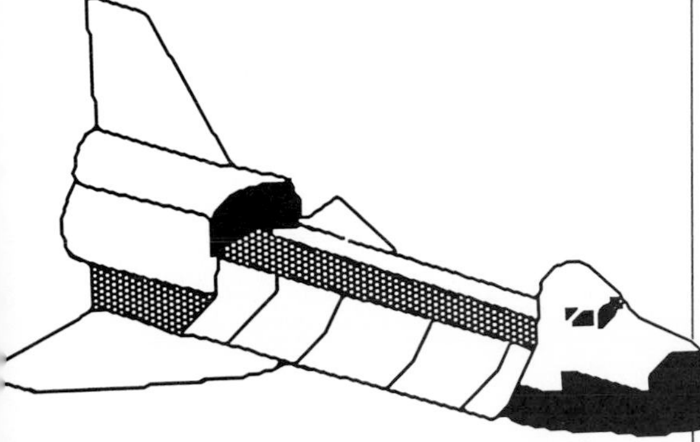

Greg Harris of the Twin Falls, Idaho, *Times-News* used the Macintosh MacPaint program to create this drawing of the shuttle that blew up on launching in 1986.

Newspapers and the new technology

It was after World War II that the old letterpress process began giving way to offset as the ideal method for printing newspapers. The smaller papers, with less investment in old equipment, took up the new process first. The big papers followed. The new process allowed cheaper and better reproduction of halftones and cheaper and more flexible typography.

But it took years before newspapers broke away from the design restrictions imposed on them by hot type and photoengraving. The typical

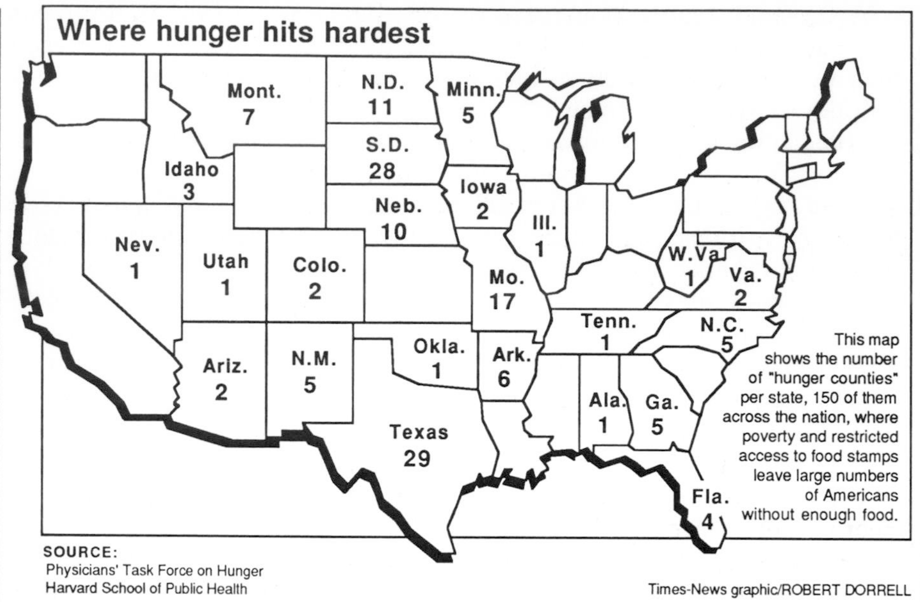

Using the Macintosh MacDraw program, Robert Dorrell, graphics editor of the Twin Falls, Idaho, *Times-News,* took about two hours to draw a somewhat abstracted map of the United States, with the states in place and a shadow to give the map a third dimension. Now he can call it up whenever he needs it and, on the computer screen, put in type and, if he wishes, add a partial box, as in this example. The numbers indicate the number of "hunger counties" in each state. The original LaserWriter printing was for 38 picas.

newspaper format still looked as though someone in the back shop, arranging metal type and cuts on a stone, did the designing. Then experimentation took hold, and some papers began to look as though high school art students were in charge, anxious to be different. Design finally grew up to take advantage of the offset without sacrificing readability.

The big idea now is to take advantage of the computer and the new technology. Since 1960 the computer has had some use—in some newsrooms—in justifying right-hand margins. Now it becomes the key to all the new systems used by newspapers.

On many of today's newspaper, reporters become directly involved in typesetting as they sit in front of video display terminals and punch out their stories. "Today's reporter is his own typesetter," observes Professor Mario R. Garcia of the University of South Flordia, "and for all practical purposes, he develops a strong link with the page designer."[21] The makeup of the paper goes on in editorial offices, not in the print shop or backshop of letterpress days.

And increasingly, papers are using pagination, a computer system by which makeup can be done on a screen. Once pagination is established, proofs of type and prints of art no longer will have to be moved around by hand and fastened to a gridded layout sheet.

In 1985 Knight-Ridder Newspapers, Inc. developed a computer graphics system that linked its twenty-nine newspapers and some others to an art supply from a central data base. Staff artists of cooperating newspapers used an Apple Macintosh to create their charts, graphs, and illustrations. Using K-RN's Vu/Text computer system, newspapers can retrieve art via telephone lines within five minutes. Local papers, using their Macintoshs, can modify the art to fit local formats. Local artists can also add their own touches to customize the art.

The Macintosh is especially suited to producing newspaper art. With the Macintosh an artist creating a chart, for example, can try several approaches in a matter of minutes and then select the approach that works best.

"Until now, the newsroom art department has been untouched by computerization," says Roger Fidler, Knight-Ridder director of graphics and newsroom technology. "Artists today are facing the same anxiety reporters and editors encountered in the 1970s when they gave up typewriters and pencils for video display terminals."[22]

Joseph M. Ungaro, executive edtior of Westchester-Rockland newspapers, New York, sees the eventual elimination of all walls between the newsroom and the production department. A number of papers will be put together by going directly from computer to plate, with laser beams used to create the plates.[23]

To illustrate a speech he was to make to a group of newspaper executives some years ago, Dan Kelly, senior vice-president and creative director of the Chicago office of Foote, Cone & Belding, asked art directors at his agency to redesign some newspaper front pages, one of which is shown here. Although the art directors admitted that their suggested formats might be impractical, they did feel that newspapers in general could be more inviting, more interesting, and more relevant to their readers. The designer of the new Knoxville *Journal* was Dave Hunter.

Redesigning the newspaper

The new technology has prompted newspapers to think about design overhauls. In many cases papers have called in outsiders to set up new patterns and new routines that staff layout people and editors can follow. Redesign of a major newspaper can cost $100,00 or more. Smaller papers can expect to pay a third to a half of that.[24]

In a redesign program every detail is considered, down to the most insignificant measurements. The redesign program anticipates every problem that may arise.

Redesign should especially consider production capabilities, including paper availability and press capacity. The goal should be to simplify procedures by standardizing them and to encourage economies in an age of rapidly rising prices and continuing shortages.

Redesign takes into account a newspaper's personality. The changes that occur should enhance that personality. The designer usually tries to

Market Active

The Knoxville Journal

City Edition

Independently Owned And Operated

Good Morning

Today's Chuckle

Rain With Snow Forecast

Science Panel Heckled

New Phone Exchange

Nixon Meets With Jews

Enemy Invades Hamlet

At Least 38 Miners Killed In SE Kentucky Explosion

Alleged Abductors

Senate Passes Money Bills

Bill Would Consolidate All Schools

U.S. Job Program Troubled

Blast Site

Basques Saved By Franco

Deadly Gas Halts Rescue

Five Eyed To Head Education

Ex-Knox Man To Operate Penn Central

Beck Sale Delayed; KHA Wants Home

Obituaries

Yablonski Murder Trial Near

OLD

The Knoxville Journal

Independently owned and operated
132nd year vol.98, no.313
Knoxville, Tennessee

City edition
Thursday, December 31, 1970
price 10cents

Senate Passes Money Bills

Yablonski Murder Trial Near

38 Miners Killed In Explosion

U.S. Job Program Troubled

Basques Saved By Franco

NEW

strengthen the personality and make it more obvious without drastically changing it.

When the Los Angeles *Times* in the early 1980s decided it needed some redesign, it called in someone with a background in book design rather than newspaper design or—as is so common now—magazine design. In their preliminary interviews *Times* executives liked what Sheila Levrant de Bretteville told them; unlike some big-name designers also interviewed, she was sympathetic to what the editors wanted—only minor or gradual change and not a startling magazine look. The editors liked the basic concept of book design, which strives for readability and does not attempt to call attention to itself. What really impressed the editors, though, was de Bretteville's promise that white space was not her god and that she would do nothing to cut down on the amount of copy to be printed.

One of her functions was to supervise the redesign of Times Roman bold as a headline face for the paper, giving it a bit more grace, and to adapt it to computer setting. She also brought back column rules to the paper.

In its redesign the *Times* looks cleaner, crisper, more contemporary; but the changes have been subtle enough that the average reader is probably only vaguely aware that they took place.[25]

"Tampering with what readers have become accustomed to always is hazardous in the newspaper business, which is why most redesign jobs do not break sharply with the past," says John Morton, newspaper analyst with Lynch Jones & Ryan, stockbrokers. He reports that some readers even objected to the recent modest changes at the Washington *Post*. "What took 50 years to establish, two 'artists' destroyed in just a year," one angry reader wrote to the editor.[26]

The look to come

Newspaper design will change as newspapering itself changes. Most journalists admit now that the electronic media do a better job with spot news than the print media. The trend in newspapers will have to be away from the "what" and the "why." TV and radio stimulate the appetite; newspapers deliver the details, the background. The interpretive newspaper will dispense with the hodgepodge and take on more and more the look of permanence and stability and, at the same time, vitality.

The computer will continue to make a difference. Reporters have already come to terms with it. Now it is the designers' turn. "The new technologies available to artists and designers are overwhelming in their complexity and sheer numbers," says *U&lc.* The publication adds, "The best of typesetters, color scanners and paginators, laser printers, slidemakers, and graphic display terminals are only as good as the people manipulating them. And therein lies the dilemma." The dilemma is that senior designers are turned off by the new devices instead of being stimulated by them. And young designers, excited by the devices, don't have much of a chance to acquaint themselves with them because their schools find them too expensive to install. *U&lc.* calls for a program through which schools and industry can come together to share their various facilities.[27]

The Courier-Journal (USPS 135-560)

For Information

Latest sports scores: 582-4871.
Want to know your congressman's address or the winner of the 21st Kentucky Derby? Our Reader's Service Department will answer your questions. It's open 9 a.m. to 5 p.m., Monday through Friday. Call 582-4545. For more extensive research on a fee basis, call the library, 582-4603.

Managing Editor

David Hawpe (in charge of The Courier-Journal news operation), 582-4613.

To report a news item or story idea

City News:
For news about the metropolitan area, except Southern Indiana, call Bill Cox, 582-4691.

Regional News:
For news about Kentucky and Southern Indiana, call Stephen Ford, 582-4657

Business News:
Phil Moeller, 582-4651.

Sports:
Stan Slusher, 582-4361.

Accent:
Maureen McNerney, 582-4667.

Weddings and Engagements:
Sandra Topy, 582-4667.

Church Notices:
George Buchanan, 582-4691.

Obituaries (call after 2 p.m.):
Bob Redmon
Louisville-area deaths, 582-4691
All other deaths,
800-292-3570 (toll free)

Pictures:
582-4680

Published by The Courier-Journal and Louisville Times Company, daily and Sunday, at 525 W. Broadway, Louisville, Ky., 40202. PHONE: Area Code 502 — 582-4011.

Consolidation of The Focus, 1826; The Louisville Daily Journal, 1830; The Morning Courier, 1837; The Daily Democrat, 1843. First issued as The Courier-Journal Nov. 8, 1868.

Editor and Publisher, Barry Bingham, Jr.; Vice President and Executive Editor, Paul Janensch; Managing Editor, David Hawpe.

Chairman of the Board, Barry Bingham, Sr.; President, George N. Gill; Senior Vice-Presidents, Cyrus MacKinnon, Bernard Block, John L. Richards, Leon Tallichet (Treasurer); Vice-President and General Manager, Maurice J. Buchart, Jr.; Vice-Presidents, Earl Bullard (Organization and Planning); Ralph L. Drury (Operations); Morris Goldstein (Information Products); Donald B. Towles (Public Affairs); Secretary, John Weeks.

The Associated Press is exclusively entitled to republish local news originated by The Courier-Journal, as well as all other AP news.

Second-class postage paid at Louisville, Ky.

Postmaster: Send address changes to The Courier-Journal & The Louisville Times, 525 W. Broadway, Louisville, Kentucky, 40202.

Have a complaint?

News

If you have a question or complaint about news coverage, call Frank Hartley, News Ombudsman, 582-4600.

If you have a specific complaint about the accuracy or fairness of news reporting, and have failed to get satisfaction from the paper, you are invited to take the complaint to the National News Council. The council is an independent, non-governmental body.

Include a copy of the article and copies of any correspondence with the newspaper. Address: 1 Lincoln Plaza, New York, N.Y. 10023. Phone: (212) 595-9411.

Circulation

If you have a problem regarding service, or if your paper is not delivered, call 582-2211.

Newspaper replacement service is available from 7 a.m. to 10 a.m. daily and 7 a.m. to 12:15 p.m. Sunday.

If you have a persistent service problem, call Circulation Ombudsman Bill Chambers, 582-4355.

Advertising

If you have a complaint about advertising, call Advertising Ombudsman Vernon Johnston, 582-4384.

To subscribe

To subscribe call 582-2211.

CARRIER DELIVERY RATES

Jefferson, Bullitt and Oldham Counties, Ky., Clark and Floyd Counties, Ind.: Daily Courier-Journal, 85c a week; daily and Sunday, $1.45; Sunday only, 60c; Morning, Evening and Sunday combination (at 20c discount) $2.10.

All other Indiana Counties and LATE KENTUCKY EDITION Counties: Daily Courier-Journal, 85c a week, daily and Sunday Courier-Journal, $1.45; Sunday only 60c.

All other Kentucky Counties (KENTUCKY EDITION): Daily Courier-Journal, $1.00 a week; daily and Sunday Courier-Journal, $1.60; Sunday only 60c.

Motor route subscriptions—Daily and Sunday 10c per week additional; Sunday only or daily only 5c per week additional.

SUBSCRIPTION RATES BY MAIL

Ky., Ind. & Tenn.	1 year	6 mos.	3 mos.	1 mo.
Daily only	$80.60	$40.30	$20.15	$7.00
Sunday only	$44.20	$22.10	$11.05	$4.25
Daily & Sunday	$124.80	$62.40	$31.20	$11.25

Ky. residents add 5% sales tax.
Rates for other states on request.

Mail orders cannot be accepted from localities served by carrier delivery. All mail subscriptions and orders for back copies are payable in advance.

Member Audit Bureau of Circulations.

To advertise

Rates-Advertising	582-4700
Classified Advertising	582-2622
Display Advertising	582-4711

Now *here* is a masthead! The Louisville *Courier-Journal* runs a box like this inside the paper every day, sometimes arranged to fit a different space, but always complete. This one is 4½ by 11. It is no work of art; but notice how sensibly things are arranged to help the reader. Main headings are "For information," "Managing Editor," "To Report a News Item or Story Idea," "Have a Complaint?" "To Advertise," and "To Subscribe." (© by the *Courier-Journal.* Reprinted by permission.)

Notes

1. Some merged newspapers adopt a hyphen for their nameplates; some don't. This paper didn't.
2. Mark Fitzgerald, "The Perception of Graphics," *Editor & Publisher,* November 3, 1984, p. 15.

3. Front Pages: How Much Have They Changed?" *Editor & Publisher,* November 2, 1985, p. 15.
4. Clive Irving, "Does God Care What the *Times* Does with Page One?" *New York,* April 14, 1975, p. 47.
5. Maureen Decker, "When Hiring Designers, Look Beyond Newspapers," *Style,* American Association of Sunday and Feature Editors, Summer 1985, pp. 4–7.
6. Martin L. Gibson, *Editing in the Electronic Era,* Iowa State University Press, Ames, Iowa, 1979, p. 215.
7. J. Clark Samuel, editor of the Foxboro, Massachusetts, *Reporter,* a weekly, wrote to *The American Press,* January 1966, to point out that, so far as he knows, his paper has used the six-column format since its founding in 1884.
8. Clive Irving, "Does God Care?" p. 44.
9. Edmund C. Arnold, "Horizontal Layouts—Whittling at Apparent Length," *Publishers' Auxiliary,* April 13, 1981, p. 5.
10. Chris Lamb, "With Malicious Intent," *Target: The Political Cartoon Quarterly,* Autumn 1985, pp. 15–21.
11. In a letter to the editor, *Editor & Publisher,* March 19, 1977, p. 7.
12. Mark Fitzgerald, "Freelance Graphics," *Editor & Publisher,* November 9, 1985, p. 18.
13. David Astor, "Exclusivity Is Debated at S. F. Meeting," *Editor & Publisher,* October 5, 1985, p. 34.
14. "Syndicates Say Industry Ever-Changing," *Publishers' Auxiliary,* August 12, 1985, p. 14.
15. "Weekly Features: Some *Do* Target Themselves to Non-dailies," *Publishers' Auxiliary,* August 12, 1985, p. 15.
16. Lee Sherman, "Avant-Garde Paper Rises from Origins in Former Porn Cinema and Aims for Big Time on the Pacific Coast," *The Business Journal Magazine,* November 12, 1984, pp. 7, 8.
17. "*Parade* Magazine Gets 129 Former *Family Weekly* Customers," *Publishers' Auxiliary,* August 12, 1985, p. 5.
18. Ad in *Advertising Age,* September 30, 1985, p. 69.
19. Ad in *Advertising Age,* September 26, 1985, p. 97.
20. Letter to the author from Roy Adams, November 5, 1985.
21. Mario R. Garcia, *Contemporary Newspaper Design,* Prentice-Hall, Englewood Cliffs, New Jersey, 1981, p. 226.
22. "Knight-Ridder Launches Computer Graphics Network," *Editor & Publisher,* September 7, 1985, p. 30.
23. "Copy Editors to Feel Automation Impact," *Editor & Publisher,* March 19, 1977, p. 16.
24. John Morton, "Improvement by Design," *Washington Journalism Review,* December 1984, p. 14.
25. Dugald Stermer, "Sheila Levrant de Bretteville," *Communication Arts,* May/June 1982, pp. 38–42.
26. John Morton, "Improvement by Design," p. 14.
27. "Now Is the Time . . . ," *U&lc.,* September 1981, p. 3.

Suggested further reading

Alexander, James P., *Programmed Journalism Editing,* Iowa State University Press, Ames, Iowa, 1980.

Allen, Wallace, *A Design for News,* Minneapolis *Tribune,* 425 Portland Ave., Minneapolis, Minn. 55488, 1981.

Arnold, Edmund C., *Designing the Total Newspaper,* Harper & Row, New York, 1981.

Baskette, Floyd K., Jack Z. Sissors, and Brian S. Brooks, *The Art of Editing,* 3d ed., Macmillan Company, New York, 1982.

Berner, R. Thomas, *Editing,* Holt, Rinehart and Winston, New York, 1982.

Computer-Assisted Layout of Newspapers, American Newspaper Publishers Association, Reston, Virginia, 1977.

Newspaper Design, American Press Institute, Reston, Virginia, 1978.

Copperud, Roy, and Roy Paul Nelson, *Editing the News,* Wm. C. Brown Company Publishers, Dubuque, Iowa, 1983.

Design: The Journal of the Society of Newspaper Design, Syracuse, New York. (Quarterly.)

Editors of the Harvard *Post, How to Produce a Small Newspaper,* 2d ed., Harvard Common Press, Harvard, Massachusetts, 1983. (With chapters on "Typography," "Pasteup," and "Design and Layout.")

Evans, Harold, *Editing and Design,* Holt, Rinehart and Winston, New York, 1973. A five-volume manual dealing with English usage, typography, and layout, put together by the editor of *The Sunday Times,* London. Useful for American as well as British editors. Volume 1, *Newsman's English:* Volume 2, *Handling Newspaper Text;* Volume 3, *News Headlines;* Volume 4, *Picture Editing;* Volume 5, *Newspaper Design.*

Garcia, Mario R., *Contemporary Newspaper Design: A Structural Approach,* Prentice-Hall, Englewood Cliffs, New Jersey, 1981.

Gibson, Martin L., *Editing in the Electronic Era,* Iowa State University Press, Ames, Iowa, 1979.

Gilmore, Gene, and Robert Root, *Modern Newspaper Editing,* 2d ed., Bond & Fraser Publishing Company, San Francisco, 1976.

Hollstein, Milton, and Larry Kurtz, *Editing with Understanding,* Macmillan Publishing Company, 1981.

Hulteng, John L., and Roy Paul Nelson, *The Fourth Estate: An Informal Appraisal of the News and Opinion Media,* 2d ed., Harper & Row Publishers, New York, 1983.

Moen, Daryl R., *Newspaper Layout and Design,* Iowa State University Press, Ames, Iowa, 1984.

Newsom, D. Earl, ed., *The Newspaper,* Prentice-Hall, Englewood Cliffs, New Jersey, 1981.

Westley, Bruce, *News Editing,* 3d ed., Houghton Mifflin, Boston, 1980.

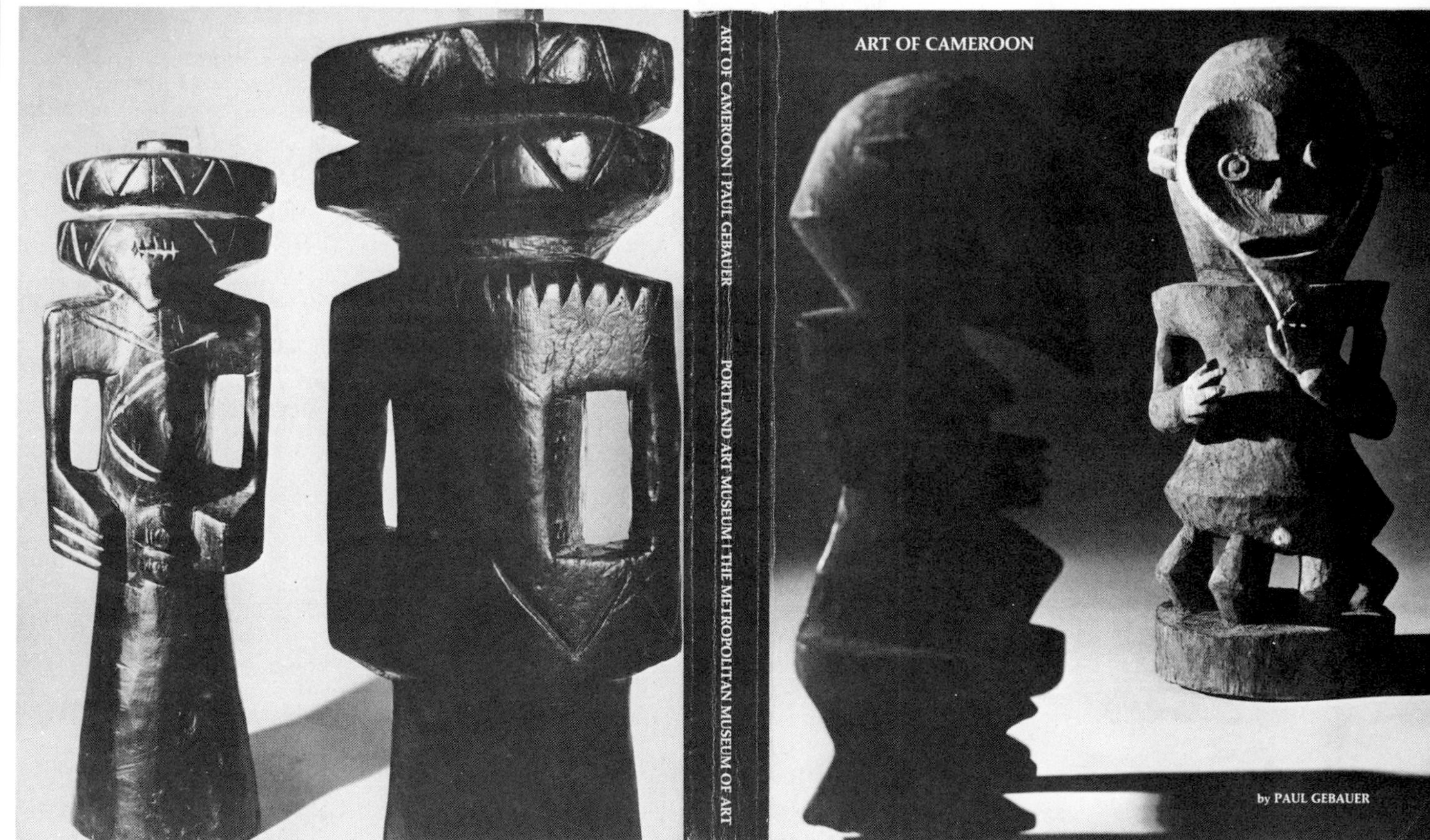

10

Book design

Charles S. Politz of Design Council, Inc. used all-caps Palatino bold in small sizes for the title and author's name, reversed on a photograph, for the cover of a handsome paperback by Paul Gebauer, *Art of Cameroon,* published by the Portland Art Museum in association with the Metropolitan Museum of Art, New York. Cover type, especially for this kind of book, does not have to be large. Placement is important to keep the type from detracting from the beauty of the photograph. You see here the front and back covers and the spine.

Think of a book publisher as essentially a middleman between the writer and the reader. It is the book publisher who arranges the details of publication and distribution of the manuscript and who finances the project.

Under the standard contract between writer and publisher, the writer gets 10 percent of the retail price of every book sold, a little more if the book goes into high sales figures. The other 90 percent is used to pay for the editing, design, production, printing, promotion, and distribution of the book and other business expenses and to provide some profit to the publisher.

More disorganized, more financially hazardous than most businesses, book publishing is unique in that its product constantly changes. Each book published—some houses publish six or seven hundred titles a year—must be separately designed, produced, and promoted.

The book publishing industry tends to divide most of its output into two broad categories: trade books and textbooks. Textbooks are those volumes, mostly nonfiction, published to meet the specific needs of students at all levels. Sales depend upon adoptions by teachers, departments, and boards of education. Trade books include most other books, fiction as well as nonfiction. They do not serve a captive audience; sales must be made on an individual basis and often depend upon impulse buying. For this reason trade books, unlike textbooks, require jackets as an aid in selling. Sales are made through retail stores, through mail order, through book clubs.

Textbooks and trade books use different pricing structures. The difference between the list price and the dealer's cost for a trade book is 40 percent. For textbooks the difference is only half that, which explains why textbooks, like this one, are hard to get at regular bookstores. Textbooks for college students must be sold by college bookstores, where large numbers are ordered for classes.

Reference books (dictionaries and encyclopedias) and children's books ("juveniles," as the trade calls them) are in categories of their own. They require different kinds of selling methods as well as different design and production approaches.

Some publishers specialize in one kind of book, some in another; and a few publishers produce books in all categories. Several hundred book

CHAPTER IV THE MAJOR ARTS

ARCHITECTURE

The human need for shelter was masterfully met by the men of old. Traditional architecture was characterized by good planning, honest workmanship, and a clever manipulation of space. Conforming to ethnic patterns, its design and materials were well adapted to local needs and life styles—a simple construction of readily available materials, built to withstand the rigors of tropical climate. With its pleasing symmetry and natural coloring, it blended into a quiet harmony with its surroundings and landscape. Neither artist nor ecologist would be able to find fault with it.

Forest Homes

The rectangular forest homes were placed individually, or more commonly as rowhouses, alongside the road. The southwestern Banyang preferred a courtlike placement of their huts, with one side of the court open to the road. Staggered gables and ochre walls broke the monotony of tropical growth. The northwestern members of the same group favored placing the huts around a rectangular courtyard dominated by the monuments for the dead. Among the Bulu of the south, one found pleasing patterns worked into the mat walls. The Bakundu of the west covered their walls with tri-colored geometric design. Mud relief patterns adorned the walls of the Mungo houses. Forest home interiors revealed tasteful arrangements of bedsteads and pottery. The deceivingly simple appearance of forest huts and forest hamlets sheltered a rich cultural heritage of long standing.

Grassland Huts

In the grasslands the square hut dominated the landscape. Here again ethnic tradition dictated outside dimensions and interior divisions. The walls, made of three layers of cane or bamboo latticework, were prefabricated on the ground, as were ceiling and roof sections. Knowledge of the principles of stress and strain was evident. All parts of the hut

(Left) Houseposts, Babanki-Kegu, Tikar Art Area.

62 ART OF CAMEROON

trained abroad, halted this experiment by declaring it disturbing to the pupils. In the Baptist chapel of the upland, Jumbam Fai continued with his interpretation of Bible stories in polychrome wall paintings. Perplexed missionaries terminated his engagement while we were on furlough in the States. We learned that local talent, free from foreign influence, can produce imaginative and exciting paintings within the framework of its own culture, as a refreshing contribution to the arts.

MUSIC

The Cameroonians, like all black Africans, are uncommonly gifted in music. From the first heartbeat of their mothers to the hour of death, their music, together with the inseparable dance, are most important parts of their existence. To them these are more than art forms or pastime. They are food for their souls; and in secular disguise, they constitute powers over good or evil, the means for overcoming witches, of fostering fertility. The music in some dances turns the performance into moving religious drama.

Differences

This music is unlike our own. It is impossible to record it by our standard notation of the eight-tone scale and fixed interval. "Our relatively simple system of time signatures, with fixed measures, is less than satisfactory when, for an example, a piece played on a xylophone must be set down that has a 4/4 beat in the left hand and a 5/4 in the right, making a 'measure' that is more than we are trained to carry as a unit." Musicologists were helped greatly by the invention of the phonograph. Phonographs allowed analysis leading to an understanding and appreciation of native music. The advent of the tape recorder gave comparative musicology the perfect tool for saving indigenous material for posterity.

The chief difference between this music and our own is found in the former's dependence on pure melody, while ours is built on harmony. The predominance of pure melody explains the acceptance of antiphony and rhythm, of variations in intervals, of the subjugation of speech forms. Elements of tonology are present but not necessarily dominant. A second difference is seen in the mastery of improvisation as a rule and not as an exception. The soloist sings a melody, inspired by the ecstacy of a moment, and the chorus responds and enlarges on it spontaneously. The dynamics of music and dance benefit immensely by the great choice of instruments.

(Right) Traditional band at Babungo Village.

THE MAJOR ARTS 63

THE ARTIST IN SOCIETY 125

Nkwen Chapel (1960) and Drum Hut (1946).

Politz often contrasted a full-page photograph with an all-type page, as in this chapter opening. He put the copy over to the outside edges to allow generous white space at the gutter. The book is set in Palatino type throughout, and in only a few sizes. Note the two levels of subheads and the subtle placement of the small caption at the bottom of the page of copy.

A photograph may occupy a page, but instead of bleeding it can surround itself with restful white.

Occasionally Politz chose to run a photograph across the gutter and far enough onto the adjoining page to temporarily suspend text matter for a spread.

publishers in the United States produce among themselves more than forty thousand different titles each year.

The typical first printing of a book comes to five to ten thousand copies. If a book sells well, the publisher may go back into a second printing, a third, and others as needed. This is not the same thing as putting out a new edition of a book. A new edition involves updating and rewriting all the chapters and probably rearranging them. It may mean dropping certain chapters and adding new ones. It involves new typesetting and design. In short, it means a brand new book but one that draws on the goodwill and promotional buildup of the first edition. The book you are reading is the fourth edition of a book that went through several printings in its first three editions. Textbooks go to new editions more frequently than trade books. Publishers decide to bring out new editions to update the material and, frankly, to fight the market in used books.

Some authors who cannot sell their books to regular book publishers turn to subsidy publishers, who charge for taking on books and publishing them. If the books happen to catch on, which is unlikely, the authors do get paid royalties. Some authors decide to publish their own books, taking care of all the details of typesetting, design, printing, advertising, and distribution. Self-publishing is becoming more popular with the availability of word processors and laser printers.

With the right idea for a book, self-publishing can be profitable. Dr. William G. Crook set up Future Health, Inc. to publish his *Yeast Connection.* Priced at $15.95, it sold twelve thousand copies a month for a time. In 1985 at least two major book publishers courted Dr. Crook for the rights to his book.

On the making of fine books

In the early years of book publishing, the publisher, printer, and seller were one and the same. As the industry grew, each became a business by itself. Today few publishers do their own printing; and, except for mail order sales, the retailing of books is also a separate business.

Specialization in book publishing has contributed to a deterioration in design. Years ago, the person who designed the book itself also designed the cover and was involved in the paper selection and other aspects of production. All of this was done with the aim of coordinating details to result in a unified book, notes Abe Lerner of Dodd, Mead's production department. Lerner thinks the industry should get away from today's "unnatural division of labor." Book designing, he says, is more than selecting typefaces and arranging them; book designing is book making.

Lerner deplores the trend toward "lively" and "jazzy" page design. "Our design and bookmaking task is to make order out of an author's manuscript, not to overpower it with distractions, no matter how well meant."[2]

A few publishers still bring out carefully crafted books with fine printing and exquisite bindings. Arion Press in San Francisco brought out a limited edition (four hundred copies) of F. Scott Fitzgerald's *The Great Gatsby* in 1985 with illustrations by architect/designer Michael Graves. Price per book was $400, but each copy was numbered and autographed by Graves.

Publishers of such books are small, and their press runs are modest. Often what they do becomes a labor of love. Charles L. Lehman, an educator in Tigard, Oregon, runs Alcium Press in Portland to publish books mostly on calligraphy, a special interest of his.[3] Lehman considers calligraphy an art that is "spiritually healing in a materialistic world."[4]

A magazine published in San Francisco, *Fine Print,* covers the art of bookmaking and celebrates the fine books issued by small presses both now and in the past. It is itself an example of fine printing and design. *Small Press,* published by the publisher of *Publishers Weekly* ("the journal of the book industry") in New York, also covers small book publishers but more from a business standpoint.

The industrial revolution brought the machine to typography and design, and pages began to look less decorative and more sterile. Eduard Bendemann in Germany was one designer who kept romanticism alive on pages he controlled. He designed this one in 1840. Observe how he took the basic design of his text or blackletter type (known as Old English) and applied it to the art and border elements on the page. This is a beautifully unified page. The decorative initial *M,* which juts up above the first line of body copy rather than down into the paragraph, is drawn in outline form to match the heading in the box under the figures.

What design does for books

A publisher's attitude toward design can affect an author's decision to go with that publisher. Alan Watts, author of *Behold the Spirit* and other philosophical books, chose Pantheon Books in New York after seeing a folder announcing its founding. He was "at once struck by the sophistication of its typographic layout. It may seem uncanny, but . . . [typography] is as revealing to me as handwriting to a graphologist, and I knew at once that I would like my own books published by this firm."[5]

Does design spur the sale of a book? Probably not, admits Marshall Lee, a book design and production specialist. But poor design can hurt sales. "The general public's reaction to book design is, in most cases, subconscious," he writes. "Except where the visual aspect is spectacular, the nonprofessional browser is aware of only a general sense of pleasure or satisfaction in the presence of a well-designed book and a vague feeling of irritation when confronted by a badly designed one."[6]

Only the large houses, those publishing more than one hundred books a year, seem able to employ full-time art directors and designers. Some houses don't even have production departments, turning that job over instead to independent shops and studios.

A few houses—Alfred A. Knopf is one—use the same designer or group of designers to develop a "house style," making books from that house easily recognizable. Publishers bringing out a series of related books—for example, books covering various aspects of the law or a "college outlines" series—tie the books together with the same basic cover and interior design. The pattern on the cover may change from title to title only in the colors used.

The typical book designer is a freelancer who works for a number of houses. The book publishing industry is not noted for its lush commissions to freelancers. But there is a satisfaction in this work, designers tell themselves, that can't be found in the much higher paid area of advertising or even in the slightly higher paid field of magazine journalism.

The book designer's approach

The typical book comes in a 6 × 9 size, centers its display-type lines, uses Times Roman for body type, and maybe Helvetica for titles, runs chapter numbers up large, starts opening paragraphs of chapters flush left, and puts most margin space at the bottoms of pages. All of which works well enough. As a designer you would want to have reasons for varying this approach.

When you vary the approach, you engage in what Stanley Rice calls "design by exception." So much of book design is routine, he points out, and designers would prefer not to be bothered with some of it. There are just so many ways to take care of page after page of text material. De-

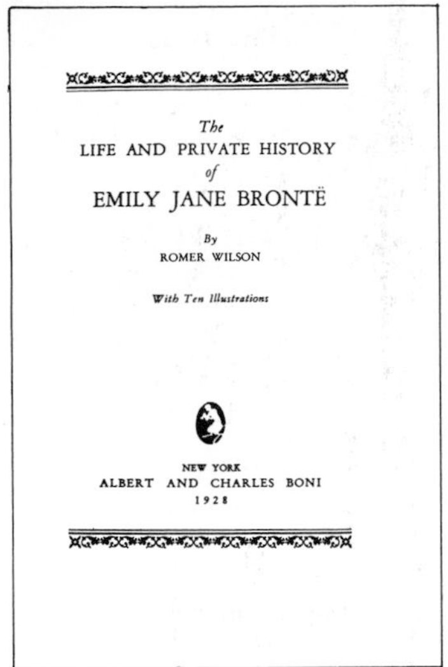
The
LIFE AND PRIVATE HISTORY
of
EMILY JANE BRONTË
By
ROMER WILSON
With Ten Illustrations
NEW YORK
ALBERT AND CHARLES BONI
1928

Well-designed title pages for books have changed little over the years. This classic design is from a 1928 book, but it would work just as well today for a quality book.

signers, he says, are beginning to ask printers and typesetters to follow standard formats except where the designers specify something else. "Design by exception can be most useful to the designer when it is conscious, systematic, and implemented by computer-controlled composition using stored format controls."[7]

You can also look at book design as involving two basic approaches, as all graphic design does. One is the *transparent* approach (Marshall Lee's term), where the design does not intrude. The designer makes reading as effortless as possible.

The other is the *mood* approach, in which the designer sets a stage for the reader. "The design of the book has to spring from its contents," says Samuel Antupit, director of art and design for Harry N. Abrams, a book publisher that brings out many art books. "There are no predetermined solutions. . . . Some books end up beautiful and elegant, some funny and jarring."[8]

When dealing with mood, the designer takes into account not only the subject matter but also the nature of the audience. Certain typefaces, for instance, are more appropriate for children than for adults (although, ironically, it is the child, whose eyes see best, that gets the larger, bolder faces). The kind of pictures used depends to a large extent on the kind of reader the book seeks to reach.

Some of the best design in publishing—certainly some of the best art—can be found in children's books. Guy Billout's children's books, published by Prentice-Hall, start out as illustrations. "They usually are based on the topic of engineering; maybe a series on monuments or bridges. I really want a reason or pretext to do the drawings. The text is just an explanation about the technical aspects."[9]

Textbooks present a special problem to the designer because they are selected or purchased, not by readers but by teachers or, worse, by committees. The designer then must satisfy two different audiences. In textbook design, writers play an important role, if not in design then in art selection. Art and copy must be integrated, and the author is in the best position to help along that integration. "Ideally, there should be no separation of author, illustrator and designer," says Alexander J. Burke, Jr., president of McGraw-Hill Book Company. "Communication through word, picture and design is, or should be, a simultaneous act of creation. Where it is, we get better education and better bookmaking."[10]

How-to books represent another challenge to designers. Usually, there are several available on the same subject on the bookstore shelves. Potential readers have only a short time to make their decisions. The name of the author is not likely to be decisive. The appearance of the book may make all the difference. Obviously, a heavily illustrated how-to will look more inviting than one with only a few illustrations. And color may also be crucial.

As a book designer you should be particularly concerned about unity. You achieve unity by keeping to the same typeface throughout, preferably for both titles and text; using the same "sink" for the beginning of each chapter; placing the page numbers and running heads at the same spot on each page; and establishing a standard copy area and staying with it throughout the book. You should insist that the printer honor your placements and measurements.

New designers hired by book publishers tend to overdesign the books assigned them. Most books cannot afford an avant-garde treatment. "Our design problem in the book industry today is not a lack of creativity—we

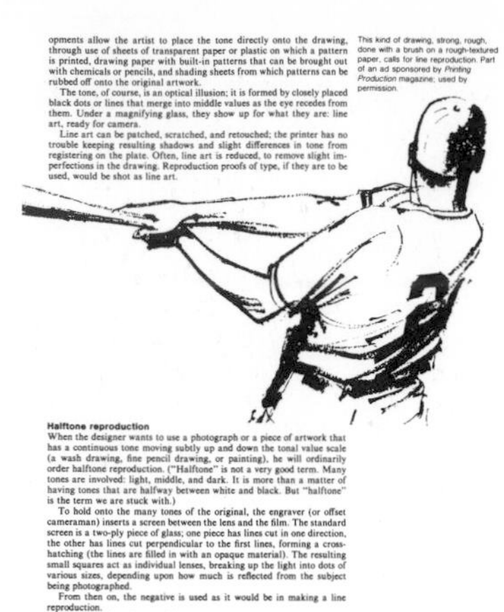

These four spreads from the heavily illustrated *The Design of Advertising* show how a grid, with single columns of copy pushed consistently to left and right outside edges, provides a concentration of white space at the gutter for a variety of arrangements of art and captions.

have more creativity than we can use," reports R. D. Scudellari, corporate art director at Random House. Rather, we need quality in execution, and our problem is to discipline young designers to the proper execution of routine tasks on which their creativity must rest if it is to produce quality end results."[11]

Production and the book designer

On magazines the art director turns over the more routine chores to a production editor, who follows through on fitting type, ordering halftones, and doing pasteups. In book publishing the art director—or the designer—may play a more subservient role. Often a production editor hires the designer and supervises the work.

The production editor, along with the editor, imposes upon the designer a number of limitations: a proposed number of pages for the printed book, some art that will have to be included, a budget.

If the book is to sell mainly in bookstores, it will need an attractive jacket, a thick or hefty appearance, and, if possible, lots of pictures. If it is a gift book, it should look large and expensive, even if it isn't. If it is a mail order book, it should be printed on lightweight paper, to save postage costs. If it is designed primarily for library sales, it should have a strong binding.

As a book designer you would read the manuscript carefully before starting your design. At the early stages you could forget the budget and come up with the ideal solution even though it might be beyond what the budget could support. You could then modify the design to fit the budget.

University presses often can experiment more than commercial publishers can. A small book Muriel Cooper designed for MIT Press, *File Under Architecture,* was set in various typewriter fonts, printed on kraft paper, and bound in covers made of corrugated boxboard. All of this was appropriate because the book challenged many principles of architecture.

Sometimes the designer is involved in the planning of the book. Samuel Antupit sits on a board at Abrams that decides what books to publish. In a few cases a book is designed first and the text then written to fit, or the design evolves as the book is written. The subject may dictate an unusual format. A book about wines may be shaped like a wine bottle, a book on

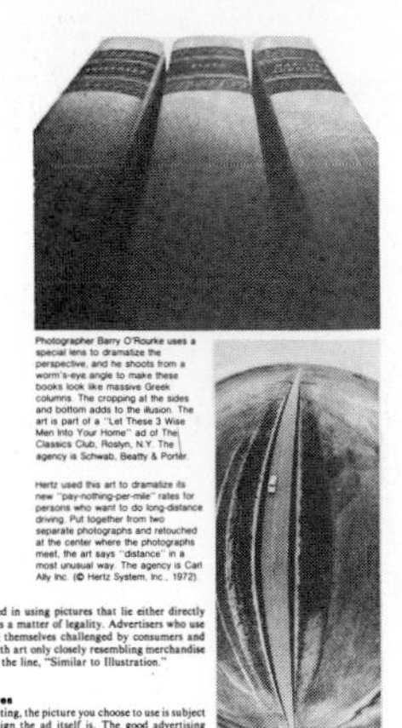

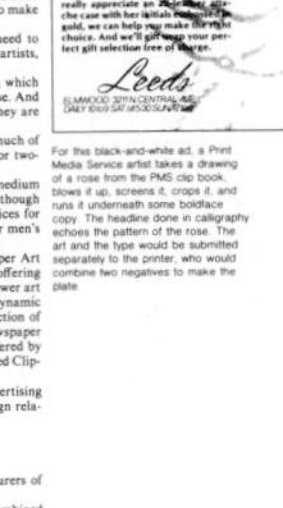

how to stop smoking like a pack of cigarettes, a kid's book like a house. Sometimes a toy or other unit is attached to the book. Die cuts and special packaging are enormously expensive, but they are novel enough to catch the most jaded book browser's attention.

A few books—juveniles and art books—are written, designed, and even illustrated by the same person. A few nonartist writers like to get in on the act, too. For instance, John Updike. "We don't always agree with him," says R. D. Scudellari, "but usually his ideas are followed."

In the course of the work the designer soon becomes an expert in production, learning how to cut costs without lowering the quality of the book. By confining color and art to certain signatures, by slightly altering page size, by omitting head- and tailbands (they pretty a book a bit at the edges of the binding but add nothing to a book's strength), by having process color reproductions tipped on rather than printed on the signatures, by avoiding multiple widths in the text—by doing many of these things, the designer can save the publisher money and still produce a handsome book.

Publishers of elementary and high school textbooks follow production guidelines set up by the Book Manufacturers Institute in collaboration with the National Association of State Textbook Administrators. These guidelines affect paper choice, binding, and margins. A textbook designer should check into these guidelines, which change from time to time.

The time needed for putting a book through production varies from as little as three weeks, for "instant" paperbacks based on news or special events, to six months, for complicated picture books. Of course, for the author, the time lag is more; before the production department gets the job, the manuscript has to be accepted, approved, and copyread—processes that can take more time than actual production.

As it has to other units of the print-medium industry, the computer has come to book publishing. Many book publishers set their type in-house now, even when their books are printed in other states and even in other countries. John Wiley & Sons, a long-established house specializing in science and technology books, worked out an arrangement with a word processing firm in 1982 for Wiley authors to use the new technology in the preparation of their manuscripts, thus doing away with many of the steps of conventional manuscript processing. The agreement included author liaison and training.

The lineup of book pages

Once in a while a designer gets a book like Stephen Schneck's *The Night Clerk* (Grove Press, 1965) to design. That book started right out on page 9, in the middle of a sentence. People who bought the book thought they had defective copies. The publisher had to send a notice around to booksellers assuring them that the book was meant to be that way.

The usual book is a little more logically planned. In fact, the lineup of pages stays pretty much the same, book after book.

Here's the lineup of pages for a nonfiction book:

- ☐ "Half" title (This page goes back to the time when books were sold without covers; the real title page was thus protected.)
- ☐ Advertising card (list of the author's previous works or of other books in the series)
- ☐ Title
- ☐ Copyright notice and catalog number
- ☐ Dedication
- ☐ Acknowledgments (Or they can follow the table of contents.)
- ☐ Preface or foreword (It's a preface if written by the author, a foreword if written by someone else.)
- ☐ Table of contents (Books without chapter titles do not need tables of contents.)
- ☐ List of illustrations
- ☐ Introduction (Or it can follow the second "half" title.)
- ☐ Second "Half" title
- ☐ Chapter 1
- ☐ Additional chapters
- ☐ Appendix
- ☐ Footnotes (if not incorporated into the text)
- ☐ Bibliography (Or it can follow the glossary.)
- ☐ Glossary
- ☐ Index
- ☐ Colophon (a paragraph or two giving design and production details about the book)

This list does not take into account blank pages in the front and back of the book. Nor does it show whether these are left- or right-hand pages. Customarily, main pages, like the title pages, are given right-hand placement.

Up through the second "half" title page, the numbering system used is small roman. From chapter 1 (or from the introduction, if it follows the second "half" title page) the numbering is arabic.

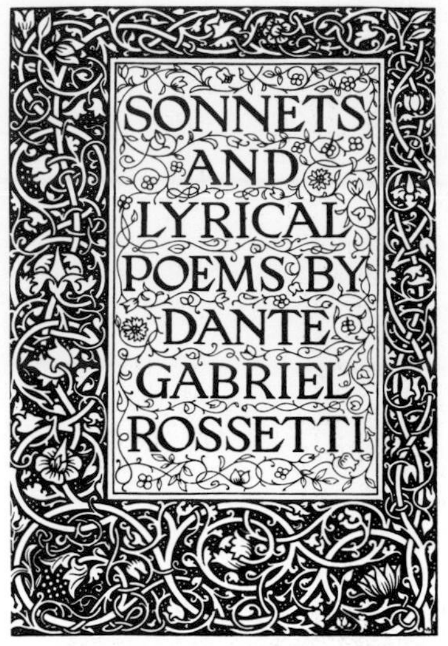

This title page was designed by England's William Morris in 1894. Morris was influenced by incunabula. He devoted himself to fighting cheapness and standardization brought on by the industrial revolution.

Laying out the book

If the book is highly illustrated and the illustrations are integrated with the text, you would, of course, design every page. But in most cases you would design only the opening and strategic pages and set basic standards for the others.

Among the pages you design are the title page or pages, table of contents pages, a chapter opening, and two facing pages inside a chapter (to show how running heads, subheads, and page numbering will look).

You also provide the printer with a specification sheet on which you list or describe the following:

Will Bradley designed this page in 1896. Bradley was one of the American book designers influenced by William Morris.

1. trim size of pages
2. size of margins
3. size of copy area
4. size and style of type and amount of leading
5. amount of paragraph indentation
6. handling of long quotes (set in different type or size? narrower width? centered or flush left or flush right?)
7. handling of footnotes
8. size and placement of page numbers (folios)
9. handling of chapter titles, subheads, running heads, and initial letters
10. amount of drop between chapter titles and beginnings of chapters
11. handling of front matter, including title page and table of contents
12. handling of back matter, including bibliography and index

The printer goes ahead and sets some sample pages according to your specifications to enable you to check them to make sure all instructions are understood and your design works. You can change your mind better at this point than after the entire book is set. The setting of the front matter of the book is deferred until last.

You start with an office-machine copy of the manuscript. The first order of business is to "cast off"—count the number of words or, better, the number of characters in the manuscript and, using standard copyfitting techniques, determine how many pages of print the characters will occupy. The longer the manuscript, the more likely you are to choose a small typeface, but you do not go smaller than 10 point, unless you choose to set the book in narrow columns. If the manuscript is short, you may use a larger face and more leading than usual, and you may choose a high-bulk paper to give extra thickness to the book. Whenever possible, you arrange the book so that the final number of pages, including front and back matter and blank pages, comes to a multiple of thirty-two.

After the editor approves your type selection and sample page layouts, the original manuscript, now copyread, goes to the printer or typographer for setting. When proofs are ready, you receive one set to use to prepare a dummy of the book. The extra number of pages remains somewhat flexible as you wrestle with fitting problems. You may have to increase or decrease some of your spacing in order to come out even on signatures. You may find it necessary to add or subtract a signature.

One way to move into the final stages is to prepare your dummy by cutting and pasting the proofs roughly into place, along with copy prints of the art. Then a pasteup artist, guided by the dummy, does a camera-ready pasteup, using reproduction proofs rather than galley proofs, and the best possible prints of the line art, if not the line art itself, along with amberlith sheets to represent the halftones, which are shot separately.

Establishing the margins

It may not seem that way, but the nontype area of a book—the white space—accounts for close to 50 percent of the total area. For art books and highly designed books, white space may account for as much as 75 percent of the total area.

Where you put this white space figures greatly in your thinking. For your all-type pages you concentrate white space on the outside edges of your spreads, but not in equal-width bands.

ORGANIZATIONAL
COMMUNICATION
TODAY AND TOMORROW
PART
V
The future is something everyone reaches at the rate of 60 minutes an hour—no more, no less. Professional communicators should anticipate the movements of the future and be ready to cope with them if they occur. Look at history, social issues, geopolitical shifts, technological advances and individual professional development as preparation for the future.

For this spread announcing the beginning of Part V of the book *Inside Organizational Communication,* put together by the International Association of Business Communicators, the designer used flat, abstract art (man on moon, eagle, globe, arrows, planets) to create a "today and tomorrow" mood.

The idea is to arrange the copy on facing pages so that the pages read as a unit. For the typical book you establish margins that tend to push the copy area of the two pages together. Book margins are like magazine margins. The narrowest margin on each page is at the gutter (but the combined space at the gutter is usually wider than other margins). The margin increases at the top, increases more at the outside edge, and increases most at the bottom. You should be careful to keep the margin at the gutter wide enough (never less than ⅝ inch for books in the 6 × 9 range) so that the type does not merge into the gutter when the book is bound. When you run a headline or title across the gutter, you allow a little extra space at the gutter to take care of space lost in the binding.

Book typography

For many books, design is almost wholly a matter of type selection and careful, consistent spacing of that type. But even that requires many agonizing decisions. For instance, how big should the paragraph indentations be? How should lists, tables, footnotes, captions, credit lines, table of contents, bibliography, glossary, and index be handled?

Your showplace pages are the title page and the pages with chapter openings. The trend is toward a two-page title spread. Why should the left-hand page be blank and the right-hand page be crowded with all the information that makes up a title page? The title, or elements of the title page, cross the gutter to unify the two pages. The effect can be dramatic, suggesting "This book is important."

Type for the chapter headings usually matches the type for the title pages. The headings seldom are larger than 18 or 24 points, and often they are smaller. Small-size type displayed with plenty of white space has just as much impact as large-size type that is crowded.

Text type in books ranges from 8 points to 12 points, depending upon the width of the column, the length of the book, the face used, the amount of leading between lines, and the age level of the reader. Body copy is leaded from 1 to 3 points. Space between words is usually ¼ em or, at most, ⅓ em.

"Widows"—last lines of paragraphs—shouldn't be any narrower than two-thirds of a column when they begin a column or page. Some publishers do not want widows of any width at the tops of pages or columns. That means as a designer you have to bring the widow and at least the one line before it to the top of a page or column when you lay out a book.

This spread is from Robert L. Tyler's *Rebel of the Woods: The I. W. W. in the Pacific Northwest.* Designer Douglas Lynch chose a condensed sans serif type for his chapter headings to give them the feel of newspaper headlines. Note his use of a vertical axis and a short, heavy horizontal rule. (Reproduced by permission of University of Oregon Books.)

You also have to make a decision about how to handle long quotations. Should they be integrated with the text, or should they be segregated, perhaps in smaller, indented type? Then how much space should go above and below them? Do you indent opening lines? Or do you handle opening lines of excerpts as you do opening lines of first paragraphs in each chapter?

Now consider the matter of how to begin the first paragraph of a chapter. There are all kinds of possibilities, with or without the use of an initial letter. In many books the first paragraph of each chapter is not indented. The display type used for the chapter title acts as the indentation, announcing to the reader a beginning. An indentation, some book designers feel, is redundant. At the other extreme, the opening paragraph may begin half way or more across the column. All or part of the opening line can be in all-caps or small-caps.

Paragraphs following subheads often go without indentations, too. For nonfiction books, and especially for textbooks, subheads are important. They help readers organize the material as they read. Subheads also break up large areas of gray type into convenient takes.

Subheads are best when kept close to the size of the body type. Sometimes they are in bold face, sometimes in all-caps, sometimes in italics. They should be accompanied by some extra white space (both above and below but mostly above) to make them stand out. Handling subheads can be a problem when they occur near or at the bottom of a page or column. Publishers like to see two or three lines of text matter under those low-lying subheads. Otherwise the subheads become isolated. Subheads can begin pages or columns, but when they are only *near* the top, at least two or three lines of text matter should go above them.

The author of a book supplies subheads with the manuscript and usually establishes the level of importance for each. Subheads can occupy up to four levels of importance. From a design standpoint, the fewer the levels the better. This book has a single level.

The designer determines the type size for each level, often choosing to keep subheads all in the same size type, centering those of the first level, running the second-level heads flush left, and indenting those of the third

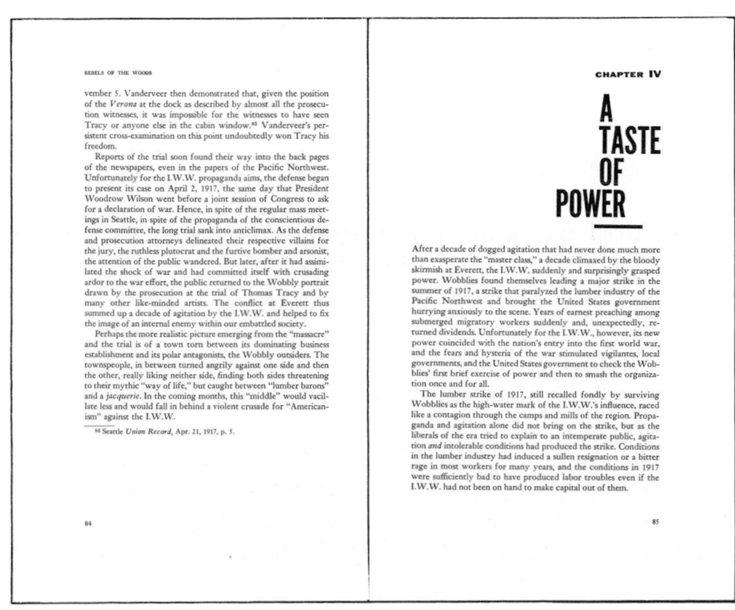
REBELS OF THE WOODS

vember 5. Vanderveer then demonstrated that, given the position of the *Verona* at the dock as described by almost all the prosecution witnesses, it was impossible for the witnesses to have seen Tracy or anyone else in the cabin window.[85] Vanderveer's persistent cross-examination on this point undoubtedly won Tracy his freedom.

Reports of the trial soon found their way into the back pages of the newspapers, even in the papers of the Pacific Northwest. Unfortunately for the I.W.W. propaganda aims, the defense began to present its case on April 2, 1917, the same day that President Woodrow Wilson went before a joint session of Congress to ask for a declaration of war. Hence, in spite of the regular mass meetings in Seattle, in spite of the propaganda of the conscientious defense committee, the long trial sank into anticlimax. As the defense and prosecution attorneys delineated their respective villains for the jury, the ruthless plutocrat and the furtive bomber and arsonist, the attention of the public wandered. But later, after it had assimilated the shock of war and had committed itself with crusading ardor to the war effort, the public returned to the Wobbly portrait drawn by the prosecution at the trial of Thomas Tracy and by many other like-minded artists. The conflict at Everett thus summed up a decade of agitation by the I.W.W. and helped to fix the image of an internal enemy within our embattled society.

Perhaps the more realistic picture emerging from the "massacre" and the trial is of a town torn between its dominating business establishment and its polar antagonists, the Wobbly outsiders. The townspeople, in between turned angrily against one side and then the other, really liking neither side, finding both sides threatening to their mythic "way of life," but caught between "lumber barons" and a *jacquerie*. In the coming months, this "middle" would vacillate less and would fall in behind a violent crusade for "Americanism" against the I.W.W.

[85] Seattle *Union Record*, Apr. 21, 1917, p. 5.

84

CHAPTER IV

A TASTE OF POWER

After a decade of dogged agitation that had never done much more than exasperate the "master class," a decade climaxed by the bloody skirmish at Everett, the I.W.W. suddenly and surprisingly grasped power. Wobblies found themselves leading a major strike in the summer of 1917, a strike that paralyzed the lumber industry of the Pacific Northwest and brought the United States government hurrying anxiously to the scene. Years of earnest preaching among submerged migratory workers suddenly and, unexpectedly, returned dividends. Unfortunately for the I.W.W., however, its new power coincided with the nation's entry into the first world war, and the fears and hysteria of the war stimulated vigilantes, local governments, and the United States government to check the Wobblies' first brief exercise of power and then to smash the organization once and for all.

The lumber strike of 1917, still recalled fondly by surviving Wobblies as the high-water mark of the I.W.W.'s influence, raced like a contagion through the camps and mills of the region. Propaganda and agitation alone did not bring on the strike, but as the liberals of the era tried to explain to an intemperate public, agitation *and* intolerable conditions had produced the strike. Conditions in the lumber industry had induced a sullen resignation or a bitter rage in most workers for many years, and the conditions in 1917 were sufficiently bad to have produced labor troubles even if the I.W.W. had not been on hand to make capital out of them.

85

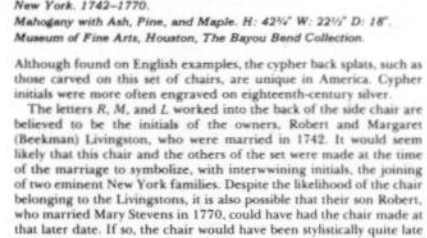

A spread from *American Furniture: 1620 to the Present* by Jonathan L. Fairbanks and Elizabeth Bidwell Bates (Richard Marek Publishers, New York, 1981) shows one way to handle illustrations in a book that is rich with them. The chairs are presented in silhouette form, with copy blocks handled as though they were captions and captions developed as short essays. Andor Braun designed the book.

level. The fourth-level heads could go in italics. Sometimes the designer runs subheads outside rather than inside the text.

You also have to decide how to handle running titles—small lines at the tops or bottoms of inside pages—along with page numbers. You want to make things easy for the reader, who should be able to see, always, the book title, the chapter title, and the page number. The book title usually goes on left-hand pages, the chapter title on right-hand pages. In some books the page numbers go to giant sizes as a design affectation.

Book art

In the well-designed book the style of art complements the style of typography. Boldface types, powerful art. Graceful types, fanciful art.

Impressionism, German expressionism, surrealism, pop art—all the various art movements have had their influence on book illustration. And with today's printing technology the designer is free to call in artists who work in any technique or any medium. Still, the predominant art form for books seems to be the line drawing done in the manner of Frederic Remington, Charles Dana Gibson, Howard Pyle, A. B. Frost, E. W. Kemble, and Rockwell Kent. One reason is that such art is the easiest to reproduce under any printing conditions. The author may supply the art, sometimes finished, sometimes only in rough form to guide the professional artist picked by the publisher.

In works of nonfiction, the photographer has taken over for the illustrator, but perhaps not to the same degree as in newspaper and magazine publishing.

Where art occupies all or most of a page, you omit the page number and the running head because these tend to detract from the art. If you feel the paper used is not opaque enough, you may decide to leave blank the side backing the printed art. For some books you may put all the art in a single signature, perhaps a glossy-stock signature, without text matter but with captions.

Publishers like to have each caption preceded by a figure number. This aids greatly in the makeup of the pages. If the text refers specifically to a picture "above" or one "below," the designer has to keep in painfully close touch with each line of copy while laying out pages and readjust material to make those descriptions really work. When the text refers instead to, say, "Fig. 5," Figure 5 can go anywhere nearby.

As in magazine design, captions for books usually are set in a face

Mary Stupp-Greer used charcoal to create illustrations like this one for her all-art book-in-progress based on an excerpt from a letter written years ago by a Chinese teacher to a missionary. The theme of the book—and of Stupp-Greer's powerful illustrations—is that people can solve conflicts through non-violent means.

smaller, lighter, or bolder than the body copy or in italics or sans serifs if the body face is roman.

Some book editors and designers avoid including credit lines in the captions, putting them instead in tiny type immediately below the art or running up the side. Or, if they can get away with it, editors may choose to bunch all credit lines and bury them somewhere in the front or back of the book.

Book paper

As much as 25 percent of the retail price of a book goes to pay for production and printing. According to an estimate by Marshall Lee, one-fifth of that 25 percent goes for paper.

More so than other designers, the book designer must know the special qualities of papers. Whereas a magazine designer usually needs to make a choice only once, the book designer must make a choice for every job. These are the four basic kinds of paper used for book printing:

1. *Antique stock.* There are many textures, finishes, and weights, but essentially these papers are soft, rough, and absorbent. They are especially good for books made up wholly of text matter; that they are nonglare makes them easy on the eyes. For quality books the designer may choose an antique stock with deckle edges.
2. *Plate or English-finish stock.* Essentially, these are antique papers that have been smoothed out, making possible sharper reproduction, especially for pictures. Paper used for the big magazines falls into this category.
3. *Coated stock.* Simple polishing (calendering) may not suffice to give the paper a finish that is smooth and slick enough. The designer, then, can choose a coated stock, smooth to the feel, rich looking, and highly desirable where maximum fidelity is desired in picture reproduction. But coated stock is expensive.
4. *Offset stock.* The offset printing process needs special papers that will resist moisture. (Offset, you'll remember, makes use of plates that carry both moisture and ink.) Untreated paper would stretch, shrink, and curl. Offset papers come in a variety of textures and finishes, but the most common is the rather smooth, severely white stock used for so many company magazines and for books that carry numerous halftones.

After the Civil War, Howard Pyle became one of America's most influential magazine illustrators. Pyle also both wrote and illustrated books. His style was rich, his design carefully controlled. This illustration is from *The Wonder Clock,* a book published in 1887.

In addition to these basic papers the designer should know about the special papers, including kraft, available for end sheets.

Doubleday once brought out a book, *The Sleeping Partner,* in a great variety of papers, a different one for each thirty-two page signature, causing William Jovanovich, president of Harcourt, Brace & World (now Harcourt Brace Jovanovich), to remark, "This is, no doubt, a way to clear out one's inventory in the name of Art."

Books these days come in a greater variety of sizes than ever, but the most common trim sizes still are 5⅜ × 8, 5½ × 8¼, and 6⅛ × 9¼. Mass paperbacks come usually in 4⅛ × 6⅜ or 4⅛ × 7 sizes. As in magazine publishing, there is a trend toward the square format, especially for volumes dealing with the fine arts. As for all printing, the designer should check with the printer on paper size available and choose a page size that can be cut with a minimum of waste.

Books meant to be kept are not lasting as long as the industry would like. The S. D. Warren Company, which offers the book trade an alkaline selection of stock that will not decay, estimates that "acid decay has rendered nearly one-third of the books in the Library of Congress too brittle for normal use. About half the books in the New York Public Library show signs of decay."[12] The book industry has adopted an infinity symbol, a figure *8* on its side enclosed in a circle, to identify books whose paper meets the tests of the American Standard for Permanence of Paper for Printed Library Materials.

Book bindings

Books come in four kinds of bindings:

1. *Sewn binding.* For this kind of binding signatures are placed next to each other. They are not nested, as for saddle-stitched maga-

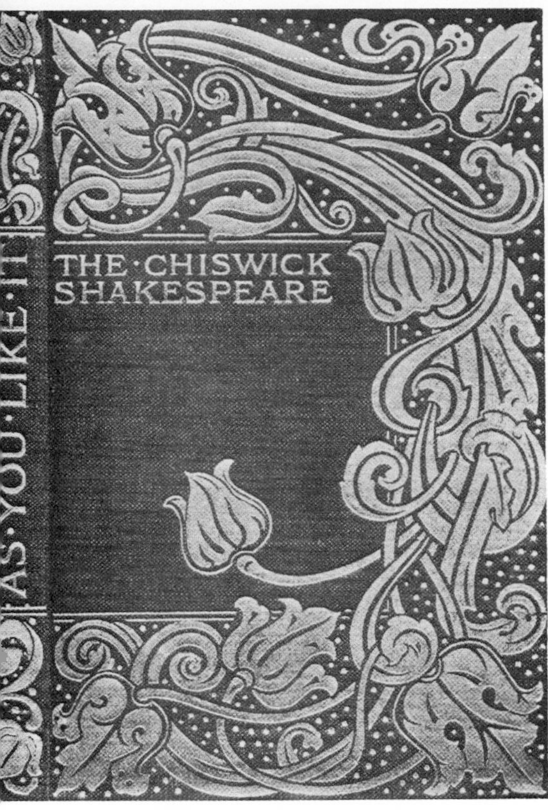

This handbound turn-of-the-century book used an Art Nouveau design for its front cover and spine. Small dots, picked up from the basic design, separate words in the titles. The small, all-caps title on the cover snuggles up in one corner of the rectangle that contains it. The designer was Gerald Moira.

zines. Open up a book and look at the binding from the top or bottom, and you can see how the signatures fit together.

Two kinds of sewing are available: (a) Smythe sewing, in which the sewing is done through the gutter of each signature and then across the back; and (b) side sewing (less common), in which the thread goes through the entire book about ⅛ inch from the gutter edge. A side-sewn book does not lie flat when opened, but the binding is sturdy. Libraries, when they find it necessary to rebind a book, frequently use side sewing.

2. *Stapled binding.* The staples can go in through the spine, if signatures are nested; or they can go in through the side. Such binding is reserved for low-budget books.
3. *Adhesive binding.* Sometimes called "perfect binding," this system brings together loose pages rather than signatures. The binding is accomplished by applying glue across the back. Cheap, mass audience paperbacks use this kind of binding. Unfortunately, the pages have a tendency to separate when subjected to constant use.
4. *Mechanical binding.* The most common mechanical binding is *spiral binding,* in which loose pages are held together by a wire that spirals along a series of punched holes. The covers of such a book can be heavy paper, cardboard, or boards covered with paper. Pages can be torn out easily. With some mechanical bindings new pages can be inserted. Mechanical binding is used for books with short press runs—books written for technical- or practical-minded audiences.

The first three binding processes—the main binding processes—can be used for paperback as well as hardbound books. Most hardbound books, however, come with sewn binding since it permits a book to lie flat when it is opened.

Fiction often comes out in hardbound form first and in paperback form later, after the must-have-it-right-away crowd has registered its approval and paid the higher prices. But textbooks and other nonfiction books frequently come out in two bindings simultaneously. The spread in prices between the two far exceeds the one or two dollars of extra cost involved in manufacturing a hardbound book. For instance, the third edition of Hugh Williamson's *Method of Book Design* (Yale University Press, 1984) cost $40 in cloth and $12.95 in paper.

The bookcover

Let's assume you are designing a hardbound book. With the kind of binding decided, you turn your attention to the cover. You must decide whether you want the boards of the cover to be wrapped fully in cloth, partially in cloth and partially in paper, or fully in paper. If the boards are to be wrapped in cloth, should the cloth be all of the same color and texture? Or should you seek a two-tone effect? And what color or colors should you use?

For many books the cover consists merely of wrapped boards with the name of the book, author, and publisher showing on the spine. But even that small amount of type should be coordinated with the other elements of the book.

The type used can be printed on the cover material before it is wrapped around the boards, or it can be stamped on afterwards.

Many hardbound books require design on the cover proper as well as on the jacket. Textbooks generally get by with cover design only. There are no jackets.

Dark colors in cloths used for hardbound books show wear at the corners more quickly than light colors do. But light-colored cloth soils more quickly. The lighter colors have the advantage of making books look bigger, suggesting to readers that they are getting a lot for their money. Textbooks tend to come out in lighter colors.

The design on hardbound covers can be printed or stamped. The stamping process, not recommended for intricate designs or small type, can make use of foils for a metallic look. The designer can also specify blind stamping, which simply depresses the surface.

For their cover material publishers once used animal skins—vellum or leather—but now they use cloth, vinyl, or paper. Cloth gained popularity as book cover material in the latter part of the nineteenth century. The cloth used today is often a cotton impregnated or coated with plastic. Paper became popular during World War II, when cloth was scarce. The paper most commonly used is kraft.

The cloth, vinyl, or paper is wrapped around binder's board (found in most textbooks), chip board (found in cheaper books), pasted board (found in most trade books), or red board (found in limp books meant to be carried around in pockets).

To keep the top edges of the book's pages from soiling, you may decide to have them stained. You can choose a color that complements the endpapers.

Endpapers in hardbacks serve more of an aesthetic than structural purpose. Their main function is to hide folded cloth and stitching. Endpapers used to be nothing more than tan kraft paper, but increasingly they have taken on color and even art.

For sets of books, hardbound as well as paperback, publishers often supply slipcases, which unite and encase the books, leaving only their spines exposed.

The cover for a paperback book represents a special challenge to the designer in that it is both a jacket and a cover. Because paperback sales are so dependent on impulse buying, the cover art must be interesting, if not compelling. For the paperback cover of *Best of The Realist,* edited by Paul Krassner (Running Press, Philadelphia, 1984), Toby Schmidt, the designer, arranged to have Michael LaRiche take a color photograph of a tiedup stack of the old magazines, with their edges yellowed and partly disintegrated by time (the irreverent magazine had been printed on cheap paper). A fresh band of white running diagonally across the middle carried the book title, byline, and blurb in black and red ink.

Like the jacket for a hardbound book, the cover for a paperback is as much an exercise in advertising design as in book design. "After all, aren't book covers packages, and isn't packaging a function of advertising?" asks Ian Summers, executive art director of Ballantine Books.

As a book publishing art director, Summers works on 150 titles at a time (Ballantine publishes 400 titles a year). As an advertising art director, by way of contrast, he worked on 10 projects at a time. Summers looks on book covers as similar to two-page advertising spreads in magazines. But the front cover is the more important part of each design. "We are in the business of making posters that are only four by seven inches tall," Summers says.

Even though Ballantine tries to be innovative, some of its covers never

The spine and front of this sixteenth century book show the high art of binding, an art pretty much lost in today's publishing rush.

In the 1920s the Bauhaus in Germany was establishing the principle that design should be simple, geometric, and above all functional. Still, some important designers of that period continued to bring to design the decorative quality of an earlier era. This is a Paul Renner book cover, so rich in personality and texture that, as designer, he was allowed to sign it.

change. People who buy gothic novels, for instance, do not respond to anything but frightened women running from castles. The only way to upgrade such covers is to hire the very best illustrators. "My ability to put the right book together with the right illustrator is probably my most important contribution," Summers declares.

Science fiction offers some of the best possibilities for high-level illustration. You look for super realism here. "The science fiction fans are probably the only category of readers who really care about the quality of art on their books. They know their artists and consider them heroes."[13]

With their heavy-paper covers paperback books have experimented with various devices to get casual browsers inside. They have used both real and fake embossing on their covers, three-dimensional pictures, and diecuts that expose part of the title page. Still, covers are largely a matter of chance. "No scientific principles guide the decisions [at Bantam Books, world's largest paperback publisher]," writes Clarence Petersen in *The Bantam Story.* "Past experience helps, but mostly publishing executives call the shots by a sort of gut reaction. Bantam knows, for instance, that the color red sells books. It is the boldest of the primary colors, which in turn are the boldest of all."[14]

The trouble is that everybody knows this, so many publishers, including Bantam, go to other colors to make their books stand out from the sea of red. Soon all puiblishers seem to settle in on some other color. In many seasons white becomes a favorite principal cover color.

Sometimes a publisher puts a book out with different covers to appeal to different buyers. Bantam's *Future Shock* by Alvin Toffler came out with six different covers. One result, Bantam discovered, was that some booksellers put all six versions on display, giving the book a big advantage over books that had a single cover.

A single paperback book, if it enjoys a long life, may go through several different cover designs before it finally goes out of print.

For some covers or jackets, type alone, carefully selected, tastefully if not unusually arranged, with strong colors, is enough to do the job. For the jacket of Heinrich Boll's novel *The Safety Net,* the *y* swings down and around to catch and hold the word *Net.* Jay A. Sigler's book on the law, *Double Jeopardy,* repeats its title on the jacket; the second one is a reflected version of the first, as from a pool of water. The jacket for *The Dangers of Nuclear War,* to demonstrate the urgency of the subject, puts on a slant giant, condensed sans serif letters that appear to be too big to be contained within the boundaries of the page. The words get successively bigger.

For other covers art is vital. Often that art becomes a visual pun. Milton Glaser's illustration for Germaine Greer's *The Female Eunuch* was a standing pair of scissors, spread open, with a woman's muscular legs for the blades.

The book jacket

Hardbound books didn't always come with jackets. The introduction of modern distribution methods required that books be protected, and the idea of the "dust" jacket was born. At first the jacket was nothing more than a plain wrapper. It did not become a display piece until after World War I. Then it helped sell the book as well as protect it.

Jacket design probably is less important to hardcover books than cover design is to paperbacks. For a hardcover book, poorly designed jackets

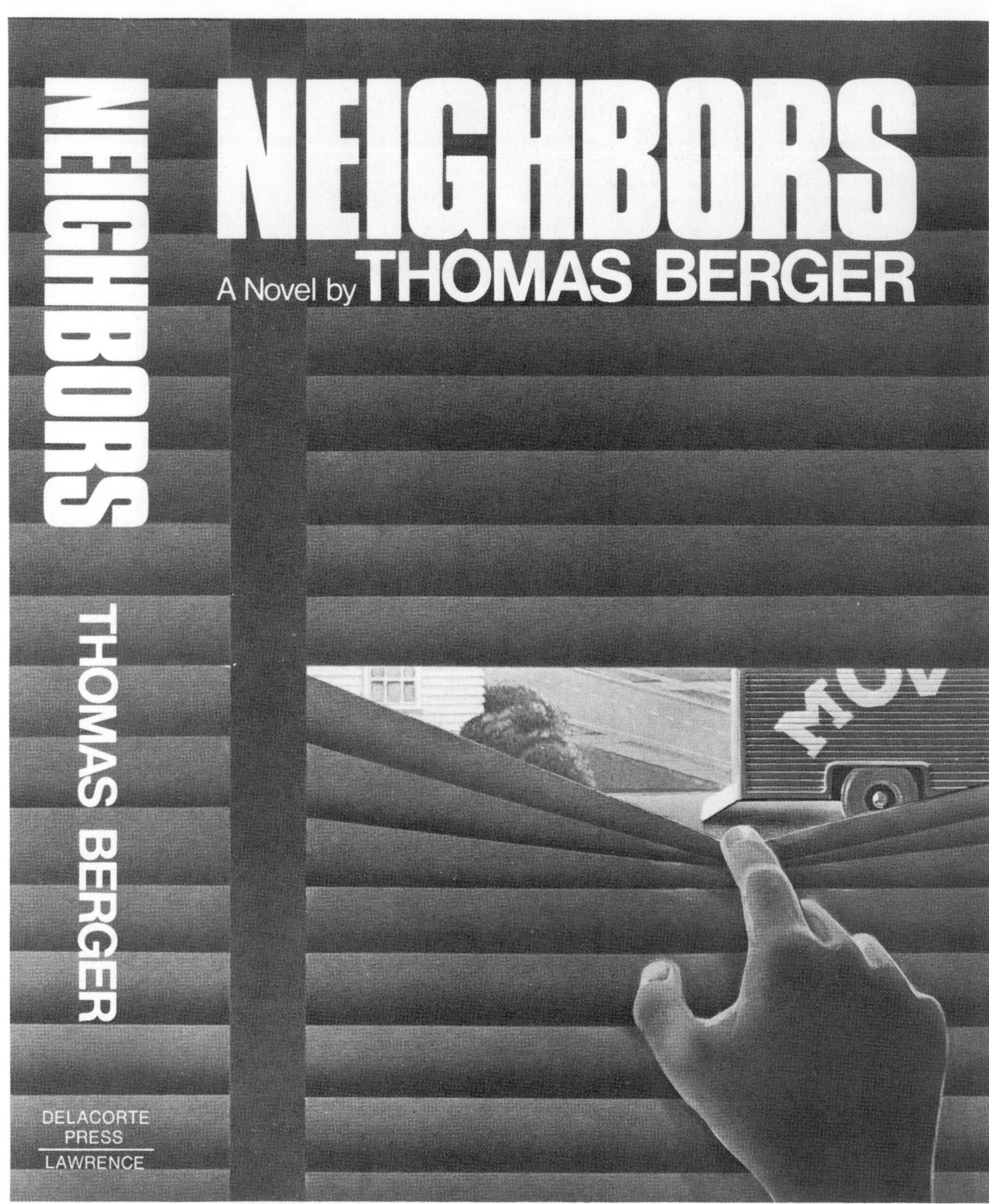

Designer-illustrator Fred Marcellino for his jacket for *Neighbors* depicts venetian blinds, which make a nice pattern on which to reverse the novel's title and the name of the author. The blinds also help say "neighbors." A hand pulls down the slats just enough to show a moving van and part of a house. You see here the jacket front and spine. (© 1980 by Fred Marcellino. Reprinted by permission of Delacorte Press/Seymour Lawrence.)

discourage buying, but well-designed jackets do not necessarily stimulate buying, says Alan Kellock, a sales manager at Harcourt Brace Jovanovich. Still, the jacket is where a book's design starts.

Once you know for sure how many pages the book will take, you ask for a bound dummy, with pages blank, so that you can get the feel of the book and can properly fit the jacket.

Ideally, you should know a great deal about a book before attempting to design its jacket. But often there is no time to give the manuscript or page proofs the reading they deserve.

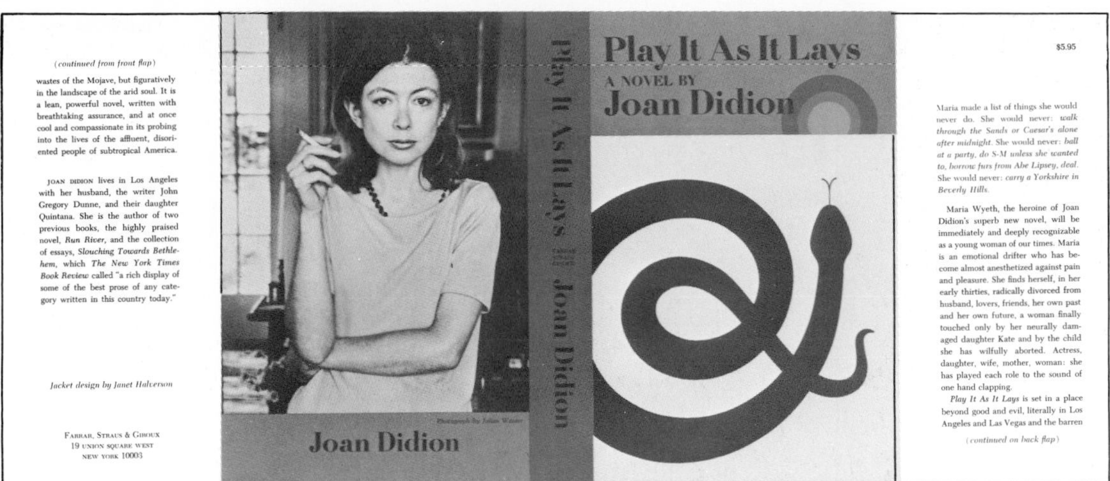

(continued from front flap)
wastes of the Mojave, but figuratively in the landscape of the arid soul. It is a lean, powerful novel, written with breathtaking assurance, and at once cool and compassionate in its probing into the lives of the affluent, disoriented people of subtropical America.
JOAN DIDION lives in Los Angeles with her husband, the writer John Gregory Dunne, and their daughter Quintana. She is the author of two previous books, the highly praised novel, Run River, and the collection of essays, Slouching Towards Bethlehem, which The New York Times Book Review called "a rich display of some of the best prose of any category written in this country today."
Jacket design by Janet Halverson
FARRAR, STRAUS & GIROUX
19 UNION SQUARE WEST
NEW YORK 10003
Joan Didion
Play It As It Lays
Joan Didion
Play It As It Lays
A NOVEL BY
Joan Didion
$5.95
Maria made a list of things she would never do. She would never: walk through the Sands or Caesar's alone after midnight. She would never: ball at a party, do S-M unless she wanted to, borrow furs from Abe Lipsey, deal. She would never: carry a Yorkshire in Beverly Hills.
Maria Wyeth, the heroine of Joan Didion's superb new novel, will be immediately and deeply recognizable as a young woman of our times. Maria is an emotional drifter who has become almost anesthetized against pain and pleasure. She finds herself, in her early thirties, radically divorced from husband, lovers, friends, her own past and her own future, a woman finally touched only by her neurally damaged daughter Kate and by the child she has wilfully aborted. Actress, daughter, wife, mother, woman: she has played each role to the sound of one hand clapping.
Play It As It Lays is set in a place beyond good and evil, literally in Los Angeles and Las Vegas and the barren
(continued on back flap)

This is Janet Halverson's jacket for Joan Didion's novel about "an emotional drifter" who has played her various roles "to the sound of one hand clapping." In black, magenta, orange, and yellow. (Reprinted by permission of Janet Halverson and Farrar, Straus & Giroux, Inc.)

The typical jacket features the name of the book and the name of the author on the front; a picture of the author on the back; and a description of the book and biographical information about the author on the inside flaps. The names of the book, author (often last name only), and publisher run from left to right across the top of the spine if the book is thick enough; if the book is too thin, the names run in a single sideways line, from top to bottom.

A jacket should emphasize a single idea, reflect the mood or character of the book, and lure the reader inside. Sometimes the name of the author is featured most prominently, sometimes the title of the book.

A question of ethics comes in when the designer gives undue play to a popular earlier work of the author, perhaps deceiving readers into thinking they are buying that earlier work. Ethics also become involved when the designer uses an illustration that promises something different from what the book actually delivers.

Because jackets serve as advertisements, advertising designers rather than book designers often create them. Sometimes the authors have a say

New American Library for its paperback release of *The Rockefellers* designed the book with two different covers so that two copies of the book, put next to each other on display in bookstores, would act as a sort of poster, with a book title looming large to catch the browser's attention. "A revolutionary new cover treatment," claimed the publisher's promotion department. The book was written by Peter Collier and David Horowitz.

The last Jewish mystic
"Rabbi Nachman of Bratzlav is perhaps the last Jewish mystic," says Martin Buber. "He stands at the end of an unbroken tradition whose beginning we do not know. For a long time men sought to deny this tradition; today it can no longer be doubted. . . . I have not translated these stories of Rabbi Nachman, but retold them in all freedom, yet out of his spirit as it is present to me."
Here is a magnificent presentation of splendid and quite unique stories which became part of the tradition of Hasidism. Martin Buber was one of the greatest of twentieth-century theologians. These tales as he has rendered them, along with his introduction and remarks on Jewish mysticism, offer a fascinating insight into his thought.
DISCUS BOOKS/PUBLISHED BY AVON
DISCUS
MARTIN BUBER
The Tales of Rabbi Nachman
AVON
380 00020 145
DISCUS/AVON/QS20/$1.45
MARTIN BUBER
The Tales of
Rabbi Nachman
A unique treasure of Hasidism recreated and introduced, and with an essay on Jewish mysticism, by one of the great thinkers of our time

Designing the cover for a paperback is a little like designing the jacket for a hardcover book. Here are the front cover, back cover, and spine for *The Tales of Rabbi Nachman* by Martin Buber (Discus Books, New York; Barbara Bertoli, art director). The publisher evidently felt that the name of the author, "one of the great thinkers of our time," was more important than the name of the book. The type and illustration form one unit. The original is in black, grayed red, and light olive.

in their design. For one of his zany books Alexander King got his publisher to wrap each copy with two jackets, an inner one that was staid and conservative and an outer one featuring one of his somewhat vulgar paintings. Tongue-in-cheek, he invited any reader who was easily offended to dispose of the outside jacket.

Grove Press, for a novel called *Commander Amanda,* produced three different jackets, all designed by Kuhlman Associates. Sets were sent to booksellers; they were invited to pick the one they wanted on copies they would be selling. This involved booksellers in the book's production and presumably made them more interested in the book. Alfred A. Knopf brought out Edward Luttwak's *Coup d'Etat* with jackets in two different color combinations: half the copies had one jacket, half the other. Booksellers were encouraged to make two-tone displays of the books to help sell them.

Most jackets come in black plus a second color. The black is for the author's portrait on the back. To save costs, some publishers run their jackets in a single color on a colored stock.

The paper used is coated or varnished only on the side on which the printing is done. The side next to the book itself is rough-finished so the jacket will cling to the book.

Stamping a design on the cover of a hardbound book requires a simple design. A type-only cover and spine may be the answer. These are some rough designs worked out by this author for an earlier hardbound edition of this book.

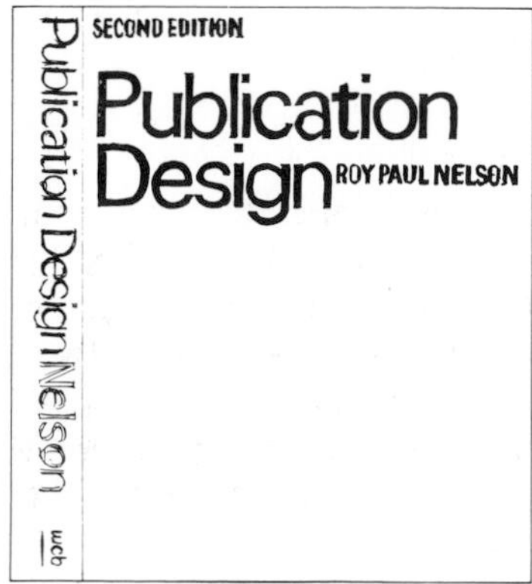

Here is one of several quick cover sketches made by the author for the fifth edition of his textbook *The Design of Advertising.* This rough uses a big rectangle to represent art for a typical ad—the kind of ad made popular by the Volkswagen Bug—and a big *5* to serve as a sort of initial letter. The vertical lines suggest columns of advertising copy, and the name at the end stands in as an ad signature or logotype.

Publishers run off more jackets than are needed to cover their books; they use the extra copies for promotion and as replacements for jackets worn and torn in shipping and handling.

First things first

All of these considerations add to the reader's enjoyment of a book, but they are as nothing compared to the Big Three contributions the designer can make.

1. Picking a paper that does not bounce the light back into the reader's eyes.
2. Picking a typeface big enough to be read without squinting.
3. Printing the text of the book far enough in from the gutter so the reader does not have to fight the binding to keep the book open.

Readers do not buy publications—books, magazines, newspapers, whatever—to admire the versatility of their art directors. They buy publications so that they can be informed; they buy them for guidance; they buy them to relax with. What they expect—what they must have—are headings and columns of type arranged for effortless assimilation, with large, clear pictures unencumbered by visual scars and typographic clutter.

What art directors must do, then, more than anything else, is make their publications useful to their readers. Design should help readers; it should not get in their way. This is not to say that art directors should shy away from imaginative approaches. Far from it. It takes imagination—more of it—to truly organize the pages of a publication rather than to merely decorate them.

Notes

1. "Cross Currents," *Publishers Weekly,* August 30, 1985, p. 310.
2. "Abe Lerner Urges Return to Design Fundamentals," *Publishers Weekly,* August 5, 1983, pp. 56, 58.
3. Lehman is also author of *Italic Handwriting and Calligraphy for the Beginner,* Taplinger, New York, 1981.
4. From a speech at the Calligraphy at the Abbey conference, Mt. Angel, Oregon, June 1, 1985.
5. Quoted by Herbert Mitgang in "Profiles: Imprint," *The New Yorker,* August 2, 1982, p. 58.
6. Marshall Lee, *Bookmaking: The Illustrated Guide to Design and Production,* R. R. Bowker Company, New York, 1965, p. 13.
7. Stanley Rice, *Book Design: Systematic Aspects,* R. R. Bowker Company, New York, 1978, p. 221.
8. "Execution," *Photo/Design,* December 1985, p. 64.
9. "Think About It," *Communication World,* September 1985, p. 23.
10. Quoted in "New Research, Team Approach Needed in Textbook Design," *Publishers Weekly,* January 3, 1977, p. 54.
11. "Interview: R. D. Scudellari," *Art Direction,* March 1979, p. 34.
12. From an ad in *Publishers Weekly,* October 4, 1985, p. 19.
13. Ian Summers, "Selling a Book by Its Cover," *Art Direction,* October 1976, pp. 59–62.
14. Clarence Petersen, *The Bantam Story,* Bantam Books, New York, 1975, p. 65.

Suggested further reading

Bailey, Herbert Smith, *The Art and Science of Book Publishing,* University of Texas Press, Austin, 1980.

Balkin, Richard, *A Writer's Guide to Book Publishing,* Hawthorn Books, New York, 1977.

Bodian, Nat G., *Book Marketing Handbook,* R. R. Bowker Company, New York, 1980.

Bonn, Thomas L., *Undercover: An Illustrated History of American Mass-Market Paperbacks,* Penguin Books, New York, 1982. (With reproductions of the 170 book covers.)
Coser, Lewis A., Charles Kadushin, and Walter W. Powell, *Books: The Culture and Commerce of Publishing,* Basic Books, New York, 1981.
Greenfield, Howard, *Books: From Writer to Reader,* Crown Publishers, New York, 1976.
Guide to Book Publishing Courses, Peterson's Guides, Princeton, New Jersey, 1979.
Judd, Karen, *Copyediting: A Practical Guide,* William Kaufmann, Los Altos, California, 1982. (Written from a book publisher's perspective.)
Lee, Marshall, *Bookmaking: The Illustrated Guide to Design and Production,* rev. ed., R. R. Bowker Company, New York, 1980.
One Book/Five Ways, William Kaufmann, Los Altos, California, 1978.
Peppin, Brigid, *Dictionary of Book Illustrators 1800–1970,* Arco, New York, 1980. (Covers 1200 artists, with samples of their work.)
Rice, Stanley, *Book Design,* 2 vols., R. R. Bowker Company, New York, 1978.
Shulevitz, Uri, *Writing with Pictures: How to Write and Illustrate Children's Books,* Watson-Guptill Publications, New York, 1985.
Thompson, Susan Otis, *American Book Design and William Morris,* R. R. Bowker Company, New York, 1977.
Williamson, Hugh, *Methods of Book Design,* 3d ed., Yale University Press, New Haven, Connecticut, 1984.
Wong, Wucius, *Principles of Three-Dimensional Design,* Van Nostrand Reinhold Company, New York, 1977.

Charles L. Lehman demonstrates the beauty of calligraphy, a beauty that can't be duplicated with type. Publishers of quality books sometimes turn to calligraphy or hand lettering for covers and jackets.

Plum Pudding

A Wodehouse Alphabet

Illustrated by Chris Marrinan

Avenue Press

San Francisco

BERTIE WOOSTER

A

A is for Aunts,
Of which Bertie has tons.
Some he greets gladly;
From others he runs.

PGW PGW PGW PGW PGW PGW PGW PGW

Everything is centered on the title page of this 4¼ × 5¼ privately published book, handset in foundry type by Douglas L. Stow and printed in letterpress on an old Chandler & Price Pilot press. Douglas and Margaret Stow of Half Moon Bay, California, designed the book for fans of P. G. Wodehouse, the late British novelist. Chris Marrinan did the illustrations. Two colors of ink were used on a quality tinted stock.

The book consists of poems about Wodehouse characters written by various friends of the Stows. Each poem takes off from a letter of the alphabet. Carl Wells wrote this one. The body type here is Bodoni bold italic. The letter *A* and the *PGW* border are in red ink.

Bookplates, printed or hand-drawn labels pasted in the front of books by book owners, show pride of ownership and identify books in case they are borrowed. Some people collect bookplates as a hobby. This turn-of-the-century Art Nouveau example is by Howard Nelson.

11

Miscellaneous publications

With a magazine or newspaper your design becomes cumulative. You see your mistakes in one issue and begin to correct them in the next. Eventually you finely tune your design to a point where, at least for the moment, it really works for you. With miscellaneous publications, as well as with books, you never know. You make your mistakes and create your triumphs, but they work only once. On the next assignment you start all over again.

Of course, some miscellaneous publications come out periodically, and so you do manage to get a handle on the design. But chances are, you work with a budget so limited you can't do what you want anyway.

Miscellaneous publications can take regular magazine and newspaper formats in addition to any of these:

1. leaflets (single sheets) or cards, loose or stapled
2. folders (sheets folded one or more times)
3. broadsides (extra large sheets like maps that are folded down for easy reading or handling)
4. booklets (similar to saddle-stapled magazines, but usually smaller—small enough, say, to fit into a No. 10 business envelope)
5. brochures (extra fancy booklets with oversize covers, die cuts, pockets, etc.)
6. yearbooks, catalogs, directories, calendars, and manuals

One estimate has one-tenth of the revenues of the typical corporation going to publications of various kinds. These include folders and leaflets, training manuals, catalogs, annual reports, and company magazines.

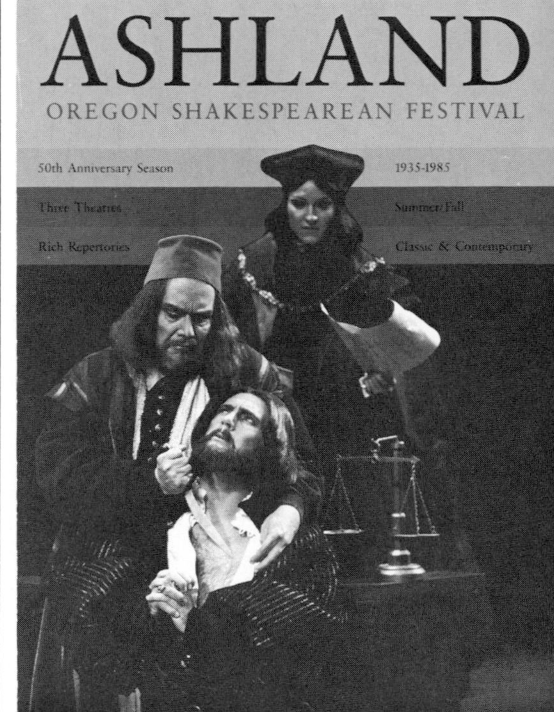

The cover for this Smythe-sewn book, published by the Oregon Shakespearean Festival, features full-color photography, depicting one of the festival's plays, and ribbons of colors at the top, into which the partially silhouetted photograph juts. Designed by Bob Reynolds of Design Council, Inc.

Moving from one format to the other

Corporate, governmental, educational, political, and other kinds of organizations using miscellaneous publications do plenty of switching back and forth with the formats. In recent years a number of company magazines decided that the traditional magazine format did not lend itself very well to news items. Something closer to a newspaper format would work better. If the magazine consisted primarily of news, it went to a newspaper format or, more commonly, to a tabloid format. Such a format

The spreads in this book vary from picture-dominated ones like this to pages that, with much to tell, carry several columns of copy.

For this spread Reynolds put the order of appearance of the photographs ahead of the problem of facing.That the photograph at the right faces off the page is not a serious matter, especially considering that it is the smaller of the two photographs on the spread. Thin red lines set off the captions at the bottom of the left page.

Reynolds offered a change of pace with this spread: a costume rendering instead of a photograph from the play. The splattering is in red, appropriate symbolism for the play.

In the back of the book Reynolds used several spreads to show actors for the season's plays along with cropped photographs of the actors in their roles. The designer allowed leftover space at the bottoms of copy blocks to determine photograph depths. The overall arrangement results, then, in a rectangle spanning the two pages.

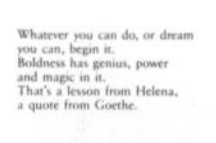

LIZZIE BORDEN IN THE LATE AFTERNOON

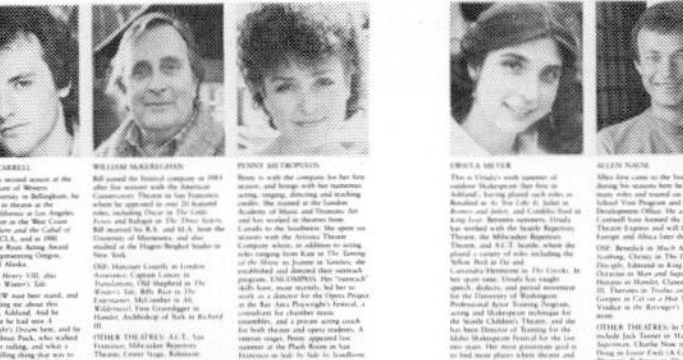

These actors play aristocrats, lawyers, playwrights, interpreters, ladies-in-waiting.

represented savings not only in paper costs (the editor could use newsprint rather than book stock) but also in binding costs. To effect further savings, some editors went to a newsletter format.

If a company magazine consisted of both feature material and news, editors—some of them—went to two formats: the magazine continued to carry feature material; the new tabloid or newsletter, perhaps issued more frequently, carried the news and chit-chat associated with the typical magazine for employees.

For publications used as sales tools, you see much experimentation with format. Sometimes the job seems to call for a simple folded sheet, sometimes something bound. A department store, for instance, instead of settling for one of those numerous tabloids we see nowadays inserted in our daily newspapers, decides on something that looks like a cheaply bound paperback book to go through the mails. Anything to get a jump on the competition.

A certificate, diploma, or award does not have to take the usual horizontal shape with calligraphic or script type, each line centered. Ernst Aufseeser designed this powerful certificate of sports achievement in the early 1930s.

Corporate design programs

Business and industrial concerns and nonprofit organizations, too, put more emphasis than ever before on the design of their publications. They have bought the concept put forth by the firms that specialize in corporate identity programs, including redesign of corporate symbols, that all printed and televised materials as well as signs on and in the company buildings should bear a family relationship and convey the impression that the firm is innovative and contemporary. It would not do, for instance, for a company to work out a beautifully designed and coordinated set of stationery and business forms and then allow the employee relations department to issue an internal magazine, newspaper, or newsletter that looks as though it was laid out by someone who couldn't make the art staff of a padded-cover yearbook put out by a rural high school.

When a company goes through a program of redesign, from trademark to company magazine, it often introduces the changes through ads and direct-mail pieces. To cite one example, when Republic Steel redesigned

Some magazine editors do it all: edit, write, design, photograph, and illustrate. Gary Olsen of *Tracks,* published by John Deere, Dubuque, Iowa, is such an editor. This is Christmas-greetings back-cover art he painted in water colors: "December Sunrise—Dubuque, Iowa." Olsen also does portraits of businesspeople for the business section of the Dubuque *Telegraph Herald.*

its logo, it issued a booklet to all employees so that they could share "the sense of pride and excitement" management felt "at the introduction of our forceful, distinctive and wholly modern appearance which portrays Republic Steel as the dynamic, forward-looking, growth-minded company we all know it to be." As the booklet explained, the new corporate identity program revolved around the company name. It stayed the same, but "Republic" grew bigger in the design "because there are many other steel companies, but only one Republic." The company also adopted a special color—"Republic Blue"—"for unique and dramatic expression." Of course, the blue was used as a second color throughout the booklet.

For management people and others involved in corporate communications, companies undergoing corporate identity redesign programs issue manuals telling exactly how to use the new symbols and signs. Placement must be just so, the manual cautions. Colors must be exact. Reading one of these manuals makes you feel as intimidated as when reading one of those mattress labels warning that "removing this label is punishable by. . . ."

Where pictorial symbols are involved in corporate design, the designer simplifies, settling for abstract shapes rather than realistic portrayals.

Central Telephone Company, Nevada, conducts a contest for local paintings and photographs to adorn the covers of its telephone directories. This directory features a highly realistic, carefully detailed painting, *Beyond the Neon,* by Anne Bridge, a blackjack dealer in Las Vegas. Bridge, one of about 100 artists to enter, won a $500 cash prize. Another artist and a photographer also won prizes. Their work was shown in a smaller size on the back cover. The theme of the competition was "The Beauty of Southern Nevada."

Sometimes initials-only do the job. A simplified logo can be reduced and repeated in a wallpaper pattern to be used as a backdrop for a booklet cover or an annual report cover.

With simplification, however, goes the risk that you are repeating someone else's design. It is almost impossible sometimes to come up with a design not used before, as NBC, to its embarrassment, discovered when it decided on its *N* logo in 1975. NBC had to settle out of court with the tiny Nebraska Educational Network, which had in use an *N* that was almost exactly the *N* that Lippincott & Margulies invented for NBC.

People who work in corporate design often face greater frustrations than exist in other design jobs, because so much is at stake and so many people are involved in decision making. Officials all along the route to production can change their minds about what may appear to be trivial matters. Each change can result in hours of additional work and revision.

Rail cars leaving for markets.

The Potash Corporation of Saskatchewan, Canada, makes a coloring book of company scenes available to school children. This is one of the 8½ × 11 pages with its heavy-outline art. "Keep your crayons nearby," advises an introductory page. "The Potash Corporation of Sasketchewan is a very busy—and very colorful—part of life in Saskatchewan." The book points out that potash is used mainly in the production of fertilizer.

One-shots

Sometimes a magazine of rather broad appeal gathers enough material on one of its areas of interest to put out a special issue apart from the regular issues. A shelter magazine, for instance, may put out a publication about furniture and distribute it to newsstands as the magazine itself is distributed. This special publication may gather together material that has already appeared in the magazine, or it may present all new material. We call the publication a one-shot, even though it may catch on and become, say, an annual publication.

Designing a one-shot could involve taking the basic design of the magazine and applying it to the special issue; or it could require a brand new design approach appropriate to the subject matter.

Any publisher can bring out a one-shot. A publisher can specialize in producing one-shots. That publisher then acts much as a book publisher would act, but the product takes on the look of a magazine instead of the look of a book.

Direct-mail pieces

The term *one-shot* can be stretched to include direct-mail pieces. Direct-mail pieces are produced by every conceivable kind of company or organization to do a public relations or selling job, and they appear only once; then they are forgotten. Unlike other one-shots they are meant mostly to be given away, not sold. The term *direct-mail* comes from their usual

This seven-fold accordion-folder publicizes Baylor University Medical Center's TelMed service, which allows people in the Dallas area to phone in for free information about medical problems and be plugged into any one of three hundred available tapes. You see here the inside spread of the folder. The opened out phone-with-cord helps unite the panels and give them visual impact.

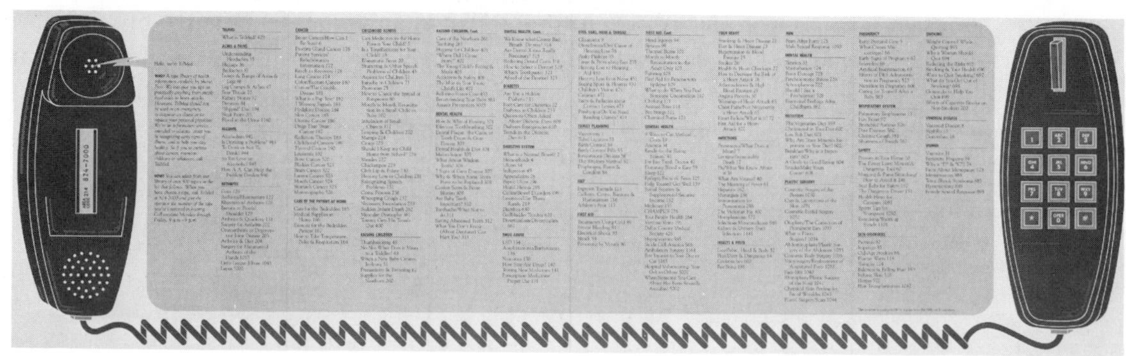

Direct-mail pieces involve a number of different formats and folds.

method of distribution; but many direct-mail pieces are handed out at doors or counters. Another term for these pieces is *direct advertising.* Still another is *direct marketing.*

The sketch above shows some of the most common direct-mail pieces, beginning with the lowly leaflet (a small single sheet, unfolded) and ending with the booklet. Items 2, 3, 4, and 5 show different folds for three-fold (eight-panel) folders. Item 4 is called a "gatefold," item 5 an "accordian fold." The next item is a "French fold," used widely for Christmas cards; printing on one side of the sheet only, you have an image on each of the four panels that show. The next-to-the-last item is a "broadside." It can fold down to folder size.

You don't have to think of the folder as strictly a vertical piece. You can turn it sideways and design the panels as horizontals. The sketch that follows shows a regular two-fold and three-fold folder turned sideways. The third horizontal folder, a two-fold, opens from the side.

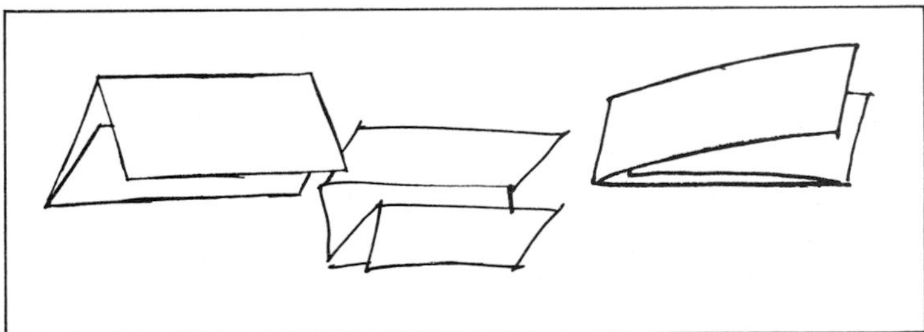

Direct-mail pieces can be designed on the horizontal as well as the vertical. The two outside pieces shown here would be considered a two-fold folder; the one in the middle is a three-fold.

In producing a folder or any direct-mail piece, the designer starts from scratch. Paper stock, format, type for headlines and body copy, even the printing process has to be selected. The designer, in effect, launches a new publication whenever designing and producing a direct-mail piece.

When you think of all the folders you see advertising and promoting products and causes and institutions, all the leaflets you see in packages, all the booklets you pick up at counters, and all the mailings you get urging you to subscribe to magazines, you begin to appreciate how massive a medium this is. In dollars spent on advertising, direct-mail ranks right up there with newspapers and TV. Certainly in dollars expended it is ahead of magazines and radio. Magazines themselves—many of them—could not exist without direct-mail advertising to gain and hold subscribers.

The trend in direct mail, as used by magazine and book publishers, is to overwhelm the potential purchaser with a variety of separate pieces crammed into one large envelope. Lately the full-color broadside has become popular to carry the principal message. The typical mailing consists of the broadside, a letter, a return card and envelope, and an extra letter wondering how on earth you can afford to pass up this bargain. All must be designed to build up to a sale. Sometimes the pieces are unified in design; sometimes the designer purposely produces a hodgepodge to overwhelm the recipient.

The biggest job of a mailing is to get the reader to open the envelope. Writers and designers of direct-mail pieces try all kinds of tricks: manila envelopes with Copperplace Gothic type to look like official government business, envelopes roughly stamped with *Urgent,* real stamps instead of postage meter prints, handwriting instead of typewriting. Sometimes a piece of intriguing art does the job. *Harper's* mailings to potential subscribers have used a question printed on the envelope, without the name of the magazine: "Should you be punished for being born with a high IQ?" Can persons who value their intelligence resist finding out what this is all about?

The advantage of direct mail is that the recipient, theoretically, reads all this material without distraction from other printed material. It is a selective medium in that a direct-mail piece can be designed and sent to a specific class of persons. But most important to the designer, the medium is flexible; it can utilize any printing process, any paper, any format, any design style. And gimmickry is limited only by the designer's lack of ingenuity.

Folders

The folder is probably the most common form of direct mail. A single cut sheet, it can be folded once, twice, three times, or more after printing; and several different kinds of folds can be used, as the previous sketches have shown. What results from the folding are panels; you would have six panels

(Opposite page)
To help employees make the move when it changed its headquarters from Washington, D.C., to nearby Oakton, Virginia, AT&T *Long Lines* produced an "Oakton in a Nutshell" kit that included a handsome full-color forty-eight page 8½ X 11 saddle-stitched booklet. This two-page spread shows the lively but orderly design created by Michael Gibbs. A light touch is provided by the noose (right page) that forms the *O* in *NOT.*

Among the items included in the help-employees-to-move kit was this envelope containing cards to fill out. This illustration shows only a few of them.

Sanders Printing Corporation, New York, as a PR stunt for art directors and other buyers of printing, put out a "Corporate Identity Manual" for the mythical David's Lemonade stand. If you've ever seen a real corporate identity manual—solemnly laying out rules on exactly how symbols, special typefaces, and signs must be used—you will appreciate the satire here. These are only three of twenty-four pages. Note especially the page dealing with "Vehicle Identification."

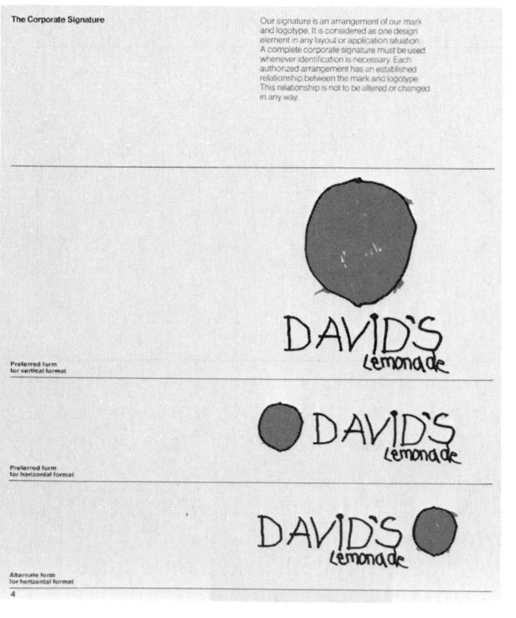
The Corporate Signature

Our signature is an arrangement of our mark and logotype. It is considered as one design element in any layout or application situation. A complete corporate signature must be used whenever identification is necessary. Each authorized arrangement has an established relationship between the mark and logotype. This relationship is not to be altered or changed in any way.

DAVID'S Lemonade

Preferred form for vertical format

DAVID'S Lemonade

Preferred form for horizontal format

DAVID'S Lemonade

Alternate form for horizontal format

4

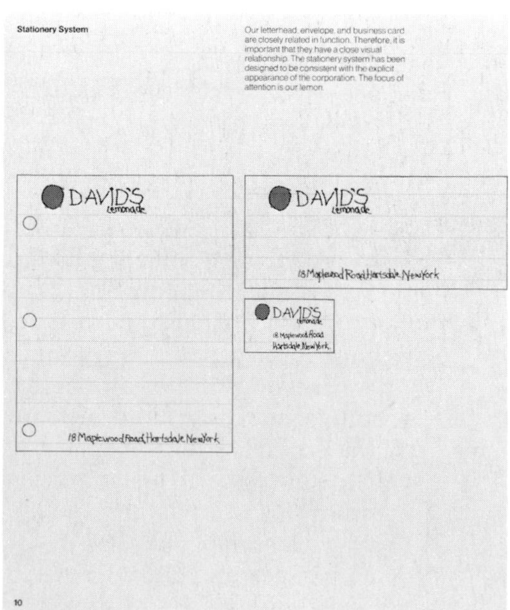
Stationery System

Our letterhead, envelope, and business card are closely related in function. Therefore, it is important that they have a close visual relationship. The stationery system has been designed to be consistent with the explicit appearance of the corporation. The focus of attention is our lemon.

DAVID'S Lemonade
18 Maplewood Road, Hartsdale New York

DAVID'S Lemonade
18 Maplewood Road Hartsdale New York

DAVID'S Lemonade
18 Maplewood Road
Hartsdale New York

10

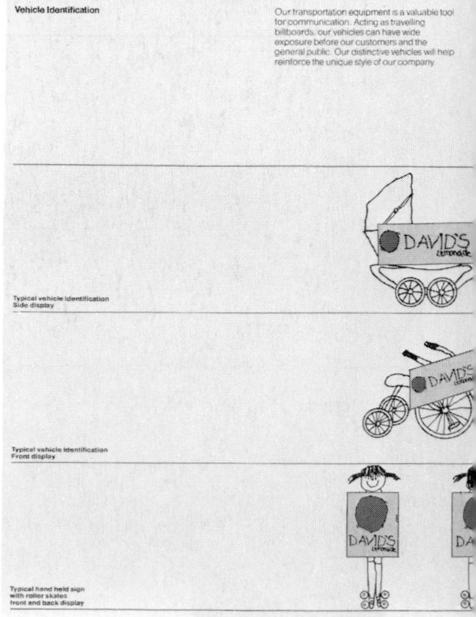
Vehicle Identification

Our transportation equipment is a valuable tool for communication. Acting as travelling billboards, our vehicles can have wide exposure before our customers and the general public. Our distinctive vehicles will help reinforce the unique style of our company.

DAVID'S Lemonade

Typical vehicle identification
Side display

Typical vehicle identification
Front display

DAVID'S

Typical hand held sign
with roller skates
front and back display

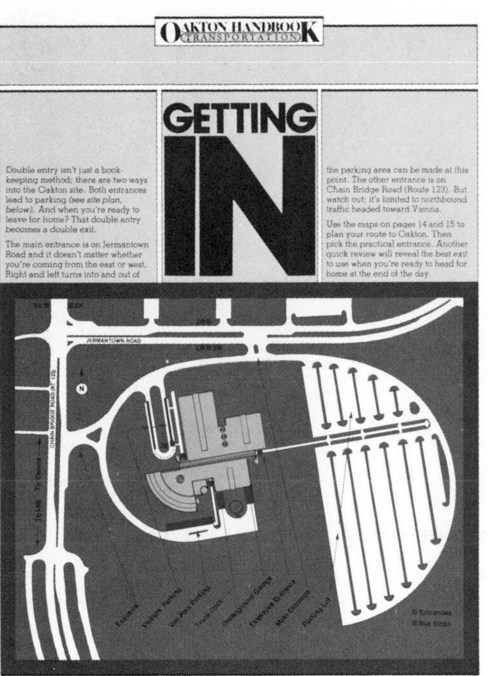

OAKTON HANDBOOK
TRANSPORTATION

GETTING IN

Double entry isn't just a bookkeeping method; there are two ways into the Oakton site. Both entrances lead to parking *(see site plan, below)*. And when you're ready to leave for home? That double entry becomes a double exit.

The main entrance is on Jermantown Road and it doesn't matter whether you're coming from the east or west. Right and left turns into and out of the parking area can be made at this point. The other entrance is on Chain Bridge Road (Route 123). But watch out; it's limited to northbound traffic headed toward Vienna.

Use the maps on pages 14 and 15 to plan your route to Oakton. Then pick the practical entrance. Another quick review will reveal the best exit to use when you're ready to head for home at the end of the day.

4

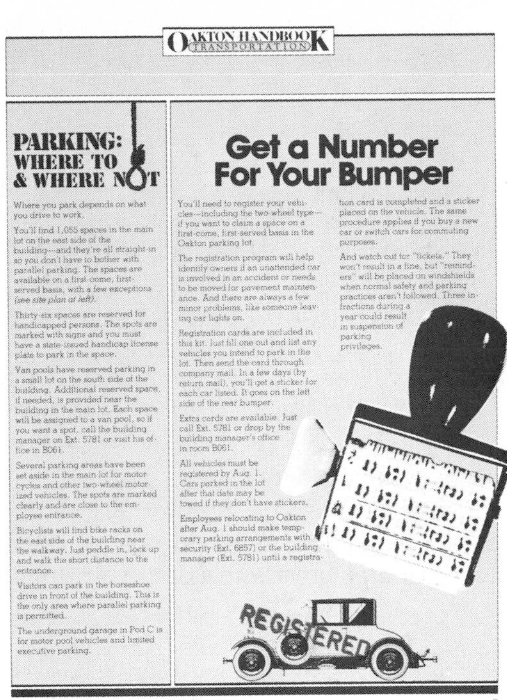

OAKTON HANDBOOK
TRANSPORTATION

PARKING: WHERE TO & WHERE NOT

Where you park depends on what you drive to work.

You'll find 1,055 spaces in the main lot on the east side of the building—and they're all straight-in so you don't have to bother with parallel parking. The spaces are available on a first-come, first-served basis, with a few exceptions *(see site plan at left)*.

Thirty-six spaces are reserved for handicapped persons. The spots are marked with signs and you must have a state-issued handicap license plate to park in the space.

Van pools have reserved parking in a small lot on the south side of the building. Additional reserved space, if needed, is provided near the building in the main lot. Each space will be assigned to a van pool, so if you want a spot, call the building manager on Ext. 5781 or visit his office in B061.

Several parking areas have been set aside in the main lot for motorcycles and other two-wheel motorized vehicles. The spots are marked clearly and are close to the employee entrance.

Bicyclists will find bike racks on the east side of the building near the walkway. Just peddle in, lock up and walk the short distance to the entrance.

Visitors can park in the horseshoe drive in front of the building. This is the only area where parallel parking is permitted.

The underground garage in Pod C is for motor pool vehicles and limited executive parking.

Get a Number For Your Bumper

You'll need to register your vehicles—including the two-wheel type—if you want to claim a space on a first-come, first-served basis in the Oakton parking lot.

The registration program will help identify owners if an unattended car is involved in an accident or needs to be moved for pavement maintenance. And there are always a few minor problems, like someone leaving car lights on.

Registration cards are included in this kit. Just fill one out and list any vehicles you intend to park in the lot. Then send the card through company mail. In a few days (by return mail), you'll get a sticker for each car listed. It goes on the left side of the rear bumper.

Extra cards are available. Just call Ext. 5781 or drop by the building manager's office in room B061.

All vehicles must be registered by Aug. 1. Cars parked in the lot after that date may be towed if they don't have stickers.

Employees relocating to Oakton after Aug. 1 should make temporary parking arrangements with security (Ext. 6857) or the building manager (Ext. 5781) until a registration card is completed and a sticker placed on the vehicle. The same procedure applies if you buy a new car or switch cars for commuting purposes.

And watch out for "tickets." They won't result in a fine, but "reminders" will be placed on windshields when normal safety and parking practices aren't followed. Three infractions during a year could result in suspension of parking privileges.

5

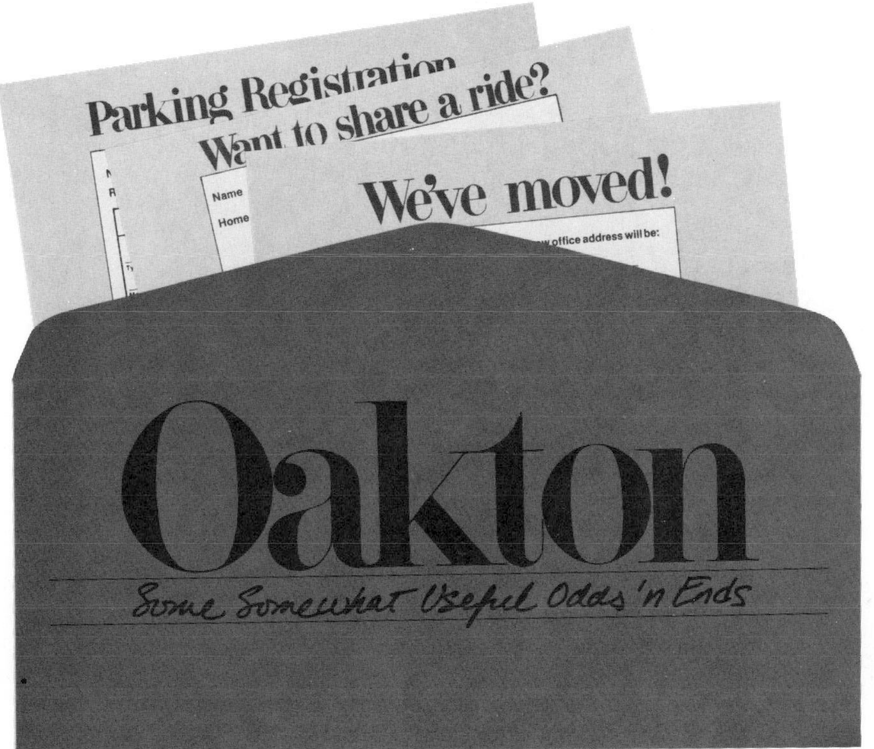

to design in a two-fold folder, three on each side of the sheet. You would have eight panels to design in a three-fold folder. The trick is to design the panels to take advantage of the sequence of the folding.

Some designers try to design folders so that each panel works separately. Other designers try to make spreads out of the panels.

A folder is cheaper to produce than a booklet because no binding costs are involved. But the design of the two involves similar problems.

The Washington Park Zoo, Portland, reversed all type and boxes and used some full-color photographs as rectangles, others as close-up silhouettes in this five-fold (twelve-panel) accordion fold. You see one side of the sheet here, the cover at the far right.

Paper choice makes a big difference to the design. For instance, some papers fold well only with the grain. Size, quality, opacity, bulk, and durability all figure in the paper choice. So do mailing factors, the printing process to be used, and the nature of the contents. An all-type piece may call for an antique (rough surface) stock, for instance, whereas a piece that is mostly photography would call for a slick, coated stock. The size of the piece would be determined by how economically it cuts from the sheets or rolls available to the printer.

Whether the folder is to be a self-mailer or a piece put inside an envelope makes a difference. A self-mailer needs one panel—or part of one panel—left blank.

As a folder designer, you would do your rough layout or comprehensive to size, trimmed and folded as the piece is to appear in print. That way the client can actually hold it, study it for design and color, and get the feel of how it folds before OKing its final printing.

Before choosing a printer, you would want to obtain some estimates of costs. For a big job you would go to two or three printers. Be sure that each printer bases the bid on the same set of specifications and the same rough layout. Price alone should not necessarily determine the successful bidder. A higher bid can turn out to be more of a bargain.

Sometimes the designer presents camera-ready copy to the successful bidder, sometimes just the rough layout. If the printer is expected to furnish the pasteup, the cost is likely to be higher.

The design of direct mail falls usually to the advertising department of the company producing it or to its advertising agency. In almost every city freelancers take on direct-mail designing assignments, too, making from $100 on up per item, depending upon whether or not they furnish camera-ready copy or just a rough. Freelancers can also work for printers.

This 5½ × 4¼ black-on-white folder uses a movie prop and Broadway-like type to invite volunteer workers to an annual American Cancer Society awards dinner in Universal City, California. The motif was used on several other pieces, including identification cards. A number of celebrities were on the program. Mary Jost was the art director, Donna Stamps the designer.

Booklets

A booklet is a bound volume of eight or more pages, often with a page size that fits a No. 10 business envelope. In an 8½ × 11 size a booklet looks like a magazine or an annual report. It is usually saddle stapled. The cover stock often is heavier than the inside pages.

Cover stock comes in a greater range of colors and surfaces than regular book stock. Some of these papers come with one color or surface on one side and a different combination on the other.

Designing a booklet is much like designing a book. You have fewer pages to deal with, and the page size may be different; but your job is to come up with a design that makes them all obviously related.

Seven reasons why it's time to switch health plans.

Sometimes as a designer you'd like to commission art for a direct-mail piece, but you're up against a deadline and you don't have the budget for it anyway. Tom Rubick did this three-fold, eight-panel folder for the Eugene Clinic Health Plan, using numbers in a dramatic way. That was his art. The arrangement has the advantage of being easy for the reader to follow. Two colors and black.

...for 20 years we've been making a world of difference. For 20 years now Peace Corps has been sending Americans to the Third World, building a tradition of people - to-people cooperation. And when you consider how the world has changed in the last two decades, that makes Peace Corps pretty special.

Today, in a single month, more than one million lives are directly affected by Peace Corps volunteers at work in over 60 countries. They treat malnourished children. Bring water to deserts. Plant forests. Help build schools and bridges.

But just as important are the bridges Peace Corps volunteers build between people. By living and working in local communities, they offer people around the world a chance to learn about Americans. And vice versa.

By becoming a member of a neighborhood, village or town, Peace Corps volunteers don't just share their work with the people they live with. They share themselves. That means they return home with a unique knowledge of other peoples and cultures. And their experiences help our nation better understand what's happening in today's world.

It also helps make the hard work, long hours and personal sacrifice worth it. Despite the rigors of Peace Corps life, more than 9 out of 10 volunteers say they'd do it again. Sound remarkable? It is. But, then, so are the people who have become Peace Corps volunteers. Since 1961 more than 80,000 Americans have served—including the 6,000 who serve today.

Twenty years ago Peace Corps was a great idea—a program that could help other nations meet their needs for skills. It was a program to promote better understanding of Americans abroad and greater knowledge of the Third World here at home.

In 1961, these were worthy objectives. But today—in an era of dwindling global resources, scarcer energy, rising international tensions and troubled economies—these Peace Corps goals have grown into prerequisites for a peaceful future.

Twenty years later, we're much more than just a good idea. We're helping to make the world work better.

fected by short-term national foreign policy objectives. Peace Corps is the only U.S. agency that places its people in the communities of developing nations to work and live with the people they're helping.

Volunteers represent the American people. They receive a monthly allowance that enables them to live at the level of their hosts. Often, in fact, they live with a host family. At the end of their service—usually two years—they get a readjustment payment of $125 for each month of service.

Peace Corps is looking for volunteers with practical experience. You don't need a special degree; we'll teach you the specific skills you don't have, or help you discover talents you do have, but don't know about. During your 8-12-week training you'll study the culture of the people with whom you'll be living, and learn to converse in the local language.

What volunteers have in common is motivation. They have a desire to work in a way that suits the local setting, and to understand and be accepted by their hosts. A volunteer might be a mid-career plumber, or a grandmother who has taught three generations of children to read and write, or a recent college graduate with a sociology degree; a printer, a lawyer, a nurse, a farmer, a doctor, a teacher.

In return you get experience—valuable professional and personal experience—and expertise in the Third World, an important asset to almost any career in the 1980s. You get a chance to travel and broaden yourself as you interact with other people, other cultures, other lifestyles. You get as much responsibility as you can handle. You get plenty of independence. You get more challenges than most people face in a lifetime. And you get a unique opportunity to see yourself, your country and the world from a new perspective.

So, then: What does Peace Corps offer? We're ready to offer you the world.

These two spreads from a Peace Corps booklet show how art can be used to cross the gutter to unite two facing pages. It is important to pick art—or crop it—so that nothing important falls at the gutter, where binding occurs.

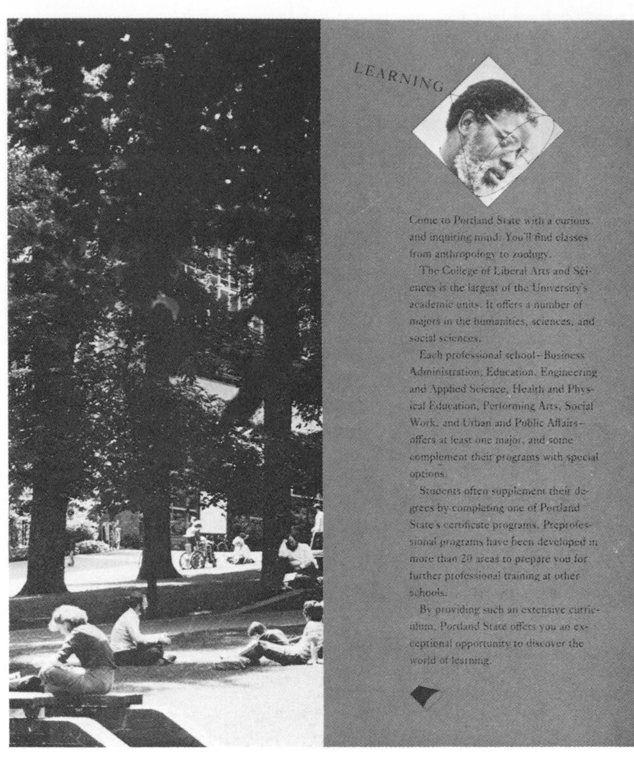

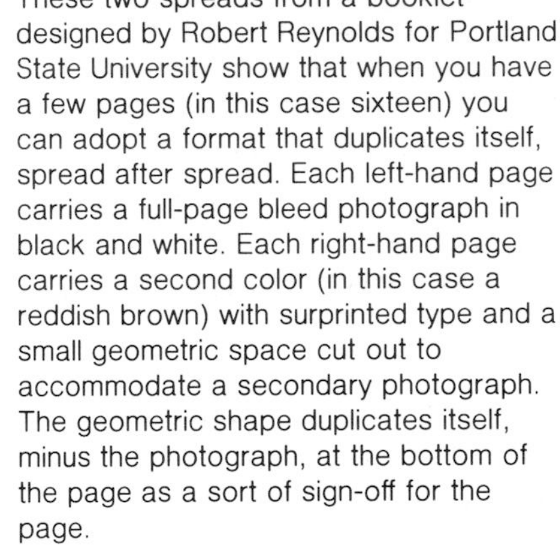
These two spreads from a booklet designed by Robert Reynolds for Portland State University show that when you have a few pages (in this case sixteen) you can adopt a format that duplicates itself, spread after spread. Each left-hand page carries a full-page bleed photograph in black and white. Each right-hand page carries a second color (in this case a reddish brown) with surprinted type and a small geometric space cut out to accommodate a secondary photograph. The geometric shape duplicates itself, minus the photograph, at the bottom of the page as a sort of sign-off for the page.

Two spreads from a full-color 8½ × 11 booklet published by the Toledo, Ohio, Chamber of Commerce show how a grid, used throughout, can bring consistency to a publication. The pattern is always evident, even with slight variations in placement.

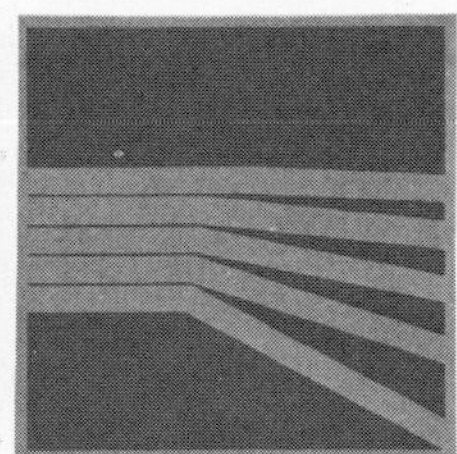

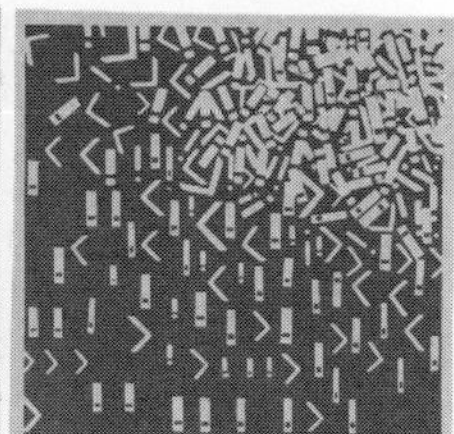

Designer James W. O'Bryan in a booklet promoting *National Review* to advertisers used small, square pieces of abstract art as a kind of chapter heading. The pieces shown here illustrate, left to right, a page saying *NR* readers are "extraordinarily activist," they are "uniquely motivated by the magazine," they travel a lot, they "entertain with zest," and they "consume books voraciously."

Catalogs

It used to be that when we thought of catalogs, we thought only of the massive "wish books" issued by Montgomery Ward, Sears Roebuck, and a few other big stores. But catalogs now come from all kinds of retailers, including those dealing in exotic and expensive merchandise. If you've ever bought anything by mail, you've found yourself swamped for years afterwards will all kinds of catalogs, expecially at Christmastime. Some firm sold your name to a mailing list broker. You became a known buyer.

Some customers or potential customers find it necessary to pay for their catalogs—to pay for being advertised to.

Designing a catalog involves presenting merchandise in the best possible light and in the most favorable setting. Pages are necessarily busy; a theme of some kind often helps to unite them.

College catalogs (or "bulletins," as they are often called) sell courses rather than merchandise, but they have some of the same problems. They may look more like a book than a catalog. The cover is particularly important. To the designers of some school catalogs, cover art boils down to the latest shot of a good-looking student reading a book, sitting under a tree with campus buildings in the background. And if the campus itself does not yield scenery attractive enough to go on the cover, the designer may choose to reproduce a picture of a nearby stream or mountain that students have been known to frequent on slow spring afternoons. Sometimes an in-classroom shot shows up with enough natural light to make good reproduction possible. Or perhaps the designer settles for a montage of faces of happy but serious-minded students, with the expected ratio of men to women and minority to majority students, of course.

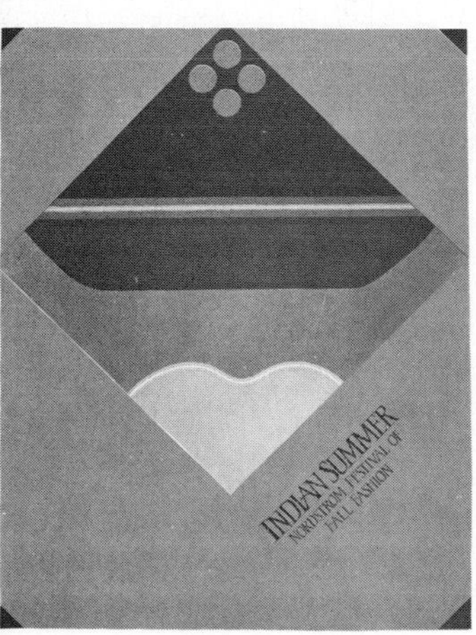

This cover for a Nordstrom "Indian Summer" catalog features a diamond-shaped painting by Neil Parsons, a noted American Indian artist. Designer Claudia Milne used triangular corners to put the art in context. The largely maroon, olive, and gold colors reflect the colors of the merchandise advertised inside. Nordstrom, Inc. is a Seattle-based fashion specialty store.

A spread from the same catalog mortises four photographs inside a two-page bleed photograph. All the rich color photographs in the catalog were taken in Santa Fe, New Mexico.

Another page from the Nordstrom catalog gives a good example of framing people in a photograph.

Lands' End, a Dodgeville, Wisconsin, mail-order house, uses a magazine approach for the cover and first few pages of one of its catalogs. This issue told the story of wool production in the British Isles in words and pictures and then, later in the catalog, showed merchandise that was available at special "exchange rate" prices. Bernie Roer art directed; Archie Lieberman designed.

Another Lands' End catalog uses a panel-less comic strip in the Jules Feiffer tradition to ready the mail-order buyer for inside pages. Note how the son's questions result in the father's abandoning a typical businessman's attire on Friday in favor of a more outdoorsy Lands' End look. Art directors, Sam Fink and Bernie Roer. Illustrator, Tom Yohe.

Calendars

The book publishing industry these days, and the book dealers, rely heavily on calendars to help them turn a profit, especially at the Christmas season. And the proliferating calendars tap every conceivable area of interest. Cat lovers, cooks, feminists, body admirers, humor buffs, word fanciers, philosophers, environmentalists, God-fearing people—all have their calendars. Some are for wall hanging, some for desk placement.

Originally only the specialty houses produced our calendars, but today most major book publishers join in the fun and profit. Even the lofty Alfred A. Knopf publishes calendars.

Georgi Publishers in New York City specializes in wall calendars featuring reproductions of impressionist and other painters. There were 27 of them for 1986, imported from West Germany. Abbeville Press in New York also publishes art calendars, including several showing Norman Rockwell's works.

Abrams, a New York art-book publisher, offered a fortieth anniversary edition of the 1946 *Esquire* Varga Girl calendar.

Workman Publishing in New York is big on calendars, including those fat, square pads that, a day at a time, teach you word definitions, provide trivia, tell your horoscope, give you Bible verses, and share jokes, puns, and riddles.

Bo-Tree Productions, Inc. in Palo Alto, California, is one of the calendar specialists. It has offered, among others, Dong Kingman's World,

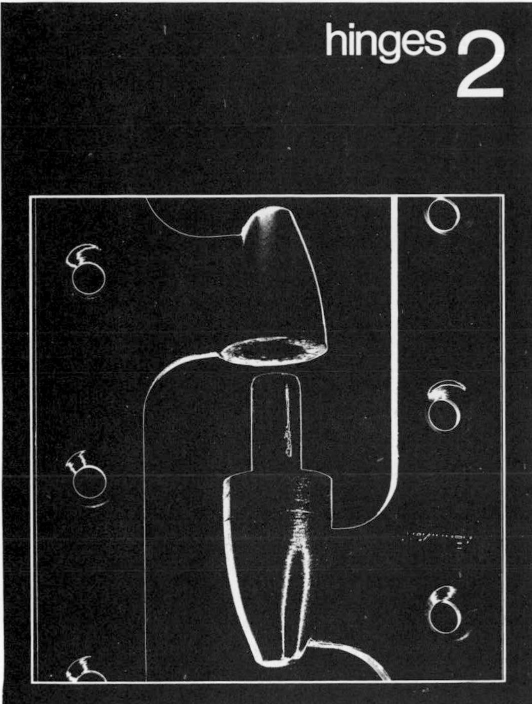

NBH

track systems 17

443

GRANT BY-PASSING PANEL SETS UP TO 30 LBS. PER PANEL

These non-adjustable panel sets are designed for by-passing doors, and are available for different panel thicknesses. When installed they allow a minimum of 1" headroom. To be used with No. 901 track.

Materials: Nylon Rollers, Steel Studs, Die Cast Aluminum Floor Guides, and Electro Zinc Plated Cold Rolled Steel Carrier Housing.

Set No. 914 is designed for 1/4" panels, and consists of 2 each No. 905 Carriers, 2 each No. 910 Carriers, 1 each No. 902 Floor Guide, necessary screws and installation instructions.

Set No. 912 is designed for 1/2" panels, and consists of 2 each No. 905 Carriers, 2 each No. 920 Carriers, 1 each No. 904 Floor Guide, necessary screws and installation instructions.

Set No. 938 is designed for 3/8" panels, and consists of 2 each No. 905 Carriers, 2 each No. 915 Carriers, 1 each No. 903 Floor Guide, necessary screws and installation instructions.

Unlike most hardware catalogs, especially wholesale hardware catalogs, National Builders Hardware Company's 532-page catalog, all black and white except for the cover, displays merchandise quietly, simply, and with an exquisite feel for design. The plan of the pages, with boxed-in art, makes for clarity and ease of ordering. Not only does the designer Charles S. Politz plan placement of the elements, but he also composes the elements in the boxes as though in each case he were creating a painting.

The boxes change size from page to page, but the sink remains the same. On this page Politz moved in close on the product, showing only part of it—but the most important part.

For Those Who Dream of Chocolate, Contemporary Women Artists, The Best Places to Play Golf, and Whales and Friends.

Cahill & Company in Dobbs Ferry, New York, has offered an Alphabets of Grace calendar that covers the history and characteristics of various typefaces. Printed by letterpress on fine stock, it was designed by Stephen Harvard.

Cartoonists have created many of the calendars. Doug Marlette's Preacher calendar (Thomas Nelson, Nashville, Tennessee) featured Rev. Will B. Dunn, who, in one drawing, advises his parishioners not to judge the very rich until they've "walked a mile in their Guccis." Gary Larson, creator of "The Far Side," produces calendars based on his popular cartoon feature. Andrew McMeel & Parker, his publisher, also offers calendars based on "Cathy," "Herman," "Ziggy," "For Better or For Worse," and other syndicated features.

A number of magazines put out calendars for their readers and potential readers. The *Arizona Highways* calendar, of course, shows beautiful full-color scenic photographs of the Southwest. *The New York Review of Books* reproduces David Levine caricatures of literary, artistic, and political figures. *Vermont Life* publishes both a wall and an engagement calendar featuring Vermont scenes. *Yankee* magazine featured selected covers in a calendar celebrating its fiftieth anniversary.

Not all calendars are meant to be sold. Banks and other organizations don't distribute calendars to customers as freely as they used to (they are too expensive to mass produce now), but manufacturers and service organizations still find them worth the expense as promotional tools. Some of the best-designed calendars come from paper manufacturers to advertising and printing people.

But promotional calendars are not always useful. Too often, says designer Byron Ferris, they represent "graphic designers trying to be playful. Designers are supposed to make things easy to read or use." With that in

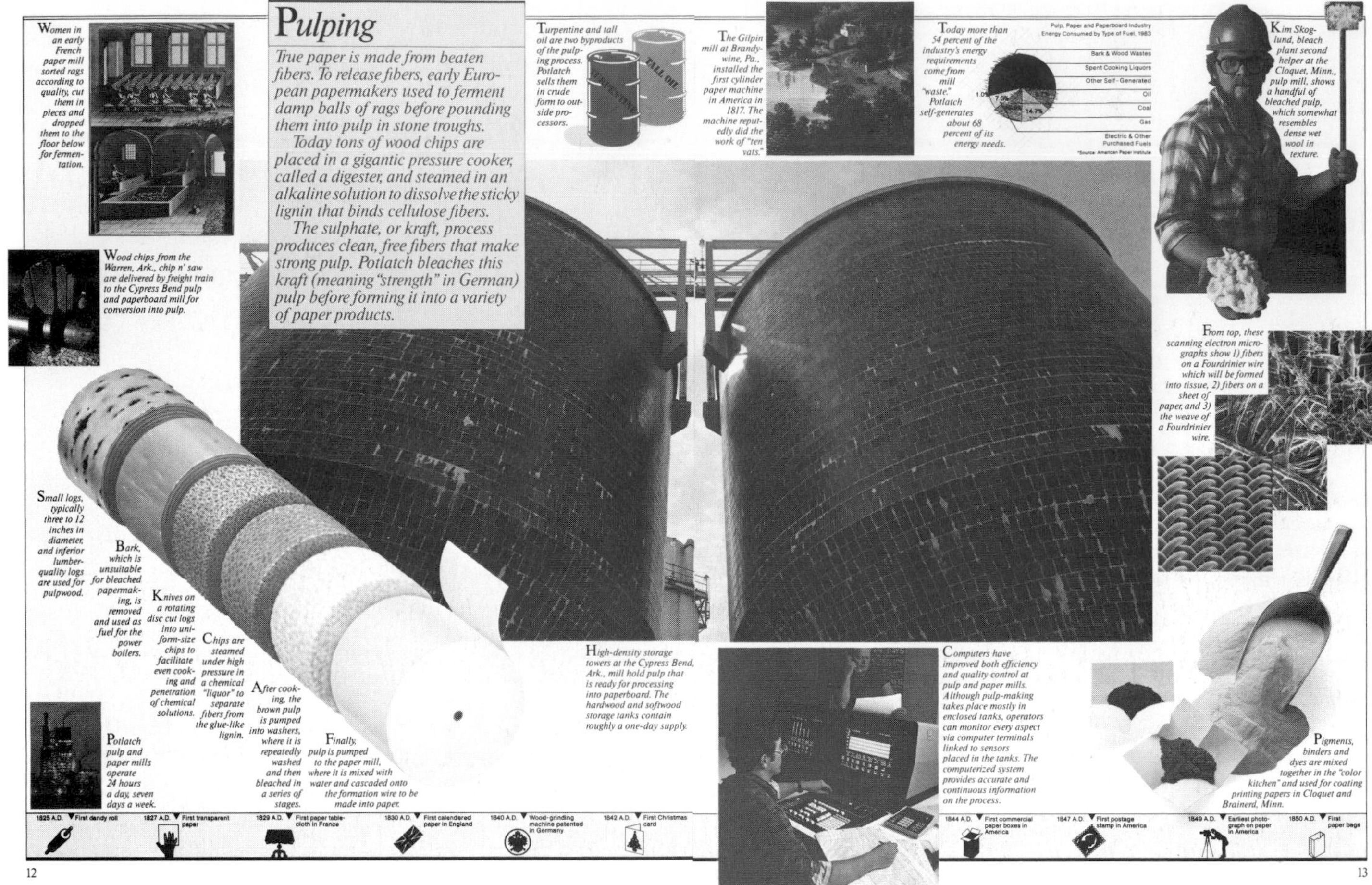

Women in an early French paper mill sorted rags according to quality, cut them in pieces and dropped them to the floor below for fermentation.

Pulping

True paper is made from beaten fibers. To release fibers, early European papermakers used to ferment damp balls of rags before pounding them into pulp in stone troughs.

Today tons of wood chips are placed in a gigantic pressure cooker, called a digester, and steamed in an alkaline solution to dissolve the sticky lignin that binds cellulose fibers.

The sulphate, or kraft, process produces clean, free fibers that make strong pulp. Potlatch bleaches this kraft (meaning "strength" in German) pulp before forming it into a variety of paper products.

Turpentine and tall oil are two byproducts of the pulping process. Potlatch sells them in crude form to outside processors.

The Gilpin mill at Brandywine, Pa., installed the first cylinder paper machine in America in 1817. The machine reputedly did the work of "ten vats."

Today more than 54 percent of the industry's energy requirements come from mill "waste." Potlatch self-generates about 68 percent of its energy needs.

Pulp, Paper and Paperboard Industry Energy Consumed by Type of Fuel, 1983

Bark & Wood Wastes
Spent Cooking Liquors
Other Self-Generated
Oil
Coal
Gas
Electric & Other Purchased Fuels

*Source: American Paper Institute

Kim Skoglund, bleach plant second helper at the Cloquet, Minn., pulp mill, shows a handful of bleached pulp, which somewhat resembles dense wet wool in texture.

Wood chips from the Warren, Ark., chip n' saw are delivered by freight train to the Cypress Bend pulp and paperboard mill for conversion into pulp.

From top, these scanning electron micrographs show 1) fibers on a Fourdrinier wire which will be formed into tissue, 2) fibers on a sheet of paper, and 3) the weave of a Fourdrinier wire.

Small logs, typically three to 12 inches in diameter, and inferior lumber-quality logs are used for pulpwood.

Bark, which is unsuitable for bleached papermaking, is removed and used as fuel for the power boilers.

Knives on a rotating disc cut logs into uniform-size chips to facilitate even cooking and penetration of chemical solutions.

Chips are steamed under high pressure in a chemical "liquor" to separate fibers from the glue-like lignin.

After cooking, the brown pulp is pumped into washers, where it is repeatedly washed and then bleached in a series of stages.

Finally, pulp is pumped to the paper mill, where it is mixed with water and cascaded onto the formation wire to be made into paper.

Potlatch pulp and paper mills operate 24 hours a day, seven days a week.

High-density storage towers at the Cypress Bend, Ark., mill hold pulp that is ready for processing into paperboard. The hardwood and softwood storage tanks contain roughly a one-day supply.

Computers have improved both efficiency and quality control at pulp and paper mills. Although pulp-making takes place mostly in enclosed tanks, operators can monitor every aspect via computer terminals linked to sensors placed in the tanks. The computerized system provides accurate and continuous information on the process.

Pigments, binders and dyes are mixed together in the "color kitchen" and used for coating printing papers in Cloquet and Brainerd, Minn.

1825 A.D. First dandy roll
1827 A.D. First transparent paper
1829 A.D. First paper tablecloth in France
1830 A.D. First calendered paper in England
1840 A.D. Wood-grinding machine patented in Germany
1842 A.D. First Christmas card
1844 A.D. First commercial paper boxes in America
1847 A.D. First postage stamp in America
1849 A.D. Earliest photograph on paper in America
1850 A.D. First paper bags

12

13

Potlatch Corporation's 1984 annual report takes several pages to tell the story of paper. One of the spreads deals with one aspect of papermaking—pulping—and, like other spreads, shows photographs and drawings arranged attractively with informative captions. The type throughout is in italics with upright starting caps. A scale across the bottoms of the pages marks important dates in the history and use of paper. Jonson Pedersen Hinrichs & Shakery, San Francisco, designed the report.

mind, Ferris designed a calendar for Teknifilm, Inc., in Portland, Oregon, to help customers plan the year in two six-month takes. (Teknifilm is the state's largest movie film and video development lab.)

Ferris's calendar was actually a small (3¼ × 7½) booklet with a twelve-page foldout. To keep the size manageable, half the calendar appeared on one side of the foldout, half on the other. Ferris's design solution considered the need of movie production people to span several months in their scheduling. The boxes he provided made room for printed reminders of convention dates and seminars appropriate to the industry.

Art directors seem to like the Graphic 365 calendar, a 45 × 32 unit with metal eyelets; it shows only dates, days, and numbers all set in giant-size close-fitting Helvetica. No illustrations. Universe in New York publishes it.

Annual reports

People read annual reports to find out about companies they have invested in or want to invest in, to check them out as places to work, to see whether they are good credit risks as buyers of services, parts, and supplies.

But research shows that the average reader devotes about five minutes to an annual report, then tosses it aside. That's why so many companies are adding visual excitement to annual reports. One way to do this, advises Delphine Hirasuna, who worked on the impressive annual reports issued by the Potlatch Corporation in San Francisco, is to use photographs

Later pages in Potlatch's annual report go to more of a magazine format, using a rich, warm gray as a background color to display four-color photographs and headings and initial letters in white.

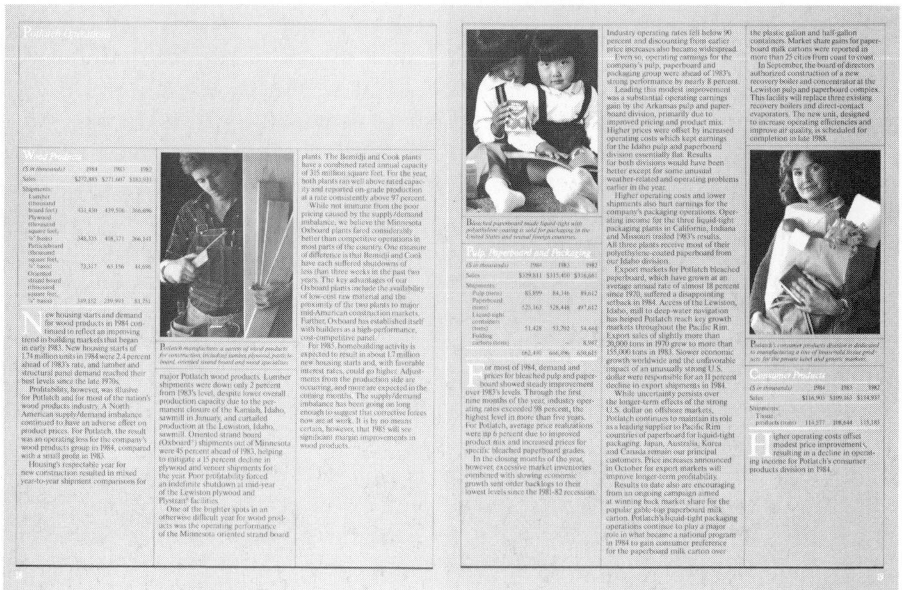

Willamette Industries, Inc., like many big companies, publishes separate annual reports for stockholders and employees. An employee annual report stresses different things and, as this one shows, sometimes makes use of a different format. Designed by Byron Ferris of Design Council, Inc., this annual report is really a huge two-fold, six-page folder. Folded out, the 32 × 17 sheet gives Ferris a chance to arrange an interesting assortment of copy blocks and art pieces, including charts and photographs. Ferris used dark brown on one side of the sheet, olive green on the other.

and illustrations "that are more than graphic elements. Develop a theme . . . that is informative, cliche-free and more than transparent self-promotion."[1]

Potlatch believes in providing information in short takes with fully explained illustrations. Its reports could be said to be encyclopedic. "Many people who read the theme section have told me they were surprised that they learned so much . . . ," Hirasuna reports. But that was because she read as many as twenty books and called dozens of experts to put together

a theme story. "Even great design can't disguise poorly researched copy."[2]

Annual reports rank among the most elaborate of the direct-mail forms. For a big company, copies of an annual report run to $5 or more each. With that kind of investment, design has to be carefully thought out. Annual reports often dazzle readers with quality art and expensive paper.

Annual reports of most corporations must conform to regulations set up by the Securities and Exchange Commission. A designer's first job is to understand current regulations, which change from time to time, and then deal with such matters as what content must be included and what type size must be used.

But even companies not bound by such regulation and nonprofit organizations, too, issue annual reports. Beginning in April of each year, which is about as early as anyone can get all the figures and features together and publish them, these booklets—some pretentious, some rather commonplace—go into the mails or over counters to people interested in what these organizations are doing.

Albany General Hospital in Albany, Oregon, gives citizens of the town an "Annual Review" as a tabloid supplement to the Albany *Democrat Herald*. Like any annual report it carries revenue and expense statements and various statistical information as well as feature material. It is generously illustrated. Saint Joseph Hospital in Joliet, Illinois, gives its annual report an added dimension and additional use by putting it in a spiral binding and making a calendar out of each two-page spread.

Although annual reports for profit-making organizations are designed primarily for stockholders, most of the nation's large manufacturing companies distribute annual-report information to employees, too. From some companies the employees get the same annual report that stockholders get; from others, regular annual reports with special sections inserted; from still others, specially prepared annual reports simplifying all those tables and financial reports. Sometimes the company magazine devotes one issue a year to the annual report.

Few companies or organizations are willing to resort to humor in annual reports—annual reports are serious business—but in recent years the reports have offered readers feature material and informal photography as well as the expected statistics and financial statements. A number of the reports revolve around themes, as yearbooks do. For instance, Time-Life, Inc. designed an annual report to look like a magazine.

The Chase Annual Report 1979

"The banking industry is burdened by anachronistic laws and regulations which are contrary to the national interest and the needs of our customers. What is needed is an environment where competitive equity exists—open, free and fair competition."

"As one of the world's premier banks, Chase's challenge in the 1980s is to continue to improve our financial performance, enhance the quality of our services and speak out for the private enterprise system."

From an Interview with David Rockefeller and Willard C. Butcher

This Chase Manhattan Corporation annual report uses nothing but type on the cover, but the type is tastefully arranged, in two colors plus black, with plenty of white space. A full interview with David Rockefeller and Willard C. Butcher appears inside. Design by Corporate Graphics, Inc., New York.

The Year

industry, leading the pack in both categories of those polled, distributor people and executives.

Fiscal 1979 marked the 25th anniversary of Star-Kist's 9-Lives canned cat food line. As if to celebrate the event, this well-established product tightened its grip upon its position as the number one canned cat food in the U.S. market, and a strong increase in sales gave 9-Lives its highest share ever of the specialty market.

No account of Star-Kist's fortunes would be complete without mention of Morris, the 9-Lives "spokesman" who, in the best show business tradition, rose from humble beginnings as an alley fighter scheduled for execution to become the darling of millions of television viewers. Morris died early in the year. He was 17. Tributes poured in honoring the memory of what was probably the world's best-known cat. Print and broadcast media saluted him, and many 9-Lives customers wrote to say they had come to know their own pets better thanks to Morris. The show-business tradition was carried on as an understudy long in training stepped out of the wings to take center stage. The new Morris, displaying the same finickiness that had made his predecessor so beloved, went to work immediately to promote the 9-Lives brand on television sets across the land.

Star-Kist enlisted the services of another four-legged celebrity—Sylvester the Cat, a cartoon character from Warner Brothers Studio—to advertise its new 9-Lives dry cat food in print and on the screen. After notable success in test markets, this entry into the competitive and fast-growing dry cat food market was launched nationally with encouraging results.

Star-Kist brand tuna also performed well, with unit sales well ahead of the previous year as meat prices rose while prices for tuna remained relatively stable. With the rise in Star-Kist unit sales came a modestly expanded share of the total tuna market.

Ore-Ida Foods marked another year of growth with powerful promotions, extension of existing product lines and a number of new product introductions. Ore-Ida brand finished the year with another all-time high share of the retail frozen potato market, registering 46.3% on the basis of volume and 51.1% on the basis of dollar sales.

Contributing to the year's excellent marketing per-

Cucumbers appealed to the Greeks and Romans of old. Emperor Tiberius, according to Pliny, liked them so much that he had them on his table every day of the year. A later emperor, Charlemagne, ordered them planted on his estates. Whatever Charlemagne ordered, Charlemagne got. /

How you use a cucumber may depend upon where you live. The British slice it paper-thin for sandwiches. The French save the smaller varieties for pickling and call upon an oval type for making perfumes. In Russia, an oval or melon-shaped cucumber goes into the popular soup known as borshch (or borsch, or borscht, or borsht; the Russians, with wonderful economy, spell it борщ). /

The temperature of cucumbers is a subject of some speculation. As early as 1615, Beaumont and Fletcher used the phrase "as cold as cucumbers." In modern parlance, a cucumber is something that the nonchalant are as cool as. But Gulliver, in his travels, visited a flying island named Laputa, ruled by abstract philosophers, and there discovered a man "of a meagre aspect, with sooty hands and face," an early pursuer of alternative energy sources:

"He had been eight years upon a project for extracting sun-beams out of cucumbers, which were to be put into vials hermetically sealed, and let out to warm the air in raw inclement summers. He told me he did not doubt in eight years more he should be able to supply the Governor's gardens with sunshine at a reasonable rate; but he complained that his stock was low, and entreated me to give him something as an encouragement to ingenuity, especially since this had been a very dear season for cucumbers."

Thus was it ever with the underfunded researcher.

10

formance was the new "All Righta" television advertising campaign, which brought awareness of the Ore-Ida brand to what were called "phenomenally high levels." The company invited a noted child psychologist to act as its new spokesman in a public relations campaign to help strengthen the brand's franchise among consumers.

Country Style dinner fries, an extra-thick French fry product, went into national distribution after it proved itself in test markets in 20% of the U.S. Continued success of this 3-pound package reflects growing consumer preference for the economies of larger-sized packaging.

Heinz brand deep fries, a premium French fry product marketed by Ore-Ida, maintained its geographical base while holding on to its share of the national market.

Mrs. Goodcookie, the frozen ready-to-bake cookie product that moved into national distribution a year earlier, made impressive gains during fiscal 1979 and is now emerging as one of the fastest-growing products in its fast-growing category. The chocolate chip variety is now the best seller in the 80% of the country where it is marketed, outperforming all other frozen cake and doughnut products. A new peanut butter variety brought out at midyear had reached number three position in the line by the end of the year.

La Pizzeria, Ore-Ida's premium frozen pizza, continued to fare exceptionally well in expanded Northeastern markets. It now holds a leading position for its category in a number of cities known for the extreme competitiveness of their pizza business.

Sales and Marketing Management magazine gave its "Distinguished Award" to the Ore-Ida marketing group for its skillful marketing of frozen food products.

New to the Heinz family of companies is Foodways National, Inc., whose acquisition was completed early in the fiscal year. At the time, Foodways was licensed to make and market a number of products in the U.S. under the Weight Watchers label, including frozen dinners, portion-controlled entrees, bouillon cubes and sugar substitutes. The Foodways subsidiary now operates as a separate entity within the Ore-Ida frozen food division.

The Hubinger Company remained in a holding pattern as sugar legislation failed to reach passage in the U.S. Congress. In only the second year since it entered the market for high fructose corn syrup (HFCS), it continued to increase its market share. It is now represented wherever this product can be used effectively to replace sugar. Chief markets for the company are soft drinks, the baking industry and processed foods. With demand for HFCS growing at 20% annually, Hubinger is moving rapidly toward full-capacity utilization of a new refinery that went into operation during the year. *(See Facilities.)* Other Hubinger products—corn syrup, starch and corn syrup solids—are being produced and sold on a full-capacity basis.

Heinz took on a new dimension when it followed the acquisition of Foodways with that of Weight Watchers International, Inc. in September of 1978.

Weight Watchers, whose business is based on an appeal to the desire for good health and good appearance, has grown steadily since its founding in May of 1963. This growth has been attributed to an increase in the number of weight-conscious consumers and to the commonsense, practical approach that underlies the Weight Watchers system. Classrooms that bring the system to the consumer are operated through franchises and by the company directly.

Company-owned domestic and foreign classroom operations generated 63% of gross revenues during the year, while franchise operations accounted for 19%. The balance came from sales of Weight Watchers foods, Weight Watchers magazine and various products and services. Classroom membership grew rapidly in the U.S. and overseas, demonstrating the fact that concern with health and appearance is opening up markets on a scale that is now worldwide.

Part of the attractiveness of the Weight Watchers program to the consumer lies in the growing number of appetizing food products that meet the company's nutritional and weight-control standards. Among items launched during the year were instant desserts and a frozen confection similar to ice cream in New Zealand, and 11 items in four new product categories—soft drinks, frozen desserts, margarine and artificial sweetener—for Canadian consumers. Introductions for the United Kingdom market included six frozen meals, while another 17 items in three product categories—canned fruit, soft drinks and ketchup—were readied for launch just after the close of the year.

11

This spread represents a continuation of a long article on "The Year" in an H. J. Heinz Company annual report. All the way through, columns are separated by thin lines, with heavy, broken bars at the top. Each spread is interrupted—and decorated—with an illustrated sidebar using a different type printed in a dark color. Corporate Graphics, Inc. did the designing.

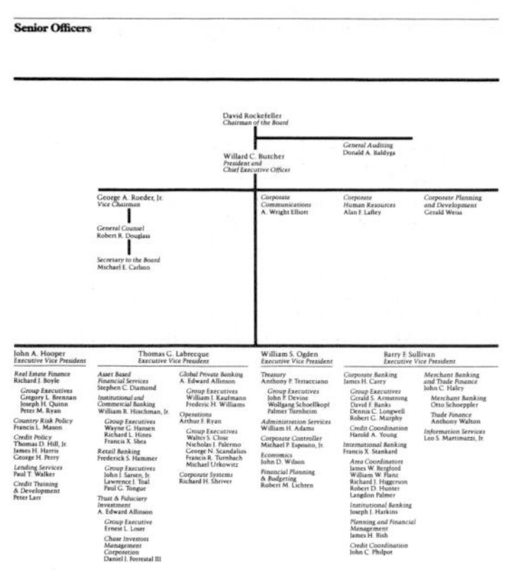

Senior Officers

This organization chart—a full page—from the Chase Manhattan annual report shows that you don't have to resort to boxes and gimmicks to show relationships of officers in an organization. The thick and thin lines here (some of them in an olive second color) pleasantly organize the spaces and help make the chart readable.

Some organizations are getting away from the usual 8½ × 11 saddle-stapled look. Their reports come in oversize or undersize formats or folders. These are fine, provided they can be filed conveniently by the recipient.

The cover can be a decisive factor in drawing the reader into the annual report and even in setting the mood. The theme, if there is one, starts here. Special papers and inks can be chosen that are appropriate to the report and the organization. Often the cover comes from a heavier stock than that used on inside pages. And the cover can come in the form of a gatefold or with an extra tissue-paper or acetate wrapper. Die cuts can also be used.

Nowhere in graphic design is white space more important. White space helps carry the concept of quality, something stockholders and members of an organization can appreciate.

Color is another important consideration. If used, it should be planned from the beginning. Color becomes especially useful in dramatizing charts and graphs.

Several organizations judge annual reports and offer rewards to those that do the best job for their sponsors. *Financial World* magazine has sponsored annual report competitions since 1941, drawing up to one thousand entries each year. Recently *Financial World* began offering a special Best of Design and Typography award.

Company magazines

Previous chapters have already dealt with company magazines, but because they come in so many varieties, some additional attention seems appropriate here. Company magazines are omnipresent, and they appear in every format imaginable. The saddle-stapled 8½ × 11 magazine is standard. Students looking forward to magazine careers no doubt will find that most opportunities lie with company magazines. In most cases the editor does it all: writes, edits, takes photographs, designs, lays out, and even pastes up. The bigger books leave the designing to an outside art director. In some cases the editing and art directing are done by the company's advertising agency.

Few company magazines carry ads. The publications are themselves advertisements—institutional advertisements—for the companies pub-

ITT Rayonier used a series of big-photograph, small-photograph pages for one of its employees' annual reports. The photographs and headings were in black, the boldface, italic, sans serif body copy was in red.

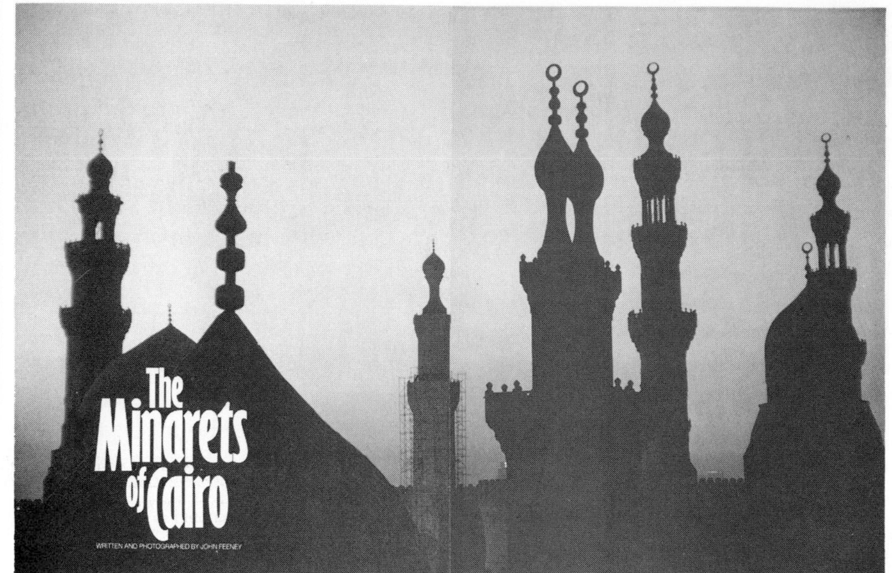

The Minarets of Cairo
WRITTEN AND PHOTOGRAPHED BY JOHN FEENEY

Recent research also shows that after several centuries, the city's medieval masons – there were no architects or town planners in those days – began to take great care in siting a new minaret; by then there were so many minarets that they could no longer be put up haphazardly. Instead, the masons tried to site them in relation to each other so as not to disturb the harmony of the area. Today, as a result, though you often find several minarets on the same street, they never seem to obstruct each other; to the contrary, they seem to come together, providing what seems to be a natural contentment in the eye of the beholder.

Egypt's internationally renowned architect, Hassan Fathy, now well into his 80's but still working, expresses this very feeling when he looks out at Cairo from his terraced rooftop and tells us: "I am surrounded by five mosques, thanks be to God, with their domes and minarets and so I say I am living in a skyscape, not a landscape. These minarets make you think that the very air around you has been given artistic expression and so the environment in which I am living makes me feel very comfortable – both physically and psychologically . . ."

The streets in Hassan Fathy's skyscape, it should be said, are narrow and crooked. But they were purposely laid out this way – to provide shade and to trap the cool night air in what by day is a harsh desert city – and as you walk through them you find your eye constantly drawn upward by yet another soaring minaret. It is this that led Fathy to describe Cairo as "a city of the perpendicular." They seem to act, he said, "as links between earth and heaven, set, as they are, against passing dawns, the circling sun, shadows, moon and stars."

The form of Cairo's minarets has not changed much over the centuries. Invariably, each minaret is made up of three or four levels – patterned, some say, after the various stages or levels of the great lighthouse at Alexandria. The base, or first level, can be either a square or an octagonal tower from which rises a second section, sometimes cylindrical, sometimes octagonal, with an encircling balcony or platform. Then comes the third stage, often a circle of small colonnades with, sometimes, a second gallery for the muezzin. At each stage, the minaret diminishes in girth until it tapers off into a small, ribbed dome, with a small crescent ring at the very tip,

lishing them. In that respect they fall under the heading of direct-mail advertising. Some company magazines communicate mostly with employees; others communicate mostly with customers, potential customers, dealers, and opinion leaders on the outside; some try to serve both internal and external audiences.

Just as general-circulation magazines have grown specialized, so have company magazines. The big companies publish a whole series of magazines, each concentrating on one aspect of the business or addressing itself to one level of employees or customers.

Aramco World Magazine bleeds John Feeney's full-color two-page photo all around to start off his article on "The Minarets of Cairo." (Minarets are high, slender towers attached to Moslem mosques.) Copy doesn't start until the next page.

Photos play an important part on all the article's fourteen pages. The first caption on the right-hand page of this spread covers both the photo at the left and the photo above. Note that the initial letter in the copy block juts up into the paragraph above, a style also seen in *Harper's. Aramco World Magazine,* published by Aramco, a corporation in Washington, D.C., is produced and designed by Scurr, Barnes & Keenan, Ltd.

If you must use a table, give it some design and surround it with a little art. This is from *Paper Times,* a magazine for employees of Boise Cascade Paper Group. The original occupied a full 8½ X 11 page.

Safety Scoreboard

Beginning with this issue, PAPER TIMES will list the continuing safety performances of Boise Cascade's 14 North American pulp and paper mills.

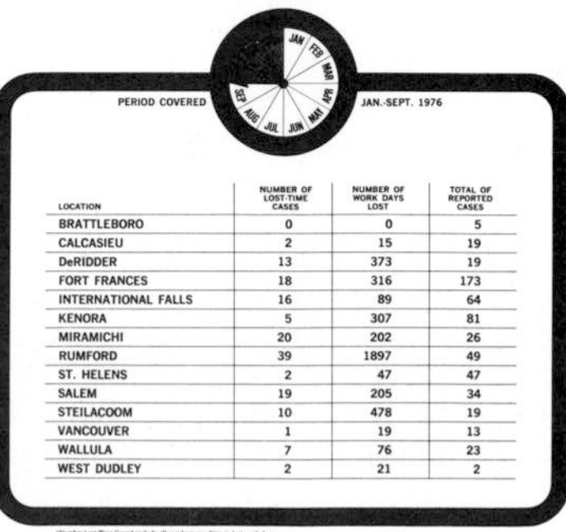

PERIOD COVERED JAN.-SEPT. 1976

LOCATION	NUMBER OF LOST-TIME CASES	NUMBER OF WORK DAYS LOST	TOTAL OF REPORTED CASES
BRATTLEBORO	0	0	5
CALCASIEU	2	15	19
DeRIDDER	13	373	19
FORT FRANCES	18	316	173
INTERNATIONAL FALLS	16	89	64
KENORA	5	307	81
MIRAMICHI	20	202	26
RUMFORD	39	1897	49
ST. HELENS	2	47	47
SALEM	19	205	34
STEILACOOM	10	478	19
VANCOUVER	1	19	13
WALLULA	7	76	23
WEST DUDLEY	2	21	2

ny amendments to the Federal ection Campaign Act that would nange the rules for corporate olitical activity.

In the political area, there are everal paths a small business can ke to become involved.

If the company doesn't want to stablish its own political action ommittee (PAC), it can work rough an already established nd credible group, e.g. the Business-Industry Political Action Com- ittee (BIPAC). A long- stablished group with high marks r electing pro-business candi- ates, BIPAC has established a rogram specifically aimed at nall business. In this program, a ompany's employees are direct- solicited for contributions to PAC. This relieves the company f the problems of establishing its wn PAC, while helping to raise nds for pro-business candidates.

If individuals in the company ould like to make contributions pro-business candidates on an dividual basis, there are pub- cations with information to help. ne **PAC-Manager,** published onthly by the NAM, places mphasis on political races involv- g pro-business candidates. De- gned to help business-associated ACs keep better informed on andidates, it is also an excellent esource for a private individual.

Another resource small usinesses shouldn't miss is state nd local trade associations. Vhile larger companies may hire eir own staff, small companies an benefit from the manpower nd information furnished by the AM and other associations to hich they belong.

It is critical that small companies ive input into the decisionmak- g process of the country. With inimal staff time, a small busi- ess can make its voice heard.■

ARRY BRUTON,
AM Public Affairs

WHERE TO GET FEDERAL DIRECTION

ARE YOU AWARE THAT EVERY FEDERAL AGENCY HAS ESTABLISHED GOALS FOR PARTICIPATION BY SMALL BUSINESS IN FEDERAL PROCUREMENT CONTRACTS OVER $10,000? IF YOU'RE NOT, YOU MAY HAVE MISSED SOME OPPORTUNITIES.

Under amendments to the Small Business Act in 1978, every agency is required to award a given percentage of procurement contracts to small business (exact figures are worked out between the agency and the Small Business Administration). Each agency also must establish an office with procurement powers, named the Office of Small and Disadvantaged Business Utilization. The director of such an office is responsible only to the ranking first or second person in the agency.

Today, these offices do exist and it's their responsibility to look after your interests. This includes making an annual report to the SBA on how well the agency has fulfilled its goals for small business participation in government procurement. The report then goes to both the Senate Select Committee on Small Business and the House Committee on Small Business for perusal and evaluation.

Though originally established just for purposes of procurement, these federal offices often assist small businesses with other actions involving their agencies. That's why we think it's worthwhile for you to know the appropriate person to contact in some of the more important agencies. NAM has put together a list of these contacts for your information. For a copy, write NAM publications coordinator, 1776 F St., N.W., Washington, D.C. 20006. Or phone (202)626-3880.■

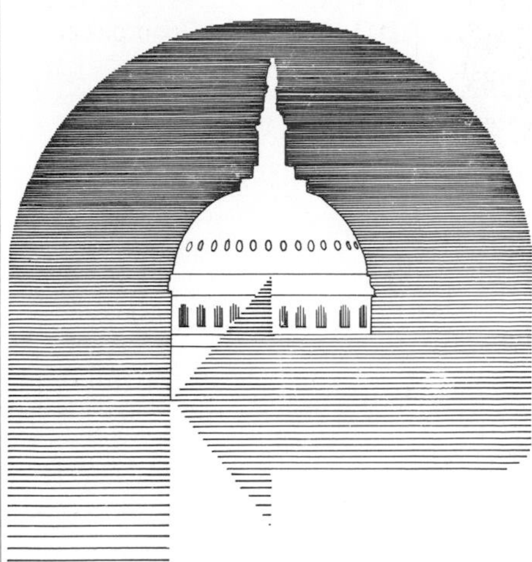

SIZING IT UP

WONDERING WHAT HAPPENED TO THE NEW SIZE STANDARDS DEVELOPED BY THE SMALL BUSINESS ADMINISTRATION? THEY'RE DONE, HAVE BEEN REVISED AND WILL BE READY TO GO PUBLIC, ACCORDING TO THE SBA, AS SOON AS THEY GET THE GO-AHEAD FROM THEIR YET-UNKNOWN ADMINISTRATOR.

SBA first came out with a new set of size standards in March 1980, but they met with strong public criticism. The criticism took the form of complaints such as failing to take into account such factors as the "absolute size" of a firm and the implications of part-time temporary workers. In total, the SBA received more than 1500 comments on the proposed rules.

The comments have been "studied, reviewed and evaluated and are reflected in a considerable amount of changes" in the standards, said Kal Skeirik, chief of the SBA Size Standards Division. Nothing will be finalized, of course, until a new Reagan appointee to the SBA has given approval. Skeirik noted that the administration has already been briefed on the new size standards and the SBA has recommended the proposed changes should not only be implemented but as quickly as possible. The standards "are an important priority in the administration," Skeirik assured NAM.

SBA size standards originated in 1953 with the establishment of the agency. They were designed to determine which businesses were eligible—in other words, which were categorized as "small business"—to participate in SBA assistance programs. Though there were some revisions of the standards in the '60s, it was not a comprehensive review. Everything was generally done on an ad hoc basis up to now, with each industry lobbying for changes to standards in just its area of concern. The only exception was an across-the-board adjustment for inflation in the mid-'70s affecting only those industries, such as retail, on a dollar-basis eligibility. So new standards will presumably be good news to the nearly 800 industries they affect.

Chief among the new changes in the proposed standards is a conversion of all industries to a number-of-employees classification system. Though manufacturing industries have always adhered to this basis, this is new for retail and service industries. They formerly were categorized by income.

The SBA has also decided it would like to use a one-size standard for eligibility purposes in its assistance programs. In the past, each program—procurement, loans, security bonds, or Small Business Investment Co. funds—warranted its own size standard.

The SBA hopes to get the standards through Congress this spring. First, of course, comes a period of public comment and then a round of House and Senate hearings after the agency has finalized its proposals. NAM will continue to keep you up-to-date on the latest progress. ■

Illustration: Kim Johnson

Enterprise

April 1981 15

You see here two pages from an "On the Move" section of *Enterprise,* a monthly publication of the National Association of Manufacturers. The special section, printed in dark green ink on cream colored stock, deals in news and features about small and medium-size businesses. This spread shows the ending of one feature and two additional features with all-cap headlines and blurbs. The type throughout is slab serif, the columns are unjustified, and the bottoms of the columns do not line up. The line drawings by Kim Johnson employ a consistent style for a highly unified look. Dean Gardei was art director.

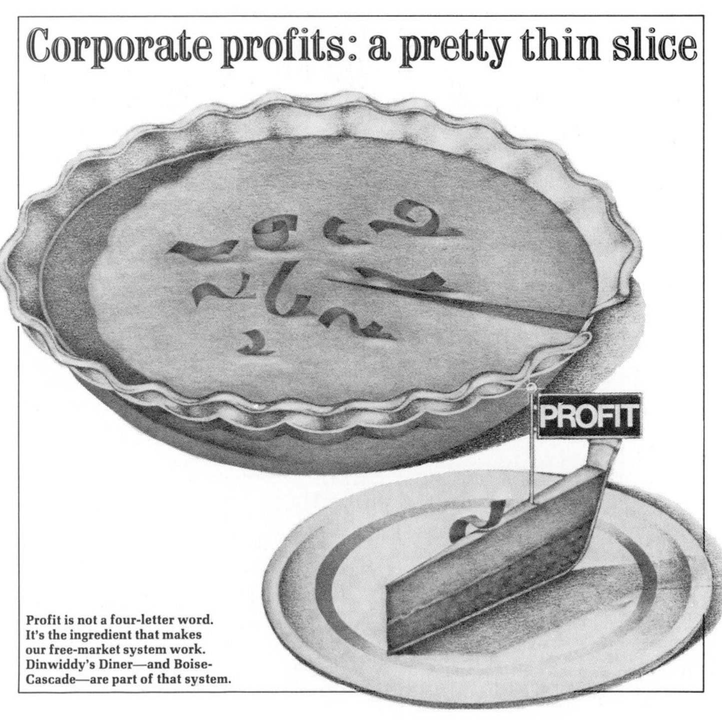

Corporate profits: a pretty thin slice
PROFIT
Profit is not a four-letter word. It's the ingredient that makes our free-market system work. Dinwiddy's Diner—and Boise-Cascade—are part of that system.

In one of its issues, *Paper Times* gave dimension and realism to a pie chart. The chart illustrated an article establishing the fact that "the average American manufacturer earns a net profit of less than *five cents on the sales dollar.* But the man on the street thinks profits are much higher."

An expert's suggestions on...

How to sing your own song

Rev. Bill Little

The Rev. Bill L. Little is a minister, author, counselor, consultant, teacher, graduate student and family man. He counsels professional baseball players, cancer patients, ranking military officers, business executives, housewives, students, his church's parishioners, and listeners to his regular family and marital relations radio program on the number one station in St. Louis.

Bill, as he prefers to be called, puts in his 19-hour days with a pace that would seem to exhaust Bruce Jenner.

What follows are highlights from a recent free-wheeling interview with Bill. As we spoke, his four-inch stack of telephone call slips mounted higher on his desk. As usual, however, Bill kept his cool and his mind on his goal at the moment: sharing some simple but eloquent truths with us in his special way. —*W. G.*

About living...

One of the things that I have learned in the last few years that has been very exciting to me about health is that there is only one valid reason for living.

The only reason for living is because you *want* to.

It's a love for life. There are three reasons people would like to live. One of them is fear of dying, one of them is a sense of obligation to others and the third one is that they just love to live and they want to sing their own song.

If you could look down into your body's immune system and the immune system looks back at you and your body's disease as you start getting sick, it may say, "Why do you want to defeat this?" And you say, "Because I'm afraid to die."

The immune system, in essence, says, "Big deal." So, in fact, fear is stress or stress-producing and retards our body's protection system. So, people who are fighting for their lives because they are afraid to die are really adding to their sickness.

The same thing is true of obligation and responsibility. You look in there and the immune system could say, "Why do you want to live?" And you say, "Because I have obligations and responsibilities." The immune system says, "I'm sorry, I don't feel up to that."

I work with cancer patients a lot. The people who do best in cancer treatment are people who really love to live and just will not quit. They are not living because they are afraid to die. They are not living because they feel they have a responsibility to their family, though some of them say that. But the person who says, "I just like to live"...that person has a better than 50 percent chance of making it longer than the other people because that's a *good* reason to live.

That's the key. That you want so much of life that it frees you from intimidation, and it frees you from the stress that usually goes on around you.

Some people respond very well under a lot of pressure and stress and other people start to make bad decisions, use poor judgement, and become accident-prone under the same amount of stress or less. But one of the things that creates stress is not having joy in what you do.

You are not going to enjoy what you're doing if you don't fit with your job. It's going to be very difficult for you. That in turn generates disease. That makes people sick. It retards the immunization system. The body becomes more susceptible to disease.

About balance...

A healthy self-concept, if you're going to have one, must be balanced with a healthy concept of others. If you're going to spend time dealing with yourself you must balance that by dealing with other people as well. Balance is one of the keys.

You have to balance dependence and independence, balance thinking and acting, balance theorizing and practicality, you have to balance individualizing and socializing. Each person has to find his own balance.

On communicating with family...

By sitting down and talking with your family, it really saves time. You can have a family problem that takes 15 minutes to work out and hassle about it, instead, for 15 hours. Or, if you want to save time, you can sit down and discuss these things once or twice or three times a week with your family. You get input from other family members and you include them in the decision-making process. You include them in planning, you distribute responsibility during that time and then there is no more hassle.

We would save ourselves a lot of time if we would spend just 30 minutes three times a week talking with our families. We would also save a lot of money in terms of divorce and sickness. We might save our families.

I talk to people who say, "I don't have time to spend an hour talking." I say, "How much time do you spend arguing with your wife or husband or your children about what you hadn't worked out with them before?" People may spend 10 minutes six times a day, five days a week doing that. And it adds up to about five to ten hours per week. You can do away with that. If you spend an hour you save nine. It's a good investment.

Even when they are communicating about problems, family members will also be wise to communicate about plans for pleasure outings and other things they can do together as a family...talking about old times and good times they have had in the past. If you only talk with your family when you have problems to work on, the focus of family life becomes a problem. So even in problem solving sessions I recommend that people spend part of that time discussing good things.

I wish I could convince this population to spend an hour twice a week or even once a week just sitting down with family members. I bet the divorce rate would go down by 40-50 percent right away. Just an hour. The average family spends about 15 minutes together seriously talking a week.

How many families do you know that even sit down together at dinner and talk? How many people sit down together without the TV going? How many people even talk to each other in the car, ride in the same car? We've gotten to the place where we are going in different directions from the time we get up in the morning till we come in at night. And we come in at different hours.

On goal-setting...

I happen to be a person who believes very strongly in setting goals. I don't believe that every person has to set them in exactly the same way. Some of us can set long range, general goals and really be motivated and pulled toward that in a sort of ideological way. I operate like that. That means I can live with a lot of ambiguity and confusion right now if I can see the eventual goal.

There are some people who function a lot better if the goal is closer to them. They look to have everything neat and ordered to get to that goal. But everyone functions better if they have some sense of direction and purpose. There are many people who have a gut feeling that short-term goals are important and their goal is to live to live fully *each* day. That's the way I look at things. I say let's plan as if we are going to live forever and live as if we are going to die today.

I have as my purpose to live my life to its fullest and to be as fully me as I can in a way that's consistent with everything else that I believe about God, about human beings, about the world, about relationships.

On Imagining

If you practice imagining a sickness long enough, you can induce real symptoms. One guy I talked about had convinced himself that his normal body temperature was 96.6. Every time he checked out with 98.6 he believed he had a fever of two degrees. He said, my gosh, when his body temperature went up to 101.6. He thought he was near death, burning up with fever, and nearly delirious because he had convinced himself that his normal was 96.6. Now there is a guy who created a symptom for himself.

About acceptance...

How do you feel when other people are doing things for you? There are a lot of us who do not mind at all doing things for other people, but we get as uncomfortable as hell when somebody else is doing something for us. If we are doing that, we're condescending. We have to be in a position of power. Let me hand it down to you, let me give you advice, but don't you give me any.

I think one of the hardest lessons I've had to learn in my whole life was how gracefully to accept advice and things from other people. I can give it and I thought I was doing it gracefully, but I never could give gracefully until I could receive it gracefully.

One of the things I have said on the air frequently is that when someone loves you, they want to give to you and it's alright to accept from someone like that. As a matter of fact, when I love someone I never feel more given to than when they take from me. When they accept they are really expressing love. I have to remember the same thing. It's easier for me to give than it is for me to receive. Receiving helps me keep balance in my life.

Ralston Purina Magazine devoted one issue to a special report "dedicated to personal well-being." This spread of two oversize pages (11 × 15½) deals with "An Expert's Suggestions on How to Sing Your Own Song." Solid blue and red blocks and initial letters help organize the materials into easy, boldface sections.

Association publications

An estimated forty thousand associations exist in this country to promote the interests of industrial, professional, educational, charitable, religious, social, and other groups; and almost all of them are involved in publishing activities. They produce magazines, newsletters, directories, manuals, annual reports, and direct-mail pieces of all descriptions.

Most of the regularly issued publications exist to educate members and keep up the funding of the organizations. Until recently these publications carried material of interest only to persons associated with or sympathetic to the associations. But they are broadening their appeal now and concerning themselves with the world outside.

The magazines issued by associations look like any other magazines, except they usually try harder to keep costs down. Many association magazines accept advertising. In that respect they differ from company magazines.

Some of the most impressive magazines now come from associations.

Man cannot live by bread alone...or carrots, peanut butter or even ice cream. Although a balanced diet is vital to good health, other factors are important, too, such as heredity, lifestyle, personality, mental attitude and environment. But good eating habits can improve your overall well-being.

Since the 1940's the United States has been trying to create a national nutrition policy. Yet after 40 years scientists are still investigating some areas.

Following are some basic recommendations which have been compiled from several sets of nutrition guidelines issued since 1980.

EAT RIGHT

Eat a variety of foods

About 40 different nutrients are needed for good health. These include vitamins and minerals, amino acids, essential fatty acids and sources of energy.

Although most foods contain more than one nutrient, no single food item contains all the essential nutrients in the amounts that you need. Therefore, you should eat a variety of foods to assure an adequate diet.

Maintain ideal weight

Obesity is linked with high blood pressure, increased levels of fats and cholesterol in the blood and diabetes. These disorders are believed to be associated with increased risks of heart attacks and strokes.

It's hard to say why some people can eat more than others and still keep within their normal weight. But one thing is certain: to lose unwanted pounds you must burn more calories than you consume.

This means you should eat less, exercise more or both. One way to eat less is to change your approach to eating. Instead of gobbling and gulping, eat slowly, chewing each mouthful thoroughly. Keep your mouth empty after each bite to talk, think or just to take your time.

If you need to lose weight, do so gradually. A steady loss of one to two pounds a week is relatively safe and more likely to be maintained. It takes time to change your eating and exercise habits. Crash diets can be dangerous and usually fail in the long run.

Since a pound of body fat contains 3,500 calories, it is possible to lose one pound a week if you decrease your daily intake to 500 calories less than you require or increase activity to burn an additional 500 calories. Do not cut your food intake so low that it is impossible to get the nutrients you need.

Avoid too much fat, saturated fat and cholesterol

Much controversy surrounds this guideline. One guideline recommends that all persons reduce their intake of total fat, cholesterol and saturated fat. But other researchers suggest that only those people with major risk factors (such as diabetes or elevated blood pressure) monitor their intake. These scientists feel that there is no evidence strong enough to recommend that these restrictions be followed by all healthy adults.

To control your consumption of fat, saturated fat and cholesterol:

- Choose lean meat, fish, poultry, beans and peas for protein.
- Moderate your use of eggs and organ meats (such as liver).
- Limit intake of butter, cream, shortening, coconut oil and foods made from these products.
- Trim excess fats off meats.
- Broil, bake or boil rather than fry.
- Read labels carefully to determine amount and types of fat in foods.

Carbohydrates and fats are the major souces of energy in U.S. diets. So if you cut back on fats you should increase your carbohydrates to supply enough energy for your body's needs.

Carbohydrates contain less than half the number of calories per ounce than fats. Although simple carbohydrates such as sugars provide calories for energy, they have few nutrients. Therefore, it is better to eat complex carbohydrates. These include beans, peas, nuts, seeds, fruits and vegetables, whole grain breads and cereals.

Increasing consumption of certain carbohydrates also can increase fiber in the diet. This tends to reduce symptoms of chronic constipation and irritable bowel.

Avoid too much sugar

Here again, researchers disagree. Many feel that most people do not need to reduce their sugar intake. The major health hazard from eating too much sugar is tooth decay. This risk of cavities is not just a matter of how much sugar you eat, but how often you eat it.

The risk increases if you eat sweets between meals and if you eat foods that stick to your teeth. Cutting down on sugar means eating less of all kinds, including white sugar, brown sugar, raw sugar, honey and syrups.

Avoid too much sodium

Although sodium is commonly associated with salt, it can be found in many other sources. Sodium is present in many foods and drinks such as condiments, sauces, pickled foods, sandwich meats and soft drinks. Baking soda, baking powder, monosodium glutamate and some medications contain sodium.

People with high blood pressure should be especially aware of the amount of sodium in their diets. About 17 percent of American adults have high blood pressure.

Americans tend to eat more sodium than they need but by using less table salt and eating sparingly of food with large amounts of sodium, they can reduce their intake.

Limit alcohol

Alcoholic beverages tend to be high in calories and low in nutrients. This makes it hard for people to drink a lot and lose or just maintain their weight and still get the nutrients they need.

Heavy drinkers may lose their appetite for certain foods with essential nutrients. Vitamin and mineral deficiencies, therefore, occur commonly in heavy drinkers. They also occur because alcohol alters the absorption and use of some essential nutrients.

Mushroom Chicken Bouillon

Light on the waistline

4 cups water
4 chicken bouillon cubes
½ teaspoon onion powder
Dash white pepper
½ pound COUNTRY STAND Fresh Mushrooms, cleaned and sliced
2 teaspoons chopped celery leaves

In large saucepan heat water, bouillon, onion powder and pepper until bouillon cubes dissolve. Stir in mushrooms and celery leaves. Heat to boiling. Reduce heat. Cover and simmer about 10 minutes or until mushrooms are tender.

Makes 4-5 servings. (18 calories per cup)

Greek Tuna Salad

1½ quarts torn salad greens washed and drained
2 cucumbers, peeled and sliced
6 green onions, thinly sliced
Salt and pepper
½ cup olive oil
3 tablespoons lemon juice
13 ounces CHICKEN OF THE SEA solid white (albacore) tuna, drained
8 radishes, cleaned
3 tomatoes, quartered
16 pitted ripe olives
½ pound feta cheese, crumbled

In a salad bowl, combine greens, cucumbers and onions. Season to taste with salt and pepper. Combine oil and lemon juice; pour on just enough to coat greens. Break up tuna slightly. Arrange it, along with remaining ingredients, over top of salad. Toss just before serving

Makes 6-8 servings.

The "Eat Right" spread from the same issue, with bold splashes of red and blue artwork and with copy wrapping around some of the art, ends with some healthful recipes. Note that the title is buried partway down on the page. It is bold enough to take such treatment.

"In field after field, the association magazine is out-pacing the commercial magazine," declares John Rogers, president of the Society of National Association Publications and editor of *Decorating Retailer.*[3]

Communication World, a prize-winning association magazine with a circulation of twelve thousand, operates with a staff of three. Gloria Gordon, managing editor, acts as art director, working closely with the pasteup artist, Heidi Sparks. Gordon has a production background and uses the help of a grid set up by a consulting art director.

Type is set in-house and sent via a modem to a typesetter in San Francisco, where the magazine's headquarters are located. The number of pages for this slick-paper monthly varies from forty-eight to seventy-two, depending on the number of ads that come in. Gordon likes a bigger book

Volcanic eruptions

Arctic soot

Nuclear winter

An article on "Climate Change" goes on for four pages before the reader comes to this spread; and the article goes on for two more pages. Each spread shows at least one photograph and carries both a heavy line across the top to unite the pages and thin lines to separate columns. The scattered abstract spot drawings, in light brown ink, act as initial letters to bring visual relief to long columns of copy. The subheads next to the drawings are in light brown, too. Linda James art directed. The publication is *The Quarterly,* published by Lawrence Livermore National Laboratory, Livermore, California.

because it gives her and the editor, Cliff McGoon, a chance to run more articles. "After laying out all the columns and departments, we have room for only three articles in a 48-page issue," she reports. "You need more articles than that if you want to guarantee yourself that you'll have at least one article that will interest every reader."[4]

Newsletters

Don't sell short the lowly all-typed newsletter. It has a no-nonsense look that sets it apart from the deluge of slick-looking magazines, folders, and brochures that executives have to wade through. It not only looks inexpensive to produce, suggesting that the company publishing it isn't wasting money; it *is* inexpensive to produce.

Often it carries a preprinted logo in color, but everything else is typewriter-produced copy (or something close to it), unjustified, with all-caps headings.

Dun and Bradstreet Corporation publishes such a letter in addition to its slicker publications. Called "Management Letter," it goes out monthly to all its managers around the world. Its pages are stapled at the upper right corner, and there are enough pages that there is a short table of contents at the top of the first page.

Large organizations as well as small offices—like those run by doctors, dentists, and lawyers—put out newsletters. Schools and churches put them out, too. So do politicians. In one of his newsletters, Senator Daniel Patrick Moynihan of New York used the line "I would . . . welcome comment about this adventure into newslettering." Professor James Q. Wilson of Harvard was displeased with the use of *newsletter* as a verb. "If my good friend, the Senator, continues to newsletter me, I shall ask my post office to deadletter him."[5]

Some newsletters do a public relations job for their publishers, or they propagandize; they go out without cost to readers. Some make money. Some cost subscribers several hundred dollars for yearly subscriptions; they carry inside information not available elsewhere.

Professor Albert Walker of Northern Illinois University calls newsletters "the number one print medium among business communicators." He estimates that fifty thousand companies and organizations issue newsletters. "Readership surveys reveal that subscribers to newspapers and magazines are scanners and skimmers. In fact, one survey revealed that many subscribers to magazines may not get around to reading some issues of the magazine they pay for. On the other hand, subscribers to newsletters are likely to read every issue from cover-to-cover."[6]

There is a close tie between newsletters and magazines. Although most newsletters have a typed-letter look, some become so polished they would qualify as magazines if they had enough pages and the right kind of binding. Some newsletters grow into full magazines. *Fine Print,* the magazine covering fine typography and printing and quality book production, started as an eight-page newsletter. *American Indian Professional,* a quarterly newsletter, went to a magazine format in 1986, at the same time changing its name to *Winds of Change.*

Some newsstand magazines offer advice or carry last-minute news items on pages that look like newsletter pages. Some company magazines find that births, deaths, advancements, retirements, bowling scores, etc., don't fit a magazine format and establish separate newsletters to carry such items.

SAN FRANCISCO
CHAMBER OF COMMERCE NEWS

JULY 15, 1985 VOL. 1, NO. 7

CHAMBER ANNUAL DINNER HONORS "THE CITY IN CINEMA"

San Francisco's frequent appearance in celebrated films, along with the importance of the film industry to this city, will be recognized at the Chamber's Annual Dinner, "The City In Cinema," on Sept. 11 at the Palace of Fine Arts.

Memorable moments from films such as "San Francisco," "The Maltese Falcon," "A View To A Kill," and "The Towering Inferno" will be included in the premiere showing of a film made for this event which will be shown at the Capital Theatre in the Palace of Fine Arts. The show was created by noted local television producer Ziggy Stone and features an original score performed by a live 23-piece orchestra. A major motion picture celebrity will be host and narrator for the evening.

The featured films, all made in San Francisco over the past 70 years, show San Francisco's special visual and scenic attractions. Besides helping the local tourist industry by capturing the city's beauty on celluloid, these film and production companies spend an estimated $75 million annually while working in San Francisco.

Tickets to the Chamber's Annual Dinner, limited to the first 500 paid reservations, are $100 per person and include a cocktail reception at the Exploratorium, formal dinner, screening of "The City In Cinema," and a post-film party. Five hundred additional tickets also are available for $50 each and include a light buffet and all other events. Patron-sponsor tickets are available for $2,000. These entitle purchasers to a table of 10 at the dinner and prominent mention on invitations, programs, and promotional materials.

Invitations to "The City In Cinema" will be mailed to all Chamber members early next month. Further information about this event is available from Chamber Special Projects Manager Jerry Armosino.

49ers Head Coach and President Bill Walsh   Dwight Clark

KICKOFF LUNCHEON PLANNED FOR 49ERS

"A Salute to the San Francisco 49ers," the Chamber's annual luncheon honoring the Super Bowl XIX champions, is planned for Aug. 29 at the Westin St. Francis.

49ers President and Head Coach Bill Walsh and team members, including Dwight Clark and Joe Montana, will attend the event. It will be a unique opportunity to meet the players and learn more about the team and the forthcoming season.

Also featured will be presentation of the 1984 Len Eshmont Award, the team's most prestigious annual honor, to linebacker Keena Turner. Presenting the award will be 1983 recipient Bill Ring. Before the noon luncheon in the St. Francis' Grand Ballroom, no-host cocktails will be served beginning at 11 a.m. in the Italian Room. The 49ers highlight film, an exciting review of the 1984 season, will be shown at 11 a.m. and again at 11:25 a.m. in the California East and West Room.

Luncheon tickets are $50 per person or $500 for a table of 10 (this can include nine guests and one 49er or 10 guests). Reservations should be made by completing the newsletter coupon and mailing it with a check to the Chamber's Accounting Department.

SCHEDULE FOR NEW COUNCILS SET

New Chamber councils, organized to represent most Chamber departments and give members the opportunity to express opinions about city and business issues, will be launched with the Oct. 4 meeting of the Government Affairs Council.

Other councils and scheduled meeting months for 1985-86 are: Planning, November; Small Business, January; Special Projects, February; Sports, March; Economic Development, April; Arts and Culture, May; Small Business, June; and International, August.

Chamber members can join as many as four of the councils. If you are interested in joining, complete the reservation coupon on page three and return it to the Chamber's Accounting Department.

ARTS COMMISSION HONORS CHAMBER FOR BVA PROGRAM

A San Francisco Arts Commission Award of Honor was presented this week to the San Francisco Chamber of Commerce for its Business Volunteers for the Arts program. The commission said BVA has established "new and exciting frontiers" for the arts and their interaction with the business community.

At the 13th annual awards program, Arts Commission President Roselyne Swig presented the Chamber's award to BVA Director Nancy Meier. It marked the first time the commission has presented the honor award to an organization.

BVA is a project of the Chamber's Arts and Culture Committee. During 1984, 89 BVA volunteers assisted 66 nonprofit arts organizations in San Francisco. Groups receiving assistance ranged from those with annual budgets as small as $5,000 to those with budgets of more than $1 million.

LUNCHEON FORUM TO FEATURE ECONOMIST HOADLEY

Noted economist Walter Hoadley will be the featured speaker at a Chamber luncheon forum planned for July 22 at noon in the Chamber boardroom. Hoadley, a Hoover Institute Senior Research Fellow and former chief economist for Bank of America, will comment on the general and specific directions of the economy. Hoadley also is known for his regular economic forecasts on KPIX, Channel 5.

Reservations for attendance at the forum should be made by calling Renee Lorda at the Chamber. There is no charge, and those attending may bring brown bag lunches.

SAN FRANCISCO
CHAMBER OF COMMERCE NEWS

APRIL 15, 1985 VOL. 1, NO. 4

This light-hearted photo is from "Creative Partnerships," one of the new NEA sponsored publications. Photo courtesy the San Francisco Symphony and the Black and White Ball.

NEW PUBLICATIONS HIGHLIGHT BAY AREA ARTS SCENE

The richness and diversity of arts activities in the Bay Area is underscored by two new publications produced through a cooperative effort of local businesses, the National Endowment for the Arts (NEA), and the Chamber's Arts and Culture Council.

The NEA selected the Bay Area as one of four regions in the nation for this special promotional effort. The new publications, presented recently at the Chamber's Business/Arts Awards Luncheon *(see page 2)* by NEA Chairman Francis S.M. Hodsoll, include a tourist guide to the arts. More than 200 arts groups in six Bay Area counties are listed, including those associated with music, dance, sculpture, film, and theater. This brochure will be sent across the United States and overseas to promote the Bay Area and its exemplary arts community.

The second publication, entitled "Creative Partnerships," is a magazine-style booklet presenting 37 case studies of exemplary support of the arts by business and the community. Both publications were supported by the Chamber through local coordination, fiscal management, and other services. A committee of business leaders, headed by McKesson CEO Neil Harlan, provided general guidance and policy.

Each publication is available in limited numbers at the Information Desk of the Chamber. Copies of the tourist guide also are available at the San Francisco Convention and Visitors Bureau. Call Nancy Meier at the Chamber for more information.

WASHINGTON FOCUSES ON U.S. BUDGET DEFICIT

The record U.S. budget deficit, now estimated at $200 billion, is currently the chief concern of the nation's leaders. This was the message received by the Chamber's recent 32-member Washington, D.C., delegation during meetings with leading officials and politicians.

The staggering budget deficit is "the theme that's going through Washington," according to Arthur V. Toupin, Bank of America's vice chairman of the board and leader of the Chamber delegation. Meetings were held with Federal Reserve Bank Chairman Paul Volcker, World Bank President A.W. Clausen, and others influential in national fiscal and monetary areas.

In addition to the budget deficit, the country's large trade deficit is another major problem leaders discussed with the Chamber group, according to Toupin. "Everyone agreed these are serious matters that need immediate attention," he said. However, 'there are very severe doubts Congress will have the political will to deal with the budget deficit in a significant way," Toupin added.

During a meeting with Secretary of the Navy John Lehman, Toupin reported there was no indication whether the Navy is favoring San Francisco or Honolulu for the homeporting of the battleship USS Missouri and its accompanying ships. A decision will be made in early July, it has been announced. Lehman did say community reaction to the presence of such a flotilla is a major factor in the forthcoming decision.

Other meetings and receptions attended by the Chamber delegation included those with Sen. Pete Wilson, Congressman Ed Zschau, Congresswoman Sala Burton, and officials at the Soviet, Egyptian, and Chinese embassies.

WORLD TRADE WEEK LUNCHEON SLATED — MAY 20

World Trade Week will be honored by the Chamber and its World Trade Association with a luncheon on May 20 featuring Bechtel Group Inc. Chairman Stephen D. Bechtel Jr. as the keynote speaker.

The third week of May has been proclaimed World Trade Week by President Ronald Reagan. The 12:15 p.m. Chamber luncheon at the Westin St. Francis Hotel will be preceded by an 11:45 a.m. hosted cocktail reception. Cost of the event is $50 for Chamber members and $55 for nonmembers. To reserve a seat, complete the newsletter coupon and return it with a check to the Chamber's Accounting Dept.

Stephen D. Bechtel Jr.

URGENT NEED FOR LETTERS SUPPORTING THE USS MISSOURI

All Chamber members are urged to take the time *now* to write a letter to Secretary of the Navy John Lehman in support of homeporting the USS Missouri in San Francisco. We were told this week that such will make a strong impression that may well win this city the 10-ship battle group.

San Francisco and Honolulu are now the two municipal contenders for the Missouri, which the Chamber estimated will create 2,500 blue-collar jobs and directly add $1.2-million annually to City revenues. Chamber Executive John H. Jacobs says this is perhaps the last opportunity San Francisco has to boost blue-collar employment. An estimated $125 million yearly payroll from the Missouri group would give the Bay Area economy a $750-million annual infusion in multiplier effect dollars, according to Chamber Economic Development Manager Bob Hayden.

Writing a personal letter in support of the Missouri homeporting here is the strongest and most effective statement that can be made, said Rear Admiral Dudley Carlson. Letters should be sent to Secretary of the Navy John Lehman, The Pentagon, Washington, D.C. 20350.

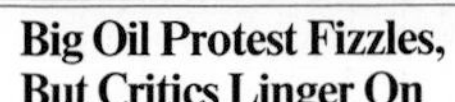

Big Oil Protest Fizzles, But Critics Linger On

Logic Lacking In Synfuel Stampede

'Wisdom' from the 'Journal'

Scrap the 'Windfall Profits' Tax

Critics Seek Change in the Economic System

How You Can Respond

Quote

The inside two pages of the four-page oversize newsletter *Re-cap,* a Mobil Corporation publication, use boxes and bars and a deep sink to nicely organize a variety of features. Only one headline face is used. Body copy is unjustified. The two line drawings add visual interest to the spread.

Newsletters come in a variety of formats, ranging from loose sheets to folded and even bound sheets. The binding can take the form of a single staple in one corner or the saddle stapling used by magazines. The distinction between newsletters and magazines, especially when you get up to eight pages, becomes blurred.

One of the most popular formats for newsletters now is the twofold folder with a total of six 8½ × 11 pages (three on each side of an 11 × 25½ sheet). The format allows the reader to turn back an illustrated cover to reveal three facing pages of important information. Then there are two more pages on the back. The newsletter becomes a sort of unbound magazine.

(Opposite page)
The issue-by-issue first-page variations in the four-page oversize newsletter published on quality, tinted, textured paper by the San Francisco Chamber of Commerce allow for a consistency in sink, typography, and use of thin lines for vertical rules and thick lines or bars for horizontal rules below the nameplate. The nameplate nicely incorporates a bit of abstract art. Thomas W. Sweeney is editor; Patricia Doherty is art director.

A newsletter often is the product of a duplicating rather than a printing process. In contrast to printing, duplicating produces only a few hundred copies per master, with quality inferior to printing but good enough to serve the purposes of the publication.

Among the duplicating processes are spirit duplicating and mimeographing. In spirit duplicating, also called fluid duplicating, the image is typed or drawn on a master backed by an aniline-dye carbon sheet. A deposit of dye is transferred to the back of the master, which is used to do the printing. In mimeographing, a stencil permits ink to pass from a cylinder to the paper. There is a process that lies somewhere between duplicating and printing, but closer to printing, called Multilith. It can re-

Women in action

RUN FOR IT

The Newsletter for City Employees of Phoenix, Arizona   October, 1985

Good for the body, bad for the sole

These four panels represent one side of a three-fold, eight-panel, folder-format newsletter published for city employees of Phoenix. The second, mostly black panel acts as the newsletter's cover when the newsletter is folded down. Lee Moore edits; Don Budd art directs.

produce photographs and art and print in color just as its big brother—offset lithography—can.

And of course for really short runs ordinary office copying machines, so readily available now, can be the quickest and cheapest and most efficient reproduction system of all.

Like other publications newsletters now make wide use of computers. "With the electronic capabilities of the word processor or a PC, we have an easy way to store a format from issue to issue and build in some unique features," says Polly Pattison, who conducts design seminars for newsletter editors. "As software programs and the electronic printers become more sophisticated, we will be able to do page formatting with little or no pasteup involved."[7] The Apple Desktop Publishing System—with a Macintosh personal computer, an Apple LaserWriter printer, and software programs like the Aldus PageMaker, MacDraw, and MacWrite—is ideally suited to newsletter publishing.

Jubilee, the monthly eight-page newsletter of a Christian organization in Washington, D.C., called Prison Fellowship, uses formal balance for its two-color cover and for some of its inside pages as well. The strong logo in maroon incorporates a symbol done in a screened version of black. The handsome publication finds it necessary to use some mundane photographs but shows them small. Mike Johnson of the Petragram Group, Virginia Beach, Virginia, does the designing.

THE MONTHLY NEWSLETTER OF PRISON FELLOWSHIP/JULY 1985

A BRUISED REED HE WILL NOT BREAK Isaiah 42:3

JUBILEE

IMPACT

FROM CRIME TO CHRIST—
FOR THESE MEN,
PRISON BROUGHT A NEW LIFE
TO CELEBRATE.

The weekend gathering had all the makings of any reunion: old friends, good food and happy memories. Yet, particularly on this Saturday morning, this reunion was different. An air of excitement, even exuberance, flowed among the 20 men grouped outside the glistening barbed wire fence at the U.S. Penitentiary in Terre Haute, Indiana. Many held Bibles. The pall of gloom hanging over the prison melted away as they greeted each other with handshakes, hugs and laughter. They were all former prisoners, waiting to go back. Why? As Chuck Eberle, of Van Wert, Ohio, explained, looking at the austere brick building: "That's where I received my life."

Many of the ex-prisoners brought their families to Terre Haute to celebrate the 19th annual reunion of "From Crime to Christ."

They call it "From Crime to Christ" and for 19 years these and other former inmates have returned each May for a spirited weekend celebration in the prison where they all served time. After a Saturday morning worship service, they speak at churches and on a local radio program of how they committed their lives to Christ in prison. They also meet to honor the man who brought them the Good News—Art Lindsey.

Seventy-five years old and little more than five feet tall, Art Lindsey is a white-haired fireball. And he is no respecter of persons—everyone is greeted with the same ferocious bear hug.

Many of this year's celebrants came in vans filled with family, friends and musical instruments, some from as far away as Atlanta, Georgia. But none came from as a remote a place as Blaze, Kentucky, where former bank robber, Ernest Carter, now lives on a farm with his wife and children. His daughter, Rachel, is named for Art Lindsey's wife.

Ernest first heard Art's Saturday afternoon radio program in 1960 while lying in his cell. Attracted to the straight-shooting preaching and gospel music, Ernest wrote Art, asking him to conduct a worship service at the prison.

The invitation appealed to Art—he longed to see the prisoners, sequestered practically in his own backyard, become whole men in Christ. He came that week and has returned every week since.

He holds no seminary degrees, just an unabashed love for the Lord who changed his life at age 39. An Indiana native, Art ran a grocery store for many years. One Sunday in 1949, his daughter, Carolyn, asked him to take her to Sunday School. The church bus had broken down and Art, touched that church meant so much to her, took her and began attending himself. Weeks later, when the pastor asked those who wanted to give their lives to the Lord to come forward, Art and his wife walked down the aisle. "I saw what a sinner I'd become," he says. "I should have been in prison myself, but never got caught."

He stayed with the grocery store a few more years, but only with half a heart. Ministry was his goal. Local businessmen and his church began supporting him in 1956. Two years later he started the radio program which is still going strong. "I didn't have any experience," he says, "but they needed someone and I knew I could talk about the Lord." The 90-minute program features local gospel musicians, guest speakers and Art's delightful presence. Yet Art never dreamed his program would launch a ministry that would change his life and countless others.

Art only met with inmate Ernest Carter a short time before his release in 1961. Five years later, Ernest returned with five others for the first reunion. The group doubled

CONTINUED ON PAGE 5

P.O. BOX 17500, WASHINGTON, D.C. 20041-0500/(703)478-0100

INSIDE AND OUT

A BUSINESSMAN, A BOY
AND A BIKE

As Paul Canada glanced through the St. Paul's Episcopal Church bulletin that December morning, he noticed an unusual request: "Male volunteer needed as big brother for nine-year-old whose father is in nearby federal prison." Months earlier, as a member of this Darien, Connecticut, church's gospel quartet, Paul had gone to the Federal Correctional Institution near Danbury. He wondered if he had met this boy's father.

With four grown children of his own, he thought the role of befriending a nine-year-old might be better suited for another man. But with the loving support of his wife, Fran, he volunteered to help Michael. His involvement quickly spread to include Michael's entire family, as well as his own. A letter Paul wrote to Prison Fellowship captures his love and concern:

"The week before I met Michael, I received a thoughtful letter from [PF Connecticut State Director] Bob Wollenweber telling about Michael's background and that he was one of four children. I then phoned his mother, Sue, and assured her I only wanted to help, not intrude. Coolness turned to warmth, and she invited Fran and me to meet the family the next evening.

Paul Canada with his special young friend, Michael.

"Michael and I hit it off right away. He agreed to spend the next night with us to start his Christmas vacation. The very next morning, I drove to a business meeting near Danbury and was determined to get into that prison and meet Michael's father. I wanted insight and perspective before picking up his son after school that day. With the Lord's help and the chaplain's, I got into the prison. Gary and I had a great talk, not only about his son but his crimes and new life in Christ. His only concerns were for the family.

"That afternoon, Michael was packed, ready and smiling when I picked him up. After supper we played Ping-Pong and board games I thought we had long disposed of. Later, I prayed with him and tucked a happy, contented nine-year-old into bed, then a very tired 57-year-old climbed into bed. I shared with Fran the blessings of the day; despite my weariness I felt better than I had in years.

"Early Saturday, we rummaged through the junk in our barn for a wheel for Michael's bike. Under the hay, he found an old yellow bike, long outgrown by my youngest son. We polished and oiled it and thanked God the old tires still held air. I'll never forget the look in Michael's clear, blue eyes as he proudly rode down our driveway.

"When I took him home that day, he excitedly showed his seven-year-old sister Katy the bike. Her eyes were like saucers. She told me she had never had a bike of her own.

"The morning before Christmas I found myself at our town dump. I told John, the bulldozer driver, the story of Michael, his father and little Katy who didn't have a bike.

"John found one. It took his bulldozer to reach it but the bike was a jewel—even under the rust. With John's mechanical skill and some tools from my trunk, we transplanted parts from other bikes and soon had a complete three-speed model. I took my prize home and with the help of my grown sons, home for Christmas, we made that bike shine like new—it's amazing what steel wool and WD-40 can do!

"It was all worth the effort to see the light of wonder and love that shone in Katy's eyes as her mother wheeled her around the yard on *her* bike. It was our best Christmas in a long, long time. Our entire family was touched.

"Though they have moved, we still see Michael and his family from time to time. It's partly selfish on my part, for every contact with that family brings an unbelievable reward. Sue frequently uses our car to take the kids to see Gary. I believe they are a happier and closer family. I know we are."

JUBILEE/JULY 1985   3

This spread appears just inside the cover of an eight-page saddle-stapled 9 × 11 newsletter, *Alum News,* published by Bristol-Myers for its retired and former employees. The front page—and all pages—look very much like these sample pages; all the stories carry headlines in a single typeface, nicely unifying the publication. Thin horizontal rules above and below the headlines give them added display. The lines of the headlines are centered. Boxes surround some of the stories. *Alum News* is one of several publications produced by Editorial Services, a division of Bristol-Myers, New York.

Lee Kleis Chairs Golf Tournament, Cancer Benefit

Directors Declare Dividend

Security Guard Now Attendant In Criminal Court

Company Reports Record Sales And Earnings for First Quarter

James Robinson Elected to Board of Directors

Pattison has developed twelve standard formats for newsletters, which she introduces to persons enrolled in her seminars. Her formats involve both one- and two-column pages. Her one-column formats usually leave generous areas of white space on the left, where headlines can be set or typed. She advocates "out-of-the-ordinary" sizes for newsletters to "increase reader interest" and French folds, gatefolds, and other folds of large sheets to avoid the costs of binding.

Like magazines and newspapers, newsletters need redesigning from time to time. Pattison says a newsletter editor can expect to pay between $500 and $3,000 for a redesign job. She suggests that a good way for an editor to approach an outside designer is to say something like "I have $1,500 to spend for a redesign job. What will that buy me?"

It is the editor who is ultimately responsible for a redesign job. This puts high stakes on picking the right designer. The job becomes more complicated when a board of directors and others, along with the editor,

Polly Pattison moved a newsletter published by Pacific Mutual from a dated look to a more contemporary look by cutting down on the size of the logo (the name was changed by the editor in the process) and going from a two-column format to a single wide column and using block rather than indented paragraphs. In the new format she put headlines at the side. The new format can also accommodate photographs when they are available. The logo and rules are preprinted in blue.

June 1983

BENEFIT DESIGN LED CC&M TOPICS AT GROUP SEMINAR IN APRIL. Says Angelo Masciantonio, head of Pacific Mutual's cost control program: "A major PM goal is to promote our cost control benefit design features. These features include pre-admission testing, ambulatory surgery, second opinions, and well-baby, convalescent, hospice, and home health care. Future options will include Preferred Provider Organizations."

PM's competitors are marketing these features as added benefits. "PM offers many of the same features in its routine benefit package. But it isn't always clear to prospective and current policyholders that we offer them," says Masciantonio. "We aren't tooting our horn enough about the richness of our benefit package."

Seminar participants were told that policyholders must choose carefully the design best suited to their needs. In the current enthusiasm to contain health-care costs, some insurance companies are selling solutions without identifying any specific problems.

PM takes a more intelligent and professional approach. "We oppose shotgunning the problem with solutions," Masciantonio says. "We want to find the right cost-management solution to a problem."

A policyholder's savings from benefit design must outweigh administrative costs before PM recommends a particular program. Some of the company's programs require special administrative procedures that make them cost-effective only to larger cases.

Without careful consideration, benefit design can end up costing policyholders more. Some of PM's competitors have allowed this to happen. PM wants to avoid costly, ineffective programs.

* * * * * * *

PACIFIC MUTUAL HAS AN INNOVATIVE CC&M PROGRAM AND WE WANT OUR TARGET MARKETS TO KNOW IT. That's why a PM ad with the headline "We're Attacking the High Cost of Group Health Insurance" began appearing in May and will continue through October. The message will appear in Fortune, Business Week, and trade publications.

The tarket markets are brokerage and business communities in the Western United States. The message is eight ways PM is working to keep group health insurance costs down: contracts with doctors who hold down costs, Benefast, second opinions for surgery, a hospital audit program, PM-MEDUSE, Employee Health and Cost

DECEMBER 1984

HEALTH COST MANAGEMENT
NEWS

PM BEGINS TO CHECK APPROPRIATE USE OF CONTRACTED HOSPTIALS

Pacific Mutual has started applying a system called Appropriateness Evaluation Protocol (AEP). The purpose of AEP? To assess unnecessary days of medical care at the hospitals where PM has contracts.

AEP was developed by Paul M. Gertman, M.D., and Joseph D. Restuccia, Dr. P.H., from research at Boston University. In a 1981 article in Medical Care the doctors defined AEP's objective: "...to develop a valid, reliable and simple technique for determining the appropriateness of hospital use, in terms of the necessity for a patient being in a hospital bed on a given day."

According to Health Data Institute (HDI), which reviews AEP data for Pacific Mutual, Appropriateness Evaluation Protocol successfully reveals unnecessary hospital use. "Among hospitals studied, the rates of inappropriate admissions have ranged from five percent to 35 percent while rates of inappropriate days have ranged from ten percent to 50 percent," reports HDI. "On average, ten percent to 15 percent of admissions and 20 percent to 30 percent of days have been found inappropriate."

As PM's contracts with hospitals reach their one-year anniversary and come up for renewal, AEP will be applied in some instances. The first hospital to use AEP was St. John's in Santa Monica. St. John's audit was not typical on two counts: St. John's helped pay the cost of the audit; and the records of patients other than PM patients were reviewed.

The only other PM-contracted hospital to use AEP has been Hoag Memorial in Newport Beach. Like St. John's, Hoag Memorial shared AEP expenses with PM.

These two hospitals helped pay AEP costs, says Bob Broaddus, VP, Group Health Management Operations, because they are interested in long-term health cost containment and want the data produced by an audit.

Although all hospitals with PM contracts have agreed to open the records of PM patients for AEP review, audits will not be required of every hospital. PM will apply AEP to hospitals that in Broaddus's words, "show that their utilization review could stand improvement."

SEVEN CALIFORNIA HOSPITALS JOIN NETWORK

The following have joined the Pacific Mutual network of contracted hospitals: Roseville Community Hospital in Roseville, Seton Medical Center in Daly City, St. Catherine Hospital on Half Moon Bay in Moss Beach, Los Alamitos Medical Center in Los Alamitos, Community Hospital of San Gabriel in San Gabriel, Henry Mayo Newhall Memorial Hospital in Valencia, and Inter-Community Medical Center, Inc. in Covina.

have to approve the new design. Pattison says she raises her bid on a job when she discovers a whole battery of people have to be satisfied.

Several newsletters serve newsletter editors. One is *The Newsletter on Newsletters* (44 West Market Street, Rhinebeck, New York 12572). There is also *The Newsletter Yearbook/Directory,* a Newsletter Clearinghouse, and a Newsletter Association of America.

Yearbooks

As a print medium, yearbooks fall somewhere in between magazines and books. Because they are permanently bound and because they serve both historical and reference purposes, they have many qualities of a book. But because they are issued periodically, they also fit the magazine category. Increasingly, they have taken on the look of a magazine.

Not all yearbooks are dominated by photographs. *Writer's Market* and similar nonschool yearbooks are really directories, with page after page of small type, hard to read but worth the trouble because of the information conveyed. *Writer's Market* comes out each year as a hardbound book with cheap newsprint pages. It is hardbound to withstand constant use, even if that use is over a short period of time. The paper is cheap because at the end of the year the information is outdated. Not that production decisions about books like this are necessarily logical. *Editor & Publisher International Year Book* is softbound and printed on a relatively high grade of paper.

Many kinds of organizations issue yearbooks, including especially schools and colleges. Although interest in yearbooks may be only moderate in large state universities, it continues strong in smaller colleges and especially in high schools, where students identify more with each other and their institutions. Many junior high schools and elementary schools publish yearbooks, too.

Some of the companies that print school yearbooks call themselves publishers, but of course the schools themselves are the publishers. Printers are only printers, despite all the good services they supply. In the school yearbook field the printers offer all kinds of aids to design, including grid sheets for pasteup, cropping devices, instructional manuals, copies of other books to emulate, and personal help from sales representatives.

The school yearbook's main offering is the photograph: the informal shot, the group shot, the mug shot. Over the years as visual sophistication has increased, editors have given more attention to the informal shot, less to the group and mug shots. But they ignore the latter at the peril of decreased sales. Yearbooking these days turns out to be something of a battle between the editor's and designer's urge to be creative and the reader's desire to have an album of portraits to file away for later perusal. There is room for experimental typography and design in the front of each book, of course, but the real challenge to the designer is to work out a readable, orderly, and attractive display of the routine lineup of same-size pictures in the back.

A yearbook with clearly defined sections may require division pages to segregate the material. Division pages can consist of heavy or colored stock.

Settling on a theme proves to be the first hurdle for editors and designers of yearbooks. The theme, an appropriate rallying point for copy and art and a unifying force in the book, sometimes gets out of hand. A theme too blatently developed can do more harm than good in a yearbook.

Newsletter Editing, Design and Production

This seminar will help you improve *all* of your publications. You'll discover ways to:

- Plan and prepare better copy
- Increase readership through writing and design techniques
- Create a format that reflects your organization's image
- Reduce typesetting and printing costs
- Get more done in less time

Register yourself—and your key employees—today.

Who Should Attend

This seminar will be valuable for anyone involved in producing newsletters, brochures and other publications—writers and editors, editorial assistants, graphic designers, publications managers, production supervisors, specialists in advertising, corporate communications, employee relations, marketing and public relations, public information officers, directors of development, administrative assistants and others.

If you're a beginner in the field of communications, you'll find this seminar packed with information and techniques to help you improve your publication and make your job easier. (And you won't have to worry about retaining the technical information that you learn. It's all explained in the seminar manual that you take back to your job.)

If you're a seasoned professional, this seminar will serve as a useful refresher course. You'll gain fresh ideas for your newsletter by viewing slides of some of the best newsletters being produced today. You'll pick up new approaches to solving some old problems. You'll have the opportunity to share ideas by talking with other professionals in your field.

If you want to expand your knowledge and your career opportunities in a growing communications field, this seminar will increase your job skills and your marketability.

What You'll Learn

At this seminar you'll learn how to:

- **Save time and money** on newsletter production without sacrificing quality.
- **Upgrade and update** your newsletter without throwing out your present format.
- **Start a new newsletter,** choose a name, develop copy, design a format.
- **Make your newsletter more readable** by understanding *how* people read.
- **Maximize the impact of photos** and illustrations with creative design techniques.
- **Talk intelligently** with graphic artists, typesetters and printers by knowing their language.
- **Control the final results** by controlling the entire newsletter production process from start to finish.
- **Produce a more successful publication** by working smarter, not harder.

Comments from Participants

"This is a great seminar. Very well planned to teach you all the basics of understanding how to put a newsletter together."
—*Andrea Sobel, Editor-in-Chief, American Express, New York, N.Y.*

"The copyfitting section will definitely aid me in being more productive. It will also help to get the company's newsletter out more efficiently and quickly, with less time spent getting typesetting done and redone."
—*Cynthia Newton, Public Relations Assistant, Johnson Controls, Inc., Milwaukee, Wis.*

"Superb job!! I usually bring back several good ideas from most seminars. But this time I've obtained enough useful ideas to fill a wheelbarrow — a very pleasant surprise. This seminar is *definitely* worth the time and money."
—*Carol Kennedy, Programmer, Standard Oil Company, Cleveland, Ohio*

"For a beginner like myself, this workshop is a lifesaver."
—*Randall Butler, Associate University Archivist, Loma Linda University, Loma Linda, Calif.*

A two-fold, six-panel folder announces a series of seminars for newsletter editors; the series is sponsored by Promotional Perspectives, Ann Arbor, Michigan. The simple, direct, full-of-copy cover is a model of how newsletters themselves should look. Kristine Moore Meves designed it.

A spread from *Volunteer,* yearbook of the University of Tennessee, takes a magazine approach. The "Special Report" deals with news items for the year. Advisor is Les Hyder.

Special Report

140/Report

Report/141

The best theme may turn out to be, simply, a consistent design style and the appearance of a single typeface throughout.

This monthly *Union Electric News* consists of one 33 × 11 sheet folded twice to make six pages (three on each side). Editor Deborah J. Walther usually uses black and one color on tinted stock. That's the cover above. The inside spread (below) shows how bars and lines and a consistent sink can be used to organize material.

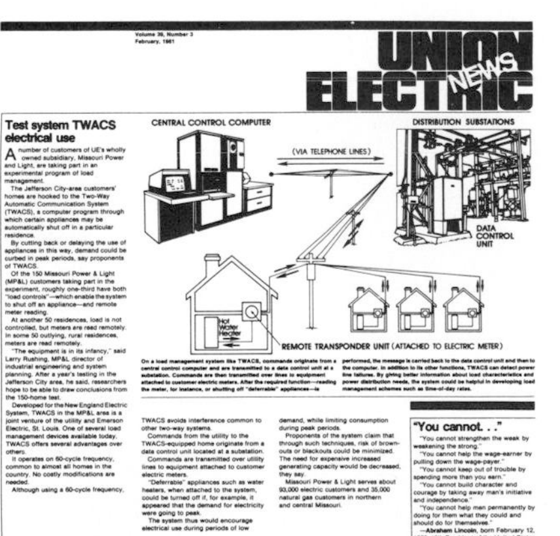
UNION ELECTRIC NEWS

Test system TWACS electrical use

"You cannot. . ."

One more thing

You started doing it, probably, back in grade school, not long after you learned to write. Right under your signature you put a wavy line and drew a couple of cross strokes in the middle. Later, while reading books, you filled in the O's with your pencil. An uncle before you no doubt drew mustaches on pictures of people on posters or in the papers.

The most persistent "improvers" are new car dealers, with their stripe tapes, luggage racks, splash guards, chrome door rims, and other affectations calculated to elevate prices. Never mind that the car's design phase was over when it left the factory. The people out at the "stores," as they call them, act as though they spent time at a college of design as they direct their hirelings to further dress up their "rigs," before slapping Additional Dealer Markup stickers on the windows.

Food manufacturers improve a product by adding preservatives and improve it further by removing the preservatives. In commercials, slice-of-life actors are so impressed by "New! Improved!" products that in their enthusiasm they fail to finish off what's left in the original packages.

Retailers constantly look for unlikely adjectives to improve the possibility of sales. So do manufacturers. Ordinary color names are not good

Christmas bills still bugging you?

Debt—and how to get out of it

Credit Buying: Better Habits

What's your opinion?

Callaway newspaper lauds UE family

The Plautzes: "do-ers" with endless energy

Patented inventor in our midst

Haynes seeks perfection for disc jockeys' device

Comment

Backward

Anti-development?

Weighing dangers

Ironic

They accept it

We've survived

enough; the colors have to be "decorator colors." In one of those *New York* magazine back-of-the-book contests, Sally Terney came up with this line: "And he made him a coat of many decorator colors."

In ads, second-hand cars become "preowned cars." Real estate agents upgrade the houses they sell by calling them "homes."

Magazine editors and designers improve their pages with ruled lines and boxes, and they improve the ruled lines by butting short bars against them. They improve the boxes by putting them inside other boxes.

Newspaper editors and magazine editors, too, improve their halftones by taping black lines around them. Sometimes they improve rectangular photos by cutting them into stars or kidneys or other imaginative shapes.

They improve the type used for headlines and titles by adding space between letters or, at the opposite extreme, moving the letters so close together that they nearly overlap. Or they fall in with trends that call for caps and small-caps or oversize opening and closing letters that extend below the baseline.

That's not really an old lady sitting there. It's a plastic casting by Duane Hanson on exhibit at the University Art Museum, Berkeley. Photographer Peter Haley for the yearbook at the University of California nicely captured the expressions of incredulity on the faces of the onlookers.

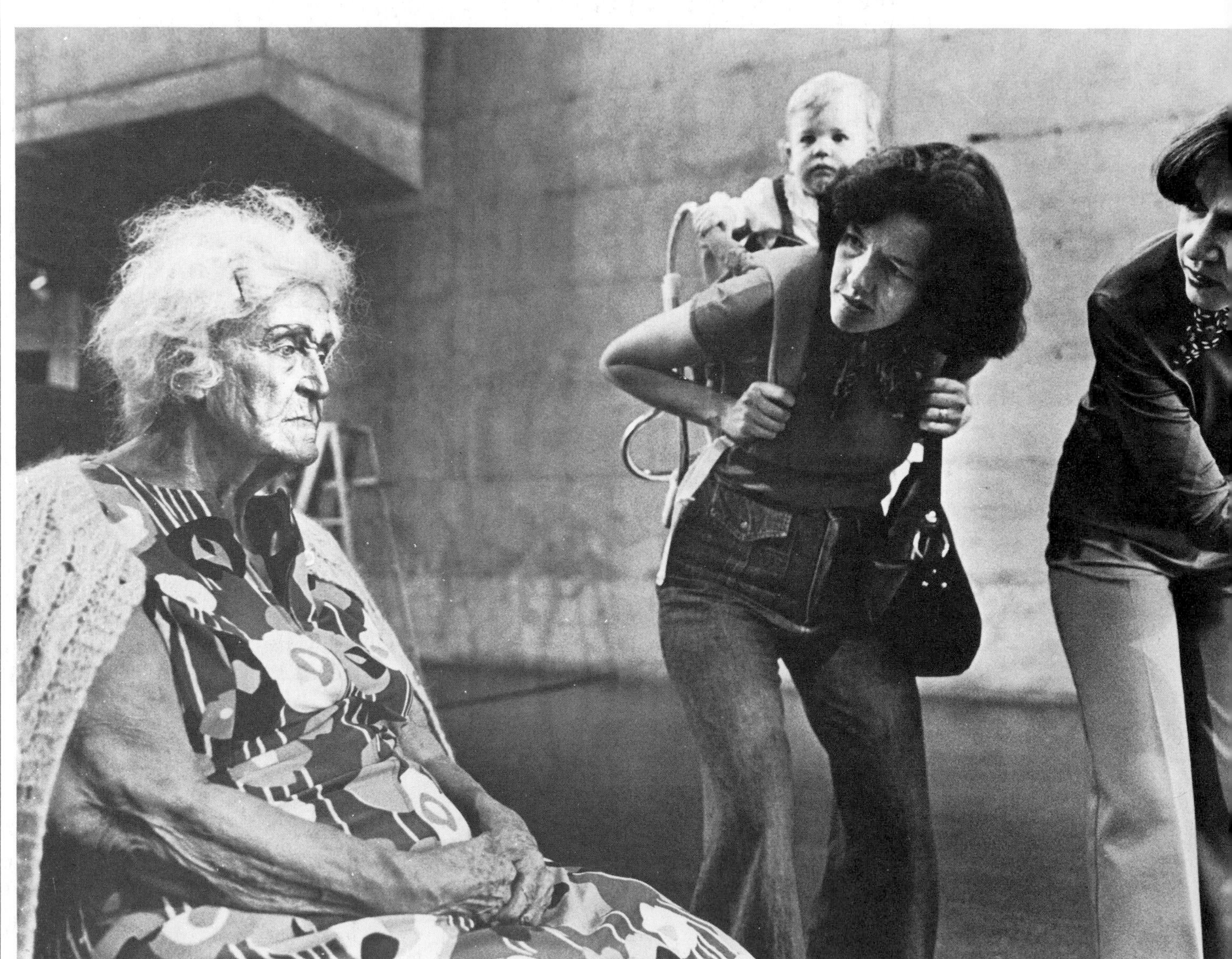

High school yearbooks, once a repository of examples of what *not* to do in graphic design, have become much more design conscious. This is the title page spread and a spread from the introduction to the *Eugenean,* the yearbook of South Eugene High School, Eugene, Oregon. The example is from 1968, but the highly ordered, modular look holds up well.

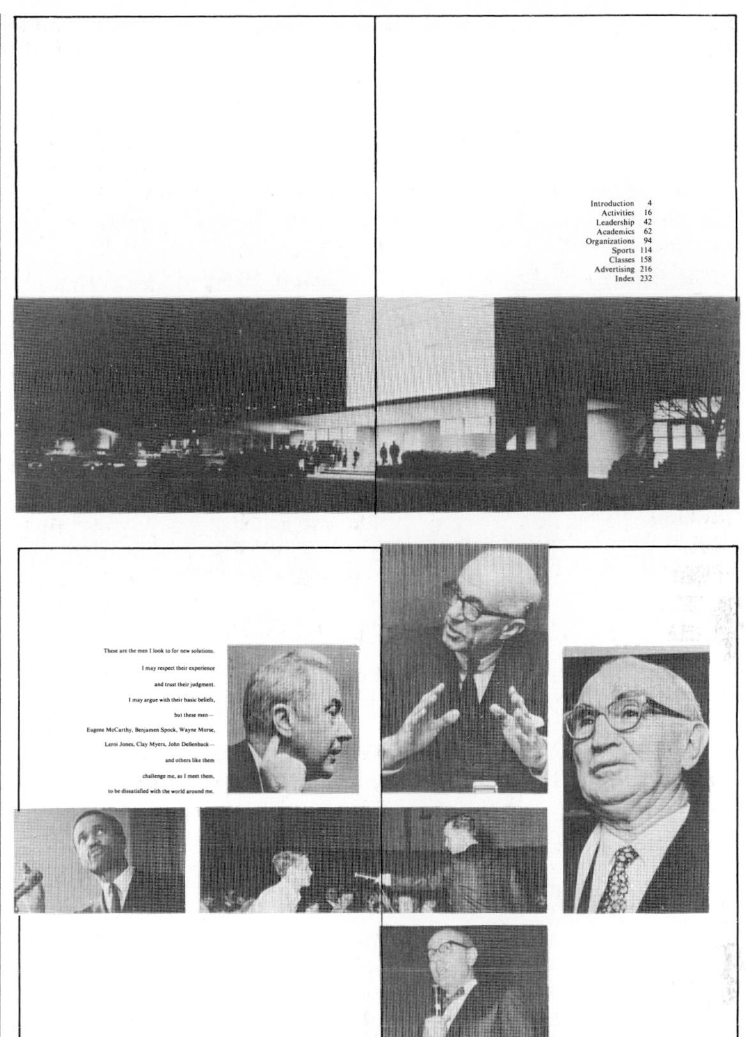

Some of this is good. A visual surprise here and there or a hint of inventiveness can add life to a page. Often the extra touches are necessary to establish an appropriate visual personality for the text. But the best design is usually the simplest. It remains in the background, taking no bows, doing its work selflessly and effortlessly.

On most pages of a well-designed publication, in-focus photographs, undoctored, appear in sizes large enough to read and appreciate. Nearby titles or headlines run in single lines of lowercase letters. Copy appears in standard typefaces, set in comfortable sizes and widths, with enough leading to be inviting.

If there is a design lesson left to learn, it may be knowing when to stop.

Notes

1. Delphine Hirasuna, "Ten Tips for Creating an Award Winning Annual Report," *Communication World,* December 1985, p. 20.
2. Ibid.
3. Quoted in "Association Publications: On to New Challenges," *Folio,* September 1985, p. 41.
4. Interview with Gloria Gordon, San Francisco, September 3, 1985.
5. Quoted by William Safire, "Safety Nets," *The New York Times Magazine,* March 29, 1979, p. 10.

6. Albert Walker, "Newsletters: Fastest Rising Print Medium," *Journal of Organizational Communication* 1, 1977, p. 22.

7. Polly Pattison, "Dynamic Newsletter Formats," *Step-by-Step Graphics*, premier edition, 1985, p. 75.

Suggested further reading

Arnold, Edmund C., *The Making of Flyers, Folders, and Brochures*, Lawrence Ragan communications, Chicago, 1983.

Beach, Mark, *Editing Your Newsletter: A Guide to Writing, Design and Production*, 2d ed., Coast to Coast Books, 2934 N.E. 16th Ave., Portland, Oregon 97212, 1982.

Brigham, Nancy, *How to Do Leaflets, Newsletters and Newspapers*, New England Free Press, 60 Union Square, Somerville, Massachusetts 02143, 1976.

Creative Newsletter Graphics, Creative Communications, Suite 530, One Dupont Circle, Washington, D.C. 20036, 1976. (Expensive.)

Denton, Mary Raye, *A Blueprint for Yearbooks Today*, Crescendo Publications, P.O. Box 28218, Dallas, Texas 75228, 1976.

Dorn, Raymond, *Tabloid Design for the Organizational Press*, Lawrence Ragan Communications, Chicago, 1983.

Gross, Fred, *Success in Newsletter Publishing: A Practical Guide*, 2d ed., Newsletter Association, Colorado Building, Suite 700, 1341 G St., N.W., Washington, D.C. 20005, 1985.

Hodgson, Richard S., *Direct Mail and Mail Order Handbook*, 2d ed., Dartnell, Chicago, 1976.

How to Create Successful Catalogs, Maxwell Sroge Publishing, 731 N. Cascade Ave., Colorado Springs, Colorado, 1985. (With contributions by 39 catalog industry experts. Expensive.)

Hudson, Howard Penn, *Publishing Newsletters*, Charles Scribner's Sons, New York, 1982.

Jones, Gerre, *How to Prepare Professional Design Brochures*, McGraw-Hill Book Company, New York, 1976.

Klemin, Diana, *The Illustrated Book: Its Art and Craft*, Murton Press, Greenwich, Connecticut, 1983.

Kliment, Stephen A., *Creative Communications for a Successful Design Practice*, Whitney Library of Design, New York, 1977.

Maas, Jane, *Better Brochures, Catalogs and Mailing Pieces*, St. Martin's Press, New York, 1981.

Moore, Charles B., and William F. Blue, Jr., *Editing and Layout Techniques for the Company Editor*, Ink Art Publications, P.O. Box 36070, Indianapolis, Indiana, 1979.

Ragan, Lawrence, *The Organizational Press*, Lawrence Ragan Communications, Chicago, Illinois, 1981.

Schuh, Colleen, *Newsletters: Designing and Producing Them*, rev. ed., Division of Program and Staff Development, University of Wisconsin–Madison, Madison, Wisconsin, 1978.

Stone, Bob, *Successful Direct Marketing Methods*, Crain Books, Chicago, 3d ed., 1984.

Success in Newsletter Publishing, Newsletter Association of America, Washington, D.C., 1985.

Sutter, Jan, *Slinging Ink: A Practical Guide to Producing Booklets, Newspapers, and Ephemeral Publications*, William Kaufmann, Los Altos, California, 1982.

Wales, LaRae H., *A Practical Guide to Newsletter Editing & Design*, Iowa State University Press, Ames, Iowa, 1976.

Williams, Patrick, *The Employee Annual Report: Purpose, Format, and Content*, Lawrence Ragan Communications, Chicago, 1984.

Winter, Elmer, *Complete Guide to Preparing a Corporate Annual Report*, Van Nostrand Reinhold Company, New York, 1985.

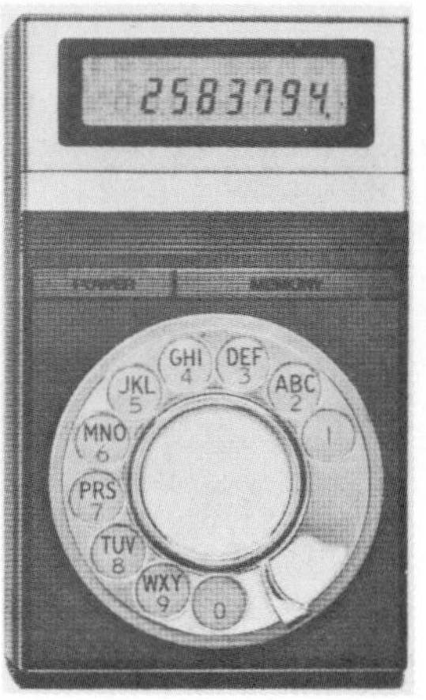

"Did you ever see a calculator with a rotary dial?" asks Pacific Northwest Bell in a letter inviting phone users to switch from rotary dialing to Touch-Tone service. The rotary-dial calculator shown at the top of the letter is a good example of double-take art, or what chapter 5 describes as a visual oxymoron.

Assignments

Chapter 1: The emergence of design

Assignment 1. Bring to class an example of a well-designed magazine, newspaper, or book. Be prepared to defend your choice. What makes the publication "well-designed"?

Assignment 2. Bring to class a magazine article that shows current design based on design of the past.

Be prepared to discuss the appropriateness of the design to the theme of the article.

Assignment 3. Get the name of the art director or designer of a magazine or newspaper published locally and arrange an interview. Find out what the art director's or designer's role is in putting out the publication. You may want to base some of your questions on information found in this chapter.

Assignment 4. Pick out a nicely designed full-page ad in a national magazine and use its basic design approach to design an opening page (a right-hand page) for a magazine article dealing with a related subject. Don't let your magazine page look like an ad.

Assignment 5. Assume that one of the women's fashion magazines—any one of them—has decided to go after a slightly more mature audience. Take an article from the current issue of the magazine and, using the same art and title, redesign it (it may run on for several pages) to appeal more to the new audience.

Assignment 6. Take a spread from any quietly designed magazine—one with, say, a gridded or Swiss Gothic look—and give it a "new wave" look.

Assignment 7. Do a single page layout for a magazine like *Parade* that likes large or playful initial letters. See whether you can design an interesting page without art, except for the art you might put into the initial letter(s). Your article, directed to young parents, bears the title "Second Thoughts on First-Born Children." Be sure to include a byline. Leave room for folios.

Chapter 2: The approach to design

Assignment 1. For an article about drug use in the schools (make up your own title and dream up your own art) do a two-page opener that puts into practice the design principles discussed in this chapter. Use black and white and one color (a "second color," as it would be called). Your work need not be finished. Your instructor will be looking for placement more than fine rendering.

Assignment 2. Design a two-page opener for the imaginary *Everybody's Magazine* for one of the following articles that will be going into a future issue:

a. "Mothers vs. Drunk Drivers" (an article about MADD)
b. "Two Cheers for the New Technology" (an article that, while admiring what the Computer Age has brought us, points up some drawbacks)
c. "Soup, Soap, and Salvation" (an article about the Salvation Army)
d. "I Hope I Break Even Because I Need the Money" (a "confession" by a confirmed gambler)

For this assignment you can become playful with typography as well as layout. And you should come up with some compelling art—art that dominates the spread. But let the copy get started on the spread (the copy should occupy no more than a single column). You have full color for this one.

Assignment 3. Find a cluttered, busy two-page spread in a magazine and see whether you can simplify it without throwing out much of its type or many of its art pieces. You can change the size of the art if you wish.

Assignment 4. See whether you can design an angry page for a magazine—a page that carries an article condemning something and calling for strong corrective action. Do it with or without art. Include a byline.

Assignment 5. Take a page from a magazine that does not now use rules and boxes and redesign the page to use one or the other—or both. Don't overdo it.

Assignment 6. Work out a grid for a magazine that doesn't now seem to have any real planning from page to page or spread to spread.

Assignment 7. Note Terry Lak's experimentation with a dragon fly in this chapter. In a similar vein pick out some other insect or an animal and see whether you can come up with a dozen variations, moving from realism to something highly abstract.

Assignment 8. Assume that an existing magazine is going from an 8½ × 11 format to a square format (about 11 × 11). Take one of its articles (three or more pages) and redesign it to fit the new format, keeping the same amount of copy. You can adjust the art sizes.

Assignment 9. Let's assume that the editor of *Popular Photography* wants to expand the two pages of "The Ups and Downs of Camera Movements" (an article shown in this chapter) to three pages, holding to the same up-and-down design approach but giving bigger play to the photographs. Do a rough layout showing how it could be done.

Chapter 3: Production

Assignment 1. Pick a page from a magazine and, through tracing and drawing, see how closely you can duplicate it. What you're doing, essentially, is creating a comprehensive rough layout. Pay particular attention to tone. For body copy use ruled lines.

Assignment 2. Make a collection of printed art pieces to illustrate the various kinds of *line reproductions* and *halftone reproductions* editors are including in their publications. For instance, include examples of grease crayon work (line), Zipatone work (line), silhouetted photographs (halftone), and wash drawings or watercolor paintings (halftone). Include descriptions of tools used by artists to create these pieces.

Assignment 3. Find some examples of flat or spot color uses (black plus one color) that create the illusion of many colors.

Assignment 4. Sherry Lee Bastion in this chapter shows what can be done with the words "Crime and Punishment" by including a piece of art. See what you can do with the same assignment. Come up with your own type arrangement and art idea. Don't let the art overpower the type.

Assignment 5. Note the simplified diagram in this chapter explaining offset lithography. Do a simplified diagram of your own, explaining one of the other printing processes. This will involve some research on your part.

Assignment 6. Pick out a line drawing from a newspaper or magazine (it could be in an ad) and adjust it by adding or subtracting something to change its meaning or impact. Assume that you are editing stock art. Explain how the new art would be used.

Assignment 7. Find a single-page feature in a magazine, make a quick tracing of it to show placement of elements, and then cut out each of the elements in the original feature, allowing only one-eighth inch of white space. Mark a big *X* on the back of each element—lightly, so it won't show through—to indicate the wrong side. Put these materials into a folder or envelope and bring it to class, where students can exchange designs to get at one they did not provide. When you have your new set of materials, do a careful pasteup of the elements, using the rough tracing as a guide.

Assignment 8. Do a dozen thumbnail sketches showing possible two-page openers for an article dealing with stress. Don't worry about the wording of the title at this point; use greeking. And don't worry about art ideas. Just show placement. Indicate to your instructor which one of the thumbnails has the best possibilities for full-size development—and tell why.

Assignment 9. You have four solid columns of copy (you're working for a three-columns-per-page magazine) and three photographs: two horizontals and one vertical. Your editor gives you three pages. The title runs to seven words. Arrange this material (be sure to include a byline, a blurb or subtitle, and picture captions) to fill the three pages, using whatever kind of sink you wish. Picture size is flexible. Use a right-hand page start.

Assignment 10. Take an existing black-and-white page from a newspaper or a spread from a magazine and see whether you can add to its impact with spot color. Be sure that in adding color you don't hurt the basic design.

Chapter 4: Typography

Assignment 1. Pick out an appropriate alphabet of type in a 36-point size or larger and, by tracing the letters, letter the title "Jogging Your Way to a Longer Life," breaking it into two or more lines. Watch your spacing. Then do the same thing using press-on letters.

Assignment 2. Find as many different examples of sans serif type as you can and point out the differences in the design of the letters for each example.

Assignment 3. Put together nine or more letters from roman alphabets of various sizes and styles to create an interesting piece of art. Don't worry about saying anything with this design. Just worry about fit and placement. Relate the letters through placement. Create ligatures if you wish. Draw the letters or cut out and paste them. (See what Joanne Hasegawa does with her drawn same-face letters.)

Assignment 4. Create a page design that uses a typeface that seems to be drawn in the same style as the accompanying art work. (See Roger Waterman's example in this chapter.)

Assignment 5. Pick out six nouns and verbs or modifiers and playfully letter them with quirks that emphasize what they are saying. (See the "DROUGHT!" example in this chapter.)

Assignment 6. Find five examples of typefaces that, simply through the design of the letters, seem to convey the following moods: restlessness, tranquility, anxiety, joy, and affection. The mood ties can be subtle. No tricks with type here, please.

Assignment 7. Collect as many different handlings of caption material as you can and evaluate them.

Assignment 8. Pick out an illustrated article from a magazine and redesign it to get rid of the art and show off new, carefully selected and placed typography. Let the beauty of the typography and wise use of white space, perhaps with some ruled lines, carry the pages.

Assignment 9. You've seen the playful typography on the Meow Mix box. Possibly you've seen similar letters on the pages of *U&lc*. For this assignment take the word *animals* and build it by using cartoon drawings of various animals as your letterstrokes. You can use a single animal or a combination of animals for each letter. Better stick to all-caps.

Chapter 5: Art

Assignment 1. Come up with a visual oxymoron for one of the following:

a. a professor and her shadow
b. a home used as an office
c. a politician courting votes from the poor
d. a country and western singer with a background in classical music

Assignment 2. Pick out a reproduction of a well-known fine-arts painting and do a parody of it to illustrate an article topic of your choosing.

Assignment 3. Find a magazine article or newspaper feature with lots of statistics and hard facts and create charts to better portray them. Better, create charts that incorporate pictures.

Assignment 4. Find examples of publication design that represent (a) Art Nouveau, (b) Art Deco, (c) Swiss gothic, and (d) new wave styles. Describe each of these art or design approaches.

Assignment 5. Make a quick rendering of Chris Craft's amusement park photo with all the gray area at the right and letter in the article title "America's Best Amusement Parks" in whatever type style and size you choose and wherever on the photo you think it belongs. Assume that the article begins just under the photo.

Assignment 6. Peter Haley's fisheye-lens shot of helmeted workers in this chapter has to be cropped to fit a deep vertical spot (one column by twelve inches) in a newspaper. Make a quick rendering of it and then show with crop marks how the picture can be cropped.

Assignment 7. Pick out a reproduction of a painting from an art book or use a postcard reproduction from an art museum and adapt its composition and proportions to a two-page spread of type and photographs that you might do for a magazine. Do not show the art itself. For this assignment you can make up an article subject and title. And of course you can visualize your own art. Perhaps you will want to go with a single photograph.

Assignment 8. Pick out a newspaper letters-to-the-editor column or section not now illustrated and describe or roughly draw a cartoon illustration for one of the letters. Hold the drawing to a single-column width.

Chapter 6: Formula and format

Assignment 1. Pick an 8½ × 11 magazine and redesign it into a pocket-size magazine. A few sample pages will be enough to show the editor what you have in mind. Hold onto the current design thinking of the magazine but do change picture sizes and edit down the copy; don't simply reduce whole pages to the smaller size.

Assignment 2. Pick a regular-size newspaper and redesign its front page to make it a tabloid. You may want to consider using boxes or ruled lines and bars on the page, along with one or two big photos. No doubt you will want to limit the number of front-page stories.

Assignment 3. Pick a magazine with a relaxed look and lots of white space and redesign it to crowd its pages. (The magazine needs to cut costs by cutting down on the number of pages.) You can change the design approach while you're at it. And where one spread has one article, it may now have two. A total of four pages is enough for this assignment. For comparison include a copy of the magazine as it now stands.

Assignment 4. Try to come up with another approach to the *Virtue* magazine assignment shown in this chapter. You'll have to use the same title, but everything else can be different. Use a second color.

Assignment 5. Finish the design of Houlihan's article in *Grace Digest*. Three more pages.

Assignment 6. Design a spread for a magazine article about newspapers that takes on a newspaper look. Make up your own title, and use greeking for any blurbs or subheads. Include art. No color.

Assignment 7. Come up with an article idea, write a title, and design a right-hand-page opener for Bob and Ray's *Wasting Time Magazine*.

Assignment 8. Assume that one of the budget-conscious opinion magazines like *The Nation* or *The Christian Century* has come upon lots of money and is going slick. Take an article from a recent issue of an opinion magazine and dress it up, adding color and art.

Assignment 9. Come up with an idea for a new, locally produced, inexpensive newsletter to be issued (possibly by your dentist, your church, or your department at school) and design the first page, with a logo but no color. Make it as handsome as you can without incurring any high costs.

Assignment 10. Take a magazine in need of redesign and redesign it. Turn in several representative pages along with the magazine itself. In an accompanying paper explain why you think your changes are necessary.

Chapter 7: The magazine cover

Assignment 1. Do a cover for *Ethics* magazine (shown in this chapter) that features the cover line "The Book Reviewer's Dilemma." (The article inside will deal with ethical problems faced by book reviewers: what to do about a book written by a friend, what to do about a book that will compete with the book reviewer's own book, how far the reviewer may wander from the book under review, etc.) The limited-circulation magazine is 8½ × 11 with some newsstand sales. Black and one color. Provide room for other cover lines if you wish. Include date (four months from the date of the assignment) and cover price ($2.50). An important part of this assignment is coming up with some art (real or abstract). And as the new art director you will want to design a new logo. Your design will set the stage for future covers.

Assignment 2. Find a printed horizontal photograph that lends itself to being divided into two equal vertical halves and render it (you'll probably have to enlarge it) to act as both the front and back covers of a company magazine (make up a name for it). Put the name on the front cover and nothing else. See whether you can come up with a clean, simple, understated, wraparound cover. The photograph should be in black and white, but the logo can be in a second color.

Assignment 3. Do a gatefold cover for any magazine that does not now use gatefolds. Let the cover foldout contain cover art half-hidden when the cover is returned to its normal position. Let the cover carry a one-two punch.

Assignment 4. Find a magazine logo that is a bit cluttered or dated and redesign it, using a recognizable typeface with only subtle changes and maybe just a hint of eccentricity. Use the *Harper's* logo as your inspiration but don't be tied down by it.

Assignment 5. Pick out a recent newspaper Sunday magazine, find a story or article in that issue that didn't make it as a cover story, get rid of the current cover story, and elevate the one you've picked. Redesign the cover to accommodate your choice. Make up some new art for the cover or use some art that went with the story.

Assignment 6. The *Sohio* cover shown in this chapter promotes a businessman-as-villain article inside. Let's say that for a future issue an entirely different cover story will deal with women who are both top business executives and mothers. Design the cover and visualize the art to dominate the page, as the original does. You have full color. Include cover lines.

Chapter 8: Inside pages

Assignment 1. Using thumbnail sketches, work out a design for a six-page article (three two-page spreads) on the growth of terrorism in the world. See whether you can come up with some kind of art device that stays in place spread after spread but changes—perhaps grows—as each spread is exposed. It should unite the pages of the spread. Use greeking for the titles and blurbs.

Assignment 2. Using thumbnail sketches again, create several approaches to the combining of two unequal-length articles in a single spread.

Assignment 3. Create a diagram of small sketches showing as many ways as you can of crossing the gutter and uniting two facing pages. Some of the crossings can be more imagined than real, as, for instance, when you repeat an element on each page.

Assignment 4. Find a poorly designed table-of-contents page and redesign it, making it not only handsome but easy to follow.

Assignment 5. Find a book of unillustrated essays by a writer like C. S. Lewis, Joseph Epstein, or Nora Ephron and pick one to be run as an article in a magazine. Estimate the number of pages the article will take, including display type and art, and design the pages in rough form. Dream up and include some art. Try to make the art symbolic or abstract rather than realistic. No color.

Assignment 6. Design a lively three-page travel article on "Things to Do and See Down Under." Include lots of illustrations, possibly a combination of photographs and cartoons. Full color available. Look up Australia in an encyclopedia for art ideas. You might want to experiment with an upside-down touch in your design.

Assignment 7. Pick out a magazine without an editorial page and design one to fit in with the magazine's basic design and, especially, its handling of standing features. The page will be mostly type. Be prepared to explain the nature of any art you might include. Be sure to include the word *Editorial* or *Editorials* somewhere on the page. (See Karen Rathe's handling of this assignment as shown in this chapter.)

Assignment 8. A company magazine asks you to design a series of interior logos or column headings. The columns cover "Promotions," "Retirements," "Honors," "Births," and "Deaths" and will appear in the back of the book. The editor would like the logos or headings to be one column wide (the magazine has three-column, 8½ × 11 pages). The logos or headings should carry the one-word names identified here along with appropriate art (not unlike the art found in the *Boys' Life* logos shown in this chapter). But to save space, these logos or headings should be horizontals rather than verticals. Don't let the art overpower the wording.

Assignment 9. Assume you have three related articles by three different writers (two men, one woman) giving their preferences for vacations. One likes the seashore; one likes the mountains; one prefers extended travel, moving by car from one spot to another. As the designer you have the articles (fairly short), an editor's note introducing them, mug shots of each writer, and one scenic shot for each article (you decide what these shots should be). You also want to include bylines for each of the three authors and brief notes (legends) describing them. Your title is "Where to Go on Your Vacation"; your subtitle is "Three Veteran Vacationers Defend Their Choices." You have five 8½ × 11 pages for the material. You can use a left- or right-hand page opener. Black plus a second color. See what kind of design you can come up with, giving each author about the same space. This is more an exercise in organization and clarity than it is an exercise in aesthetics.

Chapter 9: Newspaper design and layout

Assignment 1. Find a small daily or a weekly newspaper with indifferent or dated design and modernize its front page, giving it more of a magazine look. For this assignment you can afford to be a bit impractical. The publisher ordering the redesign is wide open to innovation. But don't get too far away from the realities of newspaper deadlines and production limitations. Pay particular attention to the nameplate.

Assignment 2. Pick a big-city daily and redesign its editorial page (and op-ed page, if it has one). Make the new page or pages inviting—and classy.

Assignment 3. Take your local newspaper and go through it. Do some sketches and make some suggestions not to completely redesign it but to clean it up a bit and make its design more consistent.

Assignment 4. Show some imaginative ways to use boxes in a newspaper. You don't have to show the boxes in context. Start with shadow boxes and boxes that enclose silhouette photographs. Then show silhouette photographs breaking out of boxes. Sketch roughly. Quantity counts in this assignment.

Assignment 5. See whether you can come up with a better way of designing the comics page of your newspaper. Get rid of a couple of the strips if necessary.

Assignment 6. Design the prototype for a locally edited Sunday magazine for your local newspaper if it does not now have one. If it does, move to the nearest daily that doesn't have such a magazine.

Assignment 7. Take a newspaper nameplate that does not now feature the day of the week in large type and redesign the nameplate to make the day as large—or almost as large—as the name of the paper. The day does not have to be on the same line as the name.

Assignment 8. Assume that your city has endured a record-breaking heat wave. Redo the nameplate for your local newspaper for one-time use to make it appear as if it is melting from the sun.

Assignment 9. Take one of the rough thumbnail sketches for *The Times,* shown in this chapter, and do several variations of it, keeping the same basic design. Your designs can be rough thumbnails, too.

Chapter 10: Book design

Assignment 1. Dream up an idea for a book you'd like to write, compile, or edit. It can be a trade book or textbook. It can be a novel or a collection of your poems. It can be a collection of your photographs with commentary. It can be an adult book or a juvenile. But let it have some commercial possibilities. Design the book. That is, get together some sample pages—enough to give the publisher an idea of what the book will look like, enough to serve as a guide to the printer. This should include, at the least, a title page, a table-of-contents page, a chapter opening, and a page or spread from inside a chapter.

Assignment 2. Do a jacket for the book in the first assignment.

Assignment 3. Do a jacket for this fourth edition of *Publication Design,* as though the publisher were planning to market a hardbound version as a trade book. Same 8½ × 11 size.

Assignment 4. Assume that the publisher of *Publication Design* wants an entirely different look for a fifth edition of the book. Do six representative pages of what you see as a good new approach, bearing in mind that the ratio of art to copy will remain about the same.

Assignment 5. You have the job of designing the title page for a book called *Pages from the Past,* a collection of early magazine and newspaper pages that, with commentary by a history professor, serve as a sort of history book or book of nostalgia. Come up with a dated look if you can. And give the page a quality feel. Make up names for the author and publisher and include these on the page. Use some art or decoration if you wish.

Assignment 6. Go through some magazines, newspapers, and books to find examples of design clichés, especially clichés that don't happen to be shown in this book. Take one of the cliché-carrying pages or spreads and suggest a change to something more refreshing.

Chapter 11: Miscellaneous publications

Assignment 1. You've seen the blown-in and bound-in cards in magazines. Design a new one for your favorite magazine and make it inviting and easy to fill out. Use as much color as you wish.

Assignment 2. Design a booklet for a newspaper that gives instructions and lays down rules for the young people who deliver it. Use cartoon illustrations throughout. Eight pages. The booklet is to fit into a No. 10 business envelope. No color.

Assignment 3. Do four sample pages for a mail-order catalog likely to be used by a merchant in town with plans to go national.

Assignment 4. Come up with a design idea for a calendar that features health food recipes, along with appropriate art.

Assignment 5. Find a company magazine and critique its design, not only marking its pages with criticism but also submitting a three- or four-page report telling how the design could be improved.

Assignment 6. Find a newsletter and pretend that it has plans to go to a magazine format. In rough sketches work out the new magazine's basic design and format.

Assignment 7. You are going into business as a publications designer and design consultant. Design your letterhead and business card.

Glossary

Terminology in journalism and art varies from publication to publication and from region to region. This glossary gives meanings of terms as the author uses them in his books on graphic design.

abstract art simplified art; art reduced to fundamental parts; art that makes its point with great subtlety. Opposite of realistic or representational art.
aesthetics a philosophy that draws distinctions between beauty and ugliness.
agate type 5½-point type.
airbrush tool that uses compressed air to shoot a spray of pigment on photographs or artwork. Used for retouching.
all-caps all-capital letters.
antique paper rough-finish, high-quality paper.
area composition composition that provides a printout or proof with copy, headlines, subheads, and even illustrations in place, as opposed to composition that provides a printout or proof of copy only.
art all pictorial matter in a publication: photographs, illustrations, cartoons, charts and graphs, etc.
Art Deco the look of the 1920s and 1930s: simple line forms, geometric shapes, pastel colors, rainbow motifs.
art director person in charge of all visual aspects of a publication, including typography.
art editor see *art director.*
Art Nouveau art with decorative, curving lines and patterns taken from nature's foliage.
ascender part of lowercase letter that moves above the x-height.
asterisk small star used as a reference mark or as a footnote.
author's alterations changes made on proofs not necessitated by errors made by typesetter or printer. The author or the publisher pays for them.
axis imaginary line used to align visual elements and relate them.
back of the book section of a magazine following the main articles and stories and consisting of continuations of articles and stories, ads, and filler material.
back shop part of publishing operation where printing is done. Usually associated with newspapers.
balance stability in design; condition in which the various elements on a page or spread are at rest.
bank see *deck.*
banner main headline running across the top of a newspaper page.
bar chart art that shows statistics in bars of various lengths.
baseline imaginary line that forms the base or bottom of letters. Some letters have descending strokes that dip below the baseline.
Bauhaus school of design in Germany (1919–1933). It championed a highly ordered, functional style in architecture and applied arts.
Ben Day process by which the engraver or printer adds pattern or tone to a line reproduction.
Bible paper thin but opaque paper.
binding that part of a magazine or book that holds the pages together.
bird's-eye view view from above.
blackletter close-fitting, bold, angular type that originated in Germany. Also known as *Old English* and *text.*
bleed a picture printed to the edge of a sheet. Used also as a verb.
blind embossing embossing without printing.
blowup enlargement. *Blow up* when used as a verb.
blueline photographic proof from a negative of a page to be printed by the offset process.
blurb follow-up title for a magazine article, longer than the main title and in smaller type. Also, a title displayed on the cover. Also, copy on a book jacket.
body copy column or page of type of a relatively small size.
body type type 12 points in size or smaller.
boldface type black type; type heavier than ordinary type.
bond paper crisp paper used for business stationery, often with rag content.
book bound publication of forty-eight pages or more, usually with a stiff or heavy cover. Some magazine editors call their publications *books.*
book paper paper other than newsprint used in the printing of books and magazines. Includes many grades and finishes.
box design element composed usually of four rules, with type or art inside.
broadsheet standard-size newspaper sheet or page.
broadside direct-mail piece that folds out to a large sheet.
brownline see *blueline.*
bullet large dot used to attract attention or to set off a unit in a series.
byline the author's name set in type, usually above the story or article.
CAD computer-aided design, by which a computer processes and manipulates the design elements.
calender to polish, as in the making of paper.
calligraphy beautiful handwriting or drawn type.
camera-ready copy a pasteup ready to be photographed by the platemaker.
camp art so bad it's good.
caption text matter accompanying a photograph; newspapers use *cutlines.*
caricature drawing of a person that exaggerates or distorts the features.
cartoon humorous drawing, done usually in pen or brush and ink, or in washes.
casebound hard cover for a book.
cast off estimate the amount of copy in a book. In magazines it's *copyfit.*
centerfold center spread that opens out for two more pages.
center spread two facing pages at the center of a magazine or newspaper.
character any letter, number, punctuation mark, or space in printed matter.
circulation number of copies sold or distributed.
cliché something used too often, hence boring and no longer effective.
clipbook pages of stock art usually on slick paper, ready for photographing by the platemaker.
clipsheet see *clipbook.*
coated paper paper to which a smooth, hard coating has been applied.
cold type type composed by typewriter, computer printer, paper pasteup, or photographic means.
collage piece of art made by pasting various elements together.
colophon paragraph(s) of information about a book's design and typography, carried at the end of the book.
color separation negative made from full-color art for use in making one of the plates.
column section of a book's or magazine's text that runs from top to bottom of the page. Also, regular editorial feature in a newspaper or magazine, usually with a byline.
column inch area that is one column wide by one inch deep.
column rule thin line separating columns of type.

combination cut printing plate made from both a line and a halftone negative.
comic strip comic drawing or cartoon that appears in a newspaper on a regular basis as a series of panels.
commercial art art prepared for editorial or advertising purposes, for any of the media.
comp short for *comprehensive layout.*
company magazine magazine published by a company for public relations reasons, not to make money.
compositor typesetter.
comprehensive layout layout finished to look almost as the printed piece will look.
Compugraphic a major phototypesetting equipment manufacturer.
condensed type type series with narrow characters.
continuous-tone art photograph or painting or any piece of art in which tones merge gradually into one another. Requires halftone reproduction.
contrast quality in design that permits one element to stand out clearly from others.
copy article, story, or other written material either before or after it is set in type.
copy area see *type page.*
copyedit see *copyread.*
copyfit estimate how much space copy will take when it is set in type.
copyread check the manuscript to correct errors made by the writer or reporter.
copyright protection available to the owner of a manuscript, piece of art, or publication, preventing others from making unfair use of it or profiting from it at the expense of the owner. Also used as a verb.
copywriting writing copy for advertisements.
cover stock heavy or thick paper used as covers for magazines or paperback books.
credit line the photographer's name set in type, usually right next to the photograph.
crop cut away unwanted areas in a piece of art, usually by putting marks in the margins.
CRT cathode ray tube. Part of the typical VDT.
cursor small block of light on VDT screen that locates characters being activated by keyboard.
cut art in plate form, ready to print. For the letterpress process.
cutlines see *caption.*
daisy wheel disk with type characters.
deck portion of a headline, consisting of lines set in the same size and style of type.
deckle edge ragged, feathery edge available in some of the quality paper stocks.
descender part of a lowercase letter that dips below the baseline.
design organization; the plan and arrangement of visual elements. A broader term than *layout.* Used also as a verb.
designer person who designs pages or spreads.
desktop publishing personal computer system that sets type, combines it with art, and prints the result. The printing can serve as camera-ready copy for an offset press.
die-cut hole or other cutout punched into heavy paper.
digitized type type in dot form produced by computers.
direct-entry typesetter a single-unit system that transmits type from a keyboard directly to a printout.
direct-mail piece folder, leaflet, booklet, or other printed item issued on a one-time basis.
display type type larger than 12 points, used for titles and headlines.
double truck newspaper terminology for *spread.*
downstyle style characterized by the use of lowercase letters wherever possible.
drop see *sink.*
dropout halftone see *highlight halftone.*
drybrush art rendering in which partially inked brush is pulled across rough-textured paper.
dummy the pages of a magazine in its planning stage, often unbound, with features and pictures crudely sketched or roughly pasted into place.
duotone halftone printed in two inks, one dark (usually black) and one lighter (any color).
duplicator machine that reproduces a limited number of copies of a publication. Large press runs require regular printing presses.
dust jacket see *jacket.*
Dutch wrap in newspapering, continuation of body copy to adjacent columns not covered by the headline.
ear paragraph, line, or box on either side of a newspaper's nameplate.
edit change, manage, or supervise for publication. Also, as a noun, short for *editorial.*
editing the process by which manuscripts and art are made ready for publication.
edition part of the press run for a particular *issue* of a publication.
editorial short essay, usually unsigned, stating the position of the publication on some current event or issue. Also used to designate the nonbusiness side of a publication.
editorial cartoon single-panel cartoon of opinion found on the editorial page of a newspaper.
element copy, title or headline, art, rule or box, border, spot of color—anything to be printed on a page or spread.
elipsis omitted word(s) indicated by three or four dots in period position.
em width of capital *M* in any type size.
emboss print an image on paper and stamp it, too, so that it rises above the surface of the paper.
en width of capital *N* in any type size.
endpapers sheets that help connect the inside front and back covers to the book proper.
English finish smooth finish. English-finish papers are widely used by magazines.
expanded type type series with wider-than-normal characters.
face style or variation of type.
family subcategory of type. The name of the face.
fanzine privately circulated amateur magazine devoted to science fiction and art, often highly illustrated with imaginative art but usually cheaply printed.
feature any story, article, editorial, column, or work of art in a publication. Also used as a verb: to play up.
filler short paragraph or story used to fill a hole at the bottom of a column of type.
fine art art created primarily for aesthetic rather than commercial purposes.
first pass first proof of set copy.
fixative clear solution sprayed onto a drawing to keep it from smearing.
flag see *logo.*
flash forms signatures of four, eight, or more pages held out by the editor until the last minute. Often they are printed on different paper stock from what is used in the remainder of the magazine.
flat color see *spot color.*
FlexForm ad newspaper ad in other than the usual square or rectangular shape.
flop change the facing of a picture. A subject facing left in the

original will face right in the printed version. Not a synonym for *reverse.*

flow chart art showing a manufacturing or other process.

flush-left aligned at the left-hand margin.

flush-left-and-right aligned at both the left- and right-hand margins.

flush-right aligned at the right-hand margin.

folder a printed piece with at least one fold.

folio page number. Also, a sheet of paper folded once.

font complete set of type of a particular face and size.

foreshorten exaggerate the perspective.

format size, shape, and appearance of a publication.

formula editorial mix of a publication.

foundry type hand-set metal type.

four-color red, yellow, blue, and black used to produce effect of full color.

fourth cover back cover of a magazine.

freelancer artist, photographer, designer, writer, or copyeditor called in to do an occasional job for a publication.

French fold a fold that allows printing on one side of a sheet to create the illusion that all the pages are printed.

gag cartoon humorous drawing, usually in a single panel, with the caption, if there is one, set in type below.

galley tray on which type is asembled and proofed. Also, short for *galley proof.*

galley proof long sheet of paper containing a first printing from a tray of type.

gatefold magazine cover that opens out to two additional pages.

gingerbread design design with an overabundance of swirls and flourishes; cluttered design.

glossy print photograph with shiny finish.

gothic term applied in the past to various typefaces that have challenged the traditional. Currently, modern sans serifs.

graph see *bar chart, line chart,* and *pie chart.* Also, short for *paragraph.*

graphic design design of printed material.

gravure method of printing from incised plate. For publications a rotary press is involved, hence *rotogravure.*

grid carefully spaced vertical and horizontal lines that define areas in a layout; a plan for designing pages.

gutter separation of two facing pages.

hairline very thin rule or line.

halftone reproduction process by which the printer gets the effect of continuous tone, as when reproducing a photograph. It's done with dots.

hand lettering lettering done with pen or brush.

hanging indent the second and all subsequent lines of a unit indented a set amount, as in this glossary.

hard copy printed record produced as tape is punched. Also, printout from computer.

head short for *headline.*

headband piece of rolled, striped cloth used at the top of the binding to give a finished look to a book.

heading headline or title. Also, the standing title for a regular column or section in a publication.

headline display type above a story, feature, or editorial in a newspaper.

headline schedule chart of different headline sizes and arrangements used by a newspaper.

hed short for *head,* which is short for *heading* or *headline.* Mostly a newspaper term.

high camp see *camp.*

highlight halftone halftone in which some parts have been dropped out to show the white of the paper.

horizontal look lines of type, rules, and art arranged to make the page or spread look wide rather than deep.

hot type type made out of metal.

house ad advertisement promoting the publication in which it appears.

house organ see *company magazine.*

house style style that is peculiar to a publisher or that remains the same from issue to issue or publication to publication.

hung punctuation punctuation placed outside the copy block.

illustration drawing or painting.

illustration board cardboard or heavy paperboard made for artists, available in various weights and finishes to take various art mediums.

imprint run a print piece through another press to add information. Used also as a noun.

incunabula books printed before 1501.

index alphabetical listing of important words and names in a book or magazine, accompanied by page numbers. Found in the back of the publication. The table of contents is found in the front.

India ink permanent drawing ink.

India paper see *Bible paper.*

initial first letter of a word at the beginning of an article or paragraph, set in display size to make it stand out.

initial cap and lowercase the first word and all proper names begin with caps; all else is lowercase.

inline type with white line running through the center of the strokes.

insert separately printed piece that can be bound into a magazine with its other signatures.

intaglio see *gravure.*

interabang combination exclamation point and question mark.

Intertype linecasting machine similar to Linotype.

issue all copies of a publication for a particular date. An issue may consist of several *editions.*

italic type type that slants to the right. Used for emphasis, for captions, for names of publications, etc.

jacket paper cover that wraps around a book.

jump contine on another page.

justify align the type so that it forms an even line on the right and the left.

kerning fitting letters together tightly so that parts of some appear in the space of others.

keyline drawing single drawing that can be used to make more than one plate, including the color plate.

kicker short headline run above main headline, often underscored.

kraft paper heavy, rough, tough paper, usually tan in color.

lay out put visual elements into a pleasing and readable arrangement. Noun form is *layout.*

lead (pronounced *led*) put extra space between lines of type.

leaders repetition of a period, spaced or unspaced, to fill out a line.

leading extra space between lines of type.

legend book publishers' term for *caption.* Also, magazine term for information about an author.

legibility quality in type that makes it easy for the reader to recognize individual letters.

letterpress method of printing from a raised surface. The original and still widely used printing process.

letterspace put extra space between letters.

letterspacing extra space between letters.

libel published defamatory statement or art that injures a person's reputation.

ligature two or more characters that join or overlap on a single piece of type.

line art in its original form, art without continuous tone, done in black ink or white paper. Also, such art after it is reproduced through *line reproduction.*

linecasting machine see *Linotype* and *Intertype.*
line chart art that shows trends in statistics through a line that rises or falls on a grid.
line conversion continuous-tone art that has been changed to line art.
line feed same as *leading,* but for photocomposition.
line printer unit that produces a printout for copyediting or proofreading, but not in the typeface that eventually will be produced.
line reproduction process by which the printer reproduces a black-and-white drawing.
linespacing see *leading.*
Linotype linecasting machine that produces type for letterpress printing or type from which reproduction proofs can be pulled.
lithography process of making prints from grease drawing on stone. See also *offset lithography.*
live area area on a page or pasteup beyond which copy should not extend.
logo short for *logotype.* The name of the publication as run on the cover and sometimes on the title or editorial page. On a newspaper it is called the *flag* or *nameplate.*
lowercase small letters (as opposed to capital letters).
Ludlow machine that casts lines of display-size letters from matrices that have been assembled by hand.
magapaper magazine with a newspaper format. Or newspaper with a magazine format.
magazine publication of eight pages or more, usually bound, that is issued at least twice a year. Also, storage unit for mats for linecasting machine.
mass media units of communication: newspapers, magazines, television and radio stations, books, etc.
masthead paragraph of information about the publication. It is run on an inside page, under the table of contents, for a magazine, and on the editorial page for a newspaper.
mat short for *matrix.* Cardboard mold of a plate, from which a copy can be made. Also, brass mold from which type can be cast.
matrix see *mat.*
matte finish dull finish.
measure width of a line or column of type.
mechanical see *camera-ready copy.*
mechanical spacing nonadjusted spacing between letters; the opposite of *optical spacing.*
media see *mass media.*
medium singular for *media.* Also, paint, ink, or marking substance used in drawing or painting. In this context the plural of *medium* is *mediums.*
mezzotint halftone made with special texture screen.
minus leading less-than-normal leading between lines.
modem device that permits transmission of computer copy via telephone.
modular design highly ordered design, marked by regularity in spacing.
moiré undesirable wavy or checkered pattern resulting when a halftone print is photographed through another screen.
Monotype composing machine that casts individual letters. Used for quality composition.
montage combination of photographs or drawings into a single unit.
mortise a cut made in a picture to make room for type or another picture. Used also as a verb.
mug shot portrait.
Multilith printing process similar to offset lithography, but on a small scale.
nameplate see *logo.*
"new journalism" journalism characterized by a highly personal, subjective style.
news hole non advertising space in a newspaper.
newsprint low-quality paper lacking permanence, used for printing newspapers.
nonlining numerals numbers with ascenders and descenders as found in some old style romans.
OCR optical character reader. It converts typewritten material to electronic impulses and transmits those to a tape punch or computer. It is also called a "scanner."
offset lithography method of printing from flat surface, based on principle that grease and water don't mix. Commercial adaptation of *lithography.*
offset paper book paper made especially for offset presses.
Old English see *blackletter.*
one-shot magazine-like publication issued only once. Deals with some area of special interest.
op art geometric art that capitalizes on optical illusions.
op-ed short for "opposite the editorial page." The page across from the editorial page.
optical center a point slightly above and to the left of the geometric center.
optical spacing spacing in typesetting that takes into account the peculiarities of the letters, resulting in a more even look.
optical weight the visual impact a given element makes on the reader.
organization chart art that shows how various people or departments relate to each other.
outline letters letters in outline rather than in solid-black form. Also called *open face.*
overlay sheet of transparent plastic placed over a drawing. The overlay contains art or type of its own for a plate that will be coordinated with the original plate.
overset type set wider than the given measure. Also, excess copy that won't fit into the layout.
page one side of a sheet of paper.
page proof proof of a page to be printed by letterpress.
paginate to number pages.
pagination composition system that produces complete pages of type and art, with no pasteup of elements necessary.
painting illustration made with oil, acrylic, tempera, casein, or water color paints. Requires halftone reproduction; if color is to be retained, it requires process color plates.
paper stock paper.
pastel colors soft, weak colors.
pastel drawing drawing made with color chalks.
pasteup see *camera-ready copy.* Verb form is *paste up.*
pencil drawing drawing made with lead or graphite pencil. Usually requires halftone reproduction.
perfect binding binding that uses glue instead of stitching or stapling.
perspective quality in a photograph or illustration that creates the illusion of distance.
photocomposition composition produced by exposing negatives of type characters on paper or film.
photoengraving cut or plate made for letterpress printing.
photo essay series of photographs that make a single point.
photojournalism photography used in the mass media to report news, express opinion, or entertain.
photolettering display type produced photographically.
phototypesetting text matter produced photographically.
pic short for *picture.*
pica 12 points, or one-sixth of an inch.
Pictograph a chart or graph in picture form. A term coined by *U.S. News & World Report.*
picture photograph, drawing, or painting.
pie chart art that shows statistics—usually percentages—as wedges in a pie or circle.

pix plural of *pic.*

plate piece of metal from which printing is done. See also *cut.*

PMT photomechanical transfer. Duplicate print of the original line art.

point unit of measurement for type; there are 72 points to an inch.

pop art fine art inspired by comic strips and containers. See also *camp.*

Preprint ad in a sort of wallpaper design printed in rotogravure in another plant for insertion in a letterpress newspaper.

press run total number of copies printed during one printing.

printer person who makes up the forms or operates the presses.

printing the act of duplicating pages and arranging or binding them into copies of publications.

process color the effect of full color achieved through use of color separation plates; way to reproduce color photographs, paintings, and transparencies.

production process that readies manuscripts and art for the printer. Can also include the typesetting and printing.

progressive proofs proofs of process color plates, each color shown separately, then in combination.

proofread check galley and page proofs against the original copy to correct any mistakes the compositor made.

proportion size relationship of one part of a design to the other parts.

psychedelic art highly decorative art characterized by blobs of improbable colors, swirls, and contorted type and lettering.

publication product of the printing press.

publishing act of producing literature and journalism and making them available to the public. Printing is only one part of publishing.

race major category of typefaces.

ragged left aligned at the right but staggered at the left.

ragged right aligned at the left but staggered at the right.

readability quality in type that makes it easy for the reader to move easily from word to word and line to line. In a broader sense it is the quality in writing and design that makes it easy for the reader to understand the writer.

readership number of readers of a publication. Larger than the *circulation.*

ream five hundred sheets of printing paper.

recto a right-hand page, always odd-numbered.

register condition in printing in which various printing plates, properly adjusted, print exactly where they are supposed to print. Used also as a verb.

relief raised printing surface.

render execute, as in making a drawing.

repro short for *reproduction proof.*

reproduction a copy.

reproduction proof a carefully printed proof made from a galley, ready to paste down so that it can be photographed.

retouch strengthen or change a photograph or negative through use of art techniques.

reverse white letters in a gray, black, or color area. Mistakenly used for *flop.* Used also as a verb.

rivers of white meandering streaks of white running vertically or diagonally through body copy, caused by bad or excessive word spacing.

roman type type designed with thick and thin strokes and serifs. Some printers refer to any type that is standing upright (as opposed to type that slants) as roman.

rotogravure see *gravure.*

rough in cartooning, the first crude sketch presented to an editor to convey the gag or editorial idea. Also, *rough layout.*

rough layout crude sketch, showing where type and art are to go.

rout cut away.

rule thin line used either horizontally or vertically to separate lines of display type or columns of copy.

run-around area of body copy that wraps around an inset piece of art.

run-in let the words follow naturally, in paragraph form.

running head or title heading that repeats itself, page after page.

saddle stitch binding made through the spine of a collection of nested signatures. Also *saddle staple.*

sans serif type typeface with strokes of equal or near-equal thicknesses and without *serifs.*

scale quality in a photograph or illustration that shows size relationships.

schlock vulgar, heavy, tasteless.

score crease paper to make it easier to fold.

scratchboard drawing drawing made by scratching a knife across a previously inked surface.

screen the concentration of dots used in the halftone process. The more dots, the finer the screen.

script type that looks like handwriting.

second color one color in addition to black or the basic color.

second cover inside front cover.

self-cover cover made from stock used for inside pages.

separate cover cover made from heavier stock than that used for inside pages.

sequence series of related elements or pages arranged in logical order.

series subdivision of a type family.

serif small finishing stroke of a roman letter found at its terminals.

set size the width of the characters, which, in computer-controlled CRT typesetting systems, can be controlled separately from the vertical point size. The set size can be expanded or condensed. For instance, 10-point type can have a set size of 9 points, meaning the type is narrower than usual.

set solid set type without leading.

shelter magazine magazine that deals with the home and its surroundings.

sidebar short story related to major story and run nearby.

side stitch stitch through side of publication while it is in closed position. Also *side staple.*

signature all the pages printed on both sides of a single sheet. The sheet is folded down to page size and trimmed. Signatures usually come in multiples of sixteen pages. A magazine or book is usually made up of several signatures.

silhouette art subject with background removed.

sink distance from top of page to where copy begins.

sinkage see *sink.*

slab serif type type designed with even-thickness strokes and heavy serifs. Sometimes called "square serif" type.

slash diagonal stripe on magazine cover, put there to advertise an article inside.

slick magazine magazine printed on slick or glossy paper. Sometimes called simply "slick."

slug line of type from linecasting machine. Also, 6-point spacing material.

slug line significant word or phrase that identifies story. Found usually on galley proofs.

small caps short for *small capitals.* Capital letters smaller than regular capital letters in the same point size.

sort what a printer calls a piece of type.

SpectaColor ad printed in rotogravure in another plant for later insertion in a newspaper. Unlike a Preprint ad, a

SpectraColor ad has clearly defined margins.

spine back cover of a book or magazine, where front and back covers join.

spot color solid color used usually for accent. Less expensive, less involved than *process color.*

spot illustration drawing that stands by itself, unrelated to the text, used as a filler or for decorative purposes.

spread facing pages in a magazine or book.

stereotype plate made from mat that in turn was made from photoengraving or type.

stock paper or other material on which image is printed.

stock art art created for general use and stored until ordered for a particular job.

straight matter text that is uninterrupted by headings, tables, etc.

strike-on composition text matter produced on typewriters or typewriter like composing machines.

style distinct and consistent approach to art or design.

subhead short headline inside article or story. Also *subhed.*

surprint black letters over gray areas, as over a photograph. Used also as a verb.

swash caps capital letters in some typefaces with extra flourishes in their strokes, usually in the italic versions.

swatch color sample.

swipe file artist's or designer's library of examples of other artists' work, used for inspiration.

Swiss design design characterized by clean, simple lines and shapes, highly ordered, with lots of white space; based on a grid system.

symmetrical balance balance achieved by equal weights and matching placement on either side of an imaginary center line.

table list of names, titles, etc.

tabloid newspaper with pages half the usual size.

tailband piece of rolled, striped cloth used at the bottom of the binding to give a finished look to a book.

tape merger in typesetting, a method of combining the original tape with a second tape containing corrections, to produce a third tape.

technique method of achieving style or effect.

text see *body copy.*

text type see *blackletter.*

third cover inside back cover.

thumbnail very rough sketch in miniature.

tint weaker version of tone or color.

tint block panel of color or tone in which something else may be printed.

tip-in sheet or signature glued onto a page.

title what goes above a story or article in a magazine. On a newspaper the term is *headline.*

tombstone heads same size and style headlines, side by side.

tone the darkness of the art or type.

trade magazine magazine published for persons in a trade, business, or profession.

transparency in photography, a color positive on film rather than paper.

type printed letters and characters. Also, the metal pieces from which the printing is done.

typeface particular style or design of type.

type page that part of the page in which type is printed, inside the margins. Sometimes called "copy area."

type specimens samples of various typefaces available.

typo typographic error made by the compositor.

typography the type in a publication. Also, the art of designing and using type.

unity design principle that holds that all elements should be related.

universal characters characters not of any particular typeface that can be used with any of them. For instance, mathematical signs.

upper case capital letters.

Vandyke see *blueline.*

VDT video display terminal. It has a keyboard with a TV-like screen above. Stories can be set and corrected on VDTs.

Velox photoprint with halftone dot pattern in place of continuous tone, ready for line reproduction.

verso a left-hand page, always with an even number.

vignette oval-shaped halftone in which background fades away gradually all around.

visual having to do with the eye.

visualization the process by which an artist or designer changes an idea or concept into visual or pictorial form.

wash drawing ink drawing shaded with black-and-white water color. Requires halftone reproduction.

watermark faint design pressed into paper during its manufacture.

waxer device or machine that deposits a thin coat of wax on the backs of proofs so that they can be attached to the pasteup.

white space space on a page not occupied by type, pictures, or other elements.

widow line of type less than the full width of the column.

woodcut engraving cut in wood. Also, the impression made by such a plate.

word processor computer with keyboard, screen, and printer that produces copy or business letters. More sophisticated than an electric or electronic typewriter.

worm's-eye view view from low vantage point.

wrong font letter, number, or character in a different size or face from what was ordered.

WYSIWYG what you see is what you get; what's seen on a terminal screen—text and art—can be printed out.

x-height height of lowercase *x* in any typeface.

Zipatone transparent sheet on which is printed a pattern of dots or lines. Fastened over part of line drawing, it gives the illusion of tone. See also *Ben Day.*

Index